LONGMAN

Student Grammar

of SPOKEN

and WRITTEN

ENGLISH

Douglas Biber
Susan Conrad
Geoffrey Leech

Longman

Pearson Education Limited
Edinburgh Gate
Harlow
Essex CM20 2JE
England
and Associated Companies throughout the World.

Visit our website: http://www.longman.com/dictionaries

First published 2002

ISBN
0 582 237270 (cased edition)
0 582 237262 (paper edition)

Library of Congress Cataloguing-in-Publication Data
A catalog record for this book is available from the Library of Congress.

British Library Cataloguing-in-Publication Data
A catalogue record of this book is available from the British Library.

Designed by Sally Lace
Graphs by Robert Escott
Set in Minion and Frutiger by Mendip Communications Limited,
Frome, Somerset
Printed in China
EPC/01

Preface

This book is a coursebook and a reference grammar for students and their teachers. Although it is based on the *Longman Grammar of Spoken and Written English (LGSWE)*, the *Student Grammar* is much more than just an abbreviated *LGSWE*. Rather, we have simplified and reorganized the content of the *LGSWE*, avoiding much technical detail while retaining the strengths of the larger book. For example, like the *LGSWE*, the *Student Grammar* contains over 3,000 authentic English examples, and contrasts the major patterns of use in spoken and written registers. However, we have simplified the presentation when possible; for example, we have tried hard to find new and simpler extracts from our corpus data, often replacing more complex examples in *LGSWE*.

Of the five authors of *LGSWE*, we three owe a debt of gratitude to our two other co-authors: Stig Johansson and Ed Finegan. We benefited from the work that Stig and Ed did on the *LGSWE* during our writing of the *Student Grammar*. We would also like to thank the students in English 528 at Northern Arizona University, who used a draft of the *Student Grammar* as their grammar textbook and provided numerous helpful comments and suggestions for revision.

To support the educational use of the *Student Grammar*, we have also written a Workbook, which can be used as a classroom textbook or for self-study by students. The Workbook provides exercises based on authentic English texts and sentences, linked directly to the Grammar Bites in the present book.

DB   SC   GL

Abbreviations, symbols, and conventions

Corpus examples and data

All examples and text extracts are taken from the LSWE Corpus, and are marked as coming from one of the four main subdivisions of the corpus:

(ACAD)	academic text
(CONV)	conversation transcription
(FICT)	fiction text
(NEWS)	news text

Some examples are truncated to save space. These are marked with the † symbol:

> (ACAD†), (CONV†), (FICT†), (NEWS†)

Truncated examples, showing an incomplete sentence or conversational turn, are used only when the omitted parts are judged to have no bearing on the grammatical point being illustrated, and where overly long examples might distract rather than help the reader. For example:

1a *Every atom has a dense nucleus.* (ACAD†)
1b *Every atom has a dense nucleus that contains practically all of the mass of the atom.* (ACAD)

Example **1a** is a truncated version of the complete sentence in example **1b**. Note that even with truncation, dispensable material is almost always omitted from the beginning or end of an example, not from the middle. In this sense, virtually every example quoted is a continuous 'slice of linguistic reality'. Occasional cases of medial omission are shown by the insertion of <. . .> at the point where the omission occurs:

> <. . .>   part of an example where words have been omitted

Other abbreviations used to label examples are:

> AmE American English
> BrE British English

In a few cases, examples have been invented to show a contrast between acceptable and unacceptable usage. Such unacceptable examples are marked *:

> * [preceding]   an example which is unacceptable in English

Some examples have a following editorial comment, marked < >:

> < >   an editorial comment

Conventions within examples

Typographic features are used to highlight particular features of an example:

> **bold type**
> highlights the main item for attention
> <u>underlining</u> or brackets [ ]
> highlight further elements

A dash at the end of a word signals that it is incomplete.

Grammatical abbreviations

A	adverbial	OP	object predicative
DO	direct object	P	predicative
IO	indirect object	S	subject
LVP	long verb phrase	SP	subject predicative
NP	noun phrase	V	verb (phrase)
O	object	VP	verb phrase

Glossary terms

There is a Glossary at the end of the book, containing definitions of many grammatical terms used in the book. These terms are flagged in bold at their first instance, or at a subsequent early instance.

Corpus data

Sections of text that draw most heavily on the data from the LSWE Corpus are flagged:

   a section of text presenting corpus patterns

Contents

Preface   iii
Abbreviations, symbols, and
conventions   iv
Grammar Bites in each chapter   viii

**1   Introduction: a discourse
      perspective on grammar**   1
1.1 Introduction   2
1.2 A corpus-based grammar   3
1.3 More about language variation   4
1.4 More detail on the LSWE Corpus   7
1.5 Overview of the book   9
1.6 Conventions used in the book   10

2   Words and word classes   12
2.1 Introduction   13
2.2 What are words?   14
2.3 Survey of lexical words   20
2.4 Survey of function words   26
2.5 Special classes of words   32
2.6 Word-class ambiguities   35

**3   Introduction to phrases
      and clauses**   37
3.1 Introduction   38
3.2 Phrases and their characteristics   38
3.3 Types of phrases   41
3.4 A preview of clause patterns   46
3.5 Clause elements   47

**4   Nouns, pronouns, and the
      simple noun phrase**   55
4.1 Introduction   56
4.2 Main types of nouns   56
4.3 Proper nouns v. common nouns   59
4.4 Package nouns   60
4.5 Determiners   65
4.6 The articles   67
4.7 Other determiners   72
4.8 Number: singular and plural   78
4.9 Case: the genitive   79
4.10 Gender   85
4.11 The formation of derived nouns   88
4.12 Personal pronouns   93
4.13 Reflexive pronouns   97
4.14 Demonstrative pronouns   98

4.15 Indefinite pronouns   99
4.16 Other pronouns   101

5   Verbs   102
5.1 Introduction   103
5.2 Verb functions and classes   103
5.3 Semantic categories of lexical
     verbs   106
5.4 The most common lexical verbs   110
5.5 Regular and irregular verb
     endings   115
5.6 Verb formation   118
5.7 Valency patterns   119
5.8 Multi-word verbs: structure and
     meaning   123
5.9 Phrasal verbs   127
5.10 Prepositional verbs   129
5.11 Phrasal-prepositional verbs   132
5.12 Other multi-word verb
     constructions   134
5.13 *Be*   135
5.14 *Have*   136
5.15 *Do*   137
5.16 The copula *be*, and other copular
     verbs   140
5.17 Functions of copular verbs   141

**6   Variation in the verb
      phrase: tense, aspect,
      voice, and modal use**   148
6.1 Introduction   149
6.2 Tense and time distinctions:
     simple present and past tense   150
6.3 Perfect and progressive aspect   156
6.4 Perfect aspect in use   159
6.5 Progressive aspect   162
6.6 Active and passive voice   166
6.7 Associations between verbs and
     passive voice   170
6.8 Voice and aspect combinations   173
6.9 Modals and semi-modals   174
6.10 Personal and logical meanings of
     modals   178
6.11 *Be going to* and *used to*   182
6.12 Modals combined with aspect or
     voice   183

6.13 Sequences of modals and semi-modals 184

7 Adjectives and adverbs 186
7.1 Introduction 187
7.2 Characteristics of adjectives 188
7.3 The formation of adjectives 190
7.4 The function of adverbs 193
7.5 The formation of adverbs 193
7.6 Semantic categories of adjectives 197
7.7 More about attributive adjectives 199
7.8 More about predicative adjectives 200
7.9 Other syntactic roles of adjectives 202
7.10 Syntactic roles of adverbs 204
7.11 Semantic categories of adverbs 208
7.12 Comparative and superlative forms of adjectives 215
7.13 Comparative and superlative forms of adverbs 218
7.14 Comparative clauses and other degree complements 218

8 Exploring the grammar of the clause 221
8.1 Introduction 222
8.2 Devices of elaboration and condensation 223
8.3 Subordination and dependent clauses 224
8.4 Coordination 227
8.5 Ellipsis and structural condensation 230
8.6 The subject–verb concord rule 232
8.7 Verbs as operators 238
8.8 Negation 239
8.9 Major types of independent clause 248
8.10 Declarative clauses 249
8.11 Interrogative clauses 249
8.12 Exclamative clauses 254
8.13 Imperative clauses 254
8.14 Non-clausal material 255
8.15 Finite dependent clauses 256
8.16 Non-finite dependent clauses 259
8.17 Subjunctive verbs in dependent clauses 261
8.18 Dependent clauses with no main clause 262

9 Complex noun phrases 263
9.1 Introduction 264
9.2 Survey of noun modifier types 265
9.3 Noun phrases with premodifiers and postmodifiers across registers 267
9.4 Types of premodifiers 272
9.5 Meaning relationships expressed by noun + noun sequences 273
9.6 Noun phrases with multiple premodifiers 276
9.7 Restrictive v. non-restrictive function 279
9.8 Postmodification by relative clauses 281
9.9 Postmodification by non-finite clauses 291
9.10 Postmodification by prepositional phrase 294
9.11 Postmodification by appositive noun phrases 297
9.12 Noun phrases with multiple postmodifiers 298
9.13 Noun complement clauses 300
9.14 Head nouns with noun complement clauses 302

10 Verb and adjective complement clauses 307
10.1 Introduction 308
10.2 Types of complement clauses 308
10.3 Grammatical positions of complement clauses 310
10.4 Discourse functions of that-clauses 312
10.5 Post-predicate that-clauses 314
10.6 Verbs controlling extraposed that-clauses 317
10.7 That-clauses controlled by adjectives 317
10.8 Discourse choices with that-clauses 319
10.9 Structure and function of wh-clauses 322
10.10 Post-predicate wh-clauses controlled by verbs 324
10.11 Interrogative clauses with whether and if 326
10.12 Overview of infinitive clauses 328

10.13 Post-predicate *to*-clauses
controlled by verbs 328
10.14 Subject predicative *to*-clauses 334
10.15 Post-predicate *to*-clauses
controlled by adjectives 335
10.16 Raising 337
10.17 Extraposed *to*-clauses 338
10.18 Raising v. extraposition 341
10.19 *To*-clause types across registers 342
10.20 Overview of *ing*-clauses 344
10.21 Post-predicate *ing*-clauses 344
10.22 Ellipsis and substitution in
complement clauses 348
10.23 Choice of complement clause
type 349

11   Adverbials 353
11.1 Introduction 354
11.2 The main classes of adverbials 355
11.3 Syntactic forms of adverbials 358
11.4 Positions of adverbials 359
11.5 The relationship between
adverbials and other clause
elements 361
11.6 Semantic categories of
circumstance adverbials 362
11.7 Extremely common circumstance
adverbials in conversation 368
11.8 Positions of circumstance
adverbials 369
11.9 Additional semantic categories of
circumstance adverbial clauses 373
11.10 Syntactic forms of adverbial
clauses 376
11.11 Positions of adverbial clauses 378
11.12 Subordinators with circumstance
adverbial clauses 380
11.13 Semantic categories of stance
adverbials 382
11.14 The most common stance
adverbials 386
11.15 Positions of stance adverbials 387
11.16 Other discourse functions of
stance adverbials 388

11.17 Semantic categories of linking
adverbials 389
11.18 The most common linking
adverbials in conversation and
academic prose 393
11.19 Positions of linking adverbials 394

12   Word order choices 397
12.1 Introduction 398
12.2 Word order 400
12.3 Fronting 400
12.4 Inversion 405
12.5 Existential *there* 412
12.6 The verb in existential *there*
clauses 414
12.7 The notional subject 414
12.8 Adverbials in existential clauses 415
12.9 Simple v. complex existential
clauses 415
12.10 Discourse functions of existential
clauses 416
12.11 Dislocation 418
12.12 Clefting 419
12.13 Word order choices after the verb 423
12.14 Summary: syntactic choices in
conversation v. academic prose 425

**13   The grammar of
conversation** 427
13.1 Introduction 428
13.2 The discourse circumstances of
conversation 429
13.3 Performance phenomena in
conversation 436
13.4 Non-clausal units 440
13.5 Ellipsis 441
13.6 Lexical bundles in speech 443
13.7 Inserts 449

Glossary of terms 455
A–Z list of irregular verbs 462
Index 464

Grammar Bites in each chapter

2

A Introduction to words — 14
B Lexical word classes — 20
C Function word classes — 26

3

A Introduction to phrases — 38
B Clause elements and clause patterns — 46

4

A Types of nouns — 56
B Types of determiners — 65
C Number and case in nouns — 78
D Gender and noun formation — 85
E Types of pronouns — 92

5

A Verb functions and classes — 103
B Single-word lexical verbs — 106
C Lexical verbs: structures and patterns — 115
D Multi-word lexical verbs — 123
E Primary verbs — 135
F Copular verbs — 140

6

A Tense — 150
B Aspect — 156
C Voice — 166
D Modals and semi-modals — 174

7

A Characteristics of adjectives and adverbs — 188
B Adjectives: roles and meanings — 197
C Adverbs: roles and meanings — 204
D Comparative and superlative forms — 215

8

A Subordination, coordination, and ellipsis — 223
B Subject–verb concord — 232
C Negation — 238
D Independent clauses — 248
E Dependent clauses — 256

9

A Types of noun modification — 265
B Premodification — 272
C Relative clauses — 279
D Other postmodifier types — 291
E Noun complement clauses — 300

10

A Types and positions of complement clauses — 308
B *That*-clauses — 312
C *Wh*-clauses — 322
D Post-predicate infinitive clauses — 328
E More on infinitive clauses — 337
F *Ing*-clauses, ellipsis/substitution, and review — 344

11

A Overview of adverbials — 355
B Circumstance adverbials — 362
C Circumstance adverbials that are clauses — 373
D Stance adverbials — 382
E Linking adverbials — 389

12

A Fronting and inversion — 400
B Existential *there* clauses — 412
C Other topics in word order — 418

13

A A functional overview of conversational grammar — 429
B Grammar tailored to real-time construction — 436
C Grammar, lexis, and discourse — 443

1

Introduction: a discourse perspective on grammar

Subjects in this chapter

- ➤ Introduction to the concept of corpus-based grammar
- ➤ Language variation: registers, dialects, standard and non-standard (vernacular) English
- ➤ The Longman Spoken and Written English Corpus
- ➤ Overview of the book
- ➤ Conventions used in the book

1.1 **Introduction**

Every time we write or speak, we are faced with a large array of choices: not only choices of what to say but of how to say it. The vocabulary and grammar that we use to communicate are influenced by a number of factors, such as the reason for the communication, the setting, the people we are addressing, and whether we are speaking or writing. Taken together, these choices give rise to systematic patterns of choice in the use of English grammar.

Traditionally, such patterns have not been included as part of grammar. Most grammars have focused on structure, describing the form and (sometimes) meaning of grammatical constructions out of context. They have not described how forms and meanings are actually used in spoken and written discourse. But for someone learning about the English language for the purposes of communication, it is the real use of the language that is important. It is not enough to study just the grammatical forms, structures, and classes. These tell us what choices are available in the grammar, but we also need to understand how these choices are used to create discourse in different situations.

The year 1999 saw the publication of a large-scale grammar of English with the aim of meeting the above needs: the *Longman Grammar of Spoken and Written English* (*LGSWE*). This was the outcome of an international research project which lasted seven years. Now, we have written a revised, simplified, and shortened version of *LGSWE* for use by advanced students and their teachers.

LGSWE made important innovations in the method of grammatical study. It was based on a large, balanced corpus of spoken and written texts. These texts were electronically stored and analyzed with the aid of computers. The analysis produced information about the frequency of grammatical features in different kinds of language. (We use the term 'feature' broadly in this book, to refer to any grammatical form, structure, class, or rule.) The results of the analysis were then studied by the team of grammarians. The goal was to explain not just what is *possible* in English grammar, but what is more or less *probable* in different situations.

This book, the *Student Grammar of Spoken and Written English* (*SGSWE*), presents the insights and discoveries of *LGSWE* to advanced students of English and their teachers. *SGSWE* is designed to be used with the accompanying workbook as a textbook (for use in class or for self-study), or alternatively as a reference grammar:

- *SGSWE* **is a pedagogical textbook on grammar**. For students systematically studying English grammar, *SGSWE* begins with the 'basics' in the opening two chapters, and moves progressively into more advanced territory. It ends with a chapter devoted to the special characteristics of conversational grammar—an important topic which has generally been neglected in grammars up to now.
- *SGSWE* **can also be used as a reference grammar**. It covers all major features, structures, and classes of English grammar, together with their meaning and use. With the help of the glossary of grammatical terms and the index, students and teachers can use this book as a reference guide. For more detailed information about a feature or its use, you can consult corresponding sections in the larger *LGSWE*.

The greatest innovation of *SGSWE* is that it is a corpus-based grammar. The new methodology of large-scale corpus study developed in *LGSWE* produces results which are very useful for students. In general, advanced students of English want to understand not only the structural rules of English, but how the language is used for communication. For this purpose, new insights, explanations, and information from corpus-based studies of English are an important advantage.

1.2 A corpus-based grammar

A corpus is a large, systematic collection of texts stored on computer. The corpus used for *LGSWE* and *SGSWE*—the Longman Spoken and Written English Corpus (the LSWE Corpus)—contains approximately 40 million words of text, providing a sound basis for the analysis of grammatical patterns. Because the *SGSWE* is based on analysis of this corpus, it offers a number of advantages over traditional grammars:

- **Real examples**: The book contains over three thousand examples of English in use. These are authentic examples from the corpus, showing how real people use real language. Invented examples that sound artificial—a familiar feature of many other grammars—are entirely absent. At the same time, we have taken care to avoid corpus examples that are overly difficult because they require understanding a complicated context.

- **Coverage of language variation**: The core corpus we have used for this book represents four major registers of the language: conversation, fiction writing, news writing, and academic prose. In the past, grammars have usually presented a single view of the language, as if the grammar of English were one fixed and unchanging system. This clearly is not true. Although there is an underlying system of grammar, speakers and writers exploit that system very differently to meet their communication needs in different circumstances. The corpus-based information included in *SGSWE* describes differences between a spoken register (conversation) and three written registers (fiction, newspapers, and academic prose). In addition, our corpus contains data from both American and British conversations and newspapers. Where they occur, important differences between these geographical dialects are pointed out. (See 1.3 for more about registers and dialects.)

- **Coverage of preference and frequency**: This grammar gives information about the preferences speakers or writers have for one grammatical choice over another. Specifically, we discuss the frequency of alternative structures and the conditions that are associated with them. This is clearly a major matter of interest to advanced learners of the language and future teachers of the language. For example, it is not enough simply to describe the structural differences between active and passive constructions, because students and teachers need to know how users choose between these two options. For example, passive verbs are ten times more frequent in academic prose than they are in conversation. And there are good reasons for this, which we discuss in 6.6.1.

- **Interpretations of frequency: context and discourse**: Information about frequency needs to be explained by human interpreters. That is, a corpus grammar needs to present the evidence of the corpus as a means of exploring *why* users of English make one choice in one situation, and a different choice in another. Usually several factors are relevant, including register, expressing personal attitudes, giving informational emphasis, or other more specific contextual conditions. The *SGSWE* gives attention to the conditions under which grammatical choices are made, so the grammar has a discourse orientation.

- **Lexico-grammatical patterns**: Another distinctive feature of the *SGSWE* is that it brings together the study of grammar and vocabulary. Traditionally, both in theory and pedagogical practice, grammar has been separate from vocabulary, as if they were two totally independent aspects of language and language learning. This separation is artificial, as becomes evident to anyone who uses a large corpus for studying grammar. What becomes clear is that, when they use a language, people bring together their knowledge of word behavior (lexis) with their knowledge of grammatical patterns. These two aspects of language interact in lexico-grammatical patterns. For example, there is one set of verbs that commonly occur with a *that*-clause (e.g. *think, say, know*) and a different set of verbs that commonly occur with a *to*-clause (e.g. *want, like, seem*). In addition, each register prefers different verbs with these clause types. These patterns help to explain the typical meanings and uses of each clause type in each register.

1.3 More about language variation

We have mentioned the coverage of language variation as one of the strengths of this grammar. It is important to recognize that there are two major types of language varieties: registers and dialects.

1.3.1 Registers

Registers are varieties of language that are associated with different circumstances and purposes. For example, Table 1.1 compares the circumstances and purposes of the four registers compared in *SGSWE*.

Comparisons between registers can be made on many different levels. For example, the most general distinction can be made on the basis of mode: conversation is spoken, while the other three registers are written. If we consider a more specific characteristic—the main communicative purpose—the registers fall into three categories. Conversation focuses on personal communication,

Table 1.1 **Circumstances of the four main registers in *SGSWE***

	CONV	FICT	NEWS	ACAD
mode	spoken	written	written	written
interactiveness and real-time production	yes	restricted to fictional dialog	no	no
shared situation	yes	no	no	no
main communicative purpose/content	personal communication	pleasure reading	information/ evaluation	argumentation/ explanation
audience	individual	wide-public	wide-public	specialist

fiction on pleasure reading, and newspapers and academic prose share a more informational purpose. (We sometimes call these last two expository registers.) However, even between newspapers and academic prose there are differences. Academic prose is more concerned with building an argument than newspaper writing is. What is more, academic prose has a more specialized audience than a newspaper, which is written with a wide audience in mind.

Register variation is the main aspect of language variation we consider in this book. We choose this focus because registers differ greatly in their grammar usage, reflecting their different communication circumstances. In other words, the circumstances of a register have a direct impact on which grammar habits are common in the register. To take an easy example, consider how pronouns and nouns are used in conversation and news. Conversation is interactive as a form of personal communication. It is not surprising, then, that conversation shows a frequent use of the first-person pronouns *I* and *we*, and the second-person pronoun *you*. In contrast, newspaper writing is not directly interactive: it is not addressed to an individual reader, and it often does not have a stated author. But it has a function of conveying general information of current interest. Not surprisingly, in newspaper texts, first- and second-person pronouns are relatively rare. Instead, proper nouns, referring to people, places, and institutions, are particularly common.

The four registers that we concentrate on are, of course, far from a complete picture of register variation in English. However, they have the advantage of (a) being major registers, likely to be frequently encountered by any advanced student of the language, and (b) being sufficiently different from one another to show important differences as well as important similarities.

Within each register there are also sub-registers. For example, fiction can be broken down into different sub-categories—detective fiction, fantasy fiction, romance fiction, etc. The compilers of the LSWE Corpus took pains to represent all the categories and to obtain as good a balance as possible between different sub-varieties within each category. (More details are given in 1.4 below.) In order to limit the size of this book, though, we make only a few references to sub-registers, such as commenting on a feature common in, say, sports reporting or detective fiction.

1.3.2 Dialects

Dialect variation interacts with register variation. Dialects are varieties according to the identity of speaker(s) or writer(s)—their geographic area, gender, socio-economic class, and so on. Dialect is less important for grammatical purposes than register. From the grammatical point of view, dialect differences are arbitrary, while register differences are functional, reflecting the way that grammar varies according to communicative purpose.

Like register, dialect distinctions can be made at different levels of specificity. 'American English' or 'British English' is a very general level; 'the speech of female teenagers in the South Bronx area of New York City' would be a more specific dialect. In the *SGSWE* we focus only on the high-level distinction between American English and British English (although the spoken corpus was developed following sampling methods for geographical regions, socio-economic class, gender, and age, so more detailed dialect studies are possible).

The corpus used for this book also includes some representation of Australian, Canadian, Caribbean, Irish, and West African English in the fiction subcorpus (see details in 1.4). For full coverage of dialect variation, we would need to have coverage of many more world varieties of English. The contrasts between British and American English in this book serve as just one example of regional dialect variation. We have chosen these two dialects because they serve as a target for many learners and teachers of English.

1.3.3 Standard and non-standard (vernacular) English

There is no official academy that regulates usage for the English language, but there is still a prevailing world-wide view that there is a 'standard English': the language variety that has been codified in dictionaries, grammars, and usage handbooks. However, in the corpus, especially in conversation, usage regarded as non-standard (also called the **vernacular**) is also found. For example, consider the vernacular use of *what* as a relative pronoun in **1**, and of *ain't* and multiple negative constructions in **2** and **3**:

1 *They were by the pub **what** we stayed in.* (CONV)
2 *I **ain't** done **nothing**.* (CONV)
3 *'There **ain't nothing** we can do.'* (FICT)

As **3** shows, vernacular forms also occur in fiction texts, particularly in representing the speech of fictional characters. However, in general, vernacular forms are rare in the written corpus.

When vernacular forms are discussed or illustrated in the rest of the book, they are generally noted as 'non-standard'. In general, our description of grammar is limited to standard English. However, it is worth bearing in mind that conversation contains many vernacular features of language, and so such features can be expected in the conversation part of our corpus, whereas they are strictly avoided in written language (except where written language deliberately mimics speech, as in fictional dialog). In a similar way, conversational transcriptions often contain informal or non-standard spellings like *gonna* and *cos* (see 1.6.2 below).

A Variation in standard English

The term 'standard English' can be misleading. 'Standard' in some contexts means 'uniform, unchanging', and so it is assumed that only one form of a grammatical feature is accepted in standard English. But this is clearly false. For example, both of the following conform to standard English, even though one begins a relative clause with *that* and the other with *which*:

1 *I could give you figures **that** would shock you.* (FICT)
2 *This chapter is devoted to a discussion of various flow processes **which** occur in open systems.* (ACAD)

The relative pronouns *that* and *which* could exchange places in these sentences, although there are a number of factors that favor one over the other (see 9.7, 9.8.1).

Little of the variability within standard English is due to dialect differences between American English and British English, which actually show very few grammatical differences in their standard dialects. We point out such differences where important in *SGSWE*. For example, one well-known difference is that American English has two past participles for the verb *get* (*got* and *gotten*), whereas British English has only one:

> *Angie, I think we've **got** a leak.* (BrE CONV)
>
> *They've **got** money.* (AmE CONV)
>
> *He must have **got** to the door just as the bomb landed.* (BrE CONV†)
>
> *And we still haven't **gotten** a damn pumpkin.* (AmE CONV)

Note: Another aspect of vernacular English is illustrated by the last example: the word *damn* (or *damned*), which is a mild 'swearword' or taboo term. Swearwords can cause offence or be considered impolite, especially where used in the wrong context, and so we point them out when they occur in examples.

B Prescriptive v. descriptive grammars

Most cases of variation within standard English (e.g. *that* and *which* in **1** and **2** above) do not attract attention from ordinary language users. However, speakers do tend to be aware of some aspects of disputed usage and sometimes have strong opinions about what forms are 'correct'. Thus while the use or the omission of *that* is rarely noticed or commented on, the choice between *who* and *whom* can rouse strong feelings (see 9.8.2). Prescriptive grammars dictate how people 'should' use the language. For example, a prescriptive grammarian would insist that only *whom* should be used when the pronoun refers to a human and functions as an object or prepositional complement. In contrast, speakers in conversation regularly prefer *who* in actual usage:

> *There's a girl **who** I work with who's pregnant.* (CONV)

In fact, many speakers would find the use of *whom* unusual in any informal, conversational situation.

In this grammar, we do not argue that any one alternative is correct in cases like these. Rather than a prescriptive grammar, the *SGSWE* is a descriptive grammar. We focus on describing the actual patterns of use and the possible reasons for those patterns. However, we do refer from time to time to some cases of disputed usage. Although these may not be so important from the viewpoint of communication, they often play a significant role in people's judgments of what is 'good grammar'. These judgments, in turn, may have an influence on actual patterns of use.

1.4 More detail on the LSWE Corpus

For a corpus-based grammar, the design of the corpus is an important concern. Detailed discussion of the LSWE Corpus can be found in Chapter 1 of *LGSWE*, especially pp. 24–35. Here we give only a brief overview of the corpus.

The entire corpus contains approximately 40 million words. Most of the analyses comparing the four registers used a subcorpus of approximately 20 million words. Additional texts for the dialect comparisons and occasional comparisons with supplementary registers account for a further 20 million words. Table 1.2 provides an overview of the overall composition of the corpus.

Table 1.2 **Overall composition of the LSWE Corpus**

	number of texts	number of words
core registers		
conversation (BrE)	3,436	3,929,500
fiction (AmE & BrE)	139	4,980,000
news (BrE)	20,395	5,432,800
academic prose (AmE & BrE)	408	5,331,800
AmE texts for dialect comparisons		
conversation (AmE)	329	2,480,800
news (AmE)	11,602	5,246,500
supplementary registers		
non-conversational speech (BrE)	751	5,719,500
general prose (AmE & BrE)	184	6,904,800
total Corpus	37,244	40,025,700

The strength of the LSWE Corpus does not just lie in its size—although size can be important, especially for the study of rare grammatical features. More important qualities are the diversity and balance of the corpus. The LSWE Corpus represents a comparatively wide range of register and dialect variation within the language, and each category of texts is represented by a wide range of writers/speakers and 'sub-registers'. In 1.3.1 and 1.3.2 we mentioned some of the sub-categories within the registers and dialects of the corpus. Tables 1.3–6 provide further details.

Like the written registers, conversation is also a diverse register, but no effort was made to identify sub-registers or list all the topics of conversation. Most of the conversations in the LSWE Corpus are private (often domestic) talk. However, occasionally other kinds of talk are included, like service encounters in a store, or one side of a telephone call. Planned speech, such as lectures, speeches, and sermons, are in a separate register of 'non-conversational speech'.

Table 1.3 **Approximate numbers of speakers in the BrE and AmE conversation subcorpora by gender**

gender	BrE	AmE
female	270	292
male	225	199

Table 1.4 **Distribution of fiction texts across national varieties**

national variety	number of texts	number of words
AmE	41	1,095,200
BrE	79	3,347,100
other	19	537,700

Table 1.5 Breakdown of the British and American news subcorpora by topic

topic	BrE	AmE
arts/entertainment	418,400	325,00
business/economics	542,800	1,545,000
domestic/local/city news	1,233,900	995,000
foreign/world news	1,156,100	680,000
sports	1,218,700	260,000
all other topics (including editorials, law, social news, science/medicine/technology, etc.)	862,500	1,485,000

Table 1.6 Breakdown of the academic prose subcorpus

major categories	number of texts	number of words
academic book extracts	75	2,655,000
academic research articles	333	2,676,800

Note: Subjects included are agriculture, anthropology/archaeology, biology/ecology, chemistry/physics, computing, education, engineering/technology, geology/geography, law/history/politics, linguistics/literature, mathematics, medicine, nursing, psychology, sociology.

1.5 Overview of the book

We have organized our discussion of grammar into several major sections:

- **Chapters 2–3 Key concepts and categories in English grammar**
  These chapters present a basic introduction to English grammar, providing the foundation for our discussion of particular areas in later chapters. They introduce the basic terms for structures, rules, and classes in English grammar, illustrating them throughout with real corpus examples. It may be useful to refer back to these chapters (as well as the glossary) if you come across a puzzling term later in the grammar. Because they review all of grammar in a simplified way, these chapters have less room for the information about discourse choice found more plentifully in later chapters.

- **Chapters 4–7 A close look at the major phrase types**
  Chapters 4–7 cover the major classes of 'content words' or lexical words (noun, verbs, adjectives, and adverbs) together with the related phrases (noun phrases, verb phrases, adjective phrases, and adverb phrases):
  4 Nouns, pronouns, and the simple noun phrase
  5 Verbs
  6 Variation in the verb phrase: tense, aspect, voice, modality
  7 Adjectives and adverbs

- **Chapter 8 Clause grammar**
  This chapter introduces the structure and function of independent and dependent clauses. It is a pivotal chapter roughly half way through the book. It looks back to the phrase chapters, Chapters 4–7, showing how those phrase types are used in clauses. At the same time, it looks forward to the later clause

chapters, Chapters 9–12, which describe the use of clauses in more complex constructions.

- **Chapters 9–12 Building on the clause**
  Building on Chapter 8, these chapters explore additional clause-based or clause-derived structures. For example, complex noun phrases (Chapter 9) may not seem to involve clauses, yet in fact they do, because noun phrases can contain relative clauses and other clause-level constructions. These constructions cannot be explained properly until clauses have been covered.
  9 Complex noun phrases
  10 Verb and adjective complement clauses
  11 Adverbials
  12 Word order choices
- **Chapter 13 The grammar of conversation**
  Chapter 13 places the spotlight firmly on spoken language, and shows how the grammar of conversation is adapted to the particular demands of spontaneous spoken interaction. It also highlights some special features of conversational grammar: for example, dysfluencies, discourse markers such as *well* and *okay*, ellipsis, interjections, and taboo expressions ('swearwords').
- **Reference section**
  The book ends with a glossary of grammatical terms and an index. The reference section of the book is designed for all users, but especially to help teachers and students using it as a reference grammar.

1.6 Conventions used in the book

The list of Abbreviations, Symbols and Conventions on p. iv covers many of the conventions used in this book. But some aspects of the transcription of conversation and the use of tables and figures deserve a more detailed explanation here.

1.6.1 Transcription of speech

Spoken language must be transcribed before it can be studied. That is, the transcriber must listen to a tape recording and write down exactly what was said. For the LSWE Corpus, the transcribers produced an orthographic transcription. This transcription uses the ordinary symbols of written texts, including the conventional spellings of words (in most cases). Conventional punctuation symbols—particularly hyphens, periods, commas, and question marks—are used to reflect typical intonation associated with those symbols. Thus, a period reflects falling intonation and a question mark reflects rising intonation.

1.6.2 Spelling variations, reduced pronunciation, and limitations of the transcription

You may sometimes notice variants which are irrelevant to the study of grammar, such as variant spellings like *OK* and *okay*, or American spellings (such as *center*) in some texts and British spellings (such as *centre*) in others. These differences are not significant, and can be ignored from the grammatical point of view. More relevant linguistically are spellings of reduced pronunciations, such as *gonna*, *gotta*, and *wanna* instead of *going to*, *got to*, and *want to*, and *cos* or *cause* instead of *because*. These are semi-conventional spellings, capturing the reduced pronunciations which are very common in casual conversation. They help give an impression of what the speech was like. You will also notice 'words' like *um* and *er* signaling filled pauses (a type of dysfluency—see 13.2.5) and exclamatory words like *hm* and *ooh* which it would be rare to find in ordinary written texts. However, a strict, phonetically accurate transcription was not the goal of the corpus, nor would a phonetically detailed transcription be feasible with a corpus of this size.

Since the corpus was not transcribed phonetically, some features of speech, such as stress and intonation, are not available. In the vast majority of cases, however, the transcription provides plenty of detail for grammatical analyses.

1.6.3 Visible frequency: the use of tables and figures

We have said that frequency is important for understanding how the grammar of English is actually used in different registers, dialects, and situations. At the same time, we recognize that tables of statistics are often not useful to the average grammar student. To overcome this problem, we have used two main ways of representing frequency, both of them avoiding the use of lists of numbers:

- The first method of indicating frequency is to use ordinary words such as *often, rarely, common, uncommon*. While not precise, these terms are useful in giving a general idea of frequency differences. These generalizations are based on corpus analysis, which is often reported in *LGSWE* with tables and figures.
- The second method is to use figures (bar graphs). These figures enable you to compare frequencies in an immediately visible way, by looking at the length of the bars being compared. In these figures, the registers are always presented in the order conversation, fiction, news writing, academic writing. For an example, see Figure 2.1 on p. 23.

To make comparisons easier in the figures, frequencies are normed to the standard measure of 'occurrences per million words'. Thus, although the sizes of the registers of the corpus are somewhat different, the comparisons are based on a standard measurement of *relative* frequency. It may be difficult to envision a million words, so (although there is great diversity in print size and rate of speech) handy comparative measures are as follows:

- Books average about 350 words/page, so one million words = about 3,000 pages.
- Speakers average about 120 words/minute, so one million words = about 140 hours.

2
Words and word classes

GRAMMAR BITES in this chapter

A Introduction to words

- ➤ Lexical words, function words, and inserts
- ➤ The structure of words: morphology
- ➤ Multi-word units: idioms, collocations, and lexical bundles

B Lexical word classes

- ➤ The structure and function of lexical words: nouns, verbs, adjectives, and adverbs
- ➤ Comparing lexical word classes in use
- ➤ Borderline cases in classifying words

C Function word classes

- ➤ The structure and function of function words: determiners, pronouns, auxiliary verbs, prepositions, adverbial particles, coordinators, and subordinators
- ➤ Special classes of words

2.1 Introduction

In grammar, we first need to identify the types of grammatical units, such as words and phrases, before describing the internal structure of these units, and how they combine to form larger units. Grammatical units are meaningful elements which combine with each other in a structural pattern. Essentially, grammar is the system which organizes and controls these form-meaning relationships.

The types of grammatical units can be graded according to size of unit, as shown below:

(discourse)

1 sentence	If	I	wash	up	all	this	stuff	somebody	else	can	dry	it.
2 clauses	If	I	wash	up	all	this	stuff	somebody	else	can	dry	it.
7 phrases	If	I	wash	up	all	this	stuff	somebody	else	can	dry	it.
12 words	If	I	wash	up	all	this	stuff	somebody	else	can	dry	it.
13 morphemes	If	I	wash	up	all	this	stuff	some|body	else	can	dry	it.

(phonemes/graphemes)   (CONV)

In the simplest cases, a unit consists of one or more elements on the level below:

- A **clause** consists of one or more phrases (covered in Chapter 3, Grammar Bite B).
- A **phrase** consists of one or more words (covered in Chapter 3, Grammar Bite A).
- A **word** consists of one or more morphemes (covered in this chapter, Grammar Bites A, B and C).

Morphemes are parts of words, i.e. stems, prefixes, and suffixes. For example, *un + friend + ly* contains three morphemes: a prefix *un-*, a stem *friend* and a suffix *-ly*. The part of grammar dealing with morphemes is **morphology**. The part of grammar dealing with the other types of grammatical units shown above (i.e. words, phrases, clauses, and sentences) is known as **syntax**.

Grammatical units can be combined to form longer written texts or spoken interaction, which is known as discourse. At the other extreme, language can be analyzed in terms of its phonemes (the individual sounds which make up the language) and graphemes (the written symbols we use to communicate in language). These are the smallest units of speech and writing.

In this book, we focus mainly on the three central types of unit: word, phrase, and clause. Morphemes are also occasionally important in describing the structure of words. However, **sentences** will not be separately described because, for the purposes of this book, sentences are orthographic (or written) units, and of interest primarily in the study of the written language. (Note: in some grammars, the word 'sentence' is used in a sense close to 'clause' in this grammar.)

In general, grammatical units are described in terms of four factors: their structure, their syntactic role, their meaning, and the way they are used in discourse.

A Structure

Units can be described in terms of their internal structure: e.g words in terms of bases and affixes (2.2.4), phrases in terms of heads and modifiers (3.3), and clauses in terms of clause elements (3.5).

B Role

Units can be described in terms of their syntactic role. For example, a phrase can have the syntactic role of object in a clause:

> *In November, Susie won **those tickets**.* (CONV)

In this example, there are also other roles: *Susie* is the subject, *In November* is an adverbial.

C Meaning

Units can be described in terms of meaning. For example, adverbs (a class of words) can express information about time, place, and manner.

D Use (or discourse function)

Units can be further described in terms of how they behave in discourse. This can include their use in different registers, their frequency in those registers, and the factors which influence their use in speech or in written texts. For example, pronouns like *it* and *they* are often used to refer back to things mentioned earlier in the same discourse:

> *Isn't **Cindy** coming? Did **she** call you?* (CONV)

Such pronouns are more common in speech than in written texts.

This chapter is devoted to words, paying attention to all four factors above. We will then move on to phrases and clauses in the next chapter.

GRAMMAR BITE

A Introduction to words

2.2 What are words?

Words are generally considered to be the basic elements of language. They clearly show up in writing, and they are the items defined in dictionaries. Yet the definition of 'word' is not simple.

Words are relatively fixed in their internal form, but they are independent in their role in larger units. For example, insertions can usually be made *between* words but not *within* words:

> *There were two pedal-bins against the wall.* (FICT)
> *There were two (large new) pedal-bins (standing) against the (side) wall.*

Notice how, in the above example, it is possible to insert words between other words to form a longer sentence without losing clarity of meaning. On the other hand, we could not easily interrupt a word, by inserting another word or morpheme inside it, as in *pedal-(new)-bins.

2.2.1 Different senses of the word 'word'

The notion of 'word' is complex, and so it is useful to identify a number of slightly different senses of 'word':

- **Orthographic words:** These are the words that we are familiar with in written language, where they are separated by spaces. For example, *They wrote us a letter* contains five distinct orthographic words.
- **Grammatical words:** A word falls into one grammatical word class (or 'part of speech') or another. Thus the orthographic word *leaves* can be either of two grammatical words: a verb (the present tense *-s* form of *leave*) or a noun (the plural of *leaf*). This is the basic sense of 'word' for grammatical purposes, and the one we normally intend in this book.
- **Lexemes:** This is a set of grammatical words which share the same basic meaning, similar forms, and the same word class. For example, *leave*, *leaves*, *left*, and *leaving* are all members of the verb lexeme *leave*. This is the meaning of 'word' that is employed in dictionaries.

Each occurrence of a word in a written or spoken text is a separate **token**. For example, in the following line of conversation there are ten separate word tokens:

> *The birds and the deer and who knows what else.* (CONV)

In contrast to word tokens, word **types** are the different vocabulary items that occur in a text (such as you would look up in a wordlist). Thus, in the sentence above, there are only eight word types (*the*, *birds*, *and*, *deer*, *who*, *knows*, *what*, and *else*), since *and* and *the* occur twice. Notice the token/type distinction applies equally to orthographic words, grammatical words, and lexemes. However, our main concern will be with grammatical words, whether as types or as tokens.

In practice, it is not often necessary to distinguish between these senses, as the word 'word' is rarely ambiguous in any given context. But if there is any potential ambiguity the sense intended will be specified.

2.2.2 Three major families of words

Words can be grouped into three families, according to their main function and their grammatical behavior: **lexical words**, **function words**, and **inserts**.

A Lexical words

- Lexical words are the main carriers of information in a text or speech act.
- They can be subdivided into the following **word classes** (or **parts of speech**): nouns, lexical verbs, adjectives, and adverbs.
- Of all the word families, lexical words are the most numerous, and their number is growing all the time. In other words, they are members of **open classes**.
- They often have a complex internal structure and can be composed of several parts: e.g. *unfriendliness = un + friend + li + ness*.

- Lexical words can be heads of phrases: e.g. the noun *completion* is the head (or main word) of the noun phrase *[the **completion** of the task]*.
- They are generally the words that are stressed most in speech.
- They are generally the words that remain if a sentence is compressed in a newspaper headline: e.g. *Elderly care crisis warning.*

B Function words

- Function words can be categorized in terms of word classes such as prepositions, coordinators, auxiliary verbs, and pronouns.
- They usually indicate meaning relationships and help us to interpret units containing lexical words, by showing how the units are related to each other.
- Function words belong to **closed classes**, which have a very limited and fixed membership. For example, English has only four coordinators: *and, or, but,* and (rarely) *nor.*
- Individual function words tend to occur frequently, and in almost any type of text.

C Inserts

- Inserts are found mainly in spoken language.
- Inserts do not form an integral part of a syntactic structure, but tend to be inserted freely in a text.
- They are often marked off by a break in intonation in speech, or by a punctuation mark in writing: e.g. ***Well**, we made it.*
- They generally carry emotional and discoursal meanings, such as *oh, ah, wow,* used to express a speaker's emotional response to a situation, or *yeah, no, okay* used to signal a response to what has just been said.
- Inserts are generally simple in form, though they often have an atypical pronunciation (e.g. *hm, uh-huh, ugh, yeah*). Examples are: ***Hm hm**, very good* (CONV), ***Yeah**, I will. **Bye*** (CONV†), ***Cheers** man* (CONV).
- Because inserts are peripheral to grammar, they will not be discussed in this chapter. We describe them in more detail in 13.7.

2.2.3 Closed classes and open classes

A **closed class** contains a limited number of members, and new members cannot be easily added. For example, it is not easy to create a new coordinator or a new pronoun: those word classes have a fairly fixed set of members.

The membership of **open classes** is indefinitely large, and can be readily extended by users of the language. Lexical classes such as nouns and adjectives are open classes. For example, we can easily form new nouns with the suffix *-ee*, adjectives with *-ish*, verbs with *-ize*, and adverbs with *-wise*:

> *gossipee, franchisee, internee, retiree*
> *birdish, broadish, coquettish, heathenish*
> *bureaucratize, mythologize, periodize, solubilize*
> *crabwise, fanwise, frogwise, starwise*

In practice, the difference between open classes and closed classes is not always clear-cut. For example, new prepositions develop out of other word classes (e.g. *regarding*), and sequences of orthographic words can gradually become fixed as a single preposition (e.g. *on account of*). As a result, 'closed classes' are not completely closed, but they are extended only slowly, perhaps over centuries. In contrast, new nouns, verbs, adjectives, and adverbs—the open classes—are always being created.

2.2.4 The structure of words: morphology

Lexical words can consist of a single morpheme (a **stem**, such as *go*, *book*, *cat*), or they can have a more complex structure created by a process of **inflection**, **derivation** or **compounding**. These processes are described below.

A Inflection

Lexical words can take inflectional **suffixes** to signal meanings and roles which are important to their word class, such as 'plural' in the case of nouns, and 'past tense' in the case of verbs. The following word classes are marked by inflection:

word class	base form example	forms with inflectional suffixes
nouns	*boy*	plural (*boys*), genitive (*boy's*, *boys'*)
verbs	*live, write*	singular present tense (*lives, writes*), past tense (*lived, wrote*), past participle (*lived, written*), *ing*-participle (*living, writing*)
adjectives	*dark*	comparative (*darker*), superlative (*darkest*)
adverbs	*soon*	comparative (*sooner*), superlative (*soonest*)

Other classes of words are generally invariable. For example, prepositions (e.g. *of*, *in*, *with*), conjunctions (e.g. *if*, *while*, *unless*) and determiners (e.g. *the*, *each*, *several*) have only one form.

B Derivation

Derivation, like inflection, usually involves adding an **affix**, i.e. a morpheme attached to the beginning of a word (a **prefix**) or to the end of a word (a **suffix**). However, this process is different from inflection because inflection does not change the identity of a word (i.e. it remains the same lexeme), while derivation creates new nouns, adjectives, verbs, and adverbs. Derivation changes the meaning or word class of a word, and often both, and in effect creates a new **base** form for the word:

 prefixes: *ex* + president, *un* + kind, *re* + read, *a* + broad
 suffixes: boy + *hood*, central + *ize*, green + *ish*, exact + *ly*

Words can be built up using a number of different prefixes and suffixes, and can thus contain several morphemes:

 industri + *al*, *industri* + *al* + *ize*, *industri* + *al* + *iz* + *ation*,
 post + *industri* + *al*

Notice that inflections, such as *-ed* and *-s*, follow derivational suffixes, such as *-iz(e)*: *central* + **iz** + *ed*, *build* + **er** + *s*.

C Compounding

Inflection and derivation result in complex words, with a stem plus one or more affixes. Another form of derivation is compounding, which also leads to more complex words. Words that are compounds contain more than one stem. Examples are:

> noun + noun: *chair + man, girl + friend*
> verb + noun: *cook + book, guess + work*
> adjective + noun: *blue + bird, flat + fish*
> noun + adjective: *head + long, water + tight*

How are we to know whether two words are genuinely a compound and not simply a sequence of two words? Three tests help to show this:

- The word will be spelt as a single word, without spaces between the two forms: *goldfish*, not *gold fish*.
- It will be pronounced with the main stress on the first element: *a 'goldfish*, not *a gold 'fish*.
- It will have a meaning which cannot be determined from the individual parts: *goldfish* (= an ornamental fish of the carp family) not *gold fish* (= a fish which is made of gold).

If a word passes all three tests, there is no doubt that it is a compound. But in other cases, we may be uncertain about whether an expression is one word or two words. As an in-between category, consider words which are joined by hyphens: e.g. *gold-tipped, care-free*. This shows that the combination overall is felt to be a single word, and yet the two parts are felt to be somewhat separate. There are also words like *ice cream*, which are usually spelled as two separate orthographic words, but where the pronunciation and meaning tests suggest a single word. Like many categories in grammar, compounds are not a hard-and-fast category.

2.2.5 Multi-word units, collocations, and lexical bundles

Apart from compounds, there are sequences of words that behave as a combination:

- A **multi-word unit** is a sequence of orthographic words which functions like a single grammatical unit: e.g. the preposition *on top of* or the adverb *of course*.
- An **idiom**, like many compounds, is a multi-word unit with a meaning that cannot be predicted from the meanings of its constituent words. A typical example is a verb expression like *fall in love* or *make up (one's) mind*. However, the boundary between idioms and freely chosen combinations is not always clear.
- A **collocation** is the relationship between two or more independent words which commonly appear together (or co-occur). The adjectives *broad* and *wide*, for example, are similar in meaning, but occur in very different collocations: e.g. *broad accent, broad agreement, broad daylight, broad grin, broad shoulders*, etc.; *wide appeal, wide area, wide experience, wide interests, wide margin*, etc.

Later in this book we use a further term, **lexical bundle**, for a sequence of words which co-occur very frequently, especially when the sequence consists of more than two words. For example, bundles like *I don't think ...* and *Would you mind ...* commonly recur in conversation (see 13.6).

2.2.6 Use of lexical words, function words, and inserts

Returning to the three word families presented in 2.2.2, we will now present two passages for illustration. The three word families are distinguished as follows: capitals = lexical words; ordinary italics = function words; bold = inserts.

> A: *is that the* TIME?
> B: **Yeah**, *it's twenty* MINUTES *to four.*
> A: **Oh** *my* CLOCK IS SLOW, **yeah**.
> B: *Do you* WANT *us to* JUST GO *out* THERE *and* COME *back and* PICK *you* GUYS *up*?
> A: **Uh huh**.
> C: **Yeah**.
> A: *You can* GO *if you* WANT *to, I'll, I* THINK *I'll* <...>
> D: *He* REALLY *doesn't* TRUST *me, does he?*
> C: *That's* RIGHT, HOW *'bout I* PIN *you?*
> D: **Okay**. **Oh**, *let me* TELL *you something.*
> B: *Do you, do you* WANT *to* GO *by yourself?*
> D: **No, no, no**. *You'll* FEEL BETTER *and we'll be* FOLLOWING *you.*
> A: *Will you* FEEL BETTER?
> D: *It doesn't.*
> C: *I* NEED *three* SAFETY PINS, *you* HAD *one in your* POCKET.
> B: **Uh huh**. (CONV)

> RADIOACTIVE LEAK CONFIRMED *at* SELLAFIELD
>
> WORK *on the* DISMANTLING *of a* NUCLEAR REPROCESSING PLANT *at* SELLAFIELD CAUSED *a* LEAK *of* RADIOACTIVITY YESTERDAY. BRITISH NUCLEAR FUELS LTD SAID *the* RADIOACTIVITY REACHED *the* AIR *through a* CHIMNEY STACK *which was* STILL *in* USE. *But* SPOKESMAN BOB PHILLIPS SAID *it was not an* INCIDENT *which* REQUIRED REPORTING *to the* GOVERNMENT. *He* DISMISSED PROTESTS *from* FRIENDS *of the* EARTH *as* 'SCAREMONGERING'. HOWEVER, DR PATRICK GREEN, FRIENDS *of the* EARTH RADIATION CAMPAIGNER, SAID: 'BNF HAS *a* SCANDALOUS TRACK RECORD *of* PLAYING *down* INCIDENTS *at first, and* ONLY ADMITTING *their* SERIOUSNESS LATER.' *Three* MONTHS AGO BNF CONFIRMED *that a* LEAK *of* RADIOACTIVE PLUTONIUM SOLUTION *had been* RECLASSIFIED *as* 'a SERIOUS INCIDENT'. (NEWS)

The conversation and news sample differ strikingly in their use of the three word categories. These examples show how lexical words are used much more frequently in news writing. News writers pack their prose with lexical words to convey information. In contrast, conversation has a higher frequency of function words. Conversation also has quite a large number of inserts, while news has very few. Academic writing and fiction fall between the two extremes of news and conversation in terms of the density of lexical words.

Major points of **GRAMMAR BITE A**: Introduction to words

➤ There are three major families of words: lexical words, function words, and inserts.

➤ These families are broken down into word classes, such as nouns, verbs, adjectives, adverbs, and prepositions.

➤ Words belong to closed classes or open classes.

➤ The different word classes have different morphology—that is, different rules for how to form them.

➤ Different registers use the various classes of words to different extents.

   ➤ Newspaper writing has the highest density of lexical words, while conversation has the lowest.

   ➤ Conversation has more use of inserts than the other registers.

GRAMMAR BITE

B Lexical word classes

2.3 Survey of lexical words

As already noted, there are four main classes of lexical words: **nouns, lexical verbs, adjectives**, and **adverbs**. To decide what class a word belongs to, it is useful to apply tests of three kinds:

* **Morphological**: what forms does a word have (e.g in terms of stems and affixes)?
* **Syntactic**: what syntactic roles does a word play in phrases or other higher units?
* **Semantic**: what type(s) of meaning does a word convey?

2.3.1 Nouns

Words such as *book, girl, gold, information* are **common nouns**. Words such as *Sarah, Oslo*, and *Microsoft* (names) are **proper nouns**. Nouns have the following characteristics:

A Morphological

Nouns have inflectional suffixes for plural **number**, and for **genitive** case: *one book → two books; Sarah's book*. Many nouns, however, are **uncountable**, and cannot have a plural form (e.g. *gold, information*). Nouns quite often contain more than one morpheme:

> compound nouns: *bomb + shell, bridge + head, clothes + line*
>
> nouns with derivational suffixes: *sing + er, bright + ness, friend + ship*

B Syntactic

Nouns can occur as the **head** of a **noun phrase**: *[a new **book** about the cold war]*, *[the ugliest **person** you've ever seen]*. As these examples show, common nouns such as *book* and *person* can be modified by many kinds of words both before and after them. Proper nouns like *Sarah*, on the other hand, rarely have any modifiers.

C Semantic

Nouns commonly refer to concrete, physical entities (people, objects, substances): e.g. *book, friend, iron*. They can also denote abstract entities, such as qualities and states: e.g. *freedom, wish, friendship*.

2.3.2 Lexical verbs

Words such as *admit, build, choose, write* are **lexical verbs**. They are distinct from **auxiliary verbs** like *can* and *will*, which we treat as function words. The **primary verbs** *be, have*, and *do* (the most common verbs in English) occur as both lexical verbs and auxiliaries. Lexical verbs are identified as follows:

A Morphological

Lexical verbs have different forms signaling **tense** (present and past), **aspect** (perfect, progressive), and **voice** (active and passive). Note the five forms of the verb lexeme *write* in these examples:

example	form
*They **write** about their family.* (CONV†)	base
*He **writes** page after page about tiny details.* (FICT)	third person present (-s form)
*They **wrote** about Venus being a jungle paradise.* (FICT)	past tense
*He has **written** to an old journalist friend.* (FICT†)	ed-participle (or past participle)
*I wonder if you are **writing** any more songs?* (FICT)	ing-participle (or present participle)

The verb forms and their functions are discussed further in 5.2.

Verb lexemes quite often have a complex form with more than one morpheme. The following are examples of multi-word verbs and derived verbs: *bring **up**, rely **on**, look **forward to**, hyphenate, itemize, soften*.

B Syntactic

Lexical verbs most frequently occur on their own, as a single-word verb phrase acting as the central part of the clause:

He *[writes]* page after page about tiny details. (FICT)

They also occur in the final or **main verb** position of **verb phrases**: *[has **written**] a letter; [will be **writing**] tomorrow*. Verb phrases are explained in 3.3.2.

C Semantic

Lexical verbs denote actions, processes, and states of affairs that happen or exist in time. They also define the role of human and non-human participants in such actions, processes, or states:

> *[You] [ate] [Chinese food].* (CONV)

In this example, *ate* expresses the action performed by *you* on the *Chinese food*. The characteristics of verbs are discussed in detail in Chapters 5 and 6.

2.3.3 Adjectives

Words such as *dark, heavy, eager,* and *guilty* are adjectives. Adjectives are identified as follows:

A Morphological

Many adjectives can take the inflectional suffixes *-er* (comparative) and *-est* (superlative): *dark → darker → darkest.* Adjectives can be complex in morphology:

> derived adjectives (with suffixes in bold): *accept**able**, forget**ful**, influ**ential***
> compound adjectives: *color-blind, home-made, ice-cold.*

B Syntactic

Adjectives can occur as the head of an **adjective phrase**: *[very **dark**], [**eager** to help], [**guilty** of a serious crime].* Adjectives and adjective phrases are most commonly used as **modifiers** preceding the head of a noun phrase, or as **predicatives** following the verb in clauses:

> modifier: *Tomorrow could be [a **sunny** day].* (CONV†)
> predicative: *It's **nice** and **warm** in here. It's **sunny**.* (CONV)

C Semantic

Adjectives describe the qualities of people, things, and abstractions: *a **heavy** box, he is **guilty**, the situation is **serious**.* Many adjectives are **gradable**. That is, they can be compared and modified for the **degree** or level of the quality: *heavier, very heavy, extremely serious.* Adjectives are discussed in detail in Chapter 7.

2.3.4 Adverbs

Words such as *now, there, usually,* and *finally* are adverbs. Adverbs are a varied word class, with the following characteristics:

A Morphological

Many adverbs are formed from adjectives by adding the suffix *-ly: clearly, eagerly.* Others have no such ending: *however, just.* A few adverbs allow comparative and superlative forms like those for adjectives: *soon → sooner → soonest; fast → faster → fastest.*

B Syntactic

Adverbs occur as head of **adverb phrases**: *[very **noisily**]*, *[more **slowly** than I had expected]*. Adverbs, with or without their own modifiers, are often used as **modifiers** of an adjective or another adverb: ***really** old*, ***very** soon*. Otherwise, they can act as **adverbials** in the clause: *I'll see you **again soon**.* See 3.5.5 on adverbials.

C Semantic

As modifiers, adverbs most often express the **degree** of a following adjective or adverb: ***totally** wrong*; ***right** now*. As elements of clauses (adverbials), adverbs and adverb phrases have a wide range of meanings:

- They can modify an action, process, or state, by expressing such notions as time, place, and manner:

    *So I learned German quite **quickly**.* (CONV†)

    *She was **here earlier today**.* (CONV†)

- They can convey the speaker's or writer's attitude towards the information in the rest of the clause:

    ***Surely** that child's not mine?* (CONV)

- They can express a connection with what was said earlier:

    *It must be beautiful, **though**.* (CONV)

For a detailed account of adverbs, see Chapters 7 and 11.

2.3.5 Comparing lexical word classes in use

As Figure 2.1 shows, there are interesting similarities and contrasts in the use of the lexical word classes across the registers. Registers can be described in terms of their style by comparing their use of the lexical classes.

- Nouns and verbs are clearly the most common types of words overall.

- Conversation has a high density of verbs, unlike informative writing such as news and academic prose, which has a high density of nouns.

- Adjectives are linked to nouns, because they most frequently modify nouns. So informative writing, which has the highest density of nouns, also has the highest density of adjectives.

- Adverbs, on the other hand, are linked to verbs. They typically describe circumstances relating to actions, processes, and states that are denoted by verbs. So conversation and fiction writing, which have the highest density of verbs, also have the highest density of adverbs.

Figure 2.1

Distribution of lexical word classes across registers

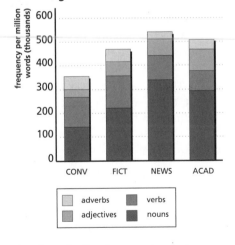

2.3.6 Borderline cases in classifying words

The categories people operate with in the real world are not clear-cut. The category of 'furniture', for example, includes clear cases, like tables and chairs, but also less clear or borderline cases, such as television sets, cookers, and electric heaters.

The same is true of word classes in grammar. For example, nouns can be more or less 'nouny'. A typical noun (e.g. *boy, car*) has singular, plural, and genitive forms (e.g. *boy, boys, boy's*). It can be preceded by *a* or *the*, and it refers to a class of people, things, or other entities. Yet in the class of nouns we find many words which have only some of these 'nouny' features: e.g. *research*, which has no plural or genitive, cannot be preceded by *a*, and refers to something abstract and intangible

As some words may be more 'borderline' than others within a word class, it is not surprising that the boundaries between two word classes may also be unclear.

As an example of borderline cases in lexical word classes, take the classification of words ending with *-ing*. Almost all of these words have a verb base, so it is easy to assume that all words ending in *-ing* are verbs. However, this conclusion is not correct. In fact, these words can belong to any of three different classes: verb (sometimes called the *ing*-participle), noun, or adjective (sometimes called participial adjective). Normally the following tests can be applied to determine the word class:

- Verbs ending in *-ing* can act as the main verb of a verb phrase, and may be followed by a noun or an adjective (underlined here): e.g. *is **eating** <u>lunch</u>; **becoming** <u>misty</u> overnight.*
- Nouns ending in *-ing* can sometimes have a plural form (e.g. *paintings*), and can usually be a head noun after *a, the,* or some other determiner: e.g. *[the **banning** of some chemicals], [her **dancing**].*
- Adjectives ending in *-ing* can appear before a noun, and can also occur after verbs such as *be* and *become*: e.g. *the **travelling** public; it was (very) **confusing**.* They are very often gradable, and can be preceded by degree adverbs such as *very, so,* and *too*: ***very** forgiving, **so** interesting, **too** boring.*

But these criteria cannot always be clearly applied. Typical borderline cases include the following:

A Nouns and verbs

The biggest problem here is the so-called **naked *ing*-form** occurring after a main verb, as in

> *The matter needed **checking**.* (NEWS†)

In this example the final word *checking* could be a verb. If one added an adverb, it would be a verb:

> *The matter needed checking **carefully**.*

In other similar cases, this form could be functioning as a noun. If it were preceded by a modifying adjective, it would clearly be a noun:

> *The matter needed **careful** checking.*

Since neither of these clues is present in the original example, the word class of *checking* is left unclear.

B Nouns and adjectives

The biggest problem here is where the *ing*-form modifies a following noun. Compare:

noun + noun	adjective + noun
living standards	*living* creatures
dancing classes	the *dancing* children
working conditions	a *working* mother

As explained in 4.11.3, both nouns and adjectives can modify a noun, so the only way to tell the difference here is to apply a 'paraphrase test': i.e. to try to express the same idea in different ways.

If a paraphrase can be found where the *ing*-form clearly has a noun-like character, the construction consists of noun + noun. For example, if a paraphrase which uses a prepositional phrase is appropriate, the construction must consist of an *ing*-noun + noun: *living standards* = *standards of living*; *dancing classes* = *classes for dancing*. In contrast, a paraphrase with a relative clause (using *that*, *which*, or *who*) shows that the construction consists of *ing*-adjective + noun: *living creatures* = *creatures which are (still) living*; *dancing children* = *children who are dancing*.

C Verbs and adjectives

Borderline cases between these categories occur where the *ing*-form follows the verb *be* without other modifiers. Consider, for example:

> *It was **embarrassing**.* (CONV)

If the *ing*-word can take an object (i.e. a following noun phrase), then it is a verb:

> *It was embarrassing (**me**).*

In contrast, if the *ing*-word is gradable and can be modified by *very*, it is an adjective:

> *It was (**very**) embarrassing.*

In some cases (like this one with *embarrassing*), both tests apply, and there is no single correct analysis. But the second analysis (adjective) is more likely.

Word classes, like virtually all grammatical categories, have uncertain boundaries; but this does not undermine their value as categories. Rather, grammar needs flexibility in its categories to enable people to communicate flexibly. In the large majority of actual instances, however, there is little ambiguity.

Review

Major points of GRAMMAR BITE B: Lexical word classes

➤ There are four lexical word classes: nouns, lexical verbs, adjectives, and adverbs.

➤ Each class can be distinguished by its morphological, syntactic, and semantic characteristics.

➤ Nouns and adjectives are more frequent in the expository or 'information-giving' registers: news and academic writing.

➤ Verbs and adverbs are more frequent in the other registers: conversation and fiction writing.

➤ The classification of lexical words is not always clear-cut, and some words have borderline status between two classes.

GRAMMAR BITE

C Function word classes

2.4 Survey of function words

Function words can also be categorized in different classes: **determiners, pronouns, auxiliary verbs, prepositions, adverbial particles, coordinators,** and **subordinators.** To distinguish these classes briefly, we will look at their semantic function and syntactic role, list their main forms, and consider their subclasses.

2.4.1 Determiners

Determiners normally precede nouns, and are used to help clarify the meaning of the noun. The most important are the following:

- The **definite article** *the* indicates that the **referent** (i.e. whatever is referred to) is assumed to be known by the speaker and the person being spoken to (or addressee).
- The **indefinite article** *a* or *an* makes it clear that the referent is one member of a class (*a book*).
- **Demonstrative determiners** indicate that the referents are 'near to' or 'away from' the speaker's immediate context (*this book, that book*, etc.).
- **Possessive determiners** tell us who or what the noun belongs to (*my book, your book, her book*, etc.).
- **Quantifiers** specify how many or how much of the noun there is (*every book, some books*, etc.).

There are also determiner-like uses of *wh***-words** and **numerals** (see 2.5).

2.4.2 Pronouns

Pronouns fill the position of a noun or a whole noun phrase. The reference of a pronoun is usually made clear by its context. There are eight major classes of pronoun:

- **Personal pronouns** refer to the speaker, the addressee(s), and other entities:

   *I won't tell **you** how **it** ended.* (CONV)

   Personal pronouns are used far more frequently than the other classes of pronouns.
- **Demonstrative pronouns** refer to entities which are 'near to' v. 'away from' the speaker's context, like demonstrative determiners (2.4.1):

> *This* is Bay City. (CONV)
>
> I like *those*. (CONV)

- **Reflexive pronouns** refer back to a previous noun phrase, usually the subject of the clause:

  > I taught *myself*. (CONV)
  >
  > She never introduced *herself*? (CONV)

- **Reciprocal pronouns**, like reflexive pronouns, refer to a previous noun phrase, but indicate that there is a mutual relationship:

  > Yeah they know *each other* pretty well. (CONV)

- **Possessive pronouns** (such as *mine, yours, his*) are closely related to possessive determiners (*my, your, his*, etc.), and usually imply a missing noun head:

  > Is this *yours*, or *mine?* (CONV)
  >
  > *Ours* is better than *theirs*. (CONV†)

  These possessive pronouns include the meaning of a head noun. For example, *yours* might refer to *your book* or *your pen*.

- **Indefinite pronouns** have a broad, indefinite meaning. Some of them are compound words consisting of quantifier + general noun (*everything, nobody, someone*, etc.). Others consist of a quantifier alone (*all, some, many*, etc.):

  > *Somebody* tricked me. (CONV)
  >
  > That's *all* I know. (CONV)

- **Relative pronouns** (*who, whom, which, that*) introduce a **relative clause** (see 9.7–8):

  > I had more friends *that* were boys. (CONV)
  >
  > He's the guy *who* told me about this. (CONV)

- **Interrogative pronouns** ask questions about unknown entities:

  > *What* did he say? (CONV)
  >
  > I just wonder *who* it was. (CONV)

Most relative and interrogative pronouns (e.g. *who, which, what*) belong to the class of *wh*-words (see 2.5.1).

2.4.3 Auxiliary verbs

There are two kinds of auxiliary verbs: **primary auxiliaries** and **modal auxiliaries**. Both are 'auxiliary verbs' in the sense that they are added to a main verb to help build verb phrases.

Auxiliary verbs precede the main or lexical verb in a verb phrase: *will arrive; has arrived; is arriving; may be arriving*, etc. (See 8.7 and 13.5.2 for cases where an auxiliary occurs without a main verb.) Some common auxiliaries have contracted forms—*'s, 're, 've, 'd, 'll*—used particularly in speech.

A Primary auxiliaries

There are three primary auxiliaries: *be, have*, and *do*. They have inflections like lexical verbs, but are normally unstressed. The same verbs *be, have*, and *do* can also act as main verbs.

base	present tense	past tense	*ing*-participle	*ed*-participle
be	*is, am, are*	*was, were*	*being*	*been*
have	*has, have*	*had*	*having*	*had*
do	*does, do*	*did*	*doing*	*done*

In various ways, the primary auxiliaries show how the main verb is to be understood (examples below are from conversation):

- The auxiliary *have* is used to form the **perfect aspect**: *I've done that once* (see 6.3, 6.4).
- The auxiliary *be* is used for the **progressive aspect** or 'continuous' aspect: *She **was** thinking about me* (see 6.3, 6.5).
- The auxiliary *be* is also used for the **passive voice**: *It **was** sent over there* (see 6.6–8).
- The auxiliary *do* is used in negative statements and in questions; this is known as **do** insertion: ***Did** he sell it? This **doesn't** make sense* (see 8.7).

B Modal auxiliaries

There are nine modal auxiliary verbs. As their name suggests, they are largely concerned with expressing 'modality', such as possibility, necessity, prediction, and volition. The modals are:

> *will   can   shall   may   must   would   could   should   might*

Each modal in the lower row is historically the past tense of the modal directly above it. For example, *would* was historically the past tense of *will*. (*Must* has no matching historical past tense.) Nowadays, though, the relationship of *will* to *would*, or *can* to *could*, etc. has less to do with tense than with modal meaning (see 6.9–10).

In practice the modals can be regarded as invariable function words, with no inflections such as *-ing* and *-ed*. The modals *will* and *would* have contracted forms (*'ll* and *'d*), and most modals have a contracted negative form ending in *n't*, such as *wouldn't*. Modals occur as the first verb in a clause, and are followed by the base form of another verb, usually the main verb (underlined below):

> *I **can** live here quietly.* (FICT†).

> *They **would** have a different view.* (ACAD†)

The modal auxiliaries, and marginal modal forms such as *be going to* (**semi-modals**), are covered in detail in 6.9–13.

2.4.4 Prepositions

Prepositions are linking words that introduce prepositional phrases. The **prepositional complement** following a preposition is generally a noun phrase, so prepositions can also be seen as linking words that connect other structures with noun phrases. For example:

> *Eleven fifty **with** the tip* (CONV)   *And she's **in** a new situation.* (CONV)

> *that picture **of** mother* (CONV)   *She's still **on** the phone.* (CONV)

Most prepositions are short, invariable forms: e.g. *about, after, around, as, at, by, down, for, from, into, like, of, off, on, round, since, than, to, towards, with, without.*

In the following examples, the preposition is in bold, and the prepositional phrase it introduces is enclosed in []. The noun phrase functioning as prepositional complement is underlined:

> He'll go [**with** <u>one of the kids</u>]. (CONV†)
>
> Late one morning [**in** <u>June</u>], [**in** <u>the thirty-first year of his life</u>], a message was brought [**to** <u>Michael K</u>] as he raked leaves [**in** <u>De Waal Park</u>]. (FICT)

Prepositions can be linked to a preceding verb, such as *rely on* and *confide in*.

> You can't, you can't **rely on** any of that information. (CONV)
>
> She **confided in** him above all others. (FICT)

These multi-word units are referred to as **prepositional verbs** (see 5.10–11).

Complex prepositions

Another set of prepositions consists of multi-word units known as **complex prepositions**, which have a meaning that cannot be derived from the meaning of the parts. Two-word complex prepositions normally end with a simple preposition:

ending in	examples
as	such as
for	as for, except for
from	apart from
of	because of, instead of, out of, regardless of
to	according to, due to, owing to

Three-word prepositions usually have the structure simple preposition + noun + simple preposition:

ending in	examples
of	by means of, in spite of, on account of, on top of
to	in addition to, with regard to
as	as far as, as well as

As with many grammatical categories, there are borderline cases with complex prepositions. It is not always clear whether a multi-word combination is a complex preposition—that is, a fixed expression with a special meaning—or a free combination of preposition (+ article) + noun + preposition. *At the expense of* is an example of an in-between case.

2.4.5 Adverbial particles

Adverbial particles are a small group of words with a core meaning of motion. The most important are: *about, across, along, around, aside*, away*, back*, by, down, forth*, home*, in, off, on, out, over, past, round, through, under, up.* All of these forms except those marked * can also be prepositions.

Adverbial particles are closely linked to verbs. They generally follow verbs, and are closely bound to them in meaning: *go away, come back, put* (something) *on,* etc. They are used to build **phrasal verbs**, such as the following:.

> **Come on**, tell me about Nick. (CONV)
>
> I just **broke down** in tears when I saw the letter. (CONV)

*Margotte rarely **turned on** the television set.* (FICT)

They are also used to build **extended prepositional phrases**, where a particle precedes the preposition. For example:

*We were going **back to the hotel** when it happened.* (NEWS)

Adverbial particles have been called 'prepositional adverbs', because of their resemblance to both prepositions (in form) and adverbs (in syntactic role). In this book, however, they are treated as a distinct word class. Phrasal verbs are considered again in 5.9, and prepositional phrases in 3.3.5.

2.4.6 Coordinators

There are two types of words traditionally called **conjunctions** in English: **coordinators** (also called coordinating conjunctions), and **subordinators** (or subordinating conjunctions), which are dealt with next, in 2.4.7.

Coordinators are used to indicate a relationship between two units such as phrases or clauses. Coordinators link elements which have the same syntactic role, and are at the same level of the syntactic hierarchy (see 2.1). Thus, in any structure [X + coordinator + Y], X and Y are equivalent. (Compare this to subordinators in the next section, which indicate that the following structure is subordinate.) The main coordinators are *and*, *but*, and *or*. In the following examples, the coordinated elements are marked by []:

*[Mother] **and** [I] saw it.* (CONV)

*[I don't want to speak too soon], **but** [I think I have been fairly consistent this season].* (NEWS)

*Is this necessarily [good] **or** [bad]?* (ACAD)

Or has a rather infrequently used negative counterpart, *nor*, which is used after negative clauses:

*[The donkeys did not come back], **nor** [did the eleven men], **nor** [did the helicopter].* (FICT)

As this example shows, coordinators can be used to connect more than two elements.

Correlative coordinators

Each simple coordinator can be combined with another word, to make a **correlative coordinator**:

both [X] **and** [Y]	**either** [X] **or** [Y]
not (only) [X] **but (also)** [Y]	**neither** [X] **nor** [Y]

For example:

*The couple were **both** [shoved] **and** [jostled].* (CONV)

*It's yes or no, isn't it? **Either** [you agree with it] **or** [you don't agree with it].* (NEWS)

*We used **not only** [the colors reflected from mineral surfaces] **but also** [the colors transmitted through minerals in microscopic thin sections].* (ACAD†)

***Neither** [Zack] **nor** [Jane] had slept that night, but they looked happy anyway.* (FICT†)

Coordination is discussed in more detail in 8.4.

2.4.7 Subordinators

Subordinators (also called subordinating conjunctions) are linking words that introduce clauses known as **dependent clauses**—clauses which cannot stand alone without another clause, called the **main clause**:

> You can hold her [*if* you want]. (CONV)

The subordinator shows the connection of meaning between the main clause and the subordinate clause. In the above example, the subordinator *if* shows a relation of 'condition'.

In the case of coordination, explained in the last section, the two elements have the same status. However, in the case of subordination, the dependent clause starting with the subordinator is embedded (or included) in the main clause. This can be shown by nested brackets *[[]]*:

> [[*As* they watched,] a flash of fire appeared.] (FICT)
>
> [A flash of fire appeared [*as* they watched.]]

Notice the dependent clause can come at the front or at the end of the main clause.

Subordinators fall into three major subclasses:

- The great majority of subordinators introduce **adverbial clauses**, adding details of time, place, reason, etc. to the main clause: *after, as, because, if, since, although, while,* etc. (see 8.15.2, 11.9–12).
- Three subordinators introduce **degree clauses**: *as, than, that* (see 7.14, 8.15.4).
- Three subordinators introduce **complement clauses** (or **nominal clauses**): *if, that, whether* (see 8.15.1, 10.1–11).

The subordinators in the first two subclasses indicate meaning relationships such as time, reason, condition, and comparison. The subordinators in the third subclass are called **complementizers** because they introduce clauses following verbs, adjectives or nouns, complementing or completing the meaning of these key words in the main clause:

> I'm glad [*that* I've found you again]. (FICT)
>
> Sometimes he did not know [*whether* he was awake or asleep]. (FICT)

Dependent clauses can also be introduced by other forms, like *wh*-words and the relative pronoun *that*. These are not subordinators.

Complex subordinators

Like prepositions, subordinators may consist of more than one word. Most of these **complex subordinators** end with *as* or *that* (often the *that* is optional, as shown by parentheses ( ) below):

ending in	examples
as	*as long as, as soon as*
that	*given (that), on condition (that), provided (that), except (that), in that, in order that, so (that), such (that)*
others	*as if, as though, even if, even though*

For examples, see 11.9–12.

2.4.8 Comparing function word classes in use

Function word classes, like lexical word classes, vary greatly in their frequency in different types of English. Figures 2.2 and 2.3 show the way frequency varies between two very different registers of English, conversation and academic prose. Notice especially the striking differences in frequency of pronouns (high in conversation) and determiners (high in academic prose). Another difference is in the frequency of adverbial particles: this is the least frequent function word class in both registers, but it is much rarer in academic prose than in conversation.

Figure 2.2
Frequency of function word classes in conversation

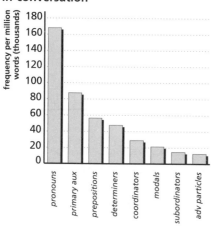

Figure 2.3
Frequency of function word classes in academic prose

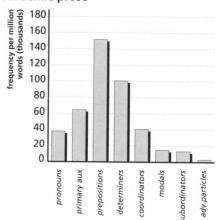

2.5 Special classes of words

A few classes of function words have special qualities: ***wh*-words**, **existential *there***, the **negator *not***, the **infinitive marker *to***, and **numerals**.

2.5.1 *Wh*-words

Wh-words, like subordinators, introduce clauses. However, *wh*-words do not form an independent word class. Instead, they are members of word classes already mentioned, especially determiners, pronouns, and adverbs. As their name suggests, *wh*-words begin with *wh*, with the single exception of *how*. They are used in two main ways: at the beginning of an **interrogative clause**, and at the beginning of a **relative clause**. Two further uses are at the beginning of a complement clause and at the beginning of an adverbial clause.

A **Introducing an interrogative clause**

What do they want? (FICT)   ***Which*** one do you mean? (FICT)
When are you leaving? (FICT)   ***Why*** should I care? (CONV†)

Interrogative *wh*-words can be:

- interrogative pronouns: *who, whom, what, which*
- interrogative determiners: *what, which, whose*
- interrogative adverbs: *when, where, how, why*

B Introducing a relative clause (relativizers)

    1 *the kind of person [**who** needs emotional space]* (NEWS†)
    2 *Graham Poole, [**whose** grandfather started the place in 1895]* (NEWS†)
    3 *a small place [**where** everyone knows everyone else]* (NEWS†)

Relativizers can be:

- relative pronouns: *who, whom, which, that*
- relative determiners: *which, whose*
- relative adverbs: *where, when, why*

Relative pronouns stand for a noun phrase, as in **1** above, where *who* refers back to *the kind of person*. Relative determiners occur before the noun, as in **2** above (***whose*** grandfather) or in the phrase *by **which** time*. Relative adverbs are used to refer to times (*when*), reasons (*why*), or places (*where*), as in **3** above (*where* refers back to *a small place*).

C Introducing a complement clause (complementizers)

    *I don't know [**what** I would have done without her].* (NEWS)
    *I give them [**whatever** I have in my pocket].* (NEWS)
    *Vada wonders [**where** she stands in her father's affections].* (NEWS)

D Adverbial clause links

    1 *They could not improve upon that, [**whatever** they might say].* (FICT)
    2 *[**However** they vary], each formation comprises a distinctive set of rock layers.* (ACAD)

In adverbial clauses as in **1** and **2**, *wh*-words combined with *-ever* express the meaning 'it doesn't matter what/when/where/. . .'. (Compare subordinators like *if* and *when* in 2.4.7 above.)

    Finally, the word *whether* is versatile: it is used as a subordinator (see 2.4.7) but it can also be classed as a *wh*-word.

2.5.2 Single-word classes

The three words considered in this group are special in that they are each unique, grammatically, and do not fit into any other class. That is, they form single-word classes.

A Existential *there*

Existential *there* is often called an anticipatory subject. No other word in English behaves in the same way, heading a clause expressing existence:

    There's a mark on this chair. (CONV)
    There were four bowls of soup. (FICT)

There are no trains on Sundays. (NEWS)

Existential *there* should not be confused with the place adverb *there*. (See the discussion of existential *there* in 12.5–10.)

B The negator *not*

The negator *not* is in some ways like an adverb, but in other respects it is unique. The main use of *not* (and its reduced form *n't*) is to make a clause negative.

*You can do this but [you **can't** do that].* (CONV) <[] marks the clause>

(Note the spelling of *can't = can + n't*.) Apart from negating whole clauses, *not* has various other negative uses (as in *not all, not many, not very,* etc.). (See 8.8.)

C The infinitive marker *to*

The infinitive marker *to* is another unique word (not to be confused with the common preposition *to*). Its chief use is as a complementizer preceding the infinitive (base) form of verbs.

*What do you want **to** drink?* (CONV)

*I'm just happy **to** be here right now.* (CONV)

In addition, infinitive *to* occurs as part of two complex subordinators expressing purpose: *in order to* and *so as to*:

*You don't have to live under the same laws as a foreigner **in order to** trade with him.* (NEWS)

*Each has the job of writing his chapter **so as to** make the novel being constructed the best it can be.* (ACAD)

2.5.3 Numerals

Numerals form a rather self-contained area of English grammar. As a word class, numerals consist of a small set of simple forms (*one, two, five,* etc.), and a large set of more complex forms which can be built up from the simple forms (e.g. *three million eight hundred and fifty-five thousand four hundred and eighteen, 3,855,418*).

They are most commonly used in the role of determiners or heads in noun phrases. There are two parallel sets of numerals, **cardinals** and **ordinals.**

A Cardinals

Cardinal numerals answer the question 'How many?' and are most commonly used like determiners, with a following noun:

Four people were arrested. (NEWS)

However, cardinals also occur as heads of noun phrases:

Four of the yen traders have pleaded guilty. (NEWS†)

In their nounlike use, cardinals can be made plural by adding *-(e)s*:

*Cops in **twos** and **threes** huddle and smile at me with benevolence.* (FICT)

*Damage is estimated at **hundreds** of **millions** of pounds.* (NEWS).

B Ordinals

Ordinal numerals answer the question 'Which?' and serve to place entities in order or in a series: *first*, *second*, *third*, etc. Similar to cardinals, they can be used either like determiners, before a noun:

> *I was doing my **third** week as a young crime reporter and had just about finished my **second** and last story of the day when the phone rang.* (FICT)

or like nouns, as head of a noun phrase:

> *Three men will appear before Belfast magistrates today on charges of intimidation. A **fourth** will be charged with having information likely to be of use to terrorists. The **fifth**, a woman, was remanded on the same charge yesterday.* (NEWS)

Ordinals are also used to form fractions. Treated as regular nouns, ordinals such as *fifth*, *tenth*, and *hundredth* can take a plural *-s* ending:

> *Probably two **thirds** of the people who live here now are not natives.* (CONV†)

> *The pupil can identify the place value of a column or a digit for values of **tenths**, **hundredths** and **thousandths**.* (ACAD†)

2.6 Word-class ambiguities

Before we leave word classes, it is important to notice that English has a large number of word forms which occur in more than one word class. In other words, the same spelling and pronunciation applies to two or more different grammatical words. Table 2.1 illustrates a range of such examples.

Some word-class ambiguities are systematic. For example, the class of quantifiers (e.g. *all*, *some*, *any*, *much*) can be seen as a 'superclass' of words which can function with similar meanings as determiners, pronouns or adverbs:

- as determiners:

> *He kept whistling at **all** the girls.* (CONV†)

> *I have **a little** money in my room.* (CONV) <note: *a little* is considered as a single determiner>

- as pronouns:

> *Is that **all** I've got dad?* (CONV)

> *'Water?' – 'Just **a little**, and a lot of ice'.* (FICT)

- as adverbs:

> *Don't get **all** mucky.* (CONV)

> *It was **a little** hard for him to understand.* (FICT†)

As these examples show, it is impossible to identify the word class of many English words without seeing them in context.

Table 2.1 **Words in more than one class**

form	noun	verb	adj	adv	prep	sub	examples
before				●			She had never asked him that **before**.
					●		He was there **before** her.
						●	They'd started leaving **before** I arrived.
early			●				Steele kicked an **early** penalty goal.
				●			He has also kicked a penalty goal **early** in the match.
fight	●						There was a hell of a **fight**.
		●					They're too big to **fight**.
narrow		●					He plans to **narrow** his focus to certain markets.
			●				Current review programs are too **narrow**.
as					●		This was the beginning of his life **as** a cultivator.
						●	**As** they watched, a flash of fire appeared.
outside			●				You can open the **outside** window.
				●			He's gone **outside**.
					●		It's sitting **outside** your house.

Review

Major points of Grammar Bite C: Function word classes

➤ There are seven classes of function words: determiners, pronouns, auxiliary verbs, prepositions, adverbial particles, coordinators, and subordinators.

➤ There are a few other word types which are not easily classified or which cut across other categories: *wh*-words, existential *there*, the negator *not*, the infinitive marker *to*, and numerals.

➤ English has a large number of words which occur in more than one grammatical category.

3
Introduction to phrases and clauses

GRAMMAR BITES in this chapter

A Introduction to phrases

- ➤ The structure of phrases
- ➤ The structure and functions of the main types of phrases: noun phrases, verb phrases, adjective phrases, adverb phrases, and prepositional phrases

B Clause elements and clause patterns

- ➤ Major clause patterns: intransitive, monotransitive, copular, ditransitive, complex transitive
- ➤ Major clause elements: subject, verb phrase, object (direct and indirect), predicative (subject and object), adverbial

3.1 Introduction

In this chapter we give you an initial survey of English grammatical structure, taking words (as classified and illustrated in Chapter 2) as the basic units. This survey progresses in two steps. The first step, in Grammar Bite A, is to see how words pattern together to form phrases. The second step, in Grammar Bite B, is to see how phrases pattern together to form clauses.

GRAMMAR BITE

A Introduction to phrases

3.2 Phrases and their characteristics

As was seen at the beginning of the last chapter, words can be organized into higher units, known as **phrases**. In 3.2 and 3.3, phrase structure and phrase types (or classes) will be examined.

The following example consists of three major phrases, as shown by bracketing [] each phrase:

1 *[The opposition][demands][a more representative government].* (NEWS†)

A phrase may consist of a single word or a group of words. Phrases can be identified by substitution—that is, by replacing one expression with another, to see how it fits into the structure. In particular, a multi-word phrase can often be replaced by a single-word phrase without changing the basic meaning:

[It]   *[demands]*   *[something].*
<The opposition>   <a more representative government.>

We can also identify phrases by movement tests. A phrase can be moved as a unit to a different position. Compare **1** above with **1a**, which has a similar meaning:

1a *[A more representative government] [is demanded] [by [the opposition]].*

When we place one set of brackets inside another, as at the end of **1a**, this means that one phrase is **embedded** (i.e. included) inside another. The possibility of embedding sometimes means that a given structure can be understood in two or more different ways. Consider the following example:

2 *They passed the table with the two men.* (FICT†)

Notice there are two possible meanings of this clause, corresponding to different ways of grouping the words (i.e. different phrase structures):

2a *[They] [passed] [the table [with [the two men]]].*
2b *[They] [passed] [the table] [with [the two men]].*

The meaning of **2a** is roughly: 'They passed the table *where the two men were sitting*'. But in **2b** the meaning is 'With (*i.e. accompanied by*) the two men, they passed the table'.

In summary:

- Words make up phrases, which behave like units.

- A phrase can consist of either one word or more than one word.
- Phrases can be identified by substitution and movement tests.
- Differences in phrase structure show up in differences of meaning.
- Phrases can be embedded (i.e. one phrase can be part of the structure of another phrase).

Phrase structure can be shown either by bracketing, as in **1–2** above, or by tree diagrams. Figures 3.1 and 3.2 correspond to the three bracketed clauses of **2a** and **2b**.

Figure 3.1
Phrase structure of 2a
(prep = prepositional)

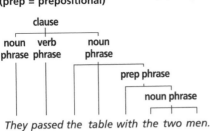

Figure 3.2
Phrase structure of 2a
(prep = prepositional)

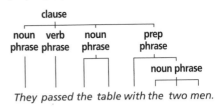

3.2.1 Syntactic roles of phrases

Phrase types differ both in their internal structure and in their syntactic roles— i.e. their relations to larger structures. Recognizing syntactic roles, like **subject** and **object**, can be crucial for the interpretation of phrases. For example, consider the difference between:

	subject	verb	object
1	[Mommy]	[loves]	[the kitty]. (CONV)
2	[The kitty]	[loves]	[Mommy].

Here the noun phrases at the beginning and end are interchanged, resulting in a clearly different meaning. Thus the first phrase in both **1** and in **2** is the subject, and the second phrase is the object. By interchanging the positions of *Mommy* and *the kitty*, we have also changed their syntactic roles.

3.2.2 Phrases in use

The use of phrases in discourse can be illustrated by comparing the two text passages presented earlier in 2.2.6. The words in these passages have been grouped into phrases (shown by brackets). Single-word phrases (which are very common) and phrases embedded within phrases are not marked. The round brackets, as in *[Do] you (want]*, signal a split (discontinuous) phrase. (That is, *you* is not part of the phrase *do want*.)

> A: Is that [the time]?
> B: Yeah, it's [twenty minutes to four].
> A: Oh [my clock] is slow, yeah.

B: [Do) you (want] us [to) just (go] out there and come back and pick [you guys] up?

A: Uh huh.

C: Yeah.

A: You [can go] if you want to, I'll, I think I'll <...>

D: He really [doesn't trust] me, does he?

C: That's right, how 'bout I pin you?

D: Okay. Oh, let me tell you something.

B: Do you, [do) you (want] to go [by yourself]?

D: No, no, no. You['ll feel] better and we['ll be following] you.

A: [Will) you (feel] better?

D: It [doesn't].

C: I need [three safety pins], you had one [in your pocket].

B: Uh huh. (CONV)

[Radioactive leak] confirmed [at Sellafield]

[Work on the dismantling of a nuclear reprocessing plant at Sellafield] caused [a leak of radioactivity] yesterday. [British Nuclear Fuels Ltd] said [the radioactivity] reached [the air] [through a chimney stack which was still in use]. But [spokesman Bob Phillips] said it was not [an incident which required reporting to the Government]. He dismissed [protests from Friends of the Earth] as 'scaremongering'. However, [Dr Patrick Green, Friends of the Earth radiation campaigner], said: 'BNF has [a scandalous track record of playing down incidents at first, and only admitting their seriousness later].' [Three months ago] BNF confirmed that [a leak of radioactive plutonium solution] [had been reclassified] [as 'a serious incident]'. (NEWS)

The length of the phrases in the two passages is very different. Generally the news story has longer phrases as well as a larger number of multi-word phrases. In fact, in the conversation sample, almost three-quarters of the phrases are only one word long, while there is only one phrase that contains four or more words. In the news sample, however, nine phrases are four or more words long, and some of these are longer than ten words.

The comparison is incomplete because it does not include phrases within phrases. These occur particularly in the news story. Using a tree diagram or brackets, the example from the beginning of the sample can be broken down as in Figure 3.3.

Noun phrases and prepositional phrases can have particularly complex structure in written texts, with several layers of phrase embedding. In fact, the complexity of phrases is a very striking measure for comparing the complexity of syntax in different registers of English. The simplest structures occur in conversation and the complexity increases through fiction and newspaper writing, with academic writing showing the greatest complexity of phrase structure.

Figure 3.3 A phrase with embedding

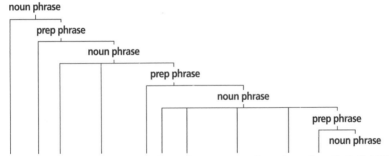

[work [on [the dismantling [of [a nuclear reprocessing plant [at [Sellafield]]]]]]]

3.3 Types of phrases

For each class of lexical word, there is a major phrase type with an example of that class as the **head**: noun phrase (3.3.1), **verb phrase** (3.3.2), **adjective phrase** (3.3.3), **adverb phrase** (3.3.4), and **prepositional phrase** (3.3.5). The head is the principal, obligatory word. In fact, each phrase type can often consist of just one word: the head.

To begin our outline of these phrase types, let's recall the procedure of word classification in 2.3, where we took account of form/structure, syntactic role, and meaning. The same three factors need to be recognized in describing phrase types:

- Form/structure: Our main test for the classification of phrases is structure, especially the word class of the head of the phrase and the other elements contained in the phrase. (This is analogous to the morphological structure of words.)
- Syntactic role: Phrases can be described according to their function or syntactic role in clauses (e.g. subject, object). (In 3.4 we outline the structure of clauses in some detail, but here we take for granted only a limited knowledge of such roles as subject and object.)
- Meaning: In general, the semantic nature of phrases is to specify and/or elaborate the meaning of the head word and its relation to other elements in the clause.

3.3.1 Noun phrases

A phrase with a noun as its head is a noun phrase. The head can be preceded by **determiners**, such as *the*, *a*, *her*, and can be accompanied by **modifiers**—elements which describe or classify whatever the head refers to. Here are some examples of noun phrases (head in bold; determiner, where present, underlined):

<u>a</u> **house**   <u>these</u> **houses**   <u>their</u> **house**   <u>many</u> **houses**
<u>his</u> bristly short **hair**   <u>her</u> below-the-knee **skirt**
<u>the</u> little **girl** next door   heavy **rain** driven by gales
<u>any</u> printed **material** discovered which might be construed as dissent

An abstract head noun can also be followed by **complements**, which complete the meaning of the noun, especially *that*-**clauses** or **infinitive** *to*-**clauses**. Noun phrases containing a complement are shown below in *[]*; heads are in bold, and complements underlined:

> **1** *[The popular* **assumption** <u>*that language simply serves to communicate 'thoughts' or 'ideas'*</u>*] is too simplistic.* (ACAD)
>
> **2** *He feels awkward about [her* **refusal** <u>*to show any sign of emotion*</u>*].* (NEWS†)

Besides common nouns, noun phrases can be headed by proper nouns (**3**), pronouns (**4–5**) and (occasionally) adjectives (**6**). (Brackets *[]* enclose noun phrases consisting of more than one word; noun phrase heads are in bold.)

> **3** **Dawn** *lives in* **Wembley**. (FICT)
>
> **4** **They** *said* **they**'*d got it.* (CONV)
>
> **5** *'Have* **you** *got [***everything** *you need]?'* (FICT)
>
> **6** *'Show me how [the* **impossible**] *can be possible!'* (FICT)

Even though these phrases do not have a common noun as head, they are noun phrases because they have the structure characteristics of a noun phrase (e.g. **5** has a modifier, *you need*, and **6** has a determiner, *the*) and they serve the same syntactic roles (e.g. acting as subject or object of a clause).

Noun phrases can take the role of subject or object in a clause. For example:

subject	verb phrase	object
I	*saw*	*a lot of Italy.* (CONV†)

Noun phrases can also take the syntactic role of predicative, adverbial, or complement (in a prepositional phrase). These roles will become clear when we introduce them in relation to other phrase types (see 3.3.5, 3.4).

3.3.2 Verb phrases

Verb phrases have a **lexical verb** or **primary verb** as their head (i.e. their **main verb**; see 2.2). The main verb can stand alone or be preceded by one or more **auxiliary verbs**. The auxiliaries further define the action, state, or process denoted by the main verb.

Finite verb phrases show distinctions of tense (present/past) and can include modal auxiliaries. **Non-finite** verb phrases do not show tense and cannot occur with modal auxiliaries, and so have fewer forms. Here we focus on finite verbs. Table 3.1 presents the range of finite verb phrases for the main verb *show* preceded by one or more auxiliary verbs.

Verb phrases are the essential part of a clause, referring to a type of state or action. The main verb determines the other clause elements that occur in the clause (e.g. the kinds of objects, see Grammar Bite B).

Verb phrases are often split into two parts (i.e. they are discontinuous). This happens in questions, where the subject is placed after the (first) auxiliary verb:

> *What's he* **doing**? (CONV) <verb phrase = *is doing*>

In addition, the parts of a verb phrase can be interrupted by adverbs or other adverbials:

able 3.1 Main forms of the verb phrase

	present tense	past tense	modal
simple	shows, show	showed	could show
perfect	has/have shown	had shown	could have shown
progressive	am/is/are showing	was/were showing	could be showing
passive	am/is/are shown	was/were shown	could be shown
perfect+progressive	has/have been showing	had been showing	could have been showing
perfect+passive	has/have been shown	had been shown	could have been shown
progressive+passive	am/is/are being shown	was/were being shown	could be being shown

Notes
a *Show*, the main verb illustrated here, has a distinct past participle form *shown*. However, occasionally *show* can also be a regular verb, so *showed* could replace *shown* in the table.
b *Could* is the only modal auxiliary illustrated here. Any modal could be substituted for it.
c In general, the verb phrases with four or more verbs (e.g. *could have been shown*) are extremely rare.

> *You know the English* **will** *always* **have** *gardens wherever they find themselves.* (FICT) <verb phrase = *will have*>
>
> *The current year* **has** *definitely* **started** *well.* (NEWS) <verb phrase = *has started*>

3.3.3 Adjective phrases

Adjective phrases have an adjective as head, and optional modifiers that can precede or follow the adjective. In these examples the head is in bold and the modifiers are in ordinary italics:

> *old   incredible   so* **lucky**   **good** *enough   desperately* **poor**

Modifiers typically answer a question about the degree of a quality (e.g. 'How lucky/poor?'). Adjective heads can also take complements. The complements are underlined below:

> **guilty** <u>of a serious crime</u>
> **subject** <u>to approval by</u>...
> **slow** <u>to respond</u>
> *more* **blatant** <u>than anything they had done in the past</u>
> *so* **obnoxious** <u>that she had to be expelled</u>

Complements often answer the question 'In what respect is the adjectival quality to be interpreted?' (e.g. 'guilty/slow in what respect?').

The structure and uses of adjective phrases are described in detail in 7.2–9. Adjectives with clauses as complements are discussed in 10.7, 10.9.2, and 10.15.

The most important roles of adjective phrases are as modifier and subject predicative:

- as a modifier before a noun, where the adjective is called an **attributive adjective** (noun phrases are marked in *[]*):

  *He's [a **deeply sick** man].* (FICT)

  *We saw [a **very good** movie] the other night.* (CONV†)

  *The European study asked [a **slightly different** question].* (ACAD)

- as a **subject predicative**, often following the verb *be*:

  *That's **right**.* (CONV)

  *He's **totally crazy**.* (CONV)

  *Gabby was **afraid to say anything more**.* (FICT)

Adjective phrases modifying nouns can be split into two parts by the noun head:

*You couldn't have a **better** name **than that**.* (FICT) <adjective phrase = better than that>

*When he plays his best, he's a **really tough** player **to beat**.* (NEWS†) <adjective phrase = really tough to beat >

3.3.4 Adverb phrases

Adverb phrases are like adjective phrases in structure, except that the head is an adverb (in bold below). Optional modifiers (in ordinary italics) may precede or follow the adverb head. They typically express degree. Complements (underlined) can also follow:

there	*quietly*
*pretty **soon***	***fortunately** enough*
*so **quickly** you don't even enjoy it*	*much more **quickly** than envisaged*

Adverb phrases should be distinguished from adverbials: adverb phrases are structures, while adverbials are clause elements. Adverb phrases, prepositional phrases, and adverbial clauses can all function as adverbials (see 3.5.5; 11.1–3).

The following syntactic roles are most usual for adverb phrases:

- as a modifier in adjective or adverb phrases (the adjective or adverb phrase modified is marked *[]*):

  *Those two were [**pretty much horribly** spoiled].* (†CONV)

  *He was an attractive little creature with a [**sweetly** expressive] face.* (FICT†)

- as an adverbial on the clause level:

  *She smiled **sweetly**.* (FICT†)

  *They sang **boomingly well**.* (FICT)

For further detail, see the treatment of adverb phrases in 7.10.5 and the extensive treatment of adverbials in Chapter 11.

3.3.5 Prepositional phrases

Prepositional phrases mostly consist of a preposition (in bold below) followed by a noun phrase, known as the **prepositional complement** (in ordinary italics). The preposition can be thought of as a link relating the noun phrase to preceding structures.

1 *to town* 3 *in the morning* 5 *on the night [of the first day]*
2 *to Sue* 4 *to him* 6 *in a street [with no name]*

Note that prepositional phrases are often embedded in larger phrases, as in **5** and **6**, where *[]* enclose an embedded prepositional phrase.

Prepositions also take **complement clauses**—clauses which have the same role as noun phrases—as complements, but normally these are only *wh*-clauses (in **7** below) and *ing*-clauses (in **8** below):

7 *Component drawings carry instructions [on **where they are used**].* (ACAD†)

8 *It was hard to live in Missouri [after **spending so much time in California**].* (CONV)

Prepositional phrases can be 'extended' by an initial **adverbial particle**, which adds a meaning such as place, direction, or degree: ***back** to the fifties*; ***down** in the south*. Another kind of extension is an adverb of degree: ***exactly** at noon*; ***nearly** till eleven*; ***considerably** to the right*.

Prepositional phrases vary in how closely they are connected with the surrounding structure. Their two major syntactic roles are:

- as an adverbial on the clause level (see Chapter 11):

   He worked [in a shop] – [probably at that time]. (CONV†)

   He retired [after three minor heart attacks] [at the age of 36]. (NEWS†)

- as a modifier or complement following a noun (the noun phrase is bracketed *{}* and the prepositional phrase is bracketed *[]*):

   He was a poet, {a teacher [of philosophy]}, and {a man [with a terrible recent history]}. (NEWS)

   Or at least that is {the ambition [of {the industrial development commission [of a small Pennsylvania steel town]}]}. (NEWS)

Prepositions also occur in prepositional verbs such as *look **at*** (see 5.10).

A preposition is said to be **stranded** if it is not followed by its prepositional complement. The prepositional complement, in such cases, is generally identified as a previous noun phrase, marked *[]* below:

9 *[What more] could a child ask **for**?* (NEWS)

10 *As soon as Unoka understood [what] his friend was driving **at**, he burst out laughing.* (FICT)

11 *Without the money to pay for your promises, your manifesto is not worth [the paper] it is written **on**.* (NEWS†)

Stranded prepositions are usually found in clauses that do not follow normal word order, such as direct questions (**9**), interrogative clauses (**10**) and relative clauses (**11**).

According to the old-fashioned 'rules' of grammar, stranded prepositions have long been considered bad style. However, in practice they frequently occur, especially in conversation. Although there is usually an alternative to stranded prepositions, in which the preposition is moved forward to precede its complement, speakers often prefer the stranded preposition. Taking **9** above as an example, the alternative of placing the preposition at the beginning of the clause (**9a**) is unlikely to occur, even in formal writing.

9 *What more could a child ask **for**?* (NEWS)
9a ***For** what more could a child ask?*

Review

Major points of **GRAMMAR BITE A**: Introduction to phrases
- ➤ Words are organized into larger units known as phrases.
- ➤ The main classes of phrases are: noun phrase, verb phrase, adjective phrase, adverb phrase, and prepositional phrase.
- ➤ The classes can be identified by their meaning, structure, and syntactic role.
- ➤ Each of these phrases has a head from the corresponding word class: e.g. noun phrases usually have a noun as their head.
- ➤ The frequency of longer and more complex phrases varies from one register to another, increasing from conversation, to fiction, to news writing, to academic prose.

GRAMMAR BITE

B Clause elements and clause patterns

3.4 A preview of clause patterns

The clause is the key unit of syntax, capable of occurring independently (i.e. without being part of any other unit). It is useful to think of the clause as a unit that can stand alone as an expression of a 'complete thought'—that is, a complete description of an event or state of affairs. Hence, many spoken utterances consist of a single clause:

Have you got an exam on Monday? (CONV)

and the same is true of many written sentences:

She smiled sweetly. (FICT)

However, not all utterances or sentences contain a complete clause. For example:

More sauce? (CONV)

Thirty pence please. (CONV)

Five years later? (FICT)

Image crisis for Clinton over haircut. (NEWS) <a headline>

Although these examples make sense as individual utterances or sentences, they do not have a verb phrase, which is the key element of a clause. However, their message could be expressed more fully as a clause:

Would you like more sauce?

Such non-clausal material will be considered further in 13.4. For the sake of clarity, we limit the discussion here to examples with a single, complete clause.

The following list presents examples of the basic clause patterns that are introduced in this section. All the examples are from conversation:

example	pattern
1 *Sarah and Michael*[S] *disappeared*[V]	subject (S) + verb phrase (V)
2 *She*[S] *changed*[V] *her dress*[DO]	subject (S) + verb phrase (V) + direct object (DO)
3 *The Swiss cheese*[S] *has gone*[V] *bad*[SP]	subject (S) + verb phrase (V) + subject predicative (SP)
4 *Marc*[S] *was*[V] *in the bathroom* [A]	subject (S) + verb phrase (V) + adverbial (A)
5 *You*[S] *gave*[V] *her*[IO] *the wrong kind of egg*[DO]	subject (S) + verb phrase (V) + indirect object (IO) + direct object (DO)
6 *That*[S] *makes*[V] *me*[DO] *so mad*[OP]	subject (S) + verb phrase (V) + direct object (DO) + object predicative (OP)
7 *They*[S] *'re sending*[V] *us*[DO] *to Disneyland*[A]	subject (S) + verb phrase (V) + direct object (DO) + adverbial (A)

The verb phrase is the central or pivotal element in each clause. The **valency** of the verb controls the kinds of elements that follow it. For example, *disappeared* in **1** cannot be followed by a noun phrase. It has the type of valency known as 'intransitive'. On the other hand, *gave* in **5** has to be followed by two noun phrases—one identifying the recipient (*her*) and the other identifying the thing that was given (*the wrong kind of egg*). Hence the verb lexeme *give* has the type of valency known as 'ditransitive'.

The clauses in the examples above illustrate the five major **valency** patterns:

- **intransitive** pattern (S + V; example **1**)
- **monotransitive** pattern (S + V + DO; example **2**)
- **copular** patterns (S + V + SP and S + V + A; examples **3** and **4**)
- **ditransitive** pattern (S + V + IO + DO; example **5**)
- **complex transitive** patterns (S + V + DO + OP and S + V + DO + A; examples **6** and **7**).

Each term is used to refer both to the clause pattern and to the valency of the verb that occurs in the pattern. So we can say clause **1** has an intransitive pattern and *disappear* is an intransitive verb. Similarly, we can say clause **5** has a ditransitive pattern and *give* is a ditransitive verb. All patterns which have an object following the verb (monotransitive, ditransitive, and complex transitive) are given the generic term **transitive**. (See the more detailed discussion of valency patterns in 5.7.)

3.5 Clause elements

Clause elements are phrases that serve syntactic roles in the clause, as introduced in Grammar Bite A. A number of tests can be applied to identify clause elements, but not all tests will apply in every case. As already noted, grammatical definitions are rarely simple and clear-cut. This is true of clause elements, too.

3.5.1 Verb phrase (V)

The verb phrase is the central element of the clause, because it expresses the action or state to which other elements relate, and it controls the other kinds of elements and meanings that can be in the clause. The verb phrase was described in 3.3.2., so nothing further needs to be said here.

3.5.2 Subject (S)

The second most important element is the subject. In syntactic terms, a number of criteria can be used to define the subject:

- The subject is a noun phrase.
- It occurs with all types of verbs.
- Subject pronouns are in the **nominative** case. For example, *he, she* are the forms of the pronouns used as subject, while the **accusative** forms *him, her* are used as object. Compare *He likes **her*** with *She likes **him***.
- The subject precedes the verb phrase (except in clauses with **inversion**, such as questions, where the subject follows the **operator**).
- The subject determines the **number** of the verb phrase, depending on whether the subject is singular or plural. Compare *She **works** late* <singular> with *They **work** late* <plural>.
- The subject noun phrase of a transitive verb can be moved after the verb, and preceded by *by* to make a clause with a **passive** verb. Compare ***Kate** saw it* with *It was seen **by Kate***.

The six criteria above deal with structure. Turning to meaning:

- The subject denotes the most important participant in the action or state denoted by the verb. With transitive verbs, this is generally the 'doer' or **agent** of the action.
- The subject generally represents the topic, i.e. the entity that the clause is about. But sometimes English requires a subject, even if the subject has no actual meaning:

    ***It**'s warm in here.* (CONV)

    ***It** never rains in Albuquerque.* (CONV)

    In these cases, English uses *it* as a pronoun that fills the place of the subject but has no content—a **dummy pronoun**.

3.5.3 Object (O)

- An object is a noun phrase.
- It usually follows the verb.
- It only occurs with transitive verbs.
- An object pronoun is in the accusative case. For example, in *He likes her* and *She likes him*, the accusative forms *her* and *him* fill the object position.
- The object noun phrase of a transitive verb can be moved to become subject of the corresponding passive clause. Compare *Everyone deserted **me*** with *I was deserted (by everyone).*

Three valency patterns contain **direct objects**: the monotransitive, ditransitive, and complex transitive patterns. The ditransitive pattern contains first an **indirect object** followed by a direct object.

A Direct objects (DO)

A direct object generally follows immediately after the verb, except where an indirect object intervenes. Its most common semantic role is to denote the entity affected by the action or process of the verb:

> *He bought **biscuits and condensed milk**.* (FICT)
>
> *We parked **the car** in the worst place.* (CONV)
>
> *Maybe you should teach **younger aged students**.* (CONV)

In these typical cases, the subject denotes the doer of the action, and the clause fits the template: '*X did something to Y*' (where *Y* is the direct object). However, there is a wide range of transitive verbs where the meanings of direct objects are less typical. Here are a few examples:

> *Oh, are you having **a lovely time**?* (CONV)
>
> *The stewards all spoke **French**.* (CONV)
>
> *We should show **understanding for the fear of our neighbours**.* (NEWS)

In these examples, the direct objects express abstractions, which are not actually affected by the action of the verb. Nevertheless, grammatically, they are direct objects.

Sometimes English verbs require a direct object even though it has no meaning. Such is the case with the verb *take*:

> *Take **it** easy Tina.* (CONV) <i.e. relax>

As with subjects, English uses *it* as the dummy pronoun for direct objects.

B Indirect objects (IO)

An indirect object occurs after ditransitive verbs such as *give* and *tell*, and comes before the direct object. It conforms to the other criteria for objects, including the formation of passives. To illustrate this last point, consider example **1**, where the indirect object is in bold and the direct object is underlined. In the passive counterpart **1a**, the indirect object *you* becomes the subject:

> **1** *Ben Franklin Transit gave **you** <u>additional funding</u>.* (CONV†)
>
> **1a** ***You** were given <u>additional funding</u> by Ben Franklin Transit.*

In contrast, the direct object *additional funding* cannot easily become the subject of a corresponding passive without the insertion of a preposition (here *to*):

> **1b** *[Additional funding] was given (**to**) you by Ben Franklin Transit.*

As for their semantic role, indirect objects generally denote people receiving something or benefiting from the action of the verb:

> *Well actually he brought **us** the big menu first.* (CONV†)
>
> *I cooked **the kids** dinner.* (CONV†)
>
> *'Agnes has been showing **me** her prize,' said Mynors.* (FICT†)

3.5.4 Predicative (P)

- A predicative can be an adjective phrase, a noun phrase, or occasionally a prepositional phrase.
- It follows the verb phrase and (if one is present) the direct object.
- It has the semantic role of characterizing a preceding noun phrase.

There are two major types of predicative, the **subject predicative** and the **object predicative**:

A Subject predicatives (SP)

Subject predicatives characterize or specify the subject noun phrase (underlined in the following examples):

1 *His skin was **very pink**.* (ACAD) <SP = adjective phrase>
2 *That tall fellow over there is **Dr Fraker**.* (FICT) <SP = noun phrase>
3 *But his wife Shelley seemed **in great shape**.* (NEWS†) <SP = prepositional phrase>

For example, in **1,** the adjective phrase *very pink* is the subject predicative, and it characterizes *his skin* (that is, it says what kind of skin he has).

Special distinguishing features of the subject predicative are:

- It immediately follows the verb phrase.
- The main verb has to be a **copular verb**, such as *be, seem,* and *become.*

Subject predicatives are also sometimes called 'subject complements'.

B Object predicatives (OP)

Object predicatives characterize or specify the direct object noun phrase (object predicatives are in bold, direct objects are underlined):

1 *Oh, I can't get this milk **open**.* (CONV) <OP = adjective phrase>
2 *Many consider these new gates **something of a menace**.* (NEWS) <OP = noun phrase>
3 *He was surprised to find himself **out of breath**.* (FICT†) <OP = prepositional phrase>

Thus in **1,** *open* characterizes *this milk.*

The distinguishing features of the object predicative are:

- It generally immediately follows the direct object.
- The main verb has to be a complex transitive verb, such as *make, find, consider,* and *name.*

The object predicative is sometimes called the 'object complement'.

3.5.5 Adverbials (A)

A Obligatory adverbials

Some verbs take an **adverbial** in order to complete their meaning. This is known as an obligatory adverbial. Obligatory adverbials can occur with two patterns: the copular pattern and the complex transitive pattern. Obligatory adverbials usually express place or direction, although they can also express time or manner meanings:

example	clause pattern
*Your toast is **on the table**.* (CONV†)	S + V + **A**
*The pleasant summer lasted **well into March**.* (FICT)	S + V + **A**
*She placed the baby **on a blanket in the living room**.* (FICT†)	S + V + DO + **A**
*I treated her **badly, very badly**.* (FICT)	S + V + DO + **A**

In these clause patterns, the adverbial has to be present in order to complete the structure and meaning of the verb. This may be tested by removing the adverbial (in bold), resulting in an incomplete clause (e.g. *your toast is* or *she placed the baby*).

B Optional adverbials

Only a few verbs require adverbials to be complete; however, adverbials occur widely in clauses as optional elements.

- Optional adverbials can be added to clauses with any type of verb.
- They are usually adverb phrases, prepositional phrases, or noun phrases.
- They can be placed in different positions within the clause—in final, initial, or medial positions.
- More than one of them can occur in a single clause.
- They are rather loosely attached to the rest of the clause. Whereas the verb phrase is central, the adverbial is relatively peripheral (except in those clause patterns that require adverbials).

Optional adverbials add additional information to the clause, covering a wide variety of meanings, such as place, time, manner, extent, and attitude.

examples	clause pattern
*I **only** bought one **today**.* (CONV)	S + (A) + V + DO + (A)
*I was here, **with Uncle Nick**, **thirty years ago**.* (FICT)	S + V + A + (A) + (A)
*They are peculiarly susceptible to drought. They **therefore** benefit **considerably from periodic submergence**.* (ACAD†)	S + (A) + V + (A) + (A)

The above examples illustrate some of the variety of adverbials, showing a range of meanings and functions, showing how a number of adverbials can co-occur in a single clause, and showing the optionality of most adverbials. However, notice that 'optionality' here means that the adverbial could be omitted *without making the clause structurally incomplete*. Of course, even optional adverbials cannot be omitted without making a difference to meaning. (Chapter 11 is devoted to adverbials.)

3.5.6 Long verb phrases

In 3.3.2 we introduced verb phrases as phrases containing a main verb sometimes preceded by one or more auxiliary verbs. There is another 'bigger' notion of verb phrase commonly used in grammar, including not only the verb phrase in this sense, but also any other clause elements which follow the main verb (object, predicative, adverbial), depending on the valency of the main verb: e.g. monotransitive, ditransitive. We will call this 'umbrella constituent' a **long verb phrase** (shown in bold below):

> *My mother **was born in Canada**.* (CONV)

Some clauses consist only of a long verb phrase, as with imperative constructions:

> ***Look at that nice dog***. (CONV)

The long verb phrase corresponds roughly to a traditional grammatical notion of 'predicate'. It is useful for analysis particularly when a complex clause consists of a subject followed by a series of conjoined long verb phrases:

> *The firefighters **grabbed me** and **pulled me up**.* (CONV†)

When we use tree diagrams in this book, we include both a long and 'short' verb phrase as separate constituents, the first including the second. It is now time to revise the tree diagrams in Figures 3.1 and 3.2, to include the added long verb phrase, which will occur in clause tree diagrams in the rest of the book; see Figures 3.4 and 3.5. Although it is important in tree diagrams, the long verb phrase will not need to be discussed in the rest of this book.

Figure 3.4 **Revision of Figure 3.1, showing the long verb phrase**
(prep = prepositional)

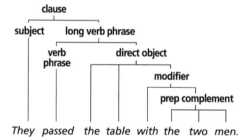

Figure 3.5 **Revision of Figure 3.2, showing the long verb phrase**
(prep = prepositional)

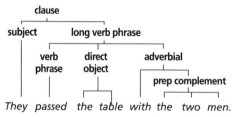

Note: Figures 3.4 and 3.5 show the same structure as Figures 3.1 and 3.2, except that (a) the long verb phrase is included and (b) the diagrams show syntactic role labels (subject, adverbial, etc.) instead of labels for phrase types (noun phrase, etc.)

3.5.7 Truly peripheral elements

Some elements are even more peripheral to the clause than adverbials. These are attached to the clause in a loose way, but do not form part of the main message of the clause. In fact, it may be unclear whether they are truly part of the clause at all. They are often set off from the rest of the clause by punctuation (in writing), intonation (in speech), or by being placed immediately before or after the clause. Sometimes these peripheral elements are complete clauses in their own right. They will simply be listed here with a brief explanation and one or two examples.

A Conjunctions

Coordinating and subordinating **conjunctions** (see 8.3–4) are fixed in initial position in the clause, even ahead of other peripheral adverbials:

> **And**, of course, now Keely doesn't have any teeth. (CONV)
>
> **Because** he and Jane aren't married. (CONV)

B Parentheticals

Parentheticals are set off from the surrounding clause by parentheses (in writing), or sometimes by dashes:

> At precisely 11.07 (**Earth time**), a message flashed up on the ITN screen. (NEWS)
>
> One of the first to make it in modern times (**some Greeks had known it long before**) was Leonardo da Vinci. (ACAD)

C Prefaces

Prefaces are noun phrases placed before the subject, which typically have the same reference as a personal pronoun in the clause. In the following examples, the preface is in bold, and the personal pronoun with the corresponding reference is underlined:

> **This woman**, <u>she</u>'s ninety years old. (CONV)
>
> But **Anna-Luise** what could have attracted <u>her</u> to a man in his fifties? (FICT)

The use of prefaces in conversation is discussed in 12.11.1 and 13.3.2.

D Tags

In contrast to prefaces, **tags** are normally added at the end of a clause, and can be either **noun phrase tags (1)**, **question tags (2)** or **declarative tags (3)**:

> 1 It's nice **that table** anyway. (CONV)
> 2 She's so generous, **isn't she?** (CONV)
> 3 Yeah I thoroughly enjoyed it **I did**. (CONV)

Noun phrase tags are comparable to prefaces, except that they follow the main part of the clause.

E Inserts

We mentioned **inserts** as a separate family of words in 2.2.2. Grammatically these are extra words which can be 'slipped into' spoken discourse, mainly to convey interactive meanings. They can occur as stand-alone elements, or as peripheral elements in a clause. Examples with clauses are:

> **Hello** *is that Cindy Jones?* (CONV)
>
> *You know who Stan is,* **right?** (CONV)

Some multi-word expressions may be considered inserts because they have become so formulaic that they seem like single units rather than syntactic constructions:

> *Er no I'll give it a – miss right now* **thank you.** (CONV)
>
> **You know** *she went all the way up to calculus in high school.* (CONV)

In 13.7, we will look at inserts in greater depth.

F Vocatives

Vocatives are nouns or noun phrases which generally refer to people, and serve to identify the person(s) being addressed:

> **Mum**, *I'm making such a big sandwich.* (CONV)
>
> *Oh, make your bloody mind up,* **boy!** (CONV) <note: *bloody* is a taboo word and may be offensive to some people>
>
> *Come on* **you reds**, *come on* **you reds**, *come on* **you reds**. (CONV) <addressing a football team during a match>

All the above types of peripherals, except for conjunctions and parentheticals, are more frequently found in spoken language.

Review

Major points in GRAMMAR BITE B: Clause elements and clause patterns

➤ Clauses (in their simplest form) are composed of phrases that function as clause elements such as subject and object.

➤ The main elements of clauses are subject, verb phrase, object (direct object or indirect object), predicative, and adverbial.

➤ These elements combine in seven basic clause patterns: intransitive, monotransitive, ditransitive, two types of copular, and two types of complex transitive patterns.

➤ Adverbials are usually optional elements. This means that they can be added to the basic clause patterns—either at the beginning, in the middle, or at the end of a clause.

➤ An 'umbrella constituent', the long verb phrase, includes the verb phrase and the clause elements which follow it.

➤ There can also be peripheral elements in a clause, such as conjunctions, tags, and vocatives.

4

Nouns, pronouns, and the simple noun phrase

GRAMMAR BITES in this chapter

A Types of nouns

- ➤ Countable and uncountable nouns
- ➤ Proper nouns
- ➤ Collective nouns, unit nouns, and species nouns

B Types of determiners

- ➤ The definite and indefinite articles *the* and *a(n)*
- ➤ Possessive and demonstrative determiners
- ➤ Quantifiers and numerals
- ➤ Semi-determiners and *wh*-determiners

C Number and case in nouns

- ➤ Number: singular and plural
- ➤ Regular and irregular plurals
- ➤ Genitives as determiner and as modifier
- ➤ Independent genitives, group genitives, and double genitives
- ➤ Genitives and *of*-phrases

D Gender and noun formation

- ➤ Masculine, feminine, personal, and neuter
- ➤ Derived nouns: common noun suffixes
- ➤ Noun compounds

E Types of pronouns

- ➤ Personal pronouns
- ➤ Possessive, reflexive, and reciprocal pronouns
- ➤ Demonstrative pronouns
- ➤ Indefinite pronouns
- ➤ Other pronouns

4.1 Introduction

Chapter 3 showed that one of the key parts of English grammar is the noun phrase. In this chapter, we focus on the simple noun phrase, which consists of a head alone, or a determiner + head. Nouns or pronouns can function as head. These components are illustrated below.

		determiner slot	head slot	
			music	← common noun
determiner	→	*the*	*friends*	← common noun
			Chicago	← proper noun
			She	← pronoun
genitive	→	*Charles's*	*grandfather*	← common noun

In addition, noun phrases can be extended by the use of modifiers and complements, which are the subject of Chapter 9.

A Types of nouns

4.2 Main types of nouns

Nouns can be grouped into a small number of classes which differ in meaning and grammatical behavior. There is first a distinction between **common** and **proper** nouns. Common nouns can be either **countable** or **uncountable**.

- Countable common nouns refer to entities which can be counted: they have both a singular and a plural form (*a cow*, *two cows*, etc.). Both in the singular and in the plural there is a contrast between **indefinite** and **definite,** signaled by **articles**: *a cow* v. *the cow*; *cows* v. *the cows*.
- Uncountable common nouns refer to something which cannot be counted: they do not vary for number. They cannot occur with the indefinite article *a(n)*, but they allow a contrast between definite and indefinite: *the milk* v. *milk*.
- Proper nouns have no contrast for number or definiteness: they are singular and definite. For example, the proper noun *Sue* has no options *a Sue, the Sue,* or *Sues*.

The differences among these noun classes are shown here:

	common countable		common uncountable		proper
	indefinite	definite	indefinite	indefinite	(definite)
singular	*a cow*	*the cow*	*milk*	*the milk*	*Sue*
plural	*cows*	*the cows*	—	—	—

Countability is partly a matter of how we view the world, rather than how the world really is. For example, *furniture* and *traffic* are uncountable nouns in English. Although they refer to sets of separate items (e.g. chairs, cars), the English language 'sees' these items as a mass.

Proper nouns need no article or plural form because they only name an individual (e.g. a specific person or place, like *Sue*, *Chicago*) whereas common nouns denote a class (like *girl*, *city*). Proper nouns are generally used in situations where the speaker and addressee know which individual is meant, without further specification.

Nevertheless, proper nouns can sometimes have modifiers like common nouns:

> *The court heard that **little** Harry's death could have been prevented if social workers had not overruled detectives.* (NEWS)

The adjective modifier here does not serve to distinguish Harry from others of that name, but adds a descriptive label to someone already identified.

Further, proper nouns sometimes have a possessive determiner:

> *I'm gonna have to phone **our** Sue.* (CONV)

> *Oh did I tell you **our** Joanie's coming over?* (CONV)

In these examples *our* signals that Sue and Joanie are members of the speaker's family. Later, in 4.3.3, it will be seen that proper nouns can also be used like common nouns.

4.2.1 Concrete v. abstract nouns

In the following text excerpt, the different kinds of noun are highlighted as follows: underlined = common countable, bold = common uncountable, capitals = proper:

> *The <u>lab</u> <u>crew</u> at CIBA-GEIGY, the Swiss <u>chemical</u> and <u>drugs</u> giant, continues to seek out <u>niche</u> <u>markets</u> with a <u>vengeance</u>. The latest <u>development</u> is a <u>drug</u> called **clomipramine** which has the endearing <u>quality</u> of reducing the <u>desire</u> to pull your **hair** out when under **stress**.* (NEWS)

This text sample illustrates another distinction:

- Concrete nouns refer to physical entities or substances.
- Abstract nouns refer to abstractions such as events, states, times, and qualities.

In the text sample, the following common nouns are concrete:

> *lab, crew, chemical, drugs, drug, clomipramine, hair*

and the following common nouns are abstract (though some of them can have concrete meanings in other sentences):

> *giant, niche, markets, vengeance, development, quality, desire, stress*

The distinction between concrete and abstract nouns is purely semantic: it has no real grammatical role, since abstract nouns, like concrete nouns, can be countable, uncountable, common, or proper. In fact, some nouns, like *thing*, cross the boundary between concrete and abstract very easily. *Thing* commonly refers to a physical object (as in **1**), but it is also widely used for abstract meanings like 'event' or 'process' (as in **2**):

> **1** *This **thing** is way too small to stick between your toes.* (CONV)
>
> **2** *I have just got it confirmed, but these **things** take time.* (CONV)

Concrete nouns are more 'physical' than abstract nouns, and the countable/ uncountable distinction can be better understood if we think of these distinctions for concrete nouns:

- Countable concrete nouns refer to persons, objects, places (e.g. *student, chair, town*).
- Uncountable concrete nouns refer to substances, materials, liquids, gases (e.g. *steel, water, air*).

However, this is just a useful guide—as the exceptional cases of *furniture* and *traffic* have already shown.

4.2.2 The same noun as countable or uncountable

Many nouns can be both countable and uncountable, but with a difference of meaning:

> *I think these are eggs from our new **chickens**.* (CONV†) <countable>
> *Would you like some **chicken** for dinner?* (CONV) <uncountable>

> *There is no way to tell how old a **rock** is merely by looking at its minerals.* (ACAD†) <countable>
> ***Rock** is defined as the inorganic mineral material covering the earth's surface.* (ACAD†) <uncountable>

Also, many basically uncountable nouns have countable uses:

> *Plant beverages include **tea**, coffee, wine, alcoholic drinks, intoxicants, and sweet beverages.* (ACAD) <uncountable>
> *Six **teas** please.* (CONV) <countable, = cups of tea>

> *I think I would like some **wine** though.* (CONV) <uncountable>
> *A lot of non-alcoholic **wines** are expensive.* (CONV†) <countable, = types of wine>

Tea and *wine*, referring to liquids or substances, are basically uncountable, but notice from these examples that *teas* (countable) can refer to cups of tea, and that *wines* can refer to types of wine.

> In a similar way, abstract nouns can have countable and uncountable uses:

> *What's your highest level of **education**?* (CONV) <uncountable>
> *Although she was a girl she wanted **an education**.* (NEWS†) <countable>

> *They had received **kindness**, thoughts and good wishes from total strangers.* (NEWS†) <uncountable>
> *It would be **a** 'cruel **kindness**' to uphold the county court order.* (NEWS) <countable>

Here the indefinite article *a/an* signals the countable use of *education* and *kindness*. The uncountable noun refers to the general abstraction, while the countable noun refers to particular instances or types of it.

4.2.3 Plural uncountable nouns

Although it may seem to be a contradiction, there are a few plural uncountable nouns:

> *She wears **those** jigsaw-type **clothes**, **trousers** usually.* (CONV)
> *She reached for the **scissors**.* (FICT)

*Letters of **thanks** have been flooding into our office.* (NEWS)

These are plural in that they have a plural ending *-s* and go with plural determiners (*those* in the first example), but they are uncountable because there is no singular form **a clothe, a thank*. (Notice that *clothes*, referring to the things people wear, is not the plural of *cloth*, which has its own plural *cloths*.)

4.3 Proper nouns v. common nouns

Important types of proper noun are:
- personal names (e.g. *Anna, Tom, Williams, Singh*)
- place names (e.g. *Australia, Karachi, Africa*)
- organization names (e.g. *Congress, Mitsubishi*)
- time names (e.g. *Saturday, July, Christmas*)

The most typical proper nouns (e.g. *Anna, Africa*) are arbitrary in form. Grammatically, these nouns have no determiner and do not have a contrast of number between singular and plural (*Annas, the Anna, an Anna* do not normally occur). In spelling, proper nouns are marked by an initial capital letter.

Yet these features of proper nouns have exceptions. Many names are actually multi-word expressions, and contain ordinary lexical words: e.g. *the Horn of Africa, the White House*. As these examples show, a name may also be preceded by *the*—something which can also occur with a single proper name as in *the Sahara (Desert), the Pacific (Ocean), the Vatican, the Kremlin*. Some proper names with *the* are plural (e.g. *the Himalayas*).

4.3.1 Initial capitals

The use of initial capitals in spelling extends beyond proper names. Uses for which the capital letter is conventional are:
- personal names (e.g. *Sam, Jones, Mandela*)
- geographical names (e.g. *Canada, Tokyo, Asia*)
- objects, especially commercial products (e.g. *Voyager, Chevrolet, Kleenex*)
- religious periods, months, and days of the week (e.g. *Ramadan, August, Friday*)
- religions and some religious concepts (e.g. *Buddhism, Islam, God, Heaven, Hell*)
- address terms for family members (e.g. *Mother, Dad, Uncle*)
- people or bodies with a unique public function (e.g. *the Pope, the President, the Senate, Parliament, the Commonwealth*)
- public buildings, institutions, laws, etc. (e.g. *the Library of Congress, Yale University, the Fire Precautions Act*)
- political parties and their members (e.g. *the Democrats, the Labour Party*)
- languages, nationalities, and ethnic groups (e.g. *Arabic, Chinese, English, Sioux*)
- adjectives and common nouns derived from proper nouns (e.g. *Marxist, Marxism, Victorian, the Victorian(s), New Yorker(s), Greek(s)*)

Not all words spelled with initial capitals are proper nouns: the last group above consists of adjectives and common nouns. They can be put in a series like this:

proper noun	adjective	singular common noun	plural common noun
Buddha, Buddhism	Buddhist	a Buddhist	Buddhists
Finland	Finnish	a Finn	Finns
Paris	Parisian	a Parisian	Parisians

In fact, there is a lot of interplay between proper nouns and common nouns. Many names are combinations of common nouns and other words with a definite article (as in *the British Library*). On the other hand, many common nouns are based on proper nouns and keep the capital letter: *the Japanese* (from *Japan*).

4.3.2 Proper nouns regularly occurring with *the*

Some proper nouns regularly occur with a definite article. Important groups are:
- geographical names, such as rivers, seas, and canals (e.g. *the Nile, the Panama Canal, the Indian Ocean*)
- plural geographical names (e.g. *the Cayman Islands, the Great Smoky Mountains*)
- buildings with public functions, such as hotels, restaurants, theatres, museums, and libraries (e.g. *the Ritz, the Metropolitan Museum*)
- names of ships (e.g. *the Titanic, the Santa Maria*)
- many newspapers and some periodicals (e.g. *The New York Times, The Guardian*)

4.3.3 Proper nouns behaving like common nouns

Sometimes proper nouns can function like common nouns. The following show typical uses:
- a person or family called X:

  *I haven't been in touch with **the Joneses** for ages.* (CONV) <the Jones family>
- a product of X

  *I got **a Bentley**, two **Cadillacs**, a Chrysler station wagon, and **an MG** for my boy.* (FICT) <makes of car>

4.4 Package nouns

Four special classes of countable common nouns are considered in this section: **collective nouns**, **unit nouns**, **quantifying nouns**, and **species nouns**. Overall, they have a function of 'packaging' together a range of entities. Package nouns are often followed by *of*-phrases: e.g. *a **load** of books*. The four different classes are sometimes difficult to separate. For example, *bunch* is a collective noun (4.4.1) but it has also become popular as a quantifying noun (= 'a quantity of') in American English conversation.

4.4.1 Collective nouns

Collective nouns refer to groups of people, animals, or things: e.g. *army, audience, committee, family, staff, team, flock, bunch.* All these nouns behave like ordinary countable nouns, varying for number and definiteness: *the team, a team, the teams, teams.* (Among collective nouns we also find proper nouns naming official bodies or organizations: *the USAF, the BBC, the Senate, the UN, NBC, Congress, Parliament.*)

One special class of collective nouns often comes before an *of*-phrase describing the members of the group:

> Two little **groups of people** stood at a respectable distance beyond the stools. (FICT)
>
> There was a small **crowd of people** around. (NEWS)
>
> The aircraft flew into a large **flock of seagulls** just after take-off. (ACAD†)

Nouns like *group, crowd,* and *flock* are called **of-collectives** because they generally precede *of* + plural noun, where the plural noun names a set of people, animals, objects, etc. Some *of*-collectives, such as *group,* are quite general in meaning, whereas others have a more specific application. Some typical **collocations** are:

collective noun	selected collocations
bunch of	idiots, thieves, roses, grapes
crowd of	demonstrators, fans, spectators, shoppers
flock of	birds, doves, geese, sheep, children
gang of	bandits, hecklers, thugs
group of	adults, girls, animals, buildings, diseases, things
set of	assumptions, characteristics, conditions

The list of collocations above suggests the range of meaning that a collective noun can cover. Other examples are: **herd** of cows, **host** of stars, **pack** of lies, **series** of accidents, **shoal** of fish, **swarm** of bees, **troop** of inspectors. Some points to note are:

- *Bunch, group,* and *set* are the most general words, allowing the widest range of collocations.
- Although many of these collectives have a specific range (e.g. *flock* refers to a group of birds and animals), they can be extended, for special effect, to other nouns (e.g. *flock of children*).
- Some of the collectives frequently have a negative effect: especially *bunch, gang,* and *pack.* Notice the contrasting effects of:

> **A group of young men** were talking eagerly. (FICT†) <neutral>
>
> **A swarm of panicked men**, most with rifles, approached the blinding, erupting generator. (FICT†) <negative>

4.4.2 Unit nouns

Unit nouns allow us to cut up a generalized mass or substance into individual units or pieces. They are countable nouns, but they are usually followed by an *of*-phrase containing an uncountable noun. Each unit noun has a specific meaning, which shows up in the different collocations it favors:

unit noun	selected collocations
a **bit** of	cake, wood, fun, luck
a **chunk** of	chocolate, concrete, gold
a **grain** of	corn, dust, salt, sand
an **item** of	clothing, equipment, news
a **lump** of	clay, coal, soil, butter, fat
a **piece** of	cake, toast, chalk, land, wood, advice, evidence
a **sheet** of	cardboard, iron, paper

Other unit nouns are illustrated by: **scrap** *of paper*, **slice** *of bread*, **speck** *of dirt*, **strip** *of cloth*.

- Like quantifying collectives, unit nouns vary in their range: **loaf** *of bread* and **rasher** *of bacon* favor only one collocation, but *bit* and *piece* can be used very generally.
- One uncountable noun can also combine with a variety of unit nouns. For example, *paper* can follow *ball of, bit of, fragment of, heap of, length of, mound of, piece of, pile of, roll of, scrap of, sheet of, wad of,* etc. depending on the meaning required.

4.4.3 Quantifying nouns

Quantifying nouns are used to refer to quantities, which are usually specified in a following *of*-phrase containing either a plural noun or an uncountable noun:

> *a pile of bricks*   *a pile of rubbish*
> *a kilo of potatoes*   *a kilo of flour*

In this section, we distinguish seven kinds of quantifying nouns:

A Nouns for a type of container

noun	selected collocations
basket of	eggs, flowers, bread, fruit
box of	books, candy, matches, soap
cup of	coffee, soup, tea

Other examples are: *bag, barrel, bottle, can, carton, crate, keg, pack, packet, sack.*

B Nouns for shape

noun	selected collocations
heap of	ashes, blankets, bones, leaves, rubble
pile of	bills, bodies, bricks, rocks, rubbish, wood

Heap and *pile* can be used more generally, to express a very large amount:

> *Oh god, I've got* **heaps of things** *to do.* (CONV†)
> *They must have cost* **a pile of money***.* (FICT)

C Measure nouns

nouns	selected collocations
pint, gallon, quart, liter/litre of	beer, blood, gas, milk, oil, wine

nouns	selected collocations
foot, inch, yard, meter/metre of	*cloth, concrete, material, wire*
ounce, pound, gram, kilo(gram) of	*butter, cheese, flour, gold,*
ton, tonne of	*aluminium, bricks, ore, sewage*

<note: *liter* and *meter* are AmE spellings; *litre* and *metre* are BrE>

Some measure nouns are used more generally: *ounce*, for example, can be used for a very small amount and *ton* for a very large amount:

> *He didn't seem to have **an ounce of grown-up character** to draw on.* (FICT)
> *He has released **tons of songs** for the consumption of the masses.* (NEWS†)

D Plural numeral nouns

Hundred, thousand, million, dozen, and *score* are nouns for precise numbers. But they can be used in the plural to express an indefinitely large number:

> *Oh goodness, darling, you've seen it **hundreds of times**.* (FICT)

E Nouns for large quantities

The nouns *load(s)* and *mass(es)* can also be used emotively and vaguely to refer to large quantities:

noun	selected collocations
a *load* of	*fuel, garbage, junk, money, stuff*
loads of	*friends, money, things, work*
a *mass* of	*blood, detail, material, stuff*
masses of	*homework, money, people*

Load(s) is found mostly in conversation, while *mass* (in the singular) is found more in written language.

F Nouns ending in *-ful*

The noun suffix *-ful* (not to be confused with the adjective suffix *-ful*, as in *careful*) can be added to almost any noun that can denote some kind of container. For example:

> *bowlful, earful, fistful, handful, mouthful, pocketful, spoonful, teaspoonful*

In their basic meaning, these nouns are similar to measure nouns (e.g. in a recipe: *Add two teaspoonfuls of olive oil*), but they can be used more imaginatively. *Handful* is the most common noun of this type, and it also stands out in being used in an extended sense, to refer to a small quantity (as in *a handful of people*).

G *Pair* and *couple*

These are both nouns referring to two people, things, etc. But they are quite different in the way they collocate with other nouns:

noun	selected collocations
pair of	*arms, eyes, glasses, gloves, hands, pants, pliers, scissors, shoes, socks*
couple of	*days, babies, balloons, boys, examples, hours, kids*

The main difference is that *pair of* applies to two things which occur together (thus it can go with plural uncountable nouns, as in *a pair of trousers*); whereas *couple of* is used more vaguely, to mean 'two or three, a very small number'. *A couple (of)* is similar to *a few*, and can be considered a plural quantifier (see 4.7.3).

Like many vague expressions, *a couple (of)* is colloquial: it occurs far more in conversation than in the written registers, and hardly occurs at all in academic writing.

4.4.4 Species nouns

Species nouns are another class of nouns often followed by an *of*-phrase, but they refer to the type rather than the quantity of something:

> *Mr. Mathew is the **sort of** character Dickens liked to create.* (NEWS)
>
> *I was 'a floater,' really. I did all **kinds of** things.* (FICT)
>
> *There are two **types of** bond energy.* (ACAD†)
>
> *The scheme covers any **make of** machine.* (NEWS†)
>
> *Limestones, one **class of** sedimentary rock, are made up of calcium carbonate.* (ACAD†)
>
> *Under these conditions certain **species of** bacteria break down the waste to form methane gas.* (ACAD)

Species nouns can be followed by countable or uncountable nouns. In the former case, there is a choice between singular and plural for both nouns:

1 *any **make** of **machine*** (NEWS) <singular + of + singular>
2 *what **sort** of **things*** (ACAD) <singular + of + plural>
3 *certain **types** of **car*** (NEWS) <plural + of + singular>
4 *these **kinds** of **questions*** (ACAD) <plural + of + plural>

The choice between **3** and **4** often makes little difference to meaning; for example, *certain types of car* and *certain types of cars* have the same meaning.

Sort (of) + noun and *kind (of)* + noun are the most common species nouns. *Sort of* + noun is particularly frequent in conversation, and *kind of* + noun in fiction. Other species nouns (*type (of)* and *species(of)*) are frequent only in academic writing. (On *sort of* and *kind of* as adverbs, see 7.11.6)

Review

Major points of **GRAMMAR BITE A**: Types of nouns

➤ The major types of noun can be categorized in two ways: countable v. uncountable nouns, and common v. proper nouns.

➤ Countable nouns have singular and plural number; uncountable nouns do not.

➤ Common nouns refer to classes, while proper nouns refer to individuals.

➤ Some nouns can switch between countable and uncountable, and some can switch between common and proper.

➤ There are also special types of package noun: collective nouns, unit nouns, quantifying nouns, and species nouns.

➤ These special noun types are often followed by of (e.g. *group of animals, cup of coffee*).

GRAMMAR BITE

B Types of determiners

4.5 Determiners

Determiners are function words used to specify the kind of reference a noun has. As Table 4.1 shows, determiners vary in the kind of noun head they occur with: the three classes in question are countable singular noun, countable plural noun, and uncountable noun.

ble 4.1 **How determiners combine with nouns**

determiner type	countable nouns		uncountable nouns (singular)
	singular nouns	plural nouns	
zero article	—	*books*	*milk*
indefinite article	*a book*	—	—
definite article	*the book*	*the books*	*the milk*
possessive	*my/your book*	*my/your books*	*my/your milk*
demonstrative	*this book* *that book*	*these books* *those books*	*this milk* *that milk*
quantifier	*every / each book*	—	—
	—	*all (the) books*	*all (the) milk*
	—	*many books*	*much milk*
	—	*some books*	*some milk*
	—	*(a) few books*	*(a) little milk*
	—	*enough books*	*enough milk*
	—	*several books*	—
	either / neither book	*both books*	—
	any book	*any books*	*any milk*
	no book	*no books*	*no milk*
numeral	*one book*	*two/three books*	—

There are other determiners, not shown in this table: e.g. *a lot of*, and the *wh-*words *what*, *which*, and *whose*. The determiner slot can also be filled by genitives (e.g. *Tanya's*)—see 4.9.2.

Sometimes more than one determiner occurs in the same noun phrase: e.g. *all the books*. In such cases, the determiners occur in a fixed order, and for this purpose we distinguish between central determiners (the most common type), predeterminers (which precede central determiners when both occur) and postdeterminers (which follow central determiners). These are shown in Table 4.2. The different slots for determiners are summarized in Table 4.3.

Table 4.2 **How determiners combine with one another**

predeterminers	central determiner	postdeterminers		head
		(1)	**(2)**	
all	the		four	(races)
all	those	other		(guys)
both	these			(problems)
half	a			(cup)
half	the			(size)
twice/double	the			(size)
	the		many/few	(occasions)
	her	first		(marriage)
	the	last	two	(years)
	the	other	two	(fellows)

Table 4.3 **Summary of the position of determiners**

predeterminers	central determiners	postdeterminers (slot 1)	postdeterminers (slot 2)
all, both, half	articles	ordinal numerals	cardinal numerals
multipliers like double, twice	demonstrative determiners possessive determiners	semi-determiners like same, other, next	quantifying determiners

4.5.1 Determiner v. noun

The special kinds of nouns introduced in 4.4.1–4 behave in a similar way to quantifying determiners and semi-determiners like *a few, a little, a lot of,* and *such* (described in 4.7.3, 4.7.5). Like these determiners, expressions like *a load of, a couple of,* and *a kind of* qualify a following noun in terms of quantity or type. Compare:

> We knew **masses of** people. (CONV†)

> There's **so many** people in that place. (CONV†)

Similarly, **this sort of** food is equivalent in meaning to **such** food, except that *sort of* occurs more in speech, and *such* more in writing.

In some ways, it is the noun following *of*, rather than the quantifying noun, that behaves like the head of the noun phrase in these expressions. We will take this topic up again under **concord** (8.6.4).

4.5.2 Determiner v. pronoun

As will be clearer in 4.12–16, there is also a strong parallel between the different types of determiner and the different types of pronoun. The main correspondences are shown in Table 4.4. Pronouns lack the referential content provided by a noun head, and therefore they depend much more on context for their interpretation than determiners.

ble 4.4 **Classes of determiners and pronouns**

determiner class	pronoun class	general name
the definite article (4.6.3): *the*	personal pronouns (4.12): *you, he, she, it,* etc.	
possessive determiners (4.7.1): *your, his, her, its,* etc.	possessive pronouns (4.12.4): *yours, his, hers, its,* etc.	possessives
demonstrative determiners (4.7.2): *this, that, these, those*	demonstrative pronouns (4.14): *this, that, these, those*	demonstratives
quantifying determiners (4.7.3): *all, some, any, no,* etc.	indefinite pronouns (4.15): *all, some, any, none,* etc.	quantifiers

4.6 **The articles**

The most common determiners are the **articles** *the* and *a/an*, which signal definite and indefinite meaning. When no determiner occurs before the noun, it is useful to say that there is a **zero article**.

The **definite article** and the **indefinite article** both take a different spoken form when the word begins with a vowel:

/ə/	*a house, a UFO*
/ən/	*an apple, an hour, an MP*
/ðə/	*the house, the union*
/ðɪ/	*the apple, the hour, the other day*

(Notice that spelling can be misleading: some words beginning with *u* have an initial consonant sound /juː../, and a few words beginning with a 'silent' *h* have an initial vowel sound.) The spelling *an* is used when the following word begins with a vowel sound.

Figure 4.1 shows that articles are much less common in conversation than in writing. This is largely because conversation uses many pronouns, which generally do not need articles. In contrast, the written registers use many more nouns, resulting in many more articles.

Figure 4.1

Distribution of definite and indefinite articles across registers

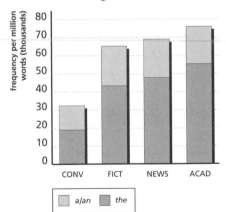

4.6.1 Indefinite meanings expressed by *a/an*

The indefinite article *a/an* is used only with singular countable nouns. It narrows down the reference of the head noun to one indefinite member of the class.

A Specific use of *a/an*

The indefinite article is often used to introduce a new specific entity into the discourse:

> 1 *A 12-year-old boy* *got mad at his parents Friday night because they refused to let **him** go fishing on the Colorado River with relatives. So, while his parents were distracted during a barbecue with eight adult friends, **he** slipped away from his sister and three brothers, snatched the keys to a Volkswagen Beetle and drove off in one of his parent's four cars, prompting fears that **he** had been kidnapped. <...> El Cajon police sent teletype descriptions of **the curly haired**, **90-pound sixth-grader** to law enforcement agencies throughout Southern California and the Arizona border area. **The boy** was found unharmed – but scared and sleepy – at about noon yesterday by San Diego County sheriff's deputies.* (NEWS†)

In **1,** the indefinite article **a** (*12-year-old boy*) introduces a specific, but unnamed and unknown boy; afterwards the boy is referred to by pronouns (*him, he*) and definite noun phrases (*the curly haired, 90-pound sixth-grader* and *the boy*).

B Unspecific use of *a/an*

The indefinite article is also used where the noun phrase does not refer to any specific individual:

> 2 *I'm looking for **a millionaire**, she says, but I don't see any around.* (CONV)
> 3 *'I feel terrible. I need **a friend**.'* (FICT)

In **2** and **3,** *a millionaire* and *a friend* are unspecific and mean 'any person of that kind'.

C Classifying or generic use of *a/an*

The indefinite article can also serve to classify an entity, as in **4,** or to refer generically to what is typical of any member of the class, as in **5:**

> 4 *My husband is **a doctor**.* (FICT) <classifying>
> 5 *A doctor* *is not better than his patient.* (FICT†) <generic>

Generic reference is described in 4.6.4 below.

4.6.2 Indefinite meaning with the zero article

Like *a/an* with singular countable nouns, the zero article signals indefiniteness with uncountable nouns (**1**) and plural countable nouns (**2**):

> 1 *We have **wine** on the table girls, drink it.* (CONV†)
> 2 *We have **telephones** and we talk to **people**.* (CONV)

The reference here is to an indefinite number or amount (often equivalent to *some*).

Zero article phrases commonly express non-specific or generic reference. But there are also some special uses of the zero article with singular countable nouns, where otherwise we expect *the* or *a/an* to occur.

A Meals as institutions

> *Are they going out for **dinner** or something?* (CONV)

B **Places as institutions**

> *The ceremony took place in* **church**. (FICT†)
>
> *They are prepared to go to* **jail** *for their cause.* (NEWS)

C **Predicatives with unique reference**

When a predicative noun phrase names a unique role or job, either a zero article or *the* is used:

> *Lukman was re-elected* **OPEC president** *in November.* (NEWS†) <with zero article>
>
> *Simon Burns is* **the chairman of the appeal fund**. (NEWS†) <with *the*>

D **Means of transport and communication**

The zero article here is found mainly after the preposition *by*:

> *travel by* **air/car/horse/rail**
>
> *send by* **mail/post/e-mail/satellite link**

E **Times of the day, days, months, and seasons**

> *Tomorrow at* **dawn** *we'll begin our journey.* (FICT)
>
> *When* **winter** *comes in 12 weeks, they will freeze.* (NEWS)

F **Parallel structures**

The zero article sometimes occurs in parallel structures like *X and Y* or *from X to Y*, where X and Y are identical or contrasting nouns:

> *He travelled from* **country** *to* **country**. (FICT)
>
> *Thankfully, it has turned out all right for* **mother** *and* **baby**. (NEWS)
>
> *This broadly relates to communications between* **lawyer** *and* **client**. (NEWS)

Examples of this kind are often fixed phrases, like *eye to eye, face to face, from start to finish*.

G **Block language**

The zero article is normal with noun phrases in **block language**, that is, abbreviated language used in newspaper headlines, labels, lists, notices (e.g. ENTRANCE, WAY OUT), etc. Compare:

> **Fire** *kills* **teenager** *after* **hoax**. (NEWS) <the headline>
>
> **A teenager** *died in* **a blaze** *at his home after firemen were diverted by a call that turned out to be* **a student prank**. (NEWS) <the news story following the headline>

Notice the headline uses the zero article for *fire, teenager,* and *hoax*, which are then mentioned in the news story as **a blaze**, **a teenager**, and **a student prank**.

H **Vocatives**

The zero article also occurs in forms of address (**vocatives**):

> *No hard feelings,* **Doctor**. (FICT)
>
> *Do you want that,* **baby**? (FICT)

With all these special uses of the zero article, it is worth noting that the same types of noun can occur with the definite article, when a more specific meaning is intended:

> **A** *Bye bye, dear, thanks for the lunch.* (CONV)
> **B** *The church serves a population of 18,000.* (NEWS)
> **D** *She took the train to the campus.* (FICT)

4.6.3 The definite article *the*

The goes with both countable and uncountable nouns. It marks the noun as referring to something or someone assumed to be known to speaker and addressee (or writer and reader).

A   Anaphoric use of *the*

After unknown entities have been introduced, they can be treated as 'known' and named by *the* in later references. This use is clear in passage **1** in 4.6.1, where we introduced the indefinite article:

> **1** *A 12-year-old boy got mad at his parents Friday night <...> and drove off in one of his parent's four cars <...> El Cajon police sent teletype descriptions of the curly haired, 90-pound sixth-grader to law enforcement agencies throughout Southern California and the Arizona border area. The boy was found unharmed <...>* (NEWS†)

This is called **anaphora**: the phrase with *the* refers back to a previously mentioned item.

B   Indirect anaphoric use of *the*

In indirect anaphora, the earlier noun is not repeated, but an associated noun is used with *the*:

> **2** *The Mercedes took a hard bounce from a pothole. 'Christ,' said Sherman, 'I didn't even see that.' He leaned forward over the steering wheel. The headlights shot across the concrete columns in a delirium.* (FICT)

We know that cars have a steering wheel and headlights, so after the Mercedes has been mentioned, 'the steering wheel' and 'the headlights' can be treated as known.

C   Use of *the* with synonyms

Sometimes, indirect anaphora involves the use of a different noun referring to the same thing or person:

> **3** *He found her blue Ford Escort in the car park. The vehicle was locked and the lights were off.* (FICT)

We know that the Ford Escort is a vehicle, and so 'the vehicle' can be treated as known. A second example is the shift from *a 12-year-old boy* to *the curly haired, 90-pound sixth-grader* in **1** above.

D Cataphoric use of *the*

Cataphora can be thought of as the opposite of anaphora. Here definite reference is established by something following later in the text, especially some modifier (marked *[]* here) of the noun (e.g. *the centre [of Bucharest]*, *the summer [of 1984]*):

4 *Another potential voter starts to tell them about **the car** [that went through his garden wall].* (NEWS)
5 *Emerson admitted that he felt like quitting for **the rest** [of the season].* (NEWS)

In **4** the defining postmodifier is a relative clause; in **5** it is an *of*-phrase.

E Situational use of *the*

The often occurs because an entity is known from the situation: either the immediate situation in which speech takes place, or the wider situation which includes knowledge of the national situation, the world, or even the universe.

6 *I think there's somebody at **the door** now.* (CONV) <immediate situation>
7 *Cos they get money off **the government**, don't they?* (CONV†) <wider situation>

Sometimes a speaker assumes situational knowledge that the hearer does not have, and so has to clarify the reference:

8 *A: Could you get me from **the shelf** the black felt pen?*
*B: **Which shelf?***
*A: **The big one**.* (CONV†)

F Other uses of *the*

The above are the major uses of the definite article, but definiteness depends on assumed shared knowledge in the minds of speaker and addressee, so some uses of *the* are more difficult to explain:

9 *A woman and a child had a narrow escape yesterday when their car left the road. **The accident** happened at about 9.25am at Marks Tey, near Colchester.* (NEWS†)

Here the reader has to infer that the event described in the first sentence is an accident. This type of usage is similar to indirect anaphora, except that we cannot point to a particular noun, like *Mercedes* in **2** above, which explains the later use of **the** *headlights*, etc.

Also, some uses of *the* are idiomatic, as part of a fixed phrase: e.g. *in the main, by the way, at the end of the day*, etc.

Finally, *the* can be used for generic reference, as in *He plays **the** trumpet*, discussed in 4.6.4 below.

As Figure 4.2 shows:

- Situational *the* is common only in conversation, where speakers rely on the context that they share with hearers.
- Anaphoric *the* is common in all registers.
- Cataphoric *the* is heavily concentrated in non-fiction writing; it is associated with complex noun phrases.

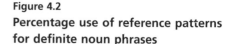

Figure 4.2

Percentage use of reference patterns for definite noun phrases

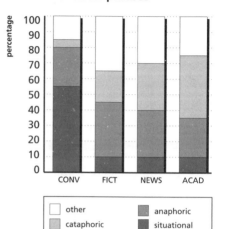

4.6.4 Generic reference

Reference is **generic** when a noun phrase refers to the whole class, rather than just one or more instances of the class. In English all three articles (*a/an*, *the*, and zero) can be used for generic reference:

- indefinite article: ***A doctor*** *is not better than his patient.* (FICT†)
- zero article: ***Doctors*** *are not better than their patients.*
- definite article: ***The doctor*** *is not better than his patient.*

All three of these sentences can be understood to express a general truth about the class of people called doctors (although **c** could also be about a particular doctor).

- *A/an* is used generically with singular countable nouns, and designates 'any person or thing of the class'.
- The zero article is used generically with plural and uncountable nouns, and refers to the class as a whole:

    *They're very nice, **cats** are.* (CONV)

    Beer *is, quite rightly, Britain's favourite Friday night drink.* (NEWS)

- In general, *the* is used generically only with singular countable nouns:

    The trumpet *is a particularly valuable instrument for **the contemporary composer**.* (NEWS†)

    *Comprehension depends on **the reader**'s ability to remember all the words in **the sentence**.* (ACAD†)

4.7 Other determiners

There are several other subclasses of determiners.

4.7.1 Possessive determiners

Possessive determiners specify the noun phrase by relating it to the speaker/ writer or other entities. The possessive determiners correspond to personal pronouns:

possessive determiner	*my*	*our*	*your*	*his*	*her*	*its*	*their*
personal pronoun	*I*	*we*	*you*	*he*	*she*	*it*	*they*

Possessive determiners make noun phrases definite:

1 ***My*** *brain was scarcely working at all.* (FICT)
2 *She didn't want to spoil **her** shoes.* (FICT†)
3 *Never hit **your** younger sister.* (CONV)

For example, ***her*** *shoes* in **2** refers to the shoes belonging to the specific woman, and not anyone else.

4.7.2 Demonstrative determiners

The **demonstrative determiners** *this/these* and *that/those* are similar to the definite article *the* in conveying definite meaning. However, they also specify whether the referent is singular or plural (*this* v. *these*) and whether the referent is 'near' or 'distant' in relation to the speaker:

	countable		uncountable
	singular	plural	singular
near	*this book*	*these books*	*this money*
distant	*that book*	*those books*	*that money*

In general, *this/these* are about twice as common as *that/those*. By far the highest frequency of *this/these* is in academic writing, where these forms are useful especially for anaphoric reference.

Like *the* (4.6.3), the demonstrative determiners can make the reference clear either by pointing to the situation (situational reference), or by referring to the neighbouring text—either preceding (anaphoric reference) or following (cataphoric reference).

A Situational reference

Situational reference is very common in conversation, where the choice between *this/these* and *that/those* reflects the speaker's perception of whether the referent is near or distant:

> ***This*** *cake's lovely.* (CONV) <the speaker is eating the cake>

> *Look at **that** man sitting there.* (CONV) <the man is sitting some distance away>

The choice of determiner can also reflect emotional distance: *this/these* can express greater sympathy than *that/those*:

> *You know I actually quite like **this** chap.* (CONV)

> A: *They're still holding **those** guys? We should have just bombed them hard right then. As soon as they tried to pull **that** hostage move.*

> B: ***Those*** *bastards.* (CONV) <note: *bastards* is a taboo word and may be offensive to some people>

B Time reference

Although the basic situational use of demonstratives is in reference to place (compare *here/there*), another kind of situational use refers to time (compare *now/then*):

> *They're buying a house **this** year in France.* (CONV) <the present year>
>
> *They started at nursery **that** summer.* (CONV) <a summer in the past>

C Anaphoric reference

In writing, demonstratives typically refer back to the preceding text:

> *In 1882 H. Weber gave [a set of postulates for abstract groups of finite order]. **These postulates** are essentially those in use today.* (ACAD)

In this example, *these postulates* in the second sentence refers back to *a set of postulates* in the first sentence.

D Cataphoric reference

Like cataphoric *the* (4.6.3), cataphoric *that* and *those* are used where a modifier following the head specifies the reference of the head noun. In these examples, the modifier is a relative clause, marked by *[]*:

> *The unit of heat was defined as **that** quantity [which would raise the temperature of unit mass of water <...>]* (ACAD†)
>
> *We apologise to **those** readers [who did not receive the Guardian on Saturday].* (NEWS†)

Here *that* and *those* are formal in style, and do not express 'distant' meaning. They could be replaced by *the*.

E Introductory *this/these*

There is a special conversational use of *this/these* to introduce a new entity into a narrative:

> *We went to **this** mall where there was **this** French restaurant.* (CONV†)

4.7.3 Quantifying determiners (quantifiers)

Some determiners specify nouns in terms of quantity or amount and are therefore called **quantifying determiners** (or simply **quantifiers**):

with uncountable nouns	with countable nouns
all money	*all girls*
much money	*many girls*

(Quantifying pronouns, discussed in 4.15.2, are related forms with similar meanings.)

Quantifiers can be broadly divided into four types:

A Inclusive

Some inclusive quantifiers are: *all, both, each, every*. *All* refers to the whole of a group or mass; *both* refers to two entities, and goes with a plural noun:

> *The testing of **all** hens will continue to be compulsory.* (NEWS†)

> ***Both** amendments were defeated.* (NEWS†)

Each and *every* refer to all the individual members of a group but, in contrast to *all*, combine only with singular countable nouns. *Each* stresses the separate individual, *every* stresses the individual as a member of the group. *Each* can denote two or more, while *every* denotes three or more.

> *We have two stations, but two people can work at **each** station.* (CONV)
>
> ***Every** minute of **every** day, hundreds of millions of tonnes of coal are burned.* (ACAD)

B Large quantity

Many and *much* denote a large quantity: *many* with plural countable nouns, and *much* with uncountable nouns. They are used especially with negatives, interrogatives, and some combinations such as *very much/many, so many/ much, too many/much, a great many, a good many*:

> *There weren't **many** people there.* (CONV†)
>
> *There's **so many** other girls wearing exactly the same thing.* (CONV†)
>
> *The girl wasn't paying **much** attention.* (FICT†)

Other determiners signifying a large amount are multi-word units, like *a lot of, lots of, plenty of, a great/good deal of. A lot of* and *lots of* often replace *much* and *many* in casual speech:

> *There were **lots of** people going through the tills.* (CONV†)
>
> *'He's had **a lot of** trouble.'* (FICT†)

In fact, *much* and *many* would be odd in these informal contexts.

C Moderate or small quantity

Some usually denotes a moderate quantity and is used with countable and uncountable nouns:

> *Insurance shares produced **some** excitement.* (NEWS)
>
> ***Some** performance curves will now be presented.* (ACAD†)

We will go into the contrast between *some* and *any* in 8.8.10–11.

Determiners denoting a small quantity are:

	plural countable	uncountable
a small number/amount	*a few, several*	*a little, a bit of*
less than expected	*few (fewer, fewest)*	*little (less, least)*

A few and *a little* are used to indicate a small amount:

> *With **a little** care he had no difficulty whatever in putting his glass back on the table.* (FICT)
>
> *There were **a few** people sitting at the tables in the back.* (FICT†)

Few and *little* (without *a*) mean 'not many' and 'not much'.

> *Very **few** women have hair that's that short.* (CONV†)
>
> *That's why I dislike plans because so much time is spent planning and so **little** time is spent doing anything.* (CONV†)

> **D** **An arbitrary or negative individual or amount**

Any denotes an arbitrary member of a group, or an arbitrary amount of a mass. *Either* has a similar meaning, but it is used to denote a member of a group of two, and occurs only with singular countable nouns:

> *There aren't **any** women.* (CONV)
>
> *Got **any** money?* (CONV)
>
> *There were no applications for bail for **either** defendant.* (NEWS†)

As these examples suggest, *any* and *either* usually occur with negatives or questions. On the other hand, *no* and *neither* have a purely negative meaning: *no* is used for countables as well as uncountables, and *neither* is used for a choice of two:

> *Next time there would be **no** mercy.* (FICT)
>
> ***Neither** method is entirely satisfactory.* (ACAD†) <comparing two methods>

There will be more to say about the relations between *some*, *any*, and *no*, and between *either* and *neither*, under the headings of **negation** (especially 8.8.7–11) and **assertive** and **non-assertive** forms (8.8.10–11).

4.7.4 Numerals as determiners

Cardinal numerals (like *two*) are similar to quantifiers, while **ordinal numerals** (like *second*) are similar to the semi-determiners (discussed below in 4.7.5). Like most quantifiers, numerals can occur in determiner position or in head position in a noun phrase:

> *You owe me **ten** bucks, Mary.* (CONV)
>
> *Tomorrow I have to get up at **seven**.* (CONV)

When the two types occur together in one noun phrase, ordinal numerals normally precede cardinal numerals:

> *The **first three** pages were stuck together with the young man's blood.* (FICT†)

Notice also that the numerals can follow the definite article—in fact this is normal with ordinal numerals.

The alphabetic form (*five*, *twenty*, etc.) is most common with numbers under ten, and with round numbers such as *a hundred*. The digital form (*5*, *20*, etc.) is more common with higher numbers:

Table 4.5 **Cardinal and ordinal numerals**

cardinal	ordinal	cardinal	ordinal
0 zero	—	10 ten	10th tenth
1 one	1st first	11 eleven	11th eleventh
2 two	2nd second	12 twelve	12th twelfth
3 three	3rd third	13 thirteen	13th thirteenth
4 four	4th fourth	14 fourteen	14th fourteenth
5 five	5th fifth	15 fifteen	15th fifteenth
6 six	6th sixth	16 sixteen	16th sixteenth
7 seven	7th seventh	17 seventeen	17th seventeenth
8 eight	8th eighth	18 eighteen	18th eighteenth
9 nine	9th ninth	19 nineteen	19th nineteenth

*Last year, **767** works were sold to **410** people in **four** days.* (NEWS)

Ordinal numbers, however, are more commonly written with the alphabetic form (*fifteenth* rather than *15th*).

4.7.5 Semi-determiners

In addition to the determiners so far mentioned, words like *same, other, another, last,* and *such* have some adjective characteristics and some determiner characteristics. These forms lack the descriptive meaning that characterizes most adjectives, and like most determiners, they can also double as pronouns (see 4.16). We call these words **semi-determiners**:

> **The same** person was there with almost exactly **the same** message. (CONV)
>
> *I saw how one fist beat into the palm of **the other** hand behind his back.* (FICT)
>
> *He's living with her and **another** girl, and **another** boy.* (CONV)
>
> *I would like to think that this is not his **last** Olympics.* (NEWS)
>
> ***Such** functions are not symmetrical.* (ACAD†)

4.7.6 *Wh*-determiners

***Wh*-determiners** are used to introduce interrogative clauses (**1**) and relative clauses (**2**):

> 1 ***Which** way are we going?* (CONV)
>
> 2 *I had a girl **whose** dog was the bridesmaid.* (NEWS)

These will be illustrated further in discussing interrogative clauses (8.11) and relative clauses (9.7–8).

Review

Major points in **GRAMMAR BITE B**: Types of determiners

➤ The most common determiners are the definite and indefinite articles (*the* and *a/an*).

➤ There is also a zero article, used with plural or uncountable nouns for indefinite meaning.

➤ All three articles can be used to express generic meaning (referring to a class as a whole).

➤ Predeterminers precede determiners in a noun phrase; postdeterminers follow determiners.

➤ Possessive and demonstrative determiners are definite in meaning (like *the*), whereas quantifying determiners are indefinite in meaning (like *a/an*).

➤ Numerals (cardinal and ordinal numbers) are grammatically like a class of determiners.

➤ Quantifying determiners and quantifying pronouns usually have the same form (e.g. *all, few*). We call both of them quantifiers.

➤ Semi-determiners, such as (*the*) *same* and *another* have characteristics of both determiners and adjectives.

GRAMMAR BITE

c Number and case in nouns

4.8 Number: singular and plural

Number is the term for the contrast between singular and plural: a contrast in English grammar affecting not only nouns, but pronouns, determiners and verbs. However, our concern now is with nouns: the singular form of nouns is the unmarked and most common form, and plural nouns are formed from the singular by inflectional change, normally the addition of a suffix.

4.8.1 Regular plurals

The overwhelming majority of nouns form their plural by adding the ending -(e)s.

A Pronunciation

Add /ɪz/ after consonants /s, z, ʃ, ʒ, tʃ, dʒ/:

> *case—cases, fuse—fuses, ash—ashes, bridge—bridges*

Add /s/ after voiceless consonants (except /s, ʃ, tʃ/):

> *cat—cats, map—maps, stick—sticks, act—acts, myth—myths*

Add /z/ after vowels and voiced consonants (except /z, ʒ, dʒ/):

> *boy—boys, dog—dogs, girl—girls, time—times, union—unions.*

B Spelling

The normal spelling is -s, but if the word ends in s, z, x, sh, or ch, the spelling is -es:

> *bus—buses, box—boxes, bush—bushes, match—matches*

If the singular ends in a consonant letter + -y, the spelling is -ies:

> *copy—copies, fly—flies, lady—ladies, army—armies*

If the singular ends in a vowel letter + -y, however, the spelling is -s:

> *boy—boys, day—days, key—keys, essay—essays*

If the singular ends in -o, the spelling of the plural is sometimes -os and sometimes -oes:

> *pianos, radios, videos* v. *heroes, potatoes, volcanoes*

4.8.2 Native irregular plurals

Irregular plurals can be divided into native English plurals and plurals borrowed from other languages. A small number of native English words have irregular plurals:

- changing the vowel:

man—men	*foot—feet*	*tooth—teeth*
woman—women	*goose—geese*	*mouse—mice*

- adding *-(r)en*:
  child—children   *ox—oxen*
- voicing the last consonant—/f/ changes to /v/:
  calf—calves   *knife—knives*   *leaf—leaves*   *life—lives*
  shelf—shelves   *thief—thieves*   *wife—wives*   *wolf—wolves*

Most nouns ending in *-f*, however, have a regular plural: *beliefs, chefs, chiefs, proofs, reefs, roofs.*

4.8.3 Latin and Greek plurals

Some words borrowed from Latin and Greek keep their original plurals, although often the regular plural is an alternative:

alumnus—alumni   *syllabus—syllabi*
curriculum—curricula   *formula—formulae*
appendix—appendices   *axis—axes*
crisis—crises   *diagnosis—diagnoses*
criterion—criteria   *phenomenon—phenomena*

4.8.4 Zero plurals

Zero plurals are plural forms which do not change from singular to plural:
- some animal nouns: *fish, sheep, deer, salmon*
- some quantifying nouns: *dozen, hundred, foot, mile* when they are used as part of a numerical quantity (e.g. *two **dozen** people, two **hundred** kids*)
- a few other zero plural nouns: *aircraft, dice, series, species.*

The sign of a zero plural is that the same form can be used with singular and plural **concord**:

*Anglers are heading for court because **fish are** too easy to catch.* (NEWS)
*Each **fish is** caught, the hook carefully removed and the weight noted before release.* (NEWS)

4.8.5 Plural-only nouns and singular nouns in *-s*

These are nouns that can be confusing because:
- they look singular but are actually plural, like *people, police, staff, cattle*
- they look plural but are actually singular, like *news, measles, mumps, checkers.*

4.9 Case: the genitive

Historically, English had **case** endings for nouns like the **nominative** and **accusative** cases of pronouns (e.g. *he—him*). However, the only case ending that survives in modern English nouns is the **genitive** ending *'s*.

4.9.1 The form of the genitive

The *-'s* genitive ending varies in pronunciation in the same way as the plural ending:

A Pronunciation

Add /ɪz/ after /s, z, ʃ, ʒ, tʃ, dʒ/:

Charles's, Liz's, George's, Cox's

Add /s/ after voiceless consonants except /s, ʃ, tʃ/:

cat's, Jack's, Philip's, Smith's, staff's

Add /z/ after vowels and voiced consonants except /z, ʒ, dʒ/:

boy's, daddy's, girl's, women's, dog's

With regular plural nouns ending in -s, e.g. *girls'*, the genitive is not pronounced.

B Spelling

The genitive is written with an apostrophe: -'s.

With regular plural nouns ending in -s, the genitive is marked by a final apostrophe: *girls'*. Thus *the girl's success* (one girl) and *the girls' success* (more than one girl) are distinguished only by the apostrophe.

For irregular plurals not ending in -s, the genitive is -'s as for singular forms: *women's rights, men's clothing*.

For singular names ending in -s, the regular genitive is usual: *Davis's, Charles's*. But sometimes these nouns are treated as if they were plural nouns: *Davis', Charles'*.

4.9.2 Genitive as determiner: specifying genitives

Genitives usually fill the determiner slot in a noun phrase: they precede the head, and like other determiners they play the role of **specifying** the reference of the head noun. In this, they have the same function as the possessive determiner. Compare:

the girl's *face*   **her** *face*   **his parents'** *home*   **their** *home*

These examples answer the question 'Whose X?'. The genitive acts as the head of its own noun phrase, which acts as determiner for the whole noun phrase. In the following, [] enclose the genitive phrase:

[the girl's] face   *[his parents'] home*   *[decent people's] feelings*

Notice that the determiner or modifier at the beginning of the three examples belongs to the genitive noun, and not to the following noun. It is often possible to use an *of*-phrase as an alternative to the genitive. Compare:

[decent people's] feelings   *the feelings [of decent people]*

This example underlines the need to see the genitive construction as a phrase, even though the genitive very frequently consists of one word, as in *[Jack's] voice*. Genitives can even have postmodifiers, as in **someone else's** *house*.

4.9.3 Genitive as modifier: classifying genitives

In contrast to specifying genitives, other genitives have the role of **classifying** the reference of the head noun: the question answered here is 'What kind of X?'. Compare these pairs of specifying and classifying genitives:

1 *Several hours later [**the bird's** relieved owner] arrived at the station.* (NEWS†)

2 *His hair felt like [**a bird's** nest]. He was a mess.* (FICT)

1 *Even [**her two children's** clothes] disappeared.* (NEWS)

2 *Hoppity in Hartlepool is one of the few nearly new shops specializing just in [**children's** clothing].* (NEWS)

In the 1 examples the reference is to the owner of a specific bird and the clothes belonging to some specific children. In the 2 examples, the genitives serve to classify the types of nest and clothes.

In many cases, a classifying genitive is equivalent to an adjective or a noun modifier, whereas this is not true of the specifying genitive. Compare the genitives in the following examples with the non-genitive modifiers which could replace them:

*the **women's** movement*	***children's** literature*	*a **summer's** day*
*(the **feminist** movement)*	*(**adult** literature)*	*(a **summer** day)*

4.9.4 Genitives of time and measure

The genitive is often used to specify time (especially in news writing):

> *Wigler's and Parsons' report appeared in **this week's** issue of Science magazine.* (NEWS)

The genitive is also used to express duration, distance/length, or value:

- duration: ***a minute's** hesitation, **a month's** holiday, **two hours'** sleep*
- distance/length: *I held the telephone at **arm's** length and stared at it.* (FICT)
- monetary value: *She had to buy **fifty pounds'** worth.* (CONV)

4.9.5 Independent genitives

Independent genitives are genitive phrases standing alone as a noun phrase. Unlike other genitives, they are not part of another (main) noun phrase. Many independent genitives involve **ellipsis** (8.5).

Elliptic genitives are genitive phrases whose main noun head can be recovered from the preceding text (see 8.5). The omitted noun is shown in *[]* below:

> *This isn't my [handwriting]. It's **Selina's**.* (FICT) <i.e. Selina's handwriting>
>
> *All the Turner girls preferred girls' [toys] to **boys'**.* (FICT†) <i.e. boys' toys>

Other independent genitives have become conventional, so that they need no supporting noun head in the context. They generally refer to people's homes (**1**), to other places such as businesses and clubs (**2**), and to commercial products and firms (**3**):

1 *She's going to **a friend's**.* (CONV†) <i.e. a friend's house>

2 *The vast main concourse had the combined appearance of a football scrimmage and Christmas Eve at **Macy's**.* (FICT) <Macy's is a department store>

3 *An open bottle of **Jack Daniel's** is on the candle table.* (FICT†) <Jack Daniel's is a type of whiskey>

4.9.6 Double genitives

The **double genitive** is a special construction in which either the independent genitive or a possessive pronoun occurs in an *of*-phrase:

> *This was **a good idea of Johnny's**.* (CONV)
>
> *There's a talk by this lady from Boulder who's **a student of Sandy's**.* (CONV)
>
> *The woman who owns Harte's is **a friend of ours**.* (FICT†)

As these examples show, the main noun phrase typically begins with the indefinite article. In fact, the definite article does not normally combine with the double genitive: **the good idea of Johnny's* is unlikely to occur.

The meaning of the double genitive can sometimes be alternatively expressed by other constructions. Thus, *a friend of ours* could alternatively be expressed as *one of our friends*.

4.9.7 Semantic types of noun taking the genitive

For the most part, the genitive inflection is used with personal nouns: that is, nouns referring to humans, including proper nouns. However, Figure 4.3 shows that the genitive is also used with other semantic types of nouns, particularly in news writing.

Apart from personal nouns, the most common genitive nouns are collective nouns, usually referring to human organizations (e.g. *the Government's denial*). Place nouns are also moderately common as genitives, usually referring to countries or other places with human populations (e.g. *Spain's inflation*). Thus, a genitive noun is very likely to have a human connection, even if it is not a personal noun.

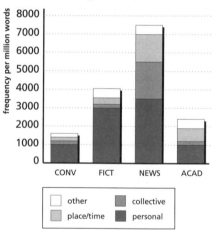

Figure 4.3

Distribution of genitive nouns

4.9.8 The choice between genitives and *of*-phrases

It is easy to find examples where the genitive construction and the *of*-phrase seem to be free variants: e.g. *the car's owner* and *the owner of the car*. Yet in practice there are several factors which favor the choice of one construction over the other. Here we briefly review those factors, considering only *of*-phrases which are in competition with the genitive (e.g. excluding *of*-phrases with special noun classes, like unit nouns and quantifying nouns—see 4.4 above).

A   The semantic class of the noun

Personal nouns, especially proper nouns, are much more likely to be used in the genitive. Inanimate and abstract nouns, on the other hand, are much more likely to be used with the *of*-construction: e.g. *the future of socialism*, rather than *socialism's future*.

B   The meaning relation between the two nouns

There are many different meaning relations that can exist between the genitive noun and the main noun (or between the corresponding nouns in an *of*-construction). Some meanings favor the genitive, while others favor the *of*-construction.

Meaning relations favoring the genitive are:

- possessive genitive:

   The family's car *was found abandoned at Andersonstown Crescent.* (NEWS)
   <the family had/owned a car>

- attributive genitive:

   On occasions, **Martha's** *courage failed her.* (FICT) <Martha was courageous>

- subjective genitive:

   Chiang's recognition *of the priority of the spoken language explained why so few characters were pictographs or ideographs.* (ACAD) <Chiang recognized something>

On the other hand, other meaning relations favour the *of*-phrase, such as the 'objective' construction where the noun after *of* has a role like the object of a verb:

   The brutal murder of a child *leaves a firm trace on the mind of a police officer like an indelible pen.* (NEWS) <someone murdered the child>

The combination of a genitive construction and an *of*-construction in the same noun phrase is illustrated in:

   The Government's denial of the need (NEWS†)   subjective + objective

   Mrs. Bidwell's description of the quarrel (FICT†)   subjective + objective

We could express the same meaning with a clause: *The Government denied the need* and *Mrs. Bidwell described the quarrel.*

C   Collocations

Genitives tend to occur in fixed collocations: *at death's door, life's work, nature's way, out of harm's way.* The genitive with *sake* is particularly productive: *for God's sake, for goodness' sake, for heaven's sake, for old time's/times' sake.*

D Length of phrases: end-weight

Genitive constructions are generally short, whereas *of*-phrases are often longer. This pattern, shown graphically in Figure 4.4, follows the general principle of **end-weight** in English (see 12.1.4).

E Information flow: end-focus

English tends to prefer **end-focus** (see 12.1.1–2): presenting given information first, and new information at the end of a construction. Thus, the genitive, coming first, tends to express given information, while the *of*-phrase, following, tends to introduce new information.

Figure 4.4

Preference for *of*-phrase v. *s*-genitives according to length

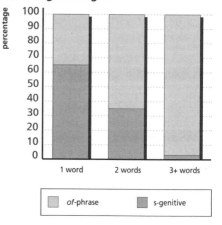

> **United's manager**, *Alex Ferguson, must despair.* (NEWS) <after Manchester United has recently been mentioned>
>
> *April 1991: Takes over as **manager of Liverpool**.* (NEWS) <after managers' jobs have recently been mentioned>

F Register distribution of genitives and *of*-phrases

A last important factor is register. Figure 4.5 shows that *of*-phrases are by far the more frequent option overall, and they are especially common in academic writing.

The proportion of genitives is much higher in news than in academic writing. News writing uses the genitive to pack information densely and concisely into noun phrases. For example:

> **Last week's** *meeting of **the borough's** policy and finance committee was all but devoid of dissenting voices.* (NEWS†)

Conversation, though, has relatively few genitives or *of*-phrases.

Figure 4.5

Distribution of *of*-phrases v. *s*-genitives across registers

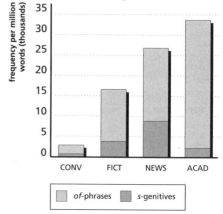

Review: Major points of GRAMMAR BITE C: Number and case in nouns

➤ Number is the term for the contrast between singular and plural in nouns.
➤ In addition to regular plurals with *-s*, English has a few classes of nouns with an irregular plural.
➤ The genitive case in nouns is used to express possession and other meanings.

➤ Genitives can have the role of either a determiner or a modifier in the larger noun phrase.
➤ Genitives can also be phrases, with their own determiners and modifiers.
➤ Genitives overlap with *of*-phrases in the range of meanings they express.

GRAMMAR BITE

D Gender and noun formation

4.10 Gender: masculine, feminine, personal, and neuter

Gender is not an important grammatical category in English: unlike many European languages, English has no masculine and feminine inflections for nouns or determiners. Yet semantically, gender is an interesting and controversial topic: for example, how do English speakers distinguish between male, female, and male-or-female reference? Gender is also an area where the language is changing. This section discusses how to signal the gender of nouns and pronouns.

Four semantic gender classes can be distinguished:

	example nouns	pronouns
masculine	*Tom, a boy, the man*	*he, him, his*
feminine	*Sue, a girl, the woman*	*she, her, hers*
personal	*a journalist, the doctor*	*who, someone*
neuter	*a house, the fish*	*it, what, which*

- **Masculine** nouns and pronouns refer primarily to male people.
- **Feminine** nouns and pronouns refer primarily to female people.
- **Personal gender** nouns and pronouns refer primarily to people, regardless of whether they are female or male.
- **Neuter gender** nouns and pronouns refer primarily to inanimates (including abstractions).

However, as the following sections show, there are special circumstances where the boundaries of these categories are fuzzy.

4.10.1 Masculine and feminine noun reference

There are four major ways of specifying masculine and feminine contrast in nouns:

- using totally different nouns:

  father—mother   son—daughter   uncle—aunt   man—woman   bull—cow

- using derived nouns with masculine and feminine suffixes -*er/or*, -*ess*:

  actor—actress   waiter—waitress   master—mistress

- using a modifier, such as *male, female; man, woman, women*:

  male nurse   female officer   woman doctor   male dancer   women priests

- using nouns in *-man, -woman*:

  chairman   Englishman   policewoman   spokeswoman

(In writing, masculine nouns consisting of noun + *man* look like compounds, but in pronunciation, *-man* is more like a derivational suffix: it is pronounced /-mən/ in both the singular and the plural.)

The derivational endings *-er/or* and *-ess* are not of equal status. While *-ess* always has female reference, *-er/or* can be used for both sexes with personal gender words like *doctor* and *teacher*. Further, *-ess* can be added to a noun without *-er/-or* to form the female variant: *lion—lioness; priest—priestess*.

Feminine nouns in *-ess* are generally used less than their masculine counterparts, because we usually use the masculine form when we do not know which sex the individual is and for plurals when we may be referring to both males and females. The most common *-ess* nouns are *princess, actress, mistress, duchess, waitress, countess, goddess, hostess,* and *stewardess.* However, all these are used less than their masculine counterparts (*prince, actor, master, duke,* etc.).

Similarly, most English speakers and writers use words ending in *-man* far more than words ending in *-woman.* Even the most common words ending in *-woman* (*spokeswoman, policewoman, chairwomen, businesswoman, congresswoman, horsewoman*) are used far less than the corresponding words ending in *-man* (*spokesman, policeman,* etc.)

4.10.2 Gender bias in nouns

There are two reasons for the preference of male terms over female terms:

- Speakers and writers refer to males more frequently than to females.
- The masculine terms are often used to refer to both sexes. For example, the masculine nouns *spokesman* and *manager* are used in the following sentences to refer to women:

  *Eyeline **spokesman** Rosie Johnson said: 'We don't need a vast sum, but without it we'll be forced to close.'* (NEWS)

  *Area **manager** Beth Robinson says: 'Our business in Finaghy has steadily increased year by year.'* (NEWS†)

Both these factors amount to a bias in favour of the masculine gender. With reference to the second factor, it is traditionally argued that a term like *chairman* or *governor* has personal gender (i.e. is sex-neutral) in addition to its masculine use. However, the fact that such roles have typically been taken by men means that these terms have strong masculine overtones.

In recent decades, efforts have been made to avoid masculine bias by using gender-neutral nouns in *-person* instead of *-man* or *-woman.* For example:

  *Mrs Ruddock said she had been nominated as **spokesperson** for the wives.* (NEWS†)

  ***Salespersons** by the thousands have been laid off in the recession.* (FICT†)

However, this trend has had limited success so far. Words in *-person* (or their plurals in *-persons* or *-people*) are rare compared with the corresponding words in *-man* or *-men.* The only moderately common words of this kind are *chairperson(s), spokesperson(s), salespeople,* and *townspeople.* (Note that both *-people* and *-persons* are used in the plural.)

4.10.3 Gender bias in pronouns

English has some personal-gender pronouns that are neutral for female/male, such as *somebody, everyone, you, they,* and *who.* But in the key case of singular third-person pronouns, there is no personal-gender form corresponding to *he* (masculine) and *she* (feminine). When there is need to refer to 'male or female', the traditional choice, again, is in favor of the masculine: using *he* to refer to both sexes or either sex:

> Each <u>novelist</u> aims to make a single novel of the material **he** has been given. (ACAD†)

Three main ways of avoiding this gender bias have been adopted in recent decades. (In the following examples, like the example above, underlining marks a personal-gender word that a pronoun co-refers to.)

A Use of coordinated pronouns and determiners

> It's the duty of every <u>athlete</u> to be aware of what **he or she** is taking. (NEWS)
>
> Thus, the <u>user</u> acts on **his/her** own responsibility when executing **his/her** functions within **his/her** task domain. (ACAD)

As the second example shows, this device can become rather clumsy through repetition. In actual practice, this strategy is restricted primarily to academic writing.

B Use of plural instead of singular pronouns

> 1 *Not <u>everybody</u> uses **their** indicator.* (CONV)
> 2 *<u>Somebody</u> left **their** keys. These aren't yours?* (CONV)
> 3 *<u>Nobody</u> likes to admit that **they** entertain very little, or that **they** rarely enjoy it when **they** do.* (NEWS)

The use of *they* referring back to a singular personal noun or pronoun is common in conversation. In serious writing, however, it is often avoided as 'incorrect', because a commonly accepted 'rule' of pronoun concord states that the pronoun should agree with its antecedent noun phrase in number, as well as in gender. However, there has been a growing adoption of this use of *they* in written texts, as in **3** above. (On concord generally, see 8.6.)

C Avoiding the problem by using the plural throughout

It is usually possible to avoid a generic singular noun phrase by converting it into the generic plural, e.g. changing **1** to **1a**:

> 1 *The <u>teacher</u> finds that **he or she needs** more time.* (ACAD†)
> 1a *<u>Teachers</u> find that **they need** more time.*

4.10.4 Personal v. neuter reference with pronouns

There is a choice between neuter *it* and personal reference by *she* or *he* in the case of babies and animals (particularly pets). Note the differences between the **a** and the **b** examples below:

1a *One three-month-old* <u>baby</u> *managed to talk **its** parents into sending Santa a letter.* (NEWS†).

1b *The* <u>baby</u> *was lying on **his** back in **his** crib, perfectly content.* (FICT)

2a *You know that* <u>cat</u>, *it scratched me.* (CONV)

2b *Only the* <u>dog's</u> *determination to be reunited with **her** master kept **her** going.* (NEWS†)

Linguistically, babies (**1**) and animals (**2**) are 'borderline beings', who may not entirely qualify as 'persons'. So *it* is a convenient way to refer to them if their sex is not known. *It*, however, may be an offensive way to refer to a child in talking (say) to its proud parents! (*She* can also be used to refer to nations and ships, as a conventional form of personification.)

It can refer to human beings when used as an introductory subject and followed by *be*:

'Who is it?' 'Me. It's me.' (FICT†)

There is nothing offensive in this usage.

4.11 The formation of derived nouns

Derived nouns are formed from other words by means of **affixation** (prefixes and suffixes), **conversion**, and **compounding**.

4.11.1 Affixation

Derivational prefixes do not normally alter the word class of the base word; that is, a prefix is added to a noun to form a new noun with a different meaning:

base noun	suffixed noun
patient	**out**patient (a patient who is not resident in a hospital)
group	**sub**group (a group which is part of a larger group)
trial	**re**trial (another trial of the same person for the same crime)

Derivational suffixes, on the other hand, usually change both the meaning and the word class; that is, a suffix is often added to a verb or adjective to form a new noun with a different meaning:

base word	suffixed noun
adjective: *dark*	*dark**ness***
verb: *agree*	*agree**ment***
noun: *friend*	*friend**ship***

A Noun prefixes

The following list shows some of the more frequent prefixes, and indicates the typical meaning signaled by each prefix.

prefix	main meaning(s)	examples
anti-	against, opposite to	*antibody, anticlimax*
arch-	supreme, most	*arch-enemy, archbishop*

prefix	main meaning(s)	examples
auto-	self	*autobiography, autograph*
bi-	two	*bicentenary, bilingualism*
bio-	of living things	*biochemistry, biomass*
co-	joint	*co-chairman, co-founder*
counter-	against	*counteract, counterclaim*
dis-	the opposite of	*disbelief, discomfort*
ex-	former	*ex-Marxist, ex-student*
fore-	ahead, before	*forefront, foreknowledge*
hyper-	extreme	*hyperinflation*
in-	inside, *or* the opposite of	*inpatient, inattention*
inter-	between, among	*interaction, intermarriage*
kilo-	a thousand	*kilobyte, kilowatt*
mal-	bad	*malfunction, malnutrition*
mega-	a million, supreme	*megawatt, megastar*
mini-	small	*minibus, mini-publication*
mis-	bad, wrong	*misconduct, mismatch*
mono-	one	*monopoly, monosyllable*
neo-	new	*neomarxist, neo-colonialism*
non-	not	*nonpayment, non-specialist*
out-	outside, separate	*outpatient, outbuilding*
poly-	many	*polysyllable, polytheism*
re-	again, back	*re-election, re-organization*
semi-	half	*semicircle, semi-darkness*
sub-	below	*subgroup, subset*
super-	more than, above, large	*superhero, supermarket*
tele-	distant	*telephone, teleshopping*
tri-	three	*tricycle, tripartism*
ultra-	beyond	*ultrafilter, ultrasound*
under-	below, too little	*underclass, underachievement*
vice-	deputy (second in command)	*vice-chairman, vice-president*

B Noun suffixes

Suffixes tend to have less specific meanings than prefixes. Grammatically speaking, their main role is to signal a change of word class, so that (for example) if you meet a word ending in *-ism*, *-ness*, or *-tion*, you can recognize it as a noun. However, some suffixes are ambiguous: e.g. *-al* and *-ful* can mark an adjective as well as a noun. (Note that the process of derivation can bring a change in the pronunciation or spelling of the base word: for example, when we add *-cy* to *infant*, the whole word is spelt *infancy*, not *infantcy*.)

The symbols V, A, and N in the list below show whether the noun is derived from a verb, an adjective, or another noun. Those that are derived from verbs and adjectives are said to be **nominalizations**. Most derived nouns are abstract in meaning.

suffix	main meaning(s)	examples
-age	(various meanings)	*baggage, wastage, postage, orphanage*
-al	action or instance of V-ing	*arrival, burial, denial, proposal*

suffix	main meaning(s)	examples
-an, -ian	nationality, language, etc.	American, historian, Korean, Victorian
-ance, -ence	action or state of V-ing,	assistance, resemblance, experience
	state of being A	dependence, difference, ignorance
-ant, -ent	a person who V-s, something used for V-ing	assistant, consultant, student, coolant, intoxicant, lubricant
-cy	state or quality of being A/N	accuracy, adequacy, infancy, lunacy
-dom	state of being A/N	boredom, freedom, stardom, wisdom
-ee	a person (various meanings)	absentee, devotee, employee, trainee
-er, -or	a person/thing that V-s,	actor, driver, filler, teacher, visitor
	a person connected with N	footballer, cottager, New Yorker
-ery, -ry	(various non-personal meanings)	bakery, bravery, refinery, robbery
-ese	nationality or language	Chinese, Japanese, journalese
-ess	a female N (see 4.10.1)	actress, baroness, tigress, waitress
-ette	a small N	cigarette, kitchenette, novelette
-ful	amount that fills a N (see 4.4.2)	handful, mouthful, spoonful
-hood	state of being A/N	childhood, falsehood, likelihood
-ician	person concerned with N	clinician, mathematician, physician
-ie, -y	a pet name for N	auntie, daddy, doggie, Johnny
-ing	action/instance of V-ing,	feeling, meeting, reading, training
	place or material	building, crossing, landing, lining
-ism	ideology, movement, tendency	atheism, criticism, capitalism, Marxism
-ist	follower of N/A-ism, specialist	atheist, capitalist, racist, physicist
-ite	citizen or follower of N	Moabite, Muscovite, Thatcherite
-ity	state or quality of being A	ability, activity, density, insanity
-let	a small N	bomblet, booklet, leaflet, piglet
-ment	action or instance of V-ing	argument, movement, statement, treatment
-ness	state or quality of being A	blindness, darkness, fairness, happiness
-ship	state or skill of being a N	friendship, membership, relationship
-tion	action or instance of V-ing	communication, education, production
-ure	action or instance of V-ing	closure, departure, exposure, pressure

Apart from -er, the most frequent noun suffixes are all abstract: -tion, -ity, -ness, -ism, -ment (see Figure 4.6). In general, these suffixes are far more frequent and productive in academic writing than in the other registers. The following is an extreme example of the use of these abstract 'nominalizations' in academic prose:

> The **conventionalist** system lacks the **capacity** to reach anything like the **flexibility** of **pragmatism**, because any **relaxation** would inevitably involve the defeat of publicly encouraged **expectation**. (ACAD)

4.11.2 Conversion

Another way to derive nouns from other word classes is known as conversion (or 'zero derivation'). In this case, no affix is added to the base, but the base itself is converted into a different word class, usually from a verb or adjective into a noun (see Table 4.6).

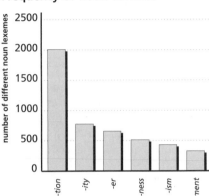

Figure 4.6
Frequency of noun suffixes

Table 4.6 Converted nouns

conversion from	base	meaning(s) of converted noun	example of converted noun
adjectives (A)	*hopeful*	someone who is A	*presidential **hopefuls***
	white	someone who is A	*they speak like the **whites** do in the South*
		something that is A	*you could see the **whites** of his eyes*
verbs (V)	*catch*	act of V-ing	*he took a brilliant **catch** <sport>*
		something that is V-ed	*they had a fine **catch** of fish*
		something used for V-ing	*he loosened the **catch** and opened the window*
	cheat	someone who V-s	*... accused him of being a **cheat***
	walk	act of V-ing	*we can go for a **walk** later*
		way of V-ing	*the **walk** of a gentleman*
		place for V-ing	*the **walk** stretched for 154 miles*

4.11.3 Compounding

Another very productive process is the formation of compound nouns. Common patterns of compounding are the following (note that the parts of the compound can be written as a single word, or else hyphenated or written as two words):

structural pattern	examples
1a noun + noun	*bar code, bathroom, database, eye-witness, lamp post, logjam, newspaper, shell-fish, suitcase, wallpaper*
1b noun + verb/noun	*gunfire, handshake, home run, landslide, moonwalk*
1c noun + verb-*er*	*dishwasher, dressmaker, eye-opener, firefighter, screwdriver*
1d noun + verb-*ing*	*fire-fighting, housekeeping, thanksgiving, window shopping*
1e verb/noun + noun	*cookbook, dipstick, playboy, swimsuit, volleyball*
1f *self* + noun	*self-control, self-esteem, self-help, self-indulgence, self-pity*

structural pattern	examples
1g verb-*ing* + noun	*filing cabinet, filling station, mockingbird, printing-press*
2 adjective + noun	*bigwig, blackbird, grandmother, highway, real estate*
3 verb + particle	*checkout, feedback, fly-over, go-between, handout, standby*
4 particle + verb/noun	*bystander, downturn, in-fighting, outfit, overcoat, upkeep*

Noun + noun combinations are the most productive type of noun compound. In fact, Patterns **1a–g** above can all be considered as special cases of noun + noun compounds. Noun compounds are especially common in news writing, where they help to pack a lot of information into a small space. (Noun + noun sequences are discussed further in 9.5.)

Review

Major points of **GRAMMAR BITE D**: Gender and the formation of nouns

➤ English nouns do not have special inflectional endings for gender; instead, gender is a semantic category in English.

➤ English speakers often show gender bias in the way they use masculine and feminine words, e.g. nouns ending in -*man* or -*woman*.

➤ Another example of gender bias is that the pronoun *he* has traditionally been used to refer to both men and women.

➤ Several strategies are used to avoid gender bias with nouns and pronouns.

➤ Derived nouns can be formed through affixation (prefixes and suffixes), conversion, and compounding.

➤ Forming new nouns with suffixes is especially common in academic writing, while compounding is especially common in news.

GRAMMAR BITE

E Types of pronouns

Most **pronouns** replace full noun phrases, and can be seen as economy devices. Personal and demonstrative pronouns, for example, serve as pointers to the neighbouring text (usually preceding text) or to the speech situation. Other pronouns have very general reference, or can be used for substitution or ellipsis (see 8.5). In this Grammar Bite, we survey the major pronoun classes: **personal pronouns, reflexive pronouns, demonstrative pronouns,** and **indefinite pronouns.**

But first, in Figure 4.7, we notice that pronouns have a very different pattern of use from nouns.

..12 **Personal pronouns**

Personal pronouns have different forms according to

- **number:** singular, plural (e.g. *I* v. *we*)
- **person:** first person, second person, third person (e.g. *I* v. *you* v. *she*)
- **case:** nominative, accusative, possessive (e.g. *I* v. *me* v. *mine*)
- **gender:** masculine, feminine, neuter (e.g. *he* v. *she* v. *it*).

These distinctions are shown in Table 4.7.

Figure 4.7

Distribution of nouns v. pronouns across registers

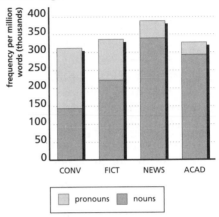

ble 4.7 Personal pronouns and corresponding possessive and reflexive forms

person	personal pronoun		possessive		reflexive pronoun
	nominative	accusative	determiner	pronoun	
1st					
singular	*I*	*me*	*my*	*mine*	*myself*
plural	*we*	*us*	*our*	*ours*	*ourselves*
2nd					
singular	*you*	*you*	*your*	*yours*	*yourself*
plural	*you*	*you*	*your*	*yours*	*yourselves*
3rd					
singular	*he*	*him*	*his*	*his*	*himself*
	she	*her*	*her*	*hers*	*herself*
	it	*it*	*its*	–	*itself*
plural	*they*	*them*	*their*	*theirs*	*themselves*

A Case forms of pronouns

The form of the personal pronoun varies according to case. Nominative personal pronouns like *I, he, she* are used for the subject of a clause, whereas accusative personal pronouns like *me, him,* and *them* are used for other positions in the clause, such as object. The possessive determiners (e.g. *my, her*) and possessive pronouns (e.g. *mine, hers*) are in effect the genitive case forms of personal pronouns.

B Person forms in pronouns

In spite of their name, personal pronouns may have both personal and non-personal reference. *I, me, you, he, she, him, her, we,* and *us* generally refer to people, while *it* has non-personal reference. The plural pronouns *they, them, theirs* can have both personal and non-personal reference, because *they* is the plural of *he, she* and *it*:

1 *You hear about <u>guys</u> beating up <u>women</u> and stuff and yet **they** love **them** so much.* (CONV) <personal reference>
2 *Those are <u>great pictures</u>, aren't **they**? Did you see **them**?* (CONV) <non-personal reference>

Person in pronouns actually relates people, things, etc. to the speech situation. The three persons (first, second, third) are generally used as follows:

- First-person pronouns refer to the speaker/writer.
- Second-person pronouns refer to the addressee(s).
- Third-person pronouns refer to other people or entities, which are neither the speaker/writer nor the addressee.

4.12.1 Person and pronoun usage

The above definitions of the first-, second- and third-person categories are clear enough and apply to the vast majority of personal pronoun uses. However, there are some problems and special cases.

A First person: *we*

While the singular pronoun *I* is unambiguous in referring to the speaker, the plural pronoun *we/us/ours* can vary according to context. *We* can be inclusive, including the addressee(s) (I + you): *What game should **we** play?.* It can also be exclusive, excluding the addressee(s) but including other people (e.g. I + my family): *Nancy, **we** love you.*

The speaker can make the reference more explicit by adding other words to *we*:

'**We all** believe in him,' said the 18-year-old chairwoman. (NEWS†)

'**We Americans** are spoilt,' he said. (NEWS)

Another more explicit method is to use *I/we* in coordination with another pronoun or proper noun:

*We've got a bond in common, **you and I**.* (FICT)

*Well, it was late, and **me and my friend Bob**, we'd been to a game.* (FICT†).

Notice that *we* in these examples is used as a subject, but is reinforced by a loosely attached coordinated phrase (see 3.5.7 on **prefaces** and **tags**). However, in general it is left to the addressee to decide the reference of *we* from the situation.

In a very different way, the meaning of *we* can also vary in academic writing. Three uses of *we* can be distinguished:

1 ***We** spoke of Dirac's piece of chalk.* (ACAD†)
2 ***We** are now able to understand why **our** information about the states of motion is so restricted in quantum mechanics.* (ACAD)
3 *When **we** start talking **we** often cease to listen.* (ACAD)

In **1**, *we* refers to the author(s) of the text. This use sometimes occurs even when there is only one author. In **2**, *we* refers to the author(s) and reader(s), assuming a common understanding shared by both. In **3**, *we* refers to people in general. *We* here is similar to the generic pronoun *one* (see 4.15.3). These meaning differences are usually implicit, so readers must decide the intended meaning in each case.

B **Second person: *you***

You is similar to *we* in inviting different interpretations. For example, since *you* can be either singular or plural, it is not always clear whether it refers to one person or more than one. As with *we*, the plural use can sometimes be specified by a following nominal expression:

> *And what did **you all** talk about?* (NEWS)
>
> ***You two** are being over optimistic.* (FICT)
>
> *Are **you guys** serious?* (FICT)

You all is particularly common, and is three times more frequent in American English conversation than in British English conversation: this form (also transcribed *y'all*) is especially a feature of southern American English.

C **Third person: *it, he, she, they***

Generally third-person pronouns are important in making referential links in a text or a conversation. In the following examples, we underline the **antecedent**, i.e. the noun phrase a pronoun refers back to:

> 1 <u>My cousin</u> works at Jones <...>. **She**'s a designer, **she**'s very famous. **She** designs a lot of clothes for Lord Browning. **Her** best friend is Princess Margaret. (CONV)
>
> 2 On **his** arrival in Hobart, <u>Mr. Bond</u> told journalists **he** was not finished yet. (NEWS)

Third-person pronouns are usually **anaphoric** as in **1**, where the antecedent precedes the pronoun. But it is also possible, as in **2**, for a pronoun to go before its antecedent. (Compare the anaphoric and cataphoric use of *the* in 4.6.3.)

It also acts as a **dummy pronoun**, which does not have a specific reference, but has the role of 'place filler', particularly as an empty subject:

> ***It**'s cold.* (CONV) <weather>
>
> ***It** is eight o'clock in the morning.* (NEWS) <time>
>
> ***It**'s a long way from here to there.* (FICT†) <distance>

Empty *it* also appears in special clause types—see extraposition (10.3.3, 10.4.3, 10.17) and clefting (12.12).

4.12.2 Generic use of personal pronouns

The personal pronouns *we*, *you*, and *they* can all be used to refer to people in general:

> ***We** cannot nibble at quantum theory. If **we** are to digest it properly it must be swallowed whole.* (ACAD)
>
> ***You**'ve got to be a bit careful when **you**'re renting out though.* (CONV)

> *Ross duly appeared in a multi-million pound advertising campaign and the rest, as **they** say, is history.* (NEWS)

These **generic** pronouns tend to retain a trace of their basic meaning as first-, second-, or third-person pronouns. Thus *we* is typical of written style, and places the focus on shared human experience or knowledge, including the speaker's. *You* is typical of spoken English; choice of this generic pronoun appeals to common human experience, inviting empathy from the hearer. *They*, also common in speech, can be roughly glossed 'people, not you or me'.

A fourth pronoun capable of expressing the meaning 'people in general' is the generic pronoun *one* (see 4.15.3): it occurs rather infrequently in formal speech or in writing.

> ***One** can have too much of a good thing.* (NEWS)

4.12.3 Case: nominative v. accusative personal pronouns

Most of the personal pronouns have a distinction between nominative and accusative case forms: *I—me, he—him, she—her, we—us, they—them*. The use of these forms is generally straightforward: the nominative is used as subject, and the accusative as object or complement of a preposition.

In some positions, however, there is variation. There is a tendency for the accusative form to spread in popular usage into contexts traditionally reserved for the nominative form:

A Variation in pronoun choice after forms of *be*

> 1 *Hello gorgeous it's **me**!* (CONV)
> 2 *So maybe it's **I**, John Isidore said to himself.* (FICT)

Although the nominative form (e.g. *I*) is traditionally considered correct after the copula *be*, the accusative form (e.g. *me*) is the normal choice in practice, in both conversation and the written registers.

B Variation in pronoun choice after *as* and *than*

We find more or less the same pattern after *as* and *than* in **comparative constructions**:

> 3 *She's as bad as **me** and you!* (CONV)
> 4 *You are closer to death than **I**.* (FICT)

The accusative form (*me*) predominates as in **3**, especially in conversation.

C Stand-alone noun phrases

Where a noun phrase stands on its own, without being integrated into a clause, the accusative forms are again commonly used:

> A: *Who told him?*
> B: ***Me**.* (CONV)

> *'**Me and my friend Bob**, we'd been to a game.'* (FICT†)

4.12.4 Possessive pronouns

The possessive pronouns (*mine, yours, his,* etc.) are like possessive determiners, except that they constitute a whole noun phrase. The antecedent is underlined in the examples below:

1 *The <u>house</u> will be* **hers** *you see when they are properly divorced.* (CONV†)
2 *Writers have produced extraordinary work in <u>conditions</u> more oppressive than* **mine**. (NEWS)

Possessive pronouns are typically used when the head noun can be found in the preceding context: thus in **1**, *hers* means 'her house', and in **2**, *mine* means 'my conditions'. Here the possessive pronoun is parallel to the elliptic use of the genitive (4.9.5).

To make the possessive noun phrase emphatic, a possessive determiner precedes *own*:

We have a wine tasting, and everybody makes **their own**. (CONV) <i.e. makes their own wine>

The possessive form with *own* typically refers back to the subject of the clause (like reflexive pronouns—see 4.13 below).

Possessive pronouns depend a great deal on context for their interpretation. Consequently they are far more common in conversation than in the written registers.

4.13 Reflexive pronouns

Reflexive pronouns end with *-self* in the singular and *-selves* in the plural. Each personal pronoun has a corresponding reflexive pronoun, and in fact *you* has two reflexive forms: *yourself* (singular) and *yourselves* (plural):

personal	*I*	*we*	*you*	*he*	*she*	*it*	*they*
reflexive	*myself*	*ourselves*	*yourself/yourselves*	*himself*	*herself*	*itself*	*themselves*

4.13.1 Reflexive pronouns in their reflexive use

The most common use of reflexive pronouns is in their basic 'reflexive' role: to mark some other element of the clause as referring back to the subject (underlined below):

1 *<u>Most consultants</u> are just selling* **themselves**. (CONV†)
2 *<u>We</u>'re all looking very sorry for* **ourselves**. (CONV)

The reflexive pronoun most commonly fills an object slot (as in **1**) or a prepositional complement slot (as in **2**) in the same clause as the **co-referential** subject (signaled here by underlining). The reflexive pronoun has to be used if co-reference is intended. For example, if *them* were used instead of *themselves* in **1** (*consultants are selling* **them**) the meaning would be different: that consultants were selling some other products.

Reflexive pronouns are used like this only when there is a co-referential subject in the same clause. Notice, in **3**, that *his big brother*, not *he*, is the subject of the non-finite clause, and therefore *him* is used instead of *himself*:

3 *<u>He</u> wanted [his big brother to treat* **him** *as an equal].* (FICT†)

4.13.2 Emphatic use of reflexive pronouns

A reflexive pronoun can be used for emphasis, immediately following the emphasized noun phrase (underlined):

1 *Unfortunately <u>I</u> **myself** did not have this chance.* (FICT)
2 *This explains why the representation of the totem is more sacred than <u>the totemic object</u> **itself**.* (ACAD)

With subject noun phrases, as in **1**, there is another variant of this construction. The reflexive pronoun is separated from its noun phrase, and placed later in the clause. This word order is preferred in conversation:

3 *<u>I</u>'ll do the preparation **myself**.* (CONV)

4.13.3 Reciprocal pronouns

The reciprocal pronouns *each other* and *one another* are similar in use to reflexive pronouns. They refer back to the subject of the clause, and occur as object or prepositional complement:

> *We always speak French to **each other**.* (CONV)
> *They got along, they admired **one another**.* (CONV)

Reciprocal pronouns express a mutual relation between two or more parties: e.g. *A and B hate each other* means *A hates B*, and *B hates A*. *Each other* is far more common than *one another*.

4.14 Demonstrative pronouns

The four words *this, that, these,* and *those* act as demonstrative determiners (as we saw in 4.7.1). They also act as demonstrative pronouns, which match the determiners in their meaning and function:

> ***That** was by far my favorite ride. It was just incredible.* (CONV)
> A: *What are **these**, mom?*
> B: ***Those** are called hot plates.* (CONV)

Like demonstrative determiners, demonstrative pronouns contrast in terms of singular (*this, that*) and plural (*these, those*), and in terms of 'near' reference (*this, these*) and 'distant' reference (*that, those*).

Demonstrative pronouns can often be considered as alternatives to the pronoun *it*. These pronouns all refer to something in the context—either in the neighbouring part of the text or the external situation. But unlike the pronoun *it*, demonstrative pronouns are usually pronounced with stress and so carry greater communicative weight.

> A: *What a neat picture.*
> B: *Yeah, I should put **that** in a frame or something – keep **it**.* (CONV)

The demonstrative pronouns are much less frequent than the personal pronouns.

That is the most common of the demonstrative pronouns. *That* is especially common in conversation, where it often has a vague reference:

> ***That**'s what I thought* (CONV).

This, on the other hand, is most frequent in academic writing. Both *this* and *these* are used commonly for textual linkage. For example:

> *We must accept that the positive part of conventionalism <...> cannot offer useful advice to judges in <u>hard cases</u>.* **These** *will inevitably be cases in which the explicit extension of the various legal conventions contains nothing decisive either way <...>.*
>
> *But it must now be said that, so far from being a depressing conclusion,* **this** *states precisely the practical importance of conventionalism in adjudication. <...>* **This** *explains why cases do not come to court <...>.*
> (ACAD†)

This passage illustrates the two major types of linkage with demonstrative pronouns. The pronoun *these* refers back to a specific noun phrase antecedent (*hard cases*). In contrast, the pronoun *this* is used here to refer back to a more extensive piece of text, which includes several preceding sentences.

4.14.1 Demonstrative pronouns referring to humans

The demonstrative pronouns are usually not used to refer to humans. A major exception to this rule, though, is when they are used in introductions:

> *Sally introduced them. 'Danny,* **this** *is my friend Sarah.'* (FICT)

Similarly, callers in a phone conversation will often identify themselves using the demonstrative pronoun *this*:

> *Hi,* **this** *is Larry.* (CONV)

4.15 Indefinite pronouns

There are three main classes of indefinite pronouns: the compound pronouns *somebody, everything, anyone,* etc.; the quantifiers *some, all, any,* etc.; and the pronoun *one*.

4.15.1 Compound pronouns

There are four groups of **compound pronouns**, beginning with the determiners *every, some, any,* and *no*:

	every-	*some-*	*any-*	*no-*
personal reference	everybody	somebody	anybody	nobody
	everyone	someone	anyone	no one
neuter reference	everything	something	anything	nothing

No one is normally spelt as two words, although the hyphenated spelling *no-one* also occurs.

The meanings of compound pronouns match the meanings of noun phrases with the corresponding determiners (4.7.3), except that they refer to indefinite persons or things. Compare:

> *'He brought me* **some natural food***.'* (FICT)
>
> *'I have brought* **something** *for you from Doctor Fischer.'* (FICT)

Compound pronouns are most common in conversation and fiction, and least common in academic writing. As the examples below show, compound pronouns have a general and often vague reference:

> *I enjoyed not having to say **anything** to **anybody**.* (CONV†)
>
> *They gutted it and they put in all new offices and **everything**. There was **nothing** in there.* (CONV)

The two personal forms in *-body* and *-one* have the same meaning, but somewhat different distributions. Pronouns ending in *-body* are most common in conversation, while pronouns in *-one* are preferred in the written registers. Pronouns ending in *-body* are also more common in American English than in British English.

4.15.2 Quantifying pronouns (quantifiers)

Quantifiers, as we have seen in 4.7.3, can act both as determiners and as pronouns. In general, the form of the word is identical for both.

Most quantifying pronouns are followed by *of* and a definite noun phrase, as in *some of the . . ., several of my . . .*:

> *some (of), both (of), each (of), either (of), neither (of), all (of), many (of), enough (of), any (of), much (of), several (of), none (of), (a) little (of), (a) few (of)*

For example:

> *Bring **all of** your friends.* (CONV†)

However, quantifying pronouns can also stand alone as a noun phrase (e.g. *all* in **1**), and they can have an elliptic meaning, referring back to some previously mentioned noun phrase (e.g. the second *some* in **2**):

> **1** *I just want to get my bonus, that's **all**.* (CONV)
>
> **2** A: *I'll eat **some of** the steak.*
> B: *I'll have **some**.* (CONV) <i.e. some of the steak>

4.15.3 The pronoun *one*

Apart from its use as a numeral (4.7.4), *one* has two uses as a pronoun:

A Substitute *one, ones*

One can replace a countable noun that has been mentioned before or is inferred from the context. A singular noun is replaced by *one*, and a plural noun by *ones*.

> *An artist cannot fail; it is success to be **one**.* (ACAD) <i.e. to be an artist>
>
> *You can test out the colors tonight and find which **ones** are best.* (CONV) <i.e. which colors>

Note that unlike other indefinite pronouns, *one* and *ones* can follow a determiner or semi-determiner: e.g. *the one, those ones, another one, the last one*. They can even follow an adjective: *the latest one*. In fact, *one* is best seen as a replacement for a noun, rather than for a whole noun phrase.

B Generic *one, one's, oneself*

One is also used as a generic pronoun (see 4.12.2) referring to people in general. In this use, *one* is singular and has no plural form. However, it has a possessive form *one's* (**2**) and a reflexive form *oneself* (**3**).

1 *One doesn't raise taxes with enthusiasm.* (NEWS†)
2 *Success and acclaim were seen as a means of validating **one's** existence.* (NEWS†)
3 ***One** does not wish to repeat **oneself** unduly.* (ACAD†)

Substitute *one* is far more common in conversation than in the written registers. Generic *one*, on the other hand, is impersonal and rather formal in tone. It is largely restricted to the written registers, especially fiction and academic writing.

.16 **Other pronouns**

There are pronoun uses corresponding to semi-determiners (see 4.7.5). For example, *others, another, the other, the latter, the last, such.*

> *Be self-reliant and helpful to **others**.* (CONV)

> *She said: 'Stilgar, I underestimated you.' '**Such** was my suspicion,' he said.* (FICT)

The *wh*-pronouns *what, which, who, whom,* and *whose* are used to form interrogative and relative clauses; these will be dealt with in later chapters (see 8.11, 9.8.2).

> ***What**'s the problem?* (NEWS)

> *But he's in the wrong, he's the one **who**'s wrong.* (FICT)

Review

Major points in **GRAMMAR BITE E**: Types of pronouns

➤ The major types of pronoun are personal, reflexive, demonstrative, and indefinite.
➤ Personal pronouns refer to people and entities in the context of discourse; they can also have generic reference.
➤ Reflexive pronouns are used to refer back to the subject, or for emphasis.
➤ Demonstrative pronouns point to entities which are 'near' or 'distant' in the context of discourse.
➤ Indefinite pronouns are mostly quantifying words, related in form and meaning to quantifying determiners.

5
Verbs

GRAMMAR BITES in this chapter

A Verb functions and classes

> ➤ Main verbs v. auxiliary verbs
> ➤ Lexical verbs v. primary verbs v. modal verbs
> ➤ Lexical verbs across registers

B Single-word lexical verbs

> ➤ The meanings that lexical verbs can express
> ➤ The different uses of the twelve most common lexical verbs

C Lexical verbs: structures and patterns

> ➤ Verbs with regular and irregular morphology
> ➤ The creation of new verbs with derivational affixes
> ➤ Verb valency patterns

D Multi-word lexical verbs

> ➤ The use of multi-word lexical verbs, including phrasal verbs, prepositional verbs, and phrasal-prepositional verbs

E Primary verbs

> ➤ The uses of the three primary verbs: *be, have,* and *do*

F Copular verbs

> ➤ The copula *be*
> ➤ Other verbs that can function as copular verbs
> ➤ The major uses and meanings of copular verbs

5.1 **Introduction**

Verbs provide the focal point of the clause. The main verb in a clause determines the other clause elements that can occur and specifies a meaning relation among those elements. However, there are many different kinds of verbs, including lexical v. auxiliary verbs, different semantic classes, and single-word v. multi-word verbs.

In the six Grammar Bites of this chapter, we describe several major classes of verbs. In Grammar Bite A, we survey the major functions and classes for verbs, considering oppositions like main v. auxiliary verb. In Grammar Bite B, we focus on single-word lexical verbs. We describe their meanings—using semantic classes—and the most common verbs in each semantic class. Then in Grammar Bite C, we discuss structural aspects of lexical verbs: their valency patterns, verbs with irregular morphology, and the creation of new verbs with derivational affixes.

In Grammar Bite D, we turn to a type of verb that is often challenging for learners of English: multi-word lexical verbs, including phrasal verbs, prepositional verbs, and phrasal-prepositional verbs. Then, in Grammar Bite E, we take a closer look at the three primary verbs (*be*, *have*, and *do*). Finally, in Grammar Bite F, we identify the verbs that function as copular verbs, illustrating their major uses and meanings.

GRAMMAR BITE

A Verb functions and classes

5.2 **Verb functions and classes**

5.2.1 **Main verbs v. auxiliary verbs**

Main verbs play a central role in clauses. They usually occur in the middle of a clause, and they are the most important element in the clause because they determine the other clause elements. The pattern of these other clause elements is called the **valency pattern**. For example, a clause with the main verb *go/went* cannot take a direct object (e.g. **I went the house*). However, *go/went* can be followed by an adverbial (underlined below):

> I **went** <u>into the empty house</u>. (FICT)

In contrast, a clause with the main verb *give* usually occurs with both a direct object and an indirect object. In the following example, *him* is the indirect object and *a message* is the direct object:

> I could **give** <u>him</u> <u>a message</u>. (FICT)

Auxiliary verbs, on the other hand, occur before a main verb and qualify the meaning of the main verb. In the following example, *could* and *be* are auxiliary verbs, and *staying* is the main verb.

> Jack the Ripper **could be staying** there. (CONV†)

In this example, *could* adds unreality to the meaning of the main verb, and *be* signals an ongoing process. The overall meaning is quite different from the sentence without auxiliary verbs, *Jack the Ripper stays there*.

5.2.2 Lexical verbs v. primary verbs v. modal verbs

Verbs can be grouped into three major classes according to their ability to function as main verbs or auxiliary verbs:

* **Lexical verbs** (e.g. *run, eat, think*) function only as main verbs.
* **Primary verbs** (*be, have,* and *do*) can function as both auxiliary and main verbs.
* **Modal verbs** (*can, could, shall, should, will, would, may, might, must*) function only as auxiliary verbs.

Lexical verbs (sometimes called 'full verbs') are used only as main verbs.

> *Children and dogs **ran** from side to side.* (FICT†)
>
> *He barely **ate** or **slept** that night.* (FICT)

The class of lexical verbs is an open class, which means that the English language is always adding new lexical verbs.

Most lexical verbs have **regular** endings for forming past and present tense (e.g. *call, calls, called*). However, many of the most common lexical verbs in English have **irregular** morphology. In the above example sentences, the verbs show irregular past tense forms: *run—ran, eat—ate,* and *sleep—slept*. (See 5.5–7.)

One distinctive feature of English grammar is that lexical verbs often occur as multi-word units (see 5.8–12):

> *He **turned on** the lights.* (FICT)
>
> *I **looked at** that one again.* (CONV)

There are only three primary verbs: *be, have,* and *do,* the most common verbs in English. These verbs form a separate class because they can be used either as a main verb or as an auxiliary verb. For example, compare the following uses of each primary verb:

* primary verbs—main verb function:

> *He **does** my washing.* (CONV)
>
> *His dad **was** an art professor.* (CONV†)
>
> *Every atom **has** a dense nucleus.* (ACAD†)

* primary verbs—auxiliary verb function (with main verb underlined):

> *He **doesn't** <u>look</u> at the numbers.* (CONV)
>
> *He **was** <u>wearing</u> a dark ski mask.* (NEWS†)
>
> *A particular combination of results **has** <u>occurred</u>.* (ACAD)

Primary verbs are described further in 5.13–15.

Finally, modal verbs are used only as auxiliary verbs. In the following examples the main verb is again underlined:

> *People thought he **might** have been <u>joking</u>.* (NEWS)
>
> *He **would** probably <u>like</u> it softer.* (NEWS)

Modal verbs and other auxiliaries are covered in detail in Chapter 6.

5.2.3 Lexical verbs across registers

Lexical verbs are much more common than primary verbs or modal verbs (see Figure 5.1). This is not surprising as there are hundreds of different lexical verbs, and most clauses occur with a lexical verb as main verb. In contrast, there are few primary verbs and modal verbs, and many clauses occur without an auxiliary verb.

When the verb *be* (*am, is, was, were*, etc.) is used as a main verb it is termed the **copula**, because of its special linking or 'coupling' function. It is the single most common verb occurring as a main verb. Interestingly, the copula *be* is more common in academic prose than in the other registers. Lexical verbs, however, are relatively rare in academic prose; they are much more common in conversation and fiction (Figure 5.2).

The following text samples illustrate the differing uses of main verbs in conversation and academic prose. Lexical verbs are in bold, and the copula *be* is underlined. Auxiliary verbs are not marked (e.g. *are* in the phrase *are taking*). (Auxiliary verbs express verb **aspect, voice,** and **modality**, which are covered in Chapter 6.)

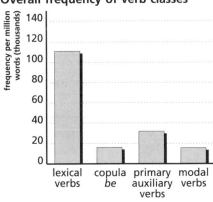

Figure 5.1
Overall frequency of verb classes

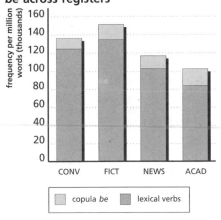

Figure 5.2
Frequency of lexical verbs and copula *be* across registers

Text sample 1: CONVERSATION

> A: Those hyacinths in the corner are **taking** *a long time to* **come** *out,* aren't *they? I'd have* **thought** *the tulips in the coal scuttle, the tulips in the cauldron, I* **thought** *they'd* **had** *it, they were* **lying** *down completely.*
> B: *I* **know***, but they've* **straightened** *out.* (CONV)

Text sample 2: ACADEMIC PROSE

> *In* **going** *from atoms to quarks there* is *a change of scale by a factor of at least 10 million. It* is *impressive that quantum mechanics can* **take** *that in its stride. The problems of interpretation* **cluster** *around two issues: the nature of reality and the nature of measurement.* (ACAD)

These two short samples illustrate important differences in the use of lexical verbs and the copula *be* across registers. Although the samples are nearly the same length, the conversation contains many more lexical verbs (eight) than the academic prose sample (three). The conversation has frequent, short clauses, and most of these clauses contain a lexical verb.

Academic prose has fewer lexical verbs for two reasons:

- First, it uses longer clauses than conversation does. Each clause has long noun phrases and prepositional phrases, but only one main verb—and with fewer clauses, there are consequently fewer main verbs.
- Second, more of the main verbs are forms of the copula *be*. These are used to state the existence of conditions (*there is a change of scale* ...) and to give evaluations (*it is impressive* ...).

Review

Major points of **GRAMMAR BITE A**: Verb functions and classes

➤ Verbs perform two major functions in clauses: main verbs v. auxiliary verbs.
  ➤ Main verbs are the central element in a clause.
  ➤ Auxiliary verbs qualify the meaning of the main verb.
➤ Verb forms can be grouped into three major classes according to their ability to function as main verbs or auxiliary verbs.
  ➤ Lexical verbs (e.g. *run, eat, think*) function only as main verbs.
  ➤ Primary verbs (*be, have,* and *do*) can function as both auxiliary and main verbs.
  ➤ Modal verbs (*can, could, shall, should, will, would, may, might, must*) function only as auxiliary verbs.
➤ Lexical verbs are much more common than primary verbs or modal verbs.
➤ Lexical verbs are most common in conversation and fiction.

GRAMMAR BITE

B Single-word lexical verbs

5.3 Semantic categories of lexical verbs

Although many verbs have more than one meaning, we find it useful to distinguish seven semantic categories: **activity verbs, communication verbs, mental verbs, causative verbs, verbs of occurrence, verbs of existence or relationship,** and **verbs of aspect.**

A Activity verbs

Activity verbs usually refer to a **volitional activity**—that is, an action performed intentionally by an **agent** or 'doer'. Thus, in the following examples, the subject (underlined below) performs the action by choice:

    Then <u>you</u> should **move** any obstacles. (CONV†)

    <u>He</u> **bought** biscuits and condensed milk. (FICT)

    In many of these jobs, <u>women</u> are **working** with women only. (ACAD)

Many commonly used verbs are activity verbs. The twenty most common, in conversation, fiction, newspaper writing, and academic prose combined, are:

bring	*buy*	*come*	*follow*
get	*give*	*go*	*leave*
make	*meet*	*move*	*pay*
play	*put*	*run*	*show*
take	*try*	*use*	*work*

Activity verbs can be **transitive**, taking a direct object, or **intransitive**, occurring without any object:

- transitive activity verbs, with the direct object underlined:

    *Well **give** <u>it</u> to the dogs, they'll **eat** <u>it</u>.* (CONV)

    *Even the smallest boys **brought** <u>little pieces of wood</u> and **threw** <u>them</u> in.* (FICT†)

- intransitive activity verbs:

    *They **ran**, on rubbery legs, through an open gate.* (FICT†)

    ***Go** to the hospital!* (CONV)

Activity verbs are also sometimes used to express events that occur without the volition of an agent. For example, *move* and *give* were used in the examples above as volitional activities. In the following examples the subjects (underlined) do not perform the activity by their will:

*During that time <u>continents, oceans, and mountain chains</u> have **moved** horizontally and vertically.* (ACAD†)

*<u>A few simple, rough calculations</u> will **give** surprisingly good estimates.* (ACAD)

B Communication verbs

Communication verbs are a special subcategory of activity verbs that involve communication activities, particularly verbs describing speech and writing:

*You **said** you didn't have it.* (CONV)

*'Stop that', he **shouted**.* (FICT)

*The organiser **asked** me if I wanted to see how the money was spent.* (NEWS)

*Too many students **write** far too little about their research methods.* (ACAD†)

The twelve most common 'communication' verbs in conversation, fiction, newspaper writing, and academic prose combined are:

ask	*call*	*claim*	*describe*
offer	*say*	*speak*	*suggest*
talk	*tell*	*thank*	*write*

C Mental verbs

Mental verbs refer to mental states and activities. For example:

*I **think** it was Freddie Kruger.* (CONV)

*I **wanted** very much to give him my orange but held back.* (FICT)

These verbs do not involve physical action. Some of the verbs convey volition; others do not. Mental verbs express a wide range of meanings:

- mental states or processes (e.g. *think, know*)
- emotions, attitudes, or desires (e.g. *love, want*)

- perceptions (e.g. *see, taste*)
- the receiving of communication (e.g. *read, hear*).

Many mental verbs describe mental activities that are relatively **dynamic** in meaning, such as the following:

> They **decided** to watch TV. (CONV)
>
> And uh then I **studied** Russian at Berkeley. (CONV)
>
> We might even **discover** that he uses a lower number of abstract nouns than other writers of his time. (ACAD)

Other mental verbs are more **stative** in meaning: that is, they describe a state rather than an action. These include verbs describing mental states, such as *believe, remember*, and *understand*, as well as many verbs describing emotions or attitudes, such as *enjoy, fear, hate*, and *prefer*:

- mental states:

> Oh yeah, right we all **believe** that. (CONV)
>
> Somehow I **doubt** it. (FICT)

- emotions/attitudes:

> He **hated** this weekly ritual of bathing. (FICT†)
>
> I **preferred** life as it was. (NEWS)

The twenty most common 'mental' verbs in conversation, fiction, newspaper writing, and academic prose combined are:

believe	*consider*	*expect*	*feel*
find	*hear*	*know*	*like*
listen	*love*	*mean*	*need*
read	*remember*	*see*	*suppose*
think	*understand*	*want*	*wonder*

D Causative verbs

Causative verbs, such as *allow, cause, force*, and *help*, indicate that some person or thing helps to bring about a new state of affairs. These verbs often occur with a derived noun (see 4.11) as the direct object, which reports the action that was facilitated. For example, *deletion* and *formulation* in the following sentences are formed from verbs (the direct objects are underlined):

> Still other rules **cause** the deletion of elements from the structure. (ACAD)
>
> This information **enables** the formulation of precise questions. (ACAD†)

The use of derived nouns with causative verbs is particularly common in academic prose. In other cases, the resulting action or event is expressed in a **complement clause** that follows the causative verb (underlined in the following examples):

> What **caused** you to be ill? (FICT)
>
> This law **enables** the volume of a gas to be calculated. (ACAD†)
>
> This would **help** protect Jaguar from fluctuations in the dollar. (NEWS†)

Complement clause structures are discussed in Chapter 10.

Compared with other semantic classes of verbs, there are only a few common causative verbs:

allow	*help*	*let*	*require*

E Verbs of occurrence

Verbs of occurrence report events that occur without an actor. Often the subjects of these verbs are affected by the event that is described by the verb, as in these examples (subjects are underlined):

> *The lights* **changed**. (CONV)
>
> *Resistant organisms* *may* **develop** *in the alimentary tract.* (ACAD†)
>
> *The term 'feature'* *has* **occurred** *many times in this chapter.* (ACAD)

Seven verbs of occurrence are especially common, in conversation, fiction, newspaper writing, and academic prose combined:

become	change	develop	die
grow	happen	occur	

F Verbs of existence or relationship

Verbs of existence or relationship report a state of existence or a logical relationship that exists between entities. Some of the most common existence verbs are **copular verbs**, such as *seem* and *appear*:

> *Witnesses said he* **appeared** *happy and relaxed.* (NEWS)
>
> *All these uses* **seem** *natural and serviceable.* (ACAD)

Copular verbs are discussed in detail in Grammar Bite F.

Other verbs in this class report a state of existence or a relationship between entities:

- state of existence:

> *I go and* **stay** *with them.* (CONV)
>
> *These varying conditions may* **exist** *in close proximity.* (ACAD†)

- relationship:

> *The exercise will* **include** *random stop checks by police, and* **involve** *special constables and traffic wardens.* (NEWS)
>
> *They* **contained** *large quantities of nitrogen.* (ACAD†)

Some common 'existence/relationship' verbs are:

appear	contain	exist	include
indicate	involve	live	look
represent	seem	stand	stay

G Verbs of aspect

Verbs of aspect characterize the stage of progress of an event or activity. These verbs usually occur with a complement clause following the verb. In the following examples the complement clause is underlined:

> *She* **kept** *running out of the room.* (CONV)
>
> *He couldn't* **stop** *talking about me.* (CONV†)
>
> *Tears* **started** *to trickle down his cheeks.* (FICT)

Complement clauses are covered in detail in Chapter 10.

Some common 'aspect' verbs are:

begin   continue   keep   start   stop

5.3.1 Verbs with multiple meanings

Many verbs have more than one meaning. In some cases, the verb's meaning covers two or more semantic categories simultaneously. For example, the verbs *hesitate* and *pretend* can convey the physical activity aspects of hesitating and pretending as well as the mental aspects.

> She **hesitated** and then said 'Why not.' (FICT)

> She can just **pretend** it's her new car. (CONV)

Also, some verbs have different meanings in different contexts. This is especially true of activity verbs, which often have secondary meanings in another category. For example, *raise* can refer to a physical activity or an act of communication (e.g. *raise your hand* or *raise the subject*) and *look* can refer to a physical action (*look down*), to a mental process (*look at the offer*), or to a state of existence (*you look happy*). These different meanings are also often associated with different valency patterns (see 5.7).

The context usually makes the intended meaning of a verb obvious. In the following pairs of examples **1** has a physical meaning, and **2** has a mental or communication meaning:

1 *Many patients are quite fit when **admitted** to the surgical ward.* (ACAD†)
2 *I must **admit** it gave me a bit of a shock.*

1 *He jumped and **raised** his right elbow so that it projected outwards.* (NEWS†)
2 *The issue was **raised** by Mr. Burns at a meeting with the Transport Secretary.* (NEWS)

1 *I think I was half ready to **follow** her.* (FICT)
2 *I don't **follow** you, begging your pardon.* (FICT)

5.4 The most common lexical verbs

The twelve most common lexical verbs in English are all activity or mental verbs, except for the verb *say*, which is the single most common lexical verb overall (see Figure 5.3):

- activity verbs: *get, go, make, come, take, give*
- mental verbs: *know, think, see, want, mean*

Figure 5.3 **Frequency of the most common lexical verbs in the LSWE Corpus (over 1,000 per million words)**

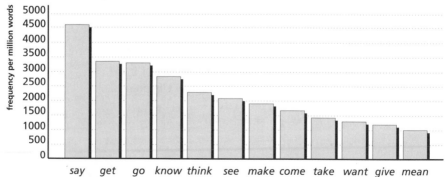

• communication verb: *say*.

(The primary verbs *be* and *have* are also extremely common expressing existence or relationship. These verbs are discussed in 5.13–14 below.)

A Say

The verb *say* is the most common lexical verb overall. Speakers and writers rely heavily on *say* to report the speech of themselves and others, rather than some communication verbs like *tell, ask, offer,* or *explain*. In all registers, this verb is most common in the past tense, in reporting a past utterance:

> You **said** you didn't have it. (CONV)
>
> No use sitting about, he **said**. (FICT)
>
> He **said** this campaign raised 'doubts about the authenticity of the eventual allegedly free choice'. (NEWS)

However, conversation differs from the written registers: it also commonly uses *say* in the present tense. Often, as in the first example below, these occurrences still report past speech, but the use of the present tense conveys a feeling of immediacy and personal involvement:

> So he **says**, Oh my God! (CONV)
>
> Rachel **says** she thinks that Pam's just acting like a spoiled brat. (CONV)

Present tense *say* is also commonly used for repeated or habitual behavior, as in:

> Look mum, he **says** horrible things to me. (CONV)

Interestingly, present tense *say* is also common in jokes, conveying a sense of immediacy:

> And the daughter comes home from school one day and **says**, mum I want to be like you. (CONV)
>
> And she **says** yes every time she's got her bubble gum in, she **says** no when she hasn't got the bubble gum in her mouth. (CONV)

See 10.5.2 for the use of *say* with complement clauses, and 12.4.3 for its use in reporting clauses.

B Get

Although it is easy to overlook, the verb *get* is more common in conversation than any other lexical verb in any register. *Get* is so common because it is extremely versatile. Although it is often used as an activity verb, it actually has a wide range of meanings and grammatical patterns. The major meanings of *get* include:

• obtaining something (activity):

> See if they can **get** some of that beer. (CONV)

• moving to or away from something (activity):

> **Get** in the car. (CONV)

• causing something to move (causative):

> We ought to **get** these wedding pictures into an album of some sort. (CONV)

• causing something to happen (causative):

> It **gets** people talking again, right. (CONV)

- changing from one state to another (occurrence):

    *She's **getting** ever so grubby-looking now.* (CONV)

    *Once you **got** to know him you liked him.* (CONV†)

- understanding something (mental):

    *Do you **get** it?* (CONV)

In addition to these meanings, *get* in the **perfect** form *have got* is equivalent to the primary verb *have* with a stative meaning, as in:

    *The Amphibicar. It's **got** little propellers in the back.* (CONV)
    <compare: *It **has** little propellers...*>

    ***Have** you **got** any plans for this weekend?* (CONV)
    <compare: *Do you **have** any plans...*>

In speech, *have* is sometimes omitted from the perfect form of *get*, as in:

    *You **got** your homework done, Jason?* (CONV)
    <compare: ***Have** you **got**...?*>

The verb *get* is also extremely versatile from a grammatical point of view. In addition to being a main verb, it functions as part of the **semi-modal** *(have) got to* (or *gotta*, see 6.9.2). It can also be used like an auxiliary verb to create a **passive** construction, the so-called '**get passive**':

    *I **got caught** once before.* (CONV†)
    <compare: *I **was caught** once before.*>

Finally, *get* occurs in idiomatic multi-word phrases:

    *He was no good she says, she **got rid of** him.* (CONV)

    *My mom loves him. He can **get away with** anything – he could **get away with** murder and my mom would still love him.* (CONV)

Given its versatility, it might seem surprising that *get* is not extremely common in all registers. However, it is relatively rare in most written registers. In general, it is considered an informal word and is therefore avoided in formal writing. In its place, written registers use a wide range of lexical verbs with more specific meanings, such as *obtain, cause, encourage, become,* and *understand.*

C Other extremely common verbs

Most of the other extremely common activity verbs are used to different extents across the registers. *Go* is extremely common in conversation and also very common in fiction:

    *We might as well **go** and see Janet.* (CONV)

    *Then they **went** and sat in rocking chairs in the front room.* (FICT)

The verb *come*, which is related to *go* in meaning, is also most common in these two registers:

    *He **came** with Alan.* (CONV)

    *'Ma, the permit isn't going to **come**', he said.* (FICT)

In fiction and news, two other activity verbs are common—*make* and *take*:

    *I thought I might **make** coffee for them all before I go.* (FICT)

    *The intruders **took** money and jewelry, commission sources said.* (NEWS)

Like *get*, both *make* and *take* commonly occur as part of idiomatic expressions. For example:

*You have to **take advantage of** every moment.* (CONV)

*Without shame he details how he came to **make a mark** in espionage history.* (NEWS)

Mental verbs, especially *know, think, see, want,* and *mean,* are particularly common in conversation. These verbs report states of awareness, certainty, perception, and desire. Mental verbs usually go with *I* or *you* as subject:

*I **think** it was a worm that it had in its mouth.* (CONV)

In many cases, these verbs occur together in the same utterance:

*I **see** what you **mean**.* (CONV)

*You **know** what I **mean**.* (CONV)

*I really **wanted** her to wear it, you **know**?* (CONV)

Fiction, too, has relatively high frequencies of the verbs *know, think,* and *see.* These verbs typically occur in the past tense, reporting the thinking and perceptions of fictional characters:

*She **knew** what had happened to them.* (FICT)

*I **thought** I would go and see the Pope.* (FICT)

*She **saw** the light again.* (FICT)

Surprisingly, the verb *see* is also relatively common in academic prose, where it is used to report scientific observations, or for references to other studies:

*The Type I disease is usually **seen** in calves grazed intensively.* (ACAD†)

*There now exists an extensive literature on the construction of social indicators (**see**, for example, Knox 1978c).* (ACAD†)

Finally, the verb *give* is relatively common in all registers. In most registers, this verb is used with activity meanings:

*He's not gonna **give** it to you twice though.* (CONV)

*She was too shy to **give** him more than a covert glance.* (FICT)

*The vehicles will be **given** to the National Association of Boys' Clubs.* (NEWS)

However, in academic prose *give* often expresses causative or existence meanings:

*A good method of analysis is one that **gives** a large correlation coefficient.* (ACAD)

*K values are **given** in Fig. 2.5.* (ACAD)

5.4.1 Repeated use of the most common verbs

Figure 5.4 (on page 114) compares the frequency of the twelve most common verbs with the frequency of all other lexical verbs. As a group, the commonest verbs occur much more frequently in conversation than in the other three registers. They are used so often that they account for nearly 45 per cent of all lexical verbs in conversation. In contrast, the commonest verbs account for only 11 per cent of all lexical verbs in academic prose.

The following two excerpts from conversations illustrate speakers' frequent use of the commonest verbs:

A: *She and Cathy might like to **come** because she did **say** to me, how is Cathy and I **said** she was <. . .>*

B: *She **knows** about Cathy's problem?*

A: *Yes, she **said** so do you* ***think** Cathy would mind if I rang her? – and I **said** no I'm sure she wouldn't.* (CONV†)

A: *I used to **get** really nervous when I came to Chinese restaurants. I never **knew** what to choose.*

B: *Really?*

A: *But gradually over the years you **get** the hang of it. Some people **get** the hang of these things more quickly than I do.*

B: *We didn't **go** often enough dear, that's the other thing.* (CONV)

Figure 5.4

Distribution of the most common lexical verbs v. other verbs

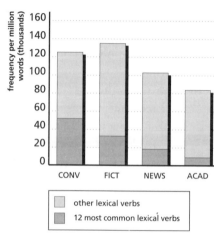

These short exchanges are typical of conversations: participants repeatedly use the most common verbs to share experiences, thoughts, and speech.

The written registers rely less on the most common verbs. In part, this might reflect a wider range of subject matter—especially in news and academic prose. It may also reflect a wish to make the text more interesting by varying vocabulary—especially in fiction. Further, varied and precise word choice is easier for writers, because they have time to plan and revise. Speakers in conversations, in contrast, have little opportunity for planning or revising, so they rely more heavily on the most common verbs (see 13.2.5 for more on the repetitiveness of conversation).

Review

Major points of **GRAMMAR BITE B**: Single-word lexical verbs

➤ Lexical verbs fall into seven major semantic categories: activity verbs, communication verbs, mental verbs, causative verbs, verbs of occurrence, verbs of existence or relationship, and verbs of aspect.

➤ Many lexical verbs have more than one meaning.

➤ Twelve verbs are especially common in English. Their main uses fall into three types:

   ➤ activity verbs: *get, go, make, come, take, give*

   ➤ mental verbs: *know, think, see, want, mean*

   ➤ communication verb: *say*.

➤ In conversation, these twelve verbs are extremely common. Written registers like academic prose tend to use a wider range of different verbs.

GRAMMAR BITE

c Lexical verbs: structures and patterns

5.5 Regular and irregular verb endings

5.5.1 Regular verbs

Inflections are morphemes that express grammatical meanings like **person** and **number**. Most verbs are **regular**, meaning that they use the same inflections to mark **person, tense, aspect,** and **voice**. For example, all regular verbs mark third person singular with an *-s* suffix and past tense with an *-ed* suffix. Yet many grammatical distinctions are not marked on verbs in English. For example, there is no difference between the verb form for first person present tense (e.g. *I walk*), second person present tense (*you walk*), and the infinitive of regular verbs (*to walk*). Some other grammatical distinctions are marked by the use of auxiliary verbs (such as *have* for perfect aspect and *be* for passive voice), rather than by inflections. Consequently, English verbs have few morphological forms. Regular verbs have only four morphological forms. These forms involve three suffixes added to a base:

form	use
base	**infinitive**, present tense except third person singular, and **subjunctive**
base + suffix *-(e)s*	third person singular present tense
base + suffix *-ing*	*ing*-participles (as in **progressive** aspect)
base + suffix *-ed*	simple past tense and *ed*-participles (or **past participle**, as in **perfect** and **passive** constructions)

For example:

base	look	move	try	push	reduce
base + *-(e)s*	looks	moves	tries	pushes	reduces
base + *-ing*	looking	moving	trying	pushing	reducing
base + *-ed*	looked	moved	tried	pushed	reduced

Pronunciation of suffixes:

- *-ing*: /ɪŋ/
- *-(e)s*: /s/ after voiceless consonants except /ʃ, ʧ, s/: *looks, hopes, laughs*
  /z/ after vowels and voiced consonants except /ʒ, ʤ, z/: *tries, moves, minds*
  /ɪz/ after /ʃ, ʧ, s, ʒ, ʤ, z/: *passes, reduces, recognizes, pushes, massages, watches, manages*
- *-ed*: /t/ after voiceless consonants except /t/: *watched, looked, pushed*
  /d/ after vowels and voiced consonants except /d/: *tried, moved*

/ɪd/ after /t, d/: *waited, wanted, included*

Spelling of suffixes:

- *-(e)s*: -*es* after the letters *s*, *z*, *x*, *sh* or *ch*: *pass—passes, push—pushes, watch—watches*
  -*s* after all other letters
- *-ing* and *-ed*: if the base of the verb ends in consonant + *e*, the final *e* is dropped before adding the suffix: *reduce—reducing—reduced*; compare a base ending in vowel + *e*: *agree—agreeing—agreed*.
- *-(es)* and *-ed*: if the verb ends in a consonant + *y*, the spellings become *-ies* and *-ied*: *copy—copies—copied, try—tries—tried*; otherwise, final *y* takes the usual endings: *play—plays—played*.

5.5.2 Irregular verbs

There is a much smaller set of **irregular** verbs—that is, they have irregular past tense and *ed*-participle forms—but these include many of the most common verbs. Note that the *ed*-participle is a good label for regular verbs, since all regular verbs have an *ed*-participle (i.e. past participle) ending in *-ed*. But it is a misleading label to use for irregular verbs, since irregular past participles (like *cut, eaten*) rarely end in *-ed*!

There are seven main patterns used to mark past tense and *ed*-participles in irregular verbs:

A Class 1

A *-t* suffix marks past tense and *ed*-participles. The *t* may replace a final *d* of the base: e.g. *build—built, send—sent, spend—spent*. Or the *t* may be added to the base: e.g. *spoil—spoilt, learn—learnt*. Some of the verbs that add *t* to the base also have a regular form: e.g. *learnt* and *learned* both occur.

B Class 2

A *-t* or *-d* suffix marks past tense and *ed*-participle, and the base vowel changes. For example:

base form	past tense	ed-participle
mean /miːn/	*meant* /ment/	*meant*
think /θɪŋk/	*thought* /θɔːt/	*thought*
sell /sɛl/	*sold* /saʊld/	*sold*
tell /tɛl/	*told* /taʊld/	*told*

C Class 3

The regular *-ed* suffix marks past tense, but an *-(e)n* suffix marks *ed*-participles. For example:

base form	past tense	ed-participle
show	*showed*	*shown* (note: *showed* also occurs)

D Class 4

No suffix is used for the past tense, but *ed*-participles have an *-(e)n* suffix; in addition, the base vowel changes in either the past tense, *ed*-participle, or both. For example:

base form	past tense	ed-participle
give /ɪ/	gave /eɪ/	given /ɪ/
know /əʊ/	knew/(j)uː/	known /əʊ/
see /iː/	saw /ɔː/	seen /iː/

E Class 5

The base vowel changes in the past tense, the *ed*-participle, or both; there are no other changes. For example:

base form	past tense	ed-participle
begin /ɪ/	began /æ/	begun /ʌ/
come /ʌ/	came /eɪ/	come /ʌ/
find /aɪ/	found /aʊ/	found /aʊ/

F Class 6

Past tense and *ed*-participle forms are identical to the base form. For example:

base form	past tense	ed-participle
cut	cut	cut
hit	hit	hit

G Class 7

One of the forms is completely different. For example:

base form	past tense	ed-participle
go /gəʊ/	went /wɛnt/	gone BrE /gɒn/ AmE /gɔn/

5.5.3 Preference for regular v. irregular endings

Many irregular verbs also have regular alternatives. For example, two different forms are used for the past tense of *speed*: the irregular *sped*, and the regular form *speeded*. In most cases, one form is used more than the other. For example, the irregular forms *hung*, *lit*, *quit*, and *sped* are more common than the regular forms *hanged*, *lighted*, *quitted*, and *speeded*. In contrast, the regular forms *dreamed*, *knitted*, and *leaned* are much more common ·than the irregular forms *dreamt*, *knit*, and *leant*.

For a few verbs, different forms are associated with different grammatical functions. For example, the regular form *spoiled* is used more commonly for past tense, but the irregular form *spoilt* is used more commonly for the *ed*-participle (in British English).

In American English, the verb *get* is unusual because it has two irregular *ed*-participle forms that occur following *have*: *got* and *gotten*. In British English, the combination *have + gotten* almost never occurs. In both American English and British English, the combination *have got* can express a meaning roughly equivalent to *have* as a lexical verb, or it can express the perfect aspect meaning of *get*:

- meanings equivalent to *have* as a lexical verb:

    *Look at that face. He **hasn't got** any teeth.* (AmE CONV)
    <compare: *He doesn't **have** any teeth.*>

    ***Have** you **got** an exam on Monday?* (BrE CONV)
    <compare: *Do you **have** an exam on Monday?*>

- perfect aspect of *get*:

    *It could **have got** put in storage or something.* (AmE CONV)

    *We **have got** ourselves into a rut.* (BrE NEWS†)

In contrast, *have gotten* in American English almost always has a perfect aspect meaning, as in:

    *I can't believe Ginger's bike **hasn't gotten** stolen yet.* (AmE CONV)

5.6 Verb formation

Derivational affixes are incomplete units of language that form a new word when they are added to an existing word (the base). **Prefixes** are attached to the front of the base, while **suffixes** are attached to the end of the base.

Verb prefixes usually do not change the word class. That is, when a prefix is attached to a verb base, the new word remains a verb. However, the meaning changes:

base verb	derived verb with prefix	base verb	derived verb with prefix
like	*dislike*	*cook*	*overcook*
lead	*mislead*	*seal*	*reseal*
do	*outdo*	*zip*	*unzip*

Verb derivational suffixes, on the other hand, are added to a noun or adjective to create a verb:

adjective base	derived verb with suffix	noun base	derived verb with suffix
active	*activate*	*assassin*	*assassinate*
simple	*simplify*	*class*	*classify*
actual	*actualize*	*alphabet*	*alphabetize*
black	*blacken*	*height*	*heighten*

5.6.1 Most common derivational affixes

There are many different derivational prefixes used to form new verbs in English. The most common derivational prefixes, in order of frequency of occurrence, are:

prefix	meaning of prefix	examples
re-	again	*reabsorb, rearm, rebuild, redefine, refinance*
dis-	opposite, apart	*disallow, disarm, disconnect, discontinue, dislike*
over-	too much, across, beyond	*overbook, overcome, overeat, overhear, overreach*
un-	opposite, in reverse	*unbend, uncouple, unfold, unload, unpack*
mis-	wrong, poorly	*misbehave, mishandle, misinform, mispronounce*
out-	beyond, further	*outbid, outdo, outgrow, outperform, outweigh*

The prefix *re-* is used most often in formal written registers, like academic prose and news. Many verbs formed with *re-* have been in use for a considerable time, but *re-* is also frequently used to create new words in technical discourse: e.g. *redeploy, redimension, retransmit*.

There are only a few derivational suffixes used for verb formation, although some of the suffixes combine with many different words. The suffixes are listed below in order of frequency of occurrence:

suffix	meaning of suffix	examples
-ize/-ise	to (cause to) become	*computerize, energize, itemize, stabilize*
-en	to (cause to) become	*awaken, flatten, lengthen, moisten*
-ate	to (cause to) become	*activate, liquidate, regulate, pollinate*
-(i)fy	to (cause to) become	*beautify, codify, exemplify, notify*

Notice that all four of the most frequent derivational suffixes have a basic meaning of 'become' or 'cause to be'. However, when different suffixes are added to the same base, separate meanings can result. For example, *liquidize* is usually used with an agent making a substance 'liquid', but *liquify* is often used without an agent, and *liquidate* is used in a financial context, when assets are 'made liquid'.

The suffix *-ize* is often spelled *-ise* in BrE.

5.7 Valency patterns

The main verb in a clause determines the other elements that are required in that clause. The pattern of the clause elements is called the **valency pattern** for the verb. The patterns are differentiated by the required clause elements that follow the verb within the clause (e.g. direct object, indirect object, subject predicative). All valency patterns include a subject, and optional adverbials can always be added.

There are five major valency patterns:

A Intransitive

Pattern: subject + verb (S + V). Intransitive verbs occur with no obligatory element following the verb:

subject	verb
More people	*came.* (FICT)

B Monotransitive

Pattern: subject + verb + direct object (S + V + DO). Monotransitive verbs occur with a single direct object:

subject	verb	direct object
She	carried	a long whippy willow twig. (FICT†)

C Ditransitive

Pattern: subject + verb + indirect object + direct object (S + V + IO + DO). Ditransitive verbs occur with two object phrases—an indirect object and a direct object:

subject	verb	indirect object	direct object
Fred Unsworth	gave	her	a huge vote of confidence. (NEWS†)

D Complex transitive

Patterns: subject + verb + direct object + object predicative (S + V + DO + OP) or subject + verb + direct object + obligatory adverbial (S + V + DO + A). Complex transitive verbs occur with a direct object (a noun phrase) which is followed by either (**1**) an object predicative (a noun phrase or adjective), or (**2**) an obligatory adverbial:

	subject	verb	direct object	object predicative
1	people	called	him	Johnny. (NEWS†)

	subject	verb	direct object	obligatory adverbial
2	He	put	his hand	on the child's shoulder. (FICT†)

E Copular

Patterns: subject + verb + subject predicative (S + V + SP) or subject + verb + obligatory adverbial (S + V + A). Copular verbs are followed by (**1**) a subject predicative (a noun, adjective, adverb or prepositional phrase) or (**2**) by an obligatory adverbial. (Copular verbs are further discussed in Grammar Bite E.)

	subject	(copular) verb	subject predicative
1	Carrie	felt	a little less bold. (FICT†)

	subject	(copular) verb	obligatory adverbial
2	I	'll keep	in touch with you. (CONV†)

F Variations on transitive patterns

The monotransitive, ditransitive, and complex transitive patterns are the **transitive** patterns; they all require some type of object. As in the above examples, the most common structure for the objects is a noun phrase. However, in some cases other structures can function as objects. For example:

- monotransitive pattern with a complement clause for the direct object:

subject	verb	direct object
He	*said*	*he was going to make a copy.* (CONV†)

- ditransitive pattern with a prepositional phrase expressing the indirect object:

subject	verb	direct object	indirect object
He	*gave*	*all that info*	*to the FBI.* (NEWS†)

<note that the indirect object prepositional phrase could also be analyzed as an adverbial>

- ditransitive pattern with a noun phrase for the indirect object and a complement clause for the direct object:

subject	verb	indirect object	direct object
Staff in the information office	*told*	*me*	*that the train had been delayed until 18.15.* (NEWS)

Verbs in all patterns can occur with optional adverbials. For example:

- intransitive with optional adverbial (S + V + (A)):

	subject	verb	optional adverbial
	He	*went*	*to the corner shop.* (FICT)
[Then]	*they*	*fell*	*in the sea.* (FICT)

- transitive with optional adverbial (S + V + O + (A)):

subject	verb	object	optional adverbial
He	*ate*	*nearly all those chips*	*tonight.* (CONV)
He	*left*	*it*	*in the bushes.* (FICT†)

5.7.1 Verbs with multiple valency patterns

Grammarians sometimes identify a verb as 'an intransitive verb' or 'a transitive verb', as if one verb normally takes just one pattern. However, the reality is different from this. Most common verbs allow more than one valency pattern, and some allow a wide range. For example, *speak* and *help* can occur with intransitive or monotransitive patterns:

intransitive	monotransitive
*Simon **spoke** first.* (FICT)	*The stewards all **spoke** French.* (NEWS)
*Money **helped**, too.* (NEWS)	*As Australia's forward coach, Evans did great work when he **helped** Alan Jones.* (NEWS)

Similarly, *find* and *make* can occur in the monotransitive or complex transitive patterns:

monotransitive	complex transitive
We might **find** a body. (NEWS†)	You might **find** these notes useful. (ACAD)
Malcolm **made** no sound. (FICT)	The sheer intensity of the thing **made** me nervous. (FICT)

Further, verbs that have the same possible valency patterns often use them with different meanings and very different frequencies. We illustrate this point below with a brief case study of three verbs.

5.7.2 Intransitive and monotransitive patterns

Many verbs can take both intransitive and monotransitive patterns, but these verbs differ in their preference for one pattern over another. For example, *stand*, *change*, and *meet* are possible with both valency patterns. However, *stand* usually occurs as an intransitive verb, while *change* and *meet* most commonly occur in the monotransitive pattern.

A Stand

The most common pattern is intransitive with an optional adverbial (S + V + (A)):

subject	adverbial	verb	optional adverbial
I	just	**stood**	there. (CONV)

Monotransitive *stand* is rare and found primarily in conversation and news in idiomatic expressions, such as *to stand a chance* or *can't stand someone or something*:

subject	verb	direct object
You don't	**stand**	a chance. (CONV†)

subject	adverbial	verb	direct object
I	really	**couldn't stand**	him. (CONV)

Monotransitive *stand* with a complement clause as the direct object is rare and found primarily in fiction:

	subject	verb	direct object (complement clause)
[Could]	you	**stand**	being alone with me for five or six days? (FICT)

B Change and meet

With these verbs, monotransitive (S + V + DO) is the most common pattern:

subject	verb	direct object
I	[want to] **change**	my clothes. (CONV)
... you	[will never] **change**	the world. (FICT†)
She	**met**	several leading actors and musicians. (NEWS†)

Intransitive (S + V) is the second most common pattern, especially for *change*:

subject	verb	
People's circumstances	*change*	[and er ... they vote differently]. (CONV)

Intransitive with optional adverbials (S + V + (A)) is also found:

subject	verb	optional adverbial
We could	*meet*	in Tucson (CONV†)
The work	had *changed*	in the post-war period. (ACAD†)

Review

Major points of **GRAMMAR BITE C**: Lexical verbs: structures and patterns
➤ Two areas are important in the structure of lexical verbs:
  ➤ their inflectional morphology, which marks person, tense, aspect, and voice.
  ➤ their derivational morphology, which shows how verbs have been created.
➤ In their inflectional morphology, most verbs occur with regular suffixes.
  ➤ Many of the most common verbs have irregular morphology.
  ➤ Some verbs allow both regular and irregular morphology.
➤ New verbs can be formed with derivational morphology.
  ➤ The prefix *re-* is frequently used for forming new words.
  ➤ The suffix *-ize* is also frequently used for forming new words.
  ➤ Four derivational suffixes are all common and are used with similar meanings: *-ize*, *-ate*, *-(i)fy*, and *-en*.
➤ The main verb determines the other elements that are necessary for the clause—i.e. the valency pattern.
  ➤ There are five major valency patterns: intransitive, monotransitive, ditransitive, complex transitive, and copular.
  ➤ Many verbs can occur with more than one valency pattern, and they often have different meanings with each pattern. Further, each verb occurs with very different frequencies for the different patterns.

GRAMMAR BITE

D Multi-word lexical verbs

5.8 Multi-word verbs: structure and meaning

Many multi-word units function like a single verb. These combinations usually have **idiomatic** meanings. That is, their meaning cannot be predicted from the meaning of each individual word.

These multi-word verbs fall into four classes:

- **phrasal verbs**
- **prepositional verbs**
- **phrasal-prepositional verbs**
- **other multi-word verb constructions.**

Phrasal verbs consist of a verb followed by an adverbial particle (e.g. *carry out*, *find out*, or *pick up*). When these adverbial particles are used independently, they have literal meanings signifying location or direction (e.g. *out*, *in*, *up*, *down*, *on*, *off*). However, in phrasal verbs they are commonly used with less literal meanings. For example, the meaning of *find out* does not include the 'place' meaning of *out*.

Prepositional verbs consist of a verb followed by a preposition, such as *look at*, *talk about*, *listen to*.

Phrasal-prepositional verbs contain both an adverbial particle and a preposition, as in *get away with*.

Because they are idiomatic in meaning, it is sometimes possible to replace multi-word verbs by single-word verbs with a similar meaning:

multi-word verb	single-word verb
carry out	undertake
look at	observe
put up with	tolerate
find out	discover
talk about	discuss
make off with	steal

In contrast to multi-word verbs, **free combinations** consist of a single-word lexical verb followed by an adverb or preposition with a separate meaning (e.g. *come down*, *go back*). In practice, it is hard to make an absolute distinction between free combinations and multi-word verbs. It is better to think of a continuum where some uses of verbs are relatively free and others relatively idiomatic.

5.8.1 Characteristics of phrasal verbs and prepositional verbs

The meanings and structures of phrasal verbs, prepositional verbs, and free combinations differ in many ways. However, just three criteria are usually sufficient for distinguishing among the types of multi-word combinations. The criteria are:

- whether or not there is an idiomatic meaning
- whether or not particle movement is possible
- how the *wh*-question is formed.

The nature of a multi-word expression is determined by whether or not there is a following noun phrase. When there is no following noun phrase (e.g. *shut up* or *go away*), there are only two possible interpretations. It must be either an intransitive phrasal verb, or a free combination of verb + adverb. If there is a following noun phrase (e.g. *find out the meaning*), there are three possible interpretations. Either it is a transitive phrasal verb, a transitive prepositional verb, or a free combination of verb + adverbial prepositional phrase.

A Idiomatic meaning

Checking for an idiomatic meaning is especially useful when there is no following noun phrase, and you wish to distinguish between an intransitive phrasal verb and a free combination. Intransitive phrasal verbs usually have an idiomatic meaning, while the words in free combinations retain their own meanings. For example, the intransitive phrasal verbs *come on*, *shut up*, *get up*, *get out*, *break down*, and *grow up* all have idiomatic meanings beyond the separate meanings of the two parts (e.g. *grow up* means to act/become more mature, not literally to grow in an upward direction). In contrast, both the verb and the adverb have separate meanings in free combinations like *come back*, *come down*, *go back*, *go in*, *look back*.

- Intransitive phrasal verbs:

    Shut up *you fool!* (CONV)

    Come on! *Tell us then!* (CONV)

- Intransitive free combinations:

    If this was new, I wouldn't let people **go in**. (CONV)

    Come back, *or I'll fire*. (FICT)

    He was afraid to **look back**. (FICT)

B Particle movement

When multi-word combinations have a following noun phrase, tests using structure are more important than those involving idiomatic meaning. The first important test is **particle movement**: that is, whether the adverbial particle can be placed both before and after the object noun phrase. Transitive phrasal verbs allow particle movement. In the following examples the object noun phrase is shown in brackets.

I went to Eddie's girl's house to **get back** *[my wool plaid shirt]*. (FICT†)

I've got to **get** *[this one]* **back** *for her mom.* (CONV)

K came back and **picked up** *[the note]*. (FICT)

He **picked** *[the phone]* **up**. (FICT)

When the object of a transitive phrasal verb is a pronoun, the adverbial particle is almost always after the object:

Yeah I'll **pick** *[them]* **up**. (CONV)

So I **got** *[it]* **back**. (CONV)

(Other factors influencing particle movement are discussed in 12.13.4.)

Particle movement is not possible with prepositional verbs. Instead, the particle (actually, a preposition) always comes before the noun phrase that is the object:

Well those kids are **waiting for** *their bus*. (CONV)

<compare: **Well those kids are* **waiting** *their bus* **for**.>

It was hard to **look at** *him.* (NEWS)

Availability **depends on** *their being close to the root.* (ACAD†)

C *Wh*-question formation

Wh-question formation is a second important structural test for deciding the type of multi-word verb. This test is especially useful for distinguishing between a transitive prepositional verb + object and a free combination of verb + adverbial prepositional phrase. In sentences with a prepositional verb, *wh*-questions are typically formed with *what* or *who*. These questions indicate that the noun phrase that follows the preposition functions as the object of the prepositional verb:

>*What are you **talking about**?* (CONV)
>*What are you **laughing at**?* (FICT)
><compare the statement: *I am **talking about** / **laughing at** something.*>
>*Who are you **working with**?* (CONV)
>*Who was he **talking to**?* (CONV)
><compare the statement: *I am **working with** / **talking to** somebody.*>

In contrast, *wh*-questions for free combinations can be formed using the adverbial *wh*-words *where* and *when*. These questions indicate that the prepositional phrase is an adverbial that follows the verb:

- place:
>*Where are you walking?* (CONV)
><compare the statement: *I am **walking to** that place.*>
>*Where will we meet?* (FICT)
><compare the statement: *We will **meet at** that place.*>

- time:
>*When are you playing?* (CONV)
><compare the statement: *I am **playing at** that time.*>
>*When are you leaving?* (FICT)
><compare the statement: *I am **leaving at** that time.*>

Comparing these features does not always result in clear-cut distinctions between all multi-word verb combinations. Many combinations can function as more than one type, depending on the context. Further, some combinations can be interpreted as belonging to more than one category. Section 5.8.2 illustrates several of these problematic cases.

5.8.2 Multi-word combinations in multiple categories

Sometimes multi-word combinations fit into more than one category. For example, the combination *fit in* can be an intransitive phrasal verb (1), or a free combination of verb + adverbial prepositional phrase (2):

  1 *He just doesn't **fit in**.* (CONV)
  2 *The mushroom was too big to **fit** [in a special dryer at Purdue University's plant and fungi collection].* (NEWS†)

In addition, some combinations have the characteristics of more than one category even in a single occurrence. For example, consider *come back*, with the meaning to 'recover' or 'resume an activity'. This combination might be analyzed as a free combination because *come* and *back* both contribute independently to the meaning. But the combination could also be regarded as an intransitive phrasal verb, because the combined meaning of the parts is idiomatic.

3 *Everton* **came back** *from a goal down to beat Blackburn 2–1.* (NEWS)

4 *When Jim went to the police station, officers told him to* **come back** *another day.* (NEWS)

Sentence **4** might seem more clearly a free combination because the adverb *back* has a literal directional meaning, while **3** has a more clearly idiomatic meaning ('recover'). However, **4** also has a meaning that can be represented by a single verb: *return*. In this sense, it, too, is idiomatic. In sum, as for many grammatical categories, the distinction is not always clear-cut.

5.8.3 Frequency of multi-word verb types

Prepositional verbs are far more common than phrasal verbs or phrasal-prepositional verbs (Figure 5.5). Both phrasal verbs and phrasal-prepositional verbs are extremely rare in academic prose, while in the other registers phrasal verbs are more common than phrasal-prepositional verbs. The greater frequency of prepositional verbs goes with the greater diversity of the meanings they express. Phrasal and phrasal-prepositional verbs are most commonly used for physical activities, while prepositional verbs cover a wide range of semantic categories.

Figure 5.5
Distribution of multi-word verbs across registers

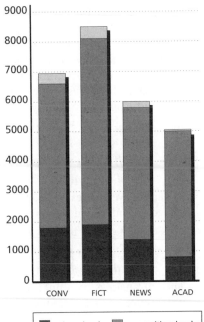

5.9 **Phrasal verbs**

There are two major subcategories of phrasal verbs: intransitive and transitive.

- Intransitive phrasal verbs:

    Come on, *tell me about Nick.* (CONV)

    Hold on! *What are you doing there?* (FICT)

    I just **broke down** *in tears when I saw the letter.* (NEWS)

- Transitive phrasal verbs:

    Did you **point out** *the faults on it then?* (CONV)

    I ventured to **bring up** *the subject of the future.* (FICT)

    I want to **find out** *the relative sizes of the most common dinosaurs.* (ACAD†)

With transitive phrasal verbs the particle can be placed after the direct object. This is the normal word order when the object is a pronoun:

*Terri **turned** it **on**.* (CONV)

*I just thought I would **point** it **out** to you.* (CONV)

*The warden said that she would **turn** the heating **on**.* (ACAD†)

In addition, a few phrasal verbs are copular, such as *turn out*, *end up*, and *wind up*. We return to these verbs in 5.16–17 below.

5.9.1 Most common phrasal verbs

A Intransitive phrasal verbs

As Figure 5.5 above shows, conversation and fiction use phrasal verbs much more frequently than news and academic prose do. This difference is especially noteworthy for intransitive phrasal verbs. They are extremely common in conversation and fiction, but extremely rare in news and academic prose. One reason for this difference is that most phrasal verbs are colloquial in tone.

In fact, the most common intransitive phrasal verbs are activity verbs that are used as directives. They often occur as imperatives. Since imperative clauses are most common in conversation and fiction, it is not surprising that these intransitive phrasal verbs are also most common in those registers:

> **Shut up!** *Just forget it.* (CONV)
>
> **Go off** *to bed now.* (CONV)
>
> **Stand up** *straight! People are looking!* (FICT)

In declarative clauses, the common intransitive phrasal verbs usually have human subjects (underlined below):

> *No, he **came over** to the study.* (CONV)
>
> *Crowe **sat up** and stared at Frederica.* (FICT)
>
> *I **sat down** behind my desk.* (FICT)

The intransitive combination *come on* in conversation is the most common phrasal verb in any register. This verb has three major functions:

* as an exclamation in a call for action:

> ***Come on**, let Andy do it.* (CONV)

* as a pre-departure summons to move:

> ***Come on**, we better go.* (CONV)

* as the main verb in a clause, meaning 'to start' or 'become activated':

> *The heating didn't **come on** this morning.* (CONV)

The intransitive phrasal verb *go on* is also extremely common. *Go on* is similar to *come on* in having a number of different functions. However, unlike *come on*, *go on* is used often in both written and spoken registers:

* as an exclamatory call for action (like *come on* above):

> *It's alright, rub it in. **Go on!*** (CONV)

* to express continuation:

> *I just ignored her and **went on**. I didn't have time to talk.* (CONV)
>
> *As time **went on**, Liebig developed his thesis.* (ACAD†)

- to mark continuation of some general action (as a transitive verb with a complement *ing-* or *to-*infinitive clause as direct object):

> Labour would **go on** getting the public's support by constructing strong unity of purpose. (NEWS†)
>
> Bjornsson **went on** to study the newspapers of 11 countries. (ACAD)

- to mark an unspecified activity, with a meaning similar to 'happen':

> Think what's **going on**. It's dreadful. (FICT)

B Transitive phrasal verbs

Transitive phrasal verbs are more evenly spread across written and spoken registers. For example, verbs such as *put on*, *make up*, and *find out* are relatively common in both conversation and the written expository registers:

> Some people they read the top bit and read the bottom bit, and sort of **make up** the bit in the middle. (CONV)
>
> Because you might **find out** it works. (CONV)
>
> Haven't you **found** that **out** yet? (FICT)
>
> For the modern mathematician these numbers would **make up** the ordered pair (V1, V2). (ACAD)

In fact, a few transitive phrasal verbs are actually more common in expository writing than in conversation. These include *carry out*, *take up*, *take on*, *set up*, and *point out*:

> It is common practice to **carry out** a series of design point calculations. (ACAD†)
>
> The rule also affected Henry Cotton, who **took up** the post at Royal Waterloo, Belgium, in 1933. (NEWS†)
>
> When the Spanish arm of the operation needed assistance he was asked to **take on** a supervisory role. (NEWS)
>
> The EIT was **set up** last year to help fund university research. (NEWS†)
>
> Gushchin (1934) **pointed out** many of the weaknesses of these attempts. (ACAD†)

Finally, the combination *turn out* is unusual in that it is a common phrasal verb that can function as a copular verb. It is discussed in 5.17.

5.10 Prepositional verbs

All prepositional verbs take a **prepositional object**, i.e. the noun phrase that occurs after the preposition. There are two major structural patterns for prepositional verbs: with a single prepositional object (Pattern 1), and with a direct object and a prepositional object (Pattern 2):

- Pattern 1: NP + V + prep + <u>NP</u> (prepositional objects are underlined)

> It just **looks like** <u>the barrel</u>. (CONV)
>
> I've never even **thought about** <u>it</u>. (CONV)

- Pattern 2: NP + V + <u>NP</u> + prep + <u>NP</u> (direct objects and prepositional objects are underlined):

*[Yeah it's really pretty]. It **reminds** <u>me</u> **of** <u>some parts of Boston</u>.* (CONV)

*He **said** <u>farewell</u> **to** <u>us</u> [on this very spot].* (FICT)

*But McGaughey **bases** <u>his prediction</u> **on** <u>first-hand experience</u>.* (NEWS†)

The two-object prepositional verb (Pattern 2) is also common with passive verbs. The noun phrase that corresponds to the direct object is placed in subject position:

<u>*The media*</u> *is falsely **accused of** <u>a lot of things</u>.* (CONV†)

*<compare the active voice: People falsely **accuse** the media **of** a lot of things.>*

<u>*The initiative*</u> *is **based on** <u>a Scottish scheme</u>.* (NEWS†)

*<compare the active voice: Someone **based** the initiative **on** a Scottish scheme.>*

Most prepositional verbs occur with only one pattern. However, some prepositional verbs occur with both Patterns 1 and 2. These include *apply* (NP) *to, connect* (NP) *with, provide* (NP) *for, ask* (NP) *for, hear* (NP) *about, know* (NP) *about*:

- *apply to* with Pattern 1:

  *The regulations also **apply to** new buildings.* (NEWS†)

- *apply to* with Pattern 2:

  *They were cosmologists wrestling to **apply** quantum mechanics **to** Einstein's general theory of relativity.* (ACAD)

- *ask for* with Pattern 1:

  *But I've **asked for** much too much already.* (FICT)

- *ask for* with Pattern 2:

  *He **asked** Stan **for** a job.* (CONV)

The structure of a prepositional verb can be analyzed in two ways. On the one hand, it can be considered a single-word lexical verb that is followed by a prepositional phrase. The prepositional phrase functions as an adverbial. This analysis is supported by the fact that it is usually possible to insert another adverbial between the verb and the prepositional phrase in Pattern 1. The adverbials *exactly* and *much* are between the verbs and prepositional phrases in these examples:

*She **looked** <u>exactly</u> [**like** Kathleen Cleaver].* (FICT)

*I never **thought** <u>much</u> [**about** it].* (FICT)

However, the verb + preposition can also be considered as a multi-word unit—a single 'prepositional verb'. This analysis is supported by the fact that prepositional verbs often have idiomatic meanings that cannot be derived from the meanings of the two parts. The two-word units can often be replaced by a single transitive verb with a similar meaning:

thought about *it* → **considered** *it*

asked for *permission* → **requested** *permission*

stand for *it* → **tolerate** *it*

Also, as explained in 5.8.1, *wh*-questions with prepositional verbs are formed using *who* or *what* (e.g. *What are your thinking about?*), rather than a *wh*-adverb *where, when,* or *how*.

5.10.1 Most common prepositional verbs

Unlike phrasal verbs, prepositional verbs are common in academic writing as well as in conversation and fiction. However, different kinds of prepositional verbs are preferred in each register.

A Conversation and fiction

Because of the typical topics and purposes in conversation and fiction, these registers have many common prepositional verbs that are activity, communication, or mental verbs. The most common prepositional verb is *look at*. It is used in two main ways:

- to direct the attention of others:

    Look at *that great big tree stuck under the bridge!* (CONV)

- to describe actions involving sight:

    The boys **looked at** *each other tearfully unbelieving.* (FICT)

The communication verb *say to* (*say* NP *to* NP) is also very common in conversation and fiction. This prepositional verb is used to report the content of speech (the direct object), while also identifying the addressee (the prepositional object):

> *She* **said** *something* **to** *mom and dad earlier on.* (CONV†)

> *I went to* **say** *thank you* **to** *Doris.* (FICT)

In many examples with *say to*, a clause is used as the direct object, to report the content of the speech. Often, following the principle of **end-weight**, such lengthy direct objects are in final position:

> *I* **said to** *John* <u>*something about the house on Frazier Street*</u>. (CONV)
> <compare: *I* **said** <u>*something about the house on Frazier Street*</u> **to** *John*.>

> *I keep* **saying to** *Michael* <u>*it's so expensive*</u>. (CONV)
> <compare: *I keep* **saying** *it's so expensive* **to** *Michael*.>

In addition to these two very frequent prepositional verbs, conversation and fiction use a number of other common prepositional verbs to indicate activities, communications, and mental processes:

- activity verbs:

    Pity we couldn't **go for** *a romp around a canal, isn't it?* (CONV)
    Patrice held her breath, **waiting for** *Lettie's reply.* (FICT)
    He **stared at** *me blankly, unbelievingly.* (FICT)

- communication verbs:

    Just **talk to** *her.* (CONV)
    I was **talking about** *the old sort of diesel multiple unit.* (CONV)
    He **spoke to** *Paul in a bitter, controlled tone.* (FICT†)

- mental verbs:

    What did they **think of** *the brochure then?* (CONV)
    I was **thinking about** *the playgroup downstairs.* (CONV)
    Since when does nobody **listen to** *you?* (CONV)

B   Academic prose

Academic prose also uses several common prepositional verbs that mark physical activities and mental states. However, these are mostly verbs that take the double object pattern (Pattern 2). They are often used in the passive voice. The most common of these is *use* NP *in*, and its passive counterpart (*be used in*):

> We will continue to **use** Table 4.2 **in** our economic analysis. (ACAD†)

> Another type of football **was used in** the second century in China to celebrate the emperor's birthday. (ACAD)

Other common prepositional verbs used in academic prose include the following:

- activity verbs:

> For example, the Message Type can **be derived from** its internal structure. (ACAD)

> Similarly other parts of the body may **be used as** bases to start from. (ACAD†)

> The method outlined could now **be applied to** a selected number of points along the blade length. (ACAD)

- mental verbs:

> This induced mustiness **is known as** Sierra rice. (ACAD)

> The electron may **be regarded as** a tiny mass carrying a negative charge. (ACAD†)

> All members of the specified Role Class **are considered as** possible senders of the received message. (ACAD†)

In general, academic prose focuses on the relations among inanimate entities, with less concern for the people who are performing actions. The preference for passive voice with prepositional verbs reflects this general focus. Thus, by using the passive, the above examples avoid mentioning the people who *derive, use, apply, know, regard,* or *consider*.

Academic prose also commonly uses prepositional verbs that express causation, existence, or simple occurrence. These verbs, too, specify relations among entities rather than describing actions:

- causative verbs:

> Further experimentation might **lead to** the identification of other difficulty factors. (ACAD†)

> Replacing the nonsense stems by English stems would have **resulted in** a grammatically correct sequence. (ACAD†)

- existence verb:

> It will **depend on** the purpose of, and audience for, the writing. (ACAD)

5.11 Phrasal-prepositional verbs

The third major type of multi-word verb shares characteristics of both phrasal and prepositional verbs. Phrasal-prepositional verbs consist of a lexical verb combined with both an adverbial particle and a preposition. For example, *look forward to* has the lexical verb *look*, the adverbial particle *forward*, and the preposition *to*:

> I'm **looking forward to** <u>the weekend</u>. (CONV)

This type of verb is similar to a prepositional verb, as the complement of the preposition (*the weekend*) functions as the prepositional object of the verb (*looking forward to*).

Here are some more examples, with the complement of the preposition underlined:

> Perhaps I can **get out of** <u>it</u> without having to tell her anything. (FICT)

> I would still **end up with** <u>a lot of money</u>. (NEWS)

A few phrasal-prepositional verbs can take two objects:

> I could **hand** <u>him</u> **over to** <u>Sadiq</u>. (FICT)

> Who **put** <u>you</u> **up to** <u>this</u>? (FICT)

Phrasal-prepositional verbs function as a semantic unit and can sometimes be replaced by a single transitive lexical verb with similar meaning. For example:

> **put up with** such treatment → **tolerate** such treatment

> **get out of** it → **avoid** it

> **come up with** a proposal → **make** a proposal

5.11.1 Most common phrasal-prepositional verbs

Like phrasal verbs, phrasal-prepositional verbs are more frequent in conversation and fiction than in expository writing. However, common phrasal-prepositional verbs are used for a limited range of meanings. Most are activity verbs.

The most frequent phrasal-prepositional verb is *get out of*. Often it is imperative (**1**) or declarative (**2**):

> 1 Just **get out of** my way. (CONV)
> 2 We have to **get out of** here. (FICT)

Several other phrasal-prepositional verbs are relatively common with activity meanings. For example:

> Stop yakking and **get on with** it! (CONV)

> He said he would **get back to** me. (FICT†)

> Burns **went up to** the soldiers and started talking. (FICT)

In news, two phrasal-prepositional verbs with activity meanings are relatively common: *get back to* and *come up with*:

> It's going to take time for you to **get back to** full strength. (NEWS)

> The panel will be asked to **come up with** the best all-time team on earth. (NEWS)

In addition, the mental verb *look forward to* is relatively common in fiction and news:

> She had been **looking forward to** this moment. (FICT)

In the case of news, *look forward to* typically occurs in direct (**1**) or reported speech (**2**):

> 1 'We are **looking forward to** the game'. (NEWS)
> 2 He said he was **looking forward to** the results of the inquiry. (NEWS†)

5.12 **Other multi-word verb constructions**

In addition to the three types of multi-word verbs discussed above, verbs are also used in relatively fixed or idiomatic multi-word constructions: verb + prepositional phrase combinations, verb + verb combinations, and verb + noun phrase combinations.

A Verb + prepositional phrase combinations

Many verb + prepositional phrase combinations are idiomatic. Such combinations function semantically as a unit that can often be replaced by a single lexical verb, as in the following sentences:

> I also have to **bear in mind** the interests of my wife and family. (NEWS†)
> <compare: remember>
>
> The triumph **came as a surprise** to many. (NEWS)
> <compare: surprised>
>
> You have to **take into account** where the younger shoots are dominant. (FICT)
> <compare: consider>

B Verb + verb combinations

A second idiomatic category involves verb + verb combinations, such as *make do (with)* and *let NP go/be*:

> Patients had to **make do with** quiche or ham salad. (NEWS†)
> He was 'very reluctant' to **let** him **go**. (NEWS†)
> I think it is time to **let** it **be**. (NEWS)

C Verb + noun phrase combinations

There are a few verbs—such as *take, make, have,* and *do*—that can be used for many meanings. These verbs can combine with noun phrases to form idiomatic verbal expressions. In many cases, the combination also includes a following preposition. For example:

> But you know how you **make fun of** me sometimes. (CONV)
> Let's **have a look at** this. (CONV)
> Do you want me to **do your hair**? (CONV)
> Yes, I'll **take care of** it. (FICT)

Review

Major points of **GRAMMAR BITE D**: Multi-word lexical verbs
➤ There are three major types of multi-word verb: phrasal verbs, prepositional verbs, and phrasal-prepositional verbs.
  ➤ Multi-word combinations can also be free combinations.
➤ Phrasal verbs consist of a verb + adverbial particle; they can be intransitive or transitive.
  ➤ Phrasal verbs are especially frequent in conversation and fiction. The most common verbs express physical activities (e.g. *come on, get up, pick up*).
  ➤ A few phrasal verbs are especially common in academic prose (e.g. *carry out*).

➤ Prepositional verbs consist of a verb + preposition. They can have one or two objects.
  ➤ Prepositional verbs are common in all registers.
  ➤ Prepositional verbs with activity and communication meanings are especially common in conversation (e.g. *look at, go for*).
  ➤ Passive voice prepositional verbs are especially common in academic prose (e.g. *be based on, be associated with*). They have causative or existence meanings.
➤ Phrasal-prepositional verbs consist of a verb + particle + preposition.
  ➤ Like phrasal verbs, phrasal-prepositional verbs are especially frequent in conversation and fiction. The most common verbs express physical activity (e.g. *get out of, get on with*).
➤ There are also other kinds of multi-word verb constructions that occur with idiomatic meanings (e.g. *bear in mind, make do* and *take time*).

GRAMMAR BITE

E Primary verbs

5.13 *Be*

5.13.1 Main verb *be*

As a main verb, *be*—the **copula**—is the most important **copular verb** in English. It links the subject noun phrase with a subject predicative (**1**) or an obligatory adverbial (**2**):

    1 *Radio waves* **are** <u>*useful*</u>. (NEWS†)
    2 *She* **was** <u>*in Olie's room*</u> *a lot.* (CONV)

The use of copula *be* is discussed further in 5.17 below.

5.13.2 Auxiliary verb *be*

As an auxiliary verb, *be* has two distinct grammatical functions:
- progressive aspect (*be* + *ing*-participle):
  The last light **was** <u>*fading*</u> *by the time he entered the town.* (FICT)
- passive voice (*be* + *ed*-participle):
  This system of intergovernmental transfers **is** <u>*called*</u> *fiscal federalism.* (ACAD)

These two auxiliary uses of *be* can occur together in the same clause (the progressive passive; see 6.8):

    A mutual investment fund for Eastern Europe **is being** <u>*launched*</u> *today with the backing of Continental Grain.* (NEWS†)

Progressive aspect and passive voice verbs are discussed further in 6.3, 6.5 and 6.6–8.

5.14 *Have*

5.14.1 Main verb *have*

Because *have* is a primary verb, we have not covered its use under our earlier discussion of lexical verbs. However, as a transitive main verb, *have* is as common as the most common lexical verbs in English. *Have* is most common in conversation and least common in academic prose. Within academic prose, though, *have* is more common than any lexical verb.

Similar to *get*, the main verb *have* can be used with many different meanings. For example:

- showing physical possession:

    *One in three of these families **has** two cars.* (NEWS)

- telling family connections:

    *Her story was this: she **had** a husband and child.* (FICT)

- describing eating or drinking:

    *The kids **had** 'superhero sundaes' which turned out to be merely ice cream.* (NEWS†)

- showing where something exists (similar to an **existential there** construction):

    *But it really would be nice to **have** a young person about the house again.* (FICT)

    <compare existential *there*: *It would be nice if **there was** a young person about the house.*>

- linking a person to an abstract quality:

    *I hope she **has** fun.* (CONV)

    *Her visitor **had** a strong pungent odor of a winter's day.* (FICT)

- linking an inanimate subject to an abstract quality:

    *Stylistics can **have** other goals than this.* (ACAD†)

    *In these extensions soil science will always **have** a major role.* (ACAD†)

- showing that someone causes something to be done:

    *Maybe you should **have** it dyed black as well.* (CONV)

In addition, the verb *have* occurs as part of the semi-modal *have to* (meaning *must*):

*I'll **have to** blank it out.* (CONV)

This semi-modal is discussed in 6.9 and 6.10.2.

Finally, *have* occurs in a number of idiomatic multi-word phrases, such as *have a look*:

*I'll **have a look**.* (CONV)

5.14.2 Auxiliary verb *have*

As an auxiliary verb, *have* is the marker of perfect aspect. Past tense *had* marks past perfect, and present *has/have* marks present perfect:

> *Twenty years before, Charlie **had** passed a whole day from rising to retiring without a drink.* (FICT)
>
> *No one **has** ever seen anything like that before.* (NEWS)

Perfect aspect verbs are discussed in 6.3–4.

5.15 *Do*

5.15.1 Main verb *do*

As a main verb in transitive constructions, *do* has an activity meaning. It can take a direct object:

> *In that moment Franklin Field **did** a wonderful thing.* (FICT)

or an indirect object + direct object:

> *Will you **do** me a favor?* (CONV)

However, *do* more commonly combines with a noun phrase to form relatively fixed, idiomatic expressions such as *do the job, do the dishes, do time* (meaning 'go to prison'), *do some work, do the wash, do your hair*. For example:

> *It **does the job**. It's not a bad little thing.* (CONV)
>
> *Well we'd better **do some work** you know.* (CONV)
>
> *I'm used to it. I **do the dishes** every day.* (CONV)

In these expressions, *do* has little lexical content. It refers to the performance of an activity that is relevant to the object noun phrase, but it does not specify that activity.

A) Main verb *do* as a transitive pro-verb

Do also commonly functions as a **pro-verb**, substituting for a lexical verb. Pro-verb *do* is especially common in conversation. It often combines with *it, this/that,* or *so,* to form a transitive pro-verb construction:

> *I didn't **do it**.* (CONV)
>
> *Well that's why he **did it**.* (CONV)
>
> *That really hurts my ears when you **do that**.* (CONV)
>
> *The Englishman, half asleep, had broken Lazzaro's right arm and knocked him unconscious. The Englishman who had **done this** was helping to carry Lazzaro in now.* (FICT)
>
> <*done this* = broken his right arm and knocked him unconscious>
>
> *'The Chancellor has had to face very difficult economic circumstances both abroad, which affects us, and at home,' he said. 'He has **done so** with great courage.'* (NEWS†)
>
> <*done so* = faced very difficult economic circumstances>

Notice that expressions like *do this* and *do so* can substitute for a large number of words.

B) Main verb *do* as an intransitive pro-verb

In British English conversation after an auxiliary verb, *do* as an intransitive pro-verb provides an alternative to **ellipsis**:

> A: *No, no signs of him resigning.*
> B: *Well they kicked him out.*
> A: *They should have* **done***, but they won't.* (CONV)
>   *<done = kicked him out>*

However, it is more common for speakers to use ellipsis rather than *do* (i.e. *they should have* rather than *they should have done*).

5.15.2 Auxiliary verb *do*

A Do-support in negatives and interrogatives

Do functions as an auxiliary verb when lexical main verbs are made negative or used in interrogatives. For example:

> negative: *He* **doesn't** *smoke or drink.* (NEWS)
>
> yes/no interrogative: **Do** *you like scallops?* (FICT)
>
> wh-interrogative: *So what* **did** *you bring for us this time?* (CONV)

This use of *do* is known as **do-support**, because *do* is added merely to support the construction of the negative or **interrogative**. The *do* does not contribute any independent meaning. In these constructions, present or past tense is marked on the verb *do*, not on the main verb. Thus compare:

negative clause	positive clause
I **didn't** realize it was from smoking. (CONV)	I realiz**ed** it was from smoking.

interrogative clause	declarative
Did you see Andy today? (CONV)	You **saw** Andy today.

Negatives are discussed further in 8.8 and interrogatives in 8.11. *Do* is here termed a 'dummy **operator**' (see 7.7), since it takes the role of an auxiliary verb where there is no auxiliary verb in the corresponding positive and declarative clause.

B Emphatic *do*

Emphatic *do* occurs as an auxiliary verb in a clause that is not negated and is not a question. It is used to emphasize that the meaning of the main verb (or the rest of the clause) is positive, in contrast with what one might expect. In speech, emphatic *do* is usually stressed. It most commonly occurs in conversation and fiction.

> 1 *I* **did have** *a protractor, but it broke.* (CONV)
> 2 *I really* **did go** *to see him.* (FICT)
> 3 *But in the final hour he* **did deliver** *the goods.* (NEWS)
> 4 *Gascoigne, though,* **does have** *a problem – his Lazio team is not a good side.* (NEWS)

Emphatic *do* cannot be combined with another auxiliary. For example, it is ungrammatical to say **It does might help.*

Emphatic *do* usually marks a state of affairs that contrasts with an expected state of affairs. The contrast is sometimes explicitly marked by connectives such as *but, however, nevertheless, though,* and *although,* as in **3** and **4** above and the following:

> *Nevertheless, great changes **do occur** and have been well documented.* (ACAD)

A special use of emphatic *do* is in commands (or suggestions/invitations that use the **imperative** form). Although this use sounds conversational, it occurs more commonly in fictional dialog than in actual conversation:

> *Oh **do shut up**!* (CONV)
> ***Do come** and see me some time.* (FICT)
> ***Do get on with** your work, Beth.* (FICT)
> *I **do beg** you to consider seriously the points I've put to you.* (FICT)

Normally the copula *be* behaves like an auxiliary, and therefore does not take emphatic *do* in declarative clauses: **They do be ...* With imperative clauses, however, *do + be* is possible:

> *'**Do be** sensible, Charles,' whispered Fiona.* (FICT)

C Auxiliary *do* as a pro-verb

Like main verb *do,* auxiliary *do* can act as a pro-verb, standing in for the whole verb phrase + complement. It is used in both positive and negative clauses:

> *A: He doesn't even know you.*
> *B: He **does**!* (CONV) <*does = does know me*>
> *I think his mom wants him to come back but his dad **doesn't**.* (CONV)
> <*doesn't = doesn't want him to come back*>

In these examples, *do* can be considered a stranded **operator** (8.7). That is, *do,* as the empty auxiliary, is left 'stranded' without the main verb which normally follows an auxiliary. The rest of the clause, as with other auxiliaries, is missing through ellipsis.

D Auxiliary *do* in question tags

Do functions as an auxiliary in **question tags**:

> *But Fanny <u>looked</u> after you, **didn't** she?* (FICT)
> *This delay <u>solves</u> nothing, **does** it?* (FICT)

This construction is obviously related to *do*-support (as in A above): it occurs where the preceding main verb (underlined above) has no auxiliary.

Review

Major points of **GRAMMAR BITE E**: Primary verbs
➤ The three primary verbs—*be, have,* and *do*—can serve as both main verbs and auxiliary verbs. They differ, however, in their specific main and auxiliary functions.
➤ *Be*:
  ➤ As copula (a main verb), *be* is the most common copular verb in English.
  ➤ As an auxiliary verb, *be* marks progressive aspect and passive voice.
➤ *Have*:
  ➤ As a main verb, *have* is one of the most common lexical verbs in English.
  ➤ It has a particularly wide range of meanings.
  ➤ As an auxiliary, *have* marks perfect aspect.

➤ *Do*:

> ➤ As a main verb, *do* is a general transitive verb of action (e.g. *do some work*).
> ➤ It often combines with a noun phrase to form idiomatic expressions (e.g. *do the dishes*).
> ➤ As a main verb, *do* can also function as a transitive pro-verb (*do it*, *do that*) or an intransitive pro-verb (e.g. *I must have done.*)
> ➤ As an auxiliary verb, *do* is used in the *do*-support construction for forming negation and questions (e.g. *Didn't you know?*).
> ➤ Auxiliary *do* is also used for emphatic meaning (e.g. *Oh do shut up!*).

GRAMMAR BITE

F Copular verbs

5.16 The copula *be*, and other copular verbs

Copular verbs are used to associate an attribute with the subject of the clause. The attribute is usually expressed by the subject predicative following the verb. For example, in the clause:

> *You're very stupid.* (CONV)

you is the subject, and the phrase *very stupid* is the subject predicative that specifies the attribute that is associated with the subject. The copula *be* (contracted as *'re*) links this attribute to the subject.

Many copular verbs are also used to locate the subject of the clause in time or space. Times and places are expressed by an obligatory adverbial of position, duration, or direction that occurs after the copula. For example:

> *I **was** in the kitchen.* (CONV)

Several verbs—like *go*, *grow*, and *come*—can function as either a copular verb or a transitive/intransitive verb, depending on the context:

* copular verb:

> *It makes your teeth and your bones **grow** strong and healthy.* (CONV)
> *It's beginning to **go** bad for you.* (FICT)
> *Your prophecy of last night has **come** true.* (FICT)

* transitive verb:

> *So you said she started to **grow** sesame herbs.* (CONV)

* intransitive verb:

> *It was when Wharton Horricker and I **went** to Mexico.* (FICT)
> *He **came** from the far north.* (FICT†)

There are many verbs that can function as copular verbs. They fall into two main categories: **current copular** verbs and **result copular** verbs.

A Current copular verbs

Current copular verbs have two subclasses. The first subclass identifies attributes that are in a continuing state of existence. This includes: *be, seem, appear, keep, remain, stay*. The other subclass reports sensory perceptions. This includes: *look, feel, sound, smell, taste*.

- state-of-existence:

    *We **are** all human.* (FICT)

    *I may have **appeared** a little short with my daughter that morning.* (FICT)

    *David Elsworth **seemed** quite satisfied with the performance of Barnbrook.* (NEWS)

- sensory perception:

    *I really do **look** awful.* (CONV)

    *Ooh that **feels** good.* (CONV)

    *They just **sound** really bad when they're recorded on.* (CONV)

B Result copular verbs

Result copular verbs identify an attribute that is the result of a process of change:

    *She'll **end up** pregnant.* (CONV)

    *His breathing **became** less frantic.* (FICT)

    *My heart **grew** sick and I couldn't eat.* (FICT)

Other result copular verbs include: *become, get, go, grow, prove, come, turn, turn out, end up, wind up.*

5.17 Functions of copular verbs

Copular verbs differ in their meanings and in the complements that they take. Overall, most copular verbs occur with an adjective phrase as the subject predicative, but some verbs are also strongly associated with other structures, such as a noun phrase or complement clause. Some verbs are limited to one type of complement, while others occur with many. In the following subsections, we review the associations between the most common copular verbs and their complements, and discuss how these associations reflect the differences in meaning and function of the verbs.

5.17.1 Current copular verbs: state of existence

A Be

The copula *be* is by far the most common verb in English. Surprisingly, the copula *be* differs from most lexical verbs because it is much more frequent in academic prose than in conversation, newspapers, or fiction. *Be* also occurs with a wide range of complements.

Unlike most copular verbs, *be* occurs most commonly with a noun phrase as subject predicative. In these structures, the noun phrase following *be* has two common functions: to characterize the subject noun phrase in some way, or to identify the subject noun phrase:

- characterizing:

    *Oh, my dad **was** <u>a great guy</u>, too.* (CONV)

    *Tomorrow could **be** <u>a sunny day</u>.* (CONV†)

- identifying:

    *That**'s** <u>our back yard</u>.* (CONV)

    *The kernel **is** <u>the part of the plant of greatest value</u>.* (ACAD†)

Adjective phrases are also very common as subject predicatives of *be*. The most common of these predicative adjectives express **stance**. In conversation, these are mostly general evaluative terms, such as *right, good, sure, nice,* and *funny*. In most cases, these adjectives occur without complements after them:

    *That **wasn't** <u>very nice</u>.* (CONV)

    *It **was** <u>funny</u> though.* (CONV)

In contrast, academic prose uses a larger range of predicative adjectives that express more specific evaluations, such as *important, possible, necessary, difficult,* and *useful*. In most cases, these adjectives occur with a complement clause or prepositional phrase. The predicative adjective expresses an evaluation that applies to the following clause or phrase:

    *It **is** also <u>important to gain the cooperation of workshop participants</u>.* (ACAD†)

    *It **is** <u>possible to have more than one major hypothesis</u>.* (ACAD†)

The common predicative adjectives occurring with *be* are described fully in 7.8.

Prepositional phrases are much less common as complements of *be*. They are used for two functions:

- as a subject predicative describing a characteristic of the subject:

    *Umuofia **was** <u>in a festival mood</u>.* (FICT)

    *The resistive voltage drop **is** <u>in phase with the current</u>.* (ACAD)

- as an adverbial expressing position or direction:

    *I wish you **were** <u>at the shack</u> with me last night.* (CONV)

    *The houses **are** <u>in a conservation area</u>.* (NEWS)

Finally, *be* sometimes occurs with a complement clause as subject predicative:

    *The capital **is** <u>to be provided by the French government</u>.* (NEWS†)

    *But the danger **was** <u>that the pound would fall further than planned</u>.* (NEWS)

B Other state-of-existence copular verbs

Table 5.1 summarizes the patterns of use for five other state-of-existence copular verbs. These verbs are all relatively common but far less common than *be*. *Seem* and *appear* have a variety of functions, while *remain, keep,* and *stay* all mark the continuation of a state.

Table 5.1   State-of-existence copular verbs (in addition to *be*)

verb	frequency	most common complements	examples
seem	most common copular verb other than *be*	*to*-complement clause	*This **seemed** <u>to work</u>.* (FICT)

le 5.1 **continued**

verb	frequency	most common complements	examples
		adjectives, especially conveying attitudes, surprise and possibility in fiction	Sometimes it **seemed** impossible that he should fail. (FICT)
			He **seemed** surprised by that. (FICT)
		adjectives of likelihood in academic prose, with extraposed that-clauses	It **seems** likely that practical work has helped to develop these skills in some students. (ACAD)
			It **seems** clear that more meals will be cooked over charcoal in the future. (ACAD†)
		noun phrase as subject predicative, especially with perceptions that are not necessarily accurate	Fijisankei, itself privately owned and independent, **seems** the ideal partner. (NEWS†)
		prepositional phrase expressing an attribute of the subject	Now he **seemed** in control. (FICT)
			Most of the time he **seems** like such a normal guy. (FICT)
appear	less common than seem	to-complement clause	The inheritance of leaf angle **appears** to be polygenic. (ACAD)
		adjectives of likelihood in academic prose and news	There was never a moment when it **appeared** likely that we could get them. (NEWS)
			The courts have **appeared** willing to go beyond the rules of neutral justice. (ACAD)
remain	most common of the three continuation verbs; particularly common in academic prose and news	adjectives, often reporting absence of change	Next Friday's date for the final **remains** unchanged. (NEWS)
		typical adjectives: unchanged, constant, intact, motionless, immobile, low, high, open, closed, controversial, uncertain, unknown, obscure	The opening of the oviduct **remains** intact. (ACAD)

Table 5.1 **continued**

verb	frequency	most common complements	examples
keep	less common than remain	typical adjectives: alive, awake, quiet, silent, secret, busy, fit, close, warm	It's funny how he manages to **keep** <u>awake</u>. (CONV)
		subject of keep is usually an animate being	He was just trying to **keep** <u>warm</u>. (FICT)
stay	least common of the three continuation verbs	typical adjectives: awake, dry, sober, alive, clear, loyal, healthy	I mean, if you **stay** <u>sober</u>. (CONV)
		subject of stay is usually human	Meanwhile, Millie's mistress **stayed** <u>loyal</u> to her husband's ambitions. (FICT)

5.17.2 Current copular verbs: sensory perceptions

The patterns of use for sensory copular verbs are summarized in Table 5.2.

Sensory copular verbs—*look, feel, sound, smell, taste*—occur with adjectival complements to report positive or negative evaluations. For example:

> Do I **look** <u>nice</u>? (CONV)

> The food **smelled** <u>good</u> to her. (FICT)

Table 5.2 **Sensory copular verbs**

verb	frequency	most common functions and complements	examples
look	very common in fiction; relatively common in conversation	often evaluates physical appearance common adjectives: awful, different, happy, lovely, pale, puzzled, sad, small, surprised, terrible, tired, well, young	Oh he does **look** <u>sad</u>, doesn't he? (CONV) Quite frankly she **looked** <u>terrible</u>. (FICT) You **look** <u>lovely</u>. (FICT)
feel	very common in fiction; moderately common in news and conversation	reports an assessment of physical or mental state of being common adjectives: ashamed, bad, better, cold, good, guilty, sick, sure, tired, uncomfortable, uneasy	It'll make you **feel** <u>better</u>. (NEWS) My hands **feel** <u>cold</u>. (FICT) I always **feel** <u>guilty</u> passing Mike's house. (CONV)
sound	most common in fiction and conversation	literal use: evaluations of sound perceptions common adjectives: good, nice, silly, stupid, interesting, awful, angry, sad, strange additional use: reactions to ideas/suggestions	She doesn't **sound** <u>angry</u> anymore. (FICT) He looked and **sounded** <u>awful</u>. (FICT) Oh how nice. That **sounds** <u>good</u> to me. (CONV)

le 5.2 continued

verb	frequency	most common functions and complements	examples
			*I know it **sounds** stupid, but I wanted to go.* (CONV)
smell	generally rare	reports evaluations of smell perceptions common adjectives: *awful, bad, funny, musty, odd, rotten, terrible, delicious, fresh, good, lovely, nice*	*It **smells** funny in here.* (CONV)
taste	rare; occasional occurrences in conversation and fiction	reports evaluations of taste perceptions common adjectives: *awful, horrible, nice, wonderful*	*They just **taste** awful.* (CONV)

Here, the copular verb identifies the sense (e.g. sight, hearing), while the predicative adjective reports the evaluation. The general evaluating adjectives *nice*, *good*, and *bad* occur commonly as subject predicative with all five sensory copular verbs.

5.17.3 Result copular verbs

The verbs *become, get, go, grow, prove, come, turn, turn out, end up,* and *wind up* are all used to describe a process of change. However, despite this general similarity, these verbs differ greatly in their specific meanings, collocational preferences, and register distributions.

A *Become*

The result copular verb *become* is especially common in academic prose and fiction. It is used to describe the process involved in changing from one state to another. In academic prose, it often refers to an impersonal process of moving from a state of ignorance or disbelief to one of knowledge or belief (i.e. without mentioning individual people who experience the change). The adjectives *clear* and *apparent* are most common with this function, but there are a number of other adjectives that occur with *become*, including *difficult, evident, important, possible*.

> *In the joint-stock company, the social character of production has **become** apparent.* (ACAD)
>
> *It soon **becomes** clear that there is much more to comprehension than vocabulary.* (ACAD†)
>
> *Performance and functionality only **become** important with Release 3.* (ACAD†)

In fiction, *become* usually refers to a specific person. It describes a change in that person's state of awareness or state of being:

> *Raymond soon **became** aware that his strategy and hard work was paying dividends.* (FICT)

> It all **became** <u>clear</u> to me when I reached street level. (FICT)
>
> I **became** <u>silent</u>, overwhelmed suddenly by the great gulf between us. (FICT†)

B Get

The result copular verb *get* is usually used to describe a person changing to a new state. *Get* is very common, especially in conversation and fiction, and it has many uses, describing both physical and mental changes. The adjectives *ready* and *worse* are the most common subject predicatives with *get*, but a number of other adjectives recur: *angry, bigger, better, bored, cold, dressed (up), drunk, lost, mad, mixed (up), old, older, pissed (off), sick, tired, upset, wet.* Many of these mark some affective or attitudinal stance. For example:

> Well he's only gonna **get** <u>worse</u>. (CONV)
>
> And if she doesn't win, she either **gets** <u>upset</u> and cries or **gets** <u>angry</u>. (CONV)
>
> And people **get** <u>pissed off</u>, don't they? (CONV) <note: *pissed off* is slang and may be offensive to some people>

C Go

The copular verb *go* is usually used to describe a change towards an undesirable state, especially in conversation and fiction. *Go* describes changes experienced by humans and other natural processes. The adjectives *crazy, mad,* and *wrong* are the most common complements of *go*, but several other adjectives recur: *bad, cold, deaf, funny, limp, quiet, red, wild.*

> You can't **go** <u>wrong</u> with that, can you? (CONV)
>
> Yeah I know. I would **go** <u>mad</u>. (CONV)
>
> Mama will **go** <u>crazy</u>. (FICT)

D Less common result copular verbs

Although *become, get,* and *go* are the most common result copular verbs, several others deserve mention. These verbs and their functions are summarized in Table 5.3.

Review

Major points of GRAMMAR BITE E: Copular verbs
➤ Copular verbs are used to express a relationship between the subject of the clause and an attribute.
➤ Copular verbs usually take an obligatory subject predicative.
➤ Some copular verbs can also occur with an obligatory adverbial.
➤ Many different verbs can function as copulas. These verbs can be grouped into two major categories: current copular verbs and result copular verbs.
  ➤ Current copular verbs express states of existence or sensory perceptions (e.g. *be, feel*).
  ➤ Result copular verbs express the result of a process of change (e.g. *become, turn out*).
➤ The copular verbs differ in their meanings and in the complements that they can take.
➤ There are highly systematic patterns of use associated with copular verbs + complements.

le 5.3   Less common result copular verbs

verb	frequency	most common functions and complements	examples
come	generally rare, occurs mainly in fiction and news	usually describes a change to a better condition	It literally is a dream **come** _true_. (NEWS†)
		recurring adjectives: _alive, awake, clean, loose, short, true, unstuck_	Slowly his face **came** _alive_ and he grinned. (FICT)
grow	primarily used in fiction	describes gradual change	We should **grow** _old_ here together. (FICT)
		often makes an implicit comparison with an earlier state through use of comparative adjective as complement	The wind dropped and it suddenly **grew** _cold_. (FICT)
			The girl's deep black eyes **grew** _darker_. (FICT)
		recurring adjectives: _angry, big, bright, cold, dark, hot, large, old, pale, tall, tired, warm, weak, bigger, darker, larger, louder, older, shorter, smaller, stronger, warmer, weaker, worse_	She continued to lose weight and **grow** _weaker_. (FICT†)
prove	used primarily in academic prose and news	reports an assessment	Looking for tourist highlights in Montepulciano can **prove** _difficult_. (NEWS)
		recurring adjectives: _costly, decisive, difficult, fatal, necessary, popular, possible, successful, suitable, useful, wrong_	He was confident the units would **prove** _popular_ with travellers. (NEWS)
			Yet it has **proved** _necessary_ to attempt this task. (ACAD†)
turn	occasionally used in fiction; rare in other registers	turn + adjective describes change in appearance; typically refers to color changes	The canals in the suburbs appear to **turn** _black_. (FICT)
		recurring adjectives: _black, brown, (bright) red, white, pale_	She had **turned** _pale_ and her voice shook. (FICT)
turn out	generally rare	emphasizes the end-point of a process with simple positive or negative evaluation	A lot of times they **turned** _out wrong_. (FICT)
		recurring adjectives: _good, nasty, nice, (all) right, wrong_	The marriage will **turn** _out all right_. (FICT)
end up and wind up	generally rare	describe an unintended negative event or state	And this argument went on. Danny **ended** _up in tears_ and I **ended** _up really angry_. (CONV)
			He says Marilyn **ended** _up pregnant_ after her affair with President Kennedy. (NEWS)
			And the young bucks who tore the place apart invariably **wound** _up dead_. (FICT†)

6

Variation in the verb phrase: tense, aspect, voice, and modal use

GRAMMAR BITES in this chapter

A Tense

- ➤ Description of past and present tenses
- ➤ Functions and meanings of past and present tenses
- ➤ The expression of future time
- ➤ Frequency of tense use for particular verbs

B Aspect

- ➤ Description of perfect and progressive aspect
- ➤ Combinations of aspects and tenses
- ➤ Functions and meanings of perfect and progressive aspect
- ➤ Most common verbs with each aspect
- ➤ Use of time adverbials and dependent clauses with past perfect

C Voice

- ➤ Forms of passive voice constructions
- ➤ Functions and frequencies of passive voice across registers
- ➤ Verbs that rarely occur in passive voice
- ➤ Voice and aspect combinations

D Modals and semi-modals

- ➤ Description of modals and semi-modals
- ➤ Functions and meanings of modals and semi-modals
- ➤ Use of modals and semi-modals across registers
- ➤ Combinations of modals, semi-modals, aspect, and voice

6.1 **Introduction**

There are six major kinds of variation in the structure of verb phrases. These are illustrated below with the verb *see*:

- **tense:**
     present (*sees*)
     past (*saw*)
- **aspect:**
     unmarked (also called **simple aspect**) (*sees*)
     perfect (*has seen*)
     progressive (*is seeing*)
     perfect progressive (*has been seeing*)
- **voice:**
     active (*sees*)
     passive (*is seen*)
- **modality:**
     unmarked (*sees*)
     with modal verb (*will/can/might see*)
- **negation:**
     positive (*sees*)
     negative (*doesn't see*)
- **finite clause type** (also called 'mood'):
     declarative (*you saw*)
     interrogative (*did you see?*)
     imperative/subjunctive (*see*)

In this chapter we concentrate on the first four kinds of variation in the verb phrase: tense, aspect, voice, and modality. (Negation and finite clause types are described in 8.8, 8.9–13 and 8.17.) These structures can be combined in numerous ways, as you will see throughout the chapter. For example, the verb phrase *will be eating* has a modal + progressive aspect, and *have been eaten* has perfect aspect + passive voice. The parts of the verb phrase—and therefore the auxiliary verbs associated with each part—follow a consistent order (optional elements are in parentheses):

	(modal)	(perfect) (form of *have*)	(progressive) (form of *be*)	(passive) (form of *be*)	main verb
example:	*will*	*have*	*been*	*being*	*eaten*

Verb phrases with all of these structures are extremely rare, but are possible.

The variations in the verb phrase are related to many differences in meanings. However, it is not possible to figure out the meaning simply by looking at the form. Rather, a single form can be used to express several meanings, and the same meaning can be expressed by more than one form.

The complex relationship between form and meaning is easy to see by contrasting verb tense and time meaning. People commonly assume that present tense verbs refer to the present time. However this is not always true. In fact, present tense verbs are sometimes used to refer to a time in the past. Compare:

- present (habitual) time with present tense:

   *He **goes** there a lot.* (CONV)

- past time with present tense (the **historic present**):

   *I wanted just a small box. He wasn't satisfied with it – He **goes** and **makes** a big one as well.* (CONV)

On the other hand, in terms of time, different forms can be used to express the same meaning. For example, in **1** below, future time is expressed with a present tense verb, while in **2**, future time is expressed with the modal *will* + infinitive:

- future time with present tense:

   1 *Goalkeeper Stephen Pears **goes** into hospital tomorrow for an operation on a cheekbone injury.* (NEWS†)

- future time with modal *will*:

   2 *This part of the project **will go** ahead extremely rapidly.* (NEWS)

The following Grammar Bites introduce the range of verb constructions used in the English verb phrase, and the meanings that each of them expresses.

GRAMMAR BITE

A Tense

6.2 Tense and time distinctions: simple present and past tense

In English, **finite verb phrases** can be marked for only two tenses: present and past. Verb phrases that are marked for **tense** are called tensed verb phrases. (See 5.5 for a discussion of verb morphology for tense with regular and irregular verbs.)

Other main verb phrases may include a modal verb. However, these two options cannot occur together: a finite verb phrase either has a modal or is marked for tense, but not both. **Non-finite phrases**, as in *to*-clauses and *ing*-clauses, do not include either tensed or modal verbs (see Fig. 6.1).

Figure 6.1 Basic choices in the verb phrase (apart from aspect and voice)

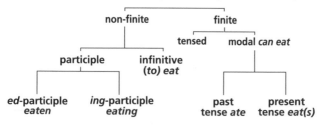

A Simple present tense and present time

Simple present tense often refers to present time, as in these examples:

1 *I **want** a packet of crisps.* (CONV)
2 *The pigment **occurs** in the epidermal cells.* (ACAD)
3 *She's vegetarian but she **eats** chicken.* (CONV)
4 *He **dances** and **moves** about a lot.* (NEWS)
5 *Here **comes** your mother.* (CONV)
6 *Oh, my goodness. There he **goes**. Look at him walk.* (CONV) <talking about a toddler>

There are three major meanings for simple present tense when it refers to present time:

- It can describe a state that exists at the present time. You can see this meaning in **1** and **2**. The state may be temporary, as in **1**, or it may last for a longer time, as in **2**.
- It can refer to a habitual action, as in **3** and **4**. In these examples, simple present tense is used to refer to an activity that is repeated on occasion, rather than to a state of being.
- It can describe an action that is happening at the present time, as in **5** and **6**.

In addition, simple present tense can sometimes be used to refer to past or future time. These special meanings are described in 6.2.1 below.

B Simple past tense and past time

Simple past tense is most often used to refer to past time. In fictional narrative and description, the use of simple past tense is common for describing imagined past states and events:

> *The clock on the tower of St Michael-in-the-Moor chimed nine as he **came** onto the road. The milkman's van **was** on the green; Mrs Southworth from the Hall **was** at the pillar box, posting a letter. He **walked** on away from the green and the houses up the bit of Jackley Road from which Tace Way **turned** off.* (FICT)

In addition, simple past tense is sometimes used for a situation at the present time. In this case, the past tense gives information about **stance**. It is usually used with verbs like *think*, *wonder*, and *want*. The clause refers to a current state of mind, but the past tense conveys tentativeness and shows that the speaker is being polite:

> ***Did** you want a cup of tea?* (CONV)
>
> *I just **wanted** to thank you guys for allowing me to tape-record you.* (CONV†)

Furthermore, in some types of dependent clauses, the simple past tense is used as the subjunctive, to show **hypothetical** or 'unreal' conditions (see 11.10.1):

> *And if you **were** in the mood we could at least go.* (CONV†)
>
> *Timothy, it's time you **got married**.* (FICT)

6.2.1 Simple present tense used for past or future time

A Simple present tense used for past time

In special cases, simple present tense is used to refer to past events or future events. When it refers to past time, it is called the historic present tense. This use is most common in conversation:

1 *No. He **says**, are you going home tonight? He thought I was going home to my parents.* (CONV)
2 *And the daughter **comes** home from school one day and **says**, mum I want to be like you. And the mum **goes**, okay dear.* (CONV†) <note: goes = says>
3 *All right. There's a fortune teller and the man **goes** to the fortune teller and the fortune teller **goes** <...> I can tell you the future.* (CONV†)

As these examples illustrate, the historic present is particularly common with verbs expressing directional movement (*come* and *go*) and with verbs that describe speaking (e.g. *say*, *go*). The verb *go* is especially interesting, because it is used to express both types of meaning. This pattern is usually found in personal stories (as in **1**) or in jokes (which are often told entirely in the historic present, as in **2** and **3**).

B Present tense used for future time

When the present tense is used to refer to future time, some other grammatical feature usually occurs in the clause:

- a time adverbial that refers to the future (see **1** below)
- an adverbial clause of time or condition that has future time reference (see **1** and **2** below):

1 *A new era **begins** for the bomb-damaged Ulster landmark [when the curtain **goes up** on Jack and the Beanstalk [in December]].* (NEWS†)
2 *[If I **refuse** to do what she says this time,] who knows where my defiance will end?* (FICT)

In **1**, the time adverbial *when the curtain goes up ... in December* pinpoints the specific future time when the new era *begins*. In addition, the time adverbial *in December* tells the specific time reference for the verb *goes up*. In **2**, the use of a present tense verb *refuse* in an *if*-clause indicates actions that might occur in future time; the modal verb *will* later in this sentence further reinforces the future time reference here.

6.2.2 Tense in reported speech

Simple past tense has a special use in reported speech or thought. The original speech or thoughts may have been in present tense, but past tense is usually used for the reports:

1 *Then the next day he **said** he no longer **loved** me.* (CONV) <direct speech: 'I no longer love you.'>
2 *And I **thought** I **was** going to go home early.* (CONV) <direct thought: 'I am going to go home early.'>

3 *Abbey* **said** *there* **was** *a meeting planned to discuss the contract this week.*
(NEWS) <direct speech: 'There is a meeting...'>

The tense of the verb in the indirect quote agrees with the past tense of the reporting verb (e.g. *said—loved* in 1). If a speaker is reporting the speech of someone else, there is also a corresponding shift in pronouns, for example from *I* to *he* in 1. Notice that the circumstances may still be continuing even though past tense is used. For example, in 3 the meeting may still be planned.

Although this use of past tense in reported speech is common, reported speech also occurs with other tenses. Consider these examples:

> *She* **said** *she* **feels** *good now.* (CONV†)

> *Graham* **said** *the owls' messy habit* **makes** *them the ideal bird for the study.* (NEWS)

Here, the reporting verb (*said*) is in the past tense, but the verb in the indirect quote remains in the present tense, emphasizing that the circumstances expressed by *feels* and *makes* are still continuing.

A further variation in tense in reported speech occasionally occurs in conversation, where present tense is used for the reporting verb and past tense for the indirect quote:

> *He says he* **bought** *another Amiga.* (CONV)

6.2.3 Future time

There is no way to mark future tense on verbs in English. That is, verbs cannot be inflected for future tense in the same way that they can be inflected for present and past tense. Instead, future time is usually marked in the verb phrase with a **modal** (such as *will or shall*) or **semi-modal** (such as *be going to*; see 6.11):

> *Even more precise coordination* **will** *be necessary.* (FICT)

> *We* **shall** *give an account of the Einstein-Podolski-Rosen paradox.* (ACAD†)

> *And he's* **going to** *see it.* (CONV)

The semi-modal *be going to* can be used for present or past tense. When the past tense is used (*was going to*), this semi-modal refers to a projected future time seen from a point in the past:

> 1 *It was in the summer holidays and Matthew* **was going to** *start school.* (CONV)

As you can see in 2, the reference can be to a situation that never actually occurred:

> 2 *I* **was going to** *be called Kate if I was a girl.* (CONV)

6.2.4 Tense use across registers

From a grammatical point of view, tense and modals belong to a single system: all finite verb phrases either have tense or a modal, but not both. As Figure 6.2 shows, tensed verb phrases are much more common than verb phrases with modals.

When modals are used, they usually express stance: the degree of certainty, or meanings such as obligation, necessity or giving or asking permission (see Grammar Bite D below). However, most clauses in English are not marked for stance. Rather, they are marked for time orientation, which requires a tensed verb. (There are other ways of marking stance with tensed verbs, such as using **stance adverbials**; see 11.2, 11.13–16.)

Figure 6.2 also shows that present tense verbs are slightly more common than past tense verbs. Present tense expresses a wider range of meanings than past tense. As we have seen, it can refer to events in the past, to present states, to habitual behaviors, and to future events. Past tense is more restricted in its meanings. It is used mainly for past time. Thus, the frequency of present tense is related to the greater variety of its uses.

However, there are important differences in the preferred tense across registers. Present tense is particularly common in both conversation and academic prose—but for very different reasons. In conversation, present tense is used to refer to the immediate context and current states or events:

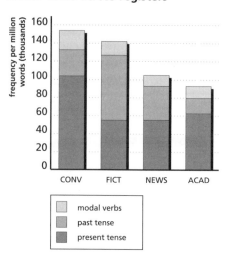

Figure 6.2

Frequency of present/past tense v. modal verbs across registers

> A: *I've done this thing today, I've to come up with, I'll do this afternoon, I'm quite proud of it.*
> B: *What **do** you do at Dudley Allen then?*
> A: *What the school?*
> B: *Yeah. **Do** you –*
> A: *No I'm, I'm only on the PTA.* <PTA = Parent-Teacher Association>
> B: *You're just on the PTA.*
> A: *That's it.* (CONV)

In this conversation, present tense is used for current states (*I'm quite proud*) as well as habitual actions (*What do you do ...*).

In academic prose, on the other hand, present tense is used to show that a proposition is true regardless of time. Consider the following:

> *A fault tree analysis **reveals** the logical connections existing between an undesired event in a technical system and component systems which **lead** to it. In the case of safety analyses for process plants, the undesired event usually **is** a fire* <...> (ACAD†)

In this example of academic prose, simple present tense is being used to convey general truths. For example, when the author writes *the analysis reveals the logical connections*, this would be true at any time.

In contrast to conversation and academic prose, fiction has a higher frequency of past tense. In fact, many fictional narratives are written entirely in the past tense, with present tense used only for the direct speech of characters. In the following example, past tense verbs are in bold and present tense verbs are underlined:

*Hurriedly draining her cup, she **frowned** at Marge, who **had** hardly touched the coffee that she just **had** to have before traveling any farther. 'Look, hon, we <u>have</u> to hurry. Mom<u>'s</u> real together about serving Thanksgiving dinner on time.' 'All right –' Marge **replied**. (FICT)*

6.2.5 Verbs that are often used in present or past tense

Many verbs are used more frequently in either simple past or simple present tense. For example, *bet* and *doubt* are usually used in the present tense, while *remark* and *sigh* are usually used in the past tense.

A Verbs that usually occur in the present tense

- Verbs that occur in the present tense over 80 per cent of the time:

   bet, doubt, know, matter, mean, mind, reckon, suppose, think

- Verbs that occur in the present tense over 70 per cent of the time:

   care, differ, fancy, imply, tend, want

Most of the verbs that usually occur in the present tense describe mental or logical states. They are often used to express emotions or attitudes, especially in conversation. For example:

   *I **don't want** one.* (CONV)

   *I **bet** he's starving for real grub.* (NEWS) <note: *grub* is an informal term for 'food'>

These verbs are also used to refer to logical thinking or analysis:

   *But I **reckon** they have got it just right with the Mondeo.* (NEWS)

   *Customs **differ**, but the meaning's the same.* (NEWS)

   *The sequence **implies** a history of Muav sedimentation and burial.* (ACAD†)

   *Transplanting **tends** to reduce lodging.* (ACAD)

B Verbs that usually occur in the past tense

- Verbs that occur in the past tense over 80 per cent of the time:

   exclaim, eye, glance, grin, nod, pause, remark, reply, shrug, sigh, smile, whisper

- Verbs that occur in the past tense over 70 per cent of the time:

   bend, bow, lean, light, park, seat, set off, shake, stare, turn away, wave, wrap

The verbs that usually occur in the past tense have very different meanings from the verbs that prefer present tense. Many of these past tense verbs are used to describe human activities: *bend, bow, eye, glance, grin, lean,* etc. A special subset of these verbs are verbs describing speaking: *exclaim, remark, reply, whisper.* All of these verbs are especially common in fiction, but they occur in other registers as well.

- Human activities:

  *She just **shrugged** her shoulders.* (CONV)

  *Rachel **glanced** at her uncle.* (FICT)

  *She **waved** to well-wishers at Sadler's Wells in London.* (NEWS†)

- Communication verbs:

  *Well he **whispered** to me last night, you know.* (CONV)

  *'A fine thing,' Dr. Saito **remarked** to me.* (FICT)

Review

Major points of **GRAMMAR BITE A**: Tense

➤ Verbs in English have only two tenses marked on them: present and past.
  ➤ Verb phrases can either be marked for tense or have a modal verb, but not both.
  ➤ Verb phrases that are marked for tense are more common than verb phrases with modal verbs.
➤ There are several different meanings expressed by present and past tense.
  ➤ Present tense verbs often refer to present time, either describing a state that exists at the present time or describing a habitual action.
  ➤ Present tense is also used to show past or future time.
  ➤ Past tense often refers to past time, but it is sometimes used to mark present time and for hypothetical conditions.
➤ Future time is usually marked in English with modals or semi-modals.
➤ Many verbs tend to occur with a particular tense.
  ➤ Verbs describing mental states are commonly in the present tense.
  ➤ Verbs about activity and communication are commonly in the past tense.

GRAMMAR BITE

B Aspect

6.3 Perfect and progressive aspect

As explained in Grammar Bite A, tense can be used to mark past and present and refer to future time. **Aspect** adds time meanings to those expressed by tense. Aspect answers the question 'Is the event/state described by the verb completed, or is it continuing?'. There are two aspects in English: **perfect** and **progressive** (sometimes known as 'continuous'). Verbs that do not have aspect marked on them are said to have simple aspect.

6.3.1 Meanings of perfect and progressive aspect

The perfect aspect most often describes events or states taking place during a preceding period of time. The progressive aspect describes an event or state of affairs in progress or continuing. Perfect and progressive aspect can be combined with either present or past tense:

- perfect aspect, present tense:

    We **have written** to Mr. Steven, but he **has ignored** our letters. (NEWS)

- perfect aspect, past tense:

    He **had seen** him picking purses. (FICT)

- progressive aspect, present tense:

    Jeff **is growing** his beard out. (CONV)

- progressive aspect, past tense:

    That's why I **was thinking** I might hang onto the Volvo. (CONV)

Present perfect verbs often refer to past actions with effects that continue up to the present time. For example, consider the sentence:

    Mr. Hawke **has embarked** on a crusade. (NEWS†)

The action (embarking on a crusade) began sometime previously, but Mr Hawke continues to be on the crusade at the time this sentence was written.

In contrast, past perfect verbs refer to actions in the past that are completed at or before a given time in the past. The actual time is often specified:

    Two brothers told a court yesterday how they watched their terminally-ill mother 'fade away' after she was given an injection. Widow Lilian Boyes, 70, **had** _earlier_ **pleaded** with doctors to 'finish her off,' Winchester Crown Court heard. (NEWS)

In this example, the events of the second sentence—the pleading—are completed by the time of the events described in the first sentence. The first sentence describes a past time with the simple past tense, and then the past perfect is used in the second sentence to refer to an even earlier time. You can find more information on past perfect and present perfect in 6.4 below.

The meaning of progressive aspect is less complicated: it is typically used to report situations or activities that are in progress at some point in time (past, present, or in the near future). For more information about the meaning and use of the progressive see 6.5 below.

6.3.2 The perfect progressive

Verb phrases can be marked for both aspects (perfect and progressive) at the same time:

- present perfect progressive:

    God knows how long I'**ve been doing** it. **Have** I **been talking** out loud? (FICT)

- past perfect progressive:

    He **had been keeping** it in a safety deposit box at the Bank of America. (FICT)

    For months she **had been waiting** for that particular corner location. (FICT)

The perfect progressive aspect is rare, occurring usually in the past tense in fiction. It combines the meaning of the perfect and the progressive, referring to a past situation or activity that was in progress for a period of time.

6.3.3 Perfect and progressive aspect across registers and dialects

A Register differences

Figure 6.3 presents the distribution of simple, perfect, and progressive aspects across registers. Perfect progressive aspect is omitted because it is too rare to show up on the chart.

The figure shows that the large majority of verb phrases are not marked for aspect. In fact, almost 90 per cent of all verbs are simple aspect. Perfect aspect is used in all registers, but it is somewhat more common in fiction and news. Progressive aspect is more common in conversation than in the written registers.

It might surprise some readers that simple aspect verbs are much more common than progressive aspect verbs in conversation, since many people believe that progressive verbs are the normal choice in conversation. It is true that progressive verbs are more common in conversation than they are in newspaper language or in academic prose. However, as Figure 6.3 shows, simple aspect verbs are the typical choice even in conversation. Progressive aspect verbs are comparatively rare, reserved for special use to express continuing action or states.

Figure 6.3

Frequency of simple, perfect and progressive aspect across registers

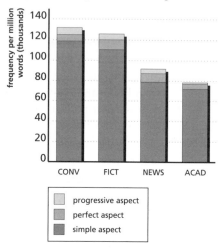

B Dialect differences

Conversation and news clearly reflect the differences between American and British English. You can see from Figure 6.4 that American English conversation uses progressive aspect much more than British English conversation does:

> *Nothing's **happening** over here.* (AmE CONV)
>
> *Oh yeah, but he's **roaming** around on the range?* (AmE CONV)
>
> *One time, I saw a seal <...> The seal **was begging**.* (AmE CONV)

Figure 6.4

Frequency of perfect and progressive aspect in AmE v. BrE conversation and news

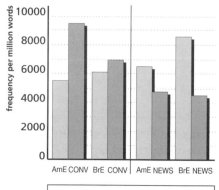

Although British English has similar constructions, they are used much less commonly.

In contrast, British English uses perfect aspect much more than American English does. American English often uses past tense in contexts where British English uses the present perfect. This difference is especially noticeable when the sentence also includes *yet* or *already*:

AmE conversation	BrE conversation
*Hey, **did** you **read** through this **yet**?*	*__Have__ you __read__ it __yet__?*
*No not **yet** I **didn't**. I **didn't** get a chance.*	*I **haven't** sold it yet.*
*We **already gave** him a down payment.*	*They've **given** me that **already**.*

Strangely, the British English preference for perfect aspect shows up most strongly in news. You can see the contrast in these examples:

> *The ceremony took place in the main State Department lobby next to the honor roll of American diplomats who gave their lives in the line of duty.* (AmE NEWS†)

> *She praised the gallantry, determination and sense of duty of the servicemen and women who **had given** their lives for their country.* (BrE NEWS)

6.4 Perfect aspect in use

The present perfect is much more common than past perfect in conversation, news, and academic prose. However, past perfect is somewhat more common in fiction. One of the easiest ways to see the functions of present and past perfect is to consider the verbs that are most common with these aspects.

6.4.1 Verbs that are common in the present perfect

A *Has/have been*

The present perfect *have/has been* is common in all registers. It often has a copular use:

> *Rowlands **has been** critical of Welsh officials.* (NEWS)

Have/has been can also have a meaning similar to *go*:

> *Where **have** you **been**?* (CONV)
> <compare: *Where did you go?*>

B *Has/have got* and *has/have had*

Two other common present perfect verbs are *has/have got* and *has/have had*. *Has/have got* is extremely common in British English conversation. It has a range of meanings similar to the simple present tense *have*:

> 1 *Jones **has got** the letter.* (BrE CONV)
> 2 *I **have got** a problem actually.* (BrE CONV)
> 3 *She's **got** blond hair.* (BrE CONV)
> 4 *He's **got** a bad temper.* (BrE CONV)

Speakers also sometimes use the *ed*-participle of the verb (*got*) but omit the perfect aspect marker (*has/have*). This expression has a meaning like the present perfect *have/has got*. It is equivalent to the present tense of *have* rather than the normal past tense meaning of *get* (that something was acquired). (Note that in formal written English, this form is considered non-standard.)

> *Oh I got loads left.* (BrE CONV)
> <compare: *I have got loads left* NOT *I acquired loads*>
>
> *And then something else I got here is peanut butter pie.* (BrE CONV)
> <compare: *Something else I have got here is peanut butter pie* NOT
> *Something else I acquired here...*>

In American English conversation, the present tense form of *have* is much more common than *has/have got* when speakers want to convey the meaning of possession:

> *This friend of mine has a vault in his house.* (AmE CONV)
> *Santa Barbara has Republican tendencies.* (AmE CONV)

In American English there is a meaning difference between *has/have got* and *has/have gotten*: *has/have got* usually refers to current possession, while *has/have gotten* means that something has been acquired or that a change of state has occurred:

> *And we still haven't gotten knobs on the doors.* (AmE CONV)

In British English, the meaning of current possession is frequently expressed by *have got*, as in examples **1–4** above. In contrast, *has/have had* expresses the current relevance of some state that came into being in the past. This expression is especially common in conversation and news:

> *No but I mean he has had a bad start.* (BrE CONV)
> *I have had a few years in which to practise cooking.* (BrE NEWS)

C Other verbs that are common in present perfect aspect

The other verbs most commonly used with present perfect aspect are some of the most common verbs overall (e.g. *gone, done, made, seen, come, said, taken, become, given, shown, thought, called*; see 5.3). Most of these are physical or communication verbs and their consequences may persist over an extended period of time:

> *He's gone home.* (CONV) <implying that he is still there>
> *Doctors in the region have called for a review of the prescription charge system.* (NEWS†) <implying that it is still expected to be done>

In academic prose, the present perfect is often used with different verbs to state that earlier findings or practices continue to be valid:

> *Experiments have shown that nitrogen deficiency tends to strengthen the lower nodes.* (ACAD†)
> *It has become the usual practice to use only maintenance applications.* (ACAD†)

6.4.2 Verbs that are rare with perfect aspect

Some verbs rarely occur with the present perfect. These are mostly verbs that describe mental or logical states:

- mental states:

    *He **needs** it for something.* (CONV)

    *But he **doubted** it.* (FICT)

- logical states:

    *Again, this **represents** a transposition of tendencies.* (ACAD†)

    *Durkheim seeks to delimit what **constitutes** crime.* (ACAD†)

You can see from the last example that academic prose writers often use simple present tense even when reporting the views and writings of scholars in the past. (Durkheim died in 1917.)

Other verbs that are rarely used in the present perfect refer to physical actions (like *glance, kiss, nod, scream, smile*). These verbs usually describe brief actions:

    *She **glanced** at him shyly.* (FICT)

    *Judge Crawford **kissed** the woman on both cheeks.* (NEWS)

6.4.3 Verbs that are common in the past perfect

Like the simple past tense, past perfect verb phrases are especially common in fiction. They are used especially for reference to an earlier period in the middle of a past tense narrative:

    *He **hadn't** even **been** jealous of her dead husband.* (FICT)

    *Nancy **had gone** with them.* (FICT)

    *He **had taken** it himself.* (FICT)

    *I kept remembering what Addy **had said**.* (FICT)

    *Rick **had seen** that before in androids.* (FICT)

The most common verbs with the past perfect are some of the most common verbs overall (see 5.3). These are mostly verbs that describe physical movements and other activities (e.g. *gone, come, left, given, got,* etc.), speech acts (*said, told*), and mental perceptions or thoughts (*see, heard, known*).

6.4.4 Choices between perfect and simple aspect

Past time can be expressed by the simple past tense, the present perfect, or the past perfect. How do speakers choose the most suitable of these three options?

A Present perfect v. simple past

Both the present perfect and the simple past tense normally refer to an event or state in the past. In addition, both can be used to refer to a state that existed over a period of time. The primary difference in meaning between the two is that the present perfect evokes a situation that continues to exist up to the present time, while the simple past tense describes an event that took place at a particular time in the past.

This meaning difference is often made explicit by time adverbials. With the simple past tense, the adverbial describes when the event or state occurred. Adverbials are underlined in the following examples:

> I **saw** him <u>yesterday</u>. (CONV)

> <u>At that moment</u>, Tony **knocked**. (FICT)

The most common time adverbial used with simple past tense is *then*. It typically describes a sequence of events:

> And <u>then</u> they **said** have you heard of the paper? And I **said** yes but not as er as a window. <u>Then</u> they **said** well and <u>then</u> I **realized** that it was Fennite. (CONV)

Other time adverbials with the simple past are used to specify a period of past time:

> <u>Throughout the rest of the week</u> we **racked** our brains. (FICT)

> I **met** Giovanni <u>during my second year in Paris</u>. (FICT)

B Past perfect v. simple past

Past perfect verb phrases look back to an extended time period that was completed in the past. In order to clarify the time reference, time adverbials are often used with verbs in past perfect:

> <u>When he returned</u> the priest **had** <u>already</u> **used** the special needle-sharp quill and ink. (FICT†)

> So he sat down and breathed deeply as the Zen teachers **had taught** him <u>years ago</u>. (FICT)

Past perfect verbs also tend to occur in dependent clauses. In this case, the simple past tense in the main clause provides the perspective for interpreting the time reference. The event in the dependent clause was completed by the time of the event in the main clause:

> 1 [When I **had sorted** that out], I <u>shrugged</u>. (FICT)
> 2 It <u>came</u> almost as a shock to realize [that her night **had been** peaceful]. (FICT)

For example, in **1**, the action described by *had sorted* was completed before the action of *shrugged* took place. In **2**, the use of *had been* shows that the night was completed by the time the narrator realized the peacefulness of it.

6.5 Progressive aspect

The progressive aspect describes activities or events in progress at a particular time, usually for a limited amount of time. The present progressive describes events that are currently in progress, or events that are going to take place in the future and about which the speaker feels quite certain:

- present progressive describing an event in progress:

> What's she **doing**? (CONV)

> I'm **looking** for an employee of yours. (FICT)

- present progressive with future time reference:

> But she's **coming** back tomorrow. (CONV)

> I'm **going** with him next week. (FICT)

Past progressive verbs describe events that were in progress at an earlier time:

> *I **was** just **coming** back from Witham.* (CONV)

> *Well he **was saying** that he's finding it a bit difficult.* (CONV)

It is sometimes assumed that the progressive aspect occurs only with dynamic verbs that describe activities. However, the progressive is also used with verbs that describe a situation or a state. In this case, the progressive refers to the ongoing continuation of the state:

> *Chris **is living** there now.* (CONV)

> *I **was sitting** in my office smoking one of James's cigarettes.* (FICT)

Some of the most common verbs occurring with the progressive aspect describe a short-term state, like most of the examples above.

6.5.1 Verbs with the progressive aspect

Progressive aspect is most common in conversation and fiction (see 6.3.3). In conversation, most progressive verb phrases are in the present tense, while past progressive verbs are preferred in fiction. There are two notable exceptions to this general trend, however: the past tense forms *was/were saying* and *was/were thinking* are more common in both registers.

Some verbs are most often used in the progressive aspect. In fact, some (e.g. *bleed* and *starve)* almost always occur as progressive verbs. The common progressive aspect verbs come from many semantic domains, including both **dynamic verbs** (e.g. *chase, shop*) and **stative verbs** (e.g. *look forward to*). Other verbs, like *arrest* or *shrug*, almost never occur as progressive verbs. These verbs have an 'instantaneous' meaning, and are difficult to use in a sense of 'ongoing progress'.

The following lists identify the verbs most strongly associated with progressive aspect and the verbs that almost never occur with progressive aspect.

- Verbs occurring over 80 per cent of the time in progressive aspect:

    activity/physical verbs: *bleed, chase, shop, starve*

    communication verbs: *chat, joke, kid, moan*

- Verbs occurring over 50 per cent of the time in progressive aspect:

    activity verbs: *dance, drip, head (for), march, pound, rain, stream, sweat*

    communication verbs: *scream, talk*

    mental/attitude verbs: *look forward, study*

- Verbs that occur less than 2 per cent of the time in the progressive aspect:

    activity verbs: *arrest, dissolve, find, invent, rule, shut, shrug, smash, swallow, throw*

    communication verbs: *accuse, communicate, disclose, exclaim, label, reply, thank*

    mental/attitude verbs: *agree, appreciate, believe, conclude, desire, know, like, want*

    perceptual states/activities: *detect, hear, perceive, see*

    facilitation/causation verbs: *convince, guarantee, initiate, oblige, prompt, provoke ·*

Many previous descriptions of progressive aspect describe it as occurring with dynamic verbs. However, it turns out that both dynamic verbs and stative verbs occur with the progressive. Similarly, verbs rarely used in the progressive form include both dynamic verbs and stative verbs.

Two characteristics determine whether a verb is commonly or rarely used in the progressive form:

• whether the subject is an **agent** or an **experiencer**
• the duration of the action described by the verb.

First, the verbs that are common with the progressive usually have a human agent as the subject of the clause. The agent actively controls the action or state expressed by the verb. In contrast, many of the verbs that rarely occur in the progressive have a human experiencer as the subject of the clause. The experiencer does not control the action or state, but experiences its effect.

This first characteristic helps to explain why some verbs that describe states and perceptions occur as progressives while others do not. For example, the perception verbs *look*, *watch*, *stare*, and *listen* are all common in progressive aspect, and the subject of the verbs is usually a human agent.

> *He's **staring** at me now.* (CONV)
>
> *I **was looking** at that one just now.* (CONV)
>
> *And the police **are** always **watching**.* (FICT†)
>
> *I felt he **wasn't listening**.* (FICT)

In contrast, the perception verbs *see* and *hear* rarely occur in the progressive. They describe perceptions which are experienced, but which are not controlled by the subject. The subject may refer to a human, but the human is an experiencer rather than an agent:

> *I **saw** him the other day.* (CONV)
>
> *Yeah, I **heard** about that.* (CONV)

You can also see the influence of the first characteristic with mental verbs. Verbs like *think* and *wonder*, which commonly occur in the progressive, involve an active agent who controls the mental activity.

> *You should **be wondering** why.* (CONV)
>
> *Oh, I **was** just **thinking**, it'd be nice to go there.* (CONV)
>
> *I **was wondering** how often she did this.* (FICT†)

In contrast, verbs like *appreciate*, *desire*, *know*, *like*, and *want* describe a state of mind rather than an activity:

> *Well I really **appreciate** your having done so much already.* (CONV)
>
> *He **didn't know** why.* (FICT)
>
> *Naturally I **want** to help.* (FICT)

Verbs that rarely have human subjects are also rare in the progressive. These are most common in academic prose, where they usually describe a relationship involving abstractions:

> *The main problem of the present investigation **concerned** the effectiveness of the game crossing sign.* (ACAD†)
>
> *Serum ferritin levels **correlate** well with the evidence of iron deficiency.* (ACAD†)

The second major characteristic that influences whether the progressive is used with a verb concerns the question 'How long does the state or action described by the verb last?'. The action, state, or situation described by common progressive verbs often extends over a substantial period of time. In contrast, the verbs that rarely occur in the progressive usually refer to an action that happens very quickly, or a temporary state of short duration.

Some mental verbs that occur with human agents fit the category of a process that extends over time. For example, verbs like *hope*, *think*, and *wonder* can signal mental processes that last for a long time. They therefore commonly occur in the progressive. Stative verbs also can refer to situations that extend over time, so they frequently occur in the progressive. Such verbs include *stay, wait, sit, stand*, and *live*. When used in the progressive, they imply that the state extends over time, but is not a permanent state. For example, 1 clearly states that Sandy is staying a few days, and 4 implies that the writer no longer lives in Furukawa:

1 *Sandy's **staying** with her for a few days.* (CONV)
2 *We **were waiting** for the train.* (CONV)
3 *I **was standing** there the other night.* (CONV)
4 *When I first came to this city as a young man, I **was living** in Furukawa.* (FICT†)

Many activity verbs (e.g. *bring, drive, move, play, walk*) also refer to an action that extends over time, and therefore they occur in the progressive:

> *He **was driving** his van, delivering copies of First Rebel.* (FICT)

> *A lot of people **are chasing** me. They're **shouting**.* (FICT)

In contrast, there are many dynamic verbs that refer to an action that takes place instantaneously. For example, *shut, smash, swallow*, and *throw* have virtually no duration. Such verbs rarely occur in the progressive:

> *The man **threw** me off the bus.* (CONV)

> *They **shut** the sliding doors behind them.* (CONV)

> *I **smashed** the electric light bulb.* (FICT)

Other verbs that rarely occur in the progressive report the end-point of a process. Consider this example:

> *A disciplinary hearing in June **ruled** that Mr. Reid should be dismissed.* (NEWS†)

The hearing may have extended over a period of time, but the ruling came at the end. Other verbs of this type include *attain, dissolve, find*, and *invent*.

The use of progressive aspect with *saying* and *thinking* often conveys a more vivid image and a greater sense of involvement than the simple past tense. This is most common in conversation, with the past progressive:

> *Aunt Margaret **was saying** it's from my great-grandmother.* (CONV†)

> *I'm **thinking** it would be a lot easier if you dropped it off on Sunday.* (CONV)

Major points in GRAMMAR BITE B: Aspect

Review

➤ There are two aspects in English: perfect and progressive.
  ➤ Each aspect can be combined with present and past tenses.
➤ Perfect aspect 'points back' to an earlier time, and usually signals that the circumstance, or its result, continued up to a given time.

➤ Perfect aspect is most common in fiction and news.
  ➤ British English newspaper writing uses perfect aspect much more than American English newspapers do.
➤ Perfect aspect verbs are often used with time adverbials that make the time reference explicit.
  ➤ Past perfect often occurs in dependent clauses, and the main clause makes the time reference clear.
➤ Progressive aspect signals an event currently in progress or an event in the future that is quite certain.
➤ Progressive aspect is used more commonly in conversation than in writing.
  ➤ American English conversation uses progressive aspect the most, far more than British English conversation.
➤ Surprisingly, the most common verbs in progressive aspect include both dynamic verbs and stative verbs.

GRAMMAR BITE

c Voice

6.6 Active and passive voice

Most transitive verbs can occur in two voices: **active voice** and **passive voice**. The active is the most common, unmarked voice. Passive verb phrases are less common and used for special discourse functions. They reduce the importance of the agent of an action and fulfill other discourse functions described in 6.6.1 and 6.6.2.

Most passive constructions are formed with the auxiliary *be* and an *ed*-participle:

> *The results of one experiment* ***are given*** *in Table 1.1.27.* (ACAD)

However, passive verb phrases can also be formed with the auxiliary verb *get*, called the ***get*-passive**:

> *It's about these people who* ***got left*** *behind in Vietnam.* (CONV)

The passive voice is possible with most transitive verbs. The subject noun phrase in the passive sentence usually corresponds to the direct object in the equivalent active voice sentence:

> 1 *[Turbofan and turboprop engines] are then discussed in turn.* (ACAD†)
>   <compare active voice: *We then discuss [turbofan and turboprop engines] in turn.*>

Passives can occur as either **short** or **long passives**. In short passives (also called **agentless passives**) the agent is not specified. Thus, in **1**, it is not stated who exactly is discussing the engines. Similarly, in **2**, the agent is an unspecified 'someone':

> 2 *To do so, [the cooling curves]* ***are plotted*** *for the two pure components.* (ACAD†)
>   <compare active voice: *Someone plotted [the cooling curves].*>

Long passives contain a *by*-phrase which, in typical cases, specifies the agent of the action. (In some cases the *by*-phrase will specify a different semantic role, such as experiencer.)

> The proposal **was approved** by the Project Coordinating Team. (ACAD)
> <compare active voice: *The Project Coordinating Team approved the proposal.*>

Short passives are about six times as frequent as long passives.

Passive constructions are also common with two-object prepositional verbs:

> [Dormancy] **is associated with** [short duration] (ACAD†)
> <compare active voice: *Researchers associate [dormancy] with [short duration].*>

> [Elements] **are** usually **classified as** [metals or non-metals]. (ACAD)
> <compare active voice: *Researchers usually classify [elements] as [metals or non-metals].*>

The subject of a passive verb can also correspond to the indirect object of a ditransitive verb:

> [Mariko] **was given** [permission to go to Osaka]. (FICT)
> <compare active voice: *Someone gave [Mariko] [permission to go to Osaka].*>

or the prepositional object of a one-object prepositional verb:

> The problem **was dealt with** by developing a reference test. (ACAD†)
> <compare active voice: *Someone dealt with [the problem] by...*>

These kinds of verbs are discussed in 5.10.

Most passive voice verbs are easy to identify. However, sometimes words look like passive verbs, but are actually predicative adjectives describing a state or quality. For example:

> We **are** <u>delighted</u> with the result. (NEWS)

> I ought to **be** <u>excited</u>. (FICT†)

These participial adjectives function as subject predicatives. They are usually gradable and can be modified by *very*.

Some participial forms (like *broken* or *frozen*) can occur as both passives and predicative adjectives. In some contexts they are clearly functioning as passive verbs, describing an action with an agent (as in **3** below). However, in other sentences the same form may express a state and behave like an adjective (**4** below):

> **3** *The silence* **was broken** *by the village crier.* (FICT)

> **4** *The wire* **is** *always* **broken.** (FICT†)

6.6.1 The use of the short passive across registers

The frequency of both forms of the passive varies greatly across registers, as shown in Figure 6.5. Passives are most common in academic prose, where they account for about 25 per cent of all finite verbs. Passives are also common in news (about 15 per cent of all finite verbs). In contrast, passive voice verbs are rare in conversation.

In many expository prose texts (such as academic research articles), passive voice verbs are especially common. For example:

*Three communities on a brackish marsh of the Rhode River, a sub-estuary of the Chesapeake Bay, **were exposed** to elevated carbon dioxide concentrations for two growing seasons beginning in April 1987. The study site and experimental design **are described** in Curtis et al. (1989a). One community **was dominated** by the perennial carbon 4 grass spartina patens.* (ACAD†)

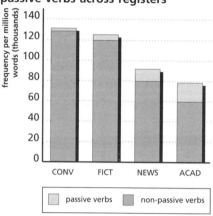

Figure 6.5

Frequency of finite passive v. non-passive verbs across registers

Often, the human actor (or **agent**) is not important in academic writing. So the passive voice is useful: it reduces the importance of the agent noun phrase by putting it in a *by*-phrase or not mentioning it at all. At the same time, the passive sentence gives the status of topic to the direct object of the corresponding active voice clause. Thus, compare the following active voice alternatives to sentences in the passage above:

> *[We, the researchers,] exposed three communities to elevated carbon dioxide concentrations.*

> *[We, the researchers,] describe the study site and experimental design in Curtis et al. (1989a).*

In an active voice clause, the agent is the subject of the clause. However, because readers already know that 'the researchers' usually do the work in a study, there is really no need to mention them. Here the short passive becomes a useful device: it allows the objects of study ('the three communities', 'the study site', and 'the experimental design') to be the subject of sentences, thereby giving them topic status.

The extensive use of passives also gives a sense of objective detachment in expository prose. This sense of objectivity is part of scientific culture, and is often expected in scientific writing.

In contrast, conversation is generally much more concerned with the experiences and actions of people. It therefore usually expresses the agent as subject, and rarely uses passive voice.

News is similar to academic writing in using the passive voice to make the agent less prominent. Often the focus of a news story is an event that involves a person or institution. The agent may be easy to guess or unimportant. Furthermore, presenting only the new information can save space, which is desirable in newspaper writing. It is natural in such cases to omit agents and use the passive voice. For example, reference to 'the police' is omitted in the following:

> *Doherty **was arrested** in New York in June.* (NEWS†)

In other cases, the agents may not be known, or they cannot be mentioned for legal reasons:

> *The officer **was beaten** and repeatedly **kicked** in the head.* (NEWS)

6.6.2 The use of the long passive across registers

Although the long passive (with a *by*-phrase) is much less common than the short passive, it is similar in being most common in academic writing, and least common in conversation.

In principle, the long passive can be replaced by an active clause with the same meaning. For example, the sentence we have just used is a long passive, and we could have used an active clause instead:

> 1a *In principle, the passive **can be replaced** by an active clause with the same meaning.* <passive>
>
> 1b *In principle, an active clause with the same meaning **can replace** the passive.* <active>

However, this active clause would have been less appropriate than the passive clause we used. Why? There are three interconnected motivations for choosing the long passive:

- Principle 1: The long passive is chosen to accord with the **information-flow** principle: the preference for presenting new information at the end of a clause (see 12.1.1). This means that given information (information already shared by the writer and the reader, often because of previous mention) is placed before new information.
- Principle 2: The long passive is chosen to accord with the **end-weight** principle (see 12.1.4). This means that a 'heavier' (or more lengthy) element of the clause, in this case the agent, is placed at the end, where it does not hold up the processing of the rest of the clause.
- Principle 3: The long passive is chosen to place initial emphasis on an element of the clause which is the topic, or theme, of the current discourse.

Example **1a** illustrates all three of these principles well:

- **1a**, unlike **1b**, begins with given information: *the passive* has already been mentioned, and the use of *the* signals its 'familiar' status in the discourse. In contrast, *an active clause with the same meaning* is new information, signalled by the indefinite article *an* and the postmodifying prepositional phrase (*with the same meaning*) which identifies the specific type of 'active clause' in question.
- **1a**, unlike **1b**, begins with a short two-word phrase as its subject (*the passive*). It ends with a longer phrase (*an active clause with the same meaning*) as its agent. This situation is reversed in **1b**.
- **1a**, unlike **1b**, begins with a reference to *the passive*, which is the current topic of the discourse, as shown, for example, by the heading of the section. In **1b**, the topic would have been placed at the end of the clause.

Although we have presented these as three factors, it is clear that they are not really separate. Principles 1 and 2 tend to support one another: a 'given' element will generally be shorter than a 'new' element. For example, in **2** below, the subject is a personal pronoun, which is a clear instance of given information, referring back to someone already mentioned; pronouns are also as short as possible, being a single word consisting of a single syllable:

> 2 *In two minutes, **he** was surrounded by [a ring of men].* (FICT)

The agent, in contrast, introduces *a ring of men* which has not been mentioned before, and which is considerably longer, consisting of four words.

Similarly Principle 3 tends to support Principle 1, because the topic of discourse is likely to be someone or something that has been already introduced to the reader.

It is important to note that the three principles mentioned above are not strict grammatical rules. Of the first two principles, the information flow principle (1) is more important than the end-weight principle (2). Thus, it is not too unusual to find examples in which the information flow principle is upheld but the end-weight principle violated:

> *The vapour at this boiling temperature* is represented by [point D]. (ACAD)
>
> *The achievement of this objective* is jeopardised by [unethical conduct]. (ACAD)

6.7 Associations between verbs and passive voice

Some verbs usually take the passive voice; other verbs are rare in the passive.

6.7.1 Verbs that are common in the passive voice

The following lists identify the verbs most strongly associated with passive voice:

- Verbs occurring over 90 per cent of the time in the passive voice:

  aligned (with), based (on), born, coupled (with), deemed, effected, entitled (to), flattened, inclined, obliged, positioned, situated, stained, subjected (to)

- Verbs occurring over 70 per cent of the time in the passive voice:

  approved, associated (with), attributed (to), classified (as), composed (of), confined (to), designed, diagnosed (as), distributed, estimated, grouped (with), intended, labelled, linked (to/with), located (at/in), plotted, recruited, stored, viewed

This shows the verbs with the strongest preference for passive voice. There are a few verbs that almost always occur in the passive, for example *be born* and *be reputed*:

> Brandon Lee **was born** in Oakland, California. (NEWS†)
>
> The deal **is reputed** to be worth £1m. (NEWS†)

Other verbs, like *be based on, be deemed, be positioned*, and *be subjected to*, are grammatical in both the active and passive voice, but they are used over 90 per cent of the time in the passive voice:

> The material **was deemed** faulty. (NEWS)
>
> Anyone found guilty of drinking alcohol **may be subjected to** 80 lashes of a cane. (NEWS)
>
> They **were based on** his book 'The Principles of Quantum Mechanics'. (ACAD†)

A Common passive verbs in academic prose

Passive voice is especially common in academic prose, and many of the common passive verbs refer to scientific methods and analysis:

> *The same mechanism **was analysed** on each.* (ACAD†)
>
> *Their occurrence **is measured** in a few parts per million.* (ACAD)
>
> *The test object clause will allow any object to **be tested**.* (ACAD)

Other passive verbs report findings or express logical relationships:

> *These effects **are believed** to **be associated with** a disturbance of auxin metabolism.* (ACAD)
>
> *The rate constant can **be interpreted** in terms of entropy.* (ACAD)

B Common passive verbs in news

In news, a different set of verbs is common in the passive voice. Many of these verbs report unpleasant or dramatic events. The agent in these clauses is unimportant, unknown, or previously mentioned:

> *He **was accused** of using threatening and insulting behavior.* (NEWS)
>
> *He **was jailed** for three months.* (NEWS)
>
> *Neither man **was injured** during the incident.* (NEWS)
>
> *Everybody remembers where they were when JFK **was shot**.* (NEWS)

C Common passive verbs in conversation

Although the passive is generally rare in conversation, a few passive verbs are more common in conversation than in the written registers. The most common is the fixed expression *can't be bothered*:

> *I can't **be bothered** really.* (CONV)
>
> *I can't **be bothered** to play the piano.* (CONV)

Be done is also relatively common:

> *It's gotta **be done**.* (CONV)

Other passive verbs in conversation are more stative in meaning and might be interpreted as predicative adjectives. These examples could be analyzed as either passives or predicative adjectives:

> *Most of our garden will **be finished** one day.* (CONV)
>
> *I might have **been concerned** about my hair or **concerned** about band or something like that.* (CONV)

6.7.2 Verbs frequently used in the *get*-passive form

The *get*-passive is rare in all registers, but is occasionally used in conversation. Only five verbs have a notable frequency with the *get*-passive:

- over 20 per million words: *get + married*
- over 5 per million words: *get + hit, involved, left, stuck*

Many of these verbs have a different emphasis when used with the *get*-passive rather than the *be*-passive. With *be*, they express a state, such as the state of 'being married' or 'being involved.' With *get*, they are more dynamic, describing the processing of getting into that state.

be passives	*get* passives
*I **was married** for a couple of years in the seventies.*	*She **got married** when she was eighteen.*
*They **weren't involved** for that long.*	*And then we start to **get involved** in local society.*
*You're gonna **be left** alone to get on with your job.*	*The one that got the short straw **got left** out or something..*
*You wouldn't **be stuck** at home.*	*My head **got stuck** up there.*

Get-passives are typical only in conversation. The written registers usually use *become* instead.

6.7.3 Verbs that are uncommon in the passive voice

There are many transitive verbs and single-object prepositional verbs that rarely occur in the passive voice:

- Verbs occurring in passive voice less than 2 per cent of the time:

    single word transitive verbs: *agree, exclaim, guess, hate, have, hesitate, joke, lack, let, like, love, mind, pretend, quit, reply, resemble, try, want, watch, wish, wonder*

    single-object prepositional verbs: *agree to/with, belong to, bet on, come across/for, compete with, cope with, correspond to, glance at, laugh about/at, listen to*

Many of these transitive verbs usually occur in the active voice. For example:

> *He **has** money.* (CONV)
>
> *Sinead **wants** a biscuit.* (CONV)
>
> *I **lacked** the courage to be alone.* (FICT)

Although these verbs are possible as passives, they simply are not used in the passive voice very often.

Some of the verbs that are rare in the passive usually take a post-predicate complement clause rather than a simple noun phrase as direct object. For example:

> *I **wished** [I had a job like that].* (CONV)
>
> *He's also **agreed** [to deal with a few other things].* (FICT)
>
> *I **pretended** [to be another friend].* (FICT)

These complement clauses make it difficult to form the passive voice. For example, we cannot say: **To be another friend was pretended by me.*

As we see from the above list, many single-object prepositional verbs rarely occur in the passive voice.

> *They're all **waiting for** me.* (CONV†)
>
> *We can **smile at** them.* (FICT)
>
> *The eigenvectors must obviously **correspond to** special states.* (ACAD)

The passive voice is awkward, if not impossible, with these verbs, because there would be a **stranded preposition** after the verb. For example: **I'm being waited for by them.*

However, a few single-object prepositional verbs do easily occur in the passive voice. The subject corresponds to the prepositional object of the active version, as in:

> *Your sister can **be relied on** to remember when your birthday is.* (FICT†)
> <compare the active: *You can **rely on** your sister to remember when your birthday is.*>

In contrast to single-object prepositional verbs, two-object prepositional verbs usually allow the passive voice. In fact, many of these verbs normally occur in the passive voice (e.g. *be associated with, be based on*). The subject is the direct object of the active form. The passive subject corresponds to the direct object of the active verb, rather than the prepositional object, so there is no stranded preposition:

> *[Some definitions of style] have **been based on** this assumption.* (ACAD)
> <compare the active: *Someone **based** [some definitions of style] **on** this assumption.*>

In general, passive subjects are easier to form from direct objects than from prepositional objects.

6.8 **Voice and aspect combinations**

In English verb phrases, the passive can combine with perfect and/or progressive aspect. In actual use, though, the perfect passive is only moderately common while the progressive passive is rare. The perfect passive with present tense is preferred in academic prose and news, while the past perfect passive is moderately common in fiction.

Perfect aspect and passive voice are both common in academic prose and news, and so it is not surprising that the two are used together in those registers. Perfect passive verb phrases with present tense typically retain the meaning of both the perfect and the passive. They show past time with present relevance (through perfect aspect) and they reduce the importance of the agent (through the passive voice):

> *He **has been jailed** for explosives offenses in Ulster and **has** previously **been denied** a visa.* (NEWS)
> *Since 1916 much government money **has been spent** on these developments.* (ACAD†)

In fiction, perfect passives are also moderately common, but they are usually in the past tense:

> *He **had been thrown** from a moving train.* (FICT)
> *Most of the lights **had been turned off**.* (FICT†)

The passive with progressive aspect is rare, but it does occur occasionally in news and academic writing:

> *A police spokesman said nobody else **was being sought** in connection with the incident.* (NEWS)

*Expenses **are** still **being incurred** while a budget for the future **is being prepared**.* (ACAD†)

Major points in **GRAMMAR BITE C**: Voice

➤ There are three types of passive voice verb phrases: short passives, long passives, and *get*-passives.

➤ Compared to active voice, passive voice reduces the importance of the agent of the action and allows the receiver of the action to become the subject of the sentence.

➤ Passive voice verbs are most common in the expository registers, where agents are often unknown or unimportant.

  ➤ In academic prose, passives often relate to scientific methods or logical relationships.

  ➤ In news, passives often report negative events that happened to someone.

➤ *Get*-passives are rare, and used almost exclusively in conversation.

➤ Some verbs usually occur as passives (e.g. *be born, be based on*). Other verbs rarely occur in the passive voice (e.g. *hate, like, want*).

➤ Voice and aspect combinations are possible; in use, the perfect passive is moderately common and the progressive passive is rare.

GRAMMAR BITE

D Modals and semi-modals

6.9 Modals and semi-modals

There are nine central modal verbs in English: *can, could, may, might, must, should, will, would,* and *shall*. Modals have several distinctive characteristics:

• They act as an auxiliary verb in verb phrases (e.g. *I can go*).

• They do not take inflections to show agreement or tense (e.g. *I can go, He/she/it can go*). That is, the form does not vary (e.g. not **He cans go*).

• They precede the negative particle in *not* negation (e.g. *I cannot go*).

• They precede the subject in yes–no questions (e.g. *Can you go?*).

• They take a bare infinitive verb as the main verb in the verb phrase (e.g. *He can go*, not **He can to go* or **He can goes* or **He can went*).

• They express stance meanings, related to possibility, necessity, obligation, etc.

In most dialects of English, only a single modal can be used in a verb phrase. However, certain regional dialects (such as southern AmE) allow some combinations of modals (e.g. *might could* or *might should*).

Semi-modals (also called 'periphrastic modals' or 'quasi-modals') are multi-word constructions that function like modal verbs: *(had) better, have to, (have) got to, ought to, be supposed to, be going to, used to*. In orthographic representations of the spoken language, *better, gotta,* and *gonna* often occur as the reduced forms of *had better, have got to,* and *be going to*.

Semi-modals express meanings that can usually be paraphrased with a central modal verb. For example:

> I **have to** read it again. (CONV) <paraphrase: I **must** read it again.>

> Mosquitoes **aren't supposed to** be inside here. (CONV) <paraphrase: Mosquitoes **should** not be inside here.>

In addition, some semi-modals are fixed expressions, which cannot be inflected for tense or person. However, some of the semi-modals, like *have to* and *be going to*, can be marked for tense and person:

- past tense:

> He **had to** call the police. (CONV)

- third-person agreement:

> Maybe she **has to** grow up a bit more. (CONV)

These semi-modals can sometimes co-occur with a central modal verb or another semi-modal, underlined in the examples:

- co-occurrence with a modal:

> I **might** **have to** tell him. (FICT)

- co-occurrence with another semi-modal:

> I think the teachers **are gonna** **have to** be there. (CONV)

There are also some lexical verbs and adjectives that have meanings similar to modal auxiliaries, in that they express stance meanings, but they are neither idiomatic nor fixed expressions. Rather, these verbs and adjectives express their core lexical meanings of desire, obligation, possibility, etc. Examples are: *need to*, *dare to*, *want to*, *be able to*, *be obliged to*, *be likely to*, *be willing to*, etc. These expressions are discussed further in 10.13.3, 10.15. (In BrE, *need* and *dare* are sometimes used in grammatical patterns similar to modal verbs; see 10.13.)

6.9.1 Time distinctions with modals and semi-modals

The central modals can be used to make time distinctions, even though they are not marked for tense. For example, the modals *will* and *shall* can be used to refer to future time. The semi-modal *be going to* is also used for future time.

> There **will** be no outcry from the corporate sector about the disarray in the accountancy profession. (NEWS)

> We **shall** deal with these questions in 4.4. (ACAD)

> It's **going to** be hot. (CONV)

In addition, it is possible to group the central modals (except *must*) into pairs with related meanings that sometimes distinguish between past time and non-past time:

modals referring to present and future time	corresponding modals that can refer to past time
can	could
may	might
shall	should
will	would

Compare the following pairs. The modal in the second example of each pair refers to a past time:

> *I think we* **can beat** *Glenavon.* (NEWS)

> *In 1971 he thought he* **could help** *his brother in his illness by writing about their childhood.* (NEWS)

> *You know he'll* **come.** (CONV)

> *I knew I* **would put** *on weight.* (CONV)

In general, though, it is misleading to describe modals as referring to past time and non-past time, as the next section explains.

6.9.2 Typical meaning distinctions for modals and semi-modals

There are many meaning distinctions made by modals beyond those of time. In fact, the main functions are related to stance: e.g. the expression of possibility or obligation. As a result, modals that can be associated with past time (like *could*) are also used for hypothetical situations with present or future time reference. In these contexts, the modals convey politeness and tentativeness:

> **Could** *I sit here a minute, Joyce?* (CONV)

> **Could** *you sign one of these too?* **Would** *you mind?* (CONV)

Each modal can have two different types of meaning: **personal** or **logical**. For example, *must* can be used to show personal obligation (*You must brush your teeth*) or logical necessity (*Today must be your birthday*, said after noticing a birthday cake). These two types of meaning are also called intrinsic and extrinsic. Personal (intrinsic) modal meaning refers to the control of actions and events by human and other agents. These meanings are personal permission, obligation, and volition (or intention). Logical (extrinsic) modal meaning refers to the logical status of states or events. It usually refers to levels of certainty, likelihood, or logical necessity.

Modals and semi-modals are grouped into three categories based on their meanings and each category contains both personal/intrinsic and logical/extrinsic meanings. (The semi-modal *used to* is excluded from these categories, being the only modal that refers primarily to past time.)

name of category	modals	meanings
permission/ability	*can, could, may, might*	personal meaning: permission or possibility, ability logical meaning: possibility
obligation/necessity	*must, should, (had) better, have (got) to, need to, ought to, be supposed to*	personal meaning: obligation logical meaning: necessity
volition/prediction	*will, would, shall, be going to*	personal meaning: volition or intention logical meaning: prediction

Often, you can tell the difference between personal and logical meanings by the structure of the clause. Personal meanings have two typical characteristics: the subject of the verb phrase usually refers to a human being, and the main verb is usually a dynamic verb that describes an activity or event that can be controlled. Consider these examples:

> You **can't mark** without a scheme. You **must make** a scheme. (CONV)
> <personal ability and obligation meanings, with human subject *you* and dynamic verbs *mark* and *make*>

> We **shall** not **attempt** a detailed account of linguistic categories in this book, but **will use** as far as possible those which are well enough known. (ACAD†)
> <personal volition or intention meanings, with human subject *we* and dynamic verbs *attempt* and *use*>

In contrast, modal verbs with logical meanings usually occur with non-human subjects and/or with main verbs that express states:

> Well, it **must be** somewhere in the office. (CONV) <necessity meaning, with stative main verb *be*>

> But in other cases his decisions **will seem** more radical. (ACAD) <prediction meaning, with non-human subject (*his decisions*) and stative verb *seem*>

The personal and logical uses of modal verbs are discussed in more detail in 6.10.

6.9.3 Modals and semi-modals across registers

Figure 6.6 shows that the nine central modals differ greatly in frequency. The modals *will*, *would*, and *can* are extremely common. *Shall* is rare. The other modals fall in between.

ᵣe 6.6 Frequency of modal auxiliary verbs in the LSWE Corpus

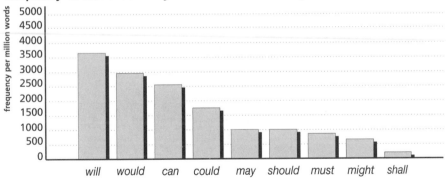

If you consider the pairs of central modals, the tentative/past time member is usually less frequent than its partner. For example, *will* is more common than *would*, and *can* more common than *could*. The exception is *shall/should*, because *should* is more common.

You can see from Figure 6.7 that modals and semi-modals are most common in conversation and least common in news and academic prose. Semi-modals are much more common in conversation than they are in the written expository registers. It is more surprising that the central modals are also more common in conversation, since researchers have often assumed that modal verbs are especially characteristic of writing. However, it turns out that both modals and semi-modals are extremely common in conversation, where they are one of several devices used to express stance.

Compare Figure 6.8 with Figure 6.6. Here you see that many individual modals—especially *will*, *can*, and *would*—are extremely common in conversation. On the other hand, the less common modal *may* is extremely rare in conversation. Academic prose, included in the figure for comparison, shows a very different set of tendencies.

Figure 6.7

Frequency of semi-modals and modals across registers

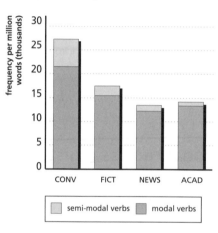

Figure 6.8

Frequency of modal verbs across registers

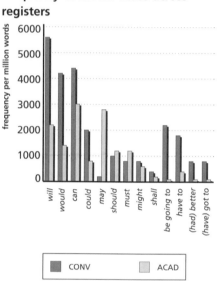

6.10 **Personal and logical meanings of modals**

In the following sections, individual modals and semi-modals are discussed in more detail, focusing on their use with personal and logical meanings. We will concentrate on conversation and academic prose because these show the clearest contrasts.

 ## 6.10.1 The permission/possibility/ability modals

Figure 6.9 summarizes the use of *can*, *could*, *may*, and *might* with permission, possibility, and ability meanings.

In academic prose, *could*, *may*, and *might* are used almost exclusively to mark logical possibility:

> *The two processes **could** well **be** independent.* (ACAD)

> *Of course, it **might be** the case that it had been settled long before that.* (ACAD)

May is especially common with this function:

re 6.9 **Frequency of permission/possibility modals with intrinsic, extrinsic, and ability meanings**

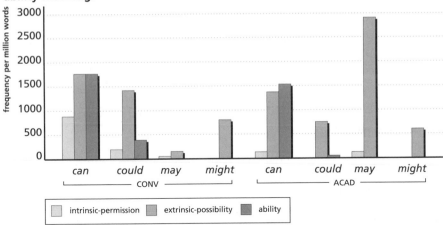

The only problem **may be** that the compound is difficult to remove. (ACAD†)

In contrast, *can* is used for both ability and logical possibility. In fact, in some cases *can* is ambiguous:

> *An isolated system is an ideal system. It **cannot be achieved** in practice.* (ACAD)

This sentence could mean that 'no one has the ability to achieve an isolated system' or that 'it is not possible that an isolated system will be achieved'.

In conversation, *could* and *might* are used most commonly for logical possibility, just as they are in academic prose. They usually express doubt, with *could* showing the greatest degree of uncertainty or tentativeness:

> *That **could be** her.* (CONV)

> *He **might relent** and show up unexpectedly but I doubt it.* (CONV)

The modal *can* usually expresses ability, but it is often ambiguous with a logical possibility meaning:

- *can* marking ability:

> *I **can hear** what she's saying to somebody.* (CONV)

> *He goes, I **can't swim**.* (CONV) <note: goes = says>

- *can* ambiguously marking ability or possibility:

> *Well you **can get** cigarettes from there, **can't** you?* (CONV)

- *can* is also relatively common with permission meanings:

> ***Can** I have* some? (CONV)

> *You **can read** my book.* (CONV)

In contrast to the other modals in this set, *may* is rarely used in conversation. When it does occur, it usually expresses logical possibility rather than permission:

> *He **may** not **see** it as a joke.* (CONV)

> *That **may be** wrong, though.* (CONV)

Despite a well-known prescription that *may* rather than *can* should be used for permission, this use of *may* is rare in the LSWE Corpus. When it does occur, *may* indicating permission is usually produced by parents or teachers talking to children. For example:

> Yes Carl. You **may do** some maths if you want to. <...> You **may do** your language work if you want to. <...> No you **may** not **draw** a picture. (CONV)

6.10.2 The obligation/necessity modals and semi-modals

Obligation/necessity modals and semi-modals are less common overall than the other modal categories. Figure 6.10 summarizes the meanings usually expressed by each modal.

Figure 6.10 Frequency of obligation/necessity modals with intrinsic and extrinsic meanings

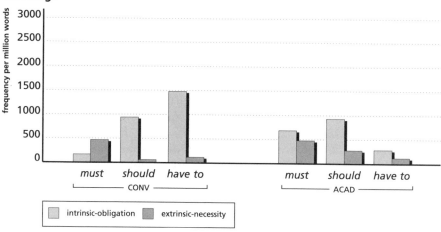

Except for the modal *must*, these modals and semi-modals usually express personal obligation. This is especially true for *should* and *have to* in conversation:

> Well I **have to** get up at ten thirty in the morning to take this thing back. (CONV)

> What do we **have to** do? (CONV)

> You **should** relax. (CONV)

Even though writers of academic prose usually suppress their own personal feelings in their writing, they also use these modals to express personal obligation rather than logical necessity:

> However one **should** not **despise** too hastily such hand-waving discussions. (ACAD)

> If the crop is to be harvested by machinery, varieties **should be cultivated** which do not readily shatter. (ACAD)

> We **have to** await the completion of David Dilks's biography. (ACAD†)

The modal *must* is particularly interesting because its distribution is the opposite of what you might expect. The logical meaning (logical necessity) is most common in conversation; the personal meaning (personal obligation) is most common in academic prose.

- *must* expressing logical necessity in conversation:

  > *Your mum **must** not **care**.* (CONV)
  >
  > *It **must have fallen** out trying to fly.* (CONV)
  >
  > *Your feet **must feel** wet now.* (CONV)

- *must* expressing personal obligation in academic prose:

  > *I **must** now **confess** something which I kept back from you in Chapter 3.* (ACAD)
  >
  > *This is the sort of case in which judges **must exercise** the discretionary power described a moment ago.* (ACAD†)

The rarity of *must* for obligation in conversation is probably due to the strong impression *must* makes when used in face-to-face interaction. *Should* and *have to* are less threatening ways to express obligation in conversation.

Both *must* and *should* are also relatively common in academic prose for expressing logical necessity. For example:

> *It **must** surely be the case that the cat is competent to act as observer of its own survival or demise.* (ACAD)
>
> *If the preceding work has been done with care there **should be** few, if any, off-types.* (ACAD)

6.10.3 The volition/prediction modals and semi-modals

These verbs all express future time meanings. The differences lie in whether the modal expresses a personal intention to perform some future act, or just the prediction of the probability of something occurring in the future. In academic prose, these modals usually express prediction:

> *Such deviations **will** often **be** the clue to special interpretations.* (ACAD)
>
> *If the marble is not moving fast enough it **will run** out of kinesic energy before it reaches the top.* (ACAD†)
>
> *Cheap money **would have** the same effect by increasing private investment.* (ACAD†)

In conversation, *will* and *would* are used for both volition and prediction, and the distinction between the two is not always clear. Utterances expressing volition usually have a first-person pronoun as subject, while those expressing prediction have other subjects:

- *will* and *would* marking volition in conversation:

  > 1 *I'**ll come** and show you it in registration Tuesday morning. <...> I **won't be** here early enough to show you before school.* (CONV)
  >
  > 2 *I think for sure I **would go** if my friends were going to go.* (CONV†)

- *will* and *would* marking prediction in conversation:

  > 3 *It **won't be** that difficult to do.* (CONV)

4 **Will** my coat **be** dry? (CONV)

5 She **would** just **feel** better if she went out. (CONV)

In the case of *would*, whether for prediction or volition, the meaning is often hypothetical. Thus, **2** implies 'I am not going because my friends are not going'. Similarly, for **5**, 'she' hasn't gone out and she might not go out at all—so the speaker's prediction is hypothetical.

The combination of first-person pronoun + *would* can also express advice. When speakers tell what they themselves would do, it may mean mean 'I think you should...'. For example:

I **would** just **read** the book as well. (CONV) <possible meaning: *I think you should just read the book as well*>

I **would** **give** it back. (CONV) <possible meaning: *I think you should give it back*>

Be going to, like *will*, can express intention or prediction, but the intention meaning is the most common one:

I**'m going to** put my feet up and rest. (CONV)

I said I **was going to** collect John's suitcase from Susan. (CONV)

This meaning, of course, is also related to future time and prediction: by showing intention, the speakers also predict future events. In contrast, *be going to* is very rare in academic prose.

Finally, *shall* is interesting because, although rare, it is used to mark personal volition in both conversation (especially BrE) and academic prose. In academic prose, this use of *shall* (**1** below) is somewhat formal and old-fashioned.

1 We **shall** here **be** concerned with only s and p orbitals. (ACAD)

2 **Shall** we **wait** for them? (BrE CONV)

Shall is typically in a question in conversation (as in **2**), where it is used to make an offer or suggestion. (This use is mainly BrE.) In both registers, *shall* is usually used with *I* or *we* as subject.

6.11 *Be going to* and *used to*

The semi-modals *be going to* and *used to* are different from the other semi-modals because they are used mostly to mark time distinctions rather than stance meanings.

The semi-modal *be going to* is a common way of marking future time in conversation and fictional dialog:

1 We**'re going to** wait. (CONV)

2 I think I**'m going to** die. (FICT)

As we saw in 6.10.3, the marking of future time often involves personal volition. In **1**, the meaning of *be going to* expresses the speaker's intention as well as a prediction of the future. In **2**, however, *be going to* is used to jokingly predict the future, with no meaning of intention.

Used to shows past habitual behavior or a past state. This semi-modal, like *be going to*, is relatively common in conversation but rare in academic prose:

Oh Nigel **used to** have a perm, didn't he? (CONV)

• He **used to** sleepwalk. (CONV)

The sequence *used to* can be confusing because it occurs with several different functions. The function described in this Grammar Bite is as a semi-modal. However, *used to* can also represent an adjective + preposition, meaning 'accustomed to'. This meaning is also common in conversation:

*I'm **used to** it. I do the dishes every day.* (CONV)

A third function of *used to* is as a passive lexical verb (*used*) followed by a *to*-clause (shown in [] below). Combinations with this meaning are pronounced differently from the other two meanings—/ju:zd.../ rather than /ju:st.../. This meaning is most common in academic prose.

*Water control may **be used** [to reduce liability to lodging].* (ACAD†)

.12 Modals combined with aspect or voice

Modals cannot combine with tense, but they can combine with aspect and voice:

- modal with perfect aspect (modal + *have* + *ed*-participle):

  *The demand for subject access **may have come** as a shock to the library profession.* (ACAD)

- modal with progressive aspect (modal + *be* + *ing*-participle):

  *Nancy **will be coming** back.* (CONV)

- modal with passive voice (modal + *be* + *ed*-participle)

  *To produce the best results the plant **should be supplied** with water which carries no contamination.* (ACAD)

The great majority of modals do not occur with marked aspect or voice. However, there are a few cases which deserve discussion.

6.12.1 Modals with perfect aspect

Perfect aspect occurs sometimes with the obligation/necessity modals *must* and *should* in fiction and news. Sometimes *should* + perfect aspect shows a past obligation (unfulfilled), as in the following:

*Papa **should have done** it long before.* (FICT†)

More commonly, however, these modals are used to mark logical necessity rather than personal obligation. In fact, with the perfect aspect, *must* is interpreted only as logical necessity. The logically necessary events occurred at some point in the past:

*So the wind **must have blown** it here.* (FICT)

*They **should have won** and would surely have done so but for a mind-boggling miss by Andy Sinton when it was 2–2.* (NEWS†)

*If they say she's made a payment, she **must have made** a payment.* (CONV)

May and *might* are used with the perfect to express a certain degree of doubt about past events or situations:

*Also he **may have had** quite a job finding it.* (FICT)

*Yesterday he confessed he **might have forgotten** one.* (NEWS)

6.12.2 Modals with progressive aspect

Relatively few modals or semi-modals occur with progressive aspect. *Will* and the obligation/necessity modals and semi-modals in conversation (and fictional dialog) are occasional exceptions to this generalization:

> He **must be running** low. (CONV)
>
> She's **supposed to be coming** in. (CONV)
>
> This **has got to be moving** around this way. (CONV†)
>
> 'May I ask who you **will be voting** for?' asked Andrew. (FICT)

Finally, although the modal *shall* is rare overall, it often occurs with progressive aspect when it is used:

> 1 We **shall be campaigning** for the survival of local government in
>   Cleveland. (NEWS)
> 2 We **shall be meeting** with all parties in the near future. (NEWS†)

Will could also be used in place of *shall* in **1** and **2**.

6.12.3 Modals with passive voice

Can and *could* are relatively common with passive voice. The use of the passive avoids identification of the agent of the main verb. As a result, the permission meaning does not occur, and the ability meaning is also less likely to occur than in the active; therefore, the possibility meaning is most common in passive:

> Each interpretation **can be seen** generally to flow through the abbreviated
> text as a whole. (ACAD) <possibility>
> <compare active voice: We can see each interpretation. . . – ability.>
>
> The methods **could be refined and made** more accurate. (ACAD)
> <possibility>
> <compare active voice: We could refine the methods. . . – ability.>

As the examples suggest, *can* + passive is most common in academic prose.

In academic prose, *must* and *should* are also relatively common with the passive voice, and are used to express a kind of collective obligation. The passive voice is useful in allowing the writer to avoid explicitly identifying who has the obligation:

> Care **must be taken** to ensure that the diffusion in stator is kept at a
> reasonable level. (ACAD)
>
> It **should be noted** that the following scenario is nothing more than one of
> many potential scenarios. (ACAD)

6.13 Sequences of modals and semi-modals

The semi-modals *have to* and *be going to* can occur in series following another modal or semi-modal:

> The researchers warn that they **will have to** treat many more patients
> before they can report a cure. (NEWS)

> *I'm gonna have to stay.* (CONV)
>
> *I thought, perhaps, you **might be going to** be married.* (FICT)

Sequences of modal + *have to* are relatively common in all four registers, especially in combination with volition/prediction modals:

> *He **would have to** wait a whole year again to taste it.* (FICT)
>
> *To succeed again they **will have to** improve their fitness and concentration.* (NEWS†)
>
> *If this programme is to make any sense we **shall have to** find a way to associate numbers with our operators.* (ACAD)

These complex verb phrases are generally less common in conversation than in the written registers, even though semi-modals are more common in conversation overall. The only complex modal combination that occurs commonly in conversation is the one that combines the two most common semi-modals, *be going to* + *have to*:

> *Because you're **going to have to** say something.* (CONV)

This combination enables speakers to express two modal meanings in one clause: future time + obligation.

Major points in GRAMMAR BITE D: Modals and semi-modals

(Review)

> ➤ There are nine central modals in English: *can, could, may, might, shall, should, will, would,* and *must.*
> ➤ In addition, there are a number of semi-modals (e.g. *be going to, have to*); these are sequences of words that function like modal verbs.
> ➤ The main function of modals and semi-modals is to convey stance.
> ➤ Modals fall into three major categories of meaning; each category combines personal (intrinsic) meanings and logical (extrinsic) meanings.
> > ➤ The categories are: permission/possibility or ability; obligation/necessity, and volition/prediction.
> ➤ Four modals and semi-modals are used primarily to express time meanings: *will, shall,* and *be going to* for future time, and *used to* for past time.
> ➤ Modals are common in all registers, but they are most common in conversation.
> ➤ Semi-modals are especially common in conversation and rare in news and academic prose.
> ➤ Modals can be used in combination with both aspects and passive voice.
> > ➤ Most modals occur with simple aspect and active voice.
> ➤ The semi-modals *have to, need to,* and *be going to* can follow a modal or other semi-modal in a series.

7
Adjectives and adverbs

GRAMMAR BITES in this chapter

A Characteristics of adjectives and adverbs

➤ Overview of typical characteristics of adjectives
➤ The forms that adjectives take
➤ Syntactic functions of adverbs
➤ The forms that adverbs take

B Adjectives: roles and meanings

➤ Semantic categories of adjectives
➤ More about attributive adjectives
➤ More about predicative adjectives
➤ Other syntactic roles of adjectives

C Adverbs: roles and meanings

➤ Syntactic roles of adverbs
➤ Semantic categories of adverbs

D Comparative and superlative forms

➤ Comparative and superlative forms of adjectives
➤ Comparative and superlative forms of adverbs
➤ Comparative constructions with clauses and phrases

7.1 **Introduction**

Adjectives and **adverbs** are two of the four lexical word classes. (As described in Chapter 2, nouns and verbs are the other two.) Adjectives and adverbs are very common in all registers, but less common than nouns and verbs. Adjectives and adverbs differ in their frequencies across registers. Like nouns, adjectives are more common in news and academic prose than in conversation. But the distribution of adverbs is like the distribution of verbs: most common in conversation and fiction.

These facts reflect the typical uses of adjectives and adverbs. Adjectives commonly modify nouns, so they add to the informational density of registers like academic prose. In contrast, adverbs often occur as clause elements (**adverbials**); they occur together with lexical verbs adding information to the short clauses of conversation and fiction.

Text sample 1 below illustrates how adjectives and nouns co-occur in academic prose. Text sample 2 illustrates how adverbs and verbs co-occur in conversation.

Text sample 1: HIV INFECTION (adjectives are in bold; nouns are underlined)

> Thus HIV infection is **likely** to remain with us for the **foreseeable** future. The **full** impact of HIV infection will be felt over decades. The virus does not need to spread rapidly in a population to have a very **marked** and gradually **expanding cumulative** effect. (ACAD)

Text sample 2: DESCRIBING A HEN (adverbs are in bold; lexical verbs are underlined)

> A: And she got her feet stuck through netting – **so** she was flapping and the net was **just** going up and down! <...>
> B: Now as she, I flapped it, I got hold of it and I flapped it **so** it, I **sort of** bounced about, she **sort of** bumped along (CONV†)

Text sample 1 illustrates the dense use of adjectives and nouns in academic prose. You can see that most of these adjectives occur as noun modifiers (e.g. **foreseeable** future, **full** impact, a very **marked** and gradually **expanding cumulative** effect). Text sample 2 has fewer nouns and adjectives, but more verbs, because the clauses are shorter. Adverbs commonly occur as adverbials in those clauses (e.g. so, just, sort of). This sample also illustrates the occurrence of adverbial particles in phrasal verbs, such as bumped along. (These particles, though, are different from adverbs and were covered in 2.4.5 and 5.8–11.)

Beyond their overall distributions, there is a great deal of variation in the form, meaning, and syntactic roles of adjectives and adverbs. Grammar Bite A introduces the characteristics and forms of these two classes. Grammar Bite B then focuses on the syntactic roles and meanings of adjectives. Grammar Bite C focuses on the syntactic roles and meanings of adverbs. Grammar Bite D then covers comparative and superlative forms of both classes.

GRAMMAR BITE

A Characteristics of adjectives and adverbs

7.2 Characteristics of adjectives

Certain characteristics are typical of adjectives, although not all adjectives have all of these characteristics. Adjectives that have these characteristics are called **central adjectives**. Adjectives with fewer of the characteristics are **peripheral adjectives**.

7.2.1 Defining characteristics of adjectives

A Morphological characteristics

Central adjectives can be inflected to show comparative and superlative degree, as with *big, bigger, biggest* (see Grammar Bite D).

B Syntactic characteristics

Central adjectives serve both **attributive** and **predicative** syntactic roles. In attributive position, an adjective is part of a noun phrase: it precedes and modifies the head noun. Most of the adjectives in Text sample 1 above—such as *foreseeable future* and *full impact*—are attributive.

Predicative adjectives are not part of a noun phrase, but instead characterize a noun phrase that is a separate clause element. Usually predicative adjectives occur as subject predicatives following a copular verb:

> *That'll be quite **impressive**.* (CONV)

Here the adjective *impressive* describes the subject *that*. Predicative adjectives also occur as object predicatives:

> *Even Oscar Wilde called it **charming**.* (NEWS)

Here the adjective *charming* describes the object *it*.

C Semantic characteristics

Central adjectives are descriptive. They typically characterize the referent of a nominal expression (e.g. **blue** and **white** *flag*, **unhappy** *childhood*). In addition, they are **gradable**, which means that they can show different degrees of a quality. Gradable adjectives can take comparative and superlative forms (e.g. *close, closer, closest*) and can be modified by an adverb of degree, such as *very*:

> *The two couples were **very close**.* (NEWS)

Many of the most common adjectives in English are central adjectives that share all of these characteristics. These include color adjectives (e.g. *red, dark*), adjectives of size and dimension (e.g. *big, long*), and adjectives of time (e.g. *new, old*).

7.2.2 Peripheral adjectives

Peripheral adjectives share some but not all of the defining characteristics of adjectives, as Table 7.1 illustrates. As the table also shows, the concept of 'central v. peripheral' is not a clear dichotomy. *Big* is a central adjective and exhibits all the characteristics listed above. Some adjectives, such as *beautiful*, have all the characteristics of central adjectives except that they cannot be inflected to show comparative or superlative degree (**beautifuller*). Other adjectives lack other characteristics. For example, *absolute* is not gradable (something cannot be more or less absolute). *Afraid* is gradable but it does not occur in attributive position, and it cannot be inflected (**afraider*). In prescriptive usage, *alive* is not a gradable adjective since something is either alive or dead. However, *alive* does sometimes occur with an adverb of degree:

> The center of the city is **very alive**. (CONV†)

Many peripheral adjectives occur in only attributive or predicative roles, but not both. For example, *unable* is used only predicatively, while *mere* is used only attributively.

> Heisenberg was totally **unable** to answer them. (ACAD) <not **an unable Heisenberg*>

> Some of them are very young, **mere** children. (FICT†) <not **children who are mere*>

ble 7.1 Variability in the defining characteristics of adjectives

morphological inflection	attributive role	predicative role	descriptive meaning	gradable	example
+	+	+	+	+	*big*
−	+	+	+	+	*beautiful*
−	+	+	?	−	*absolute*
−	−	+	+	+	*afraid*
−	−	+	+	?	*alive*
−	+	+	−	+	*different*
−	+	?	+	?	*lone*
?	+	−	−	−	*mere*

7.2.3 Frequency of attributive and predicative roles

Figure 7.1 shows how the distribution of attributive and predicative adjectives differs across registers. In news and academic prose, attributive adjectives are much more common than predicative adjectives. In conversation, both functions are relatively rare.

In news and academic prose, attributive adjectives are an important device used to add information to noun phrases. For example (adjectives are in bold, head nouns are underlined):

> With **economic** <u>specialization</u> and the development of **external economic** <u>linkages</u>, division of labor intensifies, a merchant class is added to the

political <u>elite</u>, *and* **selective** *migration* <u>streams</u> *add to the* **social** *and* **ethnic** <u>complexity</u> *of cities.* (ACAD)

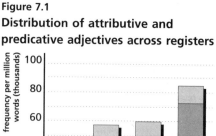

Figure 7.1
Distribution of attributive and predicative adjectives across registers

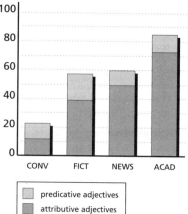

In contrast, the roughly equal frequency of predicative and attributive adjectives in conversation reflects a much greater reliance on clauses rather than noun phrases. For example, in the following conversation sample, notice how speakers use predicative adjectives to characterize events and people:

A: *Getting a B is* **good** *enough for him.*
B: *That's* **great**.
A: *Especially for people in med school – I think a lot of them are so* **used** *to being –*
B: *Super-achievers.*
A: *Super-achievers that they can't slow down, but, uh, Trey's not that way. He's real* **laid-back**. (CONV) <note: *med school* = medical school>

Specific adjectives have a strong preference for predicative or attributive position. For example, adjectives with the prefix *a-* are usually predicative. All the following adjectives occur over 98 per cent of the time in a predicative role:

abed, ablaze, abreast, afraid, aghast, aglow, alike, alive, alone, askew, asleep, aware.

In contrast, adjectives ending in *-al* show a strong preference for attributive position. All the following common adjectives occur in attributive position over 98 per cent of the time:

general, industrial, local, national, social.

7.3 The formation of adjectives

New adjectives can be formed through three processes:
• using participial forms
• adding word endings or derivational suffixes
• compounding (i.e. combining two words).

7.3.1 Participial adjectives

Both *-ing* and *-ed* participial forms can be used as adjectives. Most participial adjectives are derived from verbs (e.g. *promising, surprised, determined*). In fact, when a participle follows the verb *be*, it is sometimes difficult to know whether to analyze it as an adjective or a main verb (see 2.3.6).

New participial adjectives can also be formed by adding a negative prefix to an already existing adjective (e.g. *uninteresting* from *interesting*).

Many -*ing* and -*ed* participial forms can serve both attributive and predicative functions (e.g. *boring, thrilling, confused, excited*). However, participial adjectives are generally more common with attributive uses. Some of the most common participial adjectives are as follows:

- common -*ing* participial adjectives:

    amazing, boring, corresponding, encouraging, exciting, existing, following, increasing, interesting, leading, missing, outstanding, promising, remaining, threatening, underlying, willing, working

- common -*ed* participial adjectives:

    advanced, alleged, armed, ashamed, bored, complicated, confused, depressed, determined, disabled, disappointed, educated, excited, exhausted, frightened, interested, pleased, surprised, tired, unemployed, unexpected, worried

7.3.2 Adjectives with derivational affixes

Many adjectives are formed by adding an adjective suffix to a noun or verb. For example:

noun		suffix	derived adjective
cord	+	-less	cordless
effect	+	-ive	effective

verb		suffix	derived adjective
continue	+	-ous	continuous
elude	+	-ive	elusive

Adjectives can also be formed from other adjectives, especially by using the negative prefixes *un-*, *in-*, and *non-* (e.g. *unhappy, insensitive, nonstandard*).

Figure 7.2 shows that derived adjectives are by far most common in academic prose; they are rare in fiction and conversation. Adjectives formed with the suffix -*al* are by far more common than adjectives formed with any other suffix.

The suffix -*al* is extremely productive in academic prose; it is used to form many new adjectives, though these adjectives occur only rarely. Most of these adjectives are very specialized words, such as *adrenocortical, carpopedal,* and *tubulointerstitial*. At the same time, some -*al* adjectives are common in all registers, such as *central, final, general*.

The suffixes -*ent*, -*ive*, and -*ous* are also relatively common. Many adjectives ending in -*ent*, such as *different* and *persistent*, are derived from a verb (*differ, persist*). However,

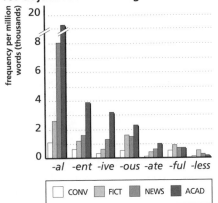

Figure 7.2

Frequency of derivational suffixes for adjectives across registers

it is hard to determine the source of adjectives like *patient, frequent, recent*. Adjectives in *-ive* also have several sources: some are formed from verbs (*active, adaptive, relative*), some are formed from nouns (*instinctive* from *instinct*), and others are more difficult to analyze (e.g. *aggressive*). Finally, most *-ous* adjectives are similar to *-al* adjectives in being highly specialized (e.g. *floriferous, umbrageous*). However, there are some more common *-ous* adjectives, like *serious, obvious, previous*.

 ## 7.3.3 Adjectival compounds

Adjectival compounds are made from a combination of more than one word, resulting in a compact expression of information. They take many forms, including:

adjective + adjective	*greyish-blue, infinite-dimensional*
adjective + noun	*full-time, cutting-edge, large-scale*
noun + adjective	*butterfly-blue, age-old, life-long*
adverb + -*ed* participle	*ill-suited, newly-restored, so-called*
adverb + -*ing* participle	*free-spending, slow-moving, tightly-fitting*
adverb + adjective	*highly-sensitive, already-tight, grimly-familiar*
reduplicative	*wishy-washy, roly-poly, goody-goody*
noun + *ed*-participle	*church-owned, classroom-based, horse-drawn*
noun + *ing*-participle	*eye-catching, law-abiding, nerve-wracking*

In some cases, the individual items in a compound can be derived from other words (e.g. *greyish* from *grey*). Some compounds would be analyzed as two words if the hyphen was omitted (e.g. *highly sensitive*).

Adjectival compounds are common in the written registers, especially news. They are most common as attributive adjectives.

Adjectival compounds present a compact form of information. Often, alternative expressions would require a full clause, usually a relative clause. Thus, *an attack that was motivated by racism* becomes *a racially-motivated attack*. Consider the following example from a news text:

1 *In a speech before the ballot, Mr Kovac – whose career includes a stint as an economic advisor to Cuban leader Fidel Castro in the 1960s – said he was in favour of '***socially-oriented***' market policies.*

2 *'I agree with the principles of a market economy **which are socially oriented**,' he told parliament.* (NEWS)

This example provides a contrast between the use of an adjectival compound in writing (**1**) and a fuller relative clause in quoted speech (**2**). The compound is used to compress information into a two-word expression, which is used as an attributive adjective in a noun phrase. In speech, without time for planning or editing, relative clauses seem easier to produce for certain kinds of information. In contrast, the more compact expression resulting from a compound attributive adjective is used by writers who have time for planning and editing.

One type of compound is more common in conversation: the reduplicative compound (e.g. *wishy-washy, roly-poly*). These compounds are different from the other compounds because the two parts rarely occur separately. They also usually play with sounds, which make them more suited to conversation.

7.4 **The function of adverbs**

Adverbs serve two major roles: they can be integrated into an element of the clause, or they themselves can be an element of the clause. In the first case, the adverb serves as a **modifier**; in the second case, the adverb is an **adverbial**.

When adverbs are modifiers, they usually modify an adjective or another adverb, as in these examples (the modified word is underlined):

> I am **almost** positive she borrowed that off Barbie! (CONV)
>
> First, health service managers must be able to price their services **reasonably accurately** for trading purposes. (NEWS)

In contrast, in the following examples, adverbs are adverbial elements of the clause:

1 *I think she'll be married **shortly**.* (CONV)
2 ***Possibly** the Wesleyan church tolerated outside unions unofficially, in a way the Anglican Church did not.* (ACAD)

These adverbs serve typical adverbial functions. In **1**, the adverb *shortly* provides information about the time when *she'll be married*. In **2**, *possibly* tells the level of certainty for the entire following clause.

It is important to note that the same adverbs can function as modifiers and adverbials. For example, the adverbs in **3** and **4** are modifiers, but the same adverbs in **5** and **6** are adverbials:

3 *To put on a grey shirt once more was **strangely** pleasing.* (FICT)
4 *This apparently complicated expression for pull-out torque gives the **surprisingly** simple characteristic shown in Fig 5.8.* (ACAD)
5 *And shortly Rabbit too is asleep. **Strangely**, he sleeps soundly, with Skeeter in the house.* (FICT)
6 ***Surprisingly**, the choked voice resumes.* (FICT)

Adverbials are covered in detail in Chapter 11. This chapter touches on adverbs as adverbials, but we concentrate here more on the structural characteristics of adverbs and on their use as modifiers.

7.5 **The formation of adverbs**

Adverbs are sometimes described as words ending in -*ly*. This is true of some adverbs, but the class is actually very diverse in form. In fact, there are four major categories for the form of adverbs.

A Simple adverbs

Simple adverbs are not derived from another word: for example, *well, too, rather, quite, soon,* and *here*. Sometimes a simple adverb form can also be used as another part of speech. For example, *fast* can be used as an adjective as well as an adverb; *down* can be used as a preposition as well as an adverb. In addition, some simple adverbs originated as compounds, but the independent meaning of the two parts has been lost (e.g. *already* from *all + ready, indeed* from *in + deed*).

B Compound adverbs

Compound adverbs are formed by combining two or more elements into a single word. Examples include adverbs such as *anyway* (*any* + *way*), *nowhere* (*no* + *where*), and *heretofore* (*here* + *to* + *fore*).

C Adverbs derived by suffixation

Many adverbs are formed by suffixing *-ly* to an adjective, such as *clearly* formed from the adjective *clear*. However, not all words ending in *-ly* are adverbs. Some adjectives end in *–ly*, such as *weekly* and *fatherly*:

> *Luzhkov is a master of populist **fatherly** gestures.* (NEWS)

Many of these words can also be used as adverbs:

> *He was smiling benignly, almost **fatherly**, at her.* (FICT)

The *-ly* suffix is very productive in forming new adverbs, resulting in unusual adverbs in both spoken and written texts:

> *Oh yes, it went very **jollily**.* (CONV)

> *Every 20 minutes or so, the play **guffawingly** alludes to the non-arrival of some long-ordered calculators.* (NEWS)

> *All phenols can act **bactericidally** or **fungicidally**.* (ACAD)

In addition to *-ly*, other suffixes are used to form adverbs. Two relatively common ones are *-wise* and *-ward(s)*. The suffix *-wise* can be added to nouns (e.g. *piecewise*) and the suffix *-ward(s)* is added to nouns (e.g. *homewards*, *seawards*) and prepositions (e.g. *onward*, *afterward*).

D Fixed phrases

Finally, some fixed phrases are used as adverbs. These phrases never vary in form, and their component words have lost their independent meaning. Examples include *of course*, *kind of*, and *at last*.

7.5.1 Distribution of adverb types

Figure 7.3 shows the preference for each adverb type in each register (based on analysis of frequently occurring adverbs). You can see that simple adverbs and *-ly* suffixes account for the majority of frequently occurring adverbs. However, the different registers have different preferences. In conversation, over 60 per cent of the common adverbs are simple forms, while about 55 per cent of the common adverbs used in academic prose are *-ly* forms.

In conversation, many simple adverbs are adverbials used to establish time and place

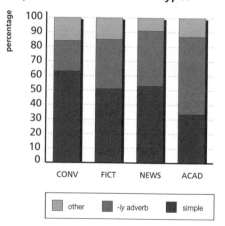

Figure 7.3
Proportional use of adverb types

CONV   FICT   NEWS   ACAD

☐ other   ▨ -ly adverb   ■ simple

relationships. They include items such as *again, always, already, far, here, never, now, soon, still, then,* and *yet*:

> But we couldn't, didn't walk too **far** today. (CONV)

Also common are some modifying adverbs, such as *very, rather, quite,* and *pretty*:

> That's **pretty** good. (CONV)

In contrast, in academic prose *-ly* adverbs derived from adjectives are commonly used, for a variety of purposes. Many function as **stance adverbials** expressing authors' attitudes (see also 11.13–16). Often these forms comment on the likelihood of an idea, with adverbs such as *possibly, probably, certainly, expectedly,* or *obviously*:

> **Obviously** this is an overstatement. (ACAD)
>
> The house is **possibly** in North America. (ACAD†)

In addition, *-ly* adverbs in academic prose are used as adverbials in descriptions of processes or conditions:

> The solubility decreases **rapidly** as the temperature falls. (ACAD)

Academic prose also commonly uses *-ly* adverbs as modifiers:

> Acclimatization is **relatively** unimportant. (ACAD)
>
> The paper by Donchin et al. is a **particularly** good methodological critique of research in this area. (ACAD)

In contrast to both conversation and academic prose, fiction uses a wide range of *-ly* adverbs, including uncommon ones, to give an apt and lively description of events:

> All three adults giggled **easily** and at everything, **absentmindedly** fingering small silver spoons. (FICT)

7.5.2 Adverbs and adjectives with the same form

Sometimes an adverb has the identical form as a related adjective. For example, *fast* is an adjective in 1 below, while in 2 it is an adverb:

> 1 **Fast** guys tire, a basketball coach once said of his own high-rise team, but big guys don't shrink. (NEWS)
>
> 2 One looter, a woman who did not run **fast** enough, was shot dead. (FICT)

In conversation, adjective forms are often used as adverbs:

> The big one went so **slow**. (CONV)

From a prescriptive point of view, *slow* is an adjective form, and its use as an adverb is classified as non-standard. However, in conversation, such uses are not unusual. For example:

> Well it was hot but it didn't come out **quick**. (CONV)
>
> They want to make sure it runs **smooth** first. (CONV†)

Good is sometimes used as an adverb in place of the prescriptively correct adverb *well*:

> They go **good** with baggy jeans. (CONV)
>
> 'It's running **good** now.' (FICT)

Many adjective forms that are used as adverbs have the function of adverbials, as in the above examples. However, other related forms occur as modifiers. A common example is the modifier *real* used in place of the prescriptively correct adverb *really*:

> *It came out **real** [good].* (CONV)

Good is commonly used as an adverb in American English conversation, but this use is rare in British English conversation and in all written registers. Clearly, this is an informal choice, favored in American English:

> *It just worked out **good**, didn't it?* (AmE CONV)

> *Bruce Jackson, In Excess' trainer said, 'He ran **good**, but he runs **good** all the time. It was easy.'* (AmE NEWS)

Figure 7.4 shows that both British and American English conversation commonly use *really* to modify adjectives, especially with the adjectives *good, nice, bad,* and *funny*:

> *This looks **really** [good] this little ... thing.* (BrE CONV)

> *You couldn't tell from looking at him but he was driving a **really** [nice] car.* (AmE CONV)

> *But he's always, he's always making **really** [funny] comments.* (BrE CONV)

On the other hand, only American English conversation frequently uses *real* to modify adjectives, especially with *good, nice, hard, bad, big, easy*:

> *It would have been **real** [bad] news.* (AmE CONV)

> *She's a **real** [nice] girl.* (AmE CONV)

Figure 7.4

Frequency of *real* and *really* as adverbs in AmE v. BrE conversation

Interestingly, the same speaker can alternate quickly between *really* and *real*:

> *I have a **really** [good] video with a **real** [good] soundtrack.* (AmE CONV)

Review

Major points of Grammar Bite A: Characteristics of adjectives and adverbs

➤ Adjectives have certain typical characteristics in their form, meaning, and use.

> ➤ Central adjectives share all of the characteristics.
> ➤ Peripheral adjectives vary in the extent to which they share the characteristics.

➤ Adjectives have two major functions: attributive and predicative.

➤ New adjectives can be formed in three ways: the use of participial forms, the use of derivational suffixes, and compounding.

➤ Adverbs have two major functions: modifier and adverbial.

➤ Adverbs have four major forms: simple, compound, forms with suffixes, and fixed phrases.

➤ Some adverbs have the same form as adjectives or, informally, adjective forms are used as adverbs (e.g. *good*).

GRAMMAR BITE

B Adjectives: roles and meanings

7.6 Semantic categories of adjectives

There are two major semantic categories of adjectives: **descriptors** and **classifiers**.

Descriptors are adjectives that describe color, size and weight, chronology and age, emotion, and other characteristics. They are typically gradable. For example:

- color descriptors: *black, white, dark, bright, blue, brown, green, grey, red*
- size/quantity/extent descriptors: *big, deep, heavy, huge, long, large, little, short, small, thin, wide*
- time descriptors describe chronology, age, and frequency: *annual, daily, early, late, new, old, recent, young*
- evaluative/emotive descriptors denote judgments, emotions, and emphasis: *bad, beautiful, best, fine, good, great, lovely, nice, poor*
- miscellaneous descriptors cover many other kinds of characteristics: *appropriate, cold, complex, dead, empty, free, hard, hot, open, positive, practical, private, serious, strange, strong, sudden.*

Classifiers limit or restrict a noun's referent, rather than describing characteristics in the way that descriptors do. For example:

- relational/classificational/restrictive classifiers limit the referent of a noun in relation to other referents: *additional, average, chief, complete, different, direct, entire, external, final, following, general, initial, internal, left, main, maximum, necessary, original, particular, previous, primary, public, similar, single, standard, top, various*
- affiliative classifiers identify the national or social group of a referent: *American, Chinese, Christian, English, French, German, Irish, United*
- topical/other classifiers give the subject area or specific type of a noun: *chemical, commercial, environmental, human, industrial, legal, medical, mental, official, oral, phonetic, political, sexual, social, visual.*

As you can see from these examples, the distinction between descriptors and classifiers is not always clear. Many topical classifiers, for instance, provide descriptive content while they also limit the reference of the head noun (e.g. *chemical, medical, political*).

Most classifiers are non-gradable. This means that they usually cannot take modifiers of degree or comparative/superlative forms. For example, we cannot say **very medical* or **more additional*.

Some adjectives can serve as both classifiers and descriptors, depending on their context of use. For example, the expressions in the left-hand column contain a descriptor, while the same adjective is a classifier in the right-hand column.

descriptor	classifier
a *popular* girl in high school	*popular* vote, *popular* opinion
criminal activity	*criminal* law
a *primary* issue	*primary* school

The most common adjectives often have a range of meanings. For example, *old* is descriptive of age (*an old radio, old newspapers*), but it can also be used to express evaluation or emotion (*poor old Rusty, good old genetics*). Even within a single category, an adjective can have more than one meaning. *Poor* as a descriptor, for instance, can mean either 'lacking financial resources' (*a poor country*) or 'not good' (*poor health*).

Meanings can also vary with syntactic role or register. For example, the predicative use of *poor* usually refers to the financial situation (*We're very poor*), while the attributive use is often associated with an emotive meaning, especially in fiction (e.g. *the poor devil, the poor little kid*).

7.6.1 Adjectives in combination

Sometimes adjectives are used in combination for a particular semantic effect.

A **Repeated comparative adjectives**

Especially in fiction, two identical comparative adjectives are sometimes joined by *and* to denote an ever-increasing degree of the adjective. For example, *funnier and funnier* is a way of saying 'increasingly funny.' Typical examples include:

 1 *His own need for food grew **slighter and slighter**.* (FICT)
 2 *Her visits to the country to see her soon became **rarer and rarer**.* (FICT)
 3 *See the branches get **smaller and smaller and smaller**.* (CONV)

Repeated adjectives typically occur after resulting copular verbs, such as *grew* in **1**, *become* in **2**, and *get* in **3**. Example **3** also shows that more than one repetition is possible.

Some adjectives make comparatives with *more* rather than with an *-er* ending (see Grammar Bite D). In this case, the structure repeats the *more* rather than the adjective itself:

 *It got **more and more popular** strangely enough.* (CONV)

B **The intensifiers *good and* and *nice and***

Sometimes adjectives are conjoined with *good* or *nice* in order to intensify the meaning of the adjective. For example, *good and sorry* intensifies the meaning of *sorry*; it does not add the individual meaning of 'good'. Sequences of this type occur in predicative rather than attributive position. They are typical of fictional dialog and natural conversation:

 *Furthermore, we'll end this conversation when I'm **good and ready**.* (FICT)

The combination *nice and* is especially common:

 *Good for your teeth. Makes your teeth **nice and strong**.* (CONV)

In contrast, similar sequences in attributive position do not intensify the meaning of the second adjective. Rather, the first adjective—*good* or *nice*—retains its meaning:

*There are many **good and prosperous** people here.* (FICT)

This example does not refer to 'very prosperous people', but rather people who are both good and prosperous.

7.7 **More about attributive adjectives**

Attributive adjectives usually modify common nouns (underlined below):

*Yes, it's a **bad** <u>attitude</u>.* (CONV)

*It had been his **favorite** <u>toy</u>.* (FICT)

Attributive adjectives can also modify proper place nouns:

old fashioned Episcopalian <u>New York</u> (NEWS)

ancient <u>Mesopotamia</u> (ACAD)

Less commonly, they modify the name of a person:

little <u>Laura Davies</u> (NEWS)

*the **late** <u>John C. Drennan</u>* (NEWS)

Attributive adjectives can also modify personal pronouns. Although these adjective + personal pronoun combinations are generally rare, they do occur occasionally in conversation and fiction, especially in exclamations. *Lucky, poor,* and *silly* are the most common adjectives modifying personal pronouns:

Lucky *you!* (CONV)

*Not like **poor** me.* (FICT)

*'**Silly** old him,' Lally laughed.* (FICT†)

7.7.1 Most common attributive adjectives in conversation and academic prose

Descriptors are relatively common in both registers, while classifiers are found much more commonly in academic prose. Most of the frequent descriptors in conversation are simple one-syllable words (see Table 7.2). Most of these adjectives describe size, time, or personal evaluations. Evaluative adjectives are the most common:

*That's a **good** film.* (CONV)

*He had this really **nice** cap.* (CONV)

Even the adjective *old*, usually classified as a time adjective, is often used for an evaluative meaning in conversation:

*The **old** pig!* (CONV)

*Yeah. Same **old** stuff.* (CONV)

Several of the most common attributive adjectives in conversation are contrasting pairs: *little/big, new/old, black/white, good/bad, same/different.*

Academic prose shows a much greater use of classifiers, especially relational and topical adjectives:

- relational adjectives: *the **same** physical units, **basic** processes, **general** method, **whole** number*

Table 7.2 **Most common attributive adjectives in conversation and academic prose**

	CONV	ACAD
descriptors		
size/amount	big, little, long	long, small, great, high, low, large
time	new, old	new, old, young
color	black, white	—
evaluative	good, bad, best, right, nice	good, best, right, important, simple, special
relational	same, whole, different	—
classifiers		
relational	—	basic, common, following, higher, individual, lower, particular, similar, specific, total, various, whole, different, full, general, major, final, main, single
topical	—	local, natural, normal, oral, physical, public, sexual, political, social, human, international, national, economic

- topical adjectives: *social* status, **human** nature, *sexual* development, **natural** law, **public** policy, **political** economy, **experimental** physics.

These adjectives are important in specifying the reference of noun phrases. In addition, academic prose writers use evaluative adjectives to express judgments of what is important, unusual, appropriate, and so on: *important* consequences, *special* cases, *appropriate* conditions, **right** level.

7.8 More about predicative adjectives

Predicative adjectives occur with two syntactic roles: **subject predicative** and **object predicative**.

A Subject predicatives

Subject predicatives complement a copular verb. They characterize the nominal expression that is in subject position (underlined):

1 <u>She</u> seems quite **nice** really. (CONV)
2 <u>That</u>'s **right**. (CONV)
3 <u>It</u> would be **easier**, **quicker**, and **cheaper**. (FICT)
4 <u>The tendencies</u> are not **significant** and get **weaker** when data are corrected for guessing. (ACAD)

For example in **1**, the predicative adjective *nice* is an evaluation characterizing the subject pronoun *she*.

Many of the most frequent predicative adjectives occur with a phrasal or clausal complement of their own. That is, they have a prepositional phrase, *to*-infinitive clause, or *that*-clause that complements their meaning. For example (complements are in *[]*):

- phrasal complements:

*Well you're **good** [at remembering numbers].* (CONV)

*That's **nice** [of you].* (FICT)

*A system concept is **subject** [to several constraints].* (ACAD†)

- clausal complements:

*'You look **good enough** [to eat],' he said.* (FICT)

*I am **sure** [the warm affinities between Scots and Jews arise out of appreciation of herrings].* (NEWS)

In general, English does not allow adjectives with prepositional or clausal complements to occur in attributive position.

B Object predicatives

Object predicatives occur with complex transitive verbs, following the direct object. Rather than characterizing the subject, they characterize the object. For example (direct objects are underlined, and the object predicative is in bold):

*I said you've got all your <u>priorities</u> **wrong**.* (CONV)

*I had <u>it</u> **right** the first time, didn't I?* (CONV)

*She had considered <u>it</u> infinitely **vulgar** and **debased**.* (FICT)

*She has since declared <u>herself</u> **bankrupt**.* (NEWS)

7.8.1 Most common predicative adjectives in conversation and academic prose

The most common predicative adjectives in conversation and academic prose are:

CONV: *able, alright, lovely, sure, right, good, nice, true, wrong, bad, fine, funny*

ACAD: *able, common, dependent, equal, equivalent, essential, greater, large, low, present, similar, useful, sure, true, difficult, different, possible, impossible, likely, important, necessary, clear, small, available, better*

Most of the common predicative adjectives are descriptors rather than classifiers. Interestingly, there is little overlap between these predicative adjectives and the common attributive adjectives. (The exceptions are *right, good, large, low, different* and *full*.)

The most common predicative adjectives in conversation tend to be evaluative and emotional: e.g. *good, lovely, bad. Right, alright,* and *sure* usually express agreement or confidence, as in *That's right*. Expressions of disagreement (e.g. *you're wrong*) are less common.

In conversation, a single common adjective can express a wide range of meanings. For example, the adjective *funny* is used for many meanings in addition to its core meaning of 'humorous'; other meanings include 'strange', 'spoiled', 'noteworthy':

*She sounds **funny** on the phone. Most odd.* (CONV)

*Told you about her having that – dish – and it went **funny**.* (CONV)

*What's **funny** about me is that I'm very much affectionate.* (CONV†)

Most predicative adjectives in conversation do not have complements:

Are you sure? (CONV)

*We'll find out what's **wrong**.* (CONV)

In contrast, predicative adjectives in academic prose are often used with complements to express intellectual claims. For example (complements are in *[]*):

   1 *It will be **clear** [that the presence of two slits is essential to give an interference pattern].* (ACAD)
   2 *The feeling of comfort is **basic** [to a sense of well-being], but it is **difficult** [to define] and is often most **notable** [in its absence].* (ACAD)

These adjectives typically provide a frame for the claim expressed in the complement. A predicative adjective such as *clear* in **1** is a kind of stance marker. It gives the author's assessment of certainty or importance. (Predicative adjectives and their complements are discussed further in 10.7.1–2, 10.15, and 10.21.3.)

7.9 Other syntactic roles of adjectives

Besides their attributive and predicative uses, adjectives can serve several other roles, including postposed modifiers, noun phrase heads, clause linkers, free modifiers, and exclamations. (Adjectives also have an important role in comparative clauses, described in Grammar Bite D.)

7.9.1 Adjectives as postposed modifiers

A **postposed** adjective is part of a noun phrase but it *follows* the head word. Postposed adjectives are most common with compound indefinite pronouns as heads, such as *no one, anything,* or *somebody*:

   *It's a shame if you haven't got <u>anyone</u> **musical** here.* (CONV)

   *I think they are doing <u>everything</u> **possible** to protect the workers.* (NEWS)

In addition, postposed adjectives appear in some fixed expressions, e.g. *attorney general, heir apparent, notary public, Asia Minor*.

   Similarly, when a modifying adjective phrase is very long, the adjective phrase will often follow the head noun:

   *It's a, a <u>lounge</u> **not much bigger than the one we've got now**.* (CONV)

   *He drew from the high soprano instrument <u>sounds</u> **totally different from what we think of as saxophone tone**.* (NEWS)

7.9.2 Adjectives as noun phrase heads

Adjectives can also function as the head of a noun phrase. Adjectives in this role can be modified by adverbs (e.g. *very* in **2** below), which is typical of adjectives but not nouns. However, these adjectives can also take premodifiers (e.g. *real working* in **3** below), which is typical of nouns:

   1 *Everyone picks on the **Welsh**, don't they?* (CONV)
   2 *I think the contrast between the <u>very</u> **rich** and the <u>very</u> **poor** in this country is disgusting.* (FICT)

3 *These people may be the <u>real working</u> **poor**, the **elderly**, the very **young**, the **unemployed**, or the **transient**.* (ACAD)

As these examples illustrate, the adjective-headed noun phrase usually refers to a group of people with the characteristic described by the adjective; thus, *the elderly* refers to 'elderly people in general'. The definite article (*the*) is typically used with adjectives as noun phrase heads.

7.9.3 Adjectives as linking expressions

An adjective sometimes serves to link clauses or sentences to one another. Adjectives in this role can also have modifiers (e.g. *still more* in **2**):

1 **Worse** *he had nothing to say.* (FICT)
2 <u>Still more</u> **important**, *children who grew up in elite homes enjoyed advantages that helped them maintain elite status.* (ACAD)

Such linking adjective phrases often express stance.

7.9.4 Adjectives as free modifiers

Adjectives can also be syntactically free modifiers of a noun phrase. These adjective phrases modify a noun phrase, but they are not syntactically part of the noun phrase; in fact, the adjective phrase has a peripheral role in the clause. These structures are most common in fiction. They typically occur in sentence-initial position. Below, the free modifiers are in bold and the noun phrases they modify are in *[]*:

Green, bronze and golden *[it] flowed though weeds and rushes.* (FICT)

Delicate and light bodied, *[it] is often confused with American blended whiskey and thus called rye.* (ACAD)

Free modifiers can also occur in sentence-final position:

[Victor chucked], **highly amused**. (FICT)

7.9.5 Adjectives as exclamations

Adjectives often serve as exclamations, especially in conversation and fictional dialog:

Great! *I need some of those.* (CONV)

Good! *I like that.* (CONV)

Other examples in conversation: *Excellent! Bloody brilliant! Sorry! Oh dear! Amazing! Wonderful! Super! Super-duper!* <note: *bloody* is a taboo word that may be offensive to some people>

Review

Major points in Grammar Bite B: Adjectives: roles and meanings
➤ Adjectives can have two different kinds of meaning: they can be descriptors or classifiers.
➤ Adjectives are sometimes combined in interesting ways: repetition of a comparative adjective shows increasing intensity (e.g. *smaller and smaller*), combination with *good and* or *nice and* intensifies the meaning (e.g. *good and ready*).

➤ Attributive adjectives occur mainly before common nouns, but they can also occur before proper nouns and personal pronouns.
  ➤ The frequency and use of attributive adjectives varies greatly between conversation and academic prose.
➤ Predicative adjectives can function as subject predicatives or object predicatives.
  ➤ Conversation and academic prose tend to use different kinds of predicative adjectives.
➤ Only a few adjectives are common in both predicative and attributive positions.
➤ Adjectives have five syntactic roles in addition to their attributive and predicative roles: postposed modifier, noun phrase head, linking expression, exclamation, and free modifier.

GRAMMAR BITE

c Adverbs: roles and meanings

7.10 Syntactic roles of adverbs

In Grammar Bite A we identified the two major roles of adverbs: modifiers and adverbials. Here we cover these roles in more detail.

7.10.1 Adverbs modifying adjectives

One of the primary functions of adverbs is modifying adjectives (the adjective is underlined below):

> I'm **rather** <u>partial</u> to parsnips. (CONV)
>
> I was **utterly, hopelessly, horribly** <u>glad</u>. (FICT)
>
> This is **slightly** <u>larger</u> than the calculated value. (ACAD†)

Usually, adverbs precede the adjectives that they modify, but the adverbs *enough* and *ago* are postposed, placed after the adjectives they modify:

> Down came the dry flakes, <u>fat</u> **enough** and <u>heavy</u> **enough** to crash like nickels on stone. (FICT)
>
> That seems <u>so long</u> **ago**. (FICT†)

Other adverbs can also be postposed:

> It is <u>rich</u> **nutritionally** with high calcium content. (ACAD)

Common adverb + adjective combinations

Registers vary greatly in their use of adverb + adjective pairs. Here we focus on the contrast between conversation and academic prose.

Conversation makes use of a few extremely frequent adverb + adjective combinations. In all cases, these most frequent combinations include a degree adverb: *real, really, too, pretty, quite,* or *very,* in combination with adjectives like *bad, good, nice, quick*. These are general evaluative expressions with vague reference. For example:

> *That looks **pretty** <u>good</u>, it's still a little high.* (CONV)

> *Really, I, I fancy Emma cos she's a **very** <u>nice</u> girl.* (CONV)

In contrast, academic prose has more diversity in adverb + adjective combinations. As in conversation, the most common adverb modifiers are degree adverbs: *more, quite, very*. However, the co-occurring adjectives express specific qualities rather than general value judgments (e.g. *different, difficult, important, large, low*). In addition, several of the common combinations in academic prose refer to statistical measurements (e.g. *significantly different/higher* and *statistically significant*).

> *He found it **very** <u>difficult</u> to regain his usual level of activity because his arthritis seemed worse after the operation.* (ACAD†)

> *The hospital mortality at 21 days for those who received streptokinase was not **significantly** <u>different</u> from the control group.* (ACAD†)

7.10.2 Adverbs modifying other adverbs

Adverbs also modify other adverbs:

> *They'll figure it out **really** <u>fast</u>.* (CONV)

> *The do-it-yourself builder **almost** <u>always</u> uses a water-repellent plywood, oil-tempered hardboard or fibre-cement sheet.* (ACAD†)

The two adverbs together (*really fast* in **1** and *almost always* in **2**) form an adverb phrase.

Common adverb + adverb combinations

Adverbs are less common as modifiers of other adverbs than as modifiers of adjectives. However, certain pairs are extremely common, especially in conversation:

pretty/so/very/too much	*pretty/really/very well*	*right now*
much better/more	*right here/there*	*pretty soon*

In both conversation and academic prose, adverb + adverb combinations are used primarily for describing amounts/intensities, or for qualifying a comparison that is being made:

> 1 *Thank you **very** <u>much</u> for listening.* (CONV)
>
> 2 *Oh, you're going to do **much** <u>better</u>.* (CONV)
>
> 3 *I admitted, however, that internal skepticism offers a **much** <u>more</u> powerful challenge to our project.* (ACAD)

As **3** illustrates, these combinations in academic prose are usually themselves modifiers of an adjective.

Adverb + adverb combinations in conversation can also be used for time and place. The modifier *right* is especially common in American English to suggest exactness:

> *I really couldn't keep him in my apartment **right** <u>now</u>.* (AmE CONV)

> *She already got a twenty percent tip **right** <u>here</u>.* (AmE CONV)

> *The whatchacallems are **right** <u>there</u>, see?* (AmE CONV†)

7.10.3 Adverbs modifying other elements

Adverbs can also modify noun phrases (or parts of noun phrases), prepositional phrases, particles, numerals, or measurements:

- modifier of noun phrase:

    *'It came as **quite** <u>a surprise</u>,' said one.* (NEWS)

- modifier of pronoun:

    ***Almost** <u>nobody</u>, it seemed, could eat what they were given.* (FICT)

- modifier of predeterminer:

    *I've done **about** <u>half</u> a side.* (CONV)

- modifier of prepositional phrase:

    *But there's a hell of a lot – **well** <u>into their seventies</u>.* (CONV)

- modifier of particle of phrasal verb:

    *It's really filled the room **right** <u>up</u>.* (CONV)

- modifier of numeral:

    *It is still not clear whether the **approximately** <u>250</u> people still listed as missing include those whom ex-detainees say were still alive in May.* (NEWS)

- modifier of other measurement expressions:

    *Tosi (1984:27–34, fig. 3) estimates that **roughly** <u>one-quarter to one-third</u> of the total surface area of four sites in 'prehistoric Turan' was devoted to different craft activities.* (ACAD)

Most of these adverbs occur as **premodifiers**. However, **postmodification** also occurs, especially when identifying the location of a noun phrase:

> *Thus, in <u>the ammonia example</u> **above**, if ammonia, NH_3, is allowed to escape from the reaction system, the reaction cannot achieve equilibrium.* (ACAD)

For some of these functions, only a small set of adverbs is used. For instance, only *right, well, straight,* and *directly* are commonly used to modify prepositions.

7.10.4 Adverbs as complements of prepositions

Another function of adverbs is to serve as the complement of a preposition. Consider the following examples, with the preposition underlined and adverb in bold:

1 <u>Before</u> **long**, *he met a pretty singing cowgirl from Texas who went by the name of Dale Evans.* (NEWS)
2 *Its importance has often been recognized <u>since</u> **then**.* (ACAD†)
3 *There's another sweatshirt lurking <u>under</u> **there** that I didn't see.* (CONV)
4 *But I'm seeing all this <u>from</u> **above**.* (FICT†)

These adverbs serving as complements of prepositions usually denote time (as in 1 and 2) or place (3 and 4).

7.10.5 Adverbs as clause elements: adverbials

An adverb (or an adverb phrase) can function as an adverbial. There are three major types of adverbials: **circumstance adverbials**, **stance adverbials**, and **linking adverbials**. Adverbs can be used for all three types of adverbials.

A Circumstance adverbials

These add information about the action or state that is described in the clause. They give details about factors such as time, manner, and place. For example:

> He took it in **slowly** but **uncomprehendingly**. (FICT†)

B Stance adverbials

These convey the speaker/writer's assessment of the proposition in the clause:

> His book **undoubtedly** fills a need. (NEWS)

C Linking adverbials

These serve to connect stretches of text:

> Most of our rural people do not have radio or television and a large proportion are illiterate. **Therefore** we had to use approaches that do not depend on the mass media or on literacy. (ACAD)

Chapter 11 gives a detailed discussion of adverbials—see especially 11.2.

7.10.6 Adverbs standing alone

In conversation, adverbs can stand alone, unconnected to other elements in a clause. They can even serve as complete utterances. In some cases, the adverbs are related by ellipsis to previous utterances. For example:

> The kitten's gone crazy. No, totally I mean it. **Totally** and **utterly**. (CONV)

Here the complete form would be *The kitten's gone totally and utterly crazy.*

Adverbs as stand-alone utterances can also serve to express—or emphasize—agreement:

> A: *What you could afford you had.*
> B: **Exactly. Exactly.**
> A: *In other words the skills of a counselor?*
> B: *Yes. Yes.*
> C: **Definitely. Definitely.**

Adverbs can also be used as questions. Often, these adverbs are stance adverbials (see 11.2, 11.13–16):

> A: *You can still vote if you lost it.*
> B: **Really?**
> A: *They should have your name on the roster.*
> A: *You're supposed to put the lid on otherwise it won't switch off.*
> B: **Seriously?**
> A: *Yeah.*

Similarly, stance adverbs can be used to answer questions:

A: *It's warm isn't it. By the radiator.*
B: ***Probably.***
A: *Are they that good?*
B: ***Definitely.*** *Only band I want to see playing – in the world.*

7.11 Semantic categories of adverbs

Adverbs cover a wide range of semantic categories. Here we identify seven main categories—place adverbs, time adverbs, manner adverbs, degree adverbs, additive/restrictive adverbs, stance adverbs, and linking adverbs—as well as other less common meanings. (The semantic classes of adverbials are discussed in more detail in 11.6, 11.9, 11.13, 11.17.)

As with verbs and adjectives, many of the most common adverbs have multiple meanings that vary with context of use. First, some adverbs have both literal and more metaphorical meanings. For example, *perfectly* can be used in its literal meaning 'in a perfect manner' (*perfectly arranged, perfectly fits the bill*). However, *perfectly* is more commonly used in a more metaphorical sense to mean 'completely' (*perfectly normal, perfectly safe*). In addition, adverbs can belong to more than one major category of meaning. *Still*, for example, can be an adverb of time (**1**) or a linking adverb (**2**):

1 *Are you **still** teaching?* (CONV)
2 *I'm doing better now.* <...> ***Still** I don't even remember how to start.* (CONV)

For further examples of ambiguous adverbs (*just, then*, and *there*) see 11.7.

7.11.1 Place adverbs

Place adverbs express distance, direction, or position:

*He loves it **there**.* (CONV) <position>
*'Don't worry, he can't have gone **far**.'* (FICT) <distance>
*It hopped **backward** among its companions.* (FICT†) <direction>

Place adverbials are further discussed in 11.6.1.

7.11.2 Time adverbs

Time adverbs express position in time, frequency, duration, and relationship:

1 *She doesn't say go away very much **now**.* (CONV) <time position>
2 *She **always** eats the onion.* (CONV) <time frequency>
3 *She will remain a happy memory with us **always**.* (NEWS) <time duration>
4 *When they took the old one out it was **already** in seven separate pieces!* (CONV) <time relationship>

These examples show how the same adverb can have different time meanings, depending on its context of use. For example, *always* in **2** refers to frequency (i.e. how often she eats the onion); while in **3**, *always* refers more to duration (= 'for ever'). Time adverbials are further illustrated in 11.6.2.

7.11.3 Manner adverbs

Manner adverbs express information about how an action is performed. Many of these adverbs have *-ly* suffixes, taking their meanings from the adjectives that they are derived from:

> **Automatically** she backed away. (FICT)

> But sentiment recovered **quickly**. (NEWS†)

Other manner adverbs are not *-ly* adverbs:

> You can run **fast** but not here. (CONV)

> To perform **well** it has to be tightly targeted to cope with quite a narrow band of frequencies. (NEWS)

In the above examples, manner adverbs are used as adverbials. But manner adverbs can also be used as modifiers, providing description that is integrated into a noun phrase:

> <...> by the dark waters of Buda, her tears dropping hotly among [the [**quietly** flowing] dead leaves]. (FICT†)

> In [a [**fast** moving] first half] the teams appeared to cancel each other out in mid-field. (NEWS)

> The Russian leader threw [the [**carefully** arranged] welcome] into chaos. (NEWS†)

These adverb + adjective combinations could also be analyzed as compound adjectives (described in 7.3.3), particularly if they were hyphenated. Manner adverbials are further discussed in 11.6.3.

7.11.4 Degree adverbs

Adverbs of degree describe the extent of a characteristic. They can be used to emphasize that a characteristic is either greater or less than some typical level:

> It's insulated **slightly** with polystyrene behind. (CONV)

> Those letters from you, it got so I **almost** believed they were really written to me. (FICT)

> They **thoroughly** deserved a draw last night. (NEWS†)

Most modifying adverbs discussed in 7.10.1–3 are adverbs of degree. Degree adverbials are discussed further in 11.6.5.

A Amplifiers/intensifiers

Degree adverbs that increase intensity are called **amplifiers** or **intensifiers**. Some of these modify gradable adjectives and indicate degrees on a scale. They include *more, very, so, extremely*:

> Our dentist was **very** good. (CONV)

> If they had not helped her **so** generously in those times, Mrs Morel would never have pulled through without incurring debts that would have dragged her down. (FICT)

> Most will be **extremely** cautious until new case law defines the extent of the new Act. (NEWS)

Other amplifiers indicate an endpoint on a scale. These include *totally, absolutely, completely,* and *quite* (in the sense of 'completely'):

> **Completely** <u>cold and unemotional.</u> (FICT)
>
> *But snow and ice accumulate in a* **totally** <u>different</u> *way from sediment.* (ACAD)

How is also used as an intensifier in exclamatory sentences:

> A: *Well it ain't the child's fault.*
> B: *No.*
> A: **How** <u>cruel!</u> (CONV)
> <note: *ain't* is a non-standard form>

Often when *how* is used as an amplifier in conversation, it is used to make an ironic comment:

> A: *This guy came reeling down the hallway completely plastered, uh, and the manager told me, oh, don't worry about him. He lives here, but he's completely harmless, and he sits out front, on the grass, right in front of the door to my apartment and drinks.*
> B: **How** <u>lovely.</u>

Some manner adverbs can lose their literal meaning to be used as amplifiers:

> 1 *New York's an* **awfully** <u>safe</u> *place.* (FICT)
> 2 *And Carl was* **perfectly** <u>awful.</u> (FICT)

In **1**, **awfully** does not mean 'in an awful way'; rather, it is a somewhat colorful way of saying 'very' or 'extremely'. Similarly in **2**, *perfectly* takes on its more metaphorical sense of 'completely'. *Dead* is another adverb used in informal situations to modify adjectives. Clearly, *dead* loses its literal meaning in such cases:

> *He is* **dead** <u>serious</u> *all the time.* (CONV)

B Diminishers/downtoners

Degree adverbs which decrease the effect of the modified item are called **diminishers** or **downtoners**. As with intensifiers, these adverbs indicate degrees on a scale and are used with gradable adjectives. They include *less, slightly, somewhat, rather,* and *quite* (in the sense of 'to some extent'):

> 1 *A* **slightly** <u>cold</u> *start gave way to wonderful contrasts of feeling.* (NEWS)
> 2 *Consequently, Marx often uses the term Klasse in a* **somewhat** <u>cavalier</u> *fashion.* (ACAD†)

Downtoners are related to **hedges** (like *kind of*; discussed below under stance adverbs). That is, they indicate that the modified item is not being used precisely. For example, in **1** and **2** above, *cold* and *cavalier* are not completely accurate descriptions of *a start* and *a fashion*.

Other degree adverbs that lessen the impact of the modified item are *almost, nearly, pretty,* and *far from*. These also occur with some non-gradable adjectives:

> *Mr Deane's glass is* **almost** <u>empty.</u> (FICT)

 ## C Choices among degree adverbs as modifiers

Conversation and academic prose have very different preferences in their choice of degree modifiers. Conversational speakers use many informal amplifiers that are avoided in academic prose; these include *bloody* (BrE), *damn*, *totally*, *absolutely*, *real*, and *really*. Forms like *bloody* and *damn* are taboo words which can be offensive in some contexts:

> *You're stupid, you're **bloody** stupid!* (CONV)

> *He'll look **really** sweet.* (CONV)

> *I got that speeding ticket and now I'm making **damn** sure I don't speed.* (CONV)

Academic prose uses more formal amplifiers, including *extremely*, *highly*, *entirely*, *fully*:

> *Indeed it is **extremely** difficult to establish any truly satisfactory system.* (ACAD†)

> *The **highly** complex process of adjustment to infection is determined by many variables.* (ACAD)

However, the two most common amplifiers for both conversation and academic prose are the same: *very* and *so* (although both tend to be more common in conversation). They occur with many different adjectives, but general positive words (*good*, *nice*) are the most common in conversation:

> *That sounds **very** good.* (CONV)

> *Oh, it's **so** nice.* (CONV)

Academic prose has a greater variety of adjectives that occur with *so* and *very*. For example:

> *It will not be **so** straightforward to achieve.* (ACAD†)

> *Racial preferences are **very** pronounced.* (ACAD)

7.11.5 Additive/restrictive adverbs

Additive adverbs show that one item is being added to another. For example:

1 *Oh, my dad was a great guy, **too**.* (CONV)
2 *The experiment **also** illustrates how thoroughgoing one has to be in applying quantum mechanics.* (ACAD)

Additive adverbs typically single out one particular part of the clause's meaning as being 'additional' to something else. However, context is often essential to determine the intended comparison. For example, 1 can mean either that my dad was a great guy in addition to having other qualities, or that someone else was also a great guy.

Restrictive adverbs such as *only* are similar to additive adverbs because they focus attention on a certain element of the clause. They serve to emphasize the importance of one part of the proposition, restricting the truth of the proposition either primarily or exclusively to that part:

> *The idea of anybody, Marge **especially**, liking that wall-eyed ox in preference to Dickie made Tom smile.* (FICT)

> ***Only** those who can afford the monthly payment of $1,210.05, plus $91.66 a month during probation, can be ordered to pay.* (NEWS)

See 11.6.6 for a fuller discussion of additive and restrictive adverbials.

7.11.6 Stance adverbs

Adverbs can be used to express three types of **stance**: epistemic, attitude, and style. These are briefly exemplified here, leaving a more detailed discussion to 11.13–16.

A Epistemic stance adverbs

These express a variety of meanings:

- showing levels of certainty or doubt:

    *No it's alright I'll **probably** manage with it.* (CONV)

- commenting on the reality or actuality of a proposition:

    ***Actually** I'm not very fussy at all.* (CONV)

- showing that a proposition is based on some evidence, without specifying the exact source:

    *The supernumerary instar is **reportedly** dependent on the density of the parental population.* (ACAD)

- showing the limitations on a proposition:

    ***Typically**, the front top six teeth will decay because of the way the child has sucked on its bottle.* (NEWS)

- conveying imprecision—these adverbs are also called **hedges**:

    *It was **kind of** strange.* (CONV)

    *I ain't seen this series – I just **sort of** remember from the last series.* (CONV)
    <note: *ain't* is a non-standard form; see 8.8.5>

Many hedges occur as adverbials. However, hedges are also common as modifiers of phrases and words. In conversation, hedges are often used to show imprecision of word choice. In the following example *a little flaming fire thing* is marked as imprecise by the use of *like* as a hedge:

    *They'd bring **like** <u>a little flaming fire thing</u>.* (CONV†)

Hedges are also common with numbers, measurements, and quantities. These hedges are also called **approximators**:

    *They were suing Kurt for **like** <u>seventy thousand</u> dollars.* (CONV)

    ***About** <u>15</u> families attended the first meeting.* (NEWS†)

    *Prices were lower across the board, with **nearly** <u>all</u> blue-chip stocks losing ground.* (NEWS)

B Attitude stance adverbs

These adverbs express a speaker's or writer's emotional attitude toward a proposition:

    *I lost the manual that goes with it, **unfortunately**.* (CONV)

    ***Surprisingly**, the dividend rates of some pretty solid companies equal and sometimes exceed rates available from bonds and certificates of deposit.* (NEWS)

C Style stance adverbs

These adverbs tell something about a speaker's manner of speaking. For example, is the speaker using language sincerely, frankly, honestly, simply, or technically?

> *Crackers she is, that woman!* **Honestly!** *She's crackers!* (CONV)

> **Frankly,** *Dee Dee suspects that in this instance she may also be a victim of lookism, i.e., discrimination against persons who do not measure up to an arbitrary, unrealistic and sexist standard of beauty.* (NEWS†)

> **Quite simply,** *life cannot be the same.* (NEWS†)

7.11.7 Linking adverbs

Linking adverbs make connections between sections of discourse. They show how the meaning of one section of text is related to another. For example:

> *They need to propel themselves upwards and it is that moment of suspension coming between their force upwards and the force of gravity downwards that is so important.* **Thus** *it is possible to fly onto and off apparatus as separate tasks.* (ACAD†)

> *And the month before he left, he had made several long distance phone calls to Arizona and Ohio. Police,* **however,** *would not say where they were concentrating their search.* (NEWS)

Linking adverbs serve as adverbials and are covered in detail in 11.17–19.

7.11.8 Other meanings

In addition to the categories specified above, adverbs occasionally realize other meanings. For example, consider the following:

1 *The technical achievement of opening a vessel measured* **angiographically** *was similarly successful for both groups of patients.* (ACAD)

2 *When there is a funeral, the body is washed* **symbolically** *as part of the service.* (NEWS)

In **1**, *angiographically* might be considered a manner adverb, but more specifically it specifies the method or **means** used to measure the vessel. In **2**, the adverb makes clear that the body washing is symbolic in intent, and it could therefore be considered an adverb of **purpose**. The semantic categories of means and purpose are more commonly realized by structures other than adverbs (see 11.6.3–4).

Another adverb which does not fit into any of the above categories is the courtesy adverb *kindly*. It functions similarly to the insert *please* to mark a request as polite. It is used most commonly in fiction, often with an ironic (i.e. impolite) meaning:

> *In any case,* **kindly** *ask the authorities to call off their search.* (FICT)

> **Kindly** *attend to what I say and not to what Mr Shelly says, sir.* (FICT)

7.11.9 Semantic domains of adverbs in conversation and academic prose

In conversation, most of the common adverbs fall into three semantic domains: time, degree, and stance. In contrast, many common adverbs in academic prose are from the semantic domains of degree and linking (see Table 7.3). These distributions are similar to the distribution of adverbials, discussed in 11.6.9. Four common adverbs in conversation refer to time and place: *here, there, then,* and *now.* These adverbs are **deictics**—i.e. they make reference to the time and place of speaking (e.g. *now* refers to the actual time of speaking). Because speakers are physically together in conversation, it is easy to use these deictics (depending on shared context; see 13.2.1).

It is also typical of conversation to use vague or general language. This can be seen in the use of the conversational adverb *else,* which modifies general pronouns like *something* and *someone:*

> If we run out of toilet rolls right, <u>someone</u> **else** can buy them cause I bought the last two lots. (CONV)

> I thought I had <u>something</u> **else** to show you up there. (CONV)

Stance adverbs are also often imprecise in conversation:

> Angie's one is really **like** <u>hot</u> and will dry things. (CONV)

> You can still find that in Mexico in **sort of** <u>hacienda-like</u> places and ranchos. (CONV)

Table 7.3 **Common adverbs in conversation and academic prose (at least 200 occurrences per million words, including both modifier and adverbial functions in AmE, BrE, or both)**

	CONV	ACAD
place	here, there, away	here
time	now, then, again, always, still, today, never, ago, ever, just, yesterday, yet (BrE), already (AmE), sometimes (AmE), later (AmE)	now, then, again, always, still, already, sometimes, often, usually
manner	together (AmE)	significantly, well
degree	very, really, too, quite (BrE), exactly (AmE), right (AmE, applied to time and place adverbials), pretty (AmE), real (AmE)	very, quite, more, relatively
additive/restrictive	just, only, even, too, else, also (AmE)	just, only, even, too, also, especially, particularly
stance	of course, probably, really, like, actually, maybe, sort of, perhaps (BrE), kind of (AmE)	of course, probably, perhaps, generally, indeed
linking	then, so, anyway, though	then, so, however, e.g., i.e., therefore, thus

> And at that stage my plaster that I'd had on after the er op had only been off **perhaps** *a fortnight.* (CONV) <note: *op* = operation>

The higher number of linking adverbs in academic prose reflects the greater importance of logical arguments and overtly marking the connections between ideas.

Review

Major points in Grammar Bite C: Adverbs: roles and meanings

➤ Adverbs have many syntactic roles: modifier of adjective, modifier of other adverb, modifier of other elements such as pronouns and prepositional phrases, complement of preposition, adverbials (element of a clause), and stand-alone adverb.

➤ Adverbs belong to seven major meaning categories: place, time, manner, degree, additive/restrictive, stance, linking.

➤ The meaning of an adverb often varies with its context of use, and sometimes meanings are blended together.

➤ The frequency and use of common adverbs differs greatly between conversation and academic prose.

GRAMMAR BITE

D Comparative and superlative forms

12 Comparative and superlative forms of adjectives

Gradable adjectives can be marked to show comparative and superlative degree. These degrees can be marked either inflectionally (using a single word) or phrasally (using a construction of more than one word):

type of marking	comparative degree	superlative degree
inflectional	*stronger, softer*	*strongest, softest*
phrasal	*more difficult, more famous*	*most difficult, most famous*

Short adjectives (one syllable) generally take an inflectional suffix, such as *strong* and *soft* above. Notice that the addition of *-er* or *-est* can involve regular spelling changes to the adjective stem. Silent *-e* is omitted before adding the suffix (e.g. *safe, safer, safest*, not *safeer, *safeest*) and final *-y* is changed to *-i* if a consonant precedes it (e.g. *tidy, tidier, tidiest*). An adjective ending with a single vowel letter followed by a single consonant usually doubles the final consonant: (e.g. *wet, wetter, wettest*, not *weter, *wetest*). Three other adjectives—*good, bad,* and *far*—have irregular comparative and superlative forms:

> *good, better, best*   *bad, worse, worst*   *far, further, furthest*

Longer adjectives often take phrasal comparison, using the degree adverbs *more* and *most*. *Difficult* and *famous* above are typical examples.

However, there is variation within these general patterns. Some two-syllable adjectives allow both types of comparison: e.g. *likelier* v. *more likely*; *narrowest* v. *most narrow*. Some short adjectives take phrasal as well as inflectional marking. For example, *fairer*, *fiercer*, and *prouder* are possible, but their phrasal alternatives also occur:

> 'Wouldn't that be **more fair**?' she asked. (FICT)
>
> Our women were **more fierce** than our men. (NEWS)
>
> 'I think this is the one she is **most proud** of.' (NEWS)

A possible reason for choosing the phrasal alternative is that it makes the comparison more prominent. In speech, the comparison can be emphasized further by stressing the word *more* or *most*.

Other general trends for the formation of comparatives and superlatives are summarized in Table 7.4.

Table 7.4 **General trends for the formation of comparative and superlative adjectives**

characteristic of adjective	form of comparative / superlative	examples
gradable adjectives of one syllable	almost always inflectional	*older, youngest*
two syllables ending in unstressed -*y*	generally inflectional	*easier, easiest, happier, happiest*
three syllables ending in -*y*	usually phrasal, sometimes inflectional	phrasal: *more unhappy*; inflectional: *almightier, almightiest*; *unhappier, unhappiest*
adjectives ending in -*ly*	varies with the adjective, some inflectional, some phrasal; many use both forms	inflectional: *earlier, earliest, likelier, likeliest*; phrasal: *more likely, most likely*
two syllables ending in unstressed vowel	usually inflectional	*mellower, narrowest, yellowest*
ending in syllabic /r/ in AmE or /ə/ in BrE or syllabic /l/	often inflectional	*cleverer, slenderest, tenderest, cruelest, feeblest, littler, nobler, simpler*
ending in -*ere* and -*ure* (stressed)	sometimes inflectional, usually phrasal	*most sincere, sincerest, most secure, securest*
gradable adjectives of two syllables with no internal morphology	usually phrasal	*more common, most common*
other adjectives longer than two syllables	almost always phrasal	*more beautiful, most incredible*
adjectives ending in derivational suffixes	almost always phrasal	*most useful, most mindless, more musical, more effective, more zealous*
adjectives formed with -*ed* and -*ing* (participial adjectives)	almost always phrasal	*more bored, most tiring*

🔍 7.12.1 The use of phrasal and inflectional markings

A Inflectional marking

Inflectionally marked comparatives and superlatives are most common in academic prose, and least common in conversation. Comparative degree is used twice as frequently as superlative.

Some common inflected comparative adjectives are:

CONV: *best, bigger, cheaper, easier, older*

FICT: *best, lower, older, younger*

NEWS: *best, better, biggest, greater, higher, highest, largest, latest, lower*

ACAD: *best, better, earlier, easier, greater, greatest, higher, highest, larger, largest, lower, older, smaller, wider*

It is striking that most of the common inflected adjectives have either an evaluative meaning (*greater, best*) or a descriptive meaning that often also implies an evaluation (e.g. *cheaper, older*).

B Phrasal comparison

In general, phrasal marking is less common than inflectional marking. Academic writing has the most occurrences of phrasal marking for comparative and superlative degree. Conversation has few occurrences.

Some common phrasally marked comparative and superlative adjectives are:

NEWS: *most important, more likely*

ACAD: *more important, most important, more likely, more difficult*

Academic prose uses more technical vocabulary, which includes longer adjectives. Because long adjectives tend to take phrasal rather than inflectional comparison, we find more phrasal marking overall in academic prose.

7.12.2 Comparatives and superlatives that are marked twice

Sometimes in conversation, adjectives are doubly marked for degree; that is, they have both inflectional and phrasal markers:

*This way, it's **more easier** to see.* (CONV)

*It's much **more warmer** in there.* (CONV)

In addition, irregular comparatives and superlatives are sometimes given the regular *-er* or *-est* ending, making *bestest* or *worser*:

*This is the **bestest** one you can read.* (CONV)

Doubly marked forms are sometimes used jokingly. In standard English they are considered unacceptable.

7.12.3 Adjectives with absolute meanings

Certain adjectives have absolute meanings: e.g. *dead, true, unique, perfect*. Degree marking seems redundant with these forms. Something is either dead or not dead, true or not—not more or less dead, or more or less true. As a result, prescriptive grammars sometimes state that these adjectives should not be made comparative or superlative, or be modified by degree adverbs such as *very*.

However, in conversation, degree marking with absolute adjectives is not unusual:

> *I'll just – trim the **very** <u>dead</u> ends off the side there.* (CONV)

> *That's **very** <u>true</u>.* (CONV)

Even in the expository registers, writers sometimes mark adjectives such as *unique* and *perfect* for comparative or superlative degree:

> *<...> the **most** <u>unique</u> transportation and distribution system for time sensitive inquiries.* (NEWS†)

> *The slates have **more** <u>perfect</u> planar partings.* (ACAD)

7.13 Comparative and superlative forms of adverbs

Like adjectives, gradable adverbs can be marked as comparative or superlative with an inflection or the use of *more* or *most* (for example, *fast, faster, fastest; frequently, more frequently, most frequently*). Inflected comparative and superlative forms are not used as often as they are with adjectives. In fact, superlative forms of adverbs are very rare, while comparative forms are only occasionally used. Examples include:

> 1 *I just kept working **harder** and **harder**.* (NEWS†)
> 2 *He went to the altar every first Friday, sometimes with her, **oftener** by himself.* (FICT)

In some cases, an adverb can be made comparative either with the use of *more* or with the *-er* inflection. For example, 2 above illustrates the use of *oftener* where *more often* could also be used. This choice appears to be related to register and author style. *Oftener* occurs primarily in fiction, and is used by only a small number of writers. In contrast, the usual choice is *more often*:

> *I love live theatre, of course, I really ought to go **more often**.* (CONV)

7.14 Comparative clauses and other degree complements

Gradable adjectives and adverbs can take clauses or phrases of degree as their complements. In these constructions, the strength of the adjective or adverb is compared against some standard or along some scale. For example:

> *Truna's only [a tiny bit **taller** **than me**].* (CONV)

Here the scale of tallness is relative to *me*. The adjective *taller* has the complement *than me*—a prepositional phrase.

7.14.1 Complements of adjectives

Comparative and degree complements of adjectives can be prepositional phrases or clauses. There are six major types of degree complements for adjectives. Two can be phrases or clauses; the final four can only be clauses. Only the first type can occur with an inflected comparative adjective (e.g. *taller*). In the following examples, the degree complement (such as a comparative clause) is enclosed in *[]*.

- **Type 1:** adjective-*er* + *than* + phrase/clause OR *more/less* + adjective + *than* + phrase/clause:

    Carrie was sure he must guess something was up but he seemed less **suspicious** *[than usual], perhaps because he was happier.* (FICT) <phrase>

    I did not want to go there if they were **poorer** *[than we were].* (FICT) <clause>

This is the most common type of comparative construction. It is particularly common in academic prose, where it is useful to help explain the nature of something by comparing or contrasting it with other things:

    But a small sample for comparison is **better** *[than nothing at all].* (ACAD)

    Distances were in fact reported as being **shorter** *[than they were in reality].* (ACAD)

- **Type 2:** *as* + adjective + *as* + phrase/clause:

    The last tinkle of the last shard died away and silence closed in **as deep** *[as ever before].* (FICT) <phrase>

    It's a good place – I mean, **as good** *[as you can get].* (CONV) <clause>

- **Type 3:** *so* + adjective + *that*-clause

    The murder investigation was **so contrived** *[that it created false testimony].* (NEWS†)

- **Type 4:** *so* + adjective + *as* + *to*-clause

    And if anybody was **so foolhardy as** *[to pass by the shrine after dusk] he was sure to see the old woman hopping about.* (FICT)

- **Type 5:** *too* + adjective + *to*-clause

    For larger systems the bundles of energy were **too numerous** *[to be countable].* (ACAD)

- **Type 6:** adjective + *enough* + *to*-clause

    1 *The stairs wouldn't be* **strong enough** *[to hold the weight].* (CONV)

Often the degree complement can be omitted. The listener or reader must then infer the comparison. For example, **1** could be reduced to:

    The stairs wouldn't be **strong enough***.*

7.14.2 Complements of adverbs

The clauses and phrases which occur as degree complements with adjectives can also occur with adverbs. The adverb phrase functions as an adverbial in all of the examples below.

- **Type 1:** adverb-*er* + *than*-phrase/clause OR *more/less* + adverb + *than*-phrase/clause

He rode it **oftener** [than ever]. (FICT†) <phrase>

Generally speaking, those higher in occupational status suffered **less acutely** [than those lower down]. (ACAD) <phrase>

We expected this to happen **much quicker** [than it did]. (NEWS) <clause>

It could happen **more quickly** [than anyone expects]. (NEWS) <clause>

- **Type 2:** as + adverb + as-phrase/clause

  The normal scan must be resumed **as quickly** [as possible]. (ACAD) <phrase>

  I didn't do **as well** [as I wish that I had]. (CONV) <clause>

- **Type 3:** so + adverb + that-clause

  Albert had spoken **so calmly** [that it made her calm too]. (FICT)

- **Type 4:** so + adverb + as to-clause (this structure occurs most commonly with the adverb far):

  He went **so far as** [to write home some vague information of his feelings about business and its prospects]. (FICT)

- **Type 5:** too + adverb + to-clause

  The situation has deteriorated **too far** [to repair]. (NEWS)

- **Type 6:** adverb + enough + to-clause

  At least four people were bitten **seriously enough** [to be hospitalized]. (NEWS)

As we saw for adjectives, the degree adverb in these constructions can usually occur without the following degree complement.

You shouldn't go to bed **too early**! (CONV)

This can be considered a type of **ellipsis** (see 8.5).

Review | Major points in Grammar Bite D: Comparative and superlative forms

➤ For gradable adjectives, comparative and superlative forms can be expressed with inflections (-er, -est) or as a phrase (with more and most).

　➤ Length, spelling, emphasis, and other factors contribute to the choice between inflection and phrase.

　➤ Comparative forms are more common than superlative.

　➤ The use of both comparatives and superlatives is more common in academic prose than conversation.

　➤ Inflectional comparison is more common than phrasal.

➤ Adjectives which are not strictly gradable (e.g. unique) are nevertheless sometimes marked for comparative or superlative degree.

➤ Adverbs can also have either inflectional comparison (-er, -est) or phrasal comparison (more, most).

➤ Adjectives and adverbs can take six different complement structures that show comparison.

8

Exploring the grammar of the clause

GRAMMAR BITES in this chapter

A Subordination, coordination, and ellipsis

- ➤ How to condense and elaborate meaning in grammar
- ➤ Subordination and dependent clauses: making grammar 'deeper'
- ➤ Coordination: making grammar 'broader'
- ➤ Ellipsis and condensation of structure: making grammar 'quicker and simpler'

B Subject–verb concord

- ➤ Concord: matching subjects and verbs in clauses
- ➤ Special cases of concord, such as collective nouns
- ➤ Notional concord v. grammatical concord
- ➤ The principle of proximity

C Negation

- ➤ Clause negation and local negation
- ➤ Negative contractions and verb contractions
- ➤ Choosing between *not*-negation and *no*-negation
- ➤ The scope of negation
- ➤ Assertive and non-assertive forms

D Independent clauses

- ➤ Declarative clauses: statements
- ➤ Interrogative clauses: questions
- ➤ Imperative clauses: directives
- ➤ Exclamative clauses and non-clausal material

E Dependent clauses

- ➤ Finite v. non-finite dependent clauses
- ➤ Finite clauses: complement, adverbial, relative, and other types
- ➤ Non-finite clauses: infinitive, *-ing*, *-ed*, and other types
- ➤ Dependent clauses without a main clause

8.1 Introduction

The **clause** is in many ways the key unit of grammar. Chapter 3 (3.4–5) surveyed simple clauses, seen as units structured around a verb phrase. In the simplest case, the chief elements of the clause—subject, verb phrase, object, predicative, and adverbial—are made up of phrases, which have been explored in some detail in Chapters 3–7.

However, we now turn to subordination: the type of syntactic structure where one clause is embedded as part of another. For example, clause elements like object or adverbial can be realized as other dependent clauses. We also need to describe how clauses can be combined by coordination, and the way simplified or condensed structures can be formed through ellipsis. The way in which clauses can be combined to make more complex structures is fundamental to grammar. The present chapter introduces the key concepts and terms. We explore the grammar of these structures in more detail in Chapters 9–13.

8.1.1 Clauses v. non-clausal material

Clauses are used very differently in different varieties of English. As a starting point, let's examine the distribution of clauses in discourse, using two text samples (the verb phrases are given in bold, and clauses are enclosed in *[]*):

Text sample 1: CONVERSATION IN A BARBER'S SHOP (*B* = barber, *C* = customer)

> B: *[I **will put**,] [I **won't smile**.] – [**Tell** me [what **would** you **like** now?]]*
> C: *Erm – [**shortened up** please Pete] – erm – [**shaved** a little at the back and sides]–[and then just sort of **brushed back** on the top a bit.]*
> B: *Right, and [when you **say** [**shaved** a little bit]]*
> C: *Yeah yo– – [you sort of just – **got** your thing] and zazoom!*
> B: *Yeah [but – **is** it that short really?]*
> C: *Yeah to–, yeah and I*
> B: *<unclear> [you **want** a number four?]*
> C: *Yeah [I **think** so]*
> . . .
> <later in the same conversation>
> B: *So yeah, [I **was** well pleased] [cos you **remember** [the time before I **said** [I **wasn't** perfect.]]]*
> C: *<unclear>*
> B: *[That's right] yeah – yeah – [[I **mean**] I'm **being** honest.]*
> C: *Yeah – mm.*
> . . .
> B: *[I **was**] – [I **thought** [it **looked** good]] – [and I **thought**,] [I **was** quite confident [that it **would stay** in very well,] [you **know**?]] –*
> C: *Mm.* (CONV)

Text sample 2: A COMPLETE NEWS STORY FROM THE *INDEPENDENT* NEWSPAPER

> *[People [who **eat** a clove or more of garlic a day] **are** less likely [to **suffer** a heart attack, high blood pressure or thrombosis,] [doctors **said** yesterday,] [**writes** Liz Hunt.]] [New clinical trials **show** [that [**including** garlic in the diet] **can** significantly **reduce** cholesterol in the blood], according to Dr Jorg*

*Grunwald, a research biologist from Berlin.] [High cholesterol levels **are associated** with atherosclerosis, or 'furring' of the arteries with fatty deposits, [which **can lead** to a heart attack.]] [Garlic **could** also [**reduce** high blood pressure] and [**prevent** blood cells sticking together,] risk factors for a heart attack, [Dr Grunwald, head of the medical and scientific department of Lichtwer Pharma, a German company that manufactures garlic pills, **said.**]] [The active ingredient in garlic **is thought** [to **be** the compound alliin.]]* (NEWS)

The differences between these two samples are striking:

The conversation text	In the newspaper text
includes non-clausal material (e.g. *right, yeah*)	all words and phrases belong to clauses
includes many single-clause units	there are no single-clause units
includes little clause embedding	the clauses contain many words

GRAMMAR BITE

A Subordination, coordination, and ellipsis

8.2 Devices of elaboration and condensation

This Grammar Bite introduces **coordination, subordination,** and **ellipsis,** three aspects of grammar which are closely interrelated, and which enable us to elaborate, combine, and reduce the structure of clauses. With coordination, two clauses are connected, with each having equal status, as in:

*It's modern **but** it's clean.* (CONV)

With subordination, on the other hand, one clause is embedded as part of another clause, as in:

***Although** it's modern, it's clean.*

Finally, ellipsis is a device of simplification: it allows us to subtract words from the complete clause structure, wherever their meaning can be 'taken for granted' (∧ marks the ellipsis):

*It's clean **although** ∧ modern.*

*It's modern **but** ∧ clean.*

8.3 Subordination and dependent clauses

We can see more exactly how subordination of clauses differs from coordination of clauses by looking at Figures 8.1 and 8.2. In the case of subordination, one clause (a dependent clause) is embedded as part of another clause (its main clause). In Figure 8.2, the dependent clause functions as an adverbial in the main clause. As shown by the repeated use of brackets in Text sample 2 (8.1.1), there can be further degrees of embedding: one dependent clause can be subordinate to another dependent clause. The following example, simplified and extracted from Text sample 2, further illustrates this:

> [New clinical trials show [that [including garlic in the diet] can reduce cholesterol.] (NEWS†)

Figure 8.1 Coordinated clauses

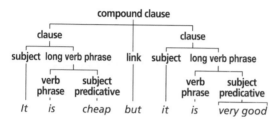

Figure 8.2 Main clause with embedded adverbial clause

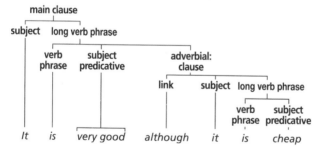

Figure 8.3 shows this complex clause as a tree diagram. In this diagram, three clauses are marked as clause$_1$, clause$_2$, and clause$_3$: clause$_2$ functions as the object of *show*, and so it is subordinate to clause$_1$; clause$_3$ functions as the subject of *can reduce*, and so it is subordinate to clause$_2$.

When we classify clauses, we draw a major distinction between **independent clauses** (those which can stand alone without being subordinate to another clause) and **dependent clauses** (those which have to be part of a larger clause). Hence clause$_1$ in Figure 8.3 is an independent clause, while clause$_2$ and clause$_3$ are dependent clauses.

e 8.3   Main clause with two degrees of embedding

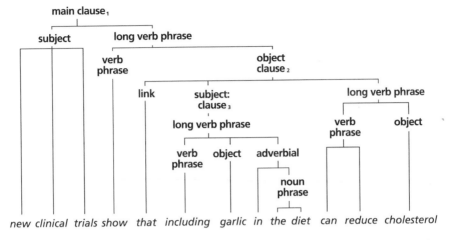

new clinical trials show that including garlic in the diet can reduce cholesterol

8.3.1 Subordinators as clause links

Subordinators differ in important ways from other clause links. Subordinators are like **coordinators**, but are different from **linking adverbials**, because they occur in a fixed position at the front of their clause. But, unlike coordinators, the clause introduced by a subordinator is always a dependent clause, and it does not necessarily follow the clause to which it is linked:

> He was screaming **because** he had to go home. (CONV)

Examples 1 and 1a illustrate how it is often possible to move a dependent clause to a different position; but 2 and 2a show this is not possible for coordinate clauses:

1   *I'm still just as afraid of her, **although** she's no longer my teacher.* (FICT)
1a   ***Although** she's no longer my teacher, I'm still just as afraid of her.*
    <equivalent to 1>

2   *She's no longer my teacher, **but** I'm still just as afraid of her.*
2a   ***But** I'm still just as afraid of her, she's no longer my teacher.*
    <not equivalent to 2>

Wh-words are like subordinators in normally being fixed at the beginning of a dependent clause. However, unlike subordinators, *wh*-words usually fill a major syntactic role (e.g. subject, object or adverbial) in the dependent clause (see 2.5.1).

8.3.2 Signals of subordination

Subordination can be signalled by:
- an overt link, in the form of a subordinator or *wh*-word
- a non-finite verb phrase, that is, by a verb phrase introduced by an infinitive, *-ing* participle or *-ed* participle.

Finite clauses are marked for tense or modality. Finite dependent clauses usually have an overt link, starting with a subordinator or a *wh*-word:

You can drink your orange [if you like]. (CONV)

Non-finite clauses have no tense and they cannot include a modal verb. Non-finite dependent clauses usually have no overt link, but the non-finite verb form itself signals that the clause is subordinate:

*[**Leaving** the road], they went into the deep darkness of the trees.* (FICT†)

Most non-finite clauses have no subject, and so the verb phrase typically begins the clause. Hence, in most cases, the listener has no problem in recognizing when the speaker is beginning a dependent clause. (For more on finite and non-finite dependent clauses, see Grammar Bite E in this chapter.)

8.3.3 Clause patterns revisited

To see in more detail how dependent clauses are embedded in main clauses, we return to the clause patterns and elements previewed in 3.4–5. At that point we introduced basic clause structures with the elements S (subject), O (object), P (predicative), and A (adverbial) realized by phrases. But now we describe how S, O, P and A can themselves be clauses. Table 8.1 identifies by # the major ways in which finite and non-finite clauses can be elements of a main clause.

Table 8.1 **Typical realizations of the clause elements S, O, P, A**

clause element	noun phrase	verb phrase	adj. phrase	adv. phrase	prep. phrase	finite clause	inf. clause	*ing-* clause	*ed-* clause
subject (S)	●					#	#	#	
verb phrase (V)		●							
subject predicative (SP)	●		●		●	#	#	#	
direct object (DO)	●					#	#	#	#
indirect object (IO)	●					#			
prep. object	●					#		#	
object predicative (OP)	●		●			#	#	#	
adverbial (A)	●			●	●	#	#	#	#

Key: adj. = adjective; adv. = adverb; prep. = prepositional; inf. = infinitive.

These dependent clause patterns are illustrated below:

- subject:

    finite clause: *That it would be unpopular with students or colleges was obvious.* (NEWS)

    infinitive clause: *To meet the lady was easy enough.* (FICT†)

    ing-clause: *Including garlic in the diet can significantly reduce cholesterol.* (NEWS†)

- subject predicative:

    finite clause: *That's what I'll do tomorrow.* (CONV)

    infinitive clause: *Their function is to detect the cries of predatory bats.* (ACAD)

- direct object:

finite clause: *She hoped **that Joe wouldn't come in drunk**.* (FICT†)

ing-clause: *Stephanie disliked **living in this unfinished mess**.* (FICT†)

infinitive clause: *'I wouldn't like **to leave him**,' Olivia said.* (FICT)

- prepositional object:

  finite clause: *Well you pay for **what you want**.* (CONV)

  ing-clause: *Please forgive me for **doubting you**.* (FICT)

- object predicative:

  infinitive clause: *No one can expect us **to sign our own death sentence**.* (NEWS†)

  ing-clause: *She watched her son George **scything the grass**.* (FICT)

  ed-clause: *I should have got my boots **mended**.* (FICT†)

- adverbial:

  finite clause: *I'm tense; excuse me **if I talk too much**.* (FICT)

  infinitive clause: *I borrowed a portable phone **to ring Waterloo**.* (NEWS)

  ing-clause: *She gazed down at the floor, **biting her lip**.* (FICT†)

  ed-clause: *I went on waiting, **tinged with doubt**.* (FICT)

8.4 Coordination

Unlike subordination, coordination can link words, phrases, or clauses:

*'No black worth [his] **or** [her] salt would touch such a [black] **and** [white] merry-go-round.* (NEWS†) <coordination linking words>

*'[A fool] **and** [his money] are soon parted,' he says.* (FICT) <coordination linking phrases>

*[He had even called her parents] **and** [they didn't know where she was], **nor** [did her friends when he called them].* (FICT) <coordination linking clauses>

In addition, the coordinators *and, or, but,* and *nor* can function as utterance- or turn-initial links in speech (see 8.4.2 below). In this case, coordinators are very close in function to linking adverbials like *however*.

A: ***And** you won't have that problem.*

B: ***But** that's a, that's a, that's a different thing.* (CONV) <turn-initial coordination>

In what follows, we survey some aspects of the use of coordinators, drawing a broad distinction between phrase-level coordination (including coordination of words) and clause-level coordination.

8.4.1 Use of coordination

There are three major coordinators in English: *and, or,* and *but*. As Figure 8.4 shows, these coordinators are not equally common: *and* is much more common than *or* or *but*. Further, although it is often supposed that *and* is especially common in conversation, Figure 8.4 shows that *and* is actually most common in academic and fiction writing.

The other major coordinators—*but* and *or*—follow very different patterns: *but* occurs most often in conversation, whereas *or* occurs most often in academic writing. There is a fourth coordinator—*nor*—which occurs much less frequently, so that it does not show up in Figure 8.4.

The registers also differ in the ways they use coordinators. Figure 8.5 shows that speakers in conversation are most likely to use *and* as a clause-level link, while in academic writing *and* is most likely to occur as a phrase-level link. Conversation often follows a simple mode of grammatical construction in simply adding one clause to another—what we later call the 'add-on' strategy (13.3.2). Hence coordinators in conversation are primarily clause-level links.

But is more frequent in conversation than the written registers, because people tend to highlight contrast and contradiction in dialog. Note the following typical use of *but* at or near the beginning of a speaker's turn:

1 A: *The golden rule is if you're reversing you must look behind you!*
   B: *Yeah,* **but** *she said she did.*
   (CONV)

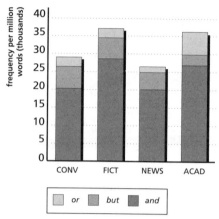

Figure 8.4

Distribution of coordinators across registers

(bar chart: frequency per million words (thousands), y-axis 0 to 40; categories CONV, FICT, NEWS, ACAD; legend: or, but, and)

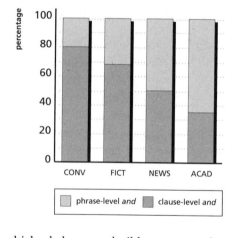

Figure 8.5

Percentage use of *and* as phrase-level v. clause-level connector

(bar chart: percentage, y-axis 0 to 100; categories CONV, FICT, NEWS, ACAD; legend: phrase-level and, clause-level and)

Academic writing contrasts very strongly with conversation in favoring phrase-level coordination, which helps to build up complex embedded structures:

2 *A distinction is needed between {₁ [elements, which include {₂ [nitrogen], [phosphorus]* **and** *[potassium]₂}], which are mobile in the phloem]* **and** *[those which are comparatively immobile, for example, {₃ [calcium], [boron]* **and** *[iron]₃}]₁} <...> An example of the {₄ [uptake]* **and** *[transfer]₄} of {₅ [nitrogen]* **and** *[phosphorus]₅} during the period of grain filling of winter wheat is given in Table 2.5.* (ACAD†)

All the instances of *and* in **2** illustrate phrase-level coordination. Example **2** also illustrates two further aspects of coordination: (a) that the coordinator can link more than two elements, as in *nitrogen, phosphorus* **and** *potassium*; and (b) that structures of coordination can be embedded, one within the other (as shown by the brackets-within-brackets in the text). Curly brackets { } are used to show whole coordinate constructions.

8.4.2 Some special uses of coordinators

Sentence-initial and turn-initial coordinators

There is a well-known prescription prohibiting the use of coordinators at the beginning of a sentence. Nevertheless, coordination often occurs in this position. Sentence-initial or turn-initial coordination is most common at the beginning of a turn in conversation:

> A: *They started late last year.*
> B: **And** *what are your academic classes you're taking next semester, you're taking the art history class?* (CONV)

However, it is also relatively common in writing.

The coordinators show different preferences for initial position: *but* and *nor*, as 'stronger' linkers, are much more likely to take this prominent position than *and* or *or*.

B **Coordination tags**

Like sentence/turn-initial coordinators, coordination tags are frowned upon in writing but popular in conversation. The most common coordination tags are the phrases *or something, and everything, and things/stuff (like that)*:

> 1 *She uses a food processor **or something**.* (CONV)
> 2 *He has a lot of contacts **and things**.* (CONV†)
> 3 *They're all sitting down **and stuff**.* (CONV)

Coordination tags are a kind of vagueness marker or **hedge**: they are a grammatical way of waving one's hand, and saying '... of course I could add more'. The coordinator *and* or *or* is followed by a general noun or pronoun. But this does not mean that the coordination is always at the word or phrase level. On the contrary, in **3** above, the coordination tag is added on to a whole clause.

In contrast to the expressions above, the tags *or so, and so on*, and *etc. (et cetera,* a Latin expression meaning 'and other things') are mainly associated with expository writing:

> *I waited for a day **or so**.* (NEWS†)
>
> *The Libertas catalogue menu offered a choice of six search modes (author and title, title, subject, **etc.**).* (ACAD)

C **Correlative coordinators**

The correlative coordinators *both ... and, either ... or, neither ... nor* were introduced in 2.4.6. They are also strongly associated with the written registers, probably because they add greater clarity and precision:

> *Symptoms may appear first in **either** younger **or** older leaves.* (ACAD)

8.5 Ellipsis and structural condensation

Ellipsis is the omission of elements which are recoverable from the linguistic context or the situation. In the following examples, the ellipted elements are re-inserted in < >:

1 *He squeezed her hand but <he> met with no response.* (FICT)
2 *He and his mate both jumped out, he <jumped out> to go to the women, his mate <jumped out> to stop other traffic on the bridge.* (FICT)
3 *Perhaps, as the review gathers steam, this can now change. It needs to <change>.* (NEWS)

Notice that the words within < >, which were not part of the original text, can be added without changing the meaning of the clause and without producing an ungrammatical structure. These are the hallmarks of ellipsis: it **condenses** (or reduces) the same meaning into a smaller number of words.

8.5.1 Types of ellipsis: initial, medial, final; textual, situational

The words omitted by ellipsis can be at the front, middle, or end of a clause. In the examples above, **1** shows initial ellipsis (omitting the subject of the second clause), **2** illustrates medial ellipsis, and **3** illustrates final ellipsis.

Another distinction is between textual ellipsis and situational ellipsis. In textual ellipsis, the missing words can be found in the nearby text. Typically, the missing words occur in the preceding text, as in **1–3** above. Thus, textual ellipsis is a means of avoiding unnecessary repetition.

In situational ellipsis, on the other hand, the missing words are clear from the situation in which language is used (^ = ellipsis)

4 ^ *Saw Susan and her boyfriend in Alder weeks ago.* (CONV)

Here the subject *I* is omitted, but it can easily be supplied from the context. Situational ellipsis usually takes the form of omitting initial function words in a clause, such as a pronoun subject, an auxiliary verb, or the initial article of a noun phrase. It is a common feature of conversation, but it also often occurs in fiction texts imitating the elliptical habits of speech:

5 *Gillespie made his examination. '^ Middle-aged man,' he said '^ anywhere between forty-five and sixty, more probably in the middle or late fifties. ^ Body seems to be in fair condition, ^ own hair, ^ not thinning. ah, yes – ^ depressed fracture of skull. He's been in the water for some time, ^ clothing ^ utterly soaked, ^ body ^ chilled.'* (FICT)

In most cases, we can easily find and fill in the gaps left by ellipsis, using grammatical and situational knowledge. (See also 8.14 on non-clausal material and block language, and 13.5 for more examples of ellipsis in conversation.)

8.5.2 Other structures with ellipsis

Ellipsis, like coordination, is a variable device which can occur in many grammatical structures. In the above paragraphs we have noted ellipsis occurring:

• in coordinate clauses

- in dependent clauses
- at the beginning of independent clauses.

Ellipsis also occurs in more specialized cases:

A Ellipsis in comparative clauses

Comparative clauses generally mirror the structure of a preceding clause. Repeated elements in the comparative clause are normally left out (or replaced by a **pro-form**). In the following examples, the ellipted elements are reinserted in < >:

> *She looks older than my mother* <does>. (CONV)
>
> *One result was that older people made greater head movements than younger people* <did>. (ACAD)

B Ellipsis in question–answer sequences

> A: *Have you got an extra exam on Monday?*
> B: <I've got> *Two exams* <on Monday>.
> A: *What exams* <have you got>?
> B: <I've got> *German, reading and French oral – French oral's a doddle.*
> A: *Is it* <a doddle>? (CONV) <note: *a doddle* = very easy>

In the quick give-and-take of conversation, speakers leave out what is easily recoverable from the linguistic context or the situation. This applies particularly to answers to questions. (On ellipsis in conversation, see further 13.5.)

C Ellipsis in noun phrases

Ellipsis is also common in noun phrases. We find ellipsis following independent genitives (**1** below), quantifiers (**2**), and semi-determiners (**3**):

> **1** *Under Reagan, everything bad that happened was either my fault or Nixon's <u>fault</u> or Congress's <u>fault</u> or some **foreigner's** ^.* (NEWS†)
>
> **2** *How's everyone's <u>champagne</u>? Tommy do you want some **more** ^?* (CONV)
>
> **3** *It gets you from one <u>place</u> to the **next** ^.* (CONV)

(Underlining shows the repeated words that have been omitted.)

8.5.3 Other forms of condensation

Pronouns and other pro-forms are similar to ellipsis in that they reduce the length and complexity of clauses. Pronouns substitute for full noun phrases that are retrievable from context, while other pro-forms, such as the substitute verb *do*, replace a whole predicate. The following examples illustrate how each of these methods can abbreviate what a person needs to say or write (the pro-form is in bold; the fuller expression is underlined):

- pronoun:

  > *We borrowed <u>the tennis racquets</u> when Bonnie and Steve were here. And we used **them** twice I think.* (CONV)

- other pro-forms:

  > A: *Who <u>took that picture</u>?*
  > B: *I **did**.* (CONV)

Another form of structural condensation occurs with non-finite clauses, which usually omit the subject and auxiliary verb. (This makes a difference to the usefulness of these clauses; see 11.10 on adverbial finite and non-finite clauses.) Compare:

> 1 *I don't know **what to write about**.* (CONV) <non-finite clause>
> 1a *I don't know **what I should write about**.* <finite clause>

Generally speaking, pronouns and pro-forms, like ellipsis, are much more common in conversation, whereas non-finite clauses are more common in the written registers.

Review

Major points of **GRAMMAR BITE A**: Subordination, coordination, and ellipsis

➤ Subordination and coordination are ways of 'deepening' and 'broadening' grammar.
➤ Subordinate clauses are embedded as part of another clause.
➤ Subordination is signaled by an overt link (such as a subordinator) or by a non-finite verb phrase.
➤ Coordinate clauses are joined, with each having equal status.
➤ Coordination can also be used to join phrases.
➤ Despite prescriptive rules, coordinators are commonly used at the beginning of a turn in conversation, and at the start of a new sentence in writing.
➤ Ellipsis is a way of simplifying grammatical structure through omission.
➤ Ellipsis is common in a wide range of contexts. A listener can usually reconstruct the missing words from the preceding text or from the situation.
➤ Pronouns and other pro-forms also reduce the length and complexity of clauses.

GRAMMAR BITE

B Subject–verb concord

8.6 The subject–verb concord rule

The rule of **subject–verb concord** is that in finite clauses, the verb phrase in a clause agrees with the subject in terms of number (singular or plural) and person (first, second or third person). Except for the verb *be*, subject–verb concord is limited to the present tense, and to the choice between the base form (e.g. *walk*) and the *s*-form (e.g. *walks*) of the finite verb. There is no subject–verb concord with modal auxiliaries, non-finite verbs, imperatives, or the subjunctive: these do not vary for number or person.

Although the rules for subject–verb concord are easy to state, in practice they are not always so easy to apply. Difficulties arise because 'singular' and 'plural' can be understood either in terms of form or in terms of meaning. We consider some special cases below.

8.6.1 Concord with plurals not ending in -s

Zero plurals, like *sheep*, do not change between singular and plural (see 4.8.4). These forms appear to break the concord rule, but in fact do not. (The subject noun phrase is marked by *[]* in examples.)

1a *[The sheep]* **is** *infected by ingesting the mollusc.* (ACAD†)

1b *In its grassy centre [the dark-wooled sheep]* **were** *grazing.* (FICT†)

The different forms of *be* used in **1a** and **1b** obey the concord rule: *sheep* in **1a** is singular, and in **1b** it is plural.

There are also some pronouns and semi-determiners which do not change between singular and plural, e.g. *which, who, the former, the latter*:

2a *He is beside* **a rock face** *[which]* **is** *like the loose side of a gigantic mule.* (FICT†)

2b *These are* **the moments** *[which]* **are** *calculable, and cannot be assessed in words.* (FICT†)

In these cases, the concord is shown by the antecedent nouns of the pro-form: e.g. singular *a rock face* in **2a** v. plural *the moments* in **2b**.

8.6.2 Concord with singular forms ending in -s

Some nouns ending in *-s* are singular (e.g. *billiards, checkers, measles,* etc.; see 4.8.5), and therefore take a singular verb. Nouns denoting fields of study (e.g. *mathematics, economics, politics*) are also singular, but they allow some variation between singular concord (in **1**) and plural concord (in **2**):

1 *[Politics]* **wishes** *to change reality, it* **requires** *power, and thus it* **is** *primarily in the service of power.* (NEWS)

2 *[The oppositionist politics] of the 1970s and early 1980s* **are** *over.* (NEWS)

In these cases the singular tends to be used where the meaning is 'field of study', and the plural where reference is to 'mode(s) of behavior'.

8.6.3 Concord with coordinated subjects

A Coordination by *and*

Subjects consisting of noun phrases coordinated by *and* take plural concord, since *and* gives these subjects plural reference:

1 *[The trees and the church]* **are** *reflected in the water.* (ACAD)

However, there are occasional exceptions to this rule. Where we find singular concord, the subject refers to something that can be viewed as a single entity:

2 *[The anxiety and anger]* **is** *then taken away and suddenly* **erupts** *in the family environment, placing stress on other members of the household.* (NEWS)

For example, in **2** *anxiety and anger* are merged into a single emotional state.

B Coordination by *or*

Subjects consisting of noun phrases coordinated by *or* generally take singular concord if both noun phrases are singular:

> *Check that [no food or drink]* **has** *been consumed.* (ACAD)

However, examples with plural concord also occur occasionally:

> *I'll wait until [my sister or mother]* **come** *down, and I'll eat with them.* (FICT)

Where one of the noun phrases linked by *or* is plural, plural concord is the rule:

> *Whether [interest rates or intervention]* **were** *the chosen instrument, and in what combination, was probably a secondary question.* (NEWS)

C Coordination by *neither ... nor*

Subjects consisting of phrases coordinated by *neither ... nor* have singular concord where both noun phrases are singular, and plural concord where both are plural:

> *[Neither geologic evidence nor physical theory]* **supports** *this conclusion.* (ACAD)

> *But [neither the pilots nor the machinists]* **appear** *interested.* (NEWS)

D Agreement of person

Coordination of different grammatical persons causes no problem with *and*, since a plural verb is used (in accordance with the general rule). Where *or* or *neither ... nor* link different grammatical persons, the verb tends to agree with the closest noun phrase:

> *Not one leaf is to go out of the garden until [either I or* **my chief taster**] **gives** *the order.* (FICT)

> *In many years of service [neither Phillips nor* **I**] **have** *seen anything like it.* (FICT)

This pattern follows the **principle of proximity** (see 8.6.7 below).

8.6.4 Concord with quantifying expressions

The indefinite pronouns *anybody/anyone, everybody/everyone, nobody/no one,* and *somebody/someone* agree with singular verb forms:

> 1 *[Everybody]'s doing what they think they're supposed to do.* (FICT)
> 2 *[Nobody]* **has** *their fridges repaired any more, they can't afford it.* (FICT)

Here subject–verb concord is singular, even though co-referent pronouns and determiners may be plural, as we notice from the forms *they* and *their* in **1** and **2** above.

Quantifying pronouns such as *all, some, any, none, a lot, most* can take either singular or plural concord, according to whether they have singular or plural reference. If an *of*-phrase follows, the noun phrase after *of* indicates whether singular or plural is required:

> 3 *[Some of it]* **is** *genuine, some of it all a smoke-screen.* (NEWS)
> 4 *[Most of the copies]* **are** *seized in raids.* (NEWS)
> 5 *Yeah all people are equal yet [some]* **are** *more equal than others.* (CONV)

In **3**, the concord is singular, as signalled by the singular pronoun *it* in the subject phrase. In **4**, the concord is plural, signalled by *copies*. Example **5** illustrates the case where there is no *of*-phrase, but the context signals a plural meaning (*some = some people*).

Singular concord is normal with *each* and *one*. Both singular and plural forms are found with *either* and *neither*, although the singular is often considered more 'correct':

> [*Neither of these words*] **is** *much help.* (FICT)

> [*Neither of us*] **believe** *in useless symbols.* (FICT)

Concord patterns also vary with *any* and *none*. With these pronouns, the singular was traditionally considered 'correct', but there is little sign of such a deliberate preference these days:

> [*None of us*] **has** *been aboard except Vinck.* (FICT)

> [*None of us*] *really* **believe** *it's ever going to happen.* (FICT†)

8.6.5 Concord with collective nouns

Singular collective nouns like *team, government, committee* allow either singular or plural concord in British English, but in American English the singular is the normal choice. Compare these examples from British English:

> [*The flock*] **is** *infected with Salmonella Typhimurium.* (BrE NEWS†)

> [*The Catholic flock – who constitute one third of Malawi's population*] – **are** *tired of dividing their loyalties.* (BrE NEWS)

Plural concord, where it occurs, puts the focus on the individuals making up the group, rather than the group as a whole. A few collective nouns, like *family* and *crew*, regularly take both singular and plural concord in British English:

> [*Her own family*] **has** *suffered the anguish of repossession.* (BrE NEWS)

> [*The family*] **are** *absolutely devastated.* (BrE NEWS)

In fact, nearly all human collective nouns occasionally occur with plural concord in British English. For example:

> [*The Government*] **have** *decreed that we will have to rebid for our betting licence.* (BrE NEWS†)

In contrast, singular concord is the norm with collective nouns in American English:

> 3 [*His committee*] **approves** *covert operations only when there's a consensus.* (AmE NEWS†)

> 4 [*The Government*] **has** *indicated it will make provision in the Bill for such an amendment.* (AmE NEWS)

8.6.6 Notional concord

Competing with the rule of grammatical concord, there is a tendency to follow **notional concord**, that is, to let the *notion* of singular/plural in the subject determine the form of the verb, rather than the grammatical *form* of the subject. Notional concord helps explain many of the special cases we have considered in 8.6.3–5. Notional concord is also behind the following cases.

A Concord with names, titles, etc.

Plural names, titles, and quotations take singular concord if the reference is to a single thing (a country, a newspaper, a dish, etc.):

> The country can ill afford an operation that would permit others to argue that [the United States] **does** not respect international law. (NEWS)
>
> [The New York Times] **was**, as usual, dryly factual. (FICT†)

B Concord with measure expressions

Plural measure expressions take singular verb forms if the reference is to a single measure (amount, weight, length, time, etc.):

> [Two pounds] **is** actually quite a lot. (CONV†)
>
> [Eighteen years] **is** a long time in the life of a motor car. (NEWS)

8.6.7 Concord and proximity

In addition to grammatical concord and notional concord, the **principle of proximity** sometimes plays a part in subject–verb agreement. This principle is the tendency, especially in speech, for the verb to agree with the closest (pro)noun, even when that (pro)noun is not the head of the subject noun phrase. For example:

> Do you think [any of them] **are** bad Claire? (CONV)
>
> [Not one of the people who'd auditioned] **were** up to par. (FICT†)

8.6.8 Concord where the subject is a clause

Singular concord is the rule when the subject is a finite or non-finite clause:

> [Carrying cases, boxes, parcels, or packages] **was** a task only for servants. (FICT)

But **nominal relative clauses** can have plural as well as singular concord:

> [What we do know] **is** this. (NEWS†)
>
> [What is needed] **are** effective regulators. (NEWS)

8.6.9 Concord with subject–verb inversion

There are some clause patterns where the subject follows, rather than precedes, the verb phrase. This pattern, known as subject–verb inversion, can give rise to opposing tendencies in the choice of subject–verb agreement.

A Existential there

With existential *there is/are*, the noun phrase which follows the main verb *be* is termed the **notional subject**. In written registers, the notional subject generally determines concord with the verb:

> There **was** [candlelight], and there **were** [bunks with quilts heaped on top]. (FICT)

However, in conversation a contrary trend is observed: the verb is likely to be singular even when the following notional subject is plural:

> *There's [so many police forces that don't even have computers yet].* (CONV†)
>
> *Gary, there's [apples] if you want one.* (CONV)

(See 12.5–10 for a full discussion of existential *there*.)

Other patterns similar to *there is/are* occur in conversation, where there is a tendency to attach the singular verb contraction *'s* to the preceding adverb:

> ***Here's*** *your shoes.* (CONV)
>
> ***Where's*** *your tapes?* (CONV)
>
> ***How's*** *mum and dad?* (CONV†)

Here again, concord in conversation is singular even where the following 'notional subject' is plural.

8.6.10 Vernacular concord in conversation

In some non-standard speech, verbs like *say*, *do*, and *be* are not inflected for number, as in:

> *She **don't** like Amanda though.* (CONV) <= *She **doesn't**...*>
>
> ***Times is*** *hard.* (CONV) <= *Times **are** ...*>

8.6.11 Concord and pronoun reference

There is normally agreement between subject–verb concord and any following personal pronouns that refer back to the subject:

> *In two short years [the government] **has** seemed to lose **its** grip.* (NEWS)

However, there are exceptions to this where the plural pronoun *they* is used as a singular reference unspecified for sex (as discussed in 4.10.3):

> *Everybody's doing what **they** think **they**'re supposed to do.* (FICT)

It is common in speech to use *they* for a person whose sex is unspecified or unknown, and this use is increasingly found in written as well as spoken registers.

Review

Major points of GRAMMAR BITE B: Subject–verb concord

➤ In finite clauses, the subject and verb need to match in terms of concord (i.e. number and person).

➤ There are a few special cases for concord, such as collective nouns, quantifiers, and coordinated noun phrases as subject.

➤ Notional concord and proximity are two factors which influence grammatical concord.

➤ There is sometimes a mismatch between subject–verb concord and pronoun reference.

C Negation

8.7 Verbs as operators

To explain negative as well as other kinds of clauses in English, it is useful to recognize the special syntactic role of the **operator**. The operator is the verb used for clause negation or for forming questions (interrogative clauses). To form a negative clause, the negative particle *not* is inserted after the operator. For interrogative clauses, the operator is placed in front of the subject noun phrase (**subject–operator inversion**). There are three major categories of operators:

A The first auxiliary verb in the verb phrase

Clause negation (the main verb is underlined below):

> They **are** not <u>forgotten</u>. (FICT)
> They **have** not <u>been</u> very helpful. (NEWS)
> I **won't** <u>fail</u>. (FICT)

Question formation:

> **Are** you <u>kidding</u>? (CONV)
> **Have** you <u>tried</u> that? (CONV)
> Where **have** you <u>been</u>? (FICT)
> What **could** I <u>do</u>? (FICT)

B The copula *be*

Clause negation:

> You're not pretty. (CONV)

Question formation:

> **Are** you serious? (CONV)

C The dummy auxiliary verb *do*

Clause negation:

> Well he **doesn't** <u>live</u> down there now. (CONV)

Question formation:

> Where **does** she <u>live</u>? (CONV)

When no operator exists (i.e. for simple present and past tenses), the dummy operator *do* is inserted to form negative and interrogative clauses:

positive	negative
I looked.	*I didn't look.*

declarative	interrogative
It makes sense.	*Does it make sense?*

(The main verb *have* and the quasi-modals *need* and *dare* are sometimes used as operators; see 8.8.6 and 8.11.7 below.)

8.7.1 Operators alone

Apart from their role in forming negation and questions, operators have another function. It is often useful to omit everything in a clause after the operator, where it would simply repeat what has already been said. This is a popular type of final ellipsis (8.5.1):

1 A: *You've <u>lost some weight since I've seen you.</u>*
   B: *I **have** ^, yes.* (CONV)

2 A: *You don't know Murphy's Law?*
   B: *Yeah, <...> if anything can <u>go wrong,</u> it **will** ^.* (CONV)

3 A: *Didn't you <u>have an aunt like that?</u>*
   B: *A great aunt.*
   A: *You **did** ^?* (CONV)

In **1–3**, the ellipsis is marked by ^, the operator is in bold, and the piece of text which is semantically repeated through the ellipsis is underlined. The operator is typically an auxiliary verb, so this is the exceptional case where an auxiliary verb occurs 'stranded', without the main verb which normally follows it. Note, in **3**, that the dummy auxiliary *do* occurs here for simple present and past tenses, just as it does in forming negation and questions.

8.8 Negation

Negation is largely a feature of clauses: a clause is either positive or negative. The most common way of making a clause negative is to insert the negative particle *not*, or its contraction *-n't*, after the operator:

negative: *I **cannot** believe it.* (NEWS†) <compare positive: *I can believe it.*>
negative: *I **haven't** eaten.* (CONV) <compare positive: *I have eaten.*>

(Note that *can* + *not* is usually written as a single word.)

There are actually two main kinds of clause negation: ***not*-negation** and ***no*-negation**. Whereas *not*-negation is formed with *not* or *-n't*, *no*-negation is formed with other negative words such as *no, nothing, none*:

> There's **nothing** you can do about it. (CONV)

As Figure 8.6 shows, *not*-negation is far more common than *no*-negation. More interestingly, negation is more than twice as common in conversation as it is in the written registers.

Figure 8.6
Distribution of negative types

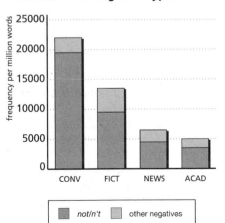

8.8.1 *Not*-negation

The negator *not/n't* is added after the operator. If there is no auxiliary verb and the main verb is not the copula *be*, the auxiliary verb *do* has to be inserted as dummy operator. Compare:

> You **can** do this but you **can't** do that. (CONV)
>
> I **remembered** it but I **didn't remember** where it burned her specifically. (CONV)

The negative of an interrogative or imperative clause is formed in the same way as the negative of a declarative clause (by adding *not/n't* after the operator):

> **Don't** you have a key? (CONV) <positive: *Do you have a key?*>
>
> Why **aren't** you working? (CONV) <positive: *Why are you working?*>
>
> **Don't** talk to me. (CONV) <positive: *Talk to me.*>

Most interrogative clauses have subject–operator inversion. If *not* is contracted to -*n't*, it is attached to the operator and comes before the subject:

> **Couldn't she** get a job like teaching? (CONV†)
>
> Hey why **isn't it** ready? (CONV)

But if *not* is a full form, it has to be placed after the subject:

> Could **she not** get a job like teaching?
>
> Hey why is **it not** ready?

This option is rare, and in general speakers choose the contracted form.

Negative imperatives with the copula *be* are exceptional because the *be* does not serve as the operator for negation; rather, *do not* or *don't* is inserted before the verb *be*:

> **Don't be** silly. (CONV)
>
> **Don't be** so hard on yourself. (FICT)

In conversation, it is usual for a negative clause to contain a contracted form attached to the immediately preceding word. This can be either a contraction of the operator (e.g. *'s, 're, 'll, 'd*) or the contraction of the negative (*n't*). The following sections discuss the choice between these alternatives.

8.8.2 Verb contraction

Verb contraction occurs with the primary verbs *be* and *have* as well as with the modal verbs *will* and *would* (see Table 8.2). The contractions *'s* and *'d* are ambiguous, with *'s* representing either *is* or *has*, and *'d* representing either *had* or

Table 8.2 Contracted forms of *be*, *have*, *will* and *would*

	present tense			past tense
	1st person sing.	2nd person sing. + plurals	3rd person sing.	
be	am → 'm	are → 're	is → 's	
have	have → 've	have → 've	has → 's	had → 'd
modals	will → 'll		would → 'd	

would (or sometimes *did*). However, the intended meaning of these contractions is generally clear in context. Here are some examples with a following *not*:

> **That's** *not true.* (CONV) <= *That is*>
>
> **It's** *not been a normal week.* (CONV) <= *It has*>
>
> **They'd** *not even washed.* (CONV) <= *They had*>
>
> **We'd** *not want your shade to plague us.* (FICT) <= *We would*>

Verb contraction needs a preceding 'host' in the clause. Usually the host is a pronoun (e.g. *I'm, you'd, she'll, that's*). But many other forms preceding a verb can serve as host, including full nouns, *wh*-words, and *there*:

> **Gerry'll** *phone you during the show.* (FICT)
>
> **Where'd** *you get that haircut?* (FICT)
>
> **How's** *it going?* (CONV)
>
> **There's** *no doubt that's going to lead to dumping.* (NEWS)
>
> **Now's** *the time to go on a seed hunting expedition in your garden.* (NEWS).

If there is no preceding host, e.g. with *yes/no* questions, then there is no possibility of verb contraction:

> **Is** *that on the sea?* (FICT) <but not: **'s that on the sea?*>

Similarly, verbs in clause-final position cannot be contracted. For example:

> *I don't know what it* **is**. (FICT†) <but not: **I don't know what it's.*>

In addition, when the noun phrase preceding the verb is complex (e.g. where it contains a postmodifier) it rarely serves as a host to a verb contraction.

Figure 8.7 shows that the registers make steeply decreasing use of contractions, in the following order: conversation > fiction > news > academic writing. In addition, contraction is favored by specific linguistic factors. For example, individual verbs are contracted with differing degrees of frequency: *be* and *will* are usually contracted in conversation, while *would* is rarely contracted. With *be*, the contraction of *am* (*'m*) is more common than *is* or *are* (*'s, 're*).

Have is much more likely to be contracted as an auxiliary verb (in the perfect aspect, as in *We've arrived*) than as a main verb (e.g. *I've no idea*). Further, the contraction of *have* is more common than *has* or *had*.

Figure 8.7

Proportional use of verbs as contractions

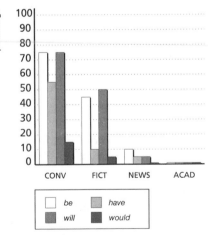

Finally, the possibility of contraction is influenced by the host: verb contraction is much more likely with a pronoun subject than with a full noun phrase.

8.8.3 Negative contraction

Negative contraction occurs when *not* is reduced and attached to a preceding primary verb (as operator) or modal auxiliary verb. The resulting negative auxiliary verb is spelled with a final *-n't*, as in:

be	*isn't, aren't, wasn't, weren't*
have	*haven't, hasn't, hadn't*
do	*don't, doesn't, didn't*
modals	*won't (= will not), wouldn't, can't (= cannot), couldn't, shan't (= shall not), shouldn't, mustn't*

Figure 8.8

Proportional use of *not* as a contraction

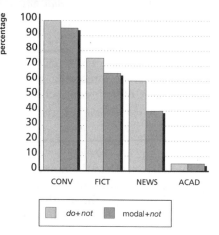

There is no contraction for *am not* (**amn't*), and although there are contractions for *may not* and *might not*, these very rarely occur.

Figure 8.8 shows a similar pattern for negative contractions as for verb contractions: the preference for contracted forms declines sharply from nearly 100 per cent in conversation to roughly 5 per cent in academic writing.

 ## 8.8.4 Negative contraction compared with verb contraction

It is impossible for negative contraction and verb contraction to co-exist in the same clause (e.g. we cannot say **It'sn't*, **We've't*), so they compete with each other where both are possible. These are the main trends:

- When *be* contraction is possible, it is strongly favored over *not* contraction: e.g. *you're not, it's not* is preferred to *you aren't, it isn't*.
- This preference is particularly strong with first- and second-person pronouns. In fact, in the case of *I'm not*, there is no alternative except for the marginally acceptable *I ain't* or *aren't I* (see 8.8.5 below).
- In contrast, with the verbs *have, will,* and *would,* there is a very strong preference for negative contraction: e.g. *I haven't, she won't, they wouldn't* are much preferred to *I've not, she'll not, they'd not*.

8.8.5 *Aren't I* and *ain't*: two rogue contractions

A *Aren't I*

Negative contraction is not a possibility with *am not* (**I amn't*), and this causes a difficulty in questions (where inversion does not allow verb contraction). In colloquial English, *aren't I* is sometimes substituted for the non-existent **amn't I*. (The full form *am I not* is generally avoided.)

> *I'm naughty **aren't** I?* (CONV)
> *'**Aren't** I supposed to understand?'* (FICT)

B Ain't

This is a very versatile negative contraction, capable of substituting for all negative contractions of *be* or the auxiliary *have*:

> *'There **ain't** nothing we can do.'* (FICT) <= *isn't*>
> *'I'm whispering now, **ain't** I?'* (FICT) <= *aren't*>
> *I **ain't** done nothing.* (CONV) <= *haven't*>

Ain't is common in the conversation of some dialects, and it occurs in representations of speech in writing. However, *ain't* is widely felt to be non-standard, and so it is generally avoided in written language, as well as in careful speech.

8.8.6 Use and non-use of dummy *do* in negation

Six verbs have variation between (**1**) acting as a lexical verb with dummy *do*, and (**2**) acting as operator themselves. For the most part, this choice exists only for British English.

A Have as a lexical verb

1 *do*-construction:	*She **doesn't** have a dime.* (FICT)
2 *have* as operator:	*I **haven't** a clue what her name was!* (BrE CONV)

Option **2** is a conservative (or even old-fashioned) choice. It occurs rarely in British English conversation and almost never in American English. (*Have got*, though, is often used as an alternative to main verb *have* in British English conversation.)

B The semi-modal *have to*

For *have to*, the same choices occur, and under similar conditions. Option **1** is again by far the most common:

1 *do*-construction:	*You **don't have to** have a conscience.* (CONV)
2 *have* as operator:	*Oh I wish I **hadn't to** go out tonight.* (BrE CONV)

C Need and dare

1 *do*-construction:	*They **do not** need to belong to the same phase.* (ACAD)
	*I **didn't** dare to mention Hella.* (FICT)
2 auxiliary construction:	*The details **need not** concern us here.* (ACAD†)
	*No, I **daren't** tell her.* (CONV)

Need and *dare* are dual-function verbs: they can behave like modal auxiliaries or like main verbs. In the auxiliary use, these verbs function as the operator for negation, as in **2**. However, this construction is restricted to British English, and even there it is relatively rare.

D *Used to* **and** *ought to*

Used to and *ought to* are two other verbs on the boundary of modal auxiliary status. They have (rare) negative contractions *usedn't* and *oughtn't*, but they also have the infinitive *to*, which aligns them with lexical verbs:

1 *do*-construction:	*We **didn't** used to see much of it.* (CONV)
	*He **didn't** ought to be doing that sort of job.* (CONV†)
2 auxiliary construction:	*Gentlemen **used not** to have any traffic with him.* (FICT†) <traffic = dealings>
	*So I think I **oughtn't** to spend more.* (CONV†)

Negation is generally rare with these verbs.

8.8.7 *No*-negation

Negation involving quantifiers can be expressed by negative words like *no*, or by a **non-assertive** word like *any* (see 8.8.10) following *not/n't*:

negative words	non-assertive words
determiners: *no, neither*	determiners: *any, either*
adverbs: *neither, nowhere, never, nor*	adverbs: *either, anywhere, ever*
pronouns: *none, neither, nobody,* *no one, nothing*	pronouns: *any, either, anybody,* *anyone, anything*

Non-assertive words can occur after *not*, where they often provide a way of expressing the same meaning as *no*-negation:

> *They had **no** sympathy for him.* (FICT)
> <compare: *They **didn't** have **any** sympathy for him.*>
> *There was **nobody** in the hut.* (FICT†)
> <compare: *There **wasn't anybody** in the hut.*>
> *I'll **never** be able to tell her.* (FICT†)
> <compare: *I **won't ever** be able to tell her.*>

When *no*-negation and *not*-negation are both possible, there is sometimes a slight difference of meaning. This is true of clauses containing *not a* v. *no*—compare **1–2** with **3–4**:

> **1** *He is ten years old, he is **not a baby**.* (FICT)
> **2** *He **wasn't a** union member.* (NEWS†)
> **3** *She was **no** great beauty.* (FICT†)
> **4** *He is **no** quitter.* (NEWS†)

While **1** and **2** can be read as factual descriptions of a person, **3** and **4** express a judgment about a person's attributes. Similarly, *She's **not a** teacher* and *She's **no** teacher* are different in that the first is a statement about her job and the second a statement about her capabilities.

8.8.8 Choosing between *not*-negation and *no*-negation

In many cases, the choice between *not*-negation and *no*-negation is just not available. For a *not*-negated clause to be equivalent to a *no*-negated clause, it has to have some indefinite form following *not*, such as *any* or *a*:

> She does**n't** have **a** car yet. (FICT)
> <compare: She has **no** car yet.>

Conversely, when a form of *no*-negation precedes the verb (usually as subject), there is no equivalent *not*-negated clause:

> '**Nobody** stole it?' said James. (FICT)
>
> Nothing can happen to you, and **nothing** can get you. (FICT)

Overall, *not*-negation is much more common than *no*-negation. As Figure 8.9 shows, *no*-negation is especially rare in conversation, but it is moderately common in the written registers. When *no*-negation does occur in conversation, it is often part of habitual collocations such as:

> There is ... no doubt/no need/ no point/no sign/no way
>
> I have ... no idea/no choice/no desire/no effect/no intention/no reason

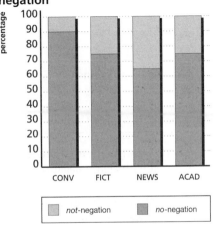

Figure 8.9

Proportional use of *not*- v. *no*-negation

8.8.9 The scope of negation

The **scope of negation** is the part of a clause that is affected by negative meaning. The scope may be restricted to a single word or phrase, in which case we consider it to be local negation rather than clause negation:

> 1 *One rabbit can finish off a few hundred young trees **in no time**.* (FICT)
> 2 *Robertson, **not unexpectedly**, claimed afterwards that his strike should have been recognised.* (NEWS)

In these examples, the negation is located in adverbials, and does not affect the interpretation of the main part of the clause. In **2,** note the 'double negative' effect of *not unexpectedly*, which actually means that Robertson's behavior was expected.

Even more local is the following use of *nowhere* and *nobody*—where in effect these words are treated like nouns:

> It's in the middle of **nowhere**, isn't it? (CONV†)
>
> He's a **nobody**, but you see I fell in love with him. (FICT)

With clause negation, the whole proposition is denied, and the scope of negation extends from the negative element to the end of the clause. Placing an adverbial before or after *not* often results in a difference of meaning. Compare **1** and **2** (the scope of negation is shown by underlining.)

1 *'Our investigations indicate that this substance was **not deliberately** administered.'* (FICT)
   <i.e. the substance was administered accidentally, not deliberately.>
2 *Alexander looked at Wilkie who **deliberately** did not see him.* (FICT)
   <i.e. he deliberately avoided seeing him.>

8.8.10 Assertive and non-assertive forms

The forms below are associated with either **assertive** or **non-assertive** contexts:

	assertive	non-assertive
adverbs	already	yet
	sometimes	ever
	somewhat	at all
	somewhere	anywhere
	still	any more
	too	either
determiners/pronouns	some	any
	somebody	anybody
	someone	anyone
	something	anything

Assertive forms are used mainly in positive clauses, whereas non-assertive forms are used with clause negation. Non-assertive forms follow the *not*, as in examples **1–3**:

1 *There aren't **any** passenger trains.* (CONV†) <negation of: *There are **some** passenger trains.*>
2 *'But he doesn't have to do **anything**.'* (FICT†) <negation of: *He has to do **something**.*>
3 *I don't think [we had **any** cheese] did we?* (CONV)

Note that the scope of negation can extend into dependent clauses, shown by [] in **3**.

   Although non-assertive forms are particularly associated with negation, they are also used in other contexts:

- interrogative clauses (**4** independent and **5** dependent):
   4 *Does **anyone ever** ring the bell Carrie?* (CONV)
   5 *Wonder if Tamsin had **any** luck selling her house.* (CONV)

- conditional clauses:
   *If there are **any** problems in performance-related pay, we can iron these out.* (NEWS)

- temporal clauses introduced by *before*:
   *I was with him before **anyone** else was.* (FICT)

- comparative and degree constructions:
   *I can trust you, Babes, more than **anybody**.* (FICT)

Another set of contexts for non-assertive forms are implicit negatives: that is, words (underlined below) which do not look negative, but convey a negative meaning.

> **6** *Most scientists, however, <u>refuse</u> to pay **any** heed or give **any** credence to Psychical Research.* (ACAD†)
>
> **7** *On the first occasion Mr Reynolds met the stoma care nurse he was very quiet and seemed <u>reluctant</u> to discuss **anything**.* (ACAD)
>
> **8** *But I very <u>rarely</u> fry **anything** anyway.* (CONV)
>
> **9** *Jane requires you to guess at and check a set of mathematical functions <u>without</u> **ever** giving you the answers.* (ACAD)

Notice that such implicit negatives belong to various word classes: *refuse* (**6**) is a verb, *reluctant* (**7**) is an adjective, *rarely* (**8**) is an adverb, and *without* (**9**) is a preposition.

8.8.11 Assertive forms used in negative clauses

Although assertive forms like *some* are strongly associated with positive clauses, they are sometimes found in negative clauses, especially if they stay outside the scope of negation:

> *For **some** reason it did not surprise him.* (FICT†)
>
> *I don't mind talking, not to **some** people.* (CONV)

8.8.12 Multiple negation

Sometimes more than one negative word occurs in the same clause. Such combinations belong to two types: dependent multiple negation and independent multiple negation.

A Dependent multiple negation

This is a common feature of conversation in some dialects, but it is generally considered to be non-standard:

> *You've **never** seen **nothing** like it.* (CONV) <meaning: *You've never seen anything like it.*>
>
> *There **ain't nothing** we can do.* (FICT) <meaning: *There isn't anything we can do.*>

The corresponding clauses in standard English have a negative form followed by a non-assertive form (as in 8.8.10).

B Independent multiple negation

We use this term for repeated negative forms which occur when a speaker reformulates a negative utterance. In these cases, the negative forms are not integrated in the same clause:

> *No, not tomorrow, she said.* (FICT)
>
> *There's **no one** to blame **not** really.* (FICT†)

We also find repeated occurrences of *not* in the same clause, each adding its own negative meaning. Here two negatives make a positive meaning:

> *Oh well you sleep on sherry though – it makes you sleepy, you* **can't not** *sleep.* (CONV) <meaning that you just have to sleep>
>
> *As it did turn out, I* **never** *did* **not** *smoke in the end. I lit a cigarette and kept them coming.* (FICT)

Independent multiple negation is generally considered to be standard.

Major points of Grammar Bite C: Negation

➤ Clauses are either positive or negative.

➤ Negative clauses are most commonly formed by using *not* or its contraction *-n't*.

➤ The verb as operator is a key tool for forming negation with *not/-n't*.

➤ Clause negation is the main type of negation, but there is also local negation.

➤ In clause negation, there is an important distinction between *not*-negation and *no*-negation.

➤ The scope of negation is important for choosing non-assertive v. assertive forms (e.g. *there aren't any. . .* v. *there are some. . .*).

➤ There are standard and non-standard forms of multiple negation.

GRAMMAR BITE

D Independent clauses

8.9 Major types of independent clause

An independent clause is a clause which is not part of any larger clause structure. However, independent clauses can be coordinated, and they can include embedded dependent clauses:

- simple independent clause (single clause):

    You can give me a cheque. (CONV)

- coordinated independent clauses (two or more coordinated clauses):

    He was crying and so I gave him back his jacket. (CONV†)

- complex independent clause (with one or more dependent clauses):

    If you pay too much they'll give us the money back. (CONV†)

All independent clauses are finite, that is, they contain a finite verb form which specifies tense (e.g. *is*, *looked*) or modality (e.g. *can*, *would*).

Independent clauses are used to perform **speech-act** functions. There is a general correspondence between four basic speech-act functions and the four structural types of independent clauses, shown in Table 8.3.

A **statement** gives information and expects no specific response from the addressee. A **question** asks for information and expects a linguistic response. A **directive** is used to give orders or requests, and expects some action from the addressee. An **exclamation** expresses the strong feelings of the speaker/writer, and expects no specific response.

le 8.3   Major classification of independent clauses

speech-act	functional	clause	structural	example
informing	statement	declarative clause	SV structure	*It's strong*
eliciting	question	interrogative clause	VS structure	*Is it strong?*
			wh-word + VS structure	*Where is she?*
			wh-word structure	*Who was there?*
directing	command	imperative clause	V structure (no S)	*Be strong!*
expressing	exclamation	exclamative clause	*wh*-word + SV structure	*How good she is!*

Structure and speech-act function do not always agree, and it is therefore useful to distinguish between the two (e.g. a declarative clause can be used as a directive). In practice, though, many grammars use the terms interchangeably, as we do when no misunderstanding can result.

The four clause types are described below, giving attention to both form and associated speech-act function.

.10 Declarative clauses

Declarative clauses have SV (subject–verb) structure and typically express statements; they are the 'default' type of independent clause, especially in writing.

Although declarative clauses normally convey information (especially in writing), they can also serve other speech-act functions in conversation and fictional dialog. For example, SV order is occasionally used in asking a question (the question status being signalled in speech by rising intonation or in writing by a question mark):

1   A: *So he's left her?*
    B: *She left him.* (CONV)
2   *'You weren't happy together?'* – *'No,'* I said. (FICT†)

These declarative questions, as they can be called, retain some of the declarative force of a statement: it is as if the speaker is testing out the truth of the statement by inviting confirmation.

.11 Interrogative clauses

As indicated in Table 8.3 above, an **interrogative clause** can be recognized by two structural clues, which often occur in combination: a VS (verb–subject) structure and an initial *wh*-word. In addition, rising intonation (in speech) and a question mark (in writing) are supplementary, non-grammatical cues.

There are three main types of independent interrogative clause: ***wh*-questions, *yes/no*-questions,** and **alternative questions.** Their basic uses are:

- to elicit missing information (*wh*-questions, 8.11.1)
- to ask whether a proposition is true or false (*yes/no* questions, 8.11.2)
- to ask which of two or more alternatives is the case (alternative questions, 8.11.3).

8.11.1 *Wh*-questions

Wh-questions begin with a *wh*-word that refers to a missing element in the clause. The missing element can be a clause element (subject, object, predicative, adverbial) or part of a phrase. Below, the role of the *wh*-word is shown within < >:

1 ***Who's** calling?* <subject> (CONV)
2 ***What** d'you mean?* <direct object> (CONV†)
3 ***Who** are you talking about?* <prepositional object> (CONV†)
4 ***How** was your trip, Nick?* <subject predicative> (CONV)
5 ***Which** photos are we going to look at?* <part of noun phrase> (CONV)
6 ***When** did you see Mark?* <adverbial, time> (CONV)
7 ***Why** did you buy that?* <adverbial, reason> (CONV)
8 ***How** old's Wendy?* <part of adjective phrase> (CONV)

Note, from 1, that the declarative order SV is preserved when the *wh*-word is the subject of the clause. All the other examples show VS order—that is, the **operator** comes before the subject. (This is known as **subject–operator inversion**.)

In informal language, the *wh*-word can be reinforced by a following expletive, signaling the speaker's strong feelings:

‘***What** the hell's the matter with you?*’ (FICT)

When the speaker asks for two pieces of information, there is more than one *wh*-word in the clause. Only one of these occurs in initial position:

***Who** is bringing **what**?* (FICT)

Very often in conversation a *wh*-question lacks a full clause structure. It may consist only of the *wh*-word:

A: *It's six o'clock isn't it?*
B: ***What?*** (CONV)

What?, as in the last example, is often a general request for repetition: an echo question. There are also echo questions where the *wh*-word is left in its regular position in the clause, instead of being fronted:

A: *And I think she's stealing stuff as well.*
B: *She's **what**?* (CONV)

More than simple requests for repetition, such echo questions can express surprise or disbelief.

Although *wh*-questions are primarily for seeking information, they can have other speech-act functions:

9 ***Who** needs sitcoms?* (NEWS)
10 ***How** dare you speak to me like that? **Who** do you think you are?* (CONV†)
11 ***Why** don't we go next week?* (CONV)

Example 9 illustrates a rhetorical question with a function close to that of a statement: ‘Nobody needs sitcoms’. Example 10 expresses a strong rebuke, and is more like an exclamation than a question. Example 11 is a suggestion, and has a function similar to a first-person imperative: ‘Let's go next week.’

8.11.2 *Yes/no* questions

Yes/no questions have VS word order: they begin with the operator followed by the subject. The addressee is expected to reply with a truth value—either *yes* or *no*. Needless to say, there are other possible answers indicating various degrees of certainly or uncertainty (*definitely, perhaps, I don't know*, etc.).

> A: *Is it Thursday today?*
> B: *No, Friday.* (CONV)
> A: *Do you think he'll be any better?*
> B: *Maybe. Yeah.* (CONV)

Casual *yes/no* questions frequently contain ellipsis:

> ∧ *You alright?* (CONV) <*are* omitted>
> ∧ *Got what you want?* (CONV) <*have you* omitted>

Like *wh*-questions, *yes/no* questions are used for purposes other than asking for information:

> 1 *Isn't that lovely?!* (CONV)
> 2 *Will you behave?!* (CONV)
> 3 *Can we turn that light off please?* (CONV)

In **1**, the interrogative structure expresses an exclamation (similar to *How lovely!*). Examples **2** and **3** function as directives: a forceful command in **2**, and a polite request in **3**.

Especially in conversation, *yes/no* questions frequently have the minimal form operator + subject:

> A: *She's a teacher.*
> B: *Oh **is she**?* (CONV)

These elliptic questions are not really asking for information: they rather function as **backchannels,** showing interest and keeping the conversation going.

8.11.3 Alternative questions

An alternative question is structurally similar to a *yes/no* question: it opens with operator + subject. But instead of expecting a *yes/no* answer, it presents alternatives for the addressee to choose between:

> A: *Do you want one **or** two?*
> B: *Two.* (CONV)
> A: *So do you like my haircut **or** not?*
> B: *It's alright.* (CONV)

An alternative question is signaled by the word *or* and by falling intonation at the end.

8.11.4 Question tags

Although **question tags** are not independent clauses, it is convenient to deal with them here. A question tag consists of operator + pronoun subject, and is used to seek confirmation of the statement the speaker has just uttered. The operator is a repetition of the operator in the preceding declarative clause; if there is no operator, the dummy operator *do* is used. The subject refers back to the subject of the preceding clause. For example:

1 *She's so generous,* **isn't she?** (CONV)
2 *She's not a lesbian,* **is she?** (CONV)
3 *She doesn't like things that blow up,* **does she?** (CONV)
4 *It seems a shame to break it up,* **doesn't it,** *when it's so good.* (CONV)

Note that the tag does not necessarily have to be placed at the very end of the clause (4), although it cannot go before the main clause verb phrase.

Question tags usually contrast with the polarity of the preceding statement. That is, a positive statement is followed by a negative question tag (**1, 4**), while a negative statement is followed by a positive question tag (**2, 3**). However, there is also a style of question tag which agrees with the preceding statement in being positive:

5 *A: She likes her granddad,* **does she?**
  B: Yeah. (CONV)
6 *A: It's my ball.*
  B: It's your ball, **is it?** (CONV)

These positive-positive question tags are similar in their effect to declarative questions (8.10): they seek confirmation of a previous statement.

8.11.5 Interrogatives across registers

Questions are many times more common in conversation than in writing, reflecting the interactive nature of conversation (see Figure 8.10). Conversation uses both *wh-* and *yes/no* questions. However, nearly half the questions in conversation consist of fragments or tags. About every fourth question in conversation is a question tag; the most common type of question tag is negative.

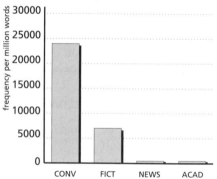

Figure 8.10

Distribution of questions

When questions are used in news or academic prose, they have rhetorical purposes, since there can be no expectation that readers will actually respond. However, these questions do help to involve the reader in the discussion. For example:

> *Sign up for the green team.* **Do you want to know what's happening to our countryside, forests, seas and seashores at home and across the world? Do you want to know how easy it is to affect the environment of the world by planting trees or buying eco-friendly products?** *If so, read this feature every week.* (NEWS)

> **How far will the magnetic flux penetrate? Is there a simple way of describing the decay of the magnetic flux mathematically?** *There is. We can use the following one-dimensional model.* (ACAD)

8.11.6 Choice between interrogative *who* and *whom*

Who is used for *wh*-questions inquiring about a person, regardless of syntactic role: that is, as subject, object, or prepositional object:

    1 **Who** *went first on the castle rock?* (FICT) <subject>
    2 **Who** *can I trust?* (CONV†) <object>
    3 *Amanda,* **who** *are you going out with?* (CONV) <prepositional object>

The traditional written form *whom* is also occasionally used for objects, but only in formal written English:

    4 '**Whom** *do you favour?*' (FICT)
    5 *I know* **whom** *she belongs to.* (FICT†)

Examples **3** and **5** illustrate preposition stranding. The alternative construction, where the preposition is fronted with the *wh*-word, is very likely to retain the form *whom*:

    For **whom** *would I be working?* (FICT)

In conversation, however, even this last-ditch refuge for *whom* is being taken over by the all-triumphant *who*:

    A: Obliged to make polite conversation all the time oh!
    B: With **who**? (CONV)

8.11.7 Use and non-use of dummy *do* in questions

As with negative clauses (8.8.6), questions show variation in the use of dummy *do* with certain verbs: *have, have to,* and the marginal modals *dare, need, ought to,* and *used to.* Apart from *have* and *have to,* these verbs are rare, especially in questions, and largely restricted to British English:

A *Have* **as a lexical verb**

    1 *do*-construction: **Did** *you have a good walk?* (CONV)
    2 with *have* as operator: **Have** *you any comments on this Mick?* (BrE CONV)

The *do*-construction **1** is virtually the only option in American English. *Have got* is preferred as an alternative to main verb *have* in British English conversation.

B **The semi-modal *have to***

    1 *do*-construction: *Look,* **do** *I* **have to** *tell you everything?* (CONV)
    2 *have* as operator: **Have** *they* **to** *pay for her to be there?* (BrE CONV)

The *do*-construction **1** is the only option in American English and the preferred option in British English.

C *Need* **and *dare***

    1 *do*-construction: **Do** *you* **need to** *go somewhere?* (CONV)
    2 auxiliary construction: *How* **dare** *you squeal like that.* (CONV)

In our corpus, option **1** is used 90 per cent of the time with *need*. The auxiliary construction with *dare* functions more like an exclamative (see 8.12) than a question.

D *Used to* and *ought to*

    1 *do*-construction: **Did** *you* **used to** *have long hair?* (FICT)
    2 auxiliary construction: *'***Ought** *I* **to** *take it?'* (FICT)

Both of these semi-modals are very rare in questions.

8.12 Exclamative clauses

Exclamations can be expressed by a range of structures, both clausal and non-clausal (see 13.2.4). Here we illustrate only independent clauses with an exclamatory function: a clause type which begins with a *wh*-word (*what* or *how*) and continues with an SV (subject–verb) pattern:

    1 *Oh,* **what a good girl you are.** (CONV)
    2 **How clever you are,** *and how beautiful.* (FICT)

8.13 Imperative clauses

Formally, most **imperative clauses** are characterized by the lack of a subject, use of the base form of the verb, and the absence of modals as well as tense and aspect markers:

    Get off *the table.* (CONV)

    Don't forget *about the deposit.* (CONV)

An imperative typically urges the addressee to do something (or not to do something): given this limited function, there is no need for tense, aspect, or modality in the imperative verb phrase.

    A special type of imperative clause contains the verb *let* followed by *us* (usually contracted to *'s*) to express a suggestion involving both the speaker and the addressee:

    Let's *catch up with Louise.* (CONV)

    Well, **let's** *try this,* **let's** *see what happens.* (CONV†)

8.13.1 The form and function of imperative clauses

Although most imperative clauses are very simple, we need to take account of some variations that occur. Optionally, the addressee of an imperative can be identified either by a subject noun phrase or a **vocative** address term:

    1 **You** *go home and go to sleep.* (CONV) <*you* as subject>
    2 *Don't* **you** *dare talk to me like that* **Clare,** *I've had enough.* (CONV)
       <*you* as subject and *Clare* as vocative>
    3 **Melissa,** *take those things away.* (CONV†) <*Melissa* as vocative>

When it occurs, the subject precedes the main verb and is not separated from it by a punctuation or intonation break. Thus, the pronoun in **1** and **2** is a subject. The distinction between a subject and a vocative is best seen in **2**, where both occur: the vocative *Clare* could be positioned at the beginning, middle or end of the vocative, and is more mobile than the subject.

Imperative clauses can also be elaborated by the addition of question tags, discourse markers like *please*, and adverbs like *just*:

4 *Pick your plates up from down there* **will you?** (CONV)
5 *Pass me his drink* **please**. (CONV†)
6 **Just** *dump it at the door there*. (CONV)

The question tag *will you* does little to soften the command in **4**. *Please* has a softening effect, but it is in some ways a minimal politeness strategy. *Just* makes the imperative seem less demanding and easier to comply with. It is clear from these and other examples that an imperative can express a range of directive speech acts, varying from commands to offers and invitations, depending on the situation and the kind of demand made on the addressee.

A different kind of function is served by the imperative clause in **7**, which is coordinated with a following declarative clause:

7 **Touch them** <tuning knobs> *and the telly goes wrong*. (CONV†)

Here the coordinated clause expresses a conditional relationship: 'if you touch them, the telly goes wrong'.

8.13.2 Imperative clauses in use

Imperatives are frequently used in conversation (see Figure 8.11) because speakers often try to direct the activity of listeners. Similarly, fiction texts use imperatives in dialog passages.

It is more surprising that the written informative registers need imperatives. In fact, imperatives are more frequent than questions in news and academic writing, presumably because writers can use them to manipulate the reaction and behavior of the reader. For example:

Figure 8.11
Distribution of imperatives

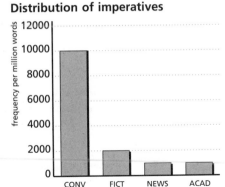

> *For full details of performances, talks, workshops, contact the Third Eye Centre.* (NEWS†)
>
> *See also Section 5.2.* (ACAD)

8.14 Non-clausal material

Conversation contains many non-clausal utterances, as shown in the comparison of two text samples early in this chapter (8.1.1; see also 13.4 and 13.7). However, non-clausal material is also found in writing, where it regularly occurs in special contexts such as public notices, headings, book titles, figure captions, and newspaper headlines (so-called *block language*). Here are some examples from headlines:

1 *Elderly care crisis warning.* (NEWS)
2 *Image crisis for Clinton over haircut.* (NEWS)

These headlines are composed of only a noun phrase. Headline **1** shows a tendency to compress meaning by stringing nouns together (four nouns occur in sequence).

In addition, non-clausal material also occurs in running text, where it adds a colloquial tone:

3 *And now for something completely different: cheap and cheerful claret.* (NEWS)

4 *Now there is no bar to having more than one particle in each state.* **Quite the contrary.** (ACAD)

Review

Major points of Grammar Bite D: Independent clauses

➤ There are four major types of independent clause: declarative, interrogative, imperative, and exclamative clauses.

➤ These correspond to four main types of speech act: statement, question, directive, and exclamation. However, there are mismatches between the clause types and the associated speech-act types.

➤ Questions are varied in form and in function.

➤ Major types of question are *wh*-questions, *yes/no* questions, and alternative questions.

➤ Question tags are also very common in conversation: e.g. *isn't it?*

➤ Grammatically, although independent clauses are the main building blocks of texts, non-clausal material is also common, particularly in conversation.

GRAMMAR BITE

E Dependent clauses

8.15 Finite dependent clauses

We now turn to dependent clauses, surveying the types of finite clause in this section, and then surveying non-finite clauses in 8.16.

8.15.1 Complement clauses

Complement clauses are controlled by a preceding verb, adjective, noun, or preposition. Complement clauses are also called **nominal clauses,** because their syntactic roles are comparable to those of a noun phrase. Thus, they are used as subject, predicative, or object in the main clause. Finite complement clauses are introduced by the subordinator *that* or by a *wh*-word.

• *that*-clauses (see 10.4–8):

> *That this was a tactical decision* <subject> *quickly became apparent.* (NEWS)

> *They believe **that the minimum wage could threaten their jobs.*** <direct object> (NEWS)

- *wh*-clauses (see 10.9–11):

    '***What I don't understand*** <subject> *is **why they don't let me know anything**.'* <subject predicative> (FICT†)

    *Perhaps it is us who made them **what they are**?* <object predicative> (FICT)

Complement clauses can also occur within phrases (marked *[]*), as complements of a noun, adjective, or preposition:

    *He was [aware **that a Garda Inquiry was being conducted**].* (NEWS)

    *There is [a fear **that such rules will be over-bureaucratic**].* (NEWS)

    *Be [very careful **what you tell me**].* (FICT)

    *She was [afraid of **what might happen if Chielo suddenly turned round and saw her**].* (FICT)

8.15.2 Adverbial clauses

Adverbial clauses are used as adverbials in the main clause. Like adverbials in general, they are normally optional elements, and can be placed either at the beginning, middle, or end of the main clause:

1 ***If you go to a bank**, they'll rip you off.* (CONV)
2 *There's a term and a half left **before he moves in**.* (CONV)
3 ***When the houses were ready**, prices of up to £51,000 were quoted.* (NEWS)
4 *Most ions are colourless, **although some have distinct colours**.* (ACAD)
5 *The conclusion, **it seems**, is intolerable.* (ACAD)
6 *He was at a tough football camp in Arkansas **I guess**.* (CONV)

Finite adverbial clauses are normally introduced by a subordinator: e.g. *if, before, when,* and *although.* (Some subordinators, like *when* in **3**, begin with *wh-,* but the clauses they introduce are not nominal *wh*-clauses like those in 8.15.1). Most adverbial clauses belong to the class of circumstance adverbials, expressing meanings like time, reason, and condition. However, **5** and **6** illustrate a type of adverbial clause called a comment clause, which normally has no subordinator. Sections 11.9–12 provide a detailed account of adverbial clauses.

8.15.3 Relative clauses

A **relative clause** is a postmodifier in a noun phrase, serving to expand the meaning and specify the reference of the head noun. It is introduced by a relativizer, which has a grammatical role (e.g. subject or direct object) in the relative clause, in addition to its linking function. The relativizer points back to its antecedent, the head of the noun phrase (the noun phrase is in *[]*; the relativizer is underlined):

    *He warned the public not to approach [the men, **who are armed and dangerous**].* (NEWS)

    *A system is [that part of the world **which we are interested in** and **which we are investigating**].* (ACAD)

Relative clauses are discussed in detail in 9.7–8.

    Nominal relative clauses are actually *wh*-complement clauses (see 8.15.1), but they are equivalent to a general noun as head + relative clause (see 10.9–11):

*Do **what you want.** (*CONV*) <= Do the thing **that you want.**>*
Whoever rents this apartment next year might have trouble. (CONV)
*<= The person **who rents this apartment next year.** . .>*

8.15.4 Comparative clauses

Comparative clauses are complements in an adjective phrase or an adverb phrase, with a gradable word as head. Comparative forms of adjectives, adverbs, pronouns, and determiners (e.g. *bigger, more carefully, less, fewer*) require a basis of comparison. For example, the use of the word *bigger* raises the question 'bigger than what?'. A comparative clause spells out the basis of this comparison, and is introduced by a conjunction (*than* for unequal comparison, and *as* for equal comparison). In **1** below the comparative clause is part of an adjective phrase; in **2** it is part of an adverb phrase (phrases are enclosed in *[ ]*):

    1 *Maybe Henry would realize she was not [as nice **as she pretended to be**].*
    (FICT)
    2 *She fled these Sunday afternoons [earlier **than she should have**].* (FICT)
Comparative clauses were described in 7.14.

8.15.5 Peripheral clauses

Two types of dependent clause have a peripheral role in the main clause: **reporting clauses** and **tag clauses**.

    Reporting clauses are on the boundary of dependent and independent status:

    1 *'Please come too,' **she begged.** – 'I'll be back when I feel like it,' **he said (to her) without emotion.** – 'I'm sorry,' **she whimpered.** (FICT†)*

A reporting clause introduces somebody's direct speech or thought. As we see in **1**, a reporting clause can report who is speaking (*she, he*), who the addressee is (*to her*), the nature of the speech act (*begged*), and the manner of speaking (*whimpered, without emotion*).

    The reporting clause often consists of just a one-word subject and a one-word verb phrase, as in the following examples. But there is variation in the ordering of S and V (see 12.4.3), and in the position of the clause relative to the quoted speech:

    2 ***They said,** 'Yes, sir,' and **saluted.*** (FICT)
    3 *'Yes,' **thought Fleury,** 'she's going at it hammer and tongs for his benefit.'*
    (FICT)
    4 *Can we do some singing? **he asks.*** (FICT)

Tag clauses are another type of peripheral clause; they are loosely attached to the end (or sometimes the middle) of another clause. They include not only **question tags** (such as *She's so generous, **isn't she**?*; see 8.11.4) but **declarative tags**, which have the effect of reinforcing the speaker's commitment to the proposition in the main clause:

    *Yeah I thoroughly enjoyed it **I did.*** (CONV)
    *He's alright **he is.*** (CONV)

Like tags in general (see 13.3.2), tag clauses are characteristic of speech.

.16 **Non-finite dependent clauses**

Non-finite clauses are regularly dependent on a main clause. They are more compact and less explicit than finite clauses: they do not have tense or modality, and they usually lack an explicit subject and subordinator (see 8.3.2). There are four major types of non-finite clause: **infinitive clauses,** *ing*-**clauses,** *ed*-**participle clauses**, and **verbless clauses.**

8.16.1 Infinitive clauses

Infinitive clauses have a wide range of syntactic roles:

- subject:

    Artificial pearls before real swine were cast by these jet-set preachers. ***To have thought this*** *made him more cheerful.* (FICT)

- extraposed subject (see 10.3.3):

    It's difficult ***to maintain a friendship.*** (CONV)
    <compare: ***To maintain a friendship*** *is difficult.*>

- subject predicative:

    '*My goal now is* ***to look to the future.***' (NEWS)

- direct object:

    He upset you very much, and I hate ***to see that***. (FICT)

- object predicative:

    Some of these issues dropped out of Marx's later works because he considered them ***to have been satisfactorily dealt with***. (ACAD†)

- adverbial:

    A little group of people had gathered by Mrs. Millings ***to watch the police activities on the foreshore***. (FICT)

- noun complement:

    They say that failure ***to take precautions against injuring others*** *is negligent.* (ACAD)

- noun postmodifier:

    It is a callous thing ***to do***. (NEWS)

- part of an adjective phrase:

    I think the old man's a bit afraid ***to go into hospital***. (CONV†)

In all these roles except object predicative and adverbial, *to*-infinitive clauses act as complement clauses (see 10.12–19).

8.16.2 *Ing*-clauses

Ing-clauses, too, have a varied range of syntactic roles:

- subject:

    Having a fever *is pleasant, vacant.* (FICT)

- extraposed subject (see 10.3.3):

    It's very difficult ***getting supplies into Sarajevo***. (NEWS†)
    <compare: ***Getting supplies into Sarajevo*** *is very difficult.*>

- subject predicative:

    *The real problem is **getting something done about cheap imports**.* (NEWS)
- direct object:

    *I started **thinking about Christmas**.* (CONV†)
- adverbial:

    *I didn't come out of it **looking particularly well**, I know.* (FICT)
- complement of a preposition (including prepositional object):

    *No-one could rely on **his going to bed early** last night.* (FICT†)
- noun postmodifier:

    *The man **making the bogus collections** was described as middle aged.* (NEWS)
- part of an adjective phrase:

    *The town is busy **taking advantage of its first City Challenge victory**.* (NEWS†)

8.16.3 *Ed*-participle clauses

Ed-participle clauses (also called past participle clauses) are less versatile than the other types of non-finite clauses. They can have the following roles:

- direct object:

    *Two-year-old Constantin will have **his cleft-palate repaired**.* (NEWS†)
- adverbial:

    *When **told by police how badly injured his victims were** he said: 'Good, I hope they die'.* (NEWS)
- noun postmodifier:

    *This, as we have seen, is the course **chosen by a large minority of households**.* (ACAD†)

Notice from this last example that the *ed*-participle form can take different forms with irregular verbs.

8.16.4 Supplement clauses

In the examples given in 8.16.1–3, the non-finite clauses are clearly integrated within the main clause. **Supplement clauses**, in contrast, are more loosely attached and can be considered a peripheral type of adverbial clause. They occur mostly in written registers, where they are usually marked off by a comma:

1 *[**Considered by many as Disney's last true classic**], The Jungle Book boasts some terrific songs.* (NEWS†)
2 *She gazed down at the floor, [**biting her lip**], [**face clouded**].* (FICT)

(Example 2 contains two supplement clauses in sequence.)

The relation between a supplement clause and its main clause is loose in meaning as well as form. By using a supplement clause, the writer marks information as supplementary background information in relation to the main clause. Supplement clauses can be *ing*-clauses or *ed*-clauses. They can also be verbless clauses.

8.16.5 Verbless clauses

Verbless clauses might be considered a special type of non-finite clause:

1 *She had also been taught,* **when in difficulty**, *to think of a good life to imitate.* (FICT)
2 **Although not a classic**, *this 90-minute video is worth watching.* (NEWS†)
3 *He does not believe celibacy should be demanded of priests* **whether gay or straight**. (NEWS)
4 *Every day,* **if possible**, *allot time at your desk to sorting and filing.* (ACAD†)

These expressions can be treated as adverbial clauses with ellipsis of the verb *be* and the subject. For example, *when in difficulty* in **1** can be decompressed as: *when she was in difficulty.*

The label 'verbless clause' seems a contradiction in terms, since we have described the clause as a unit with a verb phrase as its central element. The reason for wanting to label these units as clauses is that (a) they behave like clauses in their syntactic role, and (b) it is possible (taking account of the ellipsis of the verb *be*) to label their constituents as subordinator + subject predicative or adverbial.

8.17 Subjunctive verbs in dependent clauses

Subjunctive verb forms are rare in present-day English (although they were once much more common). Subjunctive verbs are invariable and thus do not exhibit subject–verb concord.

The present subjunctive is the base form of the verb, used where the *s*-form of the verb would occur normally. It occurs in special kinds of finite dependent clauses, particularly in some *that* complement clauses (**1**) and occasionally in some adverbial clauses (**2**):

1 *I told her she could stay with me until she found a place, but she insisted [that she* **pay** *her own way].* (FICT)
2 *The way in which we work, [whether it* **be** *in an office or on the factory floor], has undergone a major transformation in the past decade.* (NEWS)

With regular verbs, the present subjunctive is recognizable only with a singular subject. The past subjunctive is restricted to the form *were* used in the singular, especially to express unreal or hypothetical meaning:

3 *My head felt as if it* **were** *split open.* (FICT†)

Like the present subjunctive, this form is recognizable only in the singular, where it is used as an alternative to *was* as a hypothetical past tense verb.

8.18 Dependent clauses with no main clause

In special circumstances, dependent clauses can be used without being attached to a larger structure. One situation in which an unembedded dependent clause can occur is in dialog, owing to the influence of ellipsis:

> A: *You will be careful with that, won't you?*
> B: *Yeah!*
> A: **Cos it costs a lot of money.** (CONV)

However, similar phenomena occur in texts written in an informal style:

> *Sneaky, insincere? Depends how it's done.* **Which brings us onto those Americans.** *'Have a nice day.' How exaggerated, how American, we Brits recoil.* (NEWS)

Notice that the unembedded clause here is part of a passage containing non-clausal elements, and obviously imitating a spoken style.

Elsewhere, unembedded dependent clauses occur in **block language,** such as newspaper headlines:

> *Paris Transport Workers to Strike.* (NEWS)
> *Climbing High, but Feeling Low.* (NEWS)

Review

Major points of Grammar Bite E: Dependent clauses

➤ Dependent clauses are subdivided into finite and non-finite clauses (whereas independent clauses are generally finite).

➤ Finite dependent clauses include complement, adverbial, relative, comparative, and other degree clauses.

➤ There are also some clause types of borderline status: e.g. reporting clauses and question tags.

➤ Non-finite dependent clauses include infinitive clauses, *ing*-clauses, *ed*-clauses, and verbless clauses.

➤ In certain circumstances, dependent clauses are used as separate units, like independent clauses.

9
Complex noun phrases

GRAMMAR BITES in this chapter

A Types of noun modification

➤ The different structures used to modify noun phrases
➤ The patterns of use for noun modification across the registers

B Premodification

➤ Modifiers that occur in front of the head noun in a noun phrase: attributive adjectives, noun + noun sequences, and other more specialized structures

C Relative clauses

➤ Options in the structure of relative clauses, such as the choice between different relative pronouns
➤ Factors that are associated with each option

D Other postmodifier types

➤ Modifiers other than relative clauses that occur following the head noun in a noun phrase: non-finite clauses, prepositional phrases, and appositive noun phrases

E Noun complement clauses

➤ The different kinds of noun complement clauses: *that*-clauses, *to*-infinitive clauses, *of* + *ing*-clauses and *wh*-interrogative clauses
➤ The functions of the different types of noun complement clauses

9.1 **Introduction**

The basic noun phrase, which we discussed in Chapter 4, can be expanded with noun **modifiers**. **Premodifiers**, like attributive adjectives, occur before the **head** noun. **Postmodifiers**, like relative clauses, occur following the head noun. In total, noun phrases can be composed of four major components:

determiner + premodifiers + head noun + postmodifiers

All noun phrases include a head, while determiners, premodifiers, and postmodifiers are optional. This can be illustrated in the following noun phrases:

determiner	premodifiers	head (noun)	postmodifiers
	industrially advanced	countries	
a	small wooden	box	that he owned
a	market	system	that has no imperfections
the	new training	college	for teachers
		patterns	of industrial development in the United States

A pronoun can substitute for a noun or a complete noun phrase. As a result, noun phrases can have a pronoun instead of a noun as the head. Pronoun-headed phrases usually do not include a determiner or premodifiers, but they may have postmodifiers. Several pronoun-headed phrases are illustrated here:

determiner	premodifiers	head (pronoun)	postmodifiers
		I	
		she	
		anyone	who is willing to listen
		those	who take the trouble to register
the	big	one	in town

As the above examples show, noun phrases can be expanded in many ways and often involve both premodifiers and postmodifiers. As a result, noun phrases are often structurally complex, especially in written discourse.

For example, the following sentence is from a newspaper article about cellular radios. Its main clause structure is very simple: a main verb (*is*) with two noun phrase slots (marked by *[]*)—subject (*problem*) and subject predicative (*competition*).

> [The latest **problem** for the government] is [increasing **competition** for mobile cellular radio services, which have a small bunch of frequencies around 900 MHz]. (NEWS)

However, this sentence is relatively long and complex because the noun phrases have complex modification:

determiner	premodifiers	head noun	postmodifiers
The	latest	problem	for the government
	increasing	competition	for mobile cellular radio services which have a small bunch of frequencies around 900 MHz.

This example also illustrates that there are different levels of **embedding** within noun phrases. That is, postmodifiers of a first-level noun phrase can include complex noun phrases with pre- and postmodification. For example:

top-level NP:

premodifiers	head noun	postmodifiers
increasing	*competition*	*for mobile cellular radio services* ...

second-level NP (embedded within postmodifer):

premodifiers	head noun	postmodifiers
mobile cellular radio	*services*	*which have a small bunch of frequencies around 900 MHz*

Although we will stop our analysis here, we could go on to break down the noun phrase within the postmodifier *which have a small bunch of frequencies around 900 MHz*.

As this chapter will show, such complexity of noun modification is not unusual in English. In the following five Grammar Bites, we explore the major options for expanding noun phrases in English. In Grammar Bite A, we survey the structures used as noun premodifiers and postmodifiers, comparing the frequency of each type across registers. Then, in Grammar Bite B, we focus on types of premodification. In Grammar Bites C, D, and E, we turn to postnominal modifiers. Relative clauses are the most complex of these because there are many structural alternatives; these are covered in Grammar Bite C. Then, in Grammar Bite D we survey the other structures used as postnominal modifiers and discuss how sequences of postmodifiers can be used in combination. Finally, in Grammar Bite E we consider a special type of structure that occurs following noun heads: noun complement clauses. We show how noun complement clauses are different from relative clauses, and we describe the most common types of noun complement clauses.

GRAMMAR BITE

A Types of noun modification

9.2 **Survey of noun modifier types**

There are several different types of premodifiers and postmodifiers. **Premodifiers** include adjectives, participials, and other nouns:

- adjective as premodifier:

    *a **special** project* (CONV)

    *an **internal** memo* (NEWS)

- participial premodifiers:

    ***written** reasons* (NEWS)

detecting devices (ACAD)

- noun as premodifier:

    the ***bus*** strike (CONV)

    *the **police** report* (NEWS)

There are also several different types of **postmodifier**, including both clauses and phrases. Clausal postmodifiers can be either **finite** or **non-finite**. When the clauses are finite, they are **relative clauses**. Non-finite postmodifier clauses have three different forms: *to-clauses*, *ing-clauses*, and *ed-clauses*:

- relative clause as postmodifier:

    *a footpath **which disappeared in a landscape of fields and trees*** (FICT)

    *beginning students **who have had no previous college science courses*** (ACAD)

- *to*-infinitive clause as postmodifier:

    *the way **to get to our house*** (CONV)

    *enough money **to buy proper food.*** (FICT)

- *ing*-clause as postmodifier:

    *the imperious man **standing under the lamppost*** (FICT)

    *rebels **advancing rapidly southwards*** (NEWS)

- *ed*-clause as postmodifier:

    *fury **fanned by insensitive press coverage*** (NEWS)

    *products **required to support a huge and growing population*** (ACAD)

Phrasal postmodifiers consist of two main types: **prepositional phrases** and **appositive noun phrases**. **Adjective phrases** can also be postmodifiers, but they are less common.

- prepositional phrase as postmodifier:

    *doctors **at the Johns Hopkins Medical School*** (NEWS)

    *compensation **for emotional damage*** (ACAD)

- appositive noun phrase as postmodifier:

    *the Indian captain, **Mohammed Azharuddin*** (NEWS)

- adjective phrase as postmodifiers (not common):

    *President Bush will reiterate he wants a smooth transition and will co-operate in [any way **possible**].* (NEWS)

    *[The extremely short duration varieties **common in India**] were not used in West Africa.* (ACAD†)

Occasionally adverbs can also be premodifiers or postmodifiers in noun phrases:

- adverb as premodifier:

    *the **nearby** guards* (FICT†)

- adverb as postmodifier:

    *a block **behind*** (FICT†)

Noun complement clauses are different from postmodifiers in structure and meaning, although they also occur following noun heads. They involve primarily special kinds of *that-* and *to-*clauses:

*the idea **that he was completely cold and unemotional*** (FICT) *a chance **to do the right thing*** (FICT)

The special features of noun complement clauses are described in Grammar Bite E.

9.3 Noun phrases with premodifiers and postmodifiers across registers

Noun phrases with premodifiers and noun phrases with postmodifiers are about equally common in English. However, there are large differences across registers in the use of the types of modifier.

Figure 9.1 shows that the typical case in conversation is to use nouns with no modifier at all. In fact, noun phrases are often realized by a pronoun instead of a full noun. The following text sample from a conversation illustrates these patterns; all noun phrases are in [], while the head nouns and pronouns are in bold.

Figure 9.1

Distribution of noun phrases with premodifiers and postmodifiers

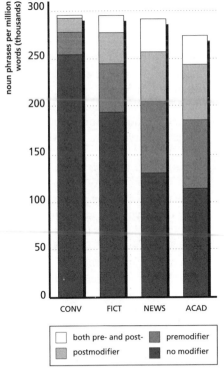

Text sample 1: PICTURES AND SLEEVES (CONV)

A: *[**Trouble**] is [**granny**] does [**it**] and [**she**]'s got [loads of **time**]. [**She**] sits there and does [**them**] twice as fast as [**me**]. [**I**] – what [**I**] like doing, [**I**] like [the **pictures**].*

B: *Yes.*

A: *So [**I**] don't mind doing [the **pictures**]. If [**she**]'d do [the **sleeves**] and [the **back**] for [**me**], [**I**]'d be very grateful.*

B: *Yeah.*

A: *Whereas [**she**] can't stand doing [the **pictures**], cos [**it**] takes [**her**] [too much **time**].*

B: *[**It**]'s like doing [**tapestry**].*

As this excerpt shows, conversation has many noun phrases, but they are usually very short and have concrete referents—specific people, places, or things. Pronouns are also extremely common in conversation. Speakers in a conversation share the same physical situation, and they often share personal knowledge about each other as well. As a result, speakers typically use noun phrases with no modification, knowing that the listener will have no trouble identifying the intended referent.

In contrast, noun phrases in academic writing usually have premodifiers or postmodifiers (or both). The following text sample illustrates these patterns, with the top-level noun phrases marked in *[]*, and the head nouns marked in bold.

Text sample 2: COLLISIONS WITH COMETS (ACAD)

> *[Professor* **H.C. Urey***] has suggested that [rare* **collisions** *between the earth and comets, recorded as scatters of tektites], must have produced [vast* **quantities** *of energy that would have been sufficient to heat up considerably both the atmosphere and the surface layers of the ocean].*

This excerpt has only three non-embedded noun phrases, but two of these have extensive modification. These two noun phrases are listed below, with premodifiers underlined and postmodifiers given in *[]*:

> <u>rare</u> **collisions** *[between the earth and comets], [recorded as scatters of tektites]*
>
> <u>vast</u> **quantities** *[of energy] [that would have been sufficient to heat up considerably both the atmosphere and the surface layers of the ocean]*

Such structures are typical of academic prose, where a majority of all noun phrases have some modification. In fact, much of the new information in academic texts occurs in the modifiers in noun phrases, resulting in a very high density of information.

It is surprising that premodifiers and postmodifiers have a similar distribution across registers. It might be expected that specific registers would tend to rely on either premodifiers or postmodifiers. Instead, we find *both* types of noun modification to be extremely common in written expository registers, while both types are relatively rare in conversation.

9.3.1 Premodifier types across registers

Adjectives are by far the most common type of noun premodifier (Figure 9.2). Adjectives come from many different semantic classes, which cover numerous concepts, including color, size/extent, time/age/frequency, and affective evaluation. Chapter 7 describes the use of these premodifying (attributive) adjectives in detail.

It is more surprising that nouns are also extremely common as noun premodifiers, especially in the written expository registers. Noun + noun sequences are used to express a wide range of meaning relationships in a succinct form. As a result, nouns as premodifiers are especially favored as a space-saving device in newspaper language. We return to a detailed discussion of noun + noun sequences in 9.5.

Figure 9.2

Frequency of premodifier types across registers

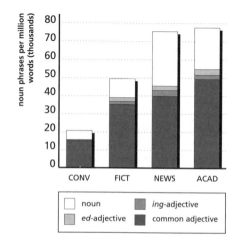

9.3.2 Postmodifier types across registers

Although relative clauses often receive the most attention in discussions of noun postmodifiers, prepositional phrases are actually much more common (Figure 9.3). Prepositional phrases as postmodifiers are especially common in news and academic prose. These structures often occur in extremely dense, embedded sequences. In the following text extract, postmodifiers are in *[]* with the associated prepositions in bold. Top-level noun phrases (i.e. those which are not part of other noun phrases) are underlined:

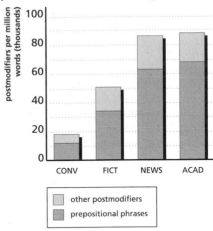

Figure 9.3

Prepositional v. other postmodification across registers

other postmodifiers

prepositional phrases

> <u>Mortality</u> [**among** stocks [**of** eggs] [stored outdoors in the ground]] averaged 70%; <u>eggs [collected the following spring from a large number [**of** natural habitats [**in** the central part [**of** the province]]] suffered <u>a 46% reduction [**in** viability]</u> [which could only be attributed to this exposure [**to** cold]]. <u>Further evidence [**of** the association [**of** winter egg mortality [**with** sub-zero temperatures and snow cover]]]</u> was reported **by** <u>Riegert</u> (1967a). (ACAD)

(Note that prepositional phrases can also function as adverbials, as in *collected . . . from.*)

In academic prose, prepositional phrases allow a very dense packaging of information in a text. They are more compact than relative clauses. For example, compare the prepositional phrase from the beginning of the last example with an alternative relative clause:

prepositional phrase postmodifier

mortality among stocks . . .

relative clause postmodifier

mortality which occurred among stocks . . .

Prepositional phrases commonly occur in sequences in academic prose, which also adds to the dense packing of information. For example, the sample above contains the sequence:

> *a large number [of natural habitats [in the central part [of the province]]]*

Relative clauses differ from prepositional phrases as postmodifiers in both their communicative function and their register distribution (see Figure 9.4). They are common in both fiction and news, where they are often used to identify or describe a person:

> *someone **whom I had never seen before*** (FICT)

> *a man on the platform **whose looks I didn't like*** (FICT)

> *a 20-year-old woman **who has been missing for a week*** (NEWS)

When they are used to characterize inanimate objects, relative clauses often link the object to a person, as in 1–3 below. Further, relative clauses in fiction and news typically use dynamic verbs describing actions, in contrast to the static presentation of information associated with prepositional phrases:

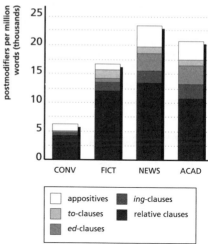

Figure 9.4

Non-prepositional postmodifier types across registers

1 *one of those mixed-up salads **which men will eat with complete docility in restaurants*** (FICT)
2 *the boiling pot of gravy **which fell upon his foot*** (FICT)
3 *the 1988 event **which left her on the verge of a nervous breakdown*** (NEWS)

All three of these examples relate an inanimate head (*salads, pot, event*) to a person (*men, his foot, her*) and use a dynamic verb (*eat, fell, left*).

The other types of clausal postmodifier are less common (although postmodifying *ed*-clauses and appositive noun phrases are relatively common in news and academic prose). Each of these postmodifier types is described in detail in Grammar Bite D.

9.3.3 Modifiers with different head noun types

In general, nouns occur freely with premodifiers and postmodifiers, while pronouns rarely occur with modification. However, there are notable exceptions to this rule. For example, proper nouns and other naming expressions usually do not occur with a modifier, since the name itself clearly refers to a specific person, place, or institution. When proper nouns do occur with a modifier, it is usually an appositive noun phrase, such as (appositive underlined):

> **Heiko**, *a 19-year-old factory worker* (NEWS)
>
> **Voronezh**, *a dour city of 850,000 people in the great Russian heartlands* (NEWS)

Personal pronouns (like *I, you, she*) follow the general rule of rarely occurring with a modifier. However, other pronoun classes behave differently. For example, the substitute pronoun *one*, which stands for a noun or noun-headed expression, is similar to common noun heads because it freely takes both premodifiers and postmodifiers. In conversation, a modifier is used to identify 'which one' is intended (premodifiers and postmodifiers underlined):

> *You know **the one** _she ran off with_.* (CONV)
>
> *He's got **a** _horrible_ **one** _that he hardly ever wears_.* (CONV)
>
> ***The** _last_ **one** _I had_ was at least four years ago.* (CONV†)

The substitute pronoun *one* in academic prose is usually directly anaphoric, substituting for a previously used noun phrase, but the modifier provides new descriptive details about that referent:

> The idea is **a** *strange* **one**. (ACAD†)

Postmodifiers are used more commonly than premodifiers to give the new information, since they can be longer and thus provide more descriptive information:

> A black body is **one** that perfectly absorbs, and then re-emits, all radiation falling upon it. (ACAD)

Indefinite pronouns can also take both premodifiers and postmodifiers. However, postmodifiers are overwhelmingly more common with this head type.

> **All** *I know* is nobody likes her. (CONV)
>
> Um, this was a surprise to **several** *of us*. (CONV)
>
> We have tried to impart **something** about the motivations of contemporary geologists. (ACAD†)
>
> But today, over thirty years after Basset's book appeared, is there **anything** new to say about 1931? (ACAD)

Demonstrative pronouns differ from other head types in that they take only postmodifiers. However, each individual pronoun shows a different pattern of use:

- The pronouns *this* and *these* are extremely rare with a modifier.
- The pronoun *that* occasionally takes a postmodifier.
- The pronoun *those* is extremely common with a postmodifier, especially in writing.

When it occurs with a modifier, the demonstrative pronoun *that* usually takes an *of* prepositional phrase as postmodifier:

> The simplest covalent structure is **that** *of diamond*. (ACAD) <i.e. the structure of diamond>

In contrast, the demonstrative pronoun *those*—referring to people or things— takes a variety of postmodifiers to identify the intended reference:

> A state may have good grounds in some special circumstances for coercing **those** who have no duty to obey. (ACAD)
>
> They sat erect, conscious of their uniforms, styled like **those** of the post-1843 Prussian army. (FICT) < = like the uniforms of the post-1843 Prussian army>
>
> This may be smugly satisfying to **those** of us who sit on the sidelines. (NEWS)

Review

Major points of **GRAMMAR BITE A:** Types of noun modification
➤ There are many different types of premodifiers and postmodifiers.
➤ Adjectives are the most common premodifier type.
  ➤ Nouns are also very common as premodifiers in the written registers.
➤ Prepositional phrases are by far the most common type of postmodifier.
  ➤ Relative clauses are also common.
➤ Premodifiers and postmodifiers are distributed in the same way across registers: rare in conversation, very common in informational writing.

> ➤ Different types of noun phrase heads (e.g. common noun, personal pronoun, indefinite pronoun) are associated with different types of modifiers.

B Premodification

9.4 Types of premodifiers

There are four major structural types of premodification in English:
- general adjective: *big pillow, new pants, official negotiations, political isolation*
- *ed*-participial modifier: *restricted area, improved growth, fixed volume, established tradition*
- *ing*-participial modifier: *flashing lights, growing problem, exhausting task*
- noun: *staff room, pencil case, market forces, maturation period*

In addition, as we showed in Chapter 4, determiners, genitives, and numerals precede the head and modifiers, and help to specify the reference of noun phrases.

Premodifiers are condensed structures. They use fewer words than postmodifiers to convey roughly the same information. Most adjectival and participial premodifiers can be re-phrased as a longer, postmodifying relative clause:

premodifiers	relative clause as postmodifier
a **big** pillow	a pillow **which is big**
a **restricted** area	an area **which is restricted**
an **established** tradition	a tradition **which has been established**
flashing lights	lights **which are flashing**

We explained in 9.3.1 that general adjectives, functioning as attributive adjectives, are the most common form of noun premodifiers.

Figure 9.2 in 9.3.1 showed that nouns are also extremely common as premodifiers, especially in newspaper language and academic prose. Noun + noun sequences can represent many different meaning relationships, but there are no signals to indicate which meaning is intended in any given case. To rephrase noun + noun sequences as postmodifiers requires a wide range of function words (different prepositions and relative pronouns) together with different verbs. Thus consider the range of meaning relationships expressed by the following noun + noun sequences:

noun + noun sequence	re-phrasing with a postmodifier
plastic trays	*trays made from plastic*
wash basins	*basins used for washing*
law report	*report about the law*

noun + noun sequence	re-phrasing with a postmodifier
company management	*the management of a company*
commission sources	*sources in the commission*
elephant boy	*boy who resembles an elephant*

In fact, such sequences often represent more than one possible meaning relationship. *Commission sources* could also be 'sources of commission', and *elephant boy* could refer to 'a boy who rides on an elephant'.

In the following section, we examine the range of meanings that noun + noun sequences can express. Then, in 9.6, we introduce more complex combinations of premodifiers.

9.5 Meaning relationships expressed by noun + noun sequences

Noun + noun sequences contain only content words, with no function word to show the meaning relationship between the two parts (see also 4.11.3). This means that they present information densely. It also means they rely heavily on implicit meaning, because the reader must infer the intended logical relationship between the modifying noun and head noun. In fact, noun + noun sequences are used to express a bewildering array of logical relations, including the following (where the head noun is labeled N2 and the premodifying noun N1):

- composition (N2 is made from N1; N2 consists of N1):

    e.g. *glass windows = windows made from glass*

    metal seat, plastic beaker, zinc supplement, protein granules, tomato sauce, satin dress, egg masses, water supplies, fact sheets

- purpose (N2 is for the purpose of N1; N2 is used for N1):

    e.g. *pencil case = case used for pencils*

    brandy bottle, patrol car, Easter eggs, picnic ham, chess board, safety device, search procedure, worship services, war fund, extortion plan

- identity (N2 has the same referent as N1 but classifies it in terms of different attributes):

    e.g. *women algebraists = women who are algebraists*

    conventionalist judge, men workers, consultant cardiologist, member country, exam papers, grant aid

- content (N2 is about N1; N2 deals with N1):

    e.g. *algebra text = a text about algebra, probability profile = profile showing probability*

    market report, sports diary, prescription chart, success rates, credit agreement, intelligence bureau

- objective (N1 is the object of the process described in N2, or of the action performed by the agent described in N2):

    e.g. *egg production = X produces eggs, taxi driver = X drives a taxi waste disposal, paddy cultivation, root development, curio sellers, corn farmer, computer users*

- subjective (N1 is the subject of the process described in N2; N2 is usually a nominalization of an intransitive verb):

  e.g. *child development = children develop*
  leaf appearance, eye movement, management buy-out

- time (N2 is found or takes place at the time given by N1):

  e.g. *summer conditions = conditions that occur during the summertime*
  Sunday school, Christmas raffle

- location (N2 is found or takes place at the location given by N1):

  e.g. *corner cupboard = a cupboard that is located in the corner*
  roof slates, Paris conference, church square, surface traction, tunnel trains

- institution (N2 identifies an institution for N1):

  e.g. *insurance companies = companies for (selling) insurance*
  ski club, egg industry

- partitive (N2 identifies parts of N1):

  e.g. *cat legs = legs of a cat*
  rifle butt, family member

- specialization (N1 identifies an area of specialization for the person or occupation given in N2; N2 is animate):

  e.g. *finance director = director who specializes in finance*
  Education Secretary, gossip columnists, football fans, estate agent, management consultant

Many sequences can be analyzed as belonging to more than one category. For example, *thigh injury* and *heart attack* could be considered as either objective (*X injured the thigh*) or location (*the injury is located at the thigh*).

In addition, many noun + noun sequences do not fit neatly into any of the above categories. For example, the expression *riot police* might be understood as expressing purpose, but there is an additional component of meaning: these are police used to control riots, not police for (creating) riots! Other noun + noun sequences express a range of meaning relationships in addition to the above major categories. For example:

noun + noun	meaning
voice communication	communication using voice
union assets	assets belonging to a union
jet streams	air streams moving like a jet
bank holiday	holiday observed by banks
pressure hose	hose able to withstand pressure
pressure ratios	ratios measuring pressure

9.5.1 Premodifying nouns that occur with many head nouns

A few premodifying nouns are especially productive in that they combine with many different head nouns. For example, the noun *family* is used with a wide range of head nouns representing many different kinds of semantic relationships:

family affair	*family barbecue*	*family doctor*
family argument	*family car*	*family entertainment*
family background	*family company*	*family friend*

In conversation, only a few nouns are productive as premodifiers. The combinations that do occur reflect the everyday-life topics of conversation. For example:

> *car* + *accident, door, insurance, keys, park, seat, wash*
>
> *school* + *book, children, clothes, fees, holidays, trips*

In contrast, newspaper language makes extensive use of noun + noun sequences. Many of the most productive premodifying nouns identify major institutions, especially government, business, and the media. For example:

> *government* + *action, agencies, approval, bonds, control, decision*
>
> *business* + *administration, cards, community, dealings, empire, ideas*
>
> *TV* + *ads, appearance, cameras, channel, crew, documentary, licence*

Some premodifiers that are productive in conversation are also productive in news. However, in news they usually have an institutional meaning. For example:

> *water* + *authorities, bill, companies, industry, levels, privatisation*

The extremely productive use of noun + noun sequences in newspaper language results in a very dense presentation of information. These forms save space, since each noun + noun sequence conveys a complex meaning in condensed form. However, the dense use of these forms can place a heavy burden on readers, who must infer the intended meaning relationship between the modifying noun and head noun.

9.5.2 Plural nouns as premodifiers

Although the singular form is usually used for premodifying nouns, plural nouns can also occur as premodifiers. Typical examples include *carpets retailer, cities correspondent, drugs business, trades union, residents association*. This pattern is much more common in British English than in American English.

Plural nouns as premodifiers occur especially in newspaper language. A few nouns are commonly found in both American and British English. For example:

> *arms* + *race, scandal, supplier, treaty*
>
> *sales* + *force, gain, increases, tax*
>
> *savings* + *account, banks, deposits, institutions*
>
> *women* + *candidates, drivers, ministers, voters*

However, there is a much larger set of plural nouns used frequently in British English but rarely in American English. For example:

> *drugs* + *administration, ban, business, companies, problem, trade*

jobs + *crisis, losses, market*

animals *shelter,* **careers** *office,* **highways** *department*

In addition to the overall dialect differences, there are two factors that are associated with the use of a plural premodifying noun. The first is when the noun premodifier only has a plural form, or has a special meaning associated with the plural:

arms *accord,* **customs** *officer,* **explosives** *factory*

However, some nouns which have only a plural form do lose the plural ending in noun + noun constructions:

scissor *kick,* **trouser** *leg*

The second factor is when the noun modifier itself contains more than one word:

1 *At Tesco's you've got fifty feet of [[**baked beans**] shelves].* (CONV†)
2 *A bit more will be said of particular features of the metalinguistic and [[**possible-worlds**] proposals].* (ACAD†)

The plural form in these sequences provides a clear signal of the structure of the complex noun phrase. In writing, some of these premodifiers are hyphenated (as in **2** above).

Some plural nouns, such as *affairs, relations, resources, rights,* and *services* are almost always premodified themselves, and retain the plural form when used in premodification:

*the State Department's [[**consular affairs**] bureau]* (NEWS)

*Labour's chief [[**foreign affairs**] spokesman]* (NEWS)

*the [[**customer relations**] department]* (CONV)

9.6 **Noun phrases with multiple premodifiers**

In written registers, many noun phrases occur with multiple premodifiers. However, it is rare for all the words in a premodification sequence to modify the head noun. Rather, premodifying sequences usually have embedded relationships, with some words modifying other premodifiers instead of the head noun. For example, consider the following noun phrases:

*[[**quite pale**] skin]*

*two [[**mutually perpendicular**] directions]*

Both of these noun phrases show an adverb (*quite* and *mutually*) modifying a following adjective (*pale* and *perpendicular*) instead of the head noun (*skin* and *directions*).

In a few cases, the meaning relationships among constituents are truly ambiguous. For example, out of context, the noun phrase *two more practical principles* has two distinct interpretations:

[two more] [practical] principles—i.e. 'two additional principles that are practical'

two [[more] practical] principles—i.e. 'two principles that are more practical'

Other noun phrases illustrate different relationships among the constituents, as in the following noun phrases with three-word premodification:

> *the [[one-time prosperous] [[market] town]]*
> *the [[controversial] [offshore investment] portfolios]*

The number of possible meaning relationships increases dramatically with each additional premodifier. Thus, noun phrases with four-word premodification can represent many different meaning relationships among constituents. For example, each of the following noun phrases with four-word premodification represents a different set of meaning relations:

> 1 *[[naked], [shameless], [direct], [brutal] exploitation]*
> 2 *[[very [finely grained]] [alluvial] material]*
> 3 *a [[totally [covered]], [uninsulated] [[pig] house]]*

In **1**, all four words in the premodification directly modify the head noun. This type of structuring is very rare, however. As **2** and **3** illustrate, multiple words in the premodification much more commonly have complex structural relationships among themselves.

9.6.1 The order of multiple premodifiers

Although there are no absolute rules, there are a few general tendencies governing the order of words in a premodification sequence:

A Adverb + adjective + head

Adverbs almost always precede adjectives. This is because adverbs usually modify the following adjective rather than the head noun directly. Examples include:

> *a **really hot** day*   *a **thoroughly satisfactory** reply*
> *a **rather blunt** penknife*   *an **extremely varied** and **immensely pleasing** exhibition*

B Adjective + noun + head

When a noun phrase has both an adjective and a noun as premodifiers, the adjective usually precedes the noun. This sequence is most common because the position closest to the head noun is filled by modifiers that are more integrated with the meaning of the head noun. The following noun phrases illustrate these tendencies:

- adjective + noun + head:
  > *mature rice grain, thick winter overcoat, true life stories, bright canvas bags*
- color adjective + noun + head:
  > *black plastic sheet, black leather jacket, red address book*
- participial adjective + noun + head:
  > *an experienced woman worker, broken bicycle wheels, an increasing mortgage burden*

This order can sometimes be reversed, especially with participial adjectives. This is when the premodifying noun modifies the participial adjective (rather than the head noun):

- noun + participial adjective + head noun:

[information processing] activities, [hypothesis testing] process

In most cases, this kind of sequence of premodifiers is hyphenated. In fact, such sequences may be considered as adjectival compounds (see 7.3.3):

English-speaking world, self-fulfilling prophecy, tree-lined avenues, egg-shaped ball

C Adjective + adjective + head

A related principle for multiple adjectives as premodifiers is that **descriptors** tend to precede **classifiers** (see 7.6.):

stronger environmental regulation, any major industrial nation

Color adjectives tend to follow other adjectives. For example:

- adjective + color adjective + head noun:

    dry white grass, clear blue eyes, shabby black clothes

9.6.2 Coordinated premodifiers

In one respect, coordinated premodifiers make the logical relationships among premodifiers explicit, since each part directly modifies the head noun:

> **black and white** *cat*
>
> **hot and hardening** *mud*
>
> **arrogant and unattractive** *man*
>
> **physical and sexual** *abuse*

However, these structures have their own kinds of indeterminacy. In most cases, premodifiers coordinated with *and* are used to identify two distinct attributes that are qualities of a single referent:

> **precise and effective** *solutions*
>
> **pleasing and efficient** *surroundings*
>
> **complex and technical** *legislation*

With plural and uncountable heads, however, *and*-coordinated premodifiers can also be used to identify two different (mutually exclusive) referents, such as:

> **spoken and written** *styles*
>
> **male and female** *workers*
>
> **British and American** *spelling*

Thus, *precise and effective solutions* refers to solutions that are both precise and effective. In contrast, *spoken and written styles* refers to two different kinds of styles—spoken style and written style—rather than to styles that are both spoken and written.

Or-coordinated premodifiers can also have two interpretations. In some cases, either one, or both, of the two attributes can be applied to a given referent:

> **racial or religious** *cohesion*
>
> **familiar or preplanned** *activities*

In other cases, though, the coordinator connects two attributes that are mutually exclusive, so that only one can characterize a given referent:

> **dead or dying** *larvae*
>
> **petroleum or coal-based** *hydrocarbon matrices*

In general, coordinated premodifiers are most common in academic writing. Certain adjective + adjective combinations are especially common, often referring to complementary demographic or institutional characteristics (e.g. *social and cultural*, *economic and political*, *mental and physical*):

> *Such a strategy assumes <...> that it will be legitimized by a range of **social and cultural** values.* (ACAD†)

In fiction, certain adjectives are common as the first member of adjective+ adjective combinations, adding descriptive details about the noun:

> ***black and ginger*** *fur* (FICT)
>
> *a **black and yellow** eel-like fish* (FICT)
>
> *this **strange and empty** country* (FICT)
>
> *this **strange and dreaded** group of men* (FICT)

Review

Major points of GRAMMAR BITE B: Premodification

➤ There are four major types of noun premodifier: general adjective, *ed*-participial modifier, *ing*-participial modifier, and noun.
  ➤ Nouns as premodifiers are especially rich in meaning because they express a wide array of logical relationships.
  ➤ A few nouns, like *car*, *school*, *government*, and *TV*, are especially productive as premodifiers.
  ➤ Plural nouns can also occur as premodifiers, as in *arms race*. This pattern is more common in British English.
➤ When noun phrases have multiple premodifiers, they tend to occur in a predictable order depending on their grammatical category: e.g. adjective + noun + head noun.
➤ Coordinated premodifiers (e.g. *male and female workers*) are found primarily in academic prose.
  ➤ Coordinated premodifiers are surprisingly complex because their meaning is not explicit.

GRAMMAR BITE

C Relative clauses

9.7 Restrictive v. non-restrictive function

Relative clauses are often classified by their function as either **restrictive** or **non-restrictive**. Restrictive relative clauses identify the intended reference of the head noun (the whole noun phrase is included in *[]*):

> *Richard hit the ball on [the car **that was going past**].* (CONV)

The relative clause in this sentence has a restrictive function. It pinpoints the particular 'car' being referred to.

In contrast, non-restrictive relative clauses add elaborating, descriptive information about a head noun that has already been identified or is assumed to be known. For example:

> He looked into [her mailbox, **which she never locked**]. (FICT)

In this example, the particular mailbox is identified by the possessive pronoun *her*, and the non-restrictive relative clause is used to provide additional, descriptive information.

In writing, non-restrictive postmodifiers are usually separated from the head noun by a comma, while no punctuation is used with a restrictive postmodifier. In spoken language, where there are no punctuation marks, intonation and pauses can differentiate restrictive and non-restrictive postmodifiers. (For the following analyses, we have used punctuation to identity non-restrictive relative clauses in the written registers.)

Overall, analyzing the frequency of relative clauses, we find that:

- Restrictive relative clauses are much more common than non-restrictive clauses.

- Newspaper stories tend to use non-restrictive clauses to a greater extent than other registers.

The information added by non-restrictive clauses is often tangential to the main point of a text. This is especially the case in news, where non-restrictive clauses are used to add information of potential interest but not directly related to the news story. For example, consider the following sentences from a news article about negotiations for the sale of the firm Whyte & Mackay by the company Brent Walker:

> Brent Walker said it expected the buyout negotiations 'would be successfully completed shortly.' Brent Walker bought Whyte & Mackay from Lonrho earlier this year for £180m in a deal that included four French vineyards, **which are also for sale for as much as £60m**. (NEWS)

In this excerpt, the fact that the French vineyards are for sale does not help the reader identify the referent of 'vineyards'. Instead, this is an extra piece of information that might be of interest to some readers.

Similar uses of non-restrictive relative clauses are also common in news when the head is a proper noun:

> American Airlines, **which began the daily flights to Chicago less than a year ago**, accused the government of being partly to blame. (NEWS†)

In constructions of this type, the identity of the head noun is well-known to readers, and the non-restrictive relative clause is used to add newsworthy but incidental information about that referent.

9.7.1 Restrictive and non-restrictive functions with other postmodifiers

Although this Grammar Bite focuses on relative clauses, it is worth noting that postmodifiers other than relative clauses can also be classified by restrictive and non-restrictive functions. The great majority of other postmodifiers are restrictive, including most of the examples you have seen earlier in this chapter. For example:

- restrictive *ed*-clause:

  > His is a fury **fanned by insensitive press coverage of homosexuality and the AIDS epidemic.** (NEWS†)

- restrictive *ing*-clause:

  > The Ethiopian army is failing to halt northern rebels **advancing rapidly southwards to the capitol.** (NEWS†)

- restrictive prepositional phrase:

  > Doctors **at the Johns Hopkins Medical School in Baltimore** say that
  > <...> (NEWS†)

In each case above, the postmodifier is important for identifying the reference of the head noun.

However, other postmodifiers do have a non-restrictive function occasionally, though much less commonly than relative clauses.

- non-restrictive *ed*-clauses:

  > A converted farm building, **donated by Mr. and Mrs. Tabor,** has been turned into a study room filled with photographs and displays. (NEWS)
  > The distinction between public and private law, **espoused in many pluralist accounts,** is largely bogus. (ACAD)

- non-restrictive *ing*-clauses:

  > Both writing and reading are enormously complex skills, **involving the coordination of sensory and cognitive processes.** (ACAD)
  > Style variation is intrinsic to the novel's satiric-epic picture of Victorian urban society, **concentrating on the capitalist house of Dombey.** (ACAD)

- non-restrictive prepositional phrases:

  > The great tall library, **with the Book of Kells and of Robert Emmet,** charmed him. (FICT)
  > The sale, **for a sum not thought to be material,** marks the final dismemberment of Metro-Cammell Weymann. (NEWS)

Appositive noun phrases are exceptional—they are usually non-restrictive:

- non-restrictive appositive noun phrases:

  > The rebels, **the Tigrayan People's Liberation Front** (TPLF) (NEWS)
  > a Soviet Deputy Defence Minister, **General Varrenikov** (NEWS)
  > both types of eggs **(diapause and non-diapause)** (ACAD)

9.8 Postmodification by relative clauses

When discussing relative clauses, we will focus on three key components: the **head** noun, the **relativizer**, and the **gap**.

- The head noun is the noun modified by the relative clause.
- The relativizer is the word, such as *who* or *that*, which introduces the relative clause. It refers to the same person or thing as the head noun.
- The gap is the location of the missing constituent in the relative clause. All relative clauses have a missing constituent, which again corresponds in meaning to the head noun.

Thus, consider the relative clause construction:

> the diamond _earrings_ **that Mama wore** ∧. (FICT)

- The head noun is _earrings_.
- The relativizer is _that_, referring to the 'earrings'.
- The gap occurs in the direct object position, after the verb _wore_. The underlying meaning of the relative clause is that 'Mama wore [the earrings]'.

There are many variations possible with relative clauses, and these are described in detail in the following sections. The most obvious of these involves the choice of relativizer (9.8.1). In addition, relative clauses can occur with different gap positions (9.8.2). Relative clauses with adverbial gaps occur with an especially wide range of variants; these are dealt with in a separate section (9.8.3).

9.8.1 The discourse choice among relativizers

In standard English, relative clauses can be formed using eight different relativizers. Five of these are **relative pronouns**: _which, who, whom, whose,_ and _that_. The other three relativizers are **relative adverbs**: _where, when,_ and _why_. In the following examples, head nouns are underlined, and relative clauses are in bold:

> The lowest pressure _ratio_ **which will give an acceptable performance** is always chosen. (ACAD†)
>
> There are plenty of existing _owners_ **who are already keen to make the move.** (NEWS)
>
> There was a slight, furtive _boy_ **whom no one knew.** (FICT)
>
> It was good for the _fans_, **whose support so far this season has been fantastic.** (NEWS)
>
> Well, I can see that this is may be the only _way_ **that I can help Neil.** (CONV)
>
> I could lead you to the _shop_ **where I bought it.** (FICT)
>
> He was born in another age, the _age_ **when we played not for a million dollars in prize money.** (NEWS)
>
> There are many _reasons_ **why we may wish to automate parts of the decision process.** (ACAD)

In addition, in many cases the relativizer can be omitted (but not with subject gaps, discussed below), resulting in a **zero relativizer** (represented as ∧ in **1** and **2**):

> 1 The next _thing_ ∧ **she knows,** she's talking to Danny. (CONV)
> 2 Gwen gave the little frowning _smile_ ∧ **she used when she was putting something to someone.** (FICT†)

Relative pronouns substitute for a noun phrase in the relative clause (subject, direct object, etc.), while relative adverbs substitute for an adverbial phrase. For example, the relative pronoun _whom_ stands for the direct object of the verb _knew_ in the following structure:

> a slight, furtive boy **whom no one knew**

Here the relative clause has the meaning of 'No one knew [the boy]'.

In contrast, the relative adverb *where* stands for an entire prepositional phrase that expresses an adverbial of place:

> the shop **where I bought it**

Here the relative clause has the meaning of 'I bought it [at the shop]'.

To some extent, the choice of relative pronoun is determined by structural factors like the position of the gap in the relative clause. The relativizers *that*, *which*, and *who* are the most flexible in their gap positions. As a result, they are by far the most frequent forms. The most common use of all three pronouns is with subject gaps:

- subject gaps:

  > *Do you want a cup of tea **that's been brewing for three days?*** (CONV)
  >
  > *The lowest pressure ratio **which will give an acceptable performance** is always chosen.* (ACAD†)
  >
  > *There are merchant bankers **who find it convenient to stir up apprehension.*** (NEWS†)

However, all three of these relative pronouns can also be used with other gap positions:

- direct object gaps:

  > *She came up with all sorts of things **that she would like for the new development.*** (CONV)
  >
  > *Ralph trotted into the forest and returned with a wide spray of green **which he dumped on the fire.*** (FICT)
  >
  > *He took an instant dislike to Leroy, **who he attacked twice.*** (FICT†)

- other gaps (circumstance adverbial or complement of preposition):

  1 *You have to pay for it in the year **that you don't make any profit.*** (CONV) <time adverbial>

  2 *Well, that's the only way **that this can be assessed.*** (CONV) <manner adverbial>

  3 <. . .> *the mustard pot, **which he had been sitting on.*** (FICT†) <complement of preposition>

  4 *They are statements of a kind **about which readers can readily agree.*** (ACAD) <complement of preposition>

  5 <. . .> *the guy **who I buy the Mega stuff off.*** (CONV†) <complement of preposition>

In contrast to *that*, *which*, and *who*, the other relativizers are rarer. They are restricted to a specific gap position:

- *Whom* occurs only with non-subject noun phrase gaps.
- *Whose* occurs only with possessive/genitive gaps.
- *Where*, *when*, and *why* occur only with adverbial gaps. The choice of the specific relative adverb is determined by the adverbial meaning of the gap: *where* for place/location; *when* for time; *why* for reason. These distinctions are described in 9.8.3.
- Zero occurs only with non-subject gaps in restrictive relative clauses. Thus, it would be impossible to omit the relative pronoun in a subject-gap relative clause such as:

> *There are merchant bankers* **who find it convenient to stir up**
> **apprehension.**
> <compare: **There are merchant bankers* **find it convenient to stir up**
> **apprehension.**>

or a non-restrictive relative clause:

> *He took an instant dislike to Leroy,* **who he attacked twice.** (FICT†)
> <compare: **He took an instant dislike to Leroy,* **he attacked twice.**>

Examples **4** and **5** above also show that when the relative pronoun is part of a prepositional phrase, speakers and writers have the choice to put the preposition before the relative pronoun (**4**) or to leave it **stranded** (**5**). Thus, **5** has the alternative form:

> **5a** *the guy* **off whom** *I bought the Mega stuff*

Although prescriptive grammarians may consider stranded prepositions incorrect, many users find that a clause like **5a** sounds overly formal or even incorrect (especially in conversation). Preposition use is discussed further with adverbial gaps (see 9.8.3).

9.8.2 Relative pronoun choices

Three relative pronouns stand out as being particularly common in English: *who*, *which*, and *that*. The zero relativizer is also relatively common. However, Figures 9.5–9.8 show that the relative pronouns are used in very different ways across registers. For example:

- *That* and zero are the preferred choices in conversation, although relative clauses are generally rare in that register.
- Fiction is similar to conversation in its preference for *that*.
- In contrast, news shows a much stronger preference for *which* and *who*, and academic prose strongly prefers *which*.

In general, the relative pronouns that begin with the letters *wh-* are considered to be more literate. In contrast, the pronoun *that* and the zero relativizer have a more colloquial flavor and are preferred in conversation.

These register differences are related to other structural and functional considerations. For example, newspaper texts commonly discuss the actions of people, resulting in a frequent use of relative clauses with *who*, such as:

> *a 20-year-old woman* **who has been missing for a week** (NEWS)

In contrast, academic prose focuses on inanimate objects or concepts, resulting in a much greater use of the relativizer *which*.

The choice among relative pronouns is influenced by a number of other factors, including gap position, and restrictive v. non-restrictive function. In general, *that* is usually used only with restrictive relative clauses, while *which* is used with both restrictive and non-restrictive clauses. The following subsections consider a number of these factors for specific sets of alternatives.

A *Who* v. *which* with human and non-human head nouns

Of the four most common relativizers (*who*, *which*, *that*, and zero), two—*who* and *which*—are most sharply distinguished:

- *Who* occurs almost exclusively after human heads.

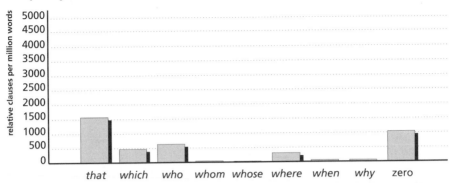

re 9.5   **Frequency of relativizers in conversation**

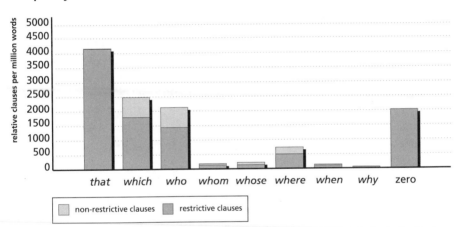

re 9.6   **Frequency of relativizers in fiction**

■ non-restrictive clauses   ■ restrictive clauses

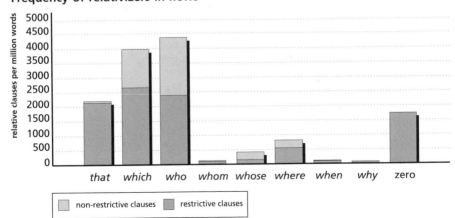

re 9.7   **Frequency of relativizers in news**

■ non-restrictive clauses   ■ restrictive clauses

Figure 9.8 Frequency of relativizers in academic prose

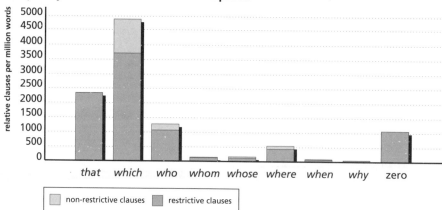

- *Which* occurs most often after inanimate heads.

Especially in the written registers, there is a very strong tendency for a relative clause with a human head noun to use *who* rather than *which* (or *that*):

> They all seemed to have relatives **who had been involved in scandals in London hotels.** (FICT)

> Team Millar rider McWilliams, **who is still looking for a 500 Grand Prix finish**, had a constructive finish. (NEWS)

B *That* and zero with human and non-human head nouns

Relative clauses with *that* or zero are flexible in that they can be used with both inanimate and animate head nouns. In conversation, *that* freely occurs with animate heads. In fact, for many head nouns referring to humans, *that* is almost as common in conversation as *who*:

> all those poor people **that died** (CONV)

> that man **that I went to that time** (CONV)

> that girl **that lives down the road** (CONV)

> all these children **that like to go to the library** (CONV)

These same head nouns also commonly take a zero relativizer in conversation:

> Who's the ugliest person **you've ever seen?** (CONV)

> I thought of a girl **I used to know called Louise.** (CONV)

C *Whom* v. *who* v. *that* with human head nouns

The relativizers *who* and *whom* are both used with animate head nouns, but the choice between them is pretty clear-cut: *who* is usually used with subject gap positions, while *whom* is used with non-subject gaps:

- *who* with subject gap:

> This gentleman is the doctor **who examined the body.** (FICT)

- *whom* with non-subject gap:

> They lived in America and had one child, a girl **whom they idolized.** (FICT)

With non-restrictive relative clauses, there is a very strong preference to use *who/whom* rather than *that* or zero:

> *Donal Lenihan,* **who had been named as captain,** *has also withdrawn after injuring a shoulder.* (NEWS)
>
> *This man,* **whom Elethia never saw,** *opened a locally famous restaurant.* (FICT†)

With restrictive relative clauses, *that* is a general-purpose relative pronoun. It occurs with animate and inanimate heads, and with gaps in subject or non-subject position. It is an alternative to *whom* for animate head nouns and non-subject gaps. The choice of *that* over *whom* is especially preferred in informal discourse (like conversation and fiction). It avoids the formal overtones of *whom*, and possibly avoids the choice between *who* and *whom*:

> *There might be people* **that we don't know of.** (CONV)
>
> *She took up with the first boy* **that she came near to liking.** (FICT)

With non-subject gaps, it is most common to completely avoid the choice among relative pronouns by omitting the relativizer altogether. With human head nouns, this alternative is the preferred choice in both spoken and written registers. See F below.

D *Which* v. *that* in detail

The relativizers *which* and *that* are similar in their grammatical potential. They are both grammatical with a wide range of gap positions and with animate or inanimate heads. However, there are a number of important differences in their actual patterns of use:

which	that
rare with animate heads	common with animate heads, especially in conversation or with non-subject gaps
common in non-restrictive relative clauses	rare in non-restrictive relative clauses
usually considered more formal	usually considered less formal
can follow a preposition (e.g. *of which*)	cannot follow a preposition (e.g. **of that*)

When *that* does introduce a non-restrictive clause, it often occurs in a series of postmodifiers and is used for special stylistic effect (especially in fiction):

> *He gazed at the yellow, stained wall [with all the spots [which dead bugs,* **that had once crawled,** *had left]].* (FICT†)

The level of formality associated with each relative pronoun is an important factor in their use. With its more formal, academic associations, *which* is preferred in academic prose. In contrast, *that* has more informal, colloquial associations and is thus preferred in conversation and most contemporary fiction:

> *An operator is simply something* **which turns one vector into another.** (ACAD)
>
> *He said something* **that she couldn't catch.** (FICT)

E Whose v. of which

The relativizer *whose* is used to mark a possessive relationship between a human head noun and some other noun phrase:

> And we also know that there's at least one and maybe two other white males **whose names we do not know.** (FICT)

Thus, the underlying meaning of the relative clause in this case, with the gap included, is: 'We do not know the males' names'.

By extension, *whose* can be used to mark possessive relationships with collective organizations, such as corporations, government agencies, clubs, societies, and committees:

> A shipping group, **whose profits dived last year by nearly a third**, has told shareholders to expect an even lower result for 1993. (NEWS)

In fact, *whose* can be used to mark possessive relationships with completely inanimate, sometimes abstract, head nouns. This use is especially common in academic prose:

> A crystal is a piece of matter **whose boundaries are naturally formed plane surfaces.** (ACAD)

> There is a way of proceeding in conceptual matters **whose method is to define away any inconvenient difficulty.** (ACAD)

An alternative to *whose* with inanimate head nouns is the phrase *of which*. This alternative is also largely restricted to academic prose:

> Some of the particles cluster into aggregates, clods or crumbs, **the size distribution of which determines the soil structure.** (ACAD)

> This wheel drives a similar but smaller wooden-toothed wheel, **the other end of which carries a large open-spoked wheel.** (ACAD†)

A variant way of introducing a relative clause with *of which* is to front only the prepositional phrase *of which*, leaving the rest of the noun phrase to follow it in its normal position in the relative clause:

> He joined a dining-club **of which the motto was, The Whole, The Good, and The Beautiful.** (FICT)

Finally, similar meanings can be expressed in two other ways: (1) a relative clause with *which* or *that* and the verb *have*, or (2) a postmodifying prepositional phrase with the preposition *with*. For example, compare:

> 1 He joined a dining-club **which had the motto** ...
> 2 He joined a dining-club **with the motto** ...

F Zero relativizer

Speakers and writers often omit the relativizer altogether in restrictive relative clauses. This alternative is possible in standard English whenever the gap is not in subject position. For example:

> the only shiny instrument **he possessed** (FICT)

> the way **the man used to watch him** (FICT)

Although the zero relativizer is found in all four registers, it has colloquial associations and is therefore especially characteristic of conversation and fiction. In conversation, the relativizer is omitted in about half of the relative clauses that permit this option:

> *the slippers **you lost*** (CONV)
>
> *that person **she was with*** (CONV)

In fiction, zero relativizer occurs both in the quoted speech of fictional characters and in fictional narrative:

- zero relativizer in fictional speech:

    > *I do beg you to consider seriously the points **I've put to you**.* (FICT)
    >
    > *I confess I have got plans **you may find a little startling**.*
    > (FICT)

- zero relativizer in fictional narrative:

    > *the names **his mother had remembered from the past*** (FICT)
    >
    > *a rather ugly tie **his father had lent him*** (FICT)

In all registers, the zero relativizer is more likely to be used when the subject of the relative clause is a personal pronoun. This is because most pronouns distinguish between subject (nominative) and object forms (e.g. *I, we, she, he* v. *me, us, her, him*), and so the presence of a subject pronoun unambiguously marks the beginning of a relative clause, even without the relativizer:

> *the only choice **we've got*** (CONV)
>
> *the kind of organisation **she likes*** (NEWS)
>
> *the way **we acquire knowledge*** (ACAD)

9.8.3 Relative clauses with adverbial gaps

When relative clauses have adverbial gaps, speakers and writers have four choices for the use of relativizers, as shown below. (The relative clause is enclosed in *[]*, and the relativizer is in bold.)

> *the time [**when** I began]*
>
> *the time [**at which** I began]*
>
> *the time [**that** I began **at**]*
>
> *the time [**that** I began]* OR *the time [**I** began]*

Each of the choices is described below.

A Relative adverbs: *where, when, why*

The first option is to use one of the three relative adverbs that specifically mark adverbial gaps: *where* for place adverbials (location or direction), *when* for time adverbials, and *why* for reason adverbials. These relative adverbs substitute for an entire adverbial phrase.

> *the area **where the chapels have closed*** (CONV)
>
> *one day **when she was at school*** (FICT)
>
> *the other reason **why the ambulance workers have lost out*** (NEWS)

Occasionally *where* and *when* are used to mark an abstract 'location' rather than physical locations or times. For example, the head noun *bit*, referring to a part of a movie or story, commonly occurs in conversation with both of these relativizers:

> *You know the bit **where the man jumps inside Whoopie Goldberg**.* (CONV)

Similar uses of *where* and *when* are especially common in academic prose:

the kind of situation **where this type of work is helpful** (ACAD)

in difficult cases **when accurate estimation of disease activity will have important therapeutic implications.** (ACAD)

The use of relative adverbs is limited because there are many types of adverbial gap that do not have a corresponding relative adverb. For example, there is no standard relative adverb for manner adverbials: *the way how I look at it.

B Preposition + relative pronoun *which*

The second option is to use the relative pronoun *which* preceded by a preposition that marks the adverbial element in the relative clause. For example:

1 *the apartments* **in which no one lives** (FICT)

2 *the endless landscape* **from which the sand is taken** (FICT)

In these constructions, the preposition + relative pronoun stands for the adverbial prepositional phrase in the relative clause. Thus, the relative clause in **1** has the meaning 'no one lives in the apartments'. This choice is recommended by many usage handbooks.

C Stranded preposition

A third option for adverbial gaps is to leave the preposition stranded in the relative clause, marking the site of the gap. The relativizer can be *which*, *that*, or zero with this option (the stranded preposition is underlined):

the one **that old James used to live <u>in</u>** (FICT)

some of the houses **I go <u>to</u>** (CONV)

D Omitted preposition

The last option is to omit the preposition altogether, providing no surface marker of the adverbial gap. The relativizer may also be omitted in these structures:

1 *the time* **that I began** (FICT)

2 *the way* **I look at it** (CONV)

3 *a place* **I would like to go** (CONV)

In these structures, the preposition has to be inferred from the information in the head noun and the main verb of the relative clause. For example, in **3** above, we can reconstruct the meaning of an adverbial *to*-phrase from the head noun *place* and the main verb *go*:

I would like to go to a place

If the verb had been *live* instead of *go*, we would have reconstructed a phrase with *in*:

I would like to live in a place

E Manner adverbial gaps and *way*

As already mentioned, there is no relative adverb available for relative clauses with manner adverbial gaps. Instead, these structures almost always use the same head noun: *way*. For example:

They're not used to the way **that we're used to living** (CONV)

*It is not the only way **in which a person can be brought before a court.***
(ACAD)

Because *way* as a head noun is so strongly associated with a manner adverbial gap, these relative clauses usually occur with both the relativizer and the preposition omitted. This tendency holds for academic prose as well as for the more colloquial registers. For example:

*That's not the way **you do that.*** (CONV)

*<. . .> the way **the book is used*** (ACAD)

Review

Major points of **GRAMMAR BITE C**: Relative clauses

➤ Relative clauses, and other postmodifiers, are classified into two main types by their function: restrictive, helping to identify the reference of the head noun, and non-restrictive, adding descriptive details about the head noun.
  ➤ In general, restrictive relative clauses are more common than non-restrictive.
  ➤ Most other postmodifier types are restrictive, but can occasionally be non-restrictive.
➤ Relative clauses have three key components: the head noun, the relativizer, and the gap.
➤ There are eight different relativizers in English. The most common ones are *which*, *who*, and *that*.
  ➤ In some cases, the relativizer can be omitted altogether, although its meaning is still implied. This is referred to as the zero relativizer.
➤ Some relativizers (such as *which* and *that*) are similar in their potential uses, but there are differences in their actual patterns of use.
➤ The gap refers to the location of a missing constituent in the relative clause. The gap can occur at almost any noun phrase position (e.g. subject, direct object, adverbial).
  ➤ Relative clauses with adverbial gaps involve special choices for the relativizer.

GRAMMAR BITE

D Other postmodifier types

9.9 Postmodification by non-finite clauses

The last Grammar Bite concentrated on relative clauses, which are finite clauses that modify a noun. However, nouns can also be modified by non-finite clauses. These constructions have non-finite verbs, which are not inflected for tense.

There are three major types of non-finite postmodifying clauses: *ing*-clauses, *ed*-clauses, and *to*-clauses. The first two types are also called participle clauses, and the third is also called an infinitive clause or a *to*-infinitive clause.

Participle clauses as postmodifiers always have subject gap positions. They can often be paraphrased as a relative clause:

*a letter **written by a member of the public*** (ACAD)

<compare: *a letter **which has been written by a member of the public***>

*young families **attending the local clinic*** (NEWS)

<compare: *families **who are attending the local clinic***>

In contrast, *to*-clause postmodifiers can have either subject or non-subject gaps:

- subject gap:

    *I haven't got friends **to beat him up** though.* (CONV)

    <compare: *Friends will beat him up*>

- non-subject gap:

    *I had a little bit **to eat**.* (CONV) <direct object: *I ate a little bit*>

    *I'll remember which way **to go**.* (CONV) <direction adverbial: *I can go that way*>

    *Get angry! We've both got a lot **to be angry about**.* (FICT) <complement of preposition: *We are angry about a lot*>

As these examples show, most non-finite clauses do not have a stated subject. However, with *to*-clauses the subject is sometimes expressed in a *for*-phrase:

*Really now is the time **for you to try and go**.* (CONV)

9.9.1 Participle clauses as postmodifiers

Both *ed*-clauses and *ing*-clauses can function as postmodifying participle clauses:

- *ed*-clauses:

    1 *The US yesterday welcomed a proposal **made by the presidents of Colombia, Peru and Bolivia**.* (NEWS)

    2 *It can be derived using the assumptions **given above**.* (ACAD)

- *ing*-clauses:

    3 *A military jeep **travelling down Beach Road at high speed** struck a youth **crossing the street**.* (FICT†)

    4 *Interest is now developing in a theoretical approach **involving reflection of Alfven waves**.* (ACAD)

The verbs in *ed*-clauses correspond to passive verbs in finite relative clauses. Thus, for **1** and **2**, equivalent relative clauses would be:

1a *a proposal **that <u>was made</u> by the presidents of Colombia, Peru and Bolivia***

2a *the assumptions **that <u>were given</u> above***

In contrast, the verbs in *ing*-clauses do not always correspond to finite progressive aspect verbs. In **3** (above), the verb *travelling* does have progressive meaning. However, in **4** the verb *involving* does not have a progressive sense. Thus, the equivalent relative clauses for **3** and **4** would be:

3a *A military jeep **that <u>was travelling</u> down Beach Road at high speed***
    <progressive>

4a *a theoretical approach **that <u>involves</u> reflection of Alfven waves**.* (ACAD)
    <not progressive>

Several patterns are important in the use of postmodifying clauses:

- Participle clauses are especially common in news and academic prose.

- In news and academic prose, *ed*-clauses are considerably more common than *ing*-clauses.
- Most *ing*-participles and passive verbs occur in participle clauses rather than relative clauses, even when relative clauses could be used. That is, a postmodifying participle clause is the expected choice whenever an *ing*-form or a passive verb occurs in a postmodifying clause.

Ing-participles expressing an abstract relationship (e.g. *consisting of*) regularly occur in a non-finite clause, even though the corresponding progressive aspect would not occur in a full relative clause (see 6.5.1):

> *a society **consisting of educated people*** (ACAD)
>
> *a matter **concerning the public interest*** (ACAD)
>
> *initiatives **involving national and local government authorities*** (ACAD)

compare:

> **a society **which is consisting of educated people***
>
> **a matter **which is concerning the public interest***
>
> **initiatives **which are involving national and local government authorities***

In contrast, *ed*-clauses can usually be rephrased as a full relative clause with a passive verb, by inserting *which is* or something similar. So participle clauses serve the interests of efficiency: they convey the same meaning in fewer words.

Passive verbs do, however, occur in finite relative clauses when tense, aspect, or modality are important. These distinctions cannot be marked in a postmodifying participle clause, so a relative clause is necessary:

> *The mistaken view is that theory refers to ideas **which have never been tested**.* (ACAD†)
>
> *Now 48 sites **which could be maintained by local authorities** have been identified.* (NEWS)

9.9.2 *To*-clauses as postmodifiers

Postmodifying *to*-clauses are more flexible than participle clauses for two reasons: they can occur with both subject and non-subject gaps, and they can occur with an overt subject noun phrase. In the following examples, the head noun (or pronoun) is underlined, and the *to*-clause is in bold:

- *to*-clauses with subject gap:

  > *Its absence was a <u>factor</u> **to be taken into account**.* (NEWS†)
  >
  > <note: this is a passive construction equivalent to 'a factor is to be taken into account'.>

- *to*-clauses with object gaps:

  > *Papa dressed in his Sunday suit and hat was a <u>sight</u> **to see**.* (FICT)
  >
  > *There is one further <u>matter</u> **to confess**.* (ACAD)

- *to*-clauses with adverbial gaps:

  > *They'd take a long <u>time</u> **to dry**.* (CONV)
  >
  > *We shall have to find a <u>way</u> **to associate numbers with our operators**.* (ACAD†)

- *to*-clauses with prepositional object gap (and stranded preposition):

    *She's had a <u>lot</u> **to put up with**.* (CONV)

- *to*-clauses with an overt subject (introduced by *for*):

    *That'll be the worst <u>thing</u> **for us to do**.* (CONV) <object gap>

    *There was no possible <u>way</u> **for the pilot to avoid it**.* (ACAD) <manner adverbial gap>

Surprisingly, a relatively high proportion of the postmodifiers in conversation are *to*-clauses. Their meaning often points to the future:

    *Father's got a lot of <u>things</u> **to tell you**.* (CONV)

The *to*-clause constructions in conversation usually have object or adverbial gap positions:

1 *Well I mean this is a horrible <u>thing</u> **to say**, but <...>* (CONV†)
2 *I've got <u>stuff</u> **to sort out** anyway.* (CONV)
3 *Friday evening I didn't have <u>a lot</u> **to drink**.* (CONV)

The most common head nouns taking a *to*-clause have general meanings. They are nouns that are especially common in conversation (e.g. *thing*, *time*, *way*). The common head nouns associated with adverbial gaps cover the three major domains of time, place, and manner:

4 *There's not enough <u>time</u> **to get it out and defrost it**.* (CONV) <time domain>
5 *But it's certainly a nice <u>place</u> **to live**.* (CONV) <place domain>
6 *That's no <u>way</u> **to talk to Sean**!* (CONV) <manner domain>

Most postmodifying *to*-clauses do not have an overt subject (as in the above examples). In these cases, the subject of the postmodifying clause is easily predicted and need not be stated. In many cases in conversation, the missing subject clearly refers to the speaker (as in examples 1–3 above). For example, 1 could be restated with the subject 'me' in a *for*-phrase:

1a *Well I mean this is a horrible <u>thing</u> **for me to say** ...*

Alternatively the subject can be interpreted as a generic reference to 'people' or 'anybody' (as in 4–6 above):

4a *There's not enough <u>time</u> **for anybody to get it out and defrost it**.*

9.10 Postmodification by prepositional phrase

9.10.1 Prepositional phrases v. relative clauses

As we explained in 9.3.2, prepositional phrases are by far the most common type of postmodifier in all registers, although they are especially common in news and academic prose.

In some cases, prepositional phrases can be re-phrased as relative clauses with nearly equivalent meaning. Prepositional phrases beginning with *with* often correspond to relative clauses with the main verb *have*:

    *feedback systems **with chaotic behaviour*** (ACAD)
    <compare the relative clause: *systems **which have chaotic behaviour***>

Some other prepositional phrases can be re-phrased as a relative clause with the copula *be* and a prepositional phrase complement:

> *documents **in his possession***
> <*compare the relative clause: documents **which were in his possession**>*
> (NEWS)

> *the car keys **on the table***
> <*compare the relative clause: the car keys **that were on the table**>* (ACAD)

In general, relative clauses with the main verb *have*, or with the copula *be* + preposition, are rare in comparison with prepositional phrase postmodifiers. Many occurrences of prepositional phrase postmodifiers, however, have specialized meanings that cannot easily be re-phrased as relative clauses:

> *the problems **at its ISC Technologies subsidiary*** (NEWS)

> *this list **of requirements*** (ACAD)

> *the same effect **on the final state*** (ACAD)

Even when a prepositional phrase and a relative clause are both possible, prepositional phrase postmodifiers are much more common. However, two factors favor the choice of a relative clause over a prepositional phrase: the need to convey non-restrictive meaning, and the need to convey past tense meaning:

- relative clauses with non-restrictive meaning.

> *Then he set off for Simon's house, **which was at the other end of the lane.*** (FICT) <with copula + preposition>

> *He said the resident, **who is in her late 70s**, had been very confused.* (NEWS†) <with copula + preposition>

> *With animals like moles, **which have tough and durable skins**, the periods involved are longer.* (ACAD†) <with *have*>

- relative clauses with past tense meaning.

> *The lower-income groups also consumed amounts of iron **that were below the standard**.* (ACAD†)

> *DMB and B Result, **which had a link with a big international agency**, went bust recently.* (NEWS†)

9.10.2 Prepositional phrases with *of*

Over half of all postmodifying prepositional phrases begin with the preposition *of*. This is due to the extremely wide range of functions for this preposition. Many functions of *of*-phrases have been discussed already in 4.4 and 4.9.8, including:

- after quantity nouns: *loads of work*
- after unit nouns: *a piece of cake*
- after container nouns: *our bottle of champagne*
- after nouns denoting shape: *a pile of money*
- after species nouns: *these kinds of question*

In addition, *of*-phrases can express many more specialized meaning relationships. Some of these could be paraphrased as noun + noun sequences:

of prepositional phrase	noun + noun sequence
ten **words of English** (FICT)	ten English words
the **color of chocolate** (FICT)	the chocolate color
the **Ministry of Defence** (NEWS)	the Defence Ministry

However, many expressions with *of*-phrases cannot be easily rephrased in this way:

> *wonderful* **contrasts of feeling** (NEWS)
>
> *a* **woman of very strong high moral values** (NEWS)
>
> *your* **style of interpretation** (ACAD)

Academic prose is noteworthy for a large number of noun + *of*-phrase expressions that are used repeatedly. Most of these **lexical bundles** convey information in one of the following areas:

- physical description: *the surface of the . . . , the shape of the . . . , the position of the . . .*
- existence or presence: *the presence of the . . . , the existence of a . . .*
- abstract qualities: *the nature of the . . . , the value of the . . . , the use of a . . .*
- long-term processes or events: *the development of an . . . , the course of the . . .*

(See 13.6 for a discussion of lexical bundles in conversation.)

9.10.3 Prepositional phrases with *in* and other prepositions

Prepositional phrases beginning with *in* are also moderately common. They express meanings that cover physical location, time meanings, and logical relationships:

- physical location:
  > *the mess* **in his bedroom** (CONV)
  >
  > *the third largest trucking firm* **in the midwest** (FICT)
- time/durational meaning:
  > *the longest touchdown* **in the history of the school** (FICT)
  >
  > *maintenance of health* **in the long term** (ACAD)
- more abstract meanings:
  > *the co-chairman's faith* **in the project** (NEWS)
  >
  > *the rapidly deteriorating trend* **in cashflow** (NEWS)
  >
  > *a resulting decrease* **in breeding performance** (ACAD)

Prepositional phrases beginning with *for, on, to,* or *with* are less common than *of* or *in*, but they are also used for a wide range of meanings:

> *a school* **for disabled children** (CONV)
>
> *the search* **for new solutions** (ACAD)
>
> *a mole* **on his head** (CONV)
>
> *his most wounding attack* **on the tabloids** (NEWS)
>
> *their first trip* **to Scotland** (NEWS)
>
> *one apparently attractive answer* **to that question** (ACAD)
>
> *some cheese* **with garlic** (CONV)

.11 Postmodification by appositive noun phrases

Appositive noun phrases have equivalent status with the preceding (head) noun phrase. That is, the order of head noun phrase + appositive noun phrase can normally be reversed to produce an equally grammatical construction with essentially the same meaning:

> *former secretary of state Jim Baker* (NEWS) = *Jim Baker former secretary of state*

Appositive noun phrases are usually non-restrictive in meaning. They provide descriptive information about the head noun, but they are not needed to identify the reference of the head noun. One exception to this is with nouns that refer to words, phrases, or expressions:

> <u>The word</u> **gossip** *itself actually means 'God's kin'.* (NEWS)

Here the appositive is restrictive in function, identifying which 'word'.

Like prepositional phrases, appositive noun phrases are an abbreviated form of postmodifier. In contrast to relative clauses, appositive noun phrases include no verbs at all. Not surprisingly, these postmodifiers are by far most common in the registers with the highest informational density. The patterns of use for appositives include:

* They are most common in news and academic prose.
* In news, appositives usually involve a proper noun with human reference.
* In academic prose, appositives usually provide information about a technical term.

In news, with its focus on the actions of human participants, appositive noun phrases provide background information about people. Most of these constructions include a proper name and a descriptive noun phrase, but these two elements can occur in either order:

* proper noun + descriptive phrase:
  > *Dr. Jan Stjernsward, chief of the World Health Organisation Cancer Unit* (NEWS)

  > *Vladimir Ashkenazy, one of the world's greatest pianists* (NEWS)

* descriptive phrase + proper noun:
  > *The editor of The Mail on Sunday, Mr Stewart Steven* (NEWS)

  > *the Labour Party's housing spokesman, Mr. Clive Soley* (NEWS)

In academic prose, appositive noun phrases have a wider range of use. In many cases, the appositive noun phrase is given in parentheses following the head noun. Appositive noun phrases are commonly used in five ways:

* to provide an explanatory gloss for a technical reference:
  > *the mill (a term introduced by Babbage)* (ACAD)

  > *the optical propagation direction (z-direction)* (ACAD)

* to introduce acronyms:
  > *IAS (Institute of Advanced Studies)* (ACAD)

  > *SLA (Second Language Acquisition)* (ACAD)

- to introduce short labels for variables, parts of diagrams, etc.:

  the valves on the pressure side (V1 and V2) (ACAD)

  a point P (ACAD)

- to name chemical or mathematical formulas:

  fayalite, Fe_2SiO_4 (ACAD)

  hydrogen chloride, HCl (ACAD)

- to list items included in some class:

  essential nutrients (manganese, copper and zinc) (ACAD)

  the various life-history events (i.e. oviposition, hatching and maturation) (ACAD)

9.12 Noun phrases with multiple postmodifiers

9.12.1 Postmodifier complexes

Noun phrases often have multiple postmodifiers, especially in academic prose. We refer to the combination of structures following a head noun as the **postmodifier complex**. The structures in a postmodifier complex can represent either a series of forms modifying a single head noun, or embeddings.

For example, the following sentence has a very simple main clause structure: NP_1 (with *chapters* as head) *consider* NP_2 (with *aspects* as head):

> [*The* <u>chapters</u> **in this section of the reader**] *consider* [*various* <u>aspects</u> **of teaching and learning that have come under increased official scrutiny by central state agencies in recent years**]. (ACAD†)

However, both NP_1 and NP_2 have postmodifier complexes, resulting in a long and complicated sentence. As Figure 9.9 shows, these two noun phrases illustrate

Figure 9.9 **Postmodifier complexes with multiple embedding v. multiple modification**

(NP = noun phrase, prep = preposition, PP = prepositional phrase, postmod = postmodifier)

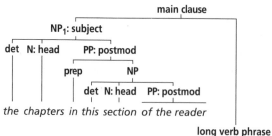

the two types of structural relationships that are possible in postmodifier complexes: multiple embedding v. multiple modification of a single head noun.

NP_1 (*chapters*) illustrates embedding. The first prepositional phrase in the postmodifier complex (*in this section*) directly modifies the head noun *chapters*, but the second prepositional phrase (*of the reader*) is embedded because it modifies the noun *section*. Thus, as Figure 9.9 shows, the head noun *chapters* has only one postmodifier: a prepositional phrase, which in turn contains a second embedded prepositional phrase.

In contrast, NP_2 (*aspects*) illustrates multiple modification of a single head noun. The prepositional phrase *of teaching and learning* directly follows *aspects* and is the first postmodifier. That prepositional phrase is then followed by a relative clause (*that have come under...*), which functions as the second postmodifier of *aspects*.

9.12.2 Common types of postmodifier complexes

In general, three patterns characterize postmodifier complexes:

- The most common type of postmodifier complex is composed of two prepositional phrases:

  *The main difficulties which are posed concern the rendition [**of culturally specific German or French terms**] [**into English**].* (ACAD)

  *A sociological description might discuss the utilisation [**of such devices**] [**for social purposes**].* (ACAD)

- When there are two postmodifiers, they are often the same structure:

  *Large clear diagrams [**drawn on sugar paper**] and [**covered with transparent film**] are particularly useful teaching aids.* (ACAD) <*ed*-clauses, co-ordinated with *and*>

  *It was spacious with a high ceiling [**painted with cherubs**] and [**decorated with flowers**].* (FICT) <*ed*-clauses, co-ordinated with *and*>

  *At the last election the Labour MP, [**Mildred Gordon**], [**a left-winger**] beat the Liberal Alliance candidate.* (NEWS†) <appositive noun phrases>

- The second postmodifier in a complex is often a relative clause, regardless of the type of first postmodifier:

  *Firemen needed police support as they tackled a car [**in the driveway**] [**which had been set on fire**].* (NEWS) <prepositional phrase + relative clause>

  *Most countries have a written document [**known as 'the constitution'**] [**which lays down the main rules**].* (ACAD†) <*ed*-clause + relative clause>

Relative clauses are particularly common as the second postmodifier in a complex because they are easily identified as a postmodifer, even when they are distant from the noun phrase head. The relativizer provides an overt surface marker of their postmodifier status.

Review

Major points of **GRAMMAR BITE D**: Other postmodifier types
➤ Postmodifiers can be clauses or phrases.
➤ In addition to relative clauses (covered in Grammar Bite C), three types of non-finite clauses can be noun postmodifiers: *ing*-clauses, *ed*-clauses, or *to*-clauses.
➤ The verbs in *ed*-clauses correspond to passive verbs in relative clauses.

➤ The verbs in *ing*-clauses sometimes correspond to progressive verbs in relative clauses, but often do not.

➤ Postmodifying *to*-clauses are more flexible than participle clauses; for example, they can have subjects that differ from the main clause subject.

➤ Prepositional phrases are by far the most common type of phrasal postmodifier.

➤ They can express an extremely wide range of meanings.

➤ Noun phrases can also be postmodifiers, called appositive noun phrases.

➤ Appositive noun phrases are non-restrictive; they are especially common in the written registers.

➤ When a noun phrase has two postmodifiers, they are usually both the same structural type (e.g. both are prepositional phrases).

➤ One exception is that relative clauses commonly occur following other structural types of postmodifier.

GRAMMAR BITE

E Noun complement clauses

9.13 Noun complement clauses

9.13.1 Noun complement clauses v. relative clauses

On the surface, **noun complement clauses**, such as the following, can appear to be identical to relative clauses with *that*:

> The fact **that it can be done** is important. (ACAD†)

However, noun complement clauses and relative clauses are actually very different structures. Their differences are summed up as follows:

	relative clause	noun complement clause
function of clause	identify reference of head noun	present the content of the head noun or add descriptive information
structure	incomplete, contains a 'gap'	complete, no 'gap'
function of *that*	relative pronoun	complementizer
omission of *that*	possible with object gaps	impossible
types of N modified	almost any noun	only a few nouns

(Noun complement clauses are similar to verb and adjective complement clauses, discussed in Chapter 10.)

Compare the following two sentences, both with the noun *report* as head:

• postmodifying relative clause:

  1 *Peter reached out for the well-thumbed <u>report</u> **that lay behind him on the cupboard top.** (FICT)*

• noun complement clause:

2 *Other semiconductor stocks eased following an industry trade group's* <u>report</u> **that its leading indicator fell in September.** (NEWS†)

The relative clause in example **1** identifies which 'report' Peter is reaching for. It has a gap in subject position, which corresponds to the head noun *report*. The underlying meaning of the relative clause is that 'the report lay behind him', but *that* takes the place of *the report* in the relative clause. (Since the gap is in subject position, omission of *that* is impossible in **1**, but it can be omitted in other relative clauses; see 9.8.2.)

In contrast, in example **2** the noun complement clause gives the actual content of the 'report': that 'the trade group's leading indicator fell'. The noun complement clause is complete structurally. It does not include a reference to the head noun in any way (i.e. it does not have a gap corresponding in meaning to the head noun). In addition, the complementizer *that* cannot be omitted in this or any other noun complement clause. Finally, *report* is one of the few nouns that can be modified by complement clauses (see 9.14 below for more on head nouns).

9.13.2 Structural types of noun complement clause

There are two main types of noun complement clause: finite *that*-clauses and non-finite *to*-infinitive clauses. In the following examples, the head is underlined and the complement clause is in bold:

- *that*-clauses:

    There were also <u>rumors</u> **that Ford had now taken its stake up to the maximum 15 per cent allowed.** (NEWS†)

    These figures lead to an <u>expectation</u> **that the main application area would be in the office environments.** (ACAD)

- *to*-clauses:

    You've been given <u>permission</u> **to wear them.** (CONV)

    Legal peers renewed their attack on the Government's <u>plans</u> **to shake up the legal profession** *yesterday.* (NEWS)

Note that while the *to*-clauses have missing subjects that can be reconstructed from the context, they do not have gaps corresponding to the heads *permission* or *plans*.

In addition, *ing*-clauses and *wh*-clauses sometimes occur as noun complement clauses:

- *of* + *ing*-clause:

    He had no <u>intention</u> **of singing at anyone's twenty-first birthday.** (FICT)

    The exchanged protons have about the same <u>chance</u> **of having the same or opposite spin orientations.** (ACAD†)

- dependent *wh*-interrogative clause:

    There was no <u>question</u> **who was the star.** (FICT)

    We always come back to the same <u>question</u> **why the devil won't he show himself.** (FICT)

In addition to the simple pattern noun + *wh*-clause shown above, there are two other structural options for *wh*-interrogative clauses. The first uses the preposition *of* followed by a *wh*-clause. The second uses the preposition *as to* followed by the *wh*-clause. This option is used primarily with the *wh*-interrogative word *whether*.

- *of + wh*-clause:

    But the <u>question</u> **of who will pay the multi-million dollar bill** *is unanswered.* (NEWS†)

    We have only the most general <u>notion</u> **of how the first continents formed.** (ACAD)

- *as to + wh*-clause:

    Masters and men were deeply divided over the substantive <u>issue</u> **as to whether women should be employed at all.** (ACAD†)

9.13.3 Restrictive and non-restrictive functions

All of the above examples have illustrated restrictive noun complement clauses. That is the most common function. However, it should be noted that noun complement clauses can be used in non-restrictive functions, where they serve a parenthetical function:

1. *Clinton's second allegation,* **that there has been collusion between the security forces and Protestant para-military groups,** *is based on a very few isolated cases.* (NEWS)

2. *The contrary assumption,* **that common sense will take wholly indistinguishable mental events to be different thoughts,** *strikes me as remarkable.* (ACAD)

In these examples, the noun complement clause still names the content of the head noun. For example in **1,** *that there has been collusion ...* is the content of *Clinton's second allegation.* These non-restrictive complement clauses are used when the writer assumes that most readers already know the content of the head noun (e.g. the 'allegation' or the 'contrary assumption'), but they want to spell it out to avoid uncertainty.

9.14 Head nouns with noun complement clauses

Unlike relative clauses, noun complement clauses occur with only a small set of head nouns. Many of the head nouns with noun complement clauses express a stance towards the proposition in the complement clause. For example, these head nouns can be used to indicate the certainty of the proposition or the source of the information: *fact, claim,* and *report.*

Noun complement clauses with head nouns that convey stance are especially common in news and academic prose. In conversation and fiction, similar functions are more commonly served by complement clauses following verbs or adjectives. In many cases, the same roots can be used to control both noun and verb complement clauses. For example:

<...> *there is every* <u>hope</u> **that this will continue.** (ACAD)

I just <u>hope</u> **that I've plugged it in properly.** (CONV)

(See 10.5, 10.7.1 on *that*-clauses following verbs and adjectives.)

Each structural type of noun complement clause occurs with a different set of head nouns. The following sections survey these head nouns and the associated functions for each type.

9.14.1 Head nouns complemented by *that*-clauses

That-clauses functioning as noun complements are one of the primary devices used to mark stance in academic prose. In these constructions, the *that*-clause reports a proposition, while the head noun reports the author's stance toward that proposition. Two main kinds of stance are expressed by the most common head nouns. The first is an assessment of the certainty of the proposition in the *that*-clause. Typical nouns are:

> *fact, possibility, claim, notion, assumption, hypothesis, rumor*

For example:

> *But there remained the very troublesome <u>fact</u> that leguminous crops required no nitrogenous manure.* (ACAD†)

> *There is a <u>possibility</u> that this morphology represents an ancestral great ape character.* (ACAD†)

The second kind of stance is an indication of the source of the information expressed in the *that*-clause. Three primary sources and their typical nouns can be distinguished:

linguistic communication	*claim, report, suggestion, proposal, remark*
cognitive reasoning	*assumption, hypothesis, idea, observation, conclusion*
personal belief	*belief, doubt, hope, opinion*

For example:

> *This conforms conveniently with Maslow's (1970) <u>suggestion</u> that human motivation is related to a hierarchy of human needs.* (ACAD)

> *The survey was aimed at testing a <u>hypothesis</u> that happily-married couples tend to vote more conservatively.* (ACAD†)

> *The traditional <u>belief</u> that veal calves should be kept in a warm environment is unscientific.* (ACAD†)

Many of these head nouns are **nominalized** equivalents of verbs or adjectives that can control *that*-complement clauses (see 9.4–8). Most of these nouns have corresponding verbs that also control *that*-clauses. For example:

> *What's your feeling about his <u>claim</u> that someone's trying to kill him?* (FICT)
> <compare: *The nuns <u>claim</u> that their eggs have never been associated with an outbreak of food poisoning.* (NEWS)>

> *There seems to be an automatic <u>assumption</u> that a single division on a scale represents a single unit of some kind.* (ACAD)
> <compare: *She had always idly <u>assumed</u> that there was some system.* (FICT)>

The only common head noun derived from an adjective is *possibility*:

> *But there remains a <u>possibility</u> that gregarious Desert Locusts might become less viable.* (ACAD†)
> <compare: *It is <u>possible</u> that she has just decided to leave the area.* (NEWS)>

As illustrated by the above examples, noun complement clauses often express stance in an abstract way, without a clear agent. With verb complement clauses, the subject of the controlling verb mentions a person, so that the stance reported by the verb can be attributed directly to that person. In contrast, the stance conveyed by a controlling head noun is not normally attributed to anyone. For example, the examples above include head nouns such as *possibility*, *belief*, *assumption* and *possibility*. Readers must infer whose attitude towards the information is reported.

Verb complement clauses are preferred in conversation while noun complement clauses are preferred in academic writing. This distribution reflects major differences between the registers in structure and function:

	conversation	academic prose
structure	preference for verbal structures	preference for integrating information in noun phrases
function	participants interested in each others' feelings and attitudes	readers/writers more interested in attitudes towards information

Conversation tends to use verb constructions that directly and prominently attribute stance to participants. Academic writing uses noun complement clauses that tend to give more prominence to the information; the stance is backgrounded and not directly attributed to the author.

9.14.2 Head nouns complemented by *to*-infinitive clauses

Unlike *that*-clauses, the head nouns with *to*-clauses do not typically present a personal stance. Instead, the nouns commonly taking *to*-clauses represent human goals, opportunities, or actions:

> *chance, attempt, effort, ability, opportunity, decision, plan, bid*

A second difference from *that*-clauses is that *to*-clauses are especially common in newspaper language (instead of academic prose). The meanings of the head nouns taking *to*-clauses fit the purposes of news, with a focus on human goals and actions rather than on stance towards propositions:

> *We need to give decent people a <u>chance</u> **to elect a sensible council**.* (NEWS)
>
> *The leader's gunshot wounds are taking their toll, complicating <u>efforts</u> **to persuade him to surrender**.* (NEWS)
>
> *Last year the society's committee made a <u>decision</u> **to relaunch** in a bid to attract more members.* (NEWS)

Yet the head nouns taking *to*-clauses are similar to those taking *that*-clauses in that many of them are nominalized equivalents of verbs or adjectives controlling *to*-complement clauses (see 9.12–15).

- nouns with corresponding verbs + *to*-clauses:

  > *attempt, decision, desire, failure, intention, permission, plan, proposal, refusal, tendency*

- nouns with corresponding adjectives + *to*-clauses:

  > *ability/inability, commitment, determination, willingness*

Thus compare:

> He chastises Renault for their <u>failure</u> **to respond to BMW's challenge.** (NEWS†)
>
> He <u>failed</u> **to notice that it made Wilson chuckle.** (FICT)
>
> Such an order should be made only where there is evidence of the defendant's <u>ability</u> **to pay.** (NEWS)
>
> I've never been <u>able</u> **to determine that for sure.** (FICT)

9.14.3 Head nouns complemented by *of-* + *ing-* clauses

Several of the head nouns that take *of-* + *ing*-clauses can also take another type of complement clause. (In contrast, there is almost no overlap between the head nouns taking *that*-clauses and the head nouns taking *to*-clauses.) Thus, the following head nouns occur with both *of-* + *ing*-clauses and with *that*-clauses:

> *idea, hope, possibility, sign, thought*

For example:

> Feynman discusses the <u>idea</u> **of putting a lamp between the two slits to illuminate the electrons.** (ACAD)
>
> <compare: *Then a door is opened for the more threatening <u>idea</u> **that some principles are part of the law because of their moral appeal.** (ACAD)>*
>
> So we have no <u>hope</u> **of finding here a common reason for rejecting checkerboard solutions.** (ACAD)
>
> <compare: *There is every <u>hope</u> **that this will continue.** (ACAD†)>*

Fewer head nouns can take both an *of-* + *ing*-clause construction and a *to*-clause, but they include two of the most common nouns with both constructions—*chance* and *intention*:

> Also one increases the <u>chance</u> **of revealing similarities between superficially distinct objects.** (ACAD)
>
> <compare: *BOAC never had a <u>chance</u> **to establish commercial operations on any scale.** (ACAD†)>*
>
> This writer has served on review teams and has had every <u>intention</u> **of giving each proposal a thorough reading.** (ACAD)
>
> <compare: *Mr. Rawlins announced his <u>intention</u> **to leave Sturge at some time in the future.** (NEWS)>*

Finally, some head nouns can control only *of* + *ing*-clauses, such as *cost, task,* and *problem*:

> They presented the move as a contribution by the Government to the huge <u>cost</u> **of improving water quality.** (NEWS)
>
> It therefore seems logical to begin the <u>task</u> **of disentangling the relationship between movement and urban structure.** (ACAD)

9.14.4 Head nouns complemented by *wh*-interrogative clauses

Wh-interrogative clauses are much less common than the other types of noun complement clause. They are restricted mostly to occurrence with the head noun *question*.

The *of-* + *wh*-clause variant is actually more common than simple *wh*-clauses as noun complements, especially in news and academic prose. Further, it occurs with a wider range of head nouns. These include nouns referring to:

speech communication	*question, story, explanation, description, account, discussion*
exemplification	*example, indication, illustration*
problems	*problem, issue*
cognitive states or processes	*knowledge, understanding, sense, analysis, idea, notion.*

For example:

> *The <u>question</u> **of how to resolve the fear which so many people have in Hong Kong** was omitted.* (NEWS)
>
> *We have no <u>knowledge</u> **of where it came from.*** (NEWS)

Review

Major points of **GRAMMAR BITE E**: Noun complement clauses

➤ Noun complement clauses can easily be confused with relative clauses.

➤ They differ in that they are structurally complete (i.e. noun complement clauses do not have a gap) and the complementizer *that* cannot be omitted.

➤ There are two main types of noun complement clause: finite *that*-clauses and non-finite *to*-clauses.

➤ *Ing*-clauses and *wh*-clauses can be used as noun complement clauses, but are less common.

➤ Noun complement clauses occur with only a few abstract head nouns.

➤ Each structural type of complement clause occurs with a different set of head nouns.

➤ The head nouns that take *that*-clauses (e.g. *fact, possibility, claim*) mark stance.

➤ The head nouns that take *to*-clauses (e.g. *chance, attempt, plan*) mark human goals or actions.

10

Verb and adjective complement clauses

GRAMMAR BITES in this chapter

A Types and positions of complement clauses

> ➤ The four major and other minor types of complement clauses
> ➤ The grammatical positions of complement clauses: subject, post-predicate, and extraposed

B *That*-clauses

> ➤ The functions of *that*-clauses in discourse
> ➤ The grammatical patterns of *that*-clauses
> ➤ Verbs and adjectives that commonly control *that*-clauses
> ➤ Choices with *that*-clauses: subject v. extraposed position, and omission of *that*

C *Wh*-clauses

> ➤ The different types of *wh*-clauses and their functions
> ➤ Grammatical patterns of *wh*-clauses
> ➤ Common verbs controlling *wh*-clauses
> ➤ *Wh*-clauses that use *whether* and *if*

D Post-predicate infinitive clauses

> ➤ Grammatical patterns of *to*-clauses controlled by verbs
> ➤ Common verbs controlling *to*-clauses
> ➤ The functions of subject predicative *to*-clauses
> ➤ Common adjectives controlling *to*-clauses

E More on infinitive clauses

> ➤ Description of raising in *to*-clauses controlled by verbs and adjectives
> ➤ The use of extraposed and subject position *to*-clauses
> ➤ The choice between raised constructions and extraposed constructions
> ➤ A summary of *to*-clause use across registers

F *Ing*-clauses, ellipsis/substitution, and review

> ➤ Grammatical patterns of *ing*-clauses
> ➤ Common verbs and adjectives controlling *ing*-clauses
> ➤ Ellipsis and substitution in *to*-, *wh*-, and *that*-clauses
> ➤ A review of complement clause use across registers

10.1 Introduction

Complement clauses are dependent clauses that complete the meaning of a verb, adjective, or noun. For example, the *that*-complement clause in the following utterance provides the content of the 'thinking':

> I <u>thought</u> **that it looked good.** (CONV†)

Here the main clause verb—*thought*—is said to control the complement clause.

Complement clauses are also called **nominal clauses**, because they often occupy a noun phrase slot in a clause, such as subject, object, or predicative. For example, the following *that*-clause is the direct object of the verb *said*:

> I <u>said</u> **that I wasn't perfect.** (CONV†)

Complement clauses can also complete the meaning of an adjective rather than a verb. In this case, a predicative adjective controls the complement clause. In the following example, the *that*-clause is a complement to the adjective *careful*:

> I've gotta be <u>careful</u> **that I don't sound too pompous.** (CONV†)

In this chapter we use the term **predicate** for the element that controls a complement clause: either a lexical verb or a predicative adjective.

Nouns can also control complement clauses. This was dealt with in the last chapter, in 9.13–14. In this chapter we focus on verb and adjective complementation.

GRAMMAR BITE

A Types and positions of complement clauses

10.2 Types of complement clauses

There are four major types of complement clauses: **that-clauses** and **wh-clauses** are finite complement clauses; **to-clauses** and **ing-clauses** are non-finite complement clauses (see 8.3.2). The clause types can be distinguished by their **complementizer**: the word that begins the complement clause (such as *that* or *to*). All four of the main types can complement both verbs and adjectives.

A That-clauses

> They <u>warned</u> him **that it's dangerous.** (CONV†)

That-clauses are finite. Therefore, they are marked for tense or modality, and they have a subject. *That*-clauses can also occur without the complementizer *that*:

> I <u>thought</u> **it was a good film.** (CONV)
> <compare: I <u>thought</u> that it was a good film.>

The absence of the complementizer does not change the structure of the clause: it is still a finite dependent clause that completes the meaning of the verb (*thought*) and functions as direct object.

B Wh-clauses

> She didn't <u>ask</u> **what my plans were.** (FICT)

Wh-clauses begin with a *wh*-word (including *how*). Like *that*-clauses, they are finite clauses, and can show tense or modality and must have a subject.

C To-infinitive clauses

> We <u>wanted</u> **to talk in front of my aunt.** (FICT)

To-infinitive clauses are non-finite complement clauses. They cannot have tense or modals (for example, you cannot say **to talked*), and usually they do not have a subject. In most cases, the assumed subject of the complement clause is the subject of the main clause.

> *To*-infinitive clauses can also occur in combination with *wh*-clauses:

> She never <u>knows</u> **how to just say no.** (CONV)

D Ing-clauses

> He <u>began</u> **crunching it gently but firmly.** (FICT†)

Ing-clauses are also non-finite; they have an *ing*-participle as their main verb form.

E Additional types of complement clause

In addition to the four major types, there are two less productive types of complement clause: **bare-infinitive clauses** and **ed-clauses**. Both of these are non-finite clauses.

> Bare infinitive clauses are a special type of infinitive clause with an infinitive verb form, but without *to*:

> Surrey police say the film would <u>help</u> **identify participants at the weekend party.** (NEWS)
> <compare: *Surrey police say the film would <u>help</u> to identify participants...*>

Ed-complement clauses are rare and very restricted in their distribution. For example:

> I <u>got</u> the door **unlocked.** (FICT†)

> Western Union must have <u>got</u> the names **reversed.** (FICT†)

> They <u>had</u> carnival rides **trucked in and installed on the great green lawns.** (FICT†)

Ed-clauses can complement only verbs, and only a few main clause verbs can control them (e.g. *get*, *have*, *want*, *need*, *see*, and *hear*). As you can see from the examples above, the *ed*-clause is separated from the controlling verb by a noun phrase.

10.3 Grammatical positions of complement clauses

There are three major grammatical positions for complement clauses: **subject** (or **pre-predicate**), **post-predicate**, and **extraposed**. Extraposed is actually an alternative to subject position.

10.3.1 Subject position

Complement clauses can occur before the verb, i.e. in subject position. This position is possible for complement clauses controlled by a verb or an adjective. This position is also sometimes called 'pre-predicate position', because the complement clause comes before the predicate.

- Subject position, verb complement clauses:

  That they are already struggling <u>*troubles*</u> *Graham Taylor.* (NEWS)

  What is good among one people <u>*is*</u> *an abomination with others.* (FICT)

  However, **to say all other courses are impossible** <u>*is*</u> *not to say this course is possible.* (NEWS)

  Walking the back nine <u>*confirms*</u> *what all the fuss is about.* (NEWS)

- Subject position, adjective complement clauses:

  That it would be unpopular with colleges or students *was* <u>*obvious*</u>. (NEWS)

  What a single mother represents *may seem touchingly* <u>*attractive*</u>. (NEWS)

  To attempt to forecast the effects of changing regulations on a national scale *is very* <u>*difficult*</u>. (ACAD)

  Her coming *was quite* <u>*useless*</u>. (FICT)

10.3.2 Post-predicate position

All complement clause types can occur after the verb or adjective that controls them. This is the post-predicate position. Post-predicate complement clauses can function as direct object (following a transitive verb), subject predicative (following a copular verb), or an adjective complement (following a predicative adjective). (Section 8.3.3 summarizes the range of syntactic roles for complement clauses.)

- Verb complement clause as direct object:

  They <u>*conclude*</u> **that the change was cynical and opportunistic.** (NEWS)

  You <u>*know*</u> **what I call my mom.** (CONV)

  They are <u>*trying*</u> **to hold it together.** (CONV†)

  I'm not going to <u>*start*</u> **going on any cross-country runs at my age.** (FICT)

- Verb complement clause as subject predicative after a copular verb:

  The industry's premise <u>*is*</u> **that we can recognize information presented below our threshold awareness.** (NEWS)

  That'<u>s</u> **what the case is all about.** (NEWS)

*The immediate reason for his return <u>is</u> **to give two charity concerts**.* (NEWS†)

*Happiness <u>is</u> **being able to assume you are happy**.* (FICT†)

- Adjective complement clause (post-predicate position):

   *I feel very <u>confident</u> **that Republican state organizations would finance an opponent**.* (NEWS†)

   *I'm not <u>sure</u> **when it's open**.* (CONV)

   *Everybody's <u>glad</u> **to have him around**.* (CONV)

   *The Prime Minister appeared <u>confident of</u> **winning an overall majority**.* (NEWS†)

10.3.3 Extraposed position

Complement clauses rarely occur in subject position. Instead, extraposed clauses are usually used to express an equivalent meaning. In an extraposed structure, dummy *it* fills the subject slot, and the complement clause occurs after the predicate. Dummy *it* does not refer to anything—it simply fills the grammatical place of subject. However, the post-predicate complement clause functions as the logical subject. For example, consider this extraposed *wh*-clause, complement to the adjective *clear*:

   *<u>It</u> was not immediately <u>clear</u> **how the Soviet leadership could enforce such a ruling**.* (NEWS†)
   <compare: *How the Soviet leadership could enforce such a ruling was not immediately clear.*>

That-clauses and *to*-clauses are the most common types of complement clauses in extraposed position. They occur as complements of both adjectives and verbs.

- Extraposed *that*-clause as verb complement:

   *It <u>appears</u> **that Big Blue does not lead the market**.* (NEWS)
   <compare: *That Big Blue does not lead the market appears (to be the case).*>

- Extraposed *that*-clause as adjective complement:

   *It seems <u>odd</u> **that I should be expected to pay for the privilege of assisting in this way**.* (NEWS)
   <compare: *That I should be expected to pay ... seems odd.*>

- Extraposed *to*-clause as verb complement:

   *It had <u>taken</u> him 26 years **to return**.* (NEWS†)
   <compare: *To return had taken him 26 years.*>

- Extraposed *to*-clause as adjective complement:

   *It's <u>good</u> **to see them in the bath**.* (CONV†)
   <compare: *To see them in the bath is good.*>

Review

Major points in **GRAMMAR BITE A**: Types and positions of complement clauses

➤ There are four major types of complement clauses: *that-*, *wh-*, *to-*, and *ing-* clauses.

   ➤ Less common types are the bare infinitive clause and *ed*-clause.

> ➤ There are three major grammatical positions for complement clauses: subject (or pre-predicate), post-predicate, and extraposed (an alternative for subject position).

B *That*-clauses

10.4 Discourse functions of *that*-clauses

Different kinds of *that*-clauses serve different functions. Their frequencies across registers—shown in Figure 10.1—reflect the communicative needs of each register in relation to these typical functions. (Subject and subject predicative *that*-clauses are relatively rare in all registers and are thus omitted from Figure 10.1.)

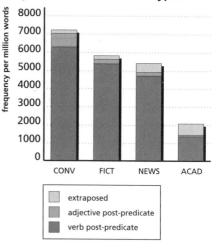

Figure 10.1
Frequencies of *that*-clause types

10.4.1 Post-predicate *that*-clauses

That-clauses in post-predicate position are by far the most common type of *that*-clause—they account for over 80 per cent of all *that*-clauses. These *that*-clauses typically report the speech and thoughts of humans. The subject of the main clause usually refers to a person, the main clause verb presents the type of reporting (e.g. speech or thought), and the *that*-clause presents the reported speech or thought. Although these structures are common in fiction and news, they are even more common in conversation, with its focus on interpersonal communication.

> I <u>think</u> **Stuart's gone a bit mad.** (CONV)
>
> Did you <u>know</u> **that Kathy Jones had a brother here?** (CONV)
>
> He <u>said</u> **that nine indictments have been returned publicly in such investigations.** (NEWS)

Post-predicate *that*-clauses controlled by adjectives are less common than those controlled by verbs. They generally tell the attitudes and emotions of speakers:

> I was quite <u>confident</u> **that it would stay in very well.** (CONV)

10.4.2 Subject predicative *that*-clauses

When a *that*-clause serves as subject predicative to a copular verb, it usually has one of three functions. First, these constructions often describe a problem of some kind:

> The problem is **that the second question cannot be answered until Washington comes up with a consensus on the first.** (NEWS)
>
> The only problem may be **that the compound is difficult to remove after use.** (ACAD)

Second, subject predicative *that*-clauses can present reasons, results, or conclusions:

> The net result is **that foreign money has frequently ended up fertilising or irrigating opium fields.** (NEWS†)
>
> Our first conclusion at this point was **that it is necessary to support the specification.** (ACAD†)

The third function is to present accepted truths or facts:

> The truth is **that the country is now specialising more in processing and marketing.** (NEWS)

> Subject predicative *that*-clauses are used mostly in news and academic prose.

10.4.3 Extraposed *that*-clauses

Extraposed *that*-clauses often involve a main clause that reports an attitude or stance without attributing it to anybody. Usually they show the attitude of the speaker or writer of the text, but the author does not assume direct responsibility:

> It is certain **that the challenges ahead are at least as daunting as anything the cold war produced.** (NEWS†)
>
> It is vitally important **that both groups are used to support one another.** (ACAD†)

Extraposed *that*-clauses are used primarily in news and academic prose. The *that*-clause usually has a non-human subject, and reports a state or relationship in an impersonal manner.

10.4.4 Embedded *that*-clauses

That-clauses often occur in complex series, using various kinds of coordination and embedding. Post-predicate clauses can be mixed with extraposed clauses. Surprisingly, complex structures of this type are found in conversation as well as in news and academic prose. Thus, the following example is quoted speech reported in a newspaper article:

> I think [**that President Reagan believed** [[**that not only was the government the problem**], but [**that it was rare indeed** [**that government could be a positive force in solving the problem**]]]]. (NEWS)

Even in this complicated sentence, you can see the *that*-clauses fulfilling their typical functions of reporting thoughts and attitudes.

10.5 Post-predicate *that*-clauses

10.5.1 Grammatical patterns

There are three major grammatical patterns for verbs that take a *that*-clause in post-predicate position:

- **Pattern 1: verb + *that*-clause** (e.g. *agree, ask*)

  1 *I didn't <u>agree</u> that he should be compelled to do singing.* (CONV)

- **Pattern 2: verb + NP + *that*-clause** (e.g. *tell, persuade*)

  2 *I <u>persuaded</u> [myself] that something awful might happen.* (FICT)

- **Pattern 3: verb + *to* NP + *that* clause** (e.g. *suggest*)

  3 *I <u>suggested</u> [to Miss Kerrison] that she sit down on the chair and wait.*
  (FICT)

All verbs that can occur in Pattern 3 can also occur in Pattern 1. For example, compare **3** to **4** below:

  4 *I <u>suggested</u> that she sit down on the chair and wait.*

(For a discussion of the subjunctive *she sit … wait* in **3** and **4**, see 8.17.)
    Many verbs can occur with both Pattern 1 and 2 (e.g. *promise*):

> *I <u>promise</u> that we will take great care of him.* (FICT†)
> <compare: *I <u>promise</u> [you] that we will take great care of him.*>

A few verbs can occur with all three patterns (e.g. *write, cable, wire*):

> *I <u>wrote</u> that I would be satisfied with any old freighter.* (FICT†)
> <compare: *I <u>wrote</u> [him] that I would be satisfied with any old freighter;*
> *I <u>wrote</u> [to him] that I would be satisfied with any old freighter.*>

Most of the verbs that take Pattern 2 can also occur in the passive voice with a *that*-clause:

> *[He] <u>was told</u> that she had checked out of the hospital.* (FICT†)
> <compare: *Someone <u>told</u> [him] that she had checked out of the hospital.*>

That-clauses do not occur following prepositions. However, some of the verbs that take *that*-clauses correspond to prepositional verbs taking noun phrases:

Pattern 1: *agree* + *that*-clause   compare: *agree to* + NP
Pattern 2: *advise* + NP + *that*-clause   compare: *advise* + NP + *of/about*
                                                      NP

For example:

> *We all <u>agree</u> that cuts are needed.* (NEWS)
> <compare: *Would she <u>agree to</u> [it]?* (CONV)>
>
> *He <u>advised</u> [them] that my stated intention would put the Prime Minister's future at risk.* (NEWS†)
> <compare: *He <u>advised</u> [the police] <u>of</u> [the first raid].* (NEWS†)>

🔎 10.5.2 Verbs controlling post-predicate *that*-clauses

Ten verbs are especially common controlling *that* post-predicate clauses: *think, say, know, see, find, believe, feel, suggest, show,* and *guess* (in American English conversation). Table 10.1 lists all common verbs controlling *that*-clauses divided into semantic domains.

▶ 10.1 The most common verbs controlling a complement *that*-clause by semantic domain and register; occurrences per million words

legend: ▬ over 600   ▬ over 200   ▪ over 100   ▮ over 20

semantic domain	CONV	FICT	NEWS	ACAD
mental/cognition				
know	over 600	over 600	over 100	over 100
think	over 600	over 600	over 200	over 20
guess (AmE)	over 200	over 100		
see	over 100	over 200	over 100	over 100
find	over 20	over 200	over 100	over 100
believe	over 20	over 100	over 200	over 20
mean	over 100	over 100	over 20	over 20
suppose	over 100	over 100		over 20
feel	over 20	over 200	over 20	over 20
realize	over 20	over 100	over 20	over 20
hear	over 20	over 100	over 20	
hope	over 20	over 100	over 20	
assume		over 20	over 20	over 100
speech act				
say	over 200	over 200	over 200	over 200
other communication				
show	over 20	over 20	over 100	over 100
suggest		over 20	over 100	over 100
ensure				over 20
indicate			over 20	over 100

A Mental verbs

Mental verbs are very common with *that*-clauses, reporting various mental states and attitudes. The verb *think* is especially common in conversation—it is frequently used in the fixed expression *I think* to report one's own thoughts and lack of certainty:

> *I* <u>*think*</u> *we picked it.* (CONV†)

> *I* <u>*think*</u> *he does too much in the furniture business.* (CONV†)

The verb *guess* + *that*-clause is very common in American English conversation and fiction:

> *I* <u>*guess*</u> *I should probably call Michele.* (AmE CONV)

> *I* <u>*guess*</u> *they didn't hear anything.* (FICT)

In general, fiction uses a wider range of mental verbs than conversation to describe characters' mental states:

> *He* <u>*knew*</u> *that if he touched it, it would be as soft as silk.* (FICT†)

> *She* <u>*saw*</u> *that it was a moose with a body as big as a truck.* (FICT)

> *He looked at the wound and* <u>*found*</u> *that it had stopped bleeding.* (FICT†)

He <u>felt</u> that something was going to happen tonight. (FICT†)

The verb *believe* also reports a cognitive state, but it is more common in news than the other registers:

The Secretary of State and Mr. Bush <u>believe</u> that there are trustworthy deals to be done. (NEWS†)

Mental verbs with *that*-clauses are an important device for expressing stance. For example, verbs such as *think, feel,* and *assume* convey a sense of possibility combined with uncertainty, while verbs such as *know, find,* and *see* convey a greater sense of certainty. Compare the level of certainty in these two examples:

I <u>think</u> it's gotta be through there. (CONV)

I <u>know</u> I told you. (CONV)

Mental verbs are less common with *that*-clauses in academic prose, because academic writers usually do not mark the reports of personal thoughts explicitly.

B Speech act and other communication verbs

The second common use of *that*-clauses is to report what someone said. For example:

She <u>said</u> that it's lovely to wear. (CONV)

Fatty had <u>told</u> him that he looked the type. (FICT†)

Besides, aid workers <u>argue</u> that cutting any aid will only result in more poppies. (NEWS)

The verb *say* is extremely common in news and conversation. Its frequent use in news reflects the fact that statements by public figures are newsworthy:

Mr. Kenneth Clarke, the Health Secretary, yesterday <u>said</u> that the latest pay offer made last Friday was worth 9 per cent. (NEWS†)

Direct speech reporting is an alternative way to express the same content as a *that*-clause with a speech act verb. The clause in direct speech gives the content of the speech, and is associated with a reporting clause containing a speech act verb (see 8.15.5):

It will be ineffective against the multi-layer reactive armour, experts <u>say</u>. (NEWS)

<compare: *Experts <u>say</u> that it will be ineffective against the multi-layer reactive armour.*>

Academic prose shows a moderately frequent use of communication verbs such as *show, ensure,* and *indicate*. These verbs are often used with a non-personal subject. Therefore, the idea expressed in the *that*-clause is not overtly attributed to anybody:

Life histories <u>show</u> that elite women also chose spouses of the same social and economic status as themselves. (ACAD)

Investigations at the Irri <u>indicate</u> that high yields and high water efficiency can be achieved with continuous flow of shallow water. (ACAD†)

Notice that many of these communication verbs also indicate the degree of certainty associated with the information. In the examples above, *indicate* is less certain than *show. Suggest* is even less certain, while *prove* expresses an extreme degree of certainty:

They *suggest* **that he could become the country's national president.**
(NEWS†)

It is extremely difficult to *prove* **that there is no gene flow between enclaves.** (ACAD†)

Finally, there are some communication verbs used with *that*-clauses to propose a potential course of action. These are not the most common verbs controlling *that*-clauses, but they are familiar verbs such as *advise, insist, order,* and *ask*:

1 *The medicine-man then* ordered **that there should be no mourning for the dead child.** (FICT)

2 *We* ask **that this food be blessed.** (CONV†)

That-clauses with this function generally occur with either the modal *should*, as in **1**, or an uninflected subjunctive verb form (e.g. *be*), as in **2**.

0.6 Verbs controlling extraposed *that*-clauses

Extraposed *that*-clauses controlled by verbs are much less common than post-predicate *that*-clauses, and many fewer verbs can control extraposed clauses. The copula *be* is most common. In these structures, the controlling predicate is the copula in combination with the following predicative noun phrase, such as *is a wonder* in the following:

It's a *wonder* **he's got any business at all!** (CONV)

It's a *wonder* **the tree's alive,** but it is. (FICT)

The copular verbs *seem* and *appear* can also take this pattern:

It *seemed* however **that in-pig sows showed more stress than empty ones.** (ACAD)

It now *appears* **that I will be expected to part with a further portion of my income.** (NEWS†)

The verb *follow* is used in an intransitive sense with extraposed *that*-clauses:

It *follows* **that metals are better conductors at lower temperatures.** (ACAD)

Extraposed *that*-clauses also occur after passive voice verbs, such as *be found, be known, be assumed, be said,* and *be shown*:

It can *be assumed* **that number of kilometers driven in one year is a fair indication of experience of driving.** (ACAD)

0.7 *That*-clauses controlled by adjectives

The adjectives that control a *that*-complement clause all convey stance. They fall into three major categories: degrees of certainty (e.g. *certain, confident, evident*); affective states (e.g. *annoyed, glad, sad*); and evaluations (e.g. *appropriate, odd, good, important, advisable*).

That-clauses controlled by adjectival predicates occur in post-predicate or extraposed position:

- post-predicate *that*-clause:

    I'm <u>glad</u> **that I found you again.** (FICT)

- extraposed *that*-clause:

    It's <u>nice</u> **that people say it to you unprompted.** (CONV)

A few adjectives, like *certain* and *sad*, can control both post-predicate and extraposed clauses. However, most adjectives can control only one type of clause. The following sections describe the adjectives that take each type.

10.7.1 Adjectives controlling post-predicate *that*-clauses

Only one adjective is especially common with post-predicate *that*-clauses: *sure*.

    I'm <u>sure</u> **that they'd got two little rooms on the ground floor.** (CONV†)

Some other adjectives controlling post-predicate *that*-clauses are:

> certainty: *certain, confident, convinced, positive, right, sure*
>
> emotive: *afraid, amazed, angry, annoyed, astonished, (un)aware, careful, concerned, depressed, disappointed, encouraged, frightened, glad, grateful, (un)happy, hopeful, hurt, irritated, mad, pleased, proud, relieved, sad, (dis)satisfied, shocked, sorry, surprised, thankful, upset, worried*

Adjectives + post-predicate *that*-clauses typically occur with a human subject, so that the associated stance is tied directly to that person:

- certainty adjective:

    The minister is <u>confident</u> **that Pakistan could deflect western pressure.** (NEWS)

- emotive adjectives:

    I'm <u>afraid</u> **it brings the caterpillars in.** (CONV)

    I'm <u>sorry</u> **I hit you just now.** (FICT)

10.7.2 Adjectives controlling extraposed *that*-clauses

Some common adjectives controlling extraposed *that*-clauses are:

> *clear, (un)likely, (im)possible, true.*

Others include:

> certainty: *certain, doubtful, evident, false, inevitable, obvious, plain, probable, right, well-known*
>
> emotion or evaluation: *amazing, astonishing, awful, curious, disappointing, embarrassing, (un)fortunate, frightening, funny, good, great, horrible, inconceivable, incredible, interesting, irritating, (un)lucky, natural, neat, nice, notable, noteworthy, odd, ridiculous, sad, shocking, silly, strange, stupid, surprising, tragic, unfair, understandable, unthinkable, unusual, upsetting, wonderful*
>
> importance: *critical, crucial, essential, important, necessary, obligatory, vital*

Adjectival predicates with extraposed *that*-clauses mark a stance or attitude towards what is in the *that*-clause. In most cases, the stance or attitude belongs to the speaker or writer, but this relationship is not overt because the subject of the main clause is the empty *it*.

The most common adjectives controlling extraposed *that*-clauses (*clear, (un)likely, (im)possible, true*) express the (un)certainty of the idea in the *that*-clause:

> It is indeed <u>possible</u> **that the results of research will lead to a reappraisal of current methods of cultivation.** (ACAD)

> It is <u>unlikely</u> **that any insect exceeds about twice this velocity.** (ACAD)

Emotion/evaluation adjectives express other positive or negative attitudes to the information in the *that*-clause: e.g. *appropriate, fortunate, great, awful, disappointing, unlucky*.

> It is <u>good</u> **that our clan holds the Ozo title in high esteem.** (FICT†)

> It's <u>horrible</u> **that he put up with Claire's nagging.** (CONV)

Other affective adjectives are not strongly positive or negative, but indicate an emotional response such as surprise, interest, or amusement:

> It's pretty <u>funny</u> **that you and Alicia were the only ones in the classroom.** (FICT†)

> It's <u>incredible</u> **that Paul is still playing.** (NEWS†)

Importance adjectives with extraposed *that*-clauses are most common in academic prose. Some evaluation and importance adjectives are used with extraposed *that*-clauses to propose a course of action. They thus have a hypothetical sense and usually occur with *should* or with subjunctive verb forms (marked *):

> It is <u>sensible</u> **that the breeding animals receive the highest protection.** (ACAD)

> It is <u>essential</u> **that the two instruments should run parallel to the microscope state.** (ACAD)

> It is <u>important</u> **that it be* well sealed from air leakage.** (ACAD)

> It is <u>desirable</u> **that it be* both lined and insulated.** (ACAD†)

0.8 Discourse choices with *that*-clauses

10.8.1 Subject position v. extraposed *that*-clauses

Subject *that*-clauses and extraposed *that*-clauses are equivalent structures. In both cases, the *that*-clause is the logical subject of the sentence.

> Maybe it <u>annoys</u> them **that you don't fit their image of a fairy princess.** (FICT)
> <compare: **That you don't fit their image of a fairy princess** annoys them.>

A third related structure has a subject noun phrase that begins with *the fact that* (see 9.13.1):

> **The fact that the medical technicians were available** does not <u>make</u> the government's conduct any less offensive. (NEWS)

Overall, extraposed *that*-clauses are far more common than subject *that*-clauses. As a result, when subject *that*-clauses are used, they serve special discourse functions. Specifically, there are four factors that are important in the choice of a subject *that*-clause over an extraposed one:

A Register

Subject *that*-clauses are rare in all registers. They occur occasionally in academic prose and news, but they are virtually non-existent in conversation.

This preference for extraposed *that*-clauses over subject *that*-clauses reflects the general preference in English to use short, simple subjects, and to use longer, more complex structures towards the end of a clause. (See 12.1.4 on the principle of end-weight.)

Subject *that*-clauses cause difficulties for both speakers and listeners: we must understand the embedded complement clause and hold it in our memory until we get to the main clause predicate. The problems caused by a subject *that*-clause are especially great in conversation, because there is no time for editing or re-hearing.

B Information structure

In almost every case where a subject *that*-clause is used, it presents information that is already presupposed as factual or generally accepted. The information in the *that*-clause is established through previously stated information. The subject *that*-clause therefore provides a link with previous discourse, and follows the information flow principle, with established information occurring before new information (see 12.1.1). For example:

> *One of the triumphs of radioactive dating emerged only gradually as more and more workers dated meteorites. It became surprisingly apparent that all meteorites are of the same age, somewhere in the vicinity of 4.5 billion years old <...>*
>
> **That there are no meteorites of any other age, regardless of when they fell to Earth,** <u>suggests</u> *strongly that all meteorites originated in other bodies of the solar system that formed at the same time the Earth did.* (ACAD)

Here the subject *that*-clause summarizes information that can be deduced from the previous paragraph. It states this known information as the subject of the sentence and moves on to the new information (*all meteorites originate in other bodies ...*).

C Grammatical factors

In most cases when a subject *that*-clause is used, the main clause predicate has a complex construction with many phrases or clauses. For example:

> **That a stimulus can be processed either verbally or non-verbally** <u>helps</u> <u>[to make sense of those otherwise anomalous findings in which verbal stimuli give rise to a LVF superiority].</u> (ACAD)

The alternative extraposed construction would be very hard to understand in cases like this.

D Topic and style

Personal style and topic can also favor the use of subject *that*-clauses. Some authors use subject *that*-clauses more than others. Sports writers as a group have a stylistic preference for them, as in:

> *That the 49ers' injury-ravaged defensive secondary was exploited by the Vikings (2–1)* <u>was</u> *no shocker.* (NEWS†)

10.8.2 Retention v. omission of *that*

Another major choice with *that*-clauses is whether to use the *that*-complementizer or not. There is no difference in meaning:

> *I* <u>hope</u> *you* <u>realized</u> *they said a few words on there.* (CONV)
> <compare: *I* <u>hope</u> *[that] you* <u>realized</u> *[that] they said a few words on there.*>

While you might guess that these options are fairly random, there are actually strong discourse factors associated with the omission or retention of *that*.

A Register factors

In conversation, omission of *that* is typical. In academic prose, on the other hand, omission of *that* is unusual. These preferences follow general patterns for the two registers: conversation often favors the reduction or omission of constituents that are not necessary; academic prose, in contrast, is carefully produced, and has elaborated structures.

B Factors favoring omission of *that*

Three grammatical factors are associated with the omission of *that*: say/think as the main clause verb, co-referential subjects in the main clause and *that*-clause, and a personal pronoun as subject of the *that*-clause. These characteristics are illustrated in **1–2**:

> 1 *I* <u>think</u> *I'll make a shopping list today.* (CONV)
> 2 *You* <u>said</u> *you didn't.* (CONV)

In **1**, the controlling verb is *think*, while in **2** it is *say*. Both examples have co-referential subjects for the main clause and *that*-clause (*I–I* in **1**, *you–you* in **2**), and the *that*-clause subjects are personal pronouns.

That-complement clauses often have these characteristics. Therefore, it is easy for hearers/readers to recognize the presence of these *that*-clauses without explicit marking with *that*.

C Factors favoring retention of *that*

Three grammatical characteristics are associated with the retention of *that*: coordinated *that*-clauses, use of passive voice, and an intervening noun phrase.

First, coordinated *that*-clauses almost always retain the *that*. It would be hard to identify the start of the second *that*-clause in **1** if *that* were omitted:

> 1 *The major conclusion of both studies* <u>was</u> *that the nation and particularly the state of Florida must quickly reduce their large reliance on foreign oil and that conservation measures and increased reliance on the abundant national supply of coal were the major alternatives.* (ACAD)

Second, when a passive voice verb is used in the main clause, *that* is usually retained:

> I <u>was told</u> **that both the new right and those who support the government's view had been excluded**. (NEWS†)

Third, if there is an intervening noun phrase (marked in *[]* below) between the main clause verb and the *that*-clause, the *that* is usually retained:

> They <u>warn</u> *[him]* **that it's dangerous**. (CONV)

The influence of these factors is strongest in conversation: omission of *that* is the norm in conversation, but when these factors occur, *that* is almost always retained.

Major points in GRAMMAR BITE B: *That*-clauses

➤ The most common type of *that*-clause is post-predicate. Its typical function is reporting the thoughts and speech of humans.
   ➤ Each of the other types of *that*-clauses has particular functions in discourse also.
➤ Mental verbs and speech act/communication verbs are the most common type of verb with a *that*-clause.
   ➤ These verbs reflect the primary function of *that*-clauses for reporting thoughts and speech.
   ➤ Many of the verb + *that*-clause combinations also convey stance.
➤ Subject-position and extraposed *that*-clauses are much less common than post-predicate *that*-clauses.
   ➤ For verbs, only *be* is common controlling extraposed *that*-clauses.
➤ The adjectives that control *that*-clauses all convey stance.
   ➤ There are three subcategories of meaning: certainty (e.g. *certain*), psychological states (e.g. *glad*, *sad*), and evaluation (e.g. *good*, *important*).
   ➤ Extraposed *that*-clauses are far more common than subject *that*-clauses.
   ➤ When subject *that*-clauses are used, they usually conform to particular characteristics of register, grammatical complexity, and information structure. In addition, some topics and individual writers favor subject *that*-clauses.
➤ Factors associated with the retention or omission of the *that*-complementizer include register, the main clause verb, and certain characteristics of the subjects in the main clause and *that*-clause.

GRAMMAR BITE

C *Wh*-clauses

10.9 Structure and function of *wh*-clauses

There are three basic types of *wh*-complement clauses: **interrogative clauses**, **nominal relative clauses**, and **exclamatives**. Interrogative clauses and nominal relative clauses use the same *wh*-words, except that *whether* is used only with interrogatives. Exclamative *wh*-clauses begin with *how* or *what*.

Interrogative clauses are used with verbs such as *ask* and *wonder* to present an indirect question:

1 *Jill was <u>asking</u> **what happened**.* (CONV†)
    <compare: *Jill asked 'What happened?'*>
2 *I <u>wonder</u> **what that could be about**.* (CONV)

Note that there is a change in word order when the *wh*-word corresponds to an object in the complement clause. For example, the complementizer *what* corresponds to the object of the preposition in **2**, but it is placed at the front of the complement clause (not: **I wonder that could be about what*).

Nominal relative clauses can be paraphrased with a general head noun + relative clause:

*Yes. Burbidge Road. Which <u>is</u> **where Carlos used to live**.* (CONV)
<paraphrase: *Which <u>is</u> **the place where Carlos used to live**.*>
***What baffles me** <u>is</u> how few of them can spell.* (NEWS)
<paraphrase: ***The thing that baffles me** <u>is</u>. . .*>

Exclamative *wh*-clauses are less common than the other types. They begin with *how* + adjective or with *what* as a predeterminer. They act as indirect exclamatives (see 8.12):

*He still <u>remembered</u> **how wonderful it had been**.* (FICT)
*I <u>was thinking</u> **how nice you are, what a good actor,** and **what a nice man**.* (FICT†)
<compare: *I was thinking 'How nice you are! . . .'*>

As these examples show, exclamative *wh*-clauses have a change in word order. The subject predicative and its *wh*-word (e.g. *how wonderful*, *how nice*) is placed at the front of the clause.

10.9.1 *Wh*-clauses controlled by verbs

With verbs, *wh*-complement clauses often occur in object position. For example:

*You <u>give</u> him **what he wants**.* (FICT)

Wh-clauses can also occur as subject:

***What could be at work there** <u>is</u> an actual enmity towards the very structure of society.* (FICT)
***How to read the record** <u>is</u> the subject of much of this book.* (ACAD)

Wh-clauses also occur as subject predicatives. These structures are particularly common in conversation, with the demonstrative pronoun *that* as subject, and the copula contracted to *'s*:

*<u>That's</u> **what I'm saying**.* (CONV)
*<u>That's</u> **why I bought the refill**.* (CONV)

10.9.2 *Wh*-clauses as complements of adjectives and prepositions

Wh-clauses can also follow adjectival predicates:

*I'm not <u>sure</u> **when it's open for anybody**.* (CONV)
*She wanted to be <u>careful</u> **what she said**.* (FICT)

Wh-clauses that are complements of adjectives can also be extraposed:

> It was <u>incredible</u> **what had happened to them.** (FICT)
>
> It was not immediately <u>clear</u> **how the Soviet leadership could enforce such a ruling.** (NEWS)

Finally, unlike *that*-clauses, *wh*-clauses can be the complement of a preposition or the object of a prepositional verb:

> She was <u>amazed at</u> **how exhausted she was.** (FICT)
>
> <compare: *She was <u>amazed</u> that she was so exhausted.*>

10.10 Post-predicate *wh*-clauses controlled by verbs

10.10.1 Grammatical patterns

There are two important grammatical patterns used with *wh*-complement clauses in post-predicate position:

- **Pattern 1: verb + *wh*-clause** (e.g. *know, remember, see*)

  > I don't <u>know</u> **what they are.** (CONV)
  >
  > I can't <u>remember</u> **how I used to be.** (FICT)

- **Pattern 2: verb + NP + *wh*-clause** (e.g. *ask, show, tell*)

  > I didn't <u>tell</u> *[you]* **what Emma thought.** (CONV)
  >
  > I want you to <u>show</u> *[me]* **where the car went off.** (FICT)

Pattern 1 has a variant with prepositional verbs:

> You actually <u>think about</u> **what you're seeing.** (CONV†)

Pattern 2 can also occur with a prepositional verb, where the preposition occurs between the NP and the *wh*-clause, e.g. *remind* + NP + *of* + *wh*-clause:

> They <u>remind</u> *[me]* <u>of</u> **when I was at school.** (CONV)

In both patterns, some verbs can take *wh*-infinitive clauses. The *wh*-word is followed by the *to* infinitive marker and the uninflected form of the verb:

> You must also <u>understand</u> **how to check their accuracy at recognised stages.** (ACAD†)
>
> I would <u>tell</u> *[them]* **where to go.** (CONV)

10.10.2 Verbs controlling *wh*-clauses

As you can see in Table 10.2, the most common verbs controlling a *wh*-clause fall into four major semantic domains: mental, speech act, other communication, and perception. In addition, the relationship verb *depend (on)* is common in conversation.

By far the most common verb controlling a *wh*-clause is *know* in conversation. Although it can be used to report what a speaker knows, it is even more commonly used to report what the speaker does not know:

> I <u>know</u> **what she said.** (CONV)

le 10.2 The most common verbs controlling a complement *wh*-clause by semantic domain and register; occurrences per million words

Legend: over 1000 | over 500 | over 200 | over 100 | over 40 | over 20

semantic domain	CONV	FICT	NEWS	ACAD
cognition				
know	over 1000	over 500	over 200	over 100
wonder	over 200	over 500		
think (about)	over 100	over 200		
remember	over 100	over 40		
understand	over 40	over 200		over 100
guess	over 100			
realize				over 100
find (out)		over 40		
speech act				
tell (NP)	over 500	over 500	over 40	
ask (NP)	over 200	over 200	over 40	
say	over 100	over 100		
explain			over 40	over 100
other communication				
show (NP)	over 40	over 40		over 40
perception				
see	over 500	over 200	over 100	over 200
look (at)	over 200			
relationship				
depend (on)	over 40			

> I <u>don't know</u> **what's happening.** (CONV)
>
> I <u>don't know</u> **where they are.** (CONV)

The verb *know* is also common in dialog in fiction and news:

> I <u>don't know</u> **how people are going to get through the winter.** (NEWS)

The verb *see* is also notably common with *wh*-clauses in conversation. Sometimes it is used for literal perceptions of seeing:

> I couldn't <u>see</u> **what they were doing.**

More commonly, however, it is used metaphorically to mean 'find out':

> I'll <u>see</u> **what cash I've got left.** (CONV)
>
> So we'll <u>see</u> **what transpires this time.** (CONV)

The expression *see what I/you mean* is particularly common in conversation:

> I can <u>see</u> **what you mean.** (CONV)
>
> Do you <u>see</u> **what I mean?** (CONV)

Other mental verbs, such as *wonder*, *think (about/of)*, *remember*, and *understand* are relatively common with *wh*-clauses in both conversation and fiction:

*I could never <u>remember</u> **how to do them**.* (CONV)

*You should <u>wonder</u> **why she wants me around**.* (FICT)

*Sethe smiled just <u>thinking about</u> **what the word could mean**.* (FICT)

Speech act verbs are also relatively common with *wh*-clauses in conversation and fiction:

*Did you <u>tell</u> him **what Greg said about your arms**?* (CONV)

*I am <u>asking</u> **what you intend to do about this man**.* (FICT)

Although these are the most common verbs with *wh*-clauses, it is important to realize that *wh*-clauses can occur with almost any transitive verb as a nominal relative clause. For example:

*The birds gathered round to <u>eat</u> **what was left**.* (FICT)

*She also <u>won</u> **what they call oratory**.* (FICT)

*He <u>dreaded</u> **what he might have to do**.* (FICT†)

*And I <u>respect</u> **what she says**.* (CONV)

Wh-clauses are generally less common in academic prose. However, there are some mental and communication verbs that are particularly useful with *wh*-clauses in academic prose. These verbs deal with discovery and description:

- mental verbs:

  *We need to <u>discover</u> **what they believe about AIDS**.* (ACAD)

  *Thus the programmer can <u>establish</u> **when a transput operation is complete**.* (ACAD†)

- communication verbs:

  *He <u>describes</u> **how the National Committee is organized**.* (ACAD)

  *An evaluation can also <u>indicate</u> **what are likely outcomes**.* (ACAD†)

10.11 Interrogative clauses with *whether* and *if*

The *wh*-word *whether* is used as a complementizer to introduce dependent *yes/no* interrogative clauses that express indirect questions. *If* can be used as a complementizer in the same way:

- *whether*-clauses:

  *He <u>wondered</u> **whether the mestizo had stolen his mule**.* (FICT†)

  *Police are not taking action until they <u>know</u> **whether the men face charges**.* (NEWS)

- *if*-clauses:

  *Ask him when they were here last. <u>See</u> **if he's got a tongue**. <u>See</u> **if he's such an idiot as he looks**.* (FICT)

  *One of the most common problems encountered is simply <u>deciding</u> **if two components in a machine clash**.* (ACAD)

In the above examples, it would be possible to change *whether* to *if*, and vice versa, without changing the meaning. Notice that this use of *if* is different from *if* as a subordinator in adverbial conditional clauses (see 11.9.1), such as the following:

> I *would've* <u>died</u> **if I was in there**. (CONV)

Adverbial *if*-clauses can be moved to initial position (e.g. **If I was in there**, *I would've died*). In contrast, interrogative *if* complement clauses cannot be moved.

With the verb *ask*, the *if/whether* clause functions as an indirect speech report of a *yes/no* question:

> I <u>asked</u> **if she needed a ride**. (FICT)
> <compare direct speech: *Do you need a ride?*>

Sometimes alternatives are offered by using *or (not)* with an *if/whether* clause:

> Mynors <u>asked</u> her **whether they should go through the marketplace or along King Street**. (FICT†) ·
> I *don't* <u>care</u> **whether you want to play an instrument or not**. (CONV)

The phrase *or not* can also directly follow the complementizer *whether*:

> We do not <u>ask</u> **whether or not** an axiom is 'true'. (ACAD†)

If is less often used with *or* + alternative expressions:

> I *don't* <u>know</u> **if she was upset or her eyes were watering because of the smoke**. (NEWS)
> It really *doesn't* <u>matter</u> **if I'm a nice guy or not**. (NEWS)

When *if* is the complementizer, *or not* cannot follow it directly: . . .* **if <u>or not</u>** *I'm a nice guy.*

As many of the above examples illustrate, *whether/if* clauses are frequently used with a negative in the main clause. The verbs *care*, *matter*, *mind*, and *know* are especially common in the negative:

> I *don't* <u>care</u> **if you're serious or not**. (CONV)
> *Doesn't* <u>matter</u> **whether – whether it's a boy or a girl**. (CONV)
> I *don't* <u>mind</u> **if the goals are spread around**. (NEWS)

10.11.1 Verbs controlling *whether-* and *if*-clauses

If-clauses are more common than *whether*-clauses as interrogative clauses. Verbs used commonly with *if*-clauses in conversation and fiction are *see*, *wonder*, and *know*; less frequent verbs include *ask*, *matter*, *mind*, *doubt*, *care*, and *remember*. *If*-clauses are generally rare in academic prose.

Whether-clauses, in contrast, occur more evenly across registers. *Know* + *whether*-clause is especially common in conversation, but many different verbs are used with moderate frequencies (e.g. *decide*, *see*, *mind*, *care*, *say*, *ask*). *Wonder* + *whether*-clause is relatively common in fiction, while *determine* + *whether*-clause is relatively common in academic prose. Several less common verbs are found primarily in academic prose with *whether*-clauses (e.g. *consider*, *establish*, *indicate*, *find out*).

If-clauses and *whether*-clauses are stylistically different. *If*-clauses are favored in more informal styles, so they are especially common in conversation and fiction, especially with *see* (= 'find out'), *wonder*, and *know*:

> Dad, try this on and <u>see</u> **if it fits**. (CONV)

> *I wonder* **if they will close our school down.** (CONV†)
>
> *I don't really* **know** **if that's such a good idea.** (CONV)

Major points in GRAMMAR BITE C: *Wh*-clauses
- ➤ There are three major types of *wh*-clauses: interrogative, nominal relative, and exclamative.
- ➤ *Wh*-clauses can be complements of verbs, adjectives, or prepositions.
- ➤ *Wh*-complements can occur with or without a noun phrase between the verb and *wh*-clause.
- ➤ There are four types of verbs that are most common with *wh*-clauses: mental, speech act, other communication, and perception.
- ➤ *Whether* and *if* are used to introduce dependent interrogative clauses.
  - ➤ *If*-clauses are more common than *whether*-clauses, especially in conversation.
  - ➤ *Whether*-clauses are used with more formal discourse and with clauses that include choices with *or* and *or not*.

GRAMMAR BITE

D Post-predicate infinitive clauses

10.12 Overview of infinitive clauses

In general, infinitive clauses are more common in the written registers than in conversation. This is the opposite of the distribution of *that*-clauses and *wh*-clauses, which are both most common in conversation.

Infinitive complement clauses serve a wide range of functions. They report speech and mental states, and they are also used to report intentions, desires, efforts, perceptions, and other general actions. They usually occur in post-predicate position, although they can also occur in subject position and in extraposed constructions. In this Grammar Bite, we concentrate on basic information about post-predicate *to*-clauses (including those that function as subject predicatives). Then, in Grammar Bite E, we describe other types of *to*-clauses.

10.13 Post-predicate *to*-clauses controlled by verbs

10.13.1 Grammatical patterns

There are five major grammatical patterns for post-predicate infinitive clauses following a verb:

- **Pattern 1: verb + *to*-clause** (e.g. *try*, *hope*)

  I'm just *trying* **to get away early.** (CONV†)

  The new promoters *hope* **to make prototypes at $299,000 each.** (NEWS)

Pattern 1 is by far the most common pattern for *to*-clauses in all registers.

- **Pattern 2: verb + NP + *to*-clause** (e.g. *tell, believe, enable, expect*)

    It <u>enables</u> *[the farmer]* **to maintain uniform and near constant conditions in the house.** (ACAD†)

Pattern 2 is moderately common in news and academic prose. Many verbs in Pattern 2 also have a corresponding passive form, which we can call **Pattern 2P: *be* verb-ed + *to*-clause**:

    PCBs *are* generally <u>considered</u> **to be carcinogenic.** (ACAD)
    <compare Pattern 2: *Researchers generally* <u>consider</u> *[PCBs]* **to be carcinogenic.**>

Pattern 2P is also moderately common in news and academic prose. In news, *be expected* is the most common verb in this pattern, while *be found* and *be required* are more common in academic prose:

    Heavy fighting with government troops <u>was expected</u> **to break out soon.** (NEWS)
    Thus, paddy soils <u>are found</u> **to be very dissimilar in chemical composition.** (ACAD†)

- **Pattern 3: verb + *for* NP + *to*-clause** (e.g. *ask, love, arrange, wait*)

    Hire a Daily Mirror van and <u>wait</u> *for [Mrs Jones]* **to arrive.** (CONV†)

Pattern 3 is most common in American English conversation.

- **Pattern 4: verb + bare infinitive clause** (e.g. *dare, help, let*)

    The police didn't <u>dare</u> **touch them** *because of United Nations.* (FICT†)

    It could have <u>helped</u> **clarify a number of issues.** (NEWS†)

This pattern is rare in all of the registers of our corpus.
Some verbs that take Pattern 4—such as *dare* and *help*—also take Pattern 1:

    It could have <u>helped</u> **to clarify a number of issues.**

- **Pattern 5: verb + NP + bare infinitive clause** (e.g. *have, feel, make, help, see*)

    I'll <u>have</u> *[Judy]* **do it.** (CONV)

    He actually <u>felt</u> *[the sweat]* **break out now on his forehead.** (FICT)

Pattern 5 is found primarily in conversation and fiction, but it is much less common than Patterns 1 and 2.

10.13.2 Meaning variations of *to*-clause patterns

> **A** **Pattern 1: verb + *to*-clause**

In this pattern, the implied subject of the *to*-clause is usually the same as the subject of the main clause. To see this, you can compare a *to*-clause with an equivalent *that*-clause:

    I didn't <u>claim</u> **to be an authority.** (CONV)
    <compare: *I didn't* <u>claim</u> **that I was an authority.**>
    Widmer said he <u>hoped</u> **to sell Brabham.** (NEWS†)
    <compare: *Widmer said he* <u>hoped</u> **that he could sell Brabham.**>

The verb *say* is unusual in this pattern, however. With *say*, the implied subject of the *to*-clause is the speaker, rather than the subject of the main clause:

Mr Bryant <u>said</u> to put it through to you. (FICT)
<compare: *Mr Bryant <u>said</u> that I <not he> should put it through to you.*>

Jerry <u>said</u> to tell you how sorry he is. (FICT)
<compare: *Jerry <u>said</u> that I <not he> should tell you how sorry he is.*>

B Pattern 2: verb + NP + *to*-clause

In Pattern 2, the roles of the NP and *to*-clause depend on the controlling verb. There are three variations.

Variation 1: This variation occurs with ditransitive verbs. In these sentences, the NP is both the indirect object of the main clause and the implied subject of the *to*-clause. The *to*-clause is the direct object of the main clause.

I <u>told</u> [grandma] to make me and Tim some more. (CONV†)

Here *grandma* is the indirect object of the main verb *told* as well as the implied subject of the *to*-clause (i.e. grandma should make me and Tim some more). Other examples of this type include:

I sprinkle a little around and <u>tell</u> [the demons] to leave. (NEWS)

He had <u>persuaded</u> [a woman] to come into the laundry room of the house. (FICT†)

Variation 2: This variation occurs with complex transitive verbs. In these sentences, the NP is the direct object of the main clause and also the implied subject of the *to*-clause. The *to*-clause is the object predicative of the main clause.

Rechem <u>believes</u> [the results] to be unscientific. (NEWS)
<compare: *Rechem <u>believes</u> that the results are unscientific.*>

Here the noun phrase *the results* functions as the direct object of *believes* as well as the implied subject of the *to*-clause. However, the *to*-clause is needed as object predicative to complete the main clause. In fact, it would give the opposite meaning to keep the direct object without the object predicative (i.e. 'Rechem believes the results').

This pattern occurs with mental verbs (e.g. *assume, believe, consider, understand*), verbs of intention, desire, and decision (e.g. *choose, expect, like, need, prefer, want, wish*), and verbs of discovery (e.g. *find*):

In a sense he <u>considered</u> [the trip] to be a medical necessity. (FICT)

She said that she would <u>like</u> [her mother] to stay with her. (ACAD)

In nylon he <u>found</u> [the Voigt average] to be closest to experimental data. (ACAD)

Variation 3: With these verbs, the NP functions as the indirect object of the main clause, but it is not the implied subject of the *to*-clause. Rather, the subject of the main clause is the implied subject of the *to*-clause. The only common verb with this pattern is *promise*:

Ollie has <u>promised</u> [Billy] to take him fishing next Sunday. (FICT)
<compare: *Ollie has <u>promised</u> Billy that he <Ollie> will take him <Billy> fishing.*>

You can see that here the implied subject of the *to*-clause is the subject of the main clause—*Ollie*.

C **Pattern 2P: NP + passive verb + *to*-clause**

We mentioned above that Pattern 2 can occur in the passive. Thus, the active voice form

$$NP_1 + verb + NP_2 + \textit{to}\text{-clause}$$

has the corresponding passive structure:

$$NP_2 + \text{passive verb} + \textit{to}\text{-clause}$$

Many verbs allow both the active and passive forms. For example:

> active: [We *NP1*] <u>assume</u> [the variable x *NP2*] **to be subjective.** (ACAD†)
> passive: [An unemployed teenager sharing a house with the family *NP2*] <u>was</u> <u>assumed</u> **to have a separate, and often lower, income.** (NEWS†)

> active: [He *NP1*] did not <u>believe</u> [this last remark *NP2*] **to be true.** (FICT)
> passive: [Tens of thousands of phantom azalea bushes and geraniums *NP2*] <u>are believed</u> **to be alive and growing in the gardens of Northern Ireland.** (NEWS)

However, no passive form is possible for some verbs that take Pattern 2, including *want*, *get*, *cause*, and *prefer*. In contrast, only the passive form is commonly used for some other verbs with *to*-clauses. These verbs include *be claimed*, *be said*, and *be thought*:

> The costs <u>are claimed</u> **to be about 2.5bn.** (NEWS†)
> In Ceausescu's Romania, even the ashtrays <u>are thought</u> **to have ears.** (NEWS†)

D **Pattern 3: verb + *for* NP + *to*-clause**

Most of the verbs that occur in Pattern 3 are prepositional verbs, such as *wait for*, *long for*, *call for*:

> She <u>waited for</u> the little antelope **to protest.** (FICT†)
> The society <u>called for</u> consumers **to take conservation measures to save water.** (NEWS†)

With these verbs, the preposition *for* is mandatory. However, a few verbs that express desire or preference can take an optional *for* + NP before the *to*-clause:

> I would <u>like</u> Sir Alec **to carry on.** (FICT)
> But I would <u>like for</u> you **to do one thing** if you would. (FICT)
> Certainly, but I should <u>hate</u> you **to forget that he has scored more runs in Test cricket than any other Englishman.** (NEWS)
> I'd <u>hate for</u> all that stuff **to go bad.** (CONV)

10.13.3 Verbs controlling post-predicate *to*-clauses

Table 10.3 lists the most common verbs with post-predicate *to*-clauses, showing their semantic categories. The written registers use verbs from many different categories. In contrast, conversation uses far fewer verbs commonly; most of those are verbs of desire (e.g. *want*, *like*), plus the verbs *seem* and *try*.

The combination *want* + *to*-clause is extremely common in conversation, where speakers often express their own desires or the desires of others:

> I don't <u>want</u> **to have a broken nose.** (CONV)

Table 10.3 **Verbs controlling infinitive clauses in post-predicate position, by semantic domain**

common = over 20 occurrences per million words
occassional = attested in corpus but less than 20 occurrences per million words

pattern	verbs
for speech act and other communication verbs:	
Pattern 1: verb + to-clause	occasional: *ask, beg, claim, decline, offer, promise, prove, request, say*
Pattern 2: verb + NP + to-clause	common: *ask, prove*
	occasional: *advise, beg, beseech, call, challenge, command, convince, invite, promise, remind, report, request, show, teach, tell, urge, warn*
Pattern 2P: passive verb + to-clause	common: *be asked*
	occasional: *be claimed, be proved/proven, be said, be told*
Pattern 3: verb + *for* NP + to-clause	occasional: *ask, call, pray*
for cognition verbs:	
Pattern 1: verb + to-clause	common: *learn*
	occasional: *expect, forget, pretend, remember*
Pattern 2: verb + NP + to-clause	common: *expect, find*
	occasional: *assume, believe, consider, estimate, imagine, judge, know, presume, suppose, take, trust, understand*
Pattern 2P: passive verb + to-clause	common: *be expected*
	occasional: *be found, be thought*
for perception verbs:	
Pattern 2: verb + NP + to-clause	occasional: *see*
Pattern 2P: passive verb + to-clause	occasional: *be felt, be heard*
Pattern 5: verb + NP + bare infinitive clause	occasional: *feel, hear, see, watch*
for verbs of desire:	
Pattern 1: verb + to-clause	common: *hope, like, need, want, wish*
	occasional: *(cannot) bear, care, dare, desire, dread, hate, love, long, prefer, regret, (cannot) stand*
Pattern 2: verb + NP + to-clause	common: *want*
	occasional: *dare, dread, hate, like, love, need, prefer, wish*
Pattern 3: verb + *for* NP + to-clause	occasional: *(cannot) bear, care, dread, hate, like, love, long, prefer, (cannot) stand*
Pattern 4: verb + bare infinitive clause	occasional: *dare*
for verbs of intention or decision:	
Pattern 1: verb + to-clause	common: *agree, decide, intend, mean, prepare*
	occasional: *aim, consent, choose, hesitate, look, plan, refuse, resolve, threaten, volunteer, wait*

ıble 10.3 **continued**

pattern	verbs
Pattern 2: verb + NP + *to*-clause	occasional: *choose, design, intend, mean, prepare, schedule*
Pattern 2P: passive verb + *to*-clause	common: *be prepared*
Pattern 3: verb + *for* NP + *to*-clause	occasional: *agree, consent, intend, look, mean, plan, wait*
for verbs of modality or causation:	
Pattern 1: verb + *to*-clause	common: *get*
	occasional: *afford, arrange, deserve, help, vote*
Pattern 2: verb + NP + *to*-clause	common: *allow, enable, require*
	occasional: *appoint, assist, authorize, cause, compel, counsel, defy, drive, elect, encourage, entitle, forbid, force, get, help, inspire, instruct, lead, leave, oblige, order, permit, persuade, prompt, raise, summon, tempt*
Pattern 2P: passive verb + *to*-clause	common: *be allowed, be enabled, be made, be required*
Pattern 3: verb + *for* NP + *to*-clause	occasional: *allow, arrange*
Pattern 4: verb + bare infinitive clause	occasional: *help, let, make to (with)*
Pattern 5: verb + NP + bare infinitive clause	occasional: *have, help, let, make*
for verbs of effort:	
Pattern 1: verb + *to*-clause	common: *attempt, fail, manage, try*
	occasional: *bother, endeavor, seek, strive, struggle, venture*
for verbs of aspect:	
Pattern 1: verb + *to*-clause	common: *begin, continue, start*
	occasional: *cease, commence, proceed*
for verbs of probability or simple fact:	
Pattern 1: verb + *to*-clause	common: *appear, seem, tend*
	occasional: *come, happen, turn out*

> *I wanted* **to go and get something.** (CONV)
>
> *He probably wants* **to speak to you.** (CONV)

Speakers also often question the desires of people they are speaking to:

> *Do you want* **to go in the water**? (CONV)

In fictional dialog, the verb *want* is also extremely common with these same functions:

> *I want* **to jump into a tub of hot water first.** (FICT)
>
> *Do you want* **to come along**? (FICT)

Verbs of effort are most common in fiction and news, where they typically report people's attempts or failures:

> *She had failed* **to appear in court.** (FICT)
>
> *Military officers have tried* **to seize power six times.** (NEWS†)

Aspectual verbs are also most common in fiction and news. They typically report the state of progression for an activity or process:

> He <u>continued</u> **to stare at her**. (FICT)
>
> Even ambulance staff not suspended are <u>beginning</u> **to feel the pinch**. (NEWS†)

The verbs *tend* and *appear*, expressing likelihood, occur most frequently in academic prose:

> The cloud <u>tended</u> **to flatten into a disk**. (ACAD)
>
> Neither the sex nor the strain of donor rats <u>appears</u> **to be important**. (ACAD)

These are **raising** structures, to be described in Grammar Bite D.

Finally, it is worth noting that verbs of modality/causation, even though they are not common overall, are common with *to*-clauses in academic prose:

> An autumn-like pattern, or even a constant day length, will <u>allow</u> the body **to develop properly before the bird starts laying**. (ACAD)

10.14 Subject predicative *to*-clauses

To-clauses acting as subject predicatives are relatively common in the written registers. They are similar to *that*-clauses as subject predicatives. They occur after a copular verb and identify or describe the subject of the main clause. The subject (marked in *[]*) is typically abstract:

> [Their hope] <u>is</u> **to succeed as the consolidator of post-Thatcherism**. (NEWS)
>
> [Their function] <u>is</u> **to detect the cries of predatory bats**. (ACAD)

There are four major uses of subject predicative *to*-clauses:

- framing points in a discussion:

> [A fourth challenge] <u>is</u> **to develop management arrangements within hospitals**. (NEWS)
>
> [The first step in any such calculation] <u>is</u> **to write the equation for the reaction**. (ACAD)

- introducing an aim, objective, plan, goal, purpose, strategy, task, or idea:

> [Our major aim] <u>is</u> **to reach beginning students in geology**. (ACAD†)
>
> [The plan] <u>is</u> **to turn Ross into a mini-conglomerate**. (NEWS†)
>
> [The purpose of this chapter] <u>is</u> **to describe some of the available techniques**. (ACAD†)

- introducing a methodology:

> [The best method for recovering eggs] <u>is</u> **to use the flushing method described in Section 2.2**. (ACAD)
>
> [An alternative technique for this stage of oocyte maturation] <u>is</u> **to collect freshly ovulated oocytes from the fallopian tubes**. (ACAD)

- making a balanced sentence structure when a *to*-clause is also subject of the main clause:

> [To be European in France] <u>is</u> **to think globally about a French-led**
> **political Europe which will challenge the power of Japan and America.**
> (NEWS)

0.15 Post-predicate *to*-clauses controlled by adjectives

Adjectives with post-predicate *to*-clauses include:
  very common: *(un)likely*
  moderately common: *(un)able, determined, difficult, due, easy, free, glad, hard,*
    ready, used, (un)willing
selected other adjectives:
  certainty: *certain, sure*
  ability or willingness: *anxious, careful, eager, fit, hesitant, inclined, obliged,*
    prepared, quick, ready, reluctant, (all) set, slow
  emotion or stance: *afraid, amazed, angry, annoyed, ashamed, astonished,*
    careful, concerned, curious, delighted, disappointed, disgusted, embarrassed,
    furious, grateful, happy, impatient, nervous, pleased, proud, sorry, surprised,
    worried
  ease or difficulty: *awkward, (un)pleasant, (im)possible, tough*
  evaluation: *bad, brave, careless, crazy, expensive, good, lucky, mad, nice, right,*
    silly, smart, (un)wise, wrong
The adjectives that control *to*-clauses fall into five semantic categories.

A Degree of certainty

These adjectives express the likelihood or certainty of the idea in the *to*-clause:

> I'm <u>certain</u> **to regret it.** (FICT)
> He's <u>liable</u> **to be a bit amorous.** (CONV)
> He was <u>sure</u> **to see the old woman hopping about.** (FICT†)

Likely and *unlikely* are the most common adjectives in this group:

> Mr. Adams said there were <u>unlikely</u> **to be enough volunteers.** (NEWS†)
> They are <u>likely</u> **to have been made by different processes.** (ACAD†)

B Ability or willingness

These adjectives express the ability, preparedness, or commitment to the action specified in the *to*-clause:

> He doesn't seem <u>willing</u> **to move out.** (CONV)
> I'm <u>ready</u> **to take over in Dave's place.** (FICT†)
> The embryos are less <u>inclined</u> **to skid about.** (ACAD†)

C Emotion or stance

These adjectives express a feeling or emotional reaction to the idea in the *to*-clause. Many different stance adjectives occur with *to*-clauses:

> Not everybody's going to be <u>glad</u> **to have him around.** (FICT†)
> I'm <u>sorry</u> **to hear about you.** (CONV)

*Gabby was <u>afraid</u> **to say anything more**.* (FICT)

D Ease or difficulty

These adjectives give the speaker's assessment of how difficult or easy a task is. The task is described in the *to*-clause. *Easy, difficult,* and *hard* are the most common adjectives in this group:

> *They're <u>easy</u> **to steal**.* (CONV)
>
> *Jobs were <u>hard</u> **to come by**.* (FICT†)
>
> *PCBs are biologically <u>difficult</u> **to degrade**.* (ACAD†)

E Evaluation

These adjectives give an evaluation of an action or situation that is described in the *to*-clause. No adjectives in this group are especially common with *to*-clauses:

> *This one is <u>nice</u> **to smell**.* (CONV†)
>
> *Katherine was <u>smart</u> **to have her wits about her**.* (FICT†)
>
> *This food wouldn't be <u>bad</u> **to wake up to**.* (FICT†)

The evaluation adjectives are slightly different from stance adjectives. Stance adjectives express the feelings of the person identified as the subject of the sentence: e.g. *glad, afraid, sorry*. Evaluation adjectives provide an external evaluation of the entire proposition. For evaluation adjectives, a paraphrase can often be given with a subject *to*-clause. For example:

> **To smell this one** *is nice*.

Review

Major points in GRAMMAR BITE D: Post-predicate infinitive clauses

➤ By far the most common position for *to*-clauses is post-predicate.
➤ There are five major patterns for *to*-clauses controlled by a verb in post-predicate position.
  ➤ The patterns vary in the way noun phrases come between the verb and *to*-clause, and in the choice of *to* or a bare infinitive.
  ➤ Some factors to consider in the grammatical patterns with *to*-clauses are: passive alternatives, the implied subject of the *to*-clause, the relationship between the object of the main clause and the *to*-clause, and prepositional verbs.
  ➤ The semantic category of a verb often influences the grammatical patterns that are possible for that verb.
➤ The verbs that are common with *to*-clauses vary across registers and cover many semantic categories.
  ➤ Conversation has the least variation. Here *want* + *to*-clause is extremely common.
  ➤ The other registers have more variation, including more verbs of effort (e.g. *try*), of aspect (e.g. *begin, continue*), of probability (e.g. *tend*), and of causation (e.g. *allow*).
➤ Subject predicative *to*-clauses have four major functions: introducing points, introducing objectives or plans, introducing methodologies, and making a balanced structure when a *to*-clause is also the subject of the main clause.
➤ *Likely/unlikely* is the only adjective that commonly controls a *to*-clause.

> Many other adjectives occur, conveying certainty, ability, stance, ease/difficulty, or evaluation.

GRAMMAR BITE

E More on infinitive clauses

.16 Raising

10.16.1 Subject-to-subject raising with *to*-clauses controlled by verbs

In Grammar Bite D, we noted that the implied subject of most post-predicate *to*-clauses is the same as the subject of the main clause. However, in some cases, the entire *to*-clause is the implied subject of the main clause. For example:

1 *The prize pupil, however, turned out **to have another side to his character**.* (NEWS)

The equivalent *that*-clause construction is an extraposed construction:

1a *It turned out **that the prize pupil had another side to his character**.*

You can see here that the grammatical subject of the main clause in 1 (*the prize pupil*) is the implied subject of the *to*-clause (the prize pupil is the one who had another side to his character). This is similar to most *to*-clauses. However, the logical subject of the main clause is the entire *to*-clause. That is, the intended meaning is not that 'the prize pupil turned out'; rather, the entire idea that 'the prize pupil had another side to his character' is the logical subject of the main clause.

This kind of structure is called subject-to-subject raising. The subject of the dependent *to*-clause is 'raised' to become the subject of the main clause. Subject-to-subject raising occurs with *to*-complement clauses controlled by verbs of probability and simple fact (e.g. *turn out, seem, tend, appear*). However, these structures occur more commonly with *to*-clauses controlled by adjectives, as described in the next section.

10.16.2 Raising with *to*-clauses controlled by adjectives

On the surface, *to*-clauses controlled by adjectives all appear the same. However, the implied subject of the *to*-clause and its relationship to the subject of the main clause can vary.

In the simplest case, the implied subject of the *to*-clause is the same as the subject of the main clause. For example:

*Millar was obstinately <u>determined</u> **to change the content of education**.* (NEWS)

However, there are two major groups of adjectives that differ from this simple case: certainty adjectives and adjectives of ease or difficulty.

A Certainty adjectives controlling subject-to-subject raising

Like the probability verbs in 10.16.1, certainty adjectives (such as *likely, unlikely, sure, certain*) occur with subject-to-subject raising. For example:

> 1 [*The government*] is <u>unlikely</u> **to meet the full cost.** (NEWS)

Here the grammatical subject of the main clause (*the government*) is the implied subject of the *to*-clause. However, the logical subject of the main clause is the entire *to*-clause. This meaning relationship becomes explicit if we paraphrase the structure with an equivalent *that*-clause. Actually, there are two possible paraphrases, one in subject position and the other extraposed:

> 1a **That the government will meet the full cost** is <u>unlikely</u>.
> 1b *It is* <u>unlikely</u> **that the government will meet the full cost.**

With both paraphrases, we see that the full complement clause functions as the logical subject of the main clause.

B Adjectives of ease or difficulty controlling object-to-subject raising

Adjectives of ease or difficulty (e.g. *difficult, easy, hard, (im)possible*) control a different type of raising. Consider this sentence:

> *Without those powers, [computer hacking] would be almost* <u>impossible</u> **to prove.** (NEWS†)

Here the grammatical subject of the main clause is the implied object of the *to*-clause. In this example, *computer hacking* (subject of the main clause) is the understood object of *prove* (the infinitive). In addition, the logical subject of the main clause is the *to*-clause. The sentence does not mean 'computer hacking would be almost impossible'. Rather, it means:

> **To prove computer hacking** *would be almost impossible.*

You can see that the subject in this restatement consists of the *to*-clause and its implied object *to prove computer hacking*.

This kind of structure is called object-to-subject raising. The object of the dependent *to*-clause is 'raised' to become the subject of the main clause.

The implied subject of the *to*-clause with these raising structures is generic. For instance, the above example means that it is impossible for *anyone* or *people generally* to prove computer hacking.

10.17 **Extraposed *to*-clauses**

There are few verbs that control extraposed *to*-clauses. The most common is the copula *be* combined with a subject predicative noun phrase or prepositional phrase:

> *It* <u>is</u> *still* <u>an adventure</u> **to travel down the canyon of the Colorado river in a small boat.** (ACAD)
> <compare: **To travel down the canyon of the Colorado river in a small boat** *is still an adventure.*>

It is for others **to offer moral guidance to the newly prosperous Pharisees.** (NEWS)

<compare: **To offer moral guidance to the newly prosperous Pharisees** *is for others.*>

In general, though, extraposed *to*-clauses controlled by verbs are rare.

In contrast, there are many adjectives that can control extraposed *to*-clauses; these forms are found especially in news and academic prose.

Adjectives taking extraposed *to*-clauses come from three major semantic domains: necessity and importance adjectives, ease and difficulty adjectives, and evaluation adjectives. The adjectives in all three classes are used to mark a stance towards the proposition in the *to*-clause.

The most common necessity or importance adjectives controlling extraposed *to*-clauses are *essential, important, interesting, necessary, vital*:

If you want peace it is <u>*important*</u> **to stay cool.** (NEWS)

I'm sure it's not <u>*necessary*</u> **to ask you not to pass any information on to the Communists.** (NEWS)

If the development of the unit spans a long period it will be <u>*essential*</u> **to make use of the new developments of this kind.** (ACAD)

Adjectives marking ease or difficulty can control extraposed *to*-clauses as well as *to*-clauses in post-predicate position (with object-to-subject raising; see 10.16.2). The most common ease or difficulty adjectives are *(im)possible, difficult, easy, easier, hard,* and *tough*:

Moreover, it is notoriously <u>*difficult*</u> **to predict the costs of major infrastructural projects.** (NEWS†)

It is <u>*easy*</u> **to see that the model ignores some fundamentally important variables.** (ACAD†)

It may be <u>*tough*</u> **to attract people.** (NEWS†)

It is <u>*possible*</u> **to love, and to aid thy neighbor, without state intervention.** (NEWS)

Evaluation adjectives come from two major subclasses: adjectives expressing general goodness or badness, and adjectives marking some specific evaluation or assessment. The border between these two semantic domains is not always clear-cut. Adjectives marking goodness or badness indicate a generalized stance towards the proposition in the extraposed *to*-clause. These adjectives include: *bad, best, better, good, nice, wonderful, worse*. For example:

It's <u>*good*</u> **to see them in the bath.** (CONV†)

It was <u>*bad*</u> **to be prodigal.** (FICT†)

Several other adjectives express more specific evaluations, including: *(in)appropriate, awkward, convenient, desirable, improper, (un)reasonable, safe, smart, stupid, surprising, useful, useless, wise, wrong*. For example:

It was <u>*awkward*</u> **to move elbows and clap in such a crowd of people.** (FICT)

For the purposes of this paper it is <u>*convenient*</u> **to consider four major categories of uncertainty.** (ACAD†)

It's not <u>*safe*</u> **to run down there.** (FICT)

However, for our purposes it is <u>*useful*</u> **to emphasize three roles.** (ACAD)

10.17.1 Extraposed v. subject position *to*-clauses

In many cases, a subject *to*-clause can be rephrased as an extraposed clause, and vice versa. In general, extraposition is the normal choice, with subject *to*-clauses being reserved for special functions. Three major factors influence this choice: register, information flow, and grammatical complexity.

A Register

Subject *to*-clauses are rare in all registers. When they do occur, they are used primarily in academic prose. Extraposed *to*-clauses are much more common, although they are also primarily used in expository writing.

B Information flow

In almost all cases, subject *to*-clauses are used for given information, creating cohesion with the previous discourse.

> *The law also allowed the seizure of all assets, not simply those related to a specific offence. 'The US law in this respect seems greatly excessive', he said.* **'To take away the profits of crime** *is one thing;* **to seize the assets that have no connection with crime** *is another.'* (NEWS†)

In this example, the ideas in the subject *to*-clauses (taking away the profits of crime and seizing the assets that have no connection with crime) directly follow from the preceding explanation of the law.

In addition, the above example shows how subject *to*-clauses are sometimes used in parallel to present a balance of connected ideas. This parallel structure can create a strong impact:

> *He advanced into the room and sat in the armchair. I felt incensed, yet helpless.* **To order him to leave** *would be overdramatic yet perhaps I should.* **To pull the bell-rope and ask for help** *would be even more so.* (FICT)

C Grammatical complexity of the rest of the clause

In most cases when a subject *to*-clause is used, the rest of the clause is a complex construction, as in:

> 1 **To accept a US mediation plan** *means [that the Israeli-Palestinian meeting is now likely in the New Year].* (NEWS)

The most common construction of this type is an equation of two *to*-clauses:

> 2 **To expect Europe to become a single warm cultural bath** *is simply [to mistake the nature of the European identity].* (NEWS†)
> 3 **To argue otherwise** *is [to betray millions of people].* (NEWS)

Extraposed constructions are usually not a practical alternative with such complex predicates, because they would be very difficult to follow. (A similar point was about subject *that*-clauses in 10.8.1.) For example, compare the following extraposed examples to 1 and 2 above:

> 1a *It means that the Israeli-Palestinian meeting is now likely in the New Year to accept a US mediation plan.*

2a *It is simply to mistake the nature of the European identity to expect Europe to become a single warm cultural bath.*

.18 Raising v. extraposition

10.18.1 Subject-to-subject raising v. extraposed *that*-clauses

Complement clauses controlled by verbs of probability and simple fact (e.g. *seem, appear*), passive voice mental verbs (e.g. *be found, be assumed*), and adjectives of certainty (e.g. *likely, unlikely, certain, sure*) have two alternative forms: a *to*-clause with subject-to-subject raising or an extraposed *that*-clause. For example:

1 *The rate for the North American continent has <u>been estimated</u> to be about 0.3 mm/year.* (ACAD)

1a *It is has been estimated that the rate for the North American continent is about 0.03 mm/year.*

In all four registers, the *to*-clause structure with subject-to-subject raising (1) is much more common. One reason for the choice of the raised *to*-clauses concerns information flow. In most constructions with subject-to-subject raising, the main clause subject (marked in *[]*) is given information that refers directly back to the topic of the previous discourse:

> *Andy really surprises me. <. . .> [Andy] <u>seems</u> to know everything.* (CONV)
> *The first thing he thought of when he woke up was Marge. <. . .> [She] wasn't <u>likely</u> to take a taxi to Naples.* (FICT)

The raised construction allows the sentence to follow the typical information pattern of English: given information comes before new, and the given information is placed in subject position (see 12.1.1).

Extraposed *that*-clauses are used when it is important to mark modality or tense in the complement clause (since these cannot be marked with a *to*-clause). For example:

> *It is <u>likely</u> that North Korea will channel investment to areas that can be contained.* (NEWS)
> *It is perhaps more <u>likely</u> that they were associated with locomotion from the beginning.* (ACAD†)

In addition, extraposed constructions are preferred when a prepositional phrase occurs between the verb and the *that*-clause:

2 *It <u>seemed</u> [to him] that his home life was disintegrating all at once.* (FICT)

3 *It <u>appears</u> [from initial observations] that the storage of viable sperm is limited to a period of two or three months.* (ACAD†)

The alternative *to*-clause constructions with raising sound more awkward, with the prepositional phrase disrupting the association between the verb and the *to*-clause:

2a *His home life seemed to him to be disintegrating all at once.*

10.18.2 Object-to-subject raising v. extraposed *to*-clauses controlled by adjectives

Adjectives of ease or difficulty are used with both post-predicate *to*-clauses and with extraposed *to*-clauses:

> 1   *They're <u>hard</u> to get.* (CONV†)
> 1a *It is <u>hard</u> to get them.*

Easy, hard, difficult, and *(im)possible* are the most common adjectives occurring in these constructions. Object-to-subject raising (**1**) and extraposition (**1a**) occur in all registers, with the raised structures being only slightly more common.

The strongest factor influencing this choice is again information flow. In almost all structures with object-to-subject raising, the implied object of the *to*-clause (which is the grammatical subject of the main clause) presents given information. It provides a link with the immediately preceding discourse:

> *A: And then I fell out of the swing.*
> *B: [That] wasn't <u>easy</u> **to do**.* (CONV)

> *The second approach <. . .> necessitates the building of special-purpose assembly and iterative routines. <. . .> [This] is <u>difficult</u> **to achieve on current commercial turnkey systems**.* (ACAD)

In contrast, extraposed structures are used when the object of the *to*-clause presents new information. The extraposed *to*-clauses also usually have long, complex objects. These structures follow the end-weight principle: longer, more complex structures tend to be placed later in a clause (see 12.1.4):

> *It is <u>difficult</u> **to imagine a direct advantage conferred by shell banding for survival in waveswept conditions**.* (ACAD†)

> *It is <u>easy</u> **to see (Figure 4–11) that for a folded sequence of layers, the oldest beds would be found at depth in the core (or central axis) of the anticline and the youngest rocks**.* (ACAD†)

10.19 *To*-clause types across registers

The distribution of *to*-clause types reflects their different discourse functions (Table 10.4). Over 60 per cent of all *to*-clauses occur in post-predicate position controlled by a verb. These *to*-clauses typically are used to report the activities, aspirations, thoughts, and emotions of human participants:

> *I <u>wanted</u> **to do it**.* (CONV)

> *Dr. Gruner <u>asked</u> Uncle Sammler **to read a few items from the Market Letter**.* (FICT)

> *Mrs. Carol Bentley <u>tried</u> **to ignore the fuss**.* (NEWS†)

> *Carpenter <u>found</u> highly nonlinear cases **to be chaotic**.* (ACAD†)

Because conversation, fiction, and news focus on such concerns, post-predicate *to*-clauses controlled by verbs are most common in those registers.

To-clauses controlled by adjectives more often describe a state, often presenting a stance toward the idea in the *to*-clause. These structures are one of the main devices for expressing stance in the written expository registers.

10.4 Types of *to*-clause complements across registers

	CONV	FICT	NEWS	ACAD
post-predicate *to*-clause complementing a verb	common	very common	very common	common
post-predicate *to*-clause complementing an adjective	rare	moderately common	common	moderately common
extraposed *to*-clause complementing a verb	rare	rare	relatively rare	rare
extraposed *to*-clause complementing an adjective	rare	moderately common	moderately common	common
subject *to*-clause	rare	rare	rare	rare
subject-predicative *to*-clause	rare	moderately common	moderately common	moderately common

Post-predicate *to*-clauses controlled by adjectives often express a person's stance towards his or her own activities. This pattern is relatively common in news:

> Sir Anthony is <u>willing</u> **to provide a focal point for discussion.** (NEWS†)
>
> Advertisers said they were <u>delighted</u> **to see many of their proposals reflected in the Government's approach.** (NEWS)

In contrast, extraposed *to*-clauses following an adjective most often present a stance that is not directly attributed to anyone. This pattern is most common in academic prose:

> It is <u>important</u> **to specify the states after the formulae in the equation.** (ACAD)
>
> It is <u>difficult</u> **to maintain a consistent level of surgical anesthesia with ether.** (ACAD†)

Review

Major points in Grammar Bite E: More on infinitive clauses

➤ Raising describes the relationship between the main clause subject and the *to*-clause.
> ➤ *To*-clauses controlled by verbs can have subject-to-subject raising.
> ➤ *To*-clauses controlled by adjectives can have subject-to-subject or object-to-subject raising.

➤ Extraposed *to*-clauses are most often controlled by an adjective.
> ➤ Extraposed clauses are more common than subject position clauses.
> ➤ The choice of subject position rather than extraposed is related to register, cohesion and information structure, the complexity of the main clause predicate, and individual style.

➤ *To*-clauses with raising are alternatives to some extraposed constructions.
> ➤ With certain verbs and adjectives, *to*-clauses with raising are more common than extraposed *that*-clauses. This choice is usually due to information structure.

➤ Adjectives of ease or difficulty are slightly more common with raised *to*-clauses than extraposed *to*-clauses. Again, information structure and cohesion are important to the choice.

➤ The different types of *to*-clauses have different frequencies across the registers, which reflect their functions.

➤ Post-predicate *to*-clauses are most common in conversation, fiction, and news. They usually report activities, desires, and thoughts of humans.

➤ *To*-clauses controlled by adjectives are most common in news and academic prose. They usually describe a state or an attitude.

GRAMMAR BITE

F *Ing*-clauses, ellipsis/substitution, and review

10.20 Overview of *ing*-clauses

Like *that*-complement clauses and *to*-complement clauses, *ing*-complement clauses serve a wide range of functions. They are used most often with verbs like *begin*, *start*, and *stop* to convey aspect, but they are also used to report speech acts, cognitive states, perceptions, emotions, and other actions. Overall, *ing*-clauses are more common in the written registers than in conversation.

Ing-clauses are most common in post-predicative position, where they can be controlled by verbs and adjectives:

> Gizmo <u>keeps</u> **trying to persuade me to go with her**. (CONV)

> I could see she was <u>confident of</u> **handling any awkward situation that might arise**. (FICT†)

In many cases the adjectives are followed by prepositions, like *confident of* in the above example.

Ing-clauses can also occur in subject position:

> **Reflecting on this and related matters** took him past his stop and almost into Dinedor itself. (FICT)

And they can occur as subject predicatives:

> Sometimes being loud is **being obnoxious**. (CONV)

10.21 Post-predicate *ing*-clauses

10.21.1 Grammatical patterns for *ing*-clauses controlled by verbs

There are three major grammatical patterns for *ing*-complement clauses in post-predicate position:

- **Pattern 1: verb + *ing*-clause** (e.g. *begin, remember*)

    1 *He <u>began</u> **paging through old newspapers**.* (FICT†)

    2 *I <u>remember</u> **reading this book**.* (CONV)

In Pattern 1, the implied subject of the *ing*-clause is the subject of the main clause. Thus, in **1**, *he* was *paging through old newspapers*, and in **2**, *I* was *reading this book*. The exception to this meaning relationship is with verbs that express a required action, such as *need*:

> *Oh you know that front room really <u>needs</u> **painting**.* (CONV)

Here the subject of the main clause (*that front room*) is the implied object of the *ing*-clause, while the implied subject of the *ing*-clause is a general noun (such as *someone*); that is, the intended meaning is that 'someone needs to paint that front room'.

- **Pattern 2: verb + NP + *ing*-clause** (e.g. *see, find*)

    3 *When you <u>see</u> [a geek] **walking down the street**, give it a good throw.* (CONV)

    4 *Don't be surprised to <u>find</u> [me] **sitting on the tee in the lotus position**.* (NEWS)

In this pattern, the noun phrase after the verb (marked in *[]* in **3** and **4**) functions as the logical subject of the *ing*-clause. For example, in **3**, *a geek* is walking down the street. The noun phrase + *ing*-clause can be considered the object of the main clause verb.

- **Pattern 2a: verb + possessive determiner + *ing*-clause**

Some Pattern 2 verbs allow a possessive determiner + *ing*-clause. Thus compare:

> *Did you <u>mind</u> [me] **saying it**, Stephen?* (FICT) <Pattern 2>
>
> *And maybe you won't <u>mind</u> [my] **saying that you're getting a little old for studying**.* (FICT) <Pattern 2a with possessive determiner>

When the possessive alternative is used, it focuses attention on the action described in the *ing*-clause. In contrast, the regular NP form puts more emphasis on the person doing the action:

> *I <u>appreciate</u> [your] **being here**.* (FICT)
>
> *We couldn't <u>picture</u> [you] **walking so far**.* (FICT)

Prescriptive tradition favors the possessive form. However, in practice over 90 per cent of Pattern 2 *ing*-clauses take the regular NP form. Further, many verbs do not allow the possessive alternative, such as *keep, have, leave, find, catch*.

- **Pattern 3: prepositional verb + *ing*-clause**

Many *ing*-clauses occur with **prepositional verbs**:

> We were <u>thinking of</u> **bringing our video camera.** (CONV)
>
> She <u>complained of</u> **feeling feverish** and went early to bed. (FICT)
>
> It also <u>assists in</u> **helping to buffer the indoor environment against sudden fluctuations outside.** (NEWS)

Here the *ing*-clause acts as object of the prepositional verb.

10.21.2 Verbs controlling *ing*-clauses

The most common verbs controlling *ing*-clauses, broken down by the four registers, are:

> CONV: *keep, start, go, stop, see NP, remember, think (about/of), get NP, sit*
>
> FICT: *keep, see NP, go, start, stop, begin, hear NP, come, spend, remember, think (about/of), get NP, sit, feel NP, stand/stood*
>
> NEWS: *start, keep, begin, see NP, go, spend, come, stop, be accused of*
>
> ACAD: *be used for, involve, be achieved by/with*

Overall, the most common verb + *ing*-clause construction is with *keep* in conversation. *Start* + *ing*-clause is also very common in conversation. In academic prose, the combination *be used for* + *ing*-clause is surprisingly common.

Verbs of aspect or manner are the most common verbs controlling *ing*-clauses, especially in conversation and fiction. The verb *keep* shows that the action in the *ing*-clause is continuous or repeated.

> She <u>keeps</u> **smelling the washing powder.** (CONV)
>
> His brake lights <u>keep</u> **flashing on.** (CONV†)

A more informal near-synonym is *go on*:

> The guard <u>went on</u> **sleeping.** (FICT†)

The verbs *start* and *stop* show the beginning or ending of an activity. They are frequent in both conversation and fiction. The more formal-sounding *begin* is common only in fiction:

> You can <u>start</u> **doing what you want then.** (CONV)
>
> A dog <u>began</u> **barking.** (FICT)
>
> Ralph had <u>stopped</u> **smiling.** (FICT†)

The verbs *go, come, sit,* and *stand* are commonly used with *ing*-clauses to describe the manner in which an action was done. They are most common in fiction. *Go* and *come* indicate the direction of movement (towards or away from a place):

> I <u>went</u> **looking for it.** (CONV)
>
> One of the children <u>came</u> **running after him.** (FICT)

Sit and *stand* denote unmoving states that are further described in the *ing*-clause:

> All morning they <u>sat</u> **waiting in the sun.** (FICT†)
>
> The two police guards <u>stood</u> **peering in the direct of the commotion.** (FICT†)

The verbs *see* and *hear* are commonly used to describe the perception of an activity:

> *I suddenly <u>saw</u> water **rushing down the wall**.* (CONV)
>
> *They could <u>hear</u> the waves **breaking on the rocks**.* (FICT)

With all the above verbs, the following *ing*-clause has a meaning of 'activity in progress', related to the use of the *ing*-form with progressive aspect (see 6.3, 6.5). For example, in the sentence *the children came running*, the verb *running* expresses the meaning of ongoing activity, similar to the main clause progressive form *the children were running*.

News and academic prose have more specialized sets of verbs that commonly control *ing*-clauses. Verbs that describe processes and states (*be used for, involve*) and effort (*be achieved by/with*) are most common:

> *Some method of refrigeration <u>is used for</u> **cooling the milk in all bulk tanks**.* (ACAD)
>
> *This <u>is achieved by</u> **saving information at the beginning of the subroutine**.* (ACAD†)

News is notable for using *ing*-clauses with verbs having to do with criminal offenses and punishments, such as *accused of* and *charged with*:

> *George Helaine, a Belgian, <u>is accused of</u> **organizing the shipment from Morocco**.* (NEWS†)
>
> *All <u>are charged with</u> **violating official secrets laws**.* (NEWS†)

Many other kinds of verbs occur with moderate frequencies controlling *ing*-clauses. For example, communication and speech act verbs give indirect reports of statements:

> *They <u>talk about</u> **building more**.* (CONV)
>
> *She had never <u>mentioned</u> **having a religion**.* (FICT)

Cognition verbs tell of a mental state or process, which is specified by the *ing*-clause:

> *I don't even <u>remember</u> **telling you that**.* (CONV)
>
> *I can't <u>conceive of</u> somebody **getting killed and injuring another person because of being too damn stupid to drive carefully**.* (FICT†) <note: *damn* is a taboo word and may be offensive to some people>

Stance verbs tell the speaker/writer's feelings or attitudes towards the idea in the *ing*-clause:

> *I <u>hate</u> **doing that**.* (CONV)
>
> *He immediately <u>regretted</u> **thinking any such thought**.* (FICT)

Finally, a few verbs show facilitation or effort:

> *Well he couldn't <u>help</u> **being a miserable sod**.* (CONV) <note: *sod* is a taboo word and may be offensive to some people>
>
> *You ought to <u>try</u> **taking some of them**.* (CONV)

10.21.3 Adjectives controlling *ing*-clauses

Most adjectives that control *ing*-clauses express a personal feeling or attitude, or some evaluation of the idea in the *ing*-clause:

> *It is true that young rabbits are great migrants and <u>capable of</u> **journeying for miles**.* (FICT)
>
> *I'm <u>sorry about</u> **being in a mood Saturday**.* (CONV)

> *These people were not <u>afraid of</u> **signing papers**.* (FICT†)
>
> *There is no reason why women should not be <u>good at</u> **selling cars**.* (NEWS)
>
> *Mineralogy and texture are also <u>useful in</u> **subdividing the sedimentary rocks**.* (ACAD)

In most cases, as in these examples, the controlling adjective is followed by a preposition.

10.22 Ellipsis and substitution in complement clauses

10.22.1 Ellipsis in post-predicate *to-* and *wh*-clauses

Various forms of ellipsis or substitution can be used with post-predicate complement clauses when the content is clear from the preceding discourse. Ellipsis can occur with *to*-clauses and *wh*-clauses, where the complement clause is omitted but the complementizer (*to* or a *wh*-word) is retained:

> *A: Are we having that tonight too?*
> *B: If you want **to**.* (CONV)
> <meaning: *If you want **to have that tonight**.*>
>
> *He feel asleep up there – I don't know **how**.* (CONV)
> <meaning: *I don't know **how he fell asleep up there**.*>

Ellipsis with complement clauses is most common in conversation. (See 13.5 for further discussion of ellipsis in conversation.) However, even though most verbs can occur with ellipsis, very few do so frequently. Each type of complement clause has a single verb that is by far most common with this type of ellipsis:

- *want + to*: *You can go if you **want to**.* (CONV)
- *know + wh*-word: *I couldn't fall asleep till four last night – I don't **know why**.* (CONV)

In addition, *try* and *like* are moderately common with an ellipted *to*-clause. *Like + to* usually follows the modal verb *would*:

> *A: Keep him in line.*
> *B: I'll **try to**.* (CONV)
>
> *A: Did you use my toothbrush again?*
> *B: Well, I **would like to**.* (CONV)

With *wh*-clause ellipsis, *wonder* and *remember* also occur:

> *A: I took a shower early this morning and I feel like I didn't shower.*
> *B: I **wonder why**.* (CONV)

With *that*-clauses, ellipsis involves the omission of the entire complement clause, including the complementizer *that*. Such ellipsis is usually found with extremely common verbs like *think*, *know*, and *guess* (in American English):

> *A: Hey, look!*
> *B: Yeah, but there's seven teams in front of them dad.*
> *A: Yeah, **I know**, but mm I don't mind that.* (CONV)

10.22.2 Substitution in post-predicate *that*-clauses

With post-predicate *that*-clauses, substitution can also occur. The substitute form *so* or *not* takes the place of the entire clause:

> A: *Oh, you tasted it before, didn't you?*
> B: *I don't think **so**.* (CONV)
> <meaning: *I don't think **that I tasted it before**.*>

> A: *Is the dog going to jump?*
> B: *I hope **not**.* (CONV)
> <meaning: *I hope **that the dog is not going to jump**.*>

Relatively few verbs permit substitution for a *that*-clause. Substitution is most common in conversation, and it occurs by far most often with *think* + *so*. Usually the subject is a first-person pronoun, and the speaker expresses a lack of certainty about the previous idea:

> A: *Have they found him?*
> B: *I don't know – I don't **think so**.* (CONV)

> *I really think your dad is going to be her executor, I'm not sure, but I really **think so**.* (CONV)

Hope, suppose, and *guess* are also used with substitution to express stance. *Suppose so* is relatively common in British English conversation, while *guess so* is more common in American English:

> A: *You have to write your name down every time.*
> B: *Yeah, I **suppose so**.* (BrE CONV)

> A: *The medicine is slowing down the disease.*
> B: *Yeah, I **guess so**.* (AmE CONV)

Say + *so* is used for indirect speech, especially in fiction:

> *But he always found fault with their effort, and he **said so** with much threatening.* (FICT)

Not is much less common for *that*-clause substitution than *so*. Only *hope* and *guess* occur frequently:

> A: *We're not having too early a lunch, are we?*
> B: *I **hope not**.* (CONV)

> A: *You don't think the Cardinals are doing very well at all, are they?*
> B: *Not that bad, I **guess not**.* (AmE CONV)

0.23 Choice of complement clause type

This chapter has discussed four types of complement clauses: *that*-clauses, *wh*-clauses, *to*-clauses, and *ing*-clauses. In many ways, the types are interchangeable: each type can complement verbs and adjectives, and each type occurs in several positions. It is natural to ask, then, how do speakers choose between them?

There are many factors that influence this choice. First, there are lexical factors, since many verbs control specific types of complement clause. Nearly any transitive verb can take a *wh*-clause, but the other clause types are more restrictive. For example, *guess* and *conclude* can control only *that*-clauses; *prepare* and *fail* can control only *to*-clauses; *keep (on)* and *finish* can control only *ing*-clauses. In addition, many other combinations occur. For example, *hope* can control *that*-clauses and *to*-clauses but not *ing*-clauses; *remember* and *believe* can control all four clause types.

There are also semantic factors. For example, some verbs have a more hypothetical meaning with a *to*-clause than an *ing*-clause. For example:

1 <u>Remember</u> **to wash your hands,** *I'll be listening.* (CONV)
2 *I* <u>remember</u> **going late at night.** (CONV)

In **1**, *remember* + *to*-clause is used to refer to a unfulfilled (but expected) future action. In **2**, *remember* + *ing*-clause is used for an event that has already occurred.

In fact, there are many subtleties concerning the meaning and structural differences among the complement clause types. Here we present only a few major points:

A Register factors

- Overall, *that*-clauses and *to*-clauses are more than twice as common as *wh*-clauses and *ing*-clauses.
- Finite complement clauses—i.e. *that*-clauses and *wh*-clauses—are most common in conversation, followed by fiction. They are relatively rare in academic prose.
- Non-finite complement clauses—i.e. *to*-clauses and *ing*-clauses—are most common in fiction, followed by news and academic prose. They are relatively rare in conversation.

B Structural factors

- The majority of *that*-clauses and *wh*-clauses occur in post-predicate position after verbs. In contrast, a much higher proportion of *to*-clauses and *ing*-clauses follow adjectives. This trend is especially strong in academic prose.
- Extraposed constructions and subject predicative constructions are more common with *to*-clauses than with *that*-clauses. For *to*-clauses, extraposed constructions are more common with adjectives than with verbs. Again, this trend is strongest in academic prose.

C Semantic factors

- *That*-clauses combine with relatively few verbs from only three semantic groups. However, individual verbs (especially *think* and *say*) are extremely common controlling *that*-clauses. In contrast, *to*-clauses and *ing*-clauses combine with a large number of different verbs expressing many different types of meaning.

The following two text samples illustrate the different uses of *that*- and *to*-clauses in conversation and academic prose. (*That*-clauses are in bold and *to*-clauses are marked in []; some *to*-clauses are embedded within *that*-clauses.)

Text sample 1: CONVERSATION

> A: *I said how's your revision going, cos I* <u>knew</u> **she was doing revision,** *she went ccccckkk I try a maths paper and I can't do that, and I <...> a chemistry paper and I can't do that and I really <growl>. I said I* <u>think</u> **you need a break** *<laugh> I* <u>think</u> **you** <u>need</u> **[to go and do something else for a little while]** *– I said cos if you keep looking over* <u>thinking</u> **you can't do it,** *have a break and go back to it afterwards. You just get really despondent*
>
> B: *Yeah.*
>
> A: *and fed up and* <u>think</u> **you can't do it** *and you go blank and then you can't touch anything you – and you* <u>know</u> **it's hard.** (CONV)

Text sample 2: ACADEMIC PROSE

> *The above means are not* <u>able</u> *[to represent an office procedure or an activity in a way which would allow automation of the co-ordination required for execution]. There are no methods for representing the interworking of the different description techniques and it should be* <u>noted</u> **that it may be** <u>necessary</u> **[to model the same activity more than once redundantly and in parallel by different means].** *In particular, it must be* <u>possible</u> *[to model the interworking of roles (to be represented by organigrams or job profiles), flow charts and forms].* (ACAD)

The conversation sample illustrates the dense use of *that*-clauses in post-predicate position. Most of the *that*-clauses are controlled by the verb *think*. The subject of *think* is typically *I* or *you*, so that the construction directly represents the thoughts of the speaker or hearer.

In contrast, the academic prose sample illustrates the different complement clauses typical of informational written prose. There are more *to*-clauses than *that*-clauses. The clauses are often controlled by adjectival predicates (e.g. *able, necessary*) with non-animate subjects (e.g. *the above means*). The controlling verbs and adjectives express many meanings (ability, communication, necessity, possibility). Finally, extraposed clauses are relatively common (*it should be noted ... and it must be possible ...*).

Review

Major points in **GRAMMAR BITE F:** *Ing*-clauses, ellipsis/substitution, and review

➤ The most common type of *ing*-clause is a post-predicate clause following a verb.
  ➤ There are two major grammatical patterns, with and without a NP between the verb and the *ing*-clause.
  ➤ The most common verbs controlling *ing*-clauses are verbs of manner or aspect (e.g. *begin, start, stop*).
  ➤ Many adjectives that control *ing*-clauses express a feeling or evaluation (e.g. *sorry, afraid, capable*).
  ➤ Many of these adjectives are followed by prepositions (e.g. *sorry about, afraid of*).

➤ Ellipsis and substitution in complement clauses is most common in conversation.
  ➤ For *to*-clauses and *wh*-clauses, the complement clause can be omitted if it is understandable from context. The complementizer *to* or *wh*-word is usually retained.

➤ With certain verbs, *so* or *not* can substitute for a *that*-clause. This substitution is most common in the expression *think so*, but occurs with several other verbs also.

➤ The types of complement clauses in this chapter are distributed differently across the registers.

➤ The patterns of use reflect register, structural factors, and semantic factors. Overall, they reflect the typical functions of the different clause types.

11

Adverbials

GRAMMAR BITES in this chapter

A Overview of adverbials

➤ The three main classes of adverbials: circumstance, stance, and linking adverbials
➤ Syntactic forms of adverbials
➤ Positions of adverbials in clauses
➤ The relationship between adverbials and other clause elements

B Circumstance adverbials

➤ Semantic categories of circumstance adverbials
➤ Syntactic forms commonly used for circumstance adverbials
➤ Some extremely common circumstance adverbials in conversation
➤ Typical positions for non-clausal circumstance adverbials

C Circumstance adverbials that are clauses

➤ Additional semantic categories for circumstance adverbials that are clauses
➤ Forms of non-finite and finite adverbial clauses
➤ Typical positions for circumstance adverbial clauses
➤ The use of subordinators with circumstance adverbial clauses

D Stance adverbials

➤ Semantic categories of stance adverbials
➤ Syntactic forms commonly used for stance adverbials
➤ The use of the most common stance adverbials
➤ Typical positions for stance adverbials
➤ Cohesive and interactive functions of stance adverbials

E Linking adverbials

➤ Semantic categories of linking adverbials
➤ Syntactic forms commonly used for linking adverbials in conversation and academic prose
➤ The most common linking adverbials in conversation and academic prose
➤ Typical positions for linking adverbials

11.1 **Introduction**

Adverbials are clause elements that serve three major functions:

- They tell the circumstances relating to the clause, such as when or where an activity took place (circumstance adverbials).
- They express a speaker's feelings, evaluation, or comments on what the clause is about (stance adverbials).
- They link the clause (or some part of it) to another clause (linking adverbials).

Adverbials can be easy to confuse with other items that have similar structures but are parts of a phrase rather than elements of a clause. For example, **1–4** below are adverbials, but **5** and **6** are not:

1 *How long have you been walking **on your two feet**?* (CONV)
2 *She grinned **widely**.* (FICT)
3 ***In all honesty**, $300 million is not going to make a fundamental change.* (NEWS)
4 ***In summary**, the Alexis apartments are of a very high standard.* (NEWS†)
5 *[The £3,000 prize **in the women's event**] went to Bev Nicholson.* (NEWS)
6 *[[**Widely** varying] types of land] are cultivated.* (ACAD)

The prepositional phrase *on your two feet* in **1** and the adverb *widely* in **2** give the circumstances relating to their main verbs (*walking* and *grinned*). In **3**, the prepositional phrase *in all honesty* gives the speaker's comment about the entire following clause. In **4**, the prepositional phrase *in summary* connects this concluding statement to the preceding discourse. All four of these examples are elements of their clauses, so they are adverbials.

In contrast, in **5** *in the women's event* modifies the noun *prize*, and in **6** *widely* modifies the adjective *varying*. Examples **5** and **6**, therefore, show elements that are only parts of phrases (marked *[]*), not adverbials.

Adverbials differ from other clause elements in several ways. Consider the following examples (*[]* shows the boundaries of adverbials in a series):

7 *As I say, we were **eleven hundred feet above sea level** and we er really · moved [**here**] [**because er I could not stand the er the bad weather**].* (CONV)
8 ***In spite of great efforts by their authors**, these books **usually** contain a number of fallacies and errors that are **in due course** passed on [**repeatedly**] [**by later writers of other books**] <...> **Unfortunately**, these authors lack <...>* (ACAD†)

The most notable point about adverbials is how varied they are. These examples illustrate many of the important characteristics of adverbials:

- **They serve a variety of functions.** Some adverbials add something about the circumstances of an activity or state (e.g. *here* in **7**, *usually* in **8**). Others give a speaker's comment about what a clause says (e.g. *unfortunately* in **8**). Still other adverbials serve a connective function (e.g. *In summary* in **4** above, connecting a concluding statement to the preceding discourse).
- **They have many semantic roles.** In the examples above, adverbials express location or place (*eleven hundred feet above sea level*, *here*); reason (*because ...*); concession (*in spite of ...*); time (*usually, in due course, repeatedly*);

agency (*by later writers*); and attitude (*unfortunately*). They are also used for many other meanings.

- **They have a wide range of syntactic forms.** The examples above include adverbs (e.g. *here, usually, unfortunately*), prepositional phrases (e.g. *in spite of great efforts, in due course*), and clauses (e.g. *as I say, because . . .*). They can also be noun phrases (e.g. *each day* or *no doubt*).
- **They occur in various positions in clauses.** The examples above illustrate adverbials in the initial position (e.g. *as I say*), medial position before the main verb but after the subject (e.g. *really, usually*), and final position (e.g. *here, repeatedly, by later writers*). Adverbials can also be placed in other medial positions.
- **Multiple adverbials can occur in a clause.** In **8**, for example, the main clause has two adverbials (*in spite of . . . , usually*) and the dependent clause has three adverbials (*in due course, repeatedly, by later writers . . .*).
- Finally, **most adverbials are optional** (the only exceptions follow certain verbs that take obligatory adverbial complementation; see 3.5.5). For example, **8** would be fine without the adverbials:

> **8a** *These books contain a number of fallacies and errors that are passed on.*

GRAMMAR BITE

A Overview of adverbials

11.2 The main classes of adverbials

We divide adverbials into three major classes by their functions: **circumstance adverbials**, **stance adverbials**, and **linking adverbials**.

A Circumstance adverbials

Circumstance adverbials are the most common type of adverbials, adding something about the action or state described in the clause. They answer questions such as 'how?', 'when?', 'where?', 'how much?', 'how long?', and 'why?'. They include both obligatory adverbials, as in **1** below, and optional adverbials, as in **2**:

> **1** *We were **at the game**.* (CONV)
> **2** *Writers on style have differed [**a great deal**] [**in their understanding of the subject**].* (ACAD)

Of the three classes, circumstance adverbials are the most integrated into the clause. However, they can vary in **scope**; that is, they can modify differing amounts of the clause (see 11.5).

B Stance adverbials

Stance adverbials add speakers' comments on what they are saying or how they are saying it. Stance adverbials fall into three categories: **epistemic**, **attitude**, and **style adverbials.**

Epistemic stance adverbials focus on the question: how true is the information in the clause. They comment on factors such as certainty, viewpoint, and limitations of truth value. For example:

> Well she **definitely** looks at her mobile. (CONV)
>
> **From my perspective**, it was a clear case of abuse. (NEWS)
>
> **On the whole**, sons-in-law were in better paid jobs than their fathers-in-law. (ACAD)

Attitude stance adverbials express speakers' evaluations and attitudes towards the content of a clause:

> **To my surprise**, the space devoted to the kinetic sculptures had a lively and progressive atmosphere. (NEWS)
>
> **Fortunately**, this is far from the truth. (ACAD)

Style stance adverbials convey a speaker's comment on the style or form of the communication. Often style stance adverbials clarify the speaker's manner of speaking or how the utterance should be understood:

> Well, yes, **technically speaking**, I guess it is burnt. (CONV)
>
> That proves at least that Cassetti was certainly alive at twenty minutes to one. At twenty-three minutes to one, **to be precise**. (FICT†)
>
> **Quite frankly**, we are having a bad year. (NEWS)

As the above examples show, stance adverbials usually have scope over the entire clause. (However, in 11.5 we discuss some special cases.) Stance adverbials are always optional.

C Linking adverbials

Linking adverbials serve a connecting function, rather than adding information to a clause. They show the relationship between two units of discourse, as in the following examples:

1. They were kid boots at eight shillings a pair. He, **however**, thought them the most dainty boots in the world, and he cleaned them with as much reverence as if they had been flowers. (FICT)
2. Some hospitals use their own ethics committees to settle such cases, but a hospital's biases could creep into its committee's decisions, Ms. Yuen says. **Furthermore**, the committee's decision wouldn't be legally binding and wouldn't shield a physician from liability. (NEWS)
3. Humanism is a positive philosophy <...> Humanists believe morality comes from within man, not from God. They believe in the pursuit of human happiness and well-being. <...> **Yet** humanism is not a soft option. It is quite hard because there are no God-given certainties. You have to make up your mind what is right and what is wrong <...> (NEWS†)
4. My objectives in this work are twofold: **first**, to set out a precise yet comprehensive analysis <...> (ACAD†)

Linking adverbials can connect units of discourse with differing sizes, as the above examples illustrate. The linked units may be sentences, as in **1** and **2**. The units may also be larger than a sentence, as in **3** where *yet* contrasts several sentences about the positive side of humanism with several sentences dealing with its negative side. The units can also be smaller than a sentence: **4** exemplifies a linking adverbial connecting a *to*-clause to the preceding main clause.

Linking adverbials also express a variety of relationships, including those illustrated above: contrast in **1**, addition in **2**, concession in **3**, and enumeration in **4**.

11.2.1 Frequency of adverbial classes

Adverbials are common in all four registers (Figure 11.1):

- Adverbials are only slightly less common than lexical verbs in conversation, fiction, and news (see 5.2.3 for the frequency of lexical verbs).
- They are actually slightly more common than lexical verbs in academic prose.
- Circumstance adverbials are by far the most common adverbials; they are particularly common in fiction writing.

It is not surprising that circumstance adverbials are so common. Although they are usually grammatically optional, they often contain information central to the message. For example, the following clauses are grammatical without their adverbials, but they would not be very informative:

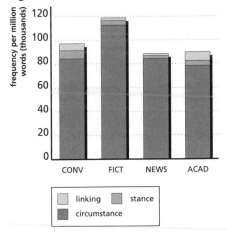

Figure 11.1
Frequency of adverbial classes across registers

> It was getting dark **when Alice awoke.** (FICT)

> Researchers use their special expertise **to exploit and test the latest technology** and **to provide much needed reliable and accurate knowledge about system performance, use, and acceptance.** (ACAD)

Circumstance adverbials have varied meanings. They cover many types of circumstantial information (place, time, process, extent, etc.; see 11.6). Fiction makes particularly frequent use of circumstance adverbials to describe the imaginary characters, events, and the setting:

> Ralph had no interest in business matters, which was evident [**at the cotton mill**] [**this morning**]. **Possessing a literary bent,** he stood out **like an abolitionist in the south.** (FICT†)

In contrast, stance adverbials and linking adverbials are much less common, accounting for less than 10 per cent of all adverbials (see Figure 11.1). When they do occur, stance adverbials are most common in conversation, while linking adverbials are most common in academic prose. The forms and functions of stance and linking adverbials are discussed in Grammar Bites D and E.

11.3 Syntactic forms of adverbials

Adverbials occur in many syntactic forms. These are exemplified below:

- single adverbs and adverb phrases:

  *Oh she **never** does anything does she?* (CONV)

  *We know each other **very well** and **frankly** we would have preferred to come out of the hat **first**.* (NEWS)

- noun phrases (including single nouns):

  *Well I went to that wedding **Saturday**.* (CONV)

  *The man came to stay with them for a few weeks **each year**.* (FICT)

- prepositional phrases:

  *The man came to stay [**with them**] [**for a few weeks**] each year.* (FICT)

  ***In this chapter** three of the most important approaches are examined.* (ACAD)

- finite clauses:

  *I had to turn it off earlier **because Rupert was shrieking**.* (CONV)

  ***If we do not act**, thousands more will come floating in on the early spring tides.* (NEWS†)

- non-finite clauses, including four major types:

ing-clauses

  *He got up and refilled the teapot, then his cup, **adding a touch of skimmed milk**.* (FICT†)

  ***Using an IBM 3090 supercomputer with 12 interconnected processing units and with a memory capacity of more than five billion characters of information**, the supercomputer center will explore new ways to connect even more advanced supercomputers.* (NEWS)

ed-clauses

  *Now **added to that** – by our wall – there was this ruddy great lorry again.* (CONV)

  *We measured a seasonal total of 56.99 cm precipitation in the two caged rain gauges, **compared to 56.78 cm on the open plots**.* (ACAD)

to-infinitive clauses

  *She called me **to say a lawyer was starting divorce proceedings**.* (FICT)

  ***To reintroduce us to the joys of story telling round the log fire**, Signals rounded up a slightly disconcerting group of five contemporary writers, all strange to me.* (NEWS)

verbless clauses

  *One practice is to designate protons **as if less than this**.* (ACAD)

  *The author apologizes **where appropriate**.* (ACAD†)

11.3.1 Frequency of the syntactic forms

In overall frequency, prepositional phrases are the most common form of adverbial (see Figure 11.2). Single adverbs are also common. Compared with these, the other types of adverbial are relatively rare.

Prepositional phrases express a wide range of meanings. They are used not only as circumstance adverbials, but as stance and linking adverbials:

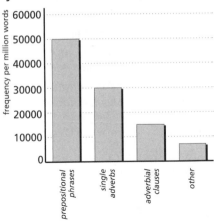

Figure 11.2
Syntactic forms of adverbials

circumstance, place: *I actually come **from the Dales**.* (CONV)
circumstance, agent: *Project topics should be organized **by the tutor**.* (ACAD†)
stance: ***In fact** I might not even need to vacuum the floor.* (CONV)
linking: *'Gossip is mischievous, light and easy to raise, but grievous to bear and hard to get rid of.' **In other words**, mud sticks.* (NEWS†)

11.4 Positions of adverbials

There are four major positions that adverbials take in a clause. It is possible for more than one adverbial to occupy each position.

A Initial

Adverbials can come before the subject or any other obligatory element:

> ***In the nature of things**, a good many somebodies are always in hospital.* (FICT)
>
> *[**Generally**], [**however**], the plants under consideration have been annuals, seedlings or cuttings of perennials.* (ACAD†)

B Medial

We can identify three specific positions within this category.

- Adverbials often occur between the subject and the beginning of the verb phrase:

> *Jean **never** put anything away.* (CONV)
>
> *I **really** don't know what they're doing.* (FICT)

- When an operator is present, the adverbial is often placed after the operator but before the main verb:

> *Carrie had **often** dreamed about coming back.* (FICT)
>
> *The utilisation of computers is not **of course** limited to business.* (ACAD)

- Adverbials can also occur after the main verb but before other obligatory elements of the clause (e.g. before the subject predicative or direct object). This placement is normal with the copula *be*:

  > It is **still** *three weeks away.* (CONV)

  > *For it is* **no longer** *a casino.* (FICT)

But adverbials are also occasionally placed after other main verbs (especially for reasons of end-weight; see 12.1.4):

> *Kathy Acker's off-the-shoulder dress displayed* **to advantage** *her collection of off-the-shoulder tattoos.* (NEWS)

C Final

And adverbs can also appear in final position in the clause, after obligatory elements:

> *And he's trailing some [***in the back window***] [***as well***].* (CONV)

> *There was an extensive literature on agriculture in Roman times which maintained a pre-eminent position* **until comparatively recently.** (ACAD)

D Other speaker's clause

In conversation and in dialog in fiction, speakers sometimes construct clauses together so that one speaker adds an adverbial to another speaker's utterance. For example:

> A: *I mean you don't have to pay for those.*
> B: *Oh* **for the films.** (CONV)

Here the complete construction would be *You don't have to pay for the films,* borrowing from the other speaker's clause.

E No clause: stand-alone adverbials

In some cases, adverbials occur without a main verb in a clause. This happens most often in conversation, which often has verbless grammatical structure (see 13.4).

> *Are you gonna have a potato fork? There you are.* **On the table.** (CONV)

11.4.1 Frequency of positions

Final position is by far the most common position of adverbials overall. Final position is over three times more common than medial position, and four times more common than initial position.

The three adverbial classes have different favorite positions:

- The most common position for circumstance adverbials is final—in fact, 70 per cent of these adverbials occur in final position.
- The most common position for stance adverbials is medial.
- The most common position for linking adverbials is initial position.

.1.5 The relationship between adverbials and other clause elements

In the introduction to this chapter, we emphasized that adverbials are elements of clauses, not parts of phrases. However, the exact relationship between adverbials and other clause elements can vary. For example, some circumstance adverbials have scope over an entire clause, while others just complete the meaning of the verb. Similarly, some linking adverbials connect whole paragraphs, while others link a main clause to a dependent clause.

All three classes (circumstance, stance, and linking) have adverbials with differing scope: they can focus on a particular part of the clause, or they can apply to the clause as a whole. Circumstance adverbials with limited scope usually restrict or minimize the meaning of some other element of the clause (scope is marked by underlining):

1 *Well you could have* **just** *one aspirin.* (CONV)
2 *I was* **only** *joking.* (CONV)
3 *The kids had 'superhero sundaes' which turned out to be* **merely** *ice cream.* (NEWS†)

In these examples, the adverbial's scope extends only to the immediately following element in the clause—*one aspirin* in **1**, *joking* in **2**, and *ice cream* in **3**. Often, this smaller scope means less choice in the placement of the adverbial. For instance, it is not acceptable to say, **Well you could have one aspirin just.* Yet these items are not simply constituents of phrases. It is possible, for example, to move *just* to precede the main verb: *Well you could* **just** *have one aspirin.*

Stance adverbials, too, can focus on a particular element in the clause:

4 *It was all that running around that made it* **sort of** *hurt.* (CONV)
5 *In short, I am* **literally** *disintegrating.* (FICT†)

In **4**, *sort of* conveys that the term *hurt* is imprecise, and in **5**, *literally* refers to the term *disintegrating.* They are thus more local in scope than many stance adverbials. However, they are not part of the structure of a phrase. It is possible to move *sort of* before the verb (*. . . that sort of made it hurt*), or to move *literally* forward (*I literally am disintegrating*) without greatly altering the meaning.

Finally, some exceptional linking adverbials can link not clauses, but phrases (signaled by *[]* in **6** and **7**):

6 *The principles of care for many of the patients in the ward may be similar,* **e.g.** *[the preparation carried out pre-operatively to ensure the safety of patients undergoing surgery].* (ACAD)
7 *He recorded what was really there in the rocks,* **that is to say** *[repeated and sudden changes in environments and extinctions of animals and plants].* (ACAD)

Adverbials such as *e.g.* and *that is to say* above are less clearly elements of a clause than many linking adverbials. Yet they continue to function as linking adverbials do—showing how the writer is connecting two units of discourse—and they are not integrated into a particular phrase.

Review

Major points of Grammar Bite A: Overview of adverbials
➤ There are three classes of adverbials: circumstance, stance, and linking.
   ➤ Circumstance adverbials are by far the most common class.
➤ Adverbials can take many forms: adverbs and adverb phrases, nouns and noun phrases, prepositional phrases, and finite and non-finite clauses.
   ➤ Prepositional phrases are the most common form overall.
➤ Adverbials can occur in three major positions in clauses: initial, final, and medial.
   ➤ Medial position has several variants.
   ➤ In conversation and fictional dialog, some adverbials are connected with another speaker's main clause.
➤ The function of adverbials in their clauses sometimes varies, depending on the scope of circumstance and stance adverbials, or the amount of text connected by linking adverbials.

GRAMMAR BITE

B Circumstance adverbials

11.6 Semantic categories of circumstance adverbials

Circumstance adverbials can be divided into the following categories and subcategories:

category	subcategories
place	distance, direction, position
time	point in time, duration, frequency, time relationship
process	manner, means, instrument, agent
contingency	cause/reason, purpose, concession, condition, result
degree	extent (amplifier, diminisher)
addition/restriction	addition, restriction
recipient	—

11.6.1 Place

Circumstance adverbials of place express distance, direction, and position.

A Distance adverbials

Distance adverbials usually answer the question 'How far?'. They include specific measurements and general descriptions of distance:

> I had to go **a long way** to put the camp behind me. (FICT)

> A woman who fell **50 feet** down a cliff was rescued by a Royal Navy helicopter. (NEWS)

B Direction adverbials

Direction adverbials describe the pathway of an action. They answer the questions 'To(wards) where?', 'From where?', or 'In what direction?'. Some give a general description (e.g. *southwards*); others describe the direction from a beginning point (e.g. *from here*) or towards a destination (e.g. *to the store*):

> And they went **from here** about – nine-ish, I suppose? (CONV)
>
> You used to walk **to the store**; now you ride. (NEWS)

C Position adverbials

Position adverbials indicate a point of location. They answer the question 'Where?'. For example:

> 1 *It would be, be cold **up there**.* (CONV)
> 2 *The implications of this comparison will be discussed further **in Section 2.4**.* (ACAD)

They commonly occur with stative verbs, such as *be* in **1**, but also occur with other verbs, such as the communication verb *discuss* in **2**.

11.6.2 Time

Adverbials of time are used for four temporal meanings: point in time, duration, frequency, and time relationships.

A Point in time adverbials

These tell when an event occurs:

> *I'll see you all **tomorrow night**.* (CONV)
>
> *Perhaps we can put that right **in January**.* (NEWS)
>
> *It is not uncommon **nowadays** to have many hundreds of cattle in one building.* (ACAD)

B Duration adverbials

These describe how long an event lasts:

> *I wouldn't like to go **for a week** in silence.* (CONV)
>
> *It lasted **years**.* (CONV)
>
> *Some observers are predicting the imminent collapse of the military regime which has ruled Ethiopia **for fifteen years**.* (NEWS)

C Frequency adverbials

These tell how often an event occurs:

> *I know but you don't have to do it **every single day**, do you?* (CONV)
>
> ***Occasionally** she would like to gaze out the window.* (FICT)
>
> *Furthermore, the term register is **sometimes** used to refer to <...>.* (ACAD†)

D Time relationships adverbials

These describe the relationship between two events, states, or times:

> *I want to er clean the floor **before I take a load of stuff in**.* (CONV)
>
> ***After this** the conversation sank for a while into mere sociability.* (FICT)

11.6.3 Process

The category of process adverbials has four subcategories: manner, means, instrument, agent.

A Manner adverbials

These, the most common subcategory of process, describe the manner or way something is done. They answer the question 'How?':

> *I found myself writing **slowly**, and rewriting, [**piecemeal**], [**endlessly**].* (FICT)
>
> *This is blue-sky country where they play their music **in that western way**.* (NEWS†)
>
> *'Where two independent doctors agree there is no hope of recovery, patients should be allowed to die **with dignity**,' she said.* (NEWS†)

Adverbials of comparison are a special type of manner adverbial. They compare the manner of one state/action to another:

> *Then I would go through the refrigerator **like a vacuum cleaner**, sucking in whatever there was* (FICT)
>
> *There are few better exponents of the art of looking **as though life is a complete grind**.* (NEWS†)

Another type of manner adverbial answers the question 'With what?' or 'With whom?' (as well as 'How?'):

> 1 *He's coming downstairs **with two sleeping bags over the top of his head**.* (CONV)
>
> 2 *I would feel safer leaving **with somebody else** anyway.* (CONV)

The *with*-adverbials illustrated by 2 can be called adverbials of accompaniment.

B Means adverbials

These describe the means by which an activity or state is accomplished:

> *The US, as the country of origin for the uranium, had originally insisted that shipments be made **by air**.* (NEWS)
>
> *We examined this question **by excluding birds for 3 years from experimental plots**.* (ACAD)

C Instrument adverbials

These mention the item that is used for a task:

> *Well you can listen to what you've taped **with headphones**.* (CONV)
>
> *She fed it **with a teaspoon**.* (FICT†)
>
> *He wrenched up a piece of the road **with splintering finger-nails**.* (FICT†)

D Agent adverbials

These tell the agent or the causer of a happening. They are used with passive constructions:

> *The fruit-pulp is also eaten **by animals**.* (ACAD)

The agent adverbial corresponds to the subject of an active voice construction, as discussed in 6.6.2.

11.6.4 Contingency

Contingency adverbials tell us how one event or state is contingent—that is, dependent—upon another. Many of the subcategories are closely related.

A Cause/reason adverbials

These answer the question 'Why?'. For example:

> *He's quite frightened **cos he doesn't know you**.* (CONV†)
>
> *He was buried under bricks, and died **of head injuries**.* (NEWS)

Traditionally, cause was considered an objective dependence of one event on another. Reason was a cognitive dependence, in terms of the way humans explain things. However, in real texts these are often hard to distinguish, so we treat them as one category.

B Purpose adverbials

These can be paraphrased as 'in order to' or 'for the purpose of'. For example:

> *I've got to talk to you **to explain what we're doing**.* (CONV)
>
> *Although some of them carried weapons, the knives were just **for show**.* (FICT†)

Purpose adverbials also answer the question 'Why?' and are closely related to reason adverbials.

C Concession adverbials

These convey an idea that contrasts with the main idea of the rest of the clause. For example:

> 1 *1700 miners have been out for seven months and, **despite intimidation**, no one has gone back to work* (NEWS)
> 2 ***Although it has been used by others**, this book is written for beginning students who have had no previous college science courses.* (ACAD†)

D Condition adverbials

These express conditions that govern the proposition of the main clause:

> *And **if you were in the mood** we could at least go.* (CONV†)

Adverbials of condition are discussed further in 11.9.1.

E Result adverbials

These adverbials tell the results of the events described in the rest of the clause or in the main clause:

*A gust of wind shook the front door, **so that Mr Harrison had to hold on to it to prevent it slamming in the policeman's face.*** (FICT)

*It has been forced to slash prices, **with the result that profits dropped 11 per cent.*** (NEWS†)

11.6.5 Degree

Degree adverbials answer the questions 'How far/much/many?' and 'To what extent?'. Sometimes they indicate amounts, either in exact terms or more generally:

*She's getting on **a bit** now.* (CONV) <i.e. she's getting rather old>

*Our estimate puts government losses in the past four weeks **at 22,000 killed, captured, or deserted.*** (NEWS)

Other degree adverbials intensify the message in the clause (these adverbials are sometimes called **amplifiers** or **intensifiers**):

*She looked **very much** like her mother.* (FICT)

*The idea is for them eventually to be restored **completely.*** (NEWS†)

Others (called **diminishers**) lower the strength of a claim made in the clause:

*You know, I think you can fix it by pulling the prongs out **a little bit.*** (CONV)

*The land tenure system varies **slightly** from place to place.* (ACAD†)

11.6.6 Addition and restriction

This category includes two opposite types of adverbials. Addition adverbials show that an idea is being added to a previous one:

1 *Some day you'll be old, **too,** Carol.* (CONV†)
2 *More than 90 minerals, including gold, silver, copper, lead, zinc and cobalt are found in Kazakhstan, which **also** has productive oil fields.* (NEWS†)

Addition adverbials often have a secondary linking function. In **1**, Carol—in addition to some other person, presumably the speaker—will be old one day. Circumstance adverbials of addition (e.g. *also, too, as well*) are similar to linking adverbials of addition (e.g. *moreover*) in that they both help build **cohesion** in a text.

Restriction adverbials emphasize that the idea in the clause is limited in some way. For example, ***only** a sick man* in **3** can be paraphrased: *a sick man and no one else.*

3 *The villagers say jokingly that **only** a sick man would choose such a remote place to build.* (FICT)
4 *So you'll have to be **especially** good, Sundays.* (FICT)
5 *Girls do have to help their mothers, sometimes; Grace **in particular** has to help her mother.* (FICT)

Unlike many other adverbials, addition and restriction adverbials cannot easily be moved without affecting their scope (see 11.5). The position of the adverbial is important in determining what element of the clause is the focus of the addition or restriction. For example, moving the restriction adverbial in **4** changes the meaning:

4a *So you'll have to be good, **especially** Sundays.*

11.6.7 Recipient

Recipient adverbials tell to whom an action was directed. Often the recipient is a person or group of people:

1 *Okay and then I'll just write the check **for you**.* (CONV)
2 *OHA will present the referendum results **to the Democrat-controlled Legislature**.* (NEWS)

However, other animals (e.g. *mice* in 3) and even inanimate objects (e.g. *house* in 4) occur in recipient adverbials:

3 *Special cages have been developed **for wild mice**.* (ACAD)
4 *I think we're getting that **for our house**.* (CONV)

The recipient adverbial can often be replaced by an indirect object (3.5.3). Compare 1 with 1a:

1a *Okay and then I'll just write **you** the check.*

Other verbs + recipient adverbials can be alternatively analyzed as a prepositional verb with an object (see 5.10).

11.6.8 Other semantic categories

Some adverbials do not fit into any of the above major semantic categories. Just to give one example, some adverbials mark perspective or respect—for example, prepositional phrases beginning with *as for, regarding, with reference to,* or *in respect of*:

> ***As for problem kids**, the association feels this is a matter for discussion with their parents.* (NEWS)
>
> *I believe that early childhood is not at all early **in respect of** learning.* (NEWS†)

11.6.9 Frequency of semantic categories

As Figure 11.3 shows, place, time, and process are generally the three most common categories of circumstance adverbials (less common types of adverbials are shown as 'other' types, including degree and recipient adverbials). In conversation, place and time adverbials are particularly common, providing down-to-earth information about where and when things happen:

> *I have to be [**at her house**] [**at seven o'clock**].* (CONV)

Adding descriptive details about place, time, and process is

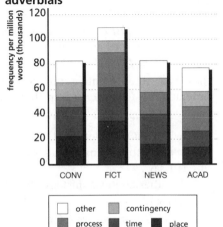

Figure 11.3
Semantic categories for circumstance adverbials

particularly important in fiction writing, for narrating actions and creating imaginary settings:

> [**Now**] [**for the first time**] *he touched her skin, the skin of her forehead* **with his fingertips.**<...> *His instinct was to lift her up and carry her* [**down the hillside**] [**to the village**]. *He was strong enough to do that* **without effort.** (FICT†)

Similarly in news reports, time, place and process adverbials typically answer the important questions of 'When?', 'Where?', and 'How?'.

Conversation has a particularly high use of *because-* and *if-*clauses:

> *I haven't been using the crutches* **because I can't walk on them very well.** (CONV)

> **If I wash up all this stuff,** *somebody else can dry it.* (CONV)

whereas academic prose has a high proportion of purpose adverbials:

> **In order to help such children**, *it is necessary to introduce novel and artificial procedures to assist learning.* (ACAD)

> *But now let us climb slowly down the stratigraphical column* **to see what other widespread facies we can find.** (ACAD)

11.7 Extremely common circumstance ⚲ adverbials in conversation

Three adverbs deserve special consideration because they are so common: *just, then, there.* These adverbs occur in conversation over 2,500 times per million words—far more than any other adverbials in other registers.

11.7.1 *Just*

Just often plays multiple roles in conversation. Its primary sense is 'only' or 'no more than', but it is also useful in focusing on the part of the clause felt to be important. For example, in the following, *just* focuses attention on the following elements: *a number on a damn computer* in 1, *crazy* in 2.

> 1 *You're* **just** *a number on a damn computer.* (CONV) <note: *damn* is a taboo word and may be offensive to some people>
> 2 *It's* **just** *crazy!* (CONV)

Just has other emotive functions that are especially useful in face-to-face interactions. Consider *just* in these imperatives:

> *Now, now* **just** *sit down!* (CONV)

> **Just** *stay there.* (CONV)

Here, *just* implies 'I'm not asking much, only this thing' or 'Don't argue; simply do as I say'.

In other contexts, *just* also has the effect of downplaying the importance of what is said:

> *She's* **just** *that way.* (CONV)

> *Let me* **just** *show you this.* (CONV)

> *I* **just** *want to show you the tape I bought.* (CONV)

Just can also be used to refer to closeness of time:

> *She'd **just** broken up with Joe.* (CONV)

11.7.2 *Then*

Then has two primary functions in conversation. First, it is often used as a deictic adverb roughly equivalent to 'at that time':

> *If I would've known **then** what I know now, I wouldn't even let you operate.* (CONV)

It is also commonly used to mark the next event in a sequence (roughly equivalent to 'after that'):

> *And **then** he goes into my bedroom and **then** he shuts the door and locks himself in.* (CONV)

(Note that *then* is also used as a linking adverb: see 11.17.4.)

11.7.3 *There*

There is also a deictic adverb, meaning 'at that place':

> *Your drink's **there**.* (CONV) <the speaker points to the drink>

There can also refer back to places that have been referred to earlier in the conversation:

> *It's gonna stay **there** until it rots.* (CONV) <*there* refers to a pond that was previously mentioned.>

> *I think I've had a meal **there** years ago.* (CONV) <*there* refers to a pub that was just described.>

11.8 Positions of circumstance adverbials

The positions of adverbials were introduced in 11.4. Figure 11.4 now shows that circumstance adverbials have a very strong preference for final position.

11.8.1 Why choose final position?

A ▸ Completing the meaning of verbs

One important factor in the preference for final position is the fact that many circumstance adverbials complete the meaning of the verbs. Some are obligatory and must be in final position:

> *I'm **at Willy's** right now.* (CONV) <verb pattern S + V + A, see 3.4 and 3.5.5>

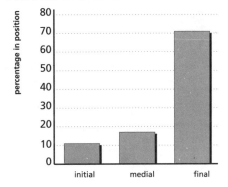

**Figure 11.4
Positions of circumstance adverbials**

> *[Whoever put this plant **on the stairs**] didn't realize we've got silly people like you in the house.* (CONV) <verb pattern S + V + DO + **A** in the clause marked *[]*>

Many optional adverbials have scope over the verb rather than the whole clause (underlining indicates the scope in the following):

1 *It was just <u>flowing along</u> **smoothly**.* (CONV) <manner adverbial>
2 *Civilized men <u>fight</u> **with gossip**.* (NEWS†) <instrument adverbial>
3 *I can't <u>get you over there</u> **in that car**.* (CONV) <means adverbial>

When an adverbial has scope over the verb, it is unusual to move it to a non-final position. For example, *In that car I can't get you over there* is hardly acceptable as an alternative to **3**.

Despite the general preference for final position, various discourse factors favor the use of initial and medial positions (see 11.8.2 and 11.8.3).

B **Ordering adverbials in final position**

It is quite common for more than one circumstance adverbial to occur in final position. The ordering of these adverbials depends in part on the semantic category of the adverbial. Consider, for example, the three common categories place, time, and manner. In general, these adverbials follow the so-called MPT rule: 'manner before place', 'place before time'—and therefore also 'manner before time'. These three orderings are illustrated below:

> *Holly had just sunk [**wearily**][**into the custom-made king-sized waterbed**].* (FICT†)
>
> *Peggy wraps the robe [**around herself**][**again**].* (FICT)
>
> *I'd been living [**independently**][**for about two years**].* (CONV)

Where examples go against the MPT rule, the ordering is often influenced by the principles of **information flow** (placing an adverbial with new information at the end) or end-weight (placing a shorter adverbial before a longer one)—see 12.1.1 and 12.1.4.

11.8.2 Why choose initial position?

A **Information flow**

Adverbials are typically placed in initial position when they contain given information. Placing them first adds to the cohesion of the discourse and keeps the expected information structure of English, with given information before new information (see 12.1.1). For example, it is obvious that *that moment* in **1** below refers back to something already mentioned. Similarly, *the circumstances* in **2** and *this act and these rules* in **3** have all been mentioned in previous text:

1 ***At that moment*** *a servant entered the library.* (FICT)
2 ***In spite of the circumstances which had brought me to Ashington Grange***, *I could not help but be thrilled.* (FICT)
3 ***For notes on this act and these rules***, *reference should be made to the eighth edition of this book.* (ACAD)

B Scope over the entire clause

When they are placed in initial position, adverbials usually have scope over the entire clause. They set up a frame for interpreting the entire proposition that follows:

> **With respect to those employees that remain technically dominant**, *Larson notes that even 'they do not control key financial decisions...'* (NEWS†)

Even when manner adverbials are placed in initial position, we also take the adverbial to have scope over the entire clause. For example:

> **Decisively**, *he pushed open the door of the florist's shop and went inside.* (FICT)

Because of its position, we attribute the decisiveness to the subject (*he*) as well as the actions of pushing open the door and going inside.

C Setting the scene (in place or time)

Initial place and time adverbials often have scope over subsequent clauses for a particular reason: they introduce a new scenario, rather like a stage setting the scene for a play:

> **On the other side of the fence**, *the upper part of the field was full of rabbit holes.* (FICT)

> **Last week**, *he promised that there would be no more boom and bust.* (NEWS)

11.8.3 Why choose medial position?

Two adverbial categories occur more often in medial position than any other position. These are adverbials of addition/restriction and degree. Often these adverbials have scope over only a particular part of the clause. Further, they are often only one- or two-word adverbials, which makes them easy to handle in medial positions. Some time adverbials are also common in medial position.

A Addition/restriction

Because they relate to a particular part of the clause, medial positions can be important for clearly showing the scope of the adverbial. For example, in the following medial examples of restriction adverbials, the placement of the adverbial highlights its relevance to the following word:

> 1 *I was **only** asking.* (CONV)
> 2 *If you read these stories day by day you **simply** don't realize how many there are.* (NEWS)

Thus, **1** downplays the speech act of asking and **2** focuses on the negative (that you do *not* realize).

Though prescriptive rules often insist that addition/restriction adverbials should immediately precede the element they focus, this is frequently not the case in real language. For example, consider the following:

> 3 *Neither Andrew nor Topaz were aware of the gloom. They **only** saw each other.* (FICT)

In **3** the context requires the meaning that 'they saw <u>each other</u> *and nobody else*', even though *only* precedes *saw*.

B Degree

Medial placement is similarly important with many degree adverbials. For example:

> 1 *Last week, Jarman hadn't **<u>quite</u> <u>decided</u>** whether they were to talk to the audience.* (NEWS†)
>
> 2 *Traditionally, with apprenticeships and jobs **almost** <u>assured</u> at 16, there was <...>* (NEWS†)

Here the underlining indicates the word most relevant to the scope of the adverb. In contrast, for other degree adverbials, final position is more common:

> *I guess I won't be able to help you **very much**.* (CONV)

C One-word adverbials of time

One-word adverbials showing time (position in time: e.g. *now, today, yesterday*; and frequency: e.g. *always, never, often, rarely*) also commonly occur in medial position. Most often they are placed before a single main verb:

> *I **always** thought that I reminded him too much of my mom.* (CONV)
>
> *Mason **now** faces a re-trial on the wounding and affray charges.* (NEWS)
>
> *Crops **rarely** experience constant environments.* (ACAD)

You may have noticed that the examples of medial adverbials tend to be short adverbials. In fact, almost 75 per cent of medial circumstance adverbials consist of only one word.

Review

Major points of **GRAMMAR BITE B**: Circumstance adverbials

➤ There are seven major semantic categories of circumstance adverbials: place, time, process, contingency, degree, addition/restriction, and recipient.

  ➤ Place, time, and process (especially manner) adverbials are most common overall.

  ➤ Three circumstance adverbials are extremely common in conversation and have important functions in spoken discourse: *just, then,* and *there*.

➤ Circumstance adverbials can appear in initial, medial, and final positions.

  ➤ Final position is the most common position for circumstance adverbials in general.

  ➤ Initial position is commonly used to maintain given/new information structure or when the adverbial has scope over a series of clauses.

  ➤ Medial position is common for addition/restriction and degree adverbs that have limited scope, and for short adverbials of time.

c Circumstance adverbials that are clauses

1.9 Additional semantic categories of circumstance adverbial clauses

Adverbial clauses fit into many of the semantic categories already presented—especially time, place, and contingency. Here are some examples:

- time:

    When the units are sold, *the city expects to recover all but its $825,000 initial investment.* (NEWS)

- place:

    Wherever your wheels take you, *cycling is serious good fun and saves you a heap of dosh!* (NEWS)

- manner (comparison):

    He smoothed the short sprays of leathery green leaves between his finger and thumb **as if their texture might tell him something.** (FICT)

- contingency (reason):

    I'll have to say I'm Rachel **because our voices sound the same.** (CONV)

- contingency (condition):

    Well, I'm going to feel lucky **if my car isn't towed,** *I think.* (CONV)

- respect:

    As dinosaurs go, *they were the biggest of the big.* (NEWS)

However, there are some additional meaning distinctions to make for circumstance adverbials that are clauses.

11.9.1 Clauses of condition

Clauses of condition can be divided into three subtypes: open, hypothetical, and rhetorical.

A Open condition

In an open condition, the clause does not say whether or not the condition is fulfilled:

1 *Read the paper* **if you don't believe me!** (FICT)
2 **If the water temperature falls below 22 °C** *there is a sharp decrease in yield of grain.* (ACAD†)
3 *He won't go with you* **unless he feels he has to.** (FICT†)

For example, in **1** you might or might not believe me, and in **2** the temperature may or may not fall below 22 degrees. These clauses do not commit themselves to the truth or falsehood of the proposition they contain.

B **Hypothetical (also called unreal) condition**

A hypothetical condition implies that the condition is not fulfilled:

> **4** *If he had had a coin* he would have tossed it. (FICT) <unfulfilled in the past>
>
> **5** *If I could correct this* I certainly would. (NEWS) <unfulfilled in the present/future>

In **4**, it is clear that he did not have a coin, and in **5** that I cannot correct this.

C **Rhetorical condition**

These clauses take the form of a condition, but combined with the main clause, they actually make a strong (unconditional) assertion. For example:

> You may think that I want to destroy the milk boards, but *if you believe that* you will believe anything. (NEWS)

The whole sentence functions as a statement meaning: 'You cannot believe that.'

11.9.2 Clauses of preference, proportion, and supplement

In addition to the semantic categories presented in 11.6, clauses can fulfill other semantic categories.

A **Preference**

Clauses can be used to show preferences:

> Victor Mason was very much the domesticated male animal who had always preferred to relax in the luxury and privacy of his own home, *rather than gallivanting in public.* (FICT)
>
> Planners working on Santa Cruz's 15-year general plan are recommending the city build more condominiums and apartments in urban areas *rather than sacrifice rural open spaces.* (NEWS)

As you can see, these preference clauses use the **subordinator** *rather than* followed by a non-finite verb.

B **Proportion**

Clauses can also be used to express proportions. These adverbial clauses often begin with *the* + comparative and require *the* + comparative in the main clause (both underlined):

> <u>The more</u> *Katheryn probed*, <u>the more</u> Sally squirmed as she gave her version of what had gone on that night. (FICT)
>
> You're out to shock and **<u>the more</u> you astound and astonish people** <u>the happier</u> you'll be. (NEWS)

C **Supplement**

These clauses supplement the information in the main clause, although the exact semantic relationship (e.g. of time, reason, or condition) varies. Usually supplement clauses are non-finite, especially *ing*-clauses and *ed*-clauses:

1 *He shook his head,* **still gazing at the patterns of sunshine on the grass outside the hut**. (FICT)
2 **Overcome by curiosity** *I stared at his odd face, at the scar, the down-weeping, blank eye, the upturned mouth, as if they could tell me something.* (FICT)

We might interpret both of these supplement clauses as time relationships (same time in **1** and a series of events in **2**). However, the adverbial in **1** could also be interpreted as a manner clause, and **2** could be interpreted as a reason clause.

11.9.3 Frequency of clausal semantic categories

Figure 11.5 shows that the distribution of adverbial clauses is similar to the distribution for all adverbials (in Figure 11.1), with fiction using the most adverbials. However, registers show interesting preferences for certain semantic categories. We discuss three of the most striking preferences here.

A **Conversation—condition clauses**

What is particularly notable in conversation is its high frequency of *if*-clauses of condition. They are used in several ways. First, there are both real and unreal conditions, as described in 11.9.1 above.

> **If we move some of these off the table** *we'll have more room to do our pictures.* (CONV) <real>
>
> **If we could afford it** *we'd get one.* (CONV) <unreal>

Conditional clauses also serve special conversational uses in suggestions, requests, and offers:

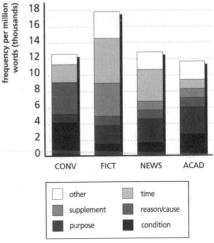

Figure 11.5
Frequencies of semantic categories of circumstance adverbial clauses

1 *You can hold her* **if you want**. (CONV)
2 *Well you can stop being a fusspot* **if you don't mind**. (CONV) <spoken to a child>
3 *You can go sit in the living room,* **if you like**. (CONV)

A conditional clause can soften the suggestion or command. It suggests that the action is the hearer's choice. But in some cases, as in **2**, the choice is not seriously meant.

B **Fiction—supplement clauses**

Compared with other registers, fiction is remarkable for its use of supplement clauses. They are very helpful for adding descriptive details to create an imaginary world. The supplement clauses often describe lesser circumstances that accompany the main narrative:

> **Dangling the keys in front of everybody's nose**, I unlocked the caddy.
> (FICT)
>
> The conductor came along the aisle, **waving his arms**. (FICT)

C Academic prose—purpose clauses

Purpose clauses are notably common in academic prose, where they help to explain procedures or recommendations:

> **In order to help such children**, it is necessary to introduce novel and artificial procedures to assist learning. (ACAD)
>
> Changing the planting date and use of shelter belts have also been suggested **to protect the crops**. (ACAD)
>
> More air must be bled from the compressor **to cool the hotter power turbine**. (ACAD)

11.10 Syntactic forms of adverbial clauses

The different forms of adverbial clauses were described in 11.3. Figure 11.6 shows that in all registers, finite clauses are more common than non-finite clauses. Finite clauses have several advantages over the other types of clauses.

First, finite clauses generally have subordinators, which allow them to cover a wide variety of semantic relationships. In comparison, non-finite clauses have a more limited range of meaning. For example, most *to*-clauses express just one kind of meaning—purpose.

In addition, the subordinators of finite clauses make the relationship between the adverbial and the main clause explicit. We have seen how some supplement clauses—which are non-finite clauses—are semantically indefinite. This can be useful for a register like fiction, but for expository writing, explicitness is an advantage.

Finite clauses also contain an overtly stated subject, which can be different from the main clause (subjects are underlined):

> **When <u>you</u>'re young,**
> <u>everything</u> seems reversible, remediable. (FICT)

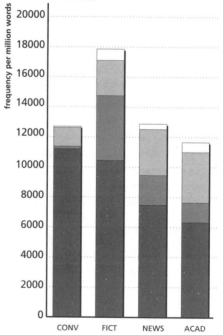

Figure 11.6

Syntactic forms of circumstance adverbial clauses

In contrast, non-finite clauses are more constrained because their subject is usually implied or understood, rather than overt. The understood subject of the adverbial clause must normally be the same as in the main clauses, as in:

> *I borrowed a portable phone* **to ring Waterloo to complain.** (NEWS)

Here we understand that *I*, not some other subject, had to 'ring Waterloo' and 'complain'.

Finally, finite adverbial clauses can have a different tense, aspect, or modality from the main clause. This is often needed for many semantic relationships, including the time and reason clauses here:

> *Last Saturday we* **were** *frantically* **doing** *that painting before it* **got** *dark.* (CONV)
> <main clause verb: past progressive; adverbial clause verb: past simple >

> *I* **like** *these foreign pictures because I* **can believe** *in them.* (FICT)
> <main clause verb: present simple; adverbial clause verb: modal>

The difference in tense and modality is essential in hypothetical conditional clauses, where modals and tenses express the unreal nature of the proposition:

> *Well you* **might get** *some facts right if you* **did!** (CONV)

> *If that* **were** *true, it* **would** *perhaps* **support** *the conclusion that* <...> (ACAD†)

Whereas finite adverbial clauses have the advantage of being more explicit and versatile, non-finite adverbial clauses have the advantage of condensing the adverbial meaning into fewer words. The use of non-finite clauses shows some strong preferences for semantic category and register. As just noted, *to*-clauses are mostly used for purpose, an especially important meaning in academic prose and news:

> **To smooth the way,** *the school has taken special steps.* (NEWS)

> *Reforming is the process whereby straight-run gasoline is cracked* **in order to raise the octane number.** (ACAD)

The only other notable use of *to*-clauses is to express result. This use is most common in news, particularly in sports reports:

> *Dick Johnson and John Bowe of Australia, in a Ford Sierra, led from the start yesterday* **to win the Bathurst 1,000-km touring car race.** (NEWS†)

> *Internazionale shrugged off defeat by Malmo* **to beat the leaders, Roma, also by 3–0.** (NEWS)

11.10.1 Dangling participles

A well-known prescriptive rule forbids the use of a **dangling** (or unattached) **participle**—i.e. an *ing*- or *ed*-clause with an understood subject that is different from the subject in the main clause. These clauses can cause absurd interpretations if they are taken literally, but readers can usually guess their intended meaning from context. Consider these two examples:

1 **Leaving the road, they went into the deep resin-scented darkness of the trees.** (FICT)
2 **Leaving the road, the deep resin-scented darkness of the trees surrounded them.**

Example **1** does not have a dangling participle because *they* is understood to be the subject of the adverbial clause (i.e. *they* left the road). But **2** has a dangling participle, because the understood subject *they* is missing from the main clause. The dangling participle structure implies that *the darkness* left the road, which is absurd.

In certain situations, the rule about dangling participles is relaxed, especially:

- when the adverbial clause is a style adverbial (see 11.13.3), and the implied subject is the speaker:

  Putting it more simply, *a racing program is always a programming error.* (ACAD†)

  <= *If I may put it more simply. . .>*

- when the main clause has a non-referential *it* as subject:

  When writing the formulae of both covalent molecules and ionic compounds, *it is often useful to use the valency of an atom, ion or group of atoms.* (ACAD)

  <= *When one is writing. . .>*

Here, we identify the subject of the adverbial clause with the researchers who *use the valency of an atom . . .*

- when the entire main clause is the implied subject of the adverbial clause:

  '**Unknown to him**, *two people were waiting for him*', *the lawyer said.* (NEWS†)

  <= *It was unknown to him that two people were waiting. . . >*

- in scientific writing when passives are used:

  Using flowing nutrient solutions, *concentrations of ions can be maintained constant at, or very close to, the root surface.* (ACAD)

Here the subject of the adverbial clause corresponds to the unstated agent of the main clause (e.g. *the researchers*).

In all of these cases, 'dangling participles' are unlikely to cause any misunderstanding.

11.11 **Positions of adverbial clauses**

Adverbial clauses usually occur in initial and final positions:

> **When you go to sleep**, *I'm gonna watch the game.* (CONV)
>
> *They stood in the passage talking about it in whispers long **after she had gone to bed**.* (FICT)
>
> *But her annoyance returned **when Jenny came in a little while later and told her that she had asked Matthew to dinner**.* (FICT)

Short clauses can also occur in medial positions, for example:

> *A numeric value stored inside a computer (after conversion **if appropriate**) consists of a series of decimal digits.* (ACAD)

In fact, the vast majority of adverbial clauses are in final position. However, a few structural and semantic categories have unusually high frequencies in initial position. There are a number of likely reasons for this choice; we cover only the two most common here. (Compare the functions of initial position discussed in 11.8.2.)

11.11.1 Common functions of initial adverbial clauses

A Cohesion and information structuring

Initial adverbial clauses can be important for the information flow of a text. They often contain given information—i.e. information already mentioned in the recently preceding discourse (see 12.1.1). This maintains the expected information structure of English, with given information before new:

> *It's not the rummy that aggravates my blood pressure.* ***If there were no cards***, *there would still be the stock market, and* ***if there weren't the stock market***, *there would be the condominium in Florida.* (FICT†) <note: 'rummy' is a card game>

Initial purpose clauses in academic prose commonly present given information:

> ***In order to achieve these growth rates*** *factors other than solar radiation must be non-limiting.* (ACAD)

In this example, the noun phrase in the initial adverbial clause (*these growth rates*) has been mentioned in the immediately preceding discourse. An initial *to*-clause can also help with cohesion by leading into the next stage of discussion, stating its purpose:

> ***To assess the impact on education***, *we turn to some specific cases.* (ACAD)

B Framing subsequent discourse

A second role that initial adverbial clauses play is framing subsequent discourse. This means that a clause 'sets the scene' for one or more following clauses. This is a particularly important function of initial time and condition clauses. They can set the scene for a series of events:

> ***When I took Katie to school this morning*** *– I had to drag her into school! She was screaming!* <...> *She was crying, I said I want to go home! I want to go home!* (CONV†)

Or they can set the scene for just one event (in this case a hypothetical one):

> ***If Senna had not either won the race or finished second***, *he would have been out of the championship.* (NEWS)

In fiction, many supplement clauses have this framing function. They often introduce a state or activity of some duration, while the main clause describes a one-time event within that time frame:

> ***Coming back across the yard*** *he heard the sound of a door swinging.* (FICT)
>
> ***Whistling***, *he began to cut new wood for the window frame.* (FICT)

In contrast to this framing effect, adverbial clauses in final position add important new circumstantial information to the end of the main clause:

> *Kerry, come back* ***when you've got some trousers that actually fit***, *okay?* (CONV)
>
> *I'm tense; excuse me* ***if I talk too much***. (FICT)
>
> *He launched into a tirade of abuse against the Government,* ***complaining that they were looking more like Tories every day***. (FICT)

11.12 Subordinators with circumstance adverbial clauses

Finite adverbial clauses usually require a **subordinator**; these are described in 11.12.1 below.

However, there are exceptions. An unreal condition can be made, for example, using subject–operator inversion rather than the subordinator *if*:

> **Should things go well**, it would be nice to see the likes of Darren Patterson and Keith Rowland getting a run. (NEWS) <= If things should go well...>

> **But were he to come**, he would most likely be invited before the summit starts. (NEWS) <= If he were to come...>

> **Had it not been for human kindness**, he would have ended up in a pork pie. (NEWS) <= If it had not been for human kindness...>

This construction is rare.

Non-finite adverbial clauses generally occur without a subordinator. For example:

> They had gone there **to liquidate his father-in-law's estate**. (FICT)

> **Given a probability sample**, well known statistical procedures can be readily applied. (ACAD)

However, they also occur (infrequently) with subordinators:

> **When asked by journalists recently about the refugee problem**, he said, 'What refugee problem?' (NEWS)

> **Before showing the use of matrices** we must first set up an algebra defining the various operations of addition, subtraction, multiplication, and so on. (ACAD)

> There are hundreds of questions to be asked **in order to find a satisfactory answer to the general question**. (ACAD)

These non-finite clauses with subordinators are found mostly in news and academic writing.

11.12.1 Most common subordinators with finite adverbial clauses

A variety of subordinators are possible in all semantic categories. However, a relatively small number are used commonly:

- common subordinators (occurring at least 200 times per million words in at least one register):

    time: *when, as, after, before, while, until, since*

    manner: *as, as if, as though*

    reason: *because (cos), since*

    concession: *though/even though, although, while*

    condition: *if, unless*

- other subordinators:

    time: *once, till, whenever, whilst, now that, immediately* (BrE), *directly* (BrE)

place: *where, wherever*

manner (including similarity and comparison): *like*

purpose: *so (that), in order that*

reason: *as, for, with, in that*

result: *so (that), such that*

concession: *whereas, whilst*

exception: *except that, save that, but that*

condition and contingency: *as long as, in case, in the event that, lest, on condition that, once, provided (that), whenever, wherever, whether*

preference: *rather than*

In two semantic categories a single subordinator predominates: *because* for reason, and *if* for condition. In contrast, time meanings vary, and specific meaning relationships are conveyed through the choice of a subordinator. Consider just a few examples:

- concurrent events:

    And **when we had that, uh, birthday party there**, *they did up her hair and put a ribbon in it and did her nails.* (CONV)

- one event after another:

    *Teenager Matthew Bown is being hailed as a hero for saving a toddler from drowning **after the child plunged into a fast-flowing stream**.* (NEWS)

- one event during another:

    *The river swilled him along, **while he whistled in happiness**.* (FICT)

As is typical, conversation tends to have one dominant subordinator in each category, while the written registers are much more diverse. For example, in conversation *when* is the only time subordinator to occur at least 200 times per million words. (In fiction *as, after, before, when* and *while* all do.) Again in conversation, *if* and *because* (often shortened to *cos* in speech) are even more frequent than *when*, dominating the condition and reason categories of adverbial clause.

11.12.2 Subordinators expressing multiple meanings

It is important to note that a single subordinator can have more than one semantic role. For example, the following common subordinators have two or three meanings:

as	manner, reason, time
since	reason, time
while	concession/contrast, time

But there are strong connections between register and the choice of subordinator meaning. Take the case of *since* in conversation and academic prose. In conversation, the subordinator *since* is most often used to indicate time:

Since Billy's come around *that's all we've been talking about.* (CONV)

*Is it six weeks **since we saw the last one** then?* (CONV)

In contrast, *since* overwhelmingly marks reason in academic prose:

Since most women did marry, most teenage girls assumed that they would do so. (ACAD†)

There can be no standard irrigation management system **since conditions under which the crop is grown vary so widely.** (ACAD)

Review

Major points of GRAMMAR BITE C: Circumstance adverbials that are clauses
> ➤ Clausal circumstance adverbials have some special types of meaning in addition to the meanings of non-clausal circumstance adverbials. For example:
>> ➤ Conditional clauses can express open, hypothetical (unreal), and rhetorical conditions.
>> ➤ Additional semantic categories are preference, proportion, and supplement.
> ➤ Finite clauses are much more common than non-finite clauses.
>> ➤ They also have a number of advantages over non-finite clauses, such as a wider range of meanings and an explicitly stated subject.
> ➤ Final position is the most common position for both finite and non-finite clauses.
> ➤ Initial position commonly serves special functions—especially signaling cohesion or information flow, and framing subsequent discourse.
> ➤ Subordinators begin the great majority of finite clauses but are rare with non-finite clauses.

GRAMMAR BITE

D Stance adverbials

11.13 Semantic categories of stance adverbials

Stance adverbials are adverbials that overtly mark a speaker's or writer's attitude to a clause or comment about its content. They can be divided into three categories: epistemic, attitude, and style.

11.13.1 Epistemic adverbials

Epistemic stance adverbials express the speaker's judgments about the information in a proposition. They have six major areas of meaning: certainty and doubt, actuality and reality, source of knowledge, limitation, viewpoint or perspective, and imprecision.

A Certainty and doubt

Some epistemic adverbials tell the speaker's level of certainty or doubt about the proposition in the clause.

• expressing certainty:

*That sort of gossip should **certainly** be condemned.* (NEWS)

*During the action the person will **undoubtedly** have certain feelings towards it and gain satisfaction from achievement.* (ACAD)

- expressing doubt:

   *In spite of that it was **probably** more comfortable than the home they'd left anyway.* (CONV)

   ***Maybe** it is true, **maybe** it isn't.* (NEWS)

Doubt/certainty adverbials include: *no doubt, certainly, undoubtedly, probably, perhaps, maybe, arguably, decidedly, definitely, incontestably, incontrovertibly, most likely, very likely, quite likely, of course, I guess, I think, I bet, I suppose, who knows.*

B Actuality and reality

Actuality and reality adverbials give the proposition the status of real-life fact, usually in contrast with what someone might have supposed:

***In fact** I'm taller than the doors.* (CONV)

*Not all the evidence by any means concurs with the view that women were **actually** superior to men in some respects.* (ACAD)

Actuality and reality adverbials include: *in fact, really, actually, in actual fact, for a fact, truly.*

C Source of knowledge

Adverbials of source of knowledge tell us where the claim reported in the proposition came from. They can allude to evidence, as with *evidently, apparently,* or *reportedly*:

***Evidently**, the stock market believes that matters will not rest there and Pearl's share price raced up 87p to 639p.* (NEWS)

They can also identify a specific source:

***According to Mr. Kandil**, nuclear power was the only clean energy alternative for Egypt.* (NEWS)

A finite clause can be used to state evidence for the truth of the main clause:

1 *It wasn't the batteries **because I tested the batteries and they were fine**.* (CONV†)

2 ***As Mr. Wardell (1986) notes**, once managerial decisions are known they then become the basis on which groups lower down the hierarchy organize their resistance and responses.* (ACAD)

In 1, the *because*-clause does not provide the reason for what is described in the main clause. Rather, it gives the source of the knowledge about the batteries: 'I know that because …'. Similarly, 'Mr. Wardell' is the source of knowledge in 2.

   Source of knowledge adverbials include: *evidently, apparently, reportedly, reputedly, according to X, as X reports/notes.*

D Limitation

Limitation stance adverbials imply that there are limits to the validity of the proposition:

***In most cases** he would have been quite right.* (FICT)

Typically there is a pair of ganglia in each segment of the body. (ACAD)

Limitation stance adverbials include: *in most cases, in most instances, mainly, typically, generally, largely, in general, on the whole.*

E Viewpoint or perspective

These adverbials mark the viewpoint or perspective from which the proposition is claimed to be true:

In our view *it would be a backward step.* (NEWS)

From our perspective, *movement success is paradoxical.* (ACAD)

Viewpoint or perspective adverbials include: *in our view, from our perspective, to my knowledge, to the best of our knowledge.*

F Imprecision

A number of stance adverbials are **hedges** (see 7.11.6) suggesting that the proposition (or part of it) is imprecise:

*Men were **like** literally throwing themselves at me.* (CONV)

*It kept **sort of** pouring out of his pocket, his brother said.* (FICT)

*Indeed, the only real drawback, **if you can call it that**, is that people are continually coming up and congratulating us on our victory over England.* (NEWS)

Hedging adverbs like *sort of, kind of,* and *like* are very common in conversation. Imprecision adverbials include: *like, sort of, kind of, so to speak, if you can call it that.*

11.13.2 Attitude adverbials

Attitude adverbials tell the speaker's attitude toward the proposition. Typically they convey an evaluation, or assessment of expectations:

1 **Fortunately**, *during my first few months here, I kept a journal.* (FICT)
2 *And **most surprising of all**, much farther away still in west Australia, we have the gingin chalk of the late cretaceous age.* (ACAD)
3 **Hopefully** *this problem will be solved when the group is thoroughly revised.* (ACAD)

Often these adverbials can be restated with *that*-clauses and adjectives describing attitudes: 1 *It is fortunate that . . .* , 2 *It is surprising that . . .* , 3 *I am hopeful that . . .* Writing manuals often warn against the use of *hopefully* as a stance adverbial, as in 3. However, this use is found in the more formal registers of news and academic prose, as well as in conversation and fiction.

Other adverbials are useful for expressing different kinds of attitude, especially in writing:

- expressing expectation: *surprisingly, not surprisingly, most surprising of all, as might be expected, as you'd expect, as you might expect, inevitably, naturally, as you might guess, to my surprise, astonishingly, of course, predictably*
- expressing evaluation: *unfortunately, conveniently, wisely, sensibly, unfortunately, quite rightly, even worse, disturbingly, ironically*
- expressing importance: *even more importantly, importantly, significantly.*

11.13.3 Style adverbials

Stance adverbials of style comment on the manner of conveying the message (e.g. *frankly, honestly, truthfully*):

   1 *Well **honestly** I, I don't know.* (CONV)
   2 ***More simply put**, a feedback system has its inputs affected by its outputs.*
     (ACAD)

Often these adverbials can be glossed as 'I am being X when I say ...'. For example, 1 means: 'I am being honest when I say I don't know.'

    Finite clauses are occasionally used as style adverbials, often with the subordinator *if*:

> *Is it a fact that you have refused to take any fee for the work you are doing, **if you don't mind my asking**?* (FICT)

> *I have to say that in terms of violent crime generally the amount of it in the United Kingdom is small compared with that in other countries and, **if I may say so**, here in Washington.* (NEWS)

These clauses suggest that the speakers view themselves as speaking in a way that might cause offence.

    Style adverbials include: *frankly, if you don't mind my saying so, literally, seriously, confidentially, to tell you the truth, technically speaking, generally speaking, to put it X* (e.g. *bluntly, charitably*).

11.13.4 Ambiguity with other adverbial classes

Some stance adverbials can have ambiguities or multiple meanings, which we now consider.

A   **Stance adverbial v. circumstance adverbial or degree modifier**

It can be difficult to tell whether a word is a stance adverbial or a circumstance adverbial (or in some cases, an adverb modifier within a phrase rather than an adverbial). The adverb *really* is particularly tricky to analyze. Some instances seem clearly to have the epistemic stance meaning of 'in reality' or 'in truth,' especially when the adverb is in initial or final position:

> ***Really**, you've noticed the difference?* (CONV)

> *I had no choice **really**.* (NEWS)

But in medial position, the meaning is less clear. In the following, *really* could have a degree meaning, or be interpreted as intensifying the (underlined) adjective or verb (roughly with the meaning of 'very (much)'):

> *It's **really** <u>wonderful</u>.* (CONV)

> *The numbers **really** <u>took off</u> in the late 1890s.* (ACAD†)

Other stance adverbials could alternatively be interpreted as circumstance adverbials of degree or time. In the following, *largely* and *mainly* could be interpreted to mean 'to a great extent' or 'usually', as well as being stance adverbials (limiting the truth of the proposition):

> *The Cranfield Institute of Technology is **mainly** engaged in post-graduate teaching and research.* (NEWS†)

> *The great scholars also are **largely** ignored for their craft skill.* (ACAD)

B ▌Stance adverbial v. linking adverbial

Some stance adverbials can also have a connecting function, overlapping with linking adverbials. *In fact* not only signals actuality, but generally indicates that what follows reinforces the point just made:

> *I went up and heard the jazz at the Crown last night. <...>* **In fact** *I was quite a busy little bee last night.* (CONV†)

> *She's never seen him on the porch.* **In fact**, *there's no chair to sit on.* (FICT)

C ▌Stance adverbial v. discourse marker

Sometimes the division between a stance adverbial and a **discourse marker** is not clear. Consider *like* in the following example:

> *She* **like** *said that they would.* (CONV)

Here it is difficult to tell whether *like* is a discourse marker (with a purely interactive function; see 13.7) or a stance adverbial suggesting that the proposition is communicated imprecisely.

11.13.5 Frequency of semantic categories

Figure 11.7 illustrates the following points about the frequency of stance adverbials across registers:

- Conversation has by far the highest frequency of stance adverbials.
- Epistemic adverbials are by far the most common meaning category in all registers.
- Style adverbials are more common in conversation than the other registers.
- Attitude adverbials are slightly more common in news and academic prose than in conversation and fiction.

Figure 11.7

Frequency of stance adverbials across registers

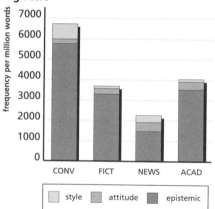

11.14 The most common stance adverbials

Very common stance adverbials that occur over 300 times per million words are:

	doubt/certainty	actuality	imprecision
CONV:	*probably, maybe*	*really, actually*	*like* (AmE), *kind of* (AmE), *sort of* (BrE)
FICT:	*probably, perhaps, maybe*	*really*	
ACAD:	*perhaps*		

('AmE' and 'BrE' here mean that the adverbials are used over 300 times per million words in those varieties. But they are also used (though not so frequently) in the other national dialect.)

The most common are all epistemic: expressing levels of doubt or certainty is important in all the registers. *Probably* and *perhaps* are especially common:

> You've **probably** wiped it off now. (CONV)
>
> Ellen thought that **perhaps** Jackie had been crazy. (FICT†)
>
> This level is **probably** sufficient to cause clinical disease. (ACAD†)

Two very common adverbials in conversation (and one in fiction) are actuality adverbials (*actually* and *really*). These are frequently used in dialog for emphasis:

> I've **actually** got very strong teeth. (CONV)
>
> That's all she could move. It **really** was. (CONV)
>
> 'I **really** have to go now.' (FICT)

Other common stance adverbials in conversation are markers of imprecision. In British English conversation, the favorite form is *sort of*:

> It's **sort of** an L in shape of an O. (BrE CONV)
>
> We **sort of** were joking about it. (BrE CONV)

In American English, the favorites are *like* and *kind of*:

> I always thought that I reminded him too much of my mom and **like** depressed him. (AmE CONV)
>
> She's **kind of** a rich, really rich woman with all this time on her hands. (AmE CONV†)

.15 Positions of stance adverbials

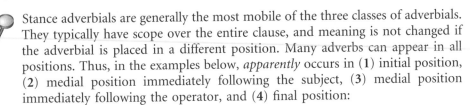

Stance adverbials are generally the most mobile of the three classes of adverbials. They typically have scope over the entire clause, and meaning is not changed if the adverbial is placed in a different position. Many adverbs can appear in all positions. Thus, in the examples below, *apparently* occurs in (**1**) initial position, (**2**) medial position immediately following the subject, (**3**) medial position immediately following the operator, and (**4**) final position:

> 1 Well **apparently** she said it stands her in good stead. (CONV)
> 2 *Arphia pseudonietana and psoleoessa texana* **apparently** were much more abundant in the wet summer of 1990. (ACAD)
> 3 The throne is **apparently** in no danger at all. (NEWS)
> 4 Words helped them, **apparently**. (FICT)

Figure 11.8
Positions of stance adverbials

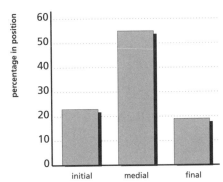

Despite this mobility, slightly over half of stance adverbials occur in medial positions (see Figure 11.8).

11.16 Other discourse functions of stance adverbials

Stance adverbials can serve a variety of discourse functions in addition to conveying epistemic, attitudinal, and style meanings.

As mentioned in 11.13.4, stance adverbials (such as *in fact, in brief, in a word*) can have a cohesive function, because they introduce a reinforcement or summary of a previous statement.

Other stance adverbials contribute to the interactive nature of conversation. For example, a speaker can use *no doubt* or *of course* to signal familiar knowledge shared with the interlocutor, as in this comment after a forecast of clear weather:

> But **no doubt** we'll have a few showers. (CONV)

Stance adverbials can also be used to soften disagreement. For instance, after one speaker lists 'Sophie' as a 'weird name', the other responds:

> Sophie. Well that's not **really** a weird name. (CONV)

Similarly, epistemic stance markers can soften a suggestion:

> Well I was thinking we could **perhaps** take her to Blagden Hall now that's open. (CONV)

Epistemic stance markers can also be used for enthusiastic emphasis:

> You've **definitely** got the right idea. (CONV)

These examples show how stance adverbials can be multi-functional in discourse—especially in conversation (compare 13.7.1, Table 13.2 on inserts).

Review

Major points of GRAMMAR BITE D: Stance adverbials

➤ There are three major types of stance adverbials: epistemic, attitude, and style.

➤ Epistemic stance adverbials convey meanings such as doubt/certainty, actuality/reality, and imprecision.

➤ Some stance adverbials overlap in their functions with circumstance adverbials, linking adverbials, and discourse markers.

➤ The highest frequency of stance adverbials overall is in conversation.

➤ Single adverbs are the most common form of stance adverbial.

➤ All of the most common stance adverbials are epistemic.

➤ Medial position is the most common position for stance adverbials.

➤ Stance adverbials have important interactional functions in conversation.

E Linking adverbials

1.17 Semantic categories of linking adverbials

The main function of linking adverbials is to clarify the connection between two units of discourse. Because they explicitly signal the link between passages of text, they are important devices for cohesion (see Chapter 12, especially 12.1.1). The six major semantic categories are: enumeration and addition, summation, apposition, result/inference, contrast/concession, and transition.

11.17.1 Enumeration and addition

Linking adverbials can be used to enumerate (list) pieces of information, or to signal the addition of items to a list. Linking adverbials for enumeration include numbering words (e.g. *first(ly)*, *second(ly)*), as well as *finally* and some prepositional phrases:

> *This new structure must accomplish two special purposes.* **First**, *as part of overcoming the division of Europe there must be an opportunity to overcome through peace and freedom the division of Berlin and Germany.* **Second**, *the architecture should reflect that America's security remains linked to Europe.* (NEWS)

> *He couldn't bring himself to say what he thought.* **For one thing**, *she seldom stopped to listen.* **For another**, *he doubted that he could make himself clear.* (FICT)

Addition linking adverbials signal that a new item of discourse is being added to previous ones:

> 1 *Each of these crystal systems is represented by a primitive lattice.* **In addition**, *there are seven multi-primitive lattices.* (ACAD)
> 2 *Feedback tends to be used to stabilize systems, not to randomize them.* **Similarly**, *natural systems would probably evolve to avoid chaos.* (ACAD)

As the use of *similarly* in **2** suggests, addition often goes with similarity of meaning.

Other typical enumerating adverbials are: *lastly, thirdly, in the first/second place, first of all, for one thing ... for another thing, to begin with, next*.

Other typical addition adverbials are: *also, by the same token, further, furthermore, likewise, moreover*.

11.17.2 Summation

Adverbials that mark summation signal that a unit of discourse concludes or sums up points made in the preceding discourse:

> **In sum**, *then, to account for a synchronic assimilation from [k] to [t] under this view, the processes of tier promotion and complex segment simplification must apply along with the spreading of the assimilation feature.* (ACAD)

> ***To conclude***, *we may place the three notions of saliency in an ordered relation as follows:* <...> (ACAD†)

Other typical summation adverbials are: *all in all, in conclusion, overall, to summarize.*

11.17.3 Apposition

Adverbials of apposition show that the following piece of text is equivalent to, or included in, the point made in the preceding discourse.

An apposition adverbial may introduce the second unit as a restatement of the first, reformulating it in some way or stating it more explicitly:

> *The current edition <...> shows that road users cover their track costs by a factor of 2.4 to 1.* ***In other words*** *users of all types pay almost two and a half times as much in taxes as is spent on all road costs from building, maintenance and signs, right down to the provision of police, traffic wardens and even grass cutting and hedge-trimming of the verges.* (NEWS†)

> *Our model allows the predefinition of who,* ***i.e.*** *which Communicator, may exchange when,* ***i.e.*** *at what point of time, what,* ***i.e.*** *which message, with whom,* ***i.e.*** *with which Communicator.* (ACAD)

In many cases, the second unit of text is an example. It is information that is logically included in part of the previous text (here marked in *[]*):

> *She understood [the parameters of the picnics] all too well.* ***E.g.*** *they could not go to the beach because of the sand.* (FICT)

> *If a population becomes highly entrained, [its diversity is greatly reduced].* ***For example***, *the age structure could become very narrow.* (ACAD)

Other typical apposition adverbials are: *which is to say, that is to say, that is, for instance, namely, specifically.* Note that some apposition adverbials used in writing are Latin abbreviations: *e.g.* ('for example'), *i.e.* ('that is'), *viz.* ('namely').

11.17.4 Result/inference

Linking adverbials of result/inference signal that the second unit of discourse states the results or consequence of the preceding discourse:

> *I once acquired a set of recordings of a Bach piano concerto. I was very fond of it, but my mother was forever criticizing and chastising my poor taste* <...> ***Consequently***, *I now hardly listen to Bach.* (FICT†)

> *As the spatial file contains all the geometric relationships necessary to specify the body, this can be used to generate any pictorial view. It is* ***thus*** *not necessary to produce an engineering drawing specifically for the purpose of showing everyone what it looks like.* (ACAD)

In conversation this category is also commonly realized by *so*. In some cases, *so* clearly marks a resultive relationship and could be replaced by *therefore*:

> *Oh well you've seen it anyway,* ***so*** *I won't put it on.* (CONV)

So does not always have such a clear role, however. At times, *so* refers to something understood from the context that is not available to readers of a written transcription. In the following example, *so* could relate to an action that is not put into words (e.g. putting away tools or closing a book) but that suggests work is finished:

*Okay **so** that's that.* (CONV)

In still other cases, *so* has little semantic content of its own. Instead, it functions more like a discourse marker (see 13.7.1, Table 13.2). For example, in the following excerpt, *so* marks the speaker's wish for an explanation of what has been said:

> A: *Uh, yeah, yeah – I'm looking forward to tomorrow night.*
> B: ***So** what are you guys doing?*
> C: *Oh, just visiting folks, pretty much.* (CONV)

Other result/inference adverbials mark one idea as an inferred result of another:

> *He works late. How am I supposed to get there **then**?* (CONV)

In this example, *then* marks the connection between the idea of the first clause (his working late) and the speaker's problem getting to another location. However, this connection is not as overt as with many resultive adverbials in writing (e.g. *He works late; **therefore**, he cannot drive me there*).

Other typical result/inference adverbials are: *hence, therefore*.

11.17.5 Contrast/concession

Here we note linking adverbials that mark some kind of contrast or conflict between information in different discourse units. Some of these adverbials clearly mark contrasting alternatives:

> *Many statutory water companies are already saddled with high borrowings. **In contrast**, the water authorities are going into the private sector flush with cash.* (NEWS)

> *All fans should be speed-controlled. **Alternatively**, a system of variable fan speed on a motorized thermostat or electronic control will give full automation on all fans.* (ACAD)

Other adverbials mark a concessive relationship: they show that the subsequent discourse expresses something contrary to the expectations raised by the preceding clause. *Though* and *anyway* are concessive adverbials:

> A: *I would love a nice new car! We won't be able to afford one for a couple years yet.*
> B: *You could afford a Mini **though**.* (CONV†)

> *Now that the lawyers have taken over, science will never be able to reach a verdict, and **anyway** it no longer matters.* (NEWS)

Other typical contrast/concession adverbials:

- focused primarily on contrast: *on the other hand, conversely, instead, on the contrary, in contrast, by comparison*
- focused primarily on concession: *anyhow, besides, nevertheless, still, in any case, at any rate, in spite of that, after all, yet*.

11.17.6 Transition

Transition adverbials mark the insertion of an item that does not follow directly from the previous discourse. The new information is signaled as only loosely connected, or unconnected, to the previous discourse, as in the following:

> A: *Yeah Guy I really don't like walking in the bathroom and seeing your underwear hanging off the mirror.*

B: *That's enough.*

C: *<laugh>*

A: *It's kind of disgusting, how do you get them to stick there **by the way**?*

D: *Velcro.* (CONV)

*It seems clear there is nothing for it but to go back and attack the first difficulties again. **Incidentally**, one way to motivate yourself if things do get sticky is to imagine that you have to explain the subject to the class the next day.* (ACAD)

Other transition adverbials are: *by the by, meanwhile, now.*

11.17.7 **Frequency of semantic categories**

Figure 11.9 shows the frequency of linking adverbials across registers. Academic prose not only has the most common use of linking adverbials; it also shows the most diversity in their meaning. Since a very important aspect of academic prose is presenting and supporting explanations and arguments, ideas often need to be overtly connected:

Figure 11.9

Frequencies of linking adverbials across registers

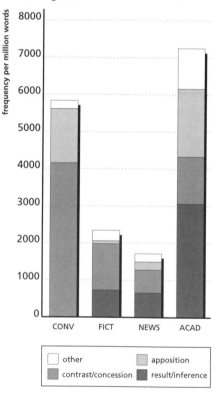

1 *To summarize, there is no class of healthy ruminant for which the direct effects of low air temperature per se are likely to cause intolerable stress in the temperate and cool zones of the world. Moreover, the effects of air temperature on food conversion efficiency below the critical temperature are likely to affect only the smallest animals and at a time when their daily intake is very small relative to lifetime requirements. Thus there are no sound economic grounds for providing any more environmental control for the healthy animal than shelter from excessive air movement and precipitation.* (ACAD)

Notice that each sentence in **1** begins with a linking adverbial. A single sentence may even contain more than one linking adverbial, as in **2**:

2 *There must, **in addition**, be some reason why water excretion by the kidney has failed, **however**, since ingestion of hypotonic fluid does not ordinarily lead to progressive dilution of body fluids.* (ACAD)

The most common types of linking adverbials in academic prose are result/inference, apposition, and contrast/concessive adverbials—all these help to structure arguments and explanations.

It may seem surprising that conversation also has a high frequency of linking adverbials (compared with news and fiction). This is mainly because of a few very high frequency items (*so, then, anyway,* and *though,* discussed in the next section). In news and fiction, on the other hand, many connections are left implicit. In the following passage, for example, the man's actions were presumably the result of the child starting to cry, but the writer uses no linking word:

> *The child had begun to cry. He went to her and bent over her, giving her a handkerchief.* (FICT)

11.18 The most common linking adverbials in conversation and academic prose

Common linking adverbials that occur over 100 times per million words are:

CONV: *so, then, though, anyway*
ACAD: *however, thus, therefore, for example, then, so, e.g., i.e., first, finally, furthermore, hence, nevertheless, rather, yet, for instance, in addition, on the other hand, that is*

The four linking adverbials commonly occurring in conversation—*so, then, though,* and *anyway*—are extremely common, averaging well over 1,000 occurrences per million words. They play important roles in the development of conversational discourse:

11.18.1 *So*

So is often used in stories in conversation. It moves the story along, making clear how one event follows from another. Some narrators use *so* repeatedly, as in the following story about a visit to the dentist:

> *He twisted it and a fragment of the tooth came off and hit me straight in the eye.* **So** *I've got I've got a little pinprick in my eye.* **So** *I'm just hoping I'm not gonna get an infection in it.* (CONV)

11.18.2 *Then*

Then is often used when one speaker sums up an inference based on another speaker's utterance:

> A: *Oh, Dad is sixty-one.*
> B: *Is he? Well* **then** *she must be sixty.* (CONV)

In some cases, particularly in British English conversation, *then* is part of a question, asking for confirmation of the inference that has been made:

> A: *Well she's gonna have that knocked into an archway through to a dining room*

B: *Oh right, lovely <...> So the third bedroom would go right across that extension **then**?* (CONV†)

Then also occurs with commands or suggestions to another participant in the conversation:

A: *It's the spears don't work – they slide off the spears that's the problem.*
B: *Well use your spoon **then**.* (CONV)

11.18.3 *Though*

Though is concessive: it is used to mark contrasts between one clause and another:

*So it should have everything, I still think that it's a bit expensive **though**.* (CONV)

*They've got loads of dressy things for girls, not for boys **though**.* (CONV)

However, *though* is also often used to establish a link between speakers. The second speaker can add a remark contrasting with the previous speaker's, while at the same time not totally disagreeing with it:

A: *That one's a nuisance.*
B: *That one's alright **though**.* (CONV)

Notice that *though* makes the disagreement much softer than a marker of direct contrast, such as *but* or *however*. (In writing, on the other hand, *though* is much more often used as a subordinator introducing an adverbial clause.)

11.18.4 *Anyway*

Anyway also has important interactional functions in conversation. It is often used by speakers as they move to their main point, dismissing preceding discourse as less important or irrelevant, especially when there has been some confusion expressed in the preceding discourse, as in the discussion of sun cream in **1**:

1   A: *cos it wasn't in the er, in the first aid drawer.*
     B: *I don't think we've unpacked it from when we went – <...>*
     A: *Can always get another one **anyway**.* (CONV†)

2   A: *When we had the er – ITV, you know, over Christmas it said in there it was on Central but when I turned it on it wasn't at all. **Anyway**, we'll see.* (CONV)

In conversation, *so, then,* and *anyway* tend to lose some of the lexical content of linking adverbials, and to resemble discourse markers with interactional functions (like *well* and *now*; see 13.7.1, Table 13.2).

11.19 Positions of linking adverbials

The most common position for linking adverbials is initial position (Figure 11.10): here, the connection between two clauses is clearly signaled as the reader or hearer is guided from the first clause to the second. In the following examples, the reader's or hearer's processing of the discourse is helped by the initial linking adverbials that specify the relationship between clauses:

1 *She knew they weren't suited to each other, really; she didn't love him, but she couldn't give him up just yet.* **Besides,** *he wasn't the sort it was easy to give up.* (FICT)

2 *The bookmakers, showing unusual generosity, gave them a 44-point advantage on the handicap betting list.* **Instead,** *with only 10 minutes left, Dewsbury led 12–6 and a genuine upset was in the offing.* (NEWS)

Figure 11.10
Positions of linking adverbials

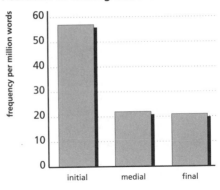

3 *One is the role of the masses of third world indigenous peoples <....>* **Secondly,** *it addressed the issue of the importance, in our models of economic development, of cultural factors.* (ACAD†)

One of the most common linking adverbials in conversation—*so*—cannot occur in any position except initial:

> *People on the West Coast are a lot more relaxed <...>* **So,** *it would be scarier to take a job on the East Coast, that's for sure.* (CONV†)

Contrast the impossibility of:

> **It would,* **so,** *be scarier to take a job ...*
> **It would be scarier to take a job ...* **so.**

Conversation has a higher proportion of linking adverbials in final position than the other registers do. This is largely due to three common adverbials—*then, anyway,* and *though*—which are often placed in final position. Examples include:

> A: *And I think she's stealing stuff <...>. From the house.*
> B: *Does she still live at home* **then**? (CONV†)
> A: *I missed it yesterday.<...>*
> B: *No well you didn't miss much* **anyway.** (CONV†)
> A: *She wasn't there.*
> B: *No she was listening* **though.** (CONV)

Many of the linking adverbials in medial positions are common linking adverbials in academic prose. *Therefore, thus,* and *however* tend to occur in medial positions when they are not in initial positions, most often after the subject or operator:

4 *Einstein,* **therefore,** *set to work to try to demolish the accepted version of quantum mechanics.* (ACAD)

5 *The support of Group Communication* **thus** *requires: the availability of already existing interchanged information <...>* (ACAD†)

6 *Monopoly was* **however** *justified by reference to universalistic and objective criteria of recruitment and achievement.* (ACAD†)

In 4 and 5 the linking adverbial follows the subject, and in 6 it follows the operator.

Review

Major points of **GRAMMAR BITE E**: Linking adverbials

➤ There are six major semantic categories of linking adverbials: enumeration/addition, summation, apposition, result/inference, contrast/concession, and transition.

➤ The greatest use and greatest diversity of linking adverbials are found in academic prose.

   ➤ Conversation has the second highest frequency of linking adverbials, due mostly to a few very common items, like *so*.

   ➤ Cohesion in news and fiction depends less on explicit linking adverbials and more on chronological order or implicit connections.

➤ Four linking adverbials are extremely common in conversation: *so, then, though, anyway*. They are important in the unfolding of conversational discourse.

➤ Initial position is the typical position for linking adverbials generally.

   ➤ Three of the common linking adverbials in conversation tend to appear in final position: *then, anyway, though*.

12

Word order choices

GRAMMAR BITES in this chapter

A Fronting and inversion

> ➤ Unmarked word order (i.e. normal word order)
> ➤ Different types of fronting and their uses across registers
> ➤ Different types of inversion and the uses of inversion across registers

B Existential *there* clauses

> ➤ *There* in existential clauses
> ➤ Subjects, verbs, and adverbials in existential clauses
> ➤ The function of existential *there* clauses

C Other topics in word order

> ➤ Types of dislocation
> ➤ Types and frequency of clefts
> ➤ Word order choices after the verb: the placement of objects
> ➤ Summary of syntactic choices in conversation and academic prose

12.1 **Introduction**

The basic word order of English is subject–verb–object (SVO), as you can see in a sentence such as:

> *Myrna*[S] *makes*[V] *the best cucumber salad*[O] . (CONV)

Myrna, the subject, precedes the verb *makes*, which precedes the object *the best cucumber salad*. However, different contexts may make it preferable to put elements of the clause in different places. For example, a speaker who wants to emphasize that Myrna, not someone else, makes the best cucumber salad might say:

> *It's Myrna who makes the best cucumber salad.*

This type of construction is called **clefting** (12.12). Or a speaker who is discussing a variety of cucumber salads might start with *the cucumber salad* and say:

> *The best cucumber salad is made by Myrna.*

This type of construction is the **passive** (discussed fully in 6.6–8). These are just two examples of ways to reorder clause elements.

In the present chapter, we discuss six grammatical devices to manipulate word order in clauses: fronting, inversion of subjects and verbs, existential *there* clauses, dislocation, clefting, and variations in the ordering of objects. Some of these devices involve simply moving elements to different positions. Others require changing the clause in more complicated ways, such as changing the verb to passive voice.

The techniques that we discuss here are used in a variety of ways to make a clause better fit its context. Four major discourse factors are important in understanding the grammatical choices that influence word order:

- information flow: given v. new information
- focus and emphasis, including end-focus and double focus
- contrast
- weight, including end-weight and balance of weight.

Because these factors are so important, we introduce them first in this chapter. However, these concepts do not explain all the reasons for word order changes. For example, irony and surprise may also be important. Also, in some registers, such as fiction, writers may simply want to make varied use of language.

12.1.1 **Information flow**

If we look at a clause in its discourse context, some elements refer back to information that is familiar due to the preceding discourse—i.e. given information—and other elements present new information. The typical word order in English is to start with given information and move to new. Thus, in the following example clause, the person *Mr Summers* and *the house* have already been introduced.

> **1** *Inside the house Mr Summers found a family of cats shut in the bathroom.*
> (NEWS)

The clause is first grounded in the situation that has already been mentioned— *the house* and *Mr Summers*. Then the communication advances with the information about what Mr Summers found. This typical ordering of information—from given to new—is the **information-flow principle**.

Given–new order of information contributes to the **cohesion** of a text. The given information is usually related to its previous mention, and the new information is often taken up in the following discourse. This order of information makes it easier for receivers to understand, because the clause starts with something that is familiar.

However, there are exceptions to the information-flow principle. For example, the needs of focus and emphasis, discussed in the next section, may be stronger than the need to follow the information-flow principle.

12.1.2 Focus and emphasis

In any clause, there is usually at least one point of focus. This point receives some prominence in the clause. It is apparent in speech because the strongest stress or intonation peak will occur at this point. Typically, the focus occurs naturally on the last lexical item in the clause (e.g. *the bathroom* in **1** above). The general principle governing focus is therefore known as the principle of **end-focus.** When the information-flow principle is being followed, new information, which occurs at the end of the clause, will be the focus.

However, there is another potential point of focus in a clause: the beginning. Many of the devices covered in this chapter increase the focus given to the beginning of the clause by starting with an element other than the subject. The result is a clause with double focus (or even more than two points of focus). For example, in **1** an adverbial occurs first. That adverbial—*Inside the house*, and more specifically the lexical item *house*—receives its own focus, in addition to the focus on *in the bathroom*.

When an initial element is the point of focus, it gains prominence. A complement of the verb in initial position is intensified, much as it is intensified by an adverb like *very*:

> *Brilliant that was!* (CONV)

Here *brilliant* is intensified by being in initial focused position, before the subject. The meaning is similar to the speaker saying *That was absolutely brilliant!* The marked word order—with the complement first—gives intensification to the complement (*brilliant*).

12.1.3 Contrast

Contrast occurs when the focused part is highlighted to show its difference from another element:

> *It's not **the bikers** – it's the **other vehicle** that's on the road.* (CONV†)

Here *the other vehicle* is focused and contrasted with *the bikers* in the preceding clause in a parallel structure. The manipulation of the sentence structure shows contrast just as the coordinator *but* and the linking adverb *however* do. The speaker, for instance, could have said: *The bikers are not a problem. However, the other vehicle is.*

12.1.4 Weight

Elements in a clause are frequently of different size and complexity, relating to their weight. For instance, a noun phrase consisting of a head noun with long premodifiers and postmodifiers is much 'heavier' than a noun phrase consisting of a single pronoun. The preferred distribution of elements in the clause is called the principle of **end-weight**: long and complex (i.e. heavier) elements are placed towards the end of the clause. This placement helps hearers and readers to follow the message more easily, because they do not have to keep in their mind complex information from the beginning of the clause as they reach the end of the clause (compare the principle of real-time processing in 13.2.5). Many heavy elements also contain a large amount of new information. The information-flow principle and end-weight principle therefore often reinforce one another.

Sometimes heavy elements are at the beginning of sentences. As described above in 12.1.2, these heavy elements then gain some prominence and they can give a clause more than one point of focus—at the end and at the beginning.

GRAMMAR BITE

A Fronting and inversion

12.2 Word order

The term 'word order' is used to refer to the order of elements in a clause: subject, verb, object, predicative, and adverbial.

The **unmarked** word order in English (i.e. clauses that contain the normal word order) has the following characteristics:

- The subject normally precedes the verb, and the verb normally precedes its complements: S + V, S + V + A, S + V + SP, S + V + DO, S + V + Prep + PO, etc.

- Independent interrogative clauses normally have subject–operator inversion (e.g. *Are you sure?*).

- All clause elements realized by *wh*-words are regularly placed in initial position. For example: *I don't know [**what** you want].* (CONV†). (Even though *what* is the object in the dependent clause (*you want what*), it is placed before the subject *you*.)

- Phrases are normally continuous. This means that a phrase is not usually broken up by another element.

12.3 Fronting

Fronting means placing in initial position a clause element which is normally found after the verb. Fronting is relatively rare in English, and it is almost always in declarative main clauses (except for the fronting of *wh*-words mentioned in the last section). However, several kinds of fronting are possible, summarized in Table 12.1.

le 12.1 **Types of fronting**

type	examples	description
fronted object	1 ***This*** *I do not understand.* (FICT) 2 ***Why he came this way*** *I will probably never know.* (FICT)	The object of the clause is in initial position. Many different structures occur as fronted objects, such as nouns, pronouns (**1**), and complement clauses (**2**).
fronted nominals other than object	***Whether Nancy was there or not****, she could not be certain.* (FICT)	A nominal structure is in initial position, such as the complement to the adjective *certain* in the example here (*She could not be certain **whether Nancy was there or not***).
fronted predicatives	1 ***Far more serious*** *were the severe head injuries.* (NEWS) 2 ***The larger*** *the base **the easier** it will be to perform the action.* (ACAD) 3 ***So preoccupied*** *was she **that** she was unaware that Diana was standing in the doorway.* (FICT†)	A subject predicative is in initial position. Many structures can occur as fronted predicatives. Special cases include **proportion** clauses with *the* (**2**) and degree clauses with *so . . . that* (**3**). Some fronted predicatives occur with inversion (**1, 3**).
fronted non-finite constructions	1 *I have said he would come down and **come down** he did.* (FICT) 2 ***Waiting below*** *was Michael Sams.* (NEWS) 3 ***Enclosed*** *is a card for our permanent signature file.* (FICT†)	An infinitive (**1**), *ing*-participle (**2**) or *ed*-participle (**3**) is in initial position. Its complements are fronted with it (e.g. *down* in *come down*). Some fronted non-finite predicates occur with inversion (**2, 3**).
fronting in dependent clauses that use *as* or *though*	1 ***Try*** *as she might to make it otherwise <. . .>* (FICT†) 2 *<. . .>* ***unsuccessful*** *though they have been in their proposals <>* (ACAD†)	Dependent clauses that use the subordinator *as* (**1**) or *though* (**2**) sometimes have an element placed before the subordinator. (**1**) illustrates fronting of a main verb and (**2**) illustrates fronting of a predicative.

12.3.1 Fronted objects and other nominals

- Noun phrases as fronted objects:
    1 *Sandy moved ahead. '**This** I do not understand,' he said.* (FICT)
    2 *Bess was satisfied with her hair, but **her freckles** she regarded as a great and unmerited affliction.* (FICT)
    3 ***Some things** you forget. **Other things** you never do.* (FICT)
- Complement clauses as fronted objects:
    4 ***What it was that changed this conclusion**, I don't remember.* (FICT)

  5 *Why he came this way* I will probably never know. (FICT)
  6 *What they can do,* we can do. (FICT)
  7 *Whether Nancy was there or not,* she could not be certain. (FICT)

- Nominals with other syntactic roles (e.g. here a subject predicative):

  8 'Pretty strange, huh?' *That it is.* I nod sadly. (FICT)

As these examples show, most occurrences of fronting put focus on both the beginning and ending of the clause. For example, in **1**, *this* gains emphasis from its initial placement, rather than the unmarked word order *I understand this*. At the same time, *understand* has its own focus because it is the last element in the clause. In addition, many instances of fronting facilitate the information-flow principle: the fronted element refers to given information. This is particularly obvious with the fronted pronouns in **1** and **8**. Finally, several fronted objects show contrasts. For example, *her freckles* are contrasted with *her hair* in **2**, *other things* are contrasted with *some things* in **3**, and *they* with *we* in **6**.

12.3.2 Fronted predicatives

Many clauses with fronted predicatives have subject–verb inversion, but some do not. Predicative fronting with subject–verb inversion can occur with comparative and superlative forms. In the following examples, underlining signals the subject, here highlighted as new information by the inversion:

  1 *The hens in the next garden: their droppings are very good dressing.* **Best of all**, though, are <u>the cattle</u>, especially when they are fed on those oilcakes. (FICT)
  2 **Far more serious** were <u>the severe head injuries</u>; in particular a bruising of the brain. (NEWS)

Usually, the predicatives which have been fronted make a comparison with some element in the preceding discourse, and form a cohesive link. In **1**, for example, the cattle are being compared with the hens. The cohesive link is also sometimes made with the words *also* and *such*:

  3 *Under stress, Sammler believed, the whole faltered, and parts (follicles, for instance) became conspicuous.* **Such** at least was <u>his observation</u>. (FICT)
  4 **Also popular for travelling** are <u>quilted, overblown pseudo-ski jackets in pink or blue that look like duvets rampant</u>. (NEWS)

The organization of these examples is consistent with the information-flow principle. In **3**, for example, *such* refers to Sammler's beliefs mentioned in the previous sentence.

There are two special cases of predicative fronting. The first contains combinations of proportion clauses (see 11.9.2) marked by pairs of phrases with *the*:

  5 *The more general the domain,* **the more general, selective and tentative** are <u>the statements about its style</u>. (ACAD) <with inversion>
  6 *The larger the base* **the easier** <u>it</u> will be to perform the action. (ACAD) <without inversion>

Heavier subjects, as in **5**, often have subject–verb inversion. Clauses with a subject pronoun, as in **6**, often do not have inversion.

The second special type of predicative fronting concerns adjectives premodified by *so* and followed by a *that*-clause of degree. For example:

So preoccupied was <u>she</u> at this moment, she was unaware that Diana was standing in the arched doorway to the sitting room. (FICT)
<compare: *She was so preoccupied at this moment that she was unaware...*>
So ruthless was <u>the IRA</u> in its all-out onslaught against the police and the Army, it didn't care who got in its way. (NEWS)
<compare: *The IRA was so ruthless in its all-out onslaught that it didn't care who got in its way.*>

In these sentences, the adjective and intensifier *so* are fronted, but the *that* comparative clause is not fronted.

When the subject is an unstressed pronoun, predicatives can still be fronted but subject–verb inversion does not take place:

   7 **Right** <u>you</u> are! (CONV)
   8 **Bloody amazing** <u>it</u> was! (CONV) <note: *bloody* is a taboo word and may be offensive to some people>
   9 **Peter Harronson**, <u>he</u> said he was called. (FICT)

Fronting has an intensifying effect, often strengthened by the choice of words (e.g. *bloody amazing*) or by emphatic stress when spoken. The fronted material is new rather than old, which makes it a marked choice with respect to the information-flow principle. In some cases, the initial predicative highlights the main purpose of the utterance; for example, in **9**, the purpose is to establish the person's name. In **9** you can also see that the fronted predicative can be an object predicative, and can actually belong to an embedded clause (signaled by [] in: *He said [he was called **Peter Harronson**]*).

12.3.3 Fronted non-finite constructions

There are three major types of fronted non-finite constructions, corresponding to the three types of non-finite verb forms: a bare infinitive, an *ing*-participle, and an *ed*-participle.

A Fronted bare infinitive constructions

In these constructions, a non-finite verb and its complements are fronted. The subject and an auxiliary verb follow in their normal position. Emphatic *do* is used if there is no other auxiliary verb (focused elements are underlined):

   1 *I had said he would come down and **come down** he <u>did</u>.* (FICT)
   2 *But, as he said, it had to be borne, and **bear it** he <u>did</u>.* (FICT†)

As these examples show, fronted bare infinitives are often associated with the echo of a previous verb. The echo is not providing new information, so the fronting serves the information-flow principle and cohesion. However, the fronting also emphasizes the repeated element. Compare **2** above with the unmarked word order and typical ellipsis (marked with ∧) of the repeated element in **3**:

   3 *I had said he would come down and he did ∧.*

Thus, the fronted infinitive predicate gives a double focus—the fronted element and the auxiliary at the end of the clause. The same is true for fronted infinitive constructions that do not echo a previous verb:

   4 **Work** *I* <u>must</u>, *and for money.* (FICT)

In **4**, both *work* and *must* are focused elements.

B   Fronted *ing-* and *ed-*constructions

Fronted *ed-* and *ing-*constructions usually occur with exceptionally long subjects. Subject–verb inversion accompanies fronted *ed-* and *ing-*constructions, so the heavy subjects (underlined below) are moved to clause-final position:

> 5 *Nothing on the walls, with one exception:* **tacked over the bed** *was <u>a yellowed, deckel-edged photograph.</u>* (FICT†)
> 6 **Enclosed** *is <u>a card for our permanent signature file which we request you to sign and return to us.</u>* (FICT)
> 7 *Billy beamed lovingly at a bright lavender farmhouse that had been spattered with machine-gun bullets.* **Standing in its cock-eyed doorway** *was <u>a German colonel.</u>* (FICT)
> 8 *<u>The money</u> was left on the parapet of a bridge carrying the track over an old dismantled railway line.* **Waiting below** *was <u>Michael Sams, who had left a tray on the bridge parapet for the money.</u>* (NEWS)

The order of the elements in these clauses agrees with the information-flow and end-weight principles. There is generally a reference to the preceding context early in the structures, and new information is introduced in the subject, which occurs at the end of the clause. The subjects are often indefinite noun phrases: the use of *a/an* shows their status as new information (*a photograph, a card, a colonel*). The fronted items contain definite noun phrases (*the bed*) and pronouns (*it, its*), showing their status as given information.

12.3.4 Fronting in dependent clauses

In dependent clauses, fronting occurs only with the subordinators *as* and *though*. For example (the dependent clause is shown in *[]*):

> 1 *[***Try*** as they <u>might</u>], no one close to Frankie Howerd could ever improve his image.* (NEWS†)
> 2 *The proponents of more traditional solutions to the problem of universals, [***unsuccessful*** though they have been <u>in their own proposals</u>], have made trouble for the solution in terms of individual properties.* (ACAD†)

Fronting the items in bold puts them in a conspicuous position before the subordinators and clearly emphasizes them. Notice that these are clauses of concession, and involve some contrast. In **2**, for example, *unsuccessful* is contrasted with the fact that they have still *made trouble*. You can also see that the end-focus falls on the underlined constituents.

12.3.5 Fronting in exclamations

Exclamative clauses with a *wh-*element (e.g. *How good she is!*) have obligatory fronting, since the *wh-*element has to occur in pre-subject position. However, there are other types of exclamations where fronting is optional. *Such* can be used like *what* in exclamations:

> **Such a gift** *he had for gesture. He looked like a king in exile.* (FICT)
> <compare: *What a gift he had for gesture;* and normal order: *He had such a gift...*>

And she thought: **Such a sure hand** *my son has with people.* (FICT)
<compare: *What a sure hand my son has with people.*>

In some cases, the exclamatory effect of the fronting is apparent from the use of exclamation marks:

Charming *you are!* (FICT)

A fine time *you picked to wake up! Where were you in my hour of need?*
(FICT)

Fronting in exclamations is often used with irony or sarcasm, as it is in these examples.

12.3.6 The use of fronting across registers

Fronting is relatively rare in all registers, although this device is used more in fiction and academic prose than conversation or news. Further, different types of fronting are preferred in each register.

In academic prose, the most common form is predicative fronting, which aids cohesion by linking clauses:

In the Peruvian case study that follows, the degree to which marketwomen are independent petty commodity traders or are undergoing proletarianization is problematic. **Also problematic** *is the degree to which gender may be playing a part in the proletarianization process.* (ACAD)

The fronting ties the sentences together through repetition (note the repetition of *problematic* above).

Conversation and fiction more commonly use fronting of objects. These elements are fronted for focus rather than for cohesion:

A: What actually does the price include?
B: **That** *I couldn't tell you.* (CONV†)

'No wet beds. **That** *I won't stand.'* (FICT)

Whether it would fire after being in the river, *I can't say.* (FICT)

In fiction, where varied sentence structure and stylistic effect are especially valued, fronting occurs more frequently than in conversation.

Although fronting is relatively rare, it is an important option for focus and cohesion; its rarity makes these effects even more conspicuous when they do occur.

2.4 Inversion

In inversion, the verb phrase or the operator comes before the subject. There are two main types of inversion (the subject is underlined):

- **subject–verb inversion** or full inversion: the subject is preceded by the entire verb phrase:

    Best of all **would be** <u>to get a job in Wellingham</u>. (FICT†)

- **subject–operator inversion** or partial inversion: the subject is preceded only by the operator rather than by the main verb or full verb phrase:

    Not before in our history **have** <u>so many strong influences</u> **united** *to produce so large a disaster.* (NEWS)

In this example, the main verb is *united* but only the auxiliary verb *have* is placed before the subject. If no other operator is present, auxiliary *do* is inserted.

*Never again **did I think** of disobedience.* (FICT†)

In general, inversion serves the following discourse functions:

- cohesion and information flow (especially subject–verb inversion)
- intensification (especially subject–operator inversion)
- placement of focus (both kinds of inversion)
- end-weight (both kinds of inversion).

The different types of inversion are summarized in Table 12.2 and explained below.

Table 12.2 Types of inversion

type of inversion	examples	conditions commonly associated with this inversion
subject–verb	*On one long wall **hung a row of van Goghs.*** (FICT†)	initial adverbial (*on one long wall*)
		short intransitive verbs (*hung*)
		long subjects (*a row of van Goghs*).
subject–operator	**1** *On no account **must he** strain.* (CONV)	negative opening elements (**1** *on no account*)
	2 *So badly **was he** affected that he had to be taught to speak again.* (NEWS)	degree expressions with *so* or *such* (**2** *so badly*)
	3 *She hadn't known much about life, nor **had he.*** (FICT)	the linking words *so, nor, neither* (**3** *nor*)
subject–verb and subject–operator in formulaic use	*So **be it**.* (FICT†) *Long **May She** Reign!* (NEWS)	archaic and formal expressions

12.4.1 Subject–verb inversion

Subject–verb inversion is most often found with an initial adverbial, a short intransitive or copular verb phrase, and a long subject that introduces new information.

A Initial adverbials

Initial place and time adverbials with subject–verb inversion are especially common.

*They found an extension to the drawing room with thigh-high cannabis plants growing in polythene bags full of compost. **Nearby** was a 400-square-yard warehouse with more plants flourishing in conditions controlled by artificial lighting and automatic watering systems.* (NEWS)

*For a moment nothing happened. **Then** came voices all shouting together.* (FICT)

> *First came the scouts, clever, graceful, quiet. They had rifles. **Next** came the antitank gunner.* (FICT)

Usually these adverbials have a cohesive function. They are often tied to previous discourse, and they often show how a scene unfolds, either in physical space or through time. *Here* and *there*, defining a place relative to the speaker, are often found with inversion:

1 *Here comes the first question.* (FICT)
2 *There's the dog. Call the dog.* (CONV)

(Notice that the place adverb *there* in 2 is different from existential *there*, explained in 12.5–10).

In academic prose, there is less need for description and time narration, but other initial adverbials are sometimes used with inversion. They usually have a clear cohesive function. For example:

> *Formaldehyde may be generated in various ways. **Among these** is heating a solution of <...>* (ACAD†)

Sometimes an adverbial particle of direction is used with inversion:

> *In came Jasper, smiling jauntily, stepping like a dancer.* (FICT)
> *Billy opened his eye, and **out** came a deep, resonant tone.* (FICT)

This type of inversion is used in dramatic narration, to emphasize a sudden happening.

B Short intransitive/copular verb phrases, and long subjects

You can see in the above examples that most of these verb phrases are short, consisting of either a copular or an intransitive main verb (e.g. *came, is, was*). As the following examples show, more complex verb phrases are possible, but here the delayed subject is heavier than the verb, thus following the principle of end-weight:

> *Among the sports **will be** <u>athletics, badminton, basketball, <...>.</u>* (NEWS†)
> *Also noted **will have been** <u>the 800 metres run by under-15 Claire Duncan at Derby and the under-17 100 metres hurdling of Jon Haslam (Liverpool) which also gained Northern silver.</u>* (NEWS)

Subject–verb inversion does not occur with a lightweight pronoun as subject:

> full noun phrase: *Then **came** <u>the turning point of the match.</u>* (NEWS)
> pronoun: *Then <u>it</u> **came** again like a whiplash.* (FICT) <but not: *Then came it.>

12.4.2 Subject–operator inversion

In subject–operator inversion, only the operator (see 8.7), rather than the whole verb phrase, is placed before the subject. Apart from its regular use in forming questions, subject–operator inversion occurs under special conditions:

A Negative and restrictive opening elements

Subject–operator inversion is found after initial negative expressions such as: *neither, nor, never, nowhere, on no condition, not only, hardly, no sooner, rarely, scarcely, seldom, little, less, only.* (Notice that *little, less,* and *only* are negative in meaning.) The negative 'trigger' for inversion is usually an adverbial or a coordinating conjunction. In the following examples, the trigger element is underlined and the operator is marked in bold:

> 1 *A: I haven't got a copy of club rules.*
>   *B: <u>Nor</u> **have** I.* (CONV)
> 2 *And she said, you know, <u>on no account</u> **must** he strain.* (CONV)
> 3 *<u>Rarely</u> **are** all the constraints on shape, function and manufacturing clearly defined at the commencement of the activity. <u>Even less</u> **are** they understood and their effect, one on another, recognized by the designer.* (ACAD)

Because of the inversion, the force of the negative element is intensified. Example **3** intensifies the force further, through use of parallel structures in the two sentences.

The expression *no way* is often found in colloquial language, triggering inversion:

> 4 *Oh <u>no way</u> **do** I want to take that.* (CONV)
> 5 *And if the case went to trial, there wasn't a damn thing Katheryn could do to stop them. And <u>no way</u> **could** she get Sarah to understand that.* (FICT)

In **4**, notice that dummy *do* is used as the operator, where *do* would be used in ordinary *not* negation: *I don't want to take that* (see 8.8.1).

Notice also that negative elements trigger subject–operator inversion only when they have scope over the entire clause (see negative scope in 8.8.9). Contrast **6** and **7**:

> 6 *<u>In no time at all</u> the hotels **would** be jammed to the doors.* (FICT)
> 7 *<u>At no time</u> **did** he indicate he couldn't cope.* (NEWS)

In **6**, *in no time* is a time adverbial roughly meaning 'very soon'; it does not affect the positive nature of the clause, and thus subject–operator inversion is not possible. But in **7**, *at no time* means that the entire clause is negative. A paraphrase would be: *He never indicated that he couldn't cope.* Thus, the opening element of **7** (but not **6**) has scope over the entire clause. Correspondingly only **7** has subject–operator inversion.

B   Degree expressions with *so* and *such, neither* and *nor*

Subject–operator inversion occurs in clauses that begin with the degree adverb *so* followed by an adjective or adverb:

> *<u>So badly</u> **was** he affected that he had to be taught to speak again.* (NEWS)

Similar constructions occur with *such ... that*:

> *<u>Such</u> **is** the gravity of the situation <u>that</u> it has already sparked an international incident.* (NEWS)

Inversion can occur after initial *so* when it is used as a pro-form pointing back to the predicate of a preceding clause:

> *A: We used to watch that on T.V.*
> *B: Yes, <u>so</u> **did** I.* (CONV) <= *and I did, too*>

> *As infections increased in women, <u>so</u> **did** infections in their babies.* (NEWS)

The initial *so* in these examples stands for given information and has a cohesive effect. The subject, containing the main new communicative point of the clause, is placed in the end-focus position after the verb.

Clauses with initial *nor* and *neither* express parallelism with a preceding negative clause. Again the inversion pattern has a cohesive effect, as the linking word refers back to given information:

> *She hadn't known much about life, <u>nor</u> **had** he.* (FICT)

> *The generalization's truth, if it is true, is not affected by how we count things in question, and <u>neither</u> **is** its falsehood if it is false.* (ACAD)

With *nor* and *neither*, subject–operator inversion is mandatory.

C Special cases of inversion

There are a few cases of inversion with formulaic expressions. Typically, these are felt to be archaic expressions with literary overtones.

Subjunctive verb forms (8.17) express a strong wish:

> *If you want to throw your life away, **so <u>be</u> it**, it is your life, not mine.* (FICT)

> *'I, Charles Seymour, do swear that I will be faithful, <. . .> so **help** me God.'* (FICT†)

Inversion combined with a subjunctive verb form (*be*, *help*) gives these expressions a solemn tone.

Clauses with inversion opening with the auxiliary *may* also express a strong wish:

> ***May God** forgive you your blasphemy, Pilot. Ye-s. **May he** forgive you and open your eyes.* (FICT)

> *The XJS may be an ageing leviathan but it is still a unique car. Long **may** it be so!* (NEWS)

12.4.3 Inversion in dependent clauses

Although inversion is most common in independent clauses, it also occurs in dependent clauses.

A Opening adverbials and opening negatives

Adverbials and negatives that begin a dependent clause (signaled by underlining in **1** and **2**) can take inversion just as they do with independent clauses. Notice the inversion after the relativizer in **1**:

> **1** *In the centre of the green was a pond, beside it was a wooden seat <u>on which</u> **sat** two men talking.* (FICT)

> **2** *Introspection suggests that <u>only rarely</u> **do** we consciously ponder the pronunciations of words.* (ACAD)

Dependent clauses also have some special cases of inversion. These are summarized in Table 12.3. The particularly interesting cases of interrogative clauses and reported clauses are discussed below.

B Dependent interrogative clauses with 'semi-direct speech'

Dependent *yes/no* interrogative clauses (marked by *[]* below) are usually introduced by *whether* or *if* and have ordinary subject–verb order, as in:

> *I asked them [if **they would** hurry it up a bit].* (FICT)

An informal alternative is to use subject–operator inversion:

Table 12.3 **Special types of inversion in dependent clauses**

type of dependent clause	examples	description
comparative clauses with as and than	Independent agencies are in a better position to offer personal service **than are those** tied to big chains. (NEWS†)	The operator follows the subordinator as or than. Usually in formal writing.
some clauses of manner	Charlotte was fascinated, **as were the other guests.** (FICT)	The operator follows the subordinator as.
conditional clauses that are hypothetical or tentative and use had, should, or were	1 **Should either of these situations** occur, wrong control actions may be taken. (ACAD) 2 **Were it** running more slowly, all geologic activity would have proceeded at a slower pace. (ACAD)	The verbs had, should, or were come before the subject. The alternative form is to use the subordinator if (1 If either of these situations occur ...).
conditional clauses that present alternatives or universals	1 When the going gets tough, it's these people who react best – **be it** a natural disaster, accident or sudden emergency. (NEWS) 2 <...> [He] has somewhat desperately tried to make up his mind to utter his whole self, **come what may.** (ACAD†)	Alternative clauses can be paraphrased with whether it/he/she/ they is/are. The subjective be is used. For (1) compare: whether it is a natural disaster. Universal clauses express a condition that is universally true. They can be paraphrased with whatever. For (2) compare: whatever may come.
interrogative clauses	And she said **would we** like these shirts. (CONV)	The inversion gives the sentence characteristics of both direct and indirect speech.
reporting clauses	'That's the whole trouble,' **said Gwen,** laughing slightly. (FICT)	The reporting clause may have subject–verb inversion. Inversion is not usual, however, when the clause subject is a pronoun (said she).

    3 *The young man who had seen Mac in Westmoreland Street asked [**was it** true that Mac had won a bet over the billiard match].* (FICT)

    4 *She needed a backing guitarist and asked Kieran, who she had met once or twice on the road, [**would he** help out].* (NEWS)

    5 *And she said [**would we** like these shirts].* (CONV)

This pattern represents a compromise between direct and indirect speech. It preserves the subject–operator inversion of the independent interrogative clause, but pronouns and verbs have been adjusted to show the reporting situation. Compare, for example, these alternatives for the semi-direct speech in example **5**:

    direct speech: *And she said, 'Would you like these shirts?'*

    indirect speech: *And she asked whether we would like these shirts.*

C Reporting clauses

Reporting clauses are direct quotations of a person's speech or thought. They are on the borderline between independent and dependent clauses. They contain some kind of reporting verb, which can be a simple verb of speaking/thinking (e.g. *say, think*) or a related verb identifying a manner of speaking (e.g. *mutter, shriek*), the type of speech act (e.g. *offer, promise*), or the phase of speaking (e.g. *begin, continue*). Such clauses often have subject–verb inversion:

> *'That's the whole trouble',* **said Gwen**, *laughing slightly.* (FICT)
>
> *Fifties and post impressionist,* **thought Alexander**, *connecting.* (FICT)
>
> *Councils,* **argues Mr Cawley**, *are being hit by an unenviable double whammy.* (NEWS)

As these examples show, quotation marks are not always present.

In news, reporting clauses can also be used for attributions of written text:

> *Where farming used to be the only viable source of income, hundreds of people have found regular work,* **reveals Plain Tales from Northern Ireland**. (NEWS†)

There is a strong preference for unmarked word order—that is, subject before verb—under any of these three conditions:

- where the subject is an unstressed pronoun:

  > *'The safety record at Stansted is first class',* **he said**. (NEWS)

- where the verb phrase is complex (containing auxiliary plus main verb):

  > *'Konrad Schneider is the only one who matters',* **Reinhold had answered**. (FICT)

- where the verb is followed by a noun or pronoun that names the addressee:

  > *There's so much to living that I did not know before,* **Jackie had told her happily**. (FICT)

The conditions of inversion in reporting clauses are similar to those for all inversion. Usually inversion is influenced by the end-weight and information-flow principles. A weighty element and/or an element deserving emphasis is last. However, inversions sometimes occur in unexpected conditions, such as with this subject pronoun:

> *'We may all be famous, then,'* **said he**. (FICT)

12.4.4 Inversion across registers

Figure 12.1 shows that inversion is a relatively rare phenomenon, although it is somewhat more common in the written registers. In fiction and in news, inversion is most common in reporting clauses, where it accounts for more than half the total occurrences.

Conversation has certain fixed patterns involving inversion, for

Figure 12.1

Approximate frequency of inversion

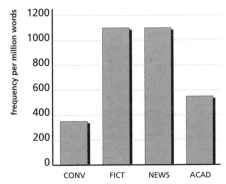

example *so am I*, and *there's/here's* . . . (where *here* and *there* are deictic adverbs, as in *Here comes your mother*). However, the time for planning and editing in the written registers makes it easier to achieve the variety of word order required for inversion.

Review

Major points of GRAMMAR BITE A: Fronting and inversion

➤ Many types of clause elements can be fronted (i.e. moved to the front of a clause): objects, nominals other than objects, predicatives, non-finite constructions, and some elements in dependent clauses.

➤ Fronting is generally infrequent, but the frequency of each type varies across the registers.

➤ Fronting is typically used for cohesion and for special emphasis and contrast.

➤ Inversion has two primary forms: subject–verb and subject–operator inversion. Other types of inversion occur in dependent clauses.

➤ Inversion can be used for cohesion, information flow, intensification and placement of focus.

GRAMMAR BITE

B Existential *there* clauses

12.5 Existential *there*

Existential *there* is a device used to state the existence or occurrence of something (or its non-existence or non-occurrence). It is used with an intransitive or copular verb. Most typically, a clause with existential *there* has the following structure:

there + be	**+ indefinite noun phrase**	**(+ place or time position adverbial)**
There's	*a bear*	*sitting in the corner.*

For example:

1 *A man goes in the pub.* **There's** *a bear sitting in the corner. He goes up to the, he goes up to the bartender. He says, why* **is there** *a bear sitting over there?* (CONV)

2 **There are** *around 6,000 accidents in the kitchens of Northern Ireland homes every year.* (NEWS)

The noun phrase following *be* is called the **notional subject**. Thus, in **1**, *a bear* is the notional subject, and in **2**, *around 6,000 accidents* is the notional subject. Typically, the notional subject is an indefinite noun phrase.

Clauses with existential *there* are called existential clauses. The main function of existential clauses is to introduce new information, which is presented in the indefinite noun phrase, the notional subject.

12.5.1 The grammatical status of existential *there*

Existential *there* is a function word. It developed from the place adverb *there*, but it no longer has a meaning of place. Existential *there* differs from the place adverb *there* in the following ways:

- Phonologically, it is normally reduced to /ðə(r)/.
- The original place meaning is lost.
- Syntactically, it functions as a subject rather than an adverbial.

You can easily see the difference between existential *there* and adverbials when existential *there* occurs in the same clause as the place adverbs *there* or *here* (underlined in these examples):

    1 **There**'s more gravy <u>here</u>. (CONV)
    2 **There**'s still no water <u>there</u>, is **there**? (CONV)

Existential there is an empty grammatical element. It has no lexical meaning. The place adverbs do have meaning and can be paraphrased: *here* = in this place, *there* = in that place.

    Syntactically, existential *there* behaves like a grammatical subject. It is placed before the verb in declarative sentences, and as **2** and **3** show, it can be used with inversion in questions and question tags.

    3 *Is **there** a microphone we can borrow?* (CONV)

Existential *there* can also occur as the subject of a non-finite clause:

    *N may be too large for [**there** to be room for that number].* (ACAD)
    *The paramedics arrived just in time, and there was some question of [**there** being brain damage this time].* (FICT)

Such non-finite existential clauses are relatively rare, however. They usually occur in academic prose.

    Place *there* and existential *there* have very different patterns of distribution across the registers, as you can see in Figure 12.2. Place *there* is very common in conversation and very rare in academic prose, reflecting differences in the importance of physical setting for the registers. In conversation, the setting is shared by speaker and addressee. It makes sense to refer to *here* and *there*. The same is true of fictional dialog. But in news and academic prose, there is no shared physical setting. The frequency of the place adverb *there* is therefore low. When place *there* does occur, it usually refers to a place in the text rather than the physical setting: e.g. <...> *references for further reading given **there*** (ACAD†).

    In contrast to place *there*, existential *there* is relatively common in all four registers.

Figure 12.2
Existential v. locative *there*

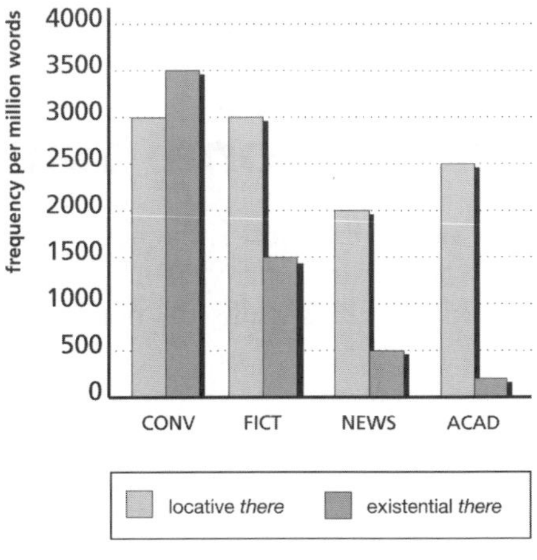

frequency per million words

CONV   FICT   NEWS   ACAD

locative *there*   existential *there*

12.6 **The verb in existential *there* clauses**

 The great majority of existential *there* clauses contain a form of the verb *be*. It may be preceded by auxiliaries or semi-modals: *has been, will be, is to be, is supposed to be, used to be,* etc. *Be* may also occur in a *to*-infinitive complement, where the controlling lexical verb expresses a kind of stance: *happen to be, tend to be, appear to be, is said to be,* etc.:

> *There **used to be** a – a house on the end of the common up at Clarendon Road.* (CONV†)

> *If you want to know, there **is supposed to be** a plot between you and me to get hold of his wealth.* (FICT)

> *There **seem to have been** a lot of people who took up painting for a while and then dropped it.* (NEWS)

> *There **is said to be** a mismatch between the mother tongue and the target language at these points.* (ACAD)

Existential clauses can also contain verbs other than *be*, usually intransitive verbs of existence or occurrence:

> *Somewhere deep inside her there **arose** a desperate hope that he would embrace here.* (FICT)

> *There **seems** no likelihood of a settlement.* (NEWS)

Existential *there* clauses with verbs other than *be* are generally rare. *Exist* is the most common alternative to *be*. It is used almost entirely in academic prose, where it has a more formal sound than *be*:

> *There **exist** innate conventions through which human artifacts convey meaning.* (ACAD†)

> *There now **exists** an extensive literature on the construction and use of social indicators in a variety of contexts.* (ACAD†)

Fiction has a greater variety of verbs in existential clauses. These include *come* and *seem* as well as a variety of less common verbs: *arise, ascend, break out, emerge, erupt, float, flow, flutter,* etc.

> *There **came** a faint stirring in his entrails.* (FICT†)

> *There **followed** a frozen pause.* (FICT†)

> *There **remained** something unmistakably clerical in his manner.* (FICT†)

12.7 **The notional subject**

The notional subject is the noun phrase that functions logically as the subject of the clause. Since *there* has no content, the notional subject is what the clause is mainly about. Usually, the notional subject is an indefinite noun phrase.

*There won't be **a mass**.* (CONV)

*There was **nobody** here yesterday.* (CONV)

Many notional subjects are structurally complex:

*There is **something extra and a little heroic about him**.* (FICT†)

*There must be **an enormous sense of isolation, of being aware of being let down**.* (NEWS)

The notional subject can also be followed by a post-modifying clause:

*There's a cow **standing in the middle of the road**.* (CONV†)
<compare: *A cow is standing in the middle of the road.*>

*There are two scales of temperature **used in science**.* (ACAD)
<compare: *Two scales of temperature are used in science.*>

Existential clauses also sometimes have notional subjects that are definite noun phrases or proper nouns. For example:

*First there was **the scandal of Fergie romping with John Bryan, pictured exclusively in the Mirror**.* (NEWS)

*There is also **the group of non-benzenoid aromatic compounds**.* (ACAD)

As in these examples, the definite noun phrases usually occur when a series of new information elements is introduced, often marked explicitly with a linking adverbial or additive adverb (e.g. *first, also*).

.2.8 Adverbials in existential clauses

Often the important information of an existential clause is not simply that something exists, but when or where it exists. Thus, existential clauses often contain a time or place adverbial.

*I said, well, there's a wheelbarrow **down there**.* (CONV)

*There are no trains **on Sundays**.* (NEWS†)

As in these examples, the adverbial is often at the end of the clause. However, initial and medial placement is also possible:

1 ***Near the peak** there were no more trees, just rocks and grass.* (FICT)
2 *There rose **to her lips** always some exclamation of triumph over life when things came together in this peace, this rest, this eternity.* (FICT)

The placement of the adverbials is affected by the same conditions as adverbials of place and time in general (see 11.8). For example, in **1**, the adverbial creates cohesion in the text because it relates to previously mentioned information. The ordering agrees with the information-flow principle, with new information at the end of the clause.

12.9 Simple v. complex existential clauses

We have just described two ways that existential clauses can be expanded: with postmodification of the notional subject and with adverbials. Figure 12.3 shows that the majority of existential clauses have one or both kinds of expansion. Two elements of existential clauses contain little or no information: the verb (*be*, in most cases) and the grammatical subject *there*. As a result, it is not surprising that most existential clauses have additional information in adverbials or postmodifiers of the notional subject.

Consider these existential clauses that have both forms of expansion— an adverbial prepositional phrase and a postmodifying relative clause:

1 *There's stuff [in here]* <u>*we need.*</u>
   (CONV)

2 *In most cases a syllable is represented by only one character, but there are many cases [among the 558]* <u>*in which the same syllable is written in more ways than one.*</u>
   (ACAD†)

Figure 12.3
Existential clauses with and without expansion

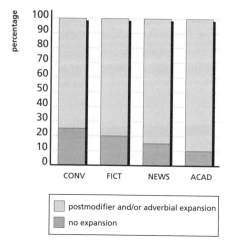

You can see that, without the expansion, the clauses would not convey much information: *There's stuff* (**1**), *There are many cases* (**2**). What is strange about **1** and **2** is that the relative clause (underlined) is separated from the rest of the notional subject by the adverbial (marked by *[]*). This is a symptom of the rather loose way in which expansions are added to the end of the notional subject.

Existential clauses without expansion occur in all four registers, but they are most common in conversation. There is a tendency in speech to present information in smaller chunks and to leave more for the listener to infer. These minimal existential clauses are often negative:

> *There's no bus.* (CONV)

> *Yeah, there really is no excuse, is there?* (CONV)

In these cases, the negative itself is important information.

12.10 Discourse functions of existential clauses

A Focusing on a new topic

It is often said that existential *there* is used to introduce new elements into the discourse. However, consider the example at the beginning of this Grammar Bite:

> *A man goes in the pub.* ***There****'s a bear sitting in the corner. He goes up to the, he goes up to the bartender. He says, why is* ***there*** *a bear sitting over there?* (CONV)

Notice that the first sentence introduces a new element: *a man*. However, this sentence does not use existential *there*. Instead, existential *there* is used twice when introducing the bear into the discourse. Significantly, the bear is the main 'character' in the story. Furthermore, when this utterance is spoken, stress falls on *bear*.

From this example, you see that existential *there* is used especially to focus on the existence or occurrence of something. Not only is this 'something new', but it is probably going to be a focus of the continuing discourse. Since existential *there* delays the new information until later in the clause, it is consistent with the information-flow principle. Often the new information comes at the end of the clause, thereby receiving end-focus.

One context where it is appropriate to focus on the existence of 'something new' is at the beginning of a story. Thus, fairytales often open with an existential clause:

> *Once upon a time* **there were** *three bears. Mama bear, Papa bear, baby bear – They all went for a walk down the woods.* (CONV) <mother reading to child>

Sometimes in informal narrative, the notional subject is further emphasized with the use of a demonstrative pronoun:

> *There was* **this really good-looking bloke** *and he was like – We, we'd given each other eyes over the bar in this pub and Lottie goes, well if you don't hurry up with him I'm gonna go and have him.* (CONV†) <note: *goes* = says>
>
> *There was* **this wonderful little old lady** *called the tissue collector. She was grey haired, quite dumpy with a white coat on and she came to collect sperm if you wanted it stored. She came up in front of my parents* <...> (NEWS†)

Again, notice that the narrative continues with further reference to the person introduced with existential *there*.

B **Introducing a series of new items**

Existential *there* is also used to develop text in another way. It is used to introduce a series of items:

> **There are** *many types of aid to medical decision making available. The earliest ones used* <...> (ACAD†)
>
> **There are** *three basic rules to consider in planning a farm enterprise*: <...> (ACAD†)

The existential clause sets up the elements that are to follow. Existential clauses also often introduce a series of 'new things' separately. For example:

1 *But* **there was** *a stillness about Ralph as he sat that marked him out:* **there was** *his size, and the attractive appearance; and most, obscurely, yet most powerfully,* **there was** *the conch.* (FICT)

2 *It was like heaven.* **There was** *candlelight, and* **there were** *bunks with quilts and blankets heaped on top.* **There was** *a table with a bottle of wine and a loaf of bread and a sausage on it.* **There were** *four bowls of soup.* **There were** *pictures of castles and lakes and pretty girls on the walls.* (FICT)

Major points of **GRAMMAR BITE B**: Existential *there* clauses

➤ Existential *there* is a grammatical subject but has no meaning content.
➤ Most existential clauses have the verb *be*, but the written registers use alternatives such as *exist, come,* and *follow.*
➤ The 'idea subject' of the existential clause is called the notional subject. It is usually an indefinite noun phrase.
➤ Many existential *there* clauses have adverbials or postmodification of the notional subject. This is because the obligatory elements of the clause usually contain little information.
➤ Existential clauses are used to introduce a new element (or series of elements) which is going to be the focus of the following discourse.

GRAMMAR BITE

C Other topics in word order

12.11 Dislocation

Dislocation has to do with how information is distributed in spoken language. It is not a simple word order option, but involves breaking up a clause-like structure into two separate chunks. A definite noun phrase is placed at one end of the clause, and a co-referential pronoun is used in the core of the clause. In the following example, | separates the two chunks, which each express an important piece of information:

> **This little shop** | *it's lovely.* (CONV)

The unmarked sentence structure would be: *This little shop is lovely.* With dislocation, *this little shop* is placed in initial position and repeated with the 'proxy' pronoun *it* in the core of the clause.

There are two types of dislocation. The above example is a **preface**: the definite noun phrase occurs in initial position. The definite noun phrase can also be after the clause—this is termed a **noun phrase tag**:

> *I think he's getting hooked on the taste of Vaseline,* **that dog.** (CONV)

12.11.1 Prefaces

Prefaces can precede both declarative and interrogative clauses. The relationship between the preface and its clause varies. In many cases, the preface is co-referential with a subject pronoun (underlined in the examples):

1 *Sharon she plays bingo on Sunday night.* (CONV)
2 *That picture of a frog, where is it?* (CONV)
3 *'That crazy Siberian, what's his name, he got one of the best houses in town.'* (FICT†)

A preface can also be co-referential with an object pronoun:

4 *Well* **Bryony** *it seemed to be a heavy cold that was making her feel miserable.* (CONV)

5 'But **Anna-Luise** – what could have attracted <u>her</u> to a man in his fifties?'
(FICT)

The pronoun can even be embedded in a dependent clause, as it is in **4** (*that was making <u>her</u> feel miserable*).

12.11.2 Noun phrase tags

Noun phrase tags may follow both declarative and interrogative clauses. The tag normally refers back to the subject of the preceding clause:

*Has <u>it</u> got double doors, **that shop**?* (CONV)

*Did <u>they</u> have any, **the kids**?* (CONV)

Sometimes the noun phrase tag is a demonstrative pronoun rather than a definite noun phrase:

*It was a good book **this**.* (CONV)

12.11.3 Functions and distribution of prefaces and noun phrase tags

Prefaces and noun phrase tags are relatively common in conversation, and they also occur occasionally in fictional dialog; they are very rare in ordinary written prose.

Prefaces serve to establish a topic. The same work can be done by separate clauses:

A: *When I went to the hospital today, **there was this girl, right**.*
B: *Yes.*
A: ***She** took an overdose.* (CONV†)

Prefaces are also a sign of the evolving nature of conversation. Notice how the first speaker appeals to the addressee by adding the discourse marker *right*. The addressee responds, and then the first speaker goes on to the main point.

The discourse functions of noun phrase tags are more difficult to pinpoint. Frequently they seem to have a clarifying function. It is possible that the speaker, after using a pronoun, may realize that the listener will not understand the referent, and thus the noun phrase tag is necessary clarification. Some noun phrases also seem to serve the principle of end-weight:

'<u>It</u> must have come as a bit of a shock, **the idea of, er, Rhiannon coming and settling down here after everything**.' (FICT)

When tags consist of a demonstrative pronoun, they obviously do not fit either the end-weight principle or the clarification function. In sentences such as the following, end-focus seems to give the noun phrase extra emphasis:

*That's marvelous **that**, isn't it yes?* (CONV)

2.12 Clefting

Clefting is similar to dislocation because information that could be given in a single simple clause is broken up. For clefting, the information is broken into two clauses, each with its own verb. There are two major types of cleft constructions: *it*-clefts and *wh*-clefts.

- *it*-cleft:

    1 *It's a man I want.* (FICT)
    <compare: *I want a man.*>

- *wh*-cleft:

    2 *What I want is something to eat, now!* (CONV)
    <compare: *I want something to eat.*>

Clefts are used to bring particular elements of the clause into additional focus, often for contrast. The extra focused element normally appears early in *it*-clefts and late in *wh*-clefts. Thus, in **1** *a man* is focused, and in **2** *something to eat* is focused. Both of these are direct objects in the basic clause structure *I want X*.

12.12.1 *It*-clefts

It-clefts consist of:

- the pronoun *it*
- a form of the verb *be*, optionally accompanied by *not* or an adverb such as *only*
- the focused element, which may be of the following types: a noun phrase, a prepositional phrase, an adverb phrase, or an adverbial clause
- a relative-like dependent clause introduced by *that*, *who/which*, or zero.

In the examples below, the specially focused element is in bold and the dependent clause is in *[]*:

- noun phrase:

    *His eyes were clear and brown and filled with an appropriate country shyness. It was **his voice** [that held me].* (FICT)

- prepositional phrase:

    *It was only **for the carrot** [that they put up with his abominable parties].* (FICT)

- adverb:

    *It is **here** [that the finite element analysis comes into its own].* (ACAD)

- adverbial clause:

    *It was **because they were frightened**, he thought, [that they had grown so small].* (FICT)

You can see that the focused element has various syntactic roles as well. For example, in **1**, *his voice* acts as subject of the dependent clause: *his voice held me*. In **2**, the focused prepositional phrase is a reason adverbial: *they put up with his abominable parties for the carrot*.

A rare variant of *it*-clefts has the focused element in initial position:

*The ceremony was in the hands of Mr Alexander Dubcek <...> **He** it was [who ushered in the new head of state to the dais] <...>* (NEWS†)

The combination of fronting and the *it*-cleft construction has a heightening effect. The meaning suggested is 'it was he and no one else'.

12.12.2 *Wh*-clefts

Wh-clefts consist of:

- a clause introduced by a *wh*-word, usually *what*; this clause has its own point of focus, usually at the end of the *wh*-clause
- a form of the verb *be*
- the specially focused nominal element: a noun phrase or a complement clause.

The specially focused element is in bold in the examples below, and the dependent *wh*-clause is placed in *[]*:

- noun phrase:

    *[What I really need] is **another credit card**.* (CONV)

- bare infinitive phrase:

    *[What you should do] is **tag them when they come in**.* (CONV)

- *to*-infinitive clause:

    *[What he did] was **to go to Holy Trinity Church**.* (FICT†)

Wh-clefts are less flexible than *it*-clefts in that they cannot be used to focus on a prepositional phrase:

> *It is **to that boy** [that she has remained faithful].* (FICT)
> <but not: **What she has remained faithful is to that boy*.>

On the other hand, *wh*-clefts have an advantage over *it*-clefts because they have a double emphasis: they give some emphasis to the opening nominal clause as well as to the element in final position.

12.12.3 Reversed and demonstrative *wh*-clefts

In general, reversed *wh*-clefts look like ordinary *wh*-clefts except that the *wh*-clause and the focused element switch positions. In the following, the reversed *wh*-clefts are underlined:

1 *There's a lot more darkness in this second TV series compared with the last one but **darkness** is <u>[what comedy is all about]</u>.* (NEWS†)
2 *'Poor Albert,' Carrie said <. . .> He heard what she said and shouted down to her, '**Help** is <u>[what I want]</u>, not your pity.'* (FICT†)

In some cases, as in **1**, the focused element is picked up from the preceding text (here, *darkness*). This accounts for its early placement. In **2** the initial placement seems to be used to emphasize the contrast between *help* and *pity*.

Another related structure has a demonstrative pronoun (usually *that*) followed by a form of *be* plus a dependent clause introduced by a *wh*-word:

> ***That**'s [how I spent my summer vacation].* (FICT)
>
> ***This** is [what it means to say such systems are effective mixing devices].* (ACAD)

These structures usually cannot be reversed (**How I spent my summer vacation is that*). Similar to many reversed *wh*-clefts, they open with a reference to preceding text. We refer to them as demonstrative *wh*-clefts.

12.12.4 Distribution of cleft constructions

Figure 12.4 shows that both conversation and the written registers use clefts, but the different types of clefts have different distributions across the registers.

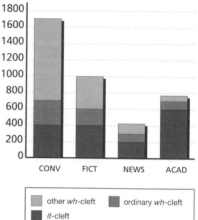

Figure 12.4
Frequency of cleft types

It-clefts are relatively common in all registers but most common in academic prose. *It*-clefts are typically contrastive:

> But it wasn't **the colour of his eyes** *[that was peculiar to him],* *it was the way he walked.* (FICT)

Because the focused elements occurs early in the sentence, the *it*-cleft is suitable for expressing a connection with the preceding discourse:

> *These are the faculties which make clerks into merchants, and merchants into millionaires. It is* **these** *[which enable the discontented clerk to earn more than eighty pounds a year].* (ACAD)

It-clefts can allow very precise statements to be made. They are also particularly useful in academic prose for presenting information as 'given', or known. Consider this example:

> *It is in fact the case that whereas not all the early investigators even tried to validate their reasoning, several, including Cauchy, Servois and Boole, certainly did. And it was* **in this connection** *[that Servois, in 1815, introduced the notions of functions which are 'distributive' and 'commutative', terms still used today].* (ACAD†)

The information in the subordinate clause is presented as known, or taken for granted. Such clefts often occur in written texts, where they help to draw the line between what is presupposed and what is treated as new information.

Wh-clefts are more associated with conversation than the written registers. The focused element in *wh*-clefts is at the end, in agreement with the information-flow principle. The purpose of the construction is to signal what is taken as background and what is the main communicative point:

> *No that's Nescafe. [What we usually have] is* **Maxwell House from work.** (CONV)

This example occurred in a context where different sorts of coffee are discussed. The main communicative point is at the end of the sentence. That is, the new information is about *Maxwell House*. *Wh*-clefts are often used in conversations as a starting point for an utterance: *what I think . . . , what I want to say . . . , what we need . . . , what this means . . .*

Demonstrative *wh*-clefts show the biggest differences across registers: relatively common in conversation but very rare in academic prose. The difference is probably one of formality and also the low information content that is common in these *wh*-clauses:

> *That's what I thought.* (CONV†)

Word order choices after the verb

In general, there is little variation in the order of the core elements towards the end of the clause. However, there are a few options worth considering.

12.13.1 The placement of direct objects and indirect objects

Ditransitive verbs often allow two options that are equivalent in meaning:

- indirect object + direct object:

  > *I'll fix [you$_{<IO>}$] [some tea$_{<DO>}$] later.* (FICT)

- direct object + preposition *to* or *for* + prepositional object:

  > *I'll fix [it$_{<DO>}$] [for [you$_{<PO>}$]].* (FICT)

For the indirect object + direct object pattern, the principle of end-weight is most important. The indirect object is very short in most cases:

> *The Academy never granted [**him**] [the membership that was his life's ambition].* (NEWS)

In the prepositional pattern, the prepositional phrase is often longer than the direct object. In addition, the prepositional phrase is often a clearer way to communicate the syntactic relationship. The prepositional phrase may even be placed before the direct object:

> *This irregularity in her features was not grotesque, but charming, and gave [to [Anastasia's face$_{<PO>}$]][a humor she herself did not possess$_{<DO>}$].* (FICT)

12.13.2 Pronoun sequences as direct and indirect objects

Where both the direct and the indirect objects are personal pronouns, there are three major patterns:

1. direct object + *to*-phrase: '*Give **it to me**, Pauli.*' (FICT)
2. indirect object + direct object: *Give **me it**, you little cow!* (CONV) <note: cow is an insult here>
3. direct object + indirect object: '*Do let me give **it him***', she said. (FICT)

The first pattern, direct object + *to*-phrase, is the most common in all the registers. This is probably because it is the clearest way to mark the syntactic relationships in the clause. In patterns **2** and **3**, there is no overt signal to show which pronoun is the indirect object and which the direct. The correct interpretation must be determined from the context. Pattern **2**, indirect object + direct object, occurs almost exclusively in conversation. Pattern **3** occurs in conversation and fiction, but is relatively rare in both.

12.13.3 Clauses with direct object and object predicative

A direct object usually precedes an object predicative. However, the object may be postponed to the end position under particular circumstances. In the following examples, the object predicative is underlined and the postponed direct object is marked in bold:

> Each region has a responsibility to create and make <u>available</u> **a collection of contemporary work.** (NEWS†)
>
> <compare: Each region has a responsibility to create a collection of contemporary work and make it <u>available.</u>>

The object predicative is light in such cases in comparison with the direct object, which is long and complex. Where the direct object is a pronoun or a short noun-headed phrase, it must precede the object predicative.

> I can make **you** <u>available to people,</u> yeah? (CONV†)
>
> <compare: *I can make <u>available to people</u> you.>
>
> He made **it** <u>impossible.</u> (FICT)
>
> <compare: *He made <u>impossible</u> it.>

12.13.4 Placement of objects of phrasal verbs

For transitive phrasal verbs, direct objects (DO) can be placed before or after the adverbial particle (AP). In the following examples, the adverbial particle is underlined, and the direct object is marked in bold:

> 1 Why do you like picking <u>up</u> **the telephone** so much? (CONV)
> 2 How fast can you pick **it** <u>up</u>? (CONV)

Where the direct object is a pronoun, it is usually placed between the verb and the particle (over 90 per cent of the time), as in **2**. However, when the direct object is an indefinite pronoun, it is often placed after the adverbial particle:

> He's going to – er – pick <u>up</u> **somebody** somewhere. (CONV†)
>
> He sent <u>out</u> **someone** to capture the bounty hunter. (FICT†)

When the direct object is a full noun, there is more variation in its placement. In conversation, over 60 per cent of the occurrences have the order direct object + adverbial particle. However, in the written registers less than 10 per cent of the occurrences have this order. In general, placement follows the principle of end-weight, with heavy direct objects placed after the adverbial particle.

Two other factors are particularly interesting in the placement of the direct object. First, the placement depends somewhat on the nature of the phrasal verb. Some phrasal verbs, such as *take up* and *make out*, are idiomatic. That is, *up* and *out* do not have their literal meanings. In these cases, adverbial particle + direct object is preferred. Other phrasal verbs can have a more literal meaning, such as *take out*, where *out* still has a spatial meaning. In these cases, direct object + adverbial particle is more usual. You can see the contrast in the following examples with *carry out*, which has both an idiomatic and literal meaning:

- idiomatic meaning, adverbial particle + direct object:

  *Now carry <u>out</u> **the instructions**.* (FICT)
- literal meaning, direct object + adverbial particle:

  *The Germans carried **the corpse** <u>out</u>.* (FICT)

The second factor is the use of adverbials. Typically, direct object + adverbial particle is preferred when the particle is followed by an adverbial. For example:

  *Paul took **his friend** <u>up</u> to the top floor.* (FICT)

  *Last week a husband took **his wife** <u>out</u> for a drive.* (NEWS†)

In these cases, the particle and adverbial are closely related in meaning and so are placed together.

2.14 Summary: syntactic choices in conversation v. academic prose

With the exception of existential clauses, the special word-order choices covered in this chapter are relatively rare. This does not mean that the devices are unimportant. When they are used well, they can contribute greatly to the coherence and effectiveness of a text. The devices that are chosen most often, however, vary across the registers. For a final review of these patterns of variation, we focus on conversation and academic prose, the registers which tend to differ the most. (Although the passive was discussed in an earlier chapter (6.6–8), we include it here. Other structures, like extraposition (Ch. 10) and adverbial position (Ch. 11) have been fully described in earlier chapters.)

In the following, + and – indicate higher v. lower relative frequency:

	CONV	ACAD
marked word order (fronting, inversion, etc.)	–	+
passive constructions	–	+
existential *there*	+	–
prefaces and noun phrase tags	+	–
demonstrative *wh*-clefts	+	–

As you can see, marked word order and passive constructions are more common in academic prose. These choices are more complex structures, reflecting the complexity of academic content and the opportunity to edit and rewrite.

Existential *there*, prefaces, noun phrase tags, and demonstrative *wh*-clefts are more common in conversation. Conversation is produced without planning and editing, and production demands are eased by the use of prefaces and tags and, in general, by shorter and simpler clauses—including short existential clauses. The language of conversation is also less varied and relies more on brief stereotyped expressions, including demonstrative *wh*-clefts such as *That's what I thought.*

Review

Major points of **GRAMMAR BITE C**: Other topics in word order

➤ There are several additional ways of manipulating word order for such purposes as focus, cohesion, contrast, and end-weight.

➤ There are two types of dislocation: prefaces and noun phrase tags.

➤ They occur almost exclusively in conversation, and help to break the discourse up into manageable 'chunks'.

➤ Clefts are another special construction type, subdivided into *it*-clefts and *wh*-clefts.

➤ Both types allow special emphasis to be put on a particular element.

➤ *It*-clefts are used especially for contrast and cohesion. They are particularly common in academic prose.

➤ *Wh*-clefts show typical information flow, though some have very little new information. They are informal and most common in conversation.

➤ There are also a few word order options following the verb: the placement of direct objects, indirect objects, object predicatives, and objects of phrasal verbs.

➤ The options for word order are used with different frequencies across the registers.

13

The grammar of conversation

GRAMMAR BITES in this chapter

A A functional overview of conversational grammar

> ➤ The special circumstances of conversation compared with other registers
> ➤ How these circumstances are reflected in conversational grammar, as contrasted with the grammar of written language

B Grammar tailored to real-time construction

> ➤ How conversational grammar is structurally adapted to real-time production
> ➤ Key aspects of this adaptation: dysfluencies, the add-on strategy, non-clausal units, and ellipsis

C Grammar, lexis, and discourse

> ➤ Lexical bundles as an interface between grammar and lexis
> ➤ Inserts as an interface between grammar and discourse

13.1 **Introduction**

Earlier chapters looked at the grammar of conversation in terms of its contrast with the three written registers of fiction, news, and academic writing. In this chapter, we focus on conversation as a variety of language worth studying in itself.

First, in Grammar Bite A, we summarize conversational features that have been covered throughout this book. This summary shows what is special about conversational grammar, compared with the written registers. We interpret conversational grammar in terms of six functional traits.

In Grammar Bite B, we concentrate on grammar construction in terms of real-time processing. We consider how grammatical structure is shaped by the fact that people have to compose and interpret spoken utterances in real time, without the leisure of revising and re-reading which writers and readers have.

Grammar Bite C finally looks at two factors of great interest which are on the boundaries of grammar, lexis, and discourse: the use of lexical bundles and of inserts.

Since almost all the examples in this chapter are from conversation, we do not mark them as '(CONV)'. However, when the dialect is important, we distinguish examples from our American and British subcorpora by using the labels '(AmE)' and '(BrE)'.

13.1.1 **An example of conversation**

To begin, we present a conversational extract which exemplifies many typical features of conversation. It will be used as an illustrative sample in the survey of features in Grammar Bite A:

Conversation sample: SERVING CHILI

(Setting: A family of four is sitting down to dinner)

(Participants: *P* = the mother, *J* = the father, *D* = their 20-year-old son, *M* = their 17-year-old son)

D1:   *Mom, I, give me a rest, give it a rest. I didn't think about you. I mean, I would rather do it.* <unclear> *some other instance in my mind.*

P1:   *Yeah, well I can understand you know, I mean* <unclear> *Hi I'm David's mother, try to ignore me.*

D2:   *I went with a girl like you once. Let's serve this damn chili.*

M1:   *Okay, let's serve the chili. Are you serving or not dad?*

J1:   *Doesn't matter.*

P2:   *Would you get those chips in there. Michael, could you put them with the crackers.*

J2:   *Here, I'll come and serve it honey if you want me to.*

P3:   *Oh wait, we still have quite a few.*

D3:   *I don't see any others.*

P4:   *I know you don't.*

D4:   *We don't have any others.*

P5:   *Yes, I got you the big bag I think it will be a help to you.*

J3:   *Here's mom's.*

M2:   *Now this isn't according to grandpa now.*

P6:   *Okay.*
M3:   *The same man who told me it's okay* <unclear>
P7:   *Are you going to put water in our cups? Whose bowl is that?*
M4:   *Mine.*
P8:   *Mike put all the water in here. Well, here we are.*
J4:   *What.*
P9:   *Will y'all turn off the TV.*
J5:   *Pie, I'll kill you, I said I'd take you to the bathroom.*
P10:   *Man, get your tail out of the soup – Oh, sorry – Did you hear I saw Sarah's sister's baby?*
M5:   *How is it?*
P11:   *She's cute, pretty really.*
       <note: *damn* is a semi-taboo word and may be offensive to some people>

This dinner table interaction touches on several apparently unrelated topics. Speakers refer to the dinner event (e.g. water, chili, crackers, cups, bowl), to other people (grandpa, Sarah's sister's baby), and to a household pet (named 'Pie'), in addition to mentioning an imaginary situation in which *P* speaks (in turn *P1*), switching off the television, and past meetings. Some lines are puzzling out of context (e.g. *No this isn't according to grandpa now; Oh sorry;* and *Man, get your tail out of the soup*). A great deal of shared background information and a shared setting are needed to understand this conversation fully. In these respects, the extract is typical of conversation.

GRAMMAR BITE

A A functional overview of conversational grammar

13.2 The discourse circumstances of conversation

In this section, we identify a range of social and situational characteristics of conversation, and discuss their association with particular grammatical traits that are common in conversation. In doing so, we pull together information about features that have been covered throughout all the chapters of this book. Our survey of linguistic features in this chapter has to be selective: there are other important linguistic features distinguishing speech from writing—such as stress and intonation—as well as additional grammatical features that we do not have space to cover here.

In the following subsections (13.2.1–6), we underline the grammatical features that are particularly characteristic of conversation, as compared with the written registers.

13.2.1 Conversation takes place in shared context

Conversation is typically carried out in face-to-face interaction with others. Speakers usually share a lot of contextual background, including a large amount of specific social, cultural, and institutional knowledge. This is one major reason why transcriptions of conversations are often difficult to understand.

Consistent with this shared knowledge, conversation has a very high frequency of pronouns and a very low frequency of nouns. The user of personal pronouns (by far the most common class of pronouns) normally assumes that we share knowledge of the intended reference of *you*, *she*, *it*, etc. First- and second-person pronouns (especially *I* and *you*), referring directly to participants in the conversation, are the most common in conversation. In fact, they account for almost two-thirds of the personal pronouns in 'Serving chili'.

The shared context of conversation is also associated with the use of substitute pro-forms and ellipsis. In **1**, *do it* substitutes for a verb phrase, and in **2** *others* substitutes for a noun phrase:

> **1** *I mean, I would rather* **do it**. (*D1*)
> **2** *I don't see any* **others**. (*D3*)

As with these examples, the meaning of pro-forms is generally impossible to tell without the context of the conversation. Some utterances with ellipsis are equally difficult to interpret without the context:

> *I know you don't* ^. (*P4*) <i.e. *I know you don't see any others*>

Ellipsis (signaled here by ^) is discussed in more detail in 13.5.

Another type of reliance on context shows in the use of deictic words (*this*, *that*, *these*, *those*, *there*, *then*, *now*, etc.), most of which are particularly common in conversation. In 'Serving chili', deictics include, for example:

> **this** *damn chili* (*D2*)   **those** *chips in* **there** (*P2*)
> **Here**'s *mom's* (*J3*)   *Whose bowl is* **that**? (*P7*)

A further context-bound factor is the use of non-clausal or fragmentary components in speech. Although such material can be found in written language (e.g. in headlines and lists), it is far more pervasive and varied in speech. **Inserts** are especially common. For example, in 'Serving chili':

> *yeah* (*P1*)   *okay* (*M1*)   *sorry* (*P10*)

These inserts rely heavily for their interpretation on situational factors. For example, *thanks* or *sorry* may be a follow-up to a non-verbal action, as well as to a verbal one, as the example *Oh, sorry* in *P10* shows. (See 13.7 for more about the functions and frequency of inserts.)

13.2.2 Conversation avoids elaboration or specification of meaning

Because it relies on context for meaning, conversation can do without the lexical and syntactic elaboration that is found in written expository registers. Conversation has a low density of lexical words in comparison with the three written registers (relying instead more on function words, especially pronouns). Similarly, it tends to have shorter phrases than the expository written registers.

This factor of syntactic non-elaboration is strongly centered on the noun phrase. Speakers in conversation make the most use of pronouns, often reducing the noun phrase to a simple monosyllable like *it* or *she*. Speakers use fewer elaborated noun phrase structures that contain modifiers and complements. Attributive adjectives, noun modifiers and relative clauses, for instance, are rare in comparison with the other registers.

In contrast to its lower lexical density generally, conversation has a higher frequency of verbs and adverbs than the other registers (especially primary and modal verbs). In a register where the noun phrase is reduced to bare essentials, verb phrases and clauses become more frequent.

The one notable exception to this general lack of syntactic elaboration is in the use of complement clauses: *that-* complement clauses and *wh-* complement clauses are actually more common in conversation than in the informational written registers:

> *Do you think **they will come back from Europe?***
>
> *I don't know **how much it costs.***

Interestingly, these dependent clause types are often used as part of relatively fixed **lexical bundles** (see 13.6 below), and they typically express meanings related to personal stance rather than the dense propositional information associated with elaborated noun phrases in news and academic prose (see 13.2.4 below).

Avoidance of elaboration of syntax is related to avoidance of specification of meaning. Just as speakers in conversation often avoid making their noun references explicit, they also tend to avoid being specific about quantity and quality. Speakers' tendency towards vagueness has been noted, and often condemned, by critics, who say the speakers are 'lazy'. The frequent use of **hedges** is an example:

> *<...> we had to **like** hold each other's hands.*
>
> *I've got order forms and **stuff like that** for music.*
>
> *And she's just turned over eighty **odd**.*

From the viewpoint of the written language, this vagueness seems to be an unacceptable lack of precision. But, from the viewpoint of speakers, greater precision is unnecessary, or even harmful because it could hold up the progress of the conversation. Hints and rough indications, relying on shared knowledge, are often just what is needed.

13.2.3 Conversation is interactive

Conversation is co-constructed by two or more people, adapting their expressions to the ongoing exchange. This is reflected in the frequency of several features:

A Negatives

Conversation has twice as many negatives as the written registers. The cognitive interaction of different speakers often results in negative utterances. For example, in 'Serving chili':

> *D3: I **don't** see any others.*
>
> *P4: I know you **don't**.*
>
> *D4: We **don't** have any others.*

B Eliciting responses

Conversation has many utterances which elicit or make a response. Sequences of question–answer are typical, as in this example from 'Serving chili':

> P3: *Whose bowl is that.*
> M4: *Mine.*

Many questions are non-clausal fragments such as *Really?* and *What for?* Such questions play an important role in the interactive nature of the conversation. In addition, about one-quarter of the questions in conversation take the form of questions tags.

> *You've got the cards, **haven't you?***
>
> *She didn't ride back, **did she?***

Question tags combine an assertion with a request for confirmation, thus illustrating the characteristic negotiation of acceptance between interlocutors. In comparison to conversation, question tags account for only about 1 in 100 questions in academic prose.

Other common features in conversation that elicit or make a response include the following:

- greetings and farewells:

> A: **Hi** Margaret.   A: *Oh.* **Goodbye** Robin.
> B: **Hi.**   B: **See you later.** *Thank you for a lift. Love you lots.*

- backchannels:

> A: *and their lawn is high up, up the road, you know*
> B: **Mm**
> C: **Yeah**
> A: *so he dug up the lawn and put a little garage in*

- response elicitors:

> *Just leave out the smutty stuff, **okay?***
>
> *It's like a magnet obviously **see?***

- imperatives:

> **Get** *on the phone and* **phone** *them up!*

C Attention-signaling forms

Conversation has a number of attention-signaling forms. For example:

> **Hey, hey** *look at all the truckers.*
>
> **Say,** *Mom, have you got any paint rollers?*

D Vocatives

Conversation commonly uses vocatives (address forms) for getting attention and managing interactions. 'Serving chili' has several clear examples: *Mom* (in *D1*), *dad* (*M1*), *Michael* (*P2*), *honey* (*J2*), *Mike* (*P8*), and *Pie* (*J5*, addressed to the dog). Vocatives often have an attitudinal function in addition to managing the discourse, especially for terms such as *honey* (discussed in 13.2.4).

E Discourse markers

Conversation has a frequent use of discourse markers and other inserts for managing interaction (see 13.7, Table 13.1).

13.2.4 Conversation expresses stance

Speakers in conversation have a primary concern for their feelings, attitudes, evaluations, and assessments of likelihood: what we have referred to as personal stance. Many of the most common grammatical features in conversation are used to express stance, including modal verbs, complement clause constructions, and stance adverbials.

Being interactive, conversation is used for polite or respectful purposes in **speech acts** such as requests, greetings, offers, and apologies. Some inserts have a stereotypical role in marking politeness: *thanks* and *thank you*, *please*, and *sorry*, for example. Vocatives such as *sir* and *madam* also have a respectful role, although these honorific forms are rare in English compared with many other languages.

More typical of English is the use of stereotypic polite openings, such as the interrogative forms *would you* and *could you*, functioning as requests in 'Serving chili':

> P2: **Would you** get those chips in there. Michael, **could you** put them with the crackers.

In other cases, the collective first-person imperative *let's* is used as a somewhat less face-threatening alternative to the second-person (*you*) imperative:

> M1: Okay, **let's** serve the chili.

However, not all forms in conversation convey respect. For example, second-person imperatives also occur in 'Serving chili' as a balder form of directive, addressed in one case by a son to his mother (**1**) and in another case to the dog (**2**):

> 1 **give** it a rest (D1)
> 2 **get** your tail out of the soup (P10)

Conversation also typically displays a varied range of attitudes. Special features used for these purposes include:

- endearments such as the following are far more common within vocatives than honorific forms such as *sir* and *madam*:

  > Yes I'm coming in a moment **darling**.

- interjections such as *ah*, *oh*, *wow*, *ugh*, and expletives, such as *bloody* and *damn*:

  > A: She burnt popcorn back there.
  > B: **Ugh** it reeks.

  > **Wow**, that's incredible.

  > **Bloody hell**! He's gone mad. (BrE) <note: *bloody*, *hell*, and *damn* are taboo words ('swearwords'), and may be offensive to some people >

- exclamations:

  > What a rip-off!
  > How wonderful! Good for you!
  > Timmy! Sit down! Good boy!

- evaluative predicative adjectives (*good, lovely, nice*, etc.):

    *I thought that was real **nice**.*

    *I don't think it's too **bad**.*

- stance adverbials:

    *P11: She's cute, pretty **really**.*

    *Well, I like the Caesar salad **actually**.*

13.2.5 Conversation takes place in real time

Speakers are under pressure in conversation to produce language quickly. There is little time for planning and no time for editing, in contrast to writing. Several characteristics of conversation reflect this real-time production pressure.

A Dysfluencies

Conversation often sounds dysfluent. For example, it is quite natural for a speaker's flow to be held up by pauses, hesitators (e.g. *er, um*), and repeats (e.g. *I – I – I*) at points where the speaker needs more time to plan ahead:

*Hopefully, **he'll, er, he'll** see the error of his ways.*

Repairs are often made; a speaker stops in the middle of saying something, and repeats it with some sort of correction. When they occur at the beginning of utterances, such repairs are also called 'false starts':

*D1: Mom, **I**, give me a rest, give it a rest.*

*Dad, **I don't think you sh–**, I think you should leave Chris home Saturday.*

Other kinds of dysfluencies are covered in 13.3.1.

B Reduced forms

To save time and energy, speakers also resort to reduction processes such as elision (omission of vowels or consonants), contractions like *it's* and *can't*, other morphologically reduced forms like *gonna*, and various types of ellipsis, which are covered in 13.5.

C Restricted and repetitive repertoire

The language used in conversation is typically repetitive in several ways.

- Local repetition: in relieving real-time planning pressure, speakers often repeat partially or exactly what has just been said in conversation. Here is an example from 'Serving chili':

    D2: <. . .> Let's serve this damn chili.

    M1: Okay, let's serve the chili

- Lexical bundles: in 13.6 we describe the use of prefabricated sequences of words, lexical bundles. Time pressure prevents speakers from exploiting the full innovative power of grammar and lexicon, and so they rely heavily on well-worn, routine word sequences, readily accessible from memory.

- Higher frequency of a few items in syntactic categories: in any syntactic category—from modals to subordinators, adverbs, and lexical verbs— conversation tends to make extremely frequent use of a small group of items, while the written registers tend to use a more diverse group of items.

For example, conversation makes repeated use of four modals *will, can, would,* and *could.* These are the only modals used in 'Serving chili'.

Other characteristics reflecting real-time processing in spoken English will be considered in Grammar Bite B (13.3–5).

13.2.6 Conversation employs a vernacular range of expression

Conversation typically takes place privately between people who know one another. It is little influenced by the traditions of prestige and correctness often associated with the printed word. Instead, the style of conversation is overwhelmingly informal. This shows in 'Serving chili' in informal lexical choice (e.g. *get, damn,* and *cute*). Reduced forms such as contractions (e.g. *it's* and *don't*) are also considered informal.

Another aspect of vernacular grammar is the occurrence of regional dialect forms. For example, in 'Serving chili', turn *P9* contains the second-person pronoun *y'all,* associated with the southern states of the USA.

Moreover, in some conversational material we find morphological forms widely regarded as non-standard, such as the multiple negative (see 8.8.12) and the concord of *he* with *don't* in:

> He **don't** have **no** manners.

Other forms are marginally non-standard, such as the negative verb form *ain't* or the combination *aren't I* (see 8.8.5). In pronoun choice, speakers often use the accusative form *me* when prescriptive rules call for the subject form *I.* In the following example, the speaker changes from *I* to *me* as he makes a coordinated noun phrase:

> But somehow I, **me and this other bloke** managed to avoid each other.

Review

Major points of **GRAMMAR BITE A**: A functional overview of conversational grammar
➤ Conversation is shaped by several discourse circumstances:
  ➤ It takes place in a shared context.
  ➤ It avoids elaboration or specification of meaning.
  ➤ It is interactive.
  ➤ It expresses politeness, emotion, attitude.
  ➤ It takes place in real time.
  ➤ It employs a vernacular range of expression.
➤ All these features of conversation show up clearly in the way grammar is used.

GRAMMAR BITE

B Grammar tailored to real-time construction

13.3 Performance phenomena in conversation

In this Grammar Bite, we take a closer look at the demands of real-time language production and processing. Speakers and listeners have no time to revise or reconsider the grammatical structures being produced during spontaneous speech; as a result, conversational grammar typically lacks much of the elaborate structure of the written sentence. In many ways, the construction of syntactic units in speech aims at simplicity—through **the add-on strategy**, through **non-clausal units**, and through **ellipsis**. However, even notions of 'simplicity' or 'complexity' need to be adjusted when applied to spoken language.

As noted above, the time pressure on speakers in conversation often results in **dysfluencies**. In extreme cases, an utterance may become almost grammatically incoherent. For example:

> *No. Do you know erm you know where the erm go over to er go over erm where the fire station is not the one that white white . . .*

Such extreme cases usually occur in extreme circumstances. Here the speaker is trying to explain to members of her family how to reach a local shopping area. Her problems are cognitive as well as syntactic. She is simultaneously building a mental map, visualizing the best route, estimating the hearer's familiarity with the area, and explaining the route.

In contrast, consider the following example, which is quite long and appears to be grammatically quite complex (the speaker is talking about his dog):

> *The trouble is if you're if you're the only one in the house he follows you and you're looking for him and every time you're moving around he's moving around behind you <laughter> so you can't find him. I thought I wonder where the hell he's gone <laughter> I mean he was immediately behind me.*

Here the only dysfluency is the initial repetition of *if you're*. It occurs because of overlapping speech from another speaker.

Thus, conversation can be characterized both by dysfluencies and by well-formed long utterances. In the next two sections, we examine some typical dysfluencies and a strategy that speakers use to adapt to real-time processing pressure.

13.3.1 More on dysfluencies

In 13.2.5 we mentioned that pauses, hesitators, and repeats are typical of conversation. Here we review two other common types of dysfluencies: incomplete utterances and syntactic blends.

A Incomplete utterances

Leaving an utterance uncompleted is not always an unplanned dysfluency, but it usually is. There are four main situations where the speaker starts to utter a grammatical unit and fails to finish, as described below.

- Incompletion followed by a fresh start. (Unlike reformulations, no part of the first start is repeated.)

  Do you know the name of the? – *I don't know what's up there.*

  That's such a neat, *it's so nice to know the history behind it.*

- Incompletion where the speaker is interrupted by another speaker. The first speaker may stop immediately, as in **1**, or there may be overlap between the speakers, as in **2** (words in curly brackets { } show overlaps):

  1 A: *There's a whole bunch of Saturdays.* **If you just put your**
     B: *This is a Sunday.*
     A: *No, no, no.*

  2 A: *So, uh, I saw him, I took him to lunch and, I, I,* **I'm surprised at how**
     {old}
     B: *{Mature he is?}*
     A: *Yeah,* **he really {has}**
     B: *{Yeah, he seemed}* *to be that way.*

- Incompletion where the hearer rather than the speaker completes the utterance.

  3 A: *I played,* **I played against erm**
     B: **Southend.**

  4 A: *She pays a certain amount,* **but erm – you get erm**
     B: **Subsidised.**
     A: *That's right. Yeah.*

In fact, utterances such as these are not incomplete, but rather show co-construction of the discourse by the participants. It can be difficult to distinguish between interruptions and cooperative co-construction. Here the co-construction seems cooperative. In **3**, the completion by B is signaled by the preceding hesitation by speaker A, who is probably having some difficulty finding the missing word. In **4**, A also seems to be having some trouble finding the right word, and accepts B's completion as appropriate.

- Abandoning the utterance, with no interruption or attempt at repair.

  A: **So it was just, you know**.
  B: *Yeah.*

The motive for incompletion in this case may not be clear. Perhaps the speaker loses the thread of what he or she is saying, or doesn't bother to complete because the hearer seems to have already understood the intention behind the utterance.

B Syntactic blends

The term **syntactic blend** is applied to a sentence or clause that finishes in a way that is grammatically inconsistent with the way it began. This type of performance error appears to be caused mainly by speakers' working memory limitations. These clauses tend to be fairly long, which suggests that the speakers suffer from a kind of syntactic memory loss in the course of production. Syntactic blends tend to be easy to understand even though they are not grammatically well-formed.

The following examples erroneously contain two verbs. After each example, we add two likely reconstructions, to show the two competing syntactic models the speaker appears to have confused:

1 *About a hundred, two hundred years ago* **we had** *ninety-five per cent of people – i– in this country* **were employed** *in farming.*
   <**a** *Ninety-five per cent of people in this country* <u>were employed</u> *in farming.*>
   <**b** <u>We had</u> *ninety-five per cent of people in this country* <u>employed</u> *in farming.*>

2 *In fact* **that's** *one of the things that there is a shortage of in this play,* **is** *people who actually care er, erm – about what happens to erm each, each other.*
   <**a** *One of the things that there is a shortage of in this play* <u>is</u> *people who actually care.*>
   <**b** <u>That's</u> *one of the things that there is a shortage of in this play, people who actually care.*>

13.3.2 The add-on strategy

Although dysfluency is normal in speech, there are many quite complex utterances which contain little or no sign of planning difficulty. This appears to be because speakers are skilled at adapting their language to the time constraints of conversation. Consider again the utterance in 13.3, with clauses now marked in brackets and the repeat omitted:

1 *[The trouble is [[if you're the only one in the house] [he follows you] [and you're looking for him] [so you can't find him]]] [I thought [I wonder [where the hell he's gone]]] [I mean [he was immediately behind me]].*

The analysis seems complex: there is a combination of eleven clauses, with six examples of embedding and one of co-ordination. How does a speaker manage to produce such a complex structure with just one small repeat?

This task is not so superhuman as it may appear. If we divide the utterance in a more basic way, simply using vertical lines for clause boundaries, the utterance neatly divides into a linear sequence of short finite-clause-like segments. These follow in line without overlap or interruption, following an add-on strategy:

1a *| The trouble is | if you're the only one in the house | he follows you | and you're looking for him | so you can't find him. | I thought | I wonder | where the hell he's gone | I mean | he was immediately behind me.|*

The semantic relationships between the clause-like units are important to the overall interpretation, but each unit expresses what can be considered a single idea, and within each unit, the processing required is simple. For example, each unit except the first has a pronoun subject.

This breakdown of speech into clause-like segments can be contrasted with an attempt to apply such an analysis to academic writing:

| *Despite the abnormal morphogenesis observed in such grafts, the range of differentiated tissues formed in such an 'experimental teratoma' can be used to provide an estimate of the developmental potential of the transferred tissue.| (ACAD)

Here there are no internal vertical lines marking the boundaries of finite clause-like segments, because there are no such boundaries. There is only one finite independent clause in the whole sentence.

Through the add-on strategy, the grammar of speech, unlike the grammar of writing, is well adapted to real-time production. It is sometimes supposed that the grammar of spoken language is simpler than the grammar of written language because of less subordination. However, this is a misleading conclusion. Some types of dependent clauses (e.g. *that*-clauses, finite adverbial clauses) are more common in speech than in writing. In subordination, as in other aspects of structure, spoken language favors the kinds of complexity that do not conflict with the add-on strategy. Consider the following:

   2 *I think [you'll find [it counts towards your income]].*

Here the double embedding (one clause within another within another) does not mean that the sentence is difficult to produce or to understand. This is clearer if we present the same sentence with the add-on strategy in mind:

   2a |*I think | you'll find | it counts towards your income.*|

Prefaces and tags

Another example of the add-on strategy is the use of prefaces and tags. These are peripheral elements that precede or follow the main body of the speaker's message. Consider:

   North and south London – they're two different worlds, aren't they? – in a way.

This utterance can be analyzed as a simple main clause with a preface and tags added on:

preface	body of message	tags
north and south London	they're two different worlds	aren't they? in a way

Using utterances with prefaces and tags, a speaker can cope with real-time production, and at the same time convey fairly complex messages. The example above is much easier to produce than this equivalent integrated structure:

   Don't you agree that north and south London are in some ways two different worlds?

Many different kinds of units can act as prefaces and tags. For example, linking or stance adverbials can be prefaces (e.g. *What's more* ... , *To be honest* ...), as can formulaic utterance launchers (e.g. *The question is* ... or *Like I say* ...). Tags can be question tags, comment clause tags (e.g. *I don't think*), or vagueness markers (e.g. ... *and stuff like that*).

13.4 Non-clausal units

As illustrated throughout this chapter, much of the discourse in conversation cannot be analyzed in terms of grammatical clauses: instead, non-clausal units play important roles. We distinguish two general kinds of non-clausal units: inserts and syntactic non-clausal units. Inserts are stand-alone words, such as interjections and discourse markers. These will be covered in 13.7. In this section we consider syntactic non-clausal units.

13.4.1 Syntactic non-clausal units

Syntactic non-clausal units are grammatical units that lack finite clause structure. Two examples are *Poor kids* (a noun phrase) and *Good for you* (an adjective phrase). The short 'fragmentary' units do not have the structure of an independent clause, nor are they a part of an independent clause. Like other performance phenomena, non-clausal units reflect the simplicity of grammatical constructions resulting from real-time production in conversation.

Syntactic non-clausal units can also be related to ellipsis. For example, *Perfect!* as a response is equivalent to the clause *That's perfect* with the subject and verb omitted. However, it is often difficult to reconstruct the full clause in these cases, because different wordings are possible (*That's perfect, It's perfect, Wasn't that perfect*). For this reason, we treat these as non-clausal units, rather than clausal units with elements omitted.

The following are some of the major types of non-clausal units.

A Condensed questions

Many questions in conversation occur as noun phrases or a verbless structure beginning with a *wh*-word:

> *More sauce?*
>
> *How about your wife?*
>
> *Now **what about a concert this Friday?***

Such question forms can also echo what has been said, requesting a clarification or expressing disbelief:

> A: *They have white chocolate. They have it for one of their mocha drinks or something, but you can get white chocolate hot cocoa.*
>
> B: <laugh>
>
> C: ***White chocolate hot cocoa?***

B Condensed directives

The following have the force of commands (addressed to children or pets) or, in the case of **3**, a piece of advice:

> 1 *No crying.*
>
> 2 *Up the stairs, now.*
>
> 3 *Careful when you pick that up*, *it's ever so slippery.*

In the following examples, the directive force of the utterance is indicated, and somewhat softened, by the use of the politeness marker *please*:

> *Hands off the jug please.*
> *Thirty pence please.* <asking for payment>

C Condensed statements

Non-clausal units which function as statements often consist of a noun phrase or an adjective phrase:

> *Very special. Prawns in it and all sorts* <in a restaurant>
> *No wonder this house i– is full of dirt!*

13.5 Ellipsis

Clausal units with ellipsis are related to the non-clausal units described in 13.4.1. Clausal units with ellipsis can be analysed in terms of the elements subject, verb, object, predicative, or adverbial, even though some of these clausal elements have been omitted. In most cases, ellipsis in conversation can be classified as initial ellipsis and final ellipsis (see 8.5.1). There is also a less frequent phenomenon of medial ellipsis.

In the examples below, ∧ marks the position of ellipted material. Ellipsis is highly characteristic of spontaneous speech, because of the need to reduce syntactic complexity due to real-time pressures. In addition, speakers respond to the impulse to speed up communication, avoiding the tedium of unnecessary repetition.

13.5.1 Initial ellipsis

In initial ellipsis, words near the beginning of the clause that have low information value are dropped. They can easily be understood from the situational context. This type of ellipsis is also called situational ellipsis.

A Ellipsis of a subject

This takes place when the subject of a declarative clause is omitted, normally at the start of a turn:

> ∧ *Must be some narky bastards in the rugby club!* <*There* is omitted>
> <note: *bastards* here is an insult and may be considered offensive>
> *A: What's concubine?*
> *B:* ∧ *Don't know, get a dictionary.* <*I* is omitted>

B Ellipsis of an initial operator in questions

> *Oh.* ∧ *You serious?* <*Are* is omitted>
> ∧ *That too early for you?* <*Is* is omitted>
> ∧ *Your Granny Iris get here?* <*Did* is omitted>

C Ellipsis of subject and operator

This type of front ellipsis can occur at the beginning of a declarative or an interrogative clause:

- declarative clauses:

  A: *I love French beaches.*
  B: *Yeah ∧ telling me.* <*You're* is omitted>

- interrogative clauses:

  ∧ *Know what I mean?* <*Do you* is omitted>
  Why aren't you working? ∧ Got a day off? <*Have you* is omitted>

13.5.2 Final (post-operator) ellipsis

Final ellipsis in a clause usually takes the form of the omission of any words following the operator:

   1 A: *I suppose Kathy is still living in that same place.*
       B: *Yeah, **she is** ∧.* <*living in that same place* omitted>
   2 A: *Do you have a couple of dollars in cash?*
       B: *Uh, no **I don't** ∧.* <*have a couple of dollars . . .* omitted>

The verb left after the rest of the clause has been ellipted—e.g. *is* in **1** and *do* in **2**—may be called a 'stranded operator' (see 8.7.1). Many examples of end ellipsis are in replies to questions. However, other contexts for final ellipsis are illustrated in this example:

    A1: *I'm not going out with her at the moment.*
    B1: *Ah!*
    A2: ***But I should be** ∧ by around Tuesday night.* <*going out with her* is omitted>
    B2: *You said by Monday last time.*
    A3: ***Did I** ∧ ? Well I lied.* <*say by Monday last time* is omitted>

The first case of ellipsis, in turn *A2*, is superficially **medial** rather than **final** ellipsis. However, it contains the omission of the main verb and complement, leaving only an optional adverbial, and so can be considered a type of final ellipsis.

    There are other kinds of final ellipsis, such as ellipsis after an infinitive *to* and after a *wh*-word:

    A: *Oh dear! – Take me home!*
    B: ***I'd love to** ∧.* <*take you home* omitted>
       *But she completely lost it. I and I still don't really know **why or how** ∧.* <*she lost it* omitted>

13.5.3 Medial ellipsis

Medial ellipsis occurs where the operator is omitted. It is particularly common with the semi-modals *had better, have got to* (often transcribed with the spelling *gotta*) and *be going to* (often spelled *gonna*):

    *Oh. Nobody would marry you. You're, **you** ∧ **better** keep the one you've got* <laugh>.
    *Yeah dude, **I** ∧ **gotta** start working.*

*<...> and **we** ^ **gonna** call it Kam.*

The American English greeting *How are you doing* (often spelt *How ya doing*) is another conventionalized context favoring medial ellipsis:

How ^ *ya doing Ms. <name>?* (AmE)

Apart from its occurrence in declarative clauses, medial ellipsis occurs in *wh-*questions, between the question word and the subject:

What ^ *she say?*

When ^ *you coming back?*

In general, medial ellipsis is found more in American English than British English, while initial and final ellipsis are found more in British English.

Review

Major points in GRAMMAR BITE B: Grammar tailored to real-time construction

➤ In conversation grammar is adapted to the needs of real-time production, aiming for simplicity.

➤ The constraints of real-time processing lead to incomplete structures and syntactic blends.

➤ Conforming to the add-on principle reduces complexity in language processing.

➤ Non-clausal units are another aspect of structural simplicity in spoken grammar.

➤ Ellipsis is a way of simplifying grammar through omission.

GRAMMAR BITE

c Grammar, lexis, and discourse

13.6 Lexical bundles in speech

As we noted in 13.2.5, the grammar of conversation reflects the repetitive and formulaic nature of speech. In this section, we focus on lexical bundles: sequences of words which are frequently re-used, and therefore become 'prefabricated chunks' that speakers and writers can easily retrieve from their memory and use again and again as text building blocks. In conversation, commonly recurring lexical bundles are sequences such as:

do you want me to ...   *going to be a ...*

I said to him ...   *I don't know what ...*

In the LSWE Corpus, it is possible to find lexical bundles simply by counting the number of times any particular sequence of words occurs per million words. For example, the bundle *do you want me to* occurs 50 times per million words in our conversation corpus. This amounts to about one occurrence per 170 minutes of conversation. This may not sound very frequent—but it is frequent enough to establish *do you want me to* as a very useful 'chunk' of language for discourse-building in speech.

13.6.1 Defining lexical bundles

To make things simpler, we defined a lexical bundle as a recurring sequence of three or four words. Two-word sequences are generally too short and numerous to be interesting. Three-word combinations are again extremely numerous, and can be considered a kind of extended **collocation**. But they are less significant as textual building blocks than four-word combinations, which are more phrasal in nature. Even longer recurrent sequences—five-word and six-word bundles—can be found, but they are much less common. Hence we focused on three-word and (particularly) four-word bundles. Figure 13.1 is a pie chart showing the relative

Figure 13.1 **Percentage of words in recurrent v. non-recurrent expressions—conversation**

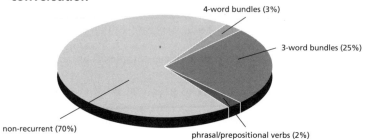

frequency of three-word and four-word bundles, compared with non-recurrent expressions.

The following three points also played a part in defining lexical bundles:

- In counting the words in lexical bundles, we relied on orthographic word units, even though these sometimes combine separate grammatical words. For example, in our analysis *into*, *cannot*, *place-name*, and *didn't* each counted as a single word.

- To be considered as a lexical bundle, a word combination had to recur at least ten times per million words, spread across at least five different conversations (this was to exclude the influence of individual speakers' habits).

- Only uninterrupted combinations were treated as lexical bundles; lexical combinations that cross a turn boundary or a punctuation mark were not counted.

On the whole, conversation is more repetitive than the written registers. This is illustrated by Figure 13.2, which shows how lexical bundles are more frequent in conversation than in academic prose. At the same time, academic prose makes considerable

Figure 13.2

Number of lexical bundles in conversation and academic prose

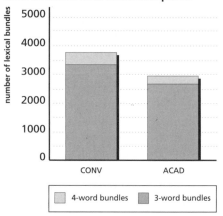

use of prefabricated blocks of text, such as:

> *in the case of the . . .*
> *it should be noted that. . .   there was no significant . . .*

Lexical bundles in academic prose typically involve parts of noun phrases and prepositional phrases, whereas lexical bundles in conversation typically involve the beginning of a finite clause—especially with a pronoun as subject followed by a frequent verb of saying or thinking: e.g. *I don't think you. . . .*

Grammatical and lexical patterning are closely interrelated aspects of language. Although lexical bundles are usually not complete grammatical units, they tend to have particular grammatical characteristics (described in 13.6.3–4).

13.6.2 Lexical bundles and local repetitions in conversation

Unlike lexical bundles, which are repeated *across* many different conversations, local repetitions occur within a single dialog. Both types of repetition are characteristic of conversation: lexical bundles show the habitual repetitiveness of speakers in general, while local repetitions tend to show the repetitiveness of speakers in a given dialog, talking about a particular topic. The following extract illustrates the difference between them: local repetitions are shown in small capitals, while lexical bundles are marked in bold italics:

> *C:* ***Did you see that*** *thing on* <unclear>
> *D: You shouldn't believe that though.*
> *B: Who's Vinnie Jones?*
> <. . .>
> *C: You like Vinnie Jones, don't you?*
> *D:* I RECKON *he er well,* <. . .> *probably* COULD –
> *A:* I DON'T RECKON *Eric* CANTONA COULD.
> *B:* DON'T RECKON CANTONA COULD *what?*
> *A:* I DON'T RECKON CANTONA COULD *beat him up.*
> *C: Yeah.*
> *B: Nor do I.*
> *A:* <unclear> *couldn't, but Mark Hughes might.*
> *B: But* ***I don't know why*** *we're talking about this.*

13.6.3 Structural aspects of lexical bundles

Although lexical bundles in conversation do not usually represent a complete grammatical unit, they fall into several grammatical types. Many of them contain a pronoun followed by a verb phrase followed by part of the verb's complement, as in *I don't know why* and *I thought that was*:

- examples building on *I don't know why*:
  > ***I don't know why*** *he didn't play much at the end of the season.*
  > ***I don't know why*** *Catherine finds that sort of thing funny.*
  > ***I don't know why*** *I did it.*

- examples building on *I thought that was*:
  > *But* ***I thought that was*** *Friday.*

> *I thought that was* going to happen.
>
> Oh *I thought that was* quite good.

Almost 90 per cent of all four-word lexical bundles in conversation are segments based on a declarative or interrogative main clause:

- declarative clause segments:

  I don't know what ... , *I don't think I* ... , *I thought it was* ... , *I said to him* ... , *I would like to* ... , *well you'll have to* ...

- interrogative clause segments:

  can I have a ... , *have you got any* ... , *do you want to* ... , *are you talking about* ... , *what's the matter with* ... , *how do you know* ...

These examples illustrate how lexical bundles tend to end with the beginning of an incomplete unit (e.g. the complement clause in *I don't know **what*** ... and the noun phrase in *have you got **any*** ...). It is also notable that such bundles tend to express particular speech acts common in conversation, such as requests (*can I have a*) and offers or suggestions (*do you want to*).

Further, lexical bundles often have set patterns which can be summarized as follows:

I don't/didn't +	*know/think/want*	+ complement clause
I want to +	*do/get/go/see/be/know*	
do you want +	*to/a/me/some/any/it/the*	

13.6.4 Common lexical bundles in conversation

The following are the most common four-word lexical bundles in conversation (all bundles listed occur more than 40 times per million words; bundles marked ° occur more than 100 times per million words):

- **Pattern 1: Personal pronoun + verb phrase +**

  °*I don't know what* ... , *well I don't know* ... , *I don't know how* ... , *I don't know if* ... , *I don't know whether* ... , *I don't know why* ... , *oh I don't know* ... , *but I don't know* ...

  I thought it was ... , *I think it was* ... , *I don't think so*

  °*I don't want to* ...

  I said to him ...

  I tell you what ...

  °*I was going to* ... , *I'm not going to* ...

  I would like to ...

  you want me to ... , *you want to go* ... , *you don't want to* ...

  you don't have to ...

  you know what I ...

  it's going to be ...

- **Pattern 2: Extended verb phrase fragments**

  have a look at . . ., let's have a look . . .

  know what I mean. . .

  going to be a . . ., going to have a . . ., going to have to . . ., was going to say . . .

  thank you very much

- **Pattern 3: Question fragments**

  °*do you want to . . . , do you want a . . . , do you want me. . .*

  °*are you going to . . . , are we going to. . .*

  do you know what . . .

  what are you doing . . ., what do you mean . . . , what do you think . . . , what do you want. . .

Most bundles are used at or near the beginning of an utterance. For the most part, the main verbs in these sequences mark personal stance, voicing the feelings, thoughts, or desires of the speaker or (less commonly) the hearer. For example:

  *No, **I thought it was** great.*

  ***I would like to** borrow a pen.*

  ***Do you want me** to send them today?*

Many of the bundles express negative meanings:

  *And **I don't know why** he didn't show up.*

  *Oh **I don't want to** hear this.*

The extended verb phrase fragments in Pattern 2 tend to show combinations of verbs with elements which complement them:

  *Oh well, let's have a look. Let's **have a look at** this.*

  *She's **going to have a** baby.*

13.6.5 Lexical bundles and idioms

Lexical bundles are distinct from **idioms**, which are word sequences whose meaning cannot be predicted from the meanings of the individual words. Examples of idioms are expressions such as:

  a piece of cake <meaning something very easy to do>

  on the double <meaning running, or moving quickly>

  step on the gas <meaning to increase speed>

Idioms vary in 'transparency': that is, whether their meaning can be derived from the literal meanings of the individual words. For example, *make up [one's] mind* is rather transparent in suggesting the meaning 'reach a decision', while *kick the bucket* is far from transparent in representing the meaning 'die'.

In contrast, lexical bundles (such as *I want to go*) do not have any metaphorical or other special interpretation. Also, whereas lexical bundles have been defined as consisting of a set of words in a fixed order, idioms often allow some variation, particularly in the function words they contain. *Make up + my/your/her/etc. + mind*, for example, is an idiom in which the third word (a possessive determiner) varies according to context:

*John, can't you ever **make up** your **mind**?*

*I can **make up** my **mind**, but it gets me into trouble.*

Although many idioms are colloquial in tone, they are not particularly common in conversation. In fact, they are less common in conversation than in fiction. Occasionally idioms are frequent enough to occur within a lexical bundle: e.g. *hang on a minute* (meaning 'wait a minute') is a lexical bundle making use of the idiom *hang on*.

13.6.6 Binomial expressions

A **binomial expression** is a special kind of lexical bundle consisting of word$_1$ + and/or + word$_2$. Word$_1$ and word$_2$ are from the same word class, and *and* is much more frequent than *or* as the linking word. The order in which the words occur is normally fixed. In conversation, the most common binomial phrases are relatively fixed expressions that commonly go together in people's experience.

A Verb *and* verb

*My dad wants to **go and see** a film.*

*Shall I **come and help** you?*

*I'm just going to **wait and see** what she says.*

*I'm going to **try and put** them up today.*

The first verb of these combinations is less variable than the second. In meaning the combination is often equivalent to using the infinitive marker *to* rather than *and*: e.g. *go and see = go to see; try and put = try to put.*

B Noun *and* noun

In conversation, most recurrent binomials of this kind refer to:
* human beings (mostly female *and* male or male *and* female):

   *My **mum and dad** went out the other day.*

   *They got **men and women** in the same dormitory.*
* food combinations:

   *Did they put **salt and vinegar** on them?*

   *Can I have two plates of **bread and butter**?*
* time expressions:

   *She's been sick continuously, **day and night**.*

   A: That's years ago.

   *B: Oh yeah, **years and years**.* <i.e. many years>

C Adverb *and* adverb

These binomials usually express directional or temporal meaning:

*Shall we count how many times Alex has been **in and out** of here saying he's going home?*

*They could have mended it **there and then**.* <i.e. at that moment, without delay>

D Adjective *and* adjective

> It was gonna be in **black and white**.

Adjective binomials (e.g. *good and strong*) were discussed in 7.6.1.

3.7 Inserts

Inserts make an important contribution to the interactive character of speech, because they signal relations between speaker, hearer(s), and discourse. Inserts are peripheral to grammar. They occur either as 'stand alone' elements or loosely attached to a clause or non-clausal structure, in which case they occur mainly in an initial position. An exception to this is hesitators, which typically occur in the middle of an utterance.

The following section describes types of inserts, their functions, and their frequency in conversation. We distinguish eight major classes of inserts: interjections (e.g. *oh*), greetings/farewells (e.g. *hi*), discourse markers (e.g. *well*), attention-getters (e.g. *hey*), response-getters (e.g. *okay?*), response forms (e.g. *right*), polite formulas (e.g. *thank you*), and expletives (e.g. *damn*—these are usually taboo words that can easily cause offence).

Throughout this discussion, it is worth remembering that the category of inserts has many ambiguities. Individual items can be used for more than one function; for example, *okay* can be a discourse marker, a response form, or a response-getter (*okay?*). The boundaries between inserts and other categories can also be fuzzy. Some items like *well*, *now*, *I mean*, and *you know* often appear to be on the borderline between inserts and adverbials.

13.7.1 Frequent inserts and their distribution

Table 13.1 illustrates the use and function of common inserts in the eight categories. Inserts are one area of grammar in which American English and British English usage tend to differ. In Figure 13.3, the overall frequencies of the most common inserts are compared in American English and British English. It is important to note, however, that many inserts are strongly preferred by particular social groups within either American or British English (distinguished by age, education, region, etc.). Table 13.2 lists inserts that are slightly less common than those in Figure 13.3.

Some interesting observations about the use of inserts in American English and British English conversation are the following:

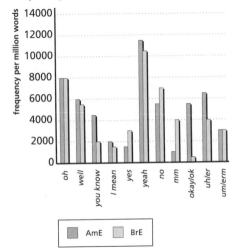

Figure 13.3
Frequency of common inserts

Table 13.1 **A survey of inserts**

individual words/expressions and examples from conversation	explanations

type of insert — interjections are words which have an exclamatory function. They usually express an emotive reaction to something that has been said, or has happened. Their pronunciation is simple and sometimes has abnormal features (e.g. *ugh, aargh, tt*)

1 *Oh how awful! How absolutely naff!* 2 A: *Nicky got that for him.* B: *Oh, did she?* A: *Yeah, I think so.*	1–2 *Oh* is by far the most common interjection. Although highly conventionalized, it has the core function of conveying some degree of surprise or emotion.
3 A: *They're chocolates.* B: *Ah isn't that nice.* 4 *Oh wow, they really did that tree nice.* *Wow.* (AmE) <admiring decorations> 5 A: *How big was it?* B: *Four pounds.* A: *Ooh, that's little.* <talking of a premature birth>	3–5 *Ah, wow,* and *ooh* also express emotional involvement, but have a more marked effect. *Wow* means that the speaker is surprised or impressed.
6 *Whoops, easy Chester. Chester down. Thank you.* <talking to a dog> 7 A: *She burnt popcorn back there.* B: *Ugh it reeks.* 8 *Ow! I've got the stomach ache.* 9 *Ouch my neck hurts.*	6 *Oops* or *whoops* signals a minor mishap, e.g. when the speaker spills something. 7–9 *Ugh, ow,* and *ouch* express negative emotions; *ugh* disgust or displeasure, and *ow* and *ouch* pain or discomfort. Other interjections expressing unpleasant or negative emotions are *aargh, tt* (pronounced as one or more alveolar clicks) and *hm*.

type of insert –– Greetings and farewells signal the beginning and end of a conversation respectively. They usually occur in symmetrical exchanges, as in these examples.

1 A: *Hi Margaret.* B: *Hi.* 2 A: *Hello, Joyce.* B: *Good morning, Bob.* 3 A: *Morning.* B: *Morning.*	1–3 As greetings, *Hi* is more casual than *Hello,* and *Hello* is more casual than forms such as *Good morning* and *Good evening.* These 'good forms' can be shortened by omission of *good,* as in 3.
4 A: *Okay.* *Bye Butch.* B: *Bye Butch, bye Marc.* 5 A: *See you.* B: *Bye bye* 6 A: *Oh.* *Goodbye Robin.* B: *See you later.* *Thank you for a lift. Love you lots.*	4–6 Farewells, like greetings, tend to become more casual and familiar as they become shorter. Thus 4 and 5 are more casual than 6. *Good night* is restricted to leave-taking at night time, especially before going to bed.

type of insert — Discourse markers tend to occur at the beginning of a turn or utterance. They signal interactively how the speaker plans to steer the dialogue.

1 A: *You are always hungry.* B: *Well, I'm not now.* 2 A: *How much rice are you supposed to have for one person?* B: *Well, I don't know.* A: *Half a cup or – well I'm asking you!*	1–2 *Well* has varied uses, but overall has the function of a 'deliberation marker', indicating the speaker's need to give brief thought to the point at issue. *Well* also often marks a contrast, as in 1 and 2, and it can also introduce an indirect or evasive answer—as in 2 again.

13.1 continued

individual words/expressions and examples from conversation	explanations
3 **Right**, are we ready? 4 A: *Get on the phone and phone them up!* B: **Right** *Claire, I will.*	**3–4** *Right* is often used at the beginning of a turn, indicating that some decision is required or accepted. As a reply, it indicates compliance, agreement, or acknowledgement.
5 A: *Alright. Have fun.* B: **Now** *does she have her dollar to buy coffee?*	**5** *Now* signals a change of topic, or a return to an earlier topic.

type of insert — Attention getters have the main function of claiming a hearer's attention.

1 **Hey**, *Raymond*, **yo**, *what's happening?* 2 **Hey**, **Hey**, *look at all the truckers.* 3 *Oh you're not,* **hey** *you're not supposed to say that.*	**1–3** *Hey* is used not only for grabbing attention, but for drawing the hearer's attention to sometimes surprising (**2**), or for making a negative comment about someone's behavior (**3**). Attention getters tend to be familiar and abrupt, and sometimes impolite.
4 **Say**, *Mom, have you got any paint rollers.* (AmE)	

type of insert — Response getters are general question tags, added at the end of a statement, question or directive.

1 *Oh hi, you're Brent's, you're Brent's older sister,* **huh**? *Your brother's so cool.* (AmE) 2 *Jordan what's the matter? What's the matter* **eh**? (BrE)	**1–2** *Huh* is AmE and *eh* (pronounced /eɪ/) is BrE.
3 *Just leave out the smutty stuff,* **okay**? 4 *You know who Stan is,* **right**?	**3–4** Some response getters, such as *okay?*, *right?*, and *alright?*, have other important functions (e.g., response forms). Unlike regular question tags (e.g. *isn't she?*), response getters have a more speaker-centred role, seeking a signal that the utterance has been understood and accepted.

type of insert — Response forms are brief responses to a previous remark by a different speaker. They are positive or negative. They are used to respond to questions, statements, or directives.

1 A: *Does somebody have a pencil?* B: **Yeah**, *here.* 2 A: *Did you have a good time <...>?* B: **Yes**. *It was very pleasant.*	**1–2** Positive response forms: *Yeah* (/jɛə/) is more common than *yes*, especially in AmE.
3 A: *You don't need it wrapped?* B: **No**, *I'm going to stick it in an envelope.*	**3–4** The usual negative response form is *no*. Abrupt positive and negative forms, spelled *yep* and *nope*, are more casual. *Unh unh* (pronounced /nʔn/) and *Huh uh* (pronounced /əʔə/) are casual forms in AmE.

Table 13.1 continued

individual words/expressions and examples from conversation	explanations
4 A: *With a cherry on top?* B: **Unh Unh.** A: *Oh, I forgot you don't like cherries.*	
5 A: *And then we stopped in Arizona to see Aunt Marie, see, on the way.* B: **Mhm.** A: *Her name was Martha* <...> B: **Uh huh.**	5 The positive response forms *Uh huh* (/əhə/) and its nasalized equivalent *mm* (/m:/) or *mhm* (/mhm/) are also used casually, especially as **backchannels** responding to assertions, to let the other speaker know that the utterance is being understood and accepted.
6 A: *Do you want to play?* B: **Okay** *come on.* A: **Okay** *you have to pick a card.*	6 *Okay* is used as a compliant response to directives, suggestions, offers, advice, and requests.

type of insert — Hesitators or 'pause fillers' signal that the speaker is hesitating, and has not yet finished what he/she wants to say.

1 *What kind of **uh** bulldog is this?*	1 The neutral vowel schwa (pronounced /ə/ and spelled *uh* or *er*) is the most common hesitator.
2 A: *How am I gonna get it back to you?* B: **Um,** *I'll come over to your house.*	2 A common alternative is the variant with a final nasal, /əm/ (spelled *um* or *erm*).
3 *And **um,** she said you were wonderful and **uh,** she's **uh,** she sends her regards.*	3 *Uh/er* and *um/erm* can occur in the same utterance, and often co-occur with other types of **dysfluency**.

type of insert — Polite formulae: here we place words like *please*, *thanks*, and *sorry*, as well as formulaic expressions like *thank you* and *excuse me*.

1 A: *Would you like another drink Adam?* B: *Yes **please** – .*	1–2 illustrate *please* (for a polite request).
2 *Can I have a – another two Diet Cokes please?* **Thank you.**	2–3 illustrate *thanks* and *thank you* (for expressing gratitude)
3 **Thanks** *Carl, I appreciate it.*	
4 *Ah!* **Beg your pardon!**	4–5 illustrate *(I) beg your pardon, pardon me*, and *excuse me* (for an apology). These forms can also be used for requesting repetition of an utterance.
5 <belch> – **Pardon me.**	

type of insert — Expletives are **taboo** expressions ('swearwords') or semi-taboo expressions used as exclamations, especially in reacting to some strongly negative experience.

1 *This is,* **God,** *a bloody afternoon wasted!*	1–6 The first six examples show swearwords,
2 *Oh* **Jesus,** *I didn't know it was that cold.*	violating the taboo on sensitive topics like
3 *I know what I forgot to get in town.* **Damn!**	religion, sex, and defecation. These terms may cause (serious) offence, especially 4 and
4 **Shit,** *play a fucking domino,* **goddamit.** (AmE)	6. (Note that 'swearwords' belonging to other word classes, such as the adjective
5 **Bloody hell!** *He's gone mad.* (BrE)	*fucking* in 6, can also cause offence.)
6 **Fuck,** *I feel fucking sweaty, I can feel it already.*	

le 13.1   **continued**

individual words/expressions and examples from conversation	explanations
7 *My gosh*, *what a great idea.*	7–11 are examples of 'semi-taboo'
8 *A: Nineteen dollars. B: Geez, that is expensive.* (AmE)	expressions. These are milder than those in 1–6, because they disguise the taboo
9 *Oh boy, gee, you've got some nice pictures.* (AmE)	meaning: e.g. *gosh* for *God*, *gee(z)* for *Jesus*. Those in **7–11** can be used to express
10 *Oh good heavens no, I mean Walt Disney.*	favourable, as well as unfavourable emotions, like interjections.
11 *Oh heck well you'll have to go on the bus.*	

le 13.2   **Less common inserts in AmE and BrE conversation**

functional type	more common in AmE (in order of frequency)	similar frequency in AmE and BrE	more common in BrE (in order of frequency)
interjections	*wow, aargh, oops, whoops*		*ah, ooh, ha, aha, tt, whoa, cor*
greetings, farewells	*hi, bye bye*	*bye*	*hello*
discourse markers			*now, you see*
attention getters	*hey*		*oi*
response getters	*huh?*		*eh?*
response forms	*uh, huh, mhm, yep, unh unh, huh uh, nope*	*alright*	*aye*
polite forms	*thank you, thanks*	*excuse me*	*please, sorry, pardon*
expletives (! = can be offensive; !! = can be deeply offensive)	*my God[!], my gosh, my goodness, geez, gee*	*gosh, shit[!!], fuck[!!], Christ[!!], damn[!], hell[!]*	*God[!]*

- The attention-getter *hey* is more frequent in American English.
- The response-getter *huh?* is more frequent in American English, whereas *eh?* is more frequent in British English.
- The response form *okay* is vastly more frequent in American English.
- American speakers show a much stronger preference for *yeah* over *yes*, although the same preference does exist for British speakers.
- The more casual greeting *Hi* is much more frequent than *Hello* (also spelled *Hullo*) in American English. Greeting formulas with 'good' (*good morning, good evening*, etc.) are surprisingly rare.
- Similarly, *good(-)bye* is surprisingly rare compared with *bye* and *bye bye*.

The tendency towards informality and phonetic reduction in conversation is strong in both varieties, but appears to be generally stronger in American English. This informality partly reflects the private nature of conversation. But it may also reflect a general drift towards familiarity in everyday speech in both British English and, more particularly, American English.

Review

Major points of **GRAMMAR BITE C**: Grammar, lexis, and discourse

➤ Lexical bundles are fixed sequences of words that are used repeatedly across texts.

> ➤ Lexical bundles are usually not idioms, and they do not have to be complete structural units.

> ➤ In conversation, most lexical bundles are clause fragments containing a finite verb.

➤ Inserts are stand-alone words such as *oh*, *okay*, or *well* that are not part of any larger syntactic unit.

> ➤ They have a wide range of discourse functions: interjections, greetings and farewells, discourse markers, attention-getters, response-getters, response forms, hesitators, polite formulae, and expletives.

> ➤ Inserts, although peripheral to grammar, have an important role in the interaction between speaker and hearer.

Glossary of terms

accusative: the morphological form, or case, associated with object syntactic roles. Accusative case is marked only on pronouns in English: *me, her, him, them*. (4.12.3)

activity verb: verbs that refer to actions and events associated with a volitional activity: *buy, go, take*. (5.3)

add-on strategy: the process of constructing conversational turns from a linear sequence of short finite clause-like segments: *I think | you'll find | it counts towards your income*. (13.3.2)

adjective: one of the four lexical word classes in English—its most common use is modifying nouns: *That's great; a bad attitude*. (2.3.3)

adjective phrase: a phrase with an adjective as its head: *very old; ready for lunch*. (3.3.3)

adverb: one of the four lexical word classes in English—its most common uses are as an adverbial and as a modifier of an adjective: *It goes fast; physically tired*. (2.3.4)

adverb phrase: a phrase with an adverb as its head: *pretty often; sooner than you think*. (3.3.4)

adverbial: a phrase or clause that functions as a clause element answering questions such as 'When?', 'Where?', 'Why?', or 'How?' (7.10.5). There are three major classes of adverbial: circumstance, stance and linking.

adverbial clause: a clause that functions as an adverbial element in a higher level clause: *You can have it if you want*. (8.15.2)

adverbial particle: a function word like *on* or *up*, that can be used as part of a phrasal and phrasal-prepositional verbs: *turn on, put up with*. (2.4.5)

affix: a cover term including both suffixes and prefixes.

affixation: the process of adding prefixes or suffixes to a word.

agent: the doer of an action: *Dad bought that for us*. This term is also used for the noun phrase following a passive + *by*: *I'm influenced by all kinds of things*. (6.6)

agentless passive: a clause with a passive voice main verb but no *by*-phrase; also called a short passive: *It was stolen*. (6.6)

alternative question: an interrogative clause that is structurally similar to a *yes/no* question but presents alternatives for the addressee to choose between: *Do you want one or two?* (8.11.3)

amplifier: an extent/degree adverb or adverbial that intensifies meaning: *totally different, restored completely*. (11.6.5)

anaphora (adjective: anaphoric): a relation between two linguistic expressions such that the second one refers back to the first: *She must have cut herself.*

antecedent: a pronoun like *he, she*, and *they* often refers back to a noun phrase occurring earlier in the same clause, utterance, or text. This noun phrase is called its antecedent. (4.12.1)

appositive noun phrase: a noun phrase that is used as a postmodifier identifying the referent of a preceding noun: *Heiko, a 19-year-old factory worker*. (9.11)

approximator: a hedge or adverb that modifies a number, measurement, or quantity: *approximately 250 people*. (7.11.6)

article: the function words that signal definite or indefinite meaning: *the, a, an*. (4.6)

aspect: a choice in the verb phrase that expresses time meanings, related to whether an action is finished or still in progress: *have eaten, was going*. (6.3)

assertive form: this term is applied to a set of words such as *some, somebody, something, somewhere, already*, which have special behavior in negative and interrogative clauses. (8.8.10)

attitude adverbial: an adverbial that conveys an evaluation or an assessment of what is said: *fortunately, surprisingly*. (11.13.2)

attributive adjective: an adjective functioning as a premodifier before a noun (occurring before the head noun in a noun phrase): *special skills, silent prayers*. (7.7)

auxiliary verb: a closed set of verbs marking meanings associated with aspect, voice, or modality: *have taken, was seen, may go*. (2.4.3)

backchannel: a word or minimal response used as an utterance to show that the listener is continuing to pay attention: *A: Her name was Martha. B: Uh huh.* (13.2.3)

bare infinitive clause: a type of complement clause with an infinitive verb form, but without the complementizer *to*: *help resettle some of the Bosnians*. (10.13.1)

base: the form of a word to which affixes are added: *friendliness* = the base *friendly* + the affix *-ness*.

binomial phrase: two words from the same grammatical category coordinated by *and* or *or*: *black and white, presence or absence*. (13.6.6)

block language: constructions typical of headlines, titles, slogans, lists, and notices, using only words essential for the message: *Waiting game. Anxious times in Middle East*. (4.6.2, 8.14)

cardinal numeral: a word (especially a postdeterminer) that states how many: *the ten books*.

case: a choice of word form marking the syntactic role of a noun or pronoun, for example as subject (*he*), object (*him*), or genitive (*John's*). (4.9, 4.12.3)

cataphora (cataphoric): a relation between two linguistic expressions such that the first one refers forward to the second: *It's nice, that table*. (4.6.3)

causative verb: a verb that indicates that some person or thing brings about, or helps to bring about, a new state of affairs: *help, let, allow, require*. (5.3)

central adjective: an adjective that has all the typical characteristics of form, meaning, and use. (7.2)

circumstance adverbial: an adverbial that describes the circumstances relating to the main clause, by answering such questions as 'Where?', 'When?', 'How?', 'Why?', 'How much?': *He'd always stay [in a small hotel] [because he prefers them]*. (11.6)

classifier: a type of adjective that limits or restricts a noun's referent: *additional money, particular facts*. (7.6)

classifying genitive: a genitive that classifies the reference of the head noun, answering the question 'What kind of X?': *a bird's nest, a girls' school*. (4.9.3)

clause: a key structural unit of grammar, normally consisting of a verb phrase plus other elements: subject, object, predicative, adverbial.

cleft: a grammatical construction with information broken into two clauses, to provide extra focus to one piece of information. It-cleft: *It was his voice that held me*. Wh-cleft: *What I want is something to eat*. (12.12)

closed class: a class of words with a small number of members, such as articles or prepositions. (2.2.2)

cohesion: the pattern of relations between structures and lexical items which combine together to form a text. Pronouns like *she*, conjunctions like *but*, and linking adverbs like *therefore* have a particular role in cohesion.

collective noun: a noun that refers to a group: *army, family, herd*. (4.4.1)

collocation: a combination of lexical words which frequently co-occur in texts: *little + baby, small + amount, make + (a) + mistake*.

common noun: a noun that refers to a class rather than a specific entity: *girl, city, grief*. (4.2)

communication verbs: verbs that refer to speaking and writing activities: *tell, shout, write*. (5.3)

comparative clause: a clause expressing comparison, normally in an adjective phrase or an adverb phrase, with a gradable word as head: *better **than it was**, **as quickly as possible***. (8.15.4)

complement: a phrase or clause that completes the meaning required by some other form. For example, *that*-clauses can be verb complements: *She said **that she has changed***.

complement clause: a dependent clause controlled by a preceding verb, adjective, noun, or preposition: *It should be easy **to remember***. (8.15.1)

complementizer: a type of subordinator that begins a complement clause: *I said **that** I wasn't perfect*. (2.4.7)

complex preposition: a preposition consisting of two or more words: *such as, in case of*. (2.4.4)

complex transitive: a transitive valency pattern that includes both a direct object and an object predicative: *Some people **call them sodas***. (3.4, 5.7)

compound pronoun: a pronoun that begins with one of the determiners *every, some, any,* or *no*: *someone, anybody, nothing*. (4.15.1)

compounding: a process that creates new words by combining two existing words: *bathroom, bittersweet*. (4.11.3)

concord (subject–verb): the requirement that the verb phrase in a finite clause agree with the subject in terms of number and person: *he is* v. *they are*. (8.6)

condensation (structural): reducing the amount of structure needed to express a given meaning, for example by using pronouns and non-finite clauses. (8.5.3)

conjunction: a type of function word that connects clauses (and sometimes phrases or words). Conjunctions are subdivided into coordinators and subordinators.

conversion: a process of creating new words by transferring an existing word to a different word class: *walk* as a verb → *a walk* as a noun. (4.11.2)

coordination: connecting two or more clauses, phrases, words, or other structures with equivalent status: *a paper in one hand **and** a bill in the other*. (8.4)

coordinator: a function word used to connect (or coordinate) two or more words, phrases, or clauses with equivalent status: *and, but, or*. (8.4)

copula: the primary verb *be* occurring as a main verb: *I am sorry*. (5.16)

copular: a valency pattern that includes a verb and a subject predicative: *He was a gambler*. (3.4, 5.7)

copular verb: any verb that occurs with a copular valency pattern, taking a subject predicative as complement: *He's American. It **tastes different***. (5.16)

co-referential: two expressions that refer to the same entity are co-referential: ***Mr. Bond** told journalists **he** was not finished yet*.

correlative coordinator: a combination of two separated words used to signal a relation of coordination: *both ... and; either ... or; neither ... nor*.

countable noun: a noun that refers to entities that can be counted: *a cow, two cows*. (4.2)

current copular verb: copular verbs that refer to a continuing state of existence or report sensory perceptions: *He **seemed** satisfied. You **stay** healthy*. (5.16)

dangling (unattached) participle: an adverbial *ing*- or *ed*-clause with an understood subject that is different from the subject in the main clause: ***Leaving the road**, the darkness of the trees surrounded them*. (11.10.1)

declarative clause: a clause (normally with subject–verb word order) that functions to make assertions or statements: *I can't pay my rent. They went to Jamaica*. (8.10)

declarative tag: a peripheral clause with subject–verb word order, added to the end of another clause: *I thoroughly enjoyed it **I did***. (8.15.5)

definite article: the determiner *the*, which signals definite meaning. (4.6)

degree clause: a complement clause of an adjective or adverb that tells the extent or degree of a characteristic: *strong enough **to hold weight**, too softly **to hear***. Comparative clauses are degree clauses, too.

deictic words: words that point to the situation (especially place or time) in which the speaker is speaking: *this, that, these, those, now, then*.

demonstrative determiner: *this/these* and *that/those* acting as determiners; they convey definite meaning, and specify whether the referent is near or distant in relation to the speaker: ***that** word, **these** pictures*. They are deictic words. (4.7.2)

demonstrative pronoun: a demonstrative form (*this, that, these, those*) functioning as a pronoun: *You will need **those***. (4.14)

dependent clause: a type of clause that is normally part of another clause, called its main clause: *I hate **to see that**. We have 30 men **who are working***. (8.15)

derivation: the process by which one word is derived from another, by affixation or conversion.

derivational affix: a prefix or suffix added to another word to form a longer word: *happy → happiness, happy → unhappy*.

descriptors: a class of adjectives that describe color, size, weight, chronology, age, emotion, and other characteristics; they are usually gradable: *red, old, sad*. (7.6)

determiner: a function word that specifies the kind of reference a noun has (e.g. definite, indefinite, negative): ***the** walls, **those** experiences, **a** bell, **no** time*. (4.5)

diminisher/downtoner: an extent/degree adverb that diminishes meaning: ***slightly** cold, **almost** empty*. (7.11.4)

direct object: a clause element that follows the main verb, typically a noun phrase referring to the entity affected by the action or process of the verb: *She broke **my favorite coffee mug***. (3.5.3)

directive: a speech act expecting some action from the addressee: *Sit down. Can you turn down the TV*.

discourse marker: a type of insert used in conversation. It signals interactively how the speaker plans to steer the dialogue: *Now, here's some ...* (13.2.3, 13.7)

dislocation: a construction with a pronoun in the main clause and a definite noun phrase before or after the main clause, used to mark the topic or for clarification: ***Sharon** she plays bingo. Did they have any, **the kids**?* (12.11)

ditransitive: a transitive valency pattern that includes both a direct object and an indirect object: *I gave **her the material***. (3.4, 5.7)

do-support (or *do*-insertion): the addition of the operator *do* when it is required for questions or negation: *Why **do** you hate it? I **do** not have my pencil*. (5.15.2, 8.7)

double genitive: A construction that includes both the genitive suffix (*'s*) and an *of*-phrase: *a good idea of Johnny's*. (4.9.6)

dummy pronoun: the pronoun *it* as a non-referential subject: ***It's** cold in here*. (3.5.2)

dynamic verbs: verbs that express action or events. (5.3)

dysfluency: the way in which unplanned speech departs from smooth flowing, grammatically well-formed utterances. (13.2.5)

ed-clause: a type of non-finite dependent clause with the *ed*-form of a verb: ***Taken together**, these things persuade many people*. (8.16.3)

ed-form, *ed*-participle: a non-finite form of verbs, which in regular verbs ends in -ed (e.g. **heated by gas**) but in irregular verbs takes various forms, including a form ending in -en: **taken, seen, sent**.

ellipsis: omission of clause or phrase elements that can be reconstructed from the context: *A: I have to appease you. B: No you don't* ∧ . (8.5)

embedded (phrase or clause): a phrase or clause that is contained within a higher-level phrase or clause: *[reduction [in the risk [of death [from job-related accidents]]]].* (9.3.2)

end-focus: the normal case in English where attention is given naturally to the last lexical item in the clause. This is signaled in speech by the strongest stress or intonation peak. (12.1.2)

end-weight: a preference in English word order, whereby more complex elements of structure tend to follow less complex ones.

epistemic adverbial: a stance adverbial that expresses the speaker's judgment about the certainty, or limited validity, of the proposition: *You are **probably** correct.* (11.13.1)

exclamation: a word, phrase or clause that functions like an exclamative clause, expressing strong feelings: *What a miracle! Great!* (3.2.4, 7.9.5, 8.9)

exclamative clause: a type of finite clause used to express strong emotion. It begins with *what* or *how*, followed by subject and verb phrase: *What a tragic death it was.* (8.12)

existential *there*: the word *there* used as subject, where it does not refer to a place, but introduces a clause expressing existence: ***There** is no answer to that question.* (12.5)

experiencer: the person who undergoes the sensory or cognitive experience expressed by a verb: *He smelled her perfume.* (6.5.1)

expletive: a 'swearword', a taboo or semi-taboo expression used as an exclamation: *God! geez! bloody hell!* (13.7)

extraposed: a complement clause is extraposed where dummy *it* fills the subject slot, and the complement clause is placed after the predicate: *It is clear **that it will not be simple**.* (10.3.3)

feminine: see gender. (4.10)

finite clause/finite verb phrase: a clause (or verb phrase) that has either present/past tense or a modal verb. (8.3.2)

free combination: a combination in which each word contributes its own meaning: *He was afraid to look back.* (5.8)

fronting: moving a clause element to initial position: ***That** I also like.* (12.3)

function words: words that express grammatical relationships and classifications, such as determiners, conjunctions, and prepositions. (2.4)

gap: the location of the missing constituent in a relative clause: *... a great athlete, which I believe I am* ∧ . (9.8)

gender: grammatical marking to signify female (feminine gender: *policewoman, she*), male (masculine gender: *businessman, he*), neither male nor female (neuter gender: *house, it*), or either male or female (personal gender: *student, who*). (4.10)

generic reference: reference to a whole class, rather than to just one or more instances of a class: ***Horses** are intelligent animals.* (4.6.4)

genitive: the marking, or case, represented by the *'s* suffix on nouns (or just by *'* in the plural): *Henry's, teachers'.* (4.9)

get-passive: a passive verb phrase marked by the auxiliary *get* rather than *be: got stolen.* (6.7.2)

gradable: quality that exists to a greater or lesser extent: e.g. *old* represents a gradable concept: *older, rather old, very old*, etc. (2.3.3)

head: the required element in any phrase that specifies the type of the phrase; for example, noun phrases have a noun (or pronoun) as the head: *the standard **rules** of behavior.* (2.8)

hedge: a word that conveys imprecision or uncertainty, often used to lessen the force of what is said: *It seems **sort of** a betrayal. I **might** need it.* (11.13.1)

historic present tense: the use of a verb phrase in the present tense to refer to an event that occurred in the past: *They went to some park and got an ice cream ... So we **get** there ...* (6.2.1)

hypothetical/unreal condition: a condition that cannot be fulfilled, expressed by the past or past perfect form of the verb phrase: *if I **had** all the money in the world ...* (11.9.1)

idiom: a fixed expression with a meaning that cannot be determined from the individual parts: *kick the bucket.* (13.6.5)

imperative clause: a clause with the base form of the verb, and usually no subject and no extended verb phrase markers (i.e. no modals or tense/aspect markers). Imperatives function as directives: *Be quiet.* (8.13, 13.2.3)

indefinite article: the determiner *a/an* that signals indefinite meaning. (4.6)

indefinite pronoun: a pronoun with indefinite meaning, e.g. compound pronouns (like *anybody*), quantifiers (like *some*), or the pronoun *one*. (4.15)

independent clause: a clause that can stand alone without being subordinate to another clause: *She has a day off school.* (8.9)

independent genitive: a genitive phrase standing alone as a noun phrase: *She's going to **a friend's**.* (4.9.5)

indirect object: a clause element that follows verbs like *give* and *tell*, referring to the recipient of the action: *Dave gave **me** this stuff.* (3.5.3)

infinitive clause: a non-finite dependent clause with the base form of a verb, usually preceded by *to: They told her **to wait six months**.* (8.16.1)

inflection: a morphological change in verbs, nouns, and some other word classes, that expresses a grammatical meaning such as number or tense: *offices, trying, came, latest.*

information flow: the normal ordering of information in English discourse, moving from given information and to new information (12.1.1)

ing-clause: a non-finite dependent clause with the *ing*-form of a verb: *I stopped **going to class**.* (8.16.2)

ing-form, *ing*-participle: a non-finite form of a verb, ending in -ing: *working, eating, discussing.* (2.3.2, 2.3.6)

insert: a general term for conversational words that can be positioned rather freely in a discourse; they usually convey emotional and discoursal meanings (e.g., *oh, yeah, hey, well*). (2.2.2, 13.2.1, 13.7)

intensifier: an alternative term for amplifier. (11.6.5)

interjection: an exclamatory insert used in speech to express emotion or attitude: *oh, ah, wow.* (13.2.4, 13.7)

interrogative clause: a clause marked in certain ways (inversion, initial *wh*-word, intonation) to show that it functions as a question: *Do you want any food? What is this?* (8.11)

interrogative pronoun: a *wh*-pronoun used (normally) at the beginning of a question or interrogative clause: *what, which, who.*

intransitive: a valency pattern with no objects: *She slept a lot. Michael disappeared.* (3.4, 5.7)

inversion: a reversal of the normal word order so that the a verb precedes the subject: *Then came the turning point of the match.* (12.4)

irregular plural: the plural form of nouns that do not follow the regular rule of just adding -(e)s to form the plural: *mouse → mice; child → children.* (4.8.2)

irregular verb: a verb which does not use the regular *-ed* inflection for past tense and/or past participle: *speak—spoke—spoken*; *send—sent—sent*. (5.5)

lexeme: a word, in the sense applicable to words listed in a dictionary—a set of grammatical words sharing the same basic lexical meaning, the same basic form and the same word class: *leave, leaves, left,* and *leaving* belong to the same lexeme. (2.2.1)

lexical bundle: a sequence of words which is used repeatedly in texts. (13.6)

lexical verb: one of the four lexical word classes in English; e.g. *come, find, overcome, magnify.* Lexical verbs act as main verbs in clauses. They cannot act as auxiliary verbs. (2.3.2)

lexical word classes: the open classes of words, used to convey content meaning: lexical verbs, nouns, adjectives, and adverbs (compare with function words).

linking adverbial: an adverbial that relates a clause to preceding (or following) clauses: *however, therefore.* (11.17–11.19)

logical modal meaning: modal verbs used to refer to the logical status of states or events, expressing certainty, likelihood, or logical necessity: *We **might** meet them.* (6.10)

long passive: a clause with a passive voice verb phrase plus a *by*-phrase as agent: *The proposal was approved by the Project Coordinating Team.* (6.6)

long verb phrase: a phrase including the verb phrase and any other clause elements which follow the main verb: *My mother **was born** in Canada.* (3.5.6)

main clause: a clause in which a dependent clause is directly embedded. In *[I think [I can fix it]]*, the dependent clause is in *[]*, and the main clause is in *[]*.

main verb: the head and final verb in a verb phrase: *told, have **had**, might **be seen**.* (3.3.2)

mark: indicate or express a given meaning: as in 'Stance adverbials overtly mark a speaker's attitude or judgments'.

marked: a pattern that is not the most typical pattern, and therefore has some special meaning or function. For example, fronting is marked in relation to regular word order: *This I do not understand* v. *I do not understand this.*

masculine: see gender. (4.10)

mental verb: a verb that refers to mental states or activities: *know, remember.* (5.3)

modal auxiliary: an alternative term for modal verb.

modal verb: a type of auxiliary verb used to express logical or personal meanings: *can, should, might.* (6.9)

modality: the expression of logical meaning or personal meaning through the use of modal auxiliary verbs. (6.9)

modifier: an omissible form that specifies further meaning about the head of its phrase: *very quickly, a social critic who wrote in 1933.*

monotransitive: a transitive valency pattern that includes only a direct object: *No one ever **saw them**.* (3.4, 5.7)

morpheme: the smallest structural unit that has meaning. Prefixes, suffixes, and stems are morphemes. (2.1)

morphology: the part of grammar explaining how morphemes are put together to construct words.

multiple negation: a construction with two or more negation markers: *You've **never** seen **nothing** like it.* (8.8.12)

negation: forming a negative clause by adding negative elements such as *not* or *no*. (8.8)

negative contraction: reduction in the spelling and/or pronunciation of *not* used in combination with the preceding verb (= operator): *isn't, can't.* (8.8.3)

neuter: see gender. (4.10)

nominal: any word, phrase, or clause filling a noun phrase slot, for example, as subject or object.

nominal clause: another term for a complement clause—a clause functioning as a nominal. (8.15.1)

nominalizations: abstract nouns formed from verbs or adjectives through derivational morphology: *educate → education, happy → happiness.*

nominative: the morphological form, or case, associated with the subject role. Nominative case is marked only on pronouns in English: *she* and *he* v. *her* and *him*. (4.12.3)

non-assertive: this term applies to a number of words such as *any, anyone, anything, ever, at all*. These are commonly used to express indefinite meaning in negative and interrogative clauses. (8.8.10)

non-clausal material: the parts of a text or discourse which do not consist of clauses. See non-clausal units.

non-clausal units: structural units (most commonly found in conversation) that are not composed of clauses: e.g. *With or without ice? How cool! Not a lot.* (13.4)

no-negation: forming a negative clause by using negative words other than *not*, such as *no, nothing, never*: *She had **no** future in Japan.* (8.8.7)

non-finite clause/non-finite verb phrase: a clause (or verb phrase) that has no tense and does not include a modal verb: *I want **to be careful**.* (8.3.2)

non-restrictive modifier: a modifier that does not restrict the reference of a head noun, but rather adds elaborating, descriptive information about the noun: *her husband, who is now remarried.* (9.7)

notional concord: subject–verb concord based on meaning rather than the actual grammatical form: ***Two pounds** is nothing. **The committee** were in there.* (8.6.6)

notional subject: the noun phrase coming after the copular verb in constructions with existential *there*; logically, it functions as the subject: *There is **no easy solution**.* (12.7)

not-negation: forming a negative clause by inserting the negative particle *not* after the operator: *It is **not** unusual.* (8.8.1)

noun complement clauses: clauses that act as complements of an abstract noun: *the expectation **that the stock will move still higher**; permission **to wear them**.* (9.13)

noun: one of the four lexical word classes in English, used to refer to concrete entities or substances, and abstract qualities or states: *pencil, bread, friendship, joy.* (2.3.1)

noun phrase: a phrase with a noun (or pronoun) as head: *the standard rules of behavior.* (3.3.1)

noun phrase tag: a definite noun phrase shifted to a position after the main clause: *Has it got double doors, that shop?* (12.11.2)

number: the choice between singular or plural forms of nouns, pronouns and other word classes: e.g. *table—tables; this—these.* (4.8)

numeral: a word that either specifies how many (cardinal numeral) or the position in a series (ordinal numeral): *the past **three** years, the **third** week.* (2.5.3)

object: a cover term for nominal clause elements occurring after the main verb, including direct objects and indirect objects. Objects can usually become the subject of a passive clause. (3.5.3)

object predicative: a clause element that occurs after the direct object and characterizes the object: *A jury found him guilty.* (3.5.4)

open class: a term describing lexical words (verbs, nouns, adjectives, or adverbs), signifying that it is not possible to list all the members of the class and that new members are regularly added. (2.2.3)

operator: the verb used to construct negative or interrogative clauses: *I **will** not allow you to go there. **Is** she walking?* (8.7)

ordinal numeral: a number word that specifies the position of items in a series: *the **first** day.*

orthographic word: a 'word' defined as such by being separated by spaces in writing. (2.2.1)

parenthetical: a element in writing 'bracketed' off by parentheses or dashes, and grammatically loosely attached to the rest of the sentence. (3.5.6)

part of speech: another term for word class.

participial: having the form of a participle: e.g. in *a sleeping child* and *He looked prepared*, *sleeping* and *prepared* are participial adjectives.

participle: the *ed-* and *ing-*forms of a verb are known as *ed-* and *ing-*participles: *was sleeping, I've prepared a brief statement.*

participle clause: a non-finite clause with an *-ing* participle or an *-ed* participle as the main verb: *I regret missing the plane. Given these obstacles, Mattel said …*

particle movement: a test for phrasal verbs, whereby the adverbial particle can be placed either before or after the following object noun phrase: *get back my shirt, get my shirt back.* (5.8.1)

passive clause: a clause containing a passive verb phrase.

passive voice, passive verb phrase: a verb construction marked by *be* + past participle, and generally used to give less prominence to the agent of the clause: *He was struck several times.* (Compare this with its active equivalent: *They struck him several times.*) (6.6)

perfect aspect: a verb construction that describes events or states taking place in the past, but linked to a subsequent time, especially the present. The perfect aspect is formed with *have* + past participle: *have seen, had driven.* (6.3)

perfect progressive: a verb construction that combines both perfect aspect and progressive aspect: *have been seeing.* (6.3.2)

peripheral adjective: an adjective with only some of the typical characteristics of adjective form, meaning, and use: *mere, awake.* (7.2.2)

peripheral clause: a clause, such as reporting clauses and tag clauses, on the boundary of. dependent and independent status. (8.15.5)

personal gender: see gender. (4.10)

personal modal meaning: modal verbs used to refer to actions and events that humans directly control, expressing personal permission, obligation, or volition (intention): *Can I follow you? We should take you there.* (6.10)

personal pronoun: the most common type of pronoun, which has different forms for first person (*I, we*) and third person (*it, they*). (4.12)

phrasal verb: a multi-word verb consisting of a lexical verb plus adverbial particle: *turn on the television set.* (5.9)

phrasal-prepositional verb: a multi-word verb consisting of a lexical verb plus adverbial particle plus preposition: *look forward to.* (5.11)

phrase: a structural unit built from words, consisting of a head plus (optionally) modifiers. (3.2)

possessive determiner: a determiner in a noun phrase that expresses possession, and is comparable to the genitive of nouns: *my, your.* (4.7.1)

possessive pronoun: a pronoun that expresses possession, and is comparable to the independent genitive of nouns: *mine, yours.* (4.12.4)

postmodification: the part of a complex noun phrase consisting of modifiers that follow it: e.g. relative clauses and prepositional phrases. (9.2, 9.3.2)

postmodifier: a modifier following a head noun: *the beginning of the program.* (9.2, 9.3.2)

postmodifier complex: the combination of all modifiers and embedded modifiers following a head noun. (9.12.1)

postposed: placed after another element that usually follows. For example, an adjective that follows the head is postposed: *everything possible.* (7.9.1)

post-predicate: a complement clauses that occur after the main verb, or after a copular verb plus predicative adjective: *I thought he was there. I'm sure she will.* (10.3.2)

predicate: the 'logical center' of a clause, consisting sometimes of a verb, and sometimes of a copular verb plus predicate adjective. The predicate determines what elements occur as complements in the clause: *I thought he was there. I'm sure she will.*

predicative adjective: an adjective that occurs in the subject predicative position, following a copular verb: *He seems tired.*

predicative: a clause element that characterizes the referent of some other clause element, either the subject (subject predicatives) or the object (object predicatives). (3.5.4)

preface: a noun phrase functioning as a dislocated peripheral element, placed before the subject of a clause: *This little shop – it's lovely.* (12.11.1)

prefix: a morpheme added to the front of a word: *reread, unsure.*

premodification: modifying structures that occur before a noun and describe it, such as attributive adjectives: *all the exciting new things.* (9.2, 9.3.1)

premodifier: an individual modifier preceding a head noun: *a homely, big child.* (9.2, 9.3.1)

preposition: a word that introduces a prepositional phrase, linking the following noun phrase to other elements of the sentence: *locked her keys in the car, your recollection about these events.* (2.4.4)

prepositional complement: the noun phrase (or nominal clause, etc.) that follows a preposition and completes the prepositional phrase: *in the car.* (2.4.4)

prepositional object: a noun phrase (or nominal clause, etc.) which normally follows the preposition of a prepositional verb, and which resembles the object of a transitive verb: *asked for permission.* (A prepositional object is a special type of prepositional complement.)

prepositional phrase: a phrase consisting of a preposition followed by a noun phrase (or a nominal clause) as prepositional complement: *to the train station, after this Monday.* (2.4.4)

prepositional verb: a multi-word verb consisting of a lexical verb plus preposition: *look at, think of.* (5.10)

primary auxiliary: a primary verb (*be, have,* or *do*) when used as an auxiliary verb.

primary verb: one of the verbs *be, have,* and *do,* which can function as either auxiliary verbs or main verbs. (5.2.2)

pro-form: a word whose function is to substitute for another, often longer, expression. (See pronoun, pro-verb.)

progressive aspect: a verb construction describing an event or state of affairs which is in progress or continuing; formed with *be* + *ing-*participle: *is staying, were flying.* (6.3)

pronoun: a function word that typically fills the position of an entire noun phrase: *a straw hat → it.* Pronouns have a substitute or co-referential function.

proper noun: a noun that names an individual, usually a specific person or place: *Sue, Chicago.* (4.2)

pro-verb: the verb *do* substituting for a lexical verb or a complete predicate: *A: He doesn't even know you. B: He does!* (5.15)

quantifier: a cover term used for quantifying determiners and quantifying pronouns.

quantifying determiner: a type of determiner that indicates the amount of something: *all the countries, some ideas.* (4.7.3)

quantifying noun: a noun that refers to quantities: *a pound of brown sugar, a pile of money.* (4.4.3)

quantifying pronoun: a type of pronoun that indicates an indefinite amount of something: *most of the people, I have some*. (4.15.2)

question: the speech act of asking for information, associated with interrogative clauses. (8.11)

question tag: a reduced interrogative clause added to the end of a declarative clause, used to seek confirmation or agreement in conversation: *This is a beautiful spot isn't it?* (8.11.4)

reciprocal pronoun: a type of pronoun that expresses a mutual relationship between two or more parties: *each other, one another*. (4.13.3)

referent: the person, entity, or group of people/entities referred to by a noun phrase.

reflexive pronoun: a type of pronoun that ends in *-self* and refers back to the subject of the clause: *myself, herself, oneself*. (4.13)

regular plural: the usual rule of adding *-(e)s* to form the plural of a noun: *cow, cows*. (4.8.1)

regular verb: a verb with the usual *-ed* endings for past tense and past participle: *walk, walked, has walked*. (5.5)

relative adverb: a relativizer *where, when*, or *why*, used when the relative clause has an adverbial gap: *that time when you got stuck on the road*. (9.8.1)

relative clause: a type of finite dependent clause used to modify a noun phrase: *the team that performed the kidney transplant*. (8.15.3)

relative pronoun: a relativizer *which, who, whom, whose*, or *that*, used when the relative clause has a non-adverbial gap: *executives who created special programs*. (9.8.1)

relativizer: the word that introduces a relative clause (either a relative pronoun or a relative adverb) and relates it to the preceding noun head. (9.8.1)

repair: an utterance in conversation where a speaker repeats what was said with some sort of correction: *I don't think you sh- I think you should leave . . .* (13.2.5)

reporting clause: a type of peripheral clause that introduces somebody's direct speech or thought: *Can we do some singing? he asks*. (8.15.5)

response form: a word like *yeah* or *no* used in speech to signal a response to the listener.

restrictive postmodifier: a postmodifier that restricts the intended reference of the head noun: *people who want Julius dead*. (9.7)

result copular verb: a copular verb that identifies an attribute that is the result of a process of change: *become, grow, come, turn out*. (5.17.3)

scope: the part of a clause whose semantic interpretation is affected by a modifier or an adverbial. See also scope of negation. (11.2, 11.5)

scope of negation: the part of a clause that becomes negative in meaning due to the occurrence of a negative word. (8.8.9)

semantic: having to do with the meaning of language forms.

semantic categories: the meaning classes of verbs, nouns, adjectives, or adverbs: e.g. activity verbs, time adverbials.

semi-determiner: words like *other* and *same*, which share properties of both determiners and adjectives. (4.7.5)

semi-modal: a multi-word verb that shares some of the grammatical and semantic properties of modal verbs: *have to, be going to*. (6.9)

sentence: a complete structure found in written texts, bounded by sentence punctuation such as '.', '!', '?'.

short passive: another term for agentless passive.

simple aspect: used for verb phrases that are not marked as either perfect aspect or progressive aspect.

species noun: a class of nouns that identify the type of something: *a kind of beer, the type of person*. (4.4.4)

specifying genitive: a genitive functioning like a determiner, and answering the question 'Whose X?' where *X* is the referent of the head noun: *the girl's name* (contrasted with classifying genitive).

speech act: the communicative function associated with an utterance: e.g. *Can you tell me what to do with this?* is a question, or request for information. (13.2.4)

stance: overt expressions of personal attitudes or feelings towards the content of a clause.

stance adverbials: adverbials that express speaker judgments of the proposition expressed by the rest of the clause: *It definitely is a trend*. (11.13, 13.2.4)

statement: a speech act used to report information, and associated with declarative clauses.

stative verbs: verbs that refer to mental states, attitudes/ emotions, perceptions, or other states of existence: *know, feel, see, exist*. (5.3)

stem: the core morpheme of a word to which affixes can be added: *saintliness* = stem *saint* + affix *-ly* + affix *-ness*.

stranded preposition: a preposition that is not followed by its prepositional complement: *Which order shall we go in?* (3.3.5)

style adverbial: a type of stance adverbial that comments on the manner of conveying the message: *But frankly I am not very impressed with it*. (11.13.3)

subject: the clause element that normally occurs before the verb phrase in a clause, and is a noun phrase identifying the agent or experiencer of the verb: *On Tuesday she sang the whole thing to us. Greenland is the place*.

subject predicative: a phrase that occurs after a copular verb and characterizes the subject of the clause: *She is a singer. It feels warm*. (3.5.4)

subject–operator inversion: a change in word order where the subject is preceded by the operator but the rest of the verb phrase (if any) follows the subject: *On no account must he strain*. (12.4)

subject–verb inversion: a change in word order where the subject is preceded by the verb phrase: *After that comes the frog*. (12.4)

subjunctive: the form of a finite verb that is sometimes used in hypothetical or non-factual cases: *whether it be in an office or on the factory floor. If I were you . . .* The subjunctive is rarely used in English. (8.17)

subordination: the type of linkage that allows one clause to be embedded in or dependent on another clause: *I thought about it after I sent the package*. (8.3)

subordinator: a function word used to introduce subordination: *because it was amazing, if he's going with me*. (2.4.6)

suffix: a morpheme added to the end of a word: *excitement, working*.

supplement clause: a peripheral type of non-finite adverbial clause that supplements the information in the main clause, without specifying the exact semantic relationship: *He shook his head, still gazing at the patterns of sunshine . . .* (11.9.2)

syntactic blend: a sentence or clause that finishes in a way that is grammatically inconsistent with the way it began: *That's one of the things that there is a shortage of in this play, is people who actually care*. This is a type of dysfluency in speech. (13.3.1)

syntactic role: the grammatical function that a unit of grammar serves in a higher unit. For example, noun phrases have roles such as subject, direct object, and indirect object in a clause. (2.1, 3.3.1)

syntax: the description of how words, phrases, and clauses are constructed and combined in a language.

tag: a peripheral element added to the end of a clause: see noun phrase tag, question tag, or declarative tag. (3.5.6)

tense: morphological marking on the verb phrase related to time distinctions: compare present tense *kick(s), do(es)* with past tense *kicked, did*. (6.2)

that-clause: a type of finite complement clause introduced by the word *that* as complementizer (although *that* is sometimes omitted): *Booker said **that I should call them up**.* (8.15.1)

to-infinitive clause: a non-finite dependent clause with the base form of a verb preceded by *to*: *They told her **to wait six months**. something **to consider**.* (8.16.1)

token: each occurrence of a word in a text is a token of that word (compare with type). (2.2)

transitive: a valency pattern that includes one or more objects. (3.4)

type: a word considered as a distinct vocabulary item (compare with token). (2.2)

uncountable noun: a type of noun that refers to things that cannot be counted, and normally has no plural form: *milk, equipment, leather*. (4.2)

unit noun: a type of noun that specifies the units used to divide up a generalized mass or substance into countable parts: ***slice** of bread, **grain** of salt*. (4.4.2)

unmarked: the grammatical choice that is most typical, such as subject–verb–object word order in English (compare with marked).

valency pattern: the pattern of clause elements that can occur with a verb: e.g. intransitive, monotransitive. (5.7)

verb: a class of words which have finite and non-finite forms, and normally vary for present and past tense: *have, take, look*. A cover term for lexical verbs and auxiliary verbs. (2.3.2, 2.4.3)

verb contraction: reduction in the spelling and/or pronunciation of verbs used in combination with adjacent words: *I'll, he's*. (8.8.2)

verb phrase: a phrase with a main verb as head: ***tells**, **was taken**, **has been answered***.

verbless clause: a type of non-finite dependent clause with no verb: *The author apologizes **where appropriate**.* (8.16.5)

verbs of aspect: verbs that characterize the stage of progress of an event or activity: *begin, continue, stop*. (5.3)

verbs of existence or relationship: verbs that report a state of existence or a logical relationship: *appear, exist, represent*. (5.3)

verbs of occurrence: verbs that report events that occur without an actor's volition: *become, happen, develop*. (5.3)

vernacular: natural spoken English associated with regional or social dialect, and often not regarded as part of the standard language.

vocative: a peripheral noun phrase used to identify the person who is being addressed: *These are good eggs **Dad**.* (3.5.7, 13.2.3)

voice: the choice in the verb phrase between active (*takes*) and passive (*was taken*) forms. (6.6)

volitional activity: an activity performed intentionally by an agent.

wh-clause: a type of finite clause introduced by a *wh*-word as complementizer: *She didn't ask **what my plans were**.* (10.9–11)

wh-determiner: a determiner which is a *wh*-word: *whose, which*. (4.7.6)

wh-interrogative clause: another term for a *wh*-question.

wh-pronoun: a pronoun which is a *wh*-word: *which, what, who*.

wh-question: a type of interrogative clause with an initial *wh*-word: ***What** are these?* (8.11.1)

wh-word: a word like *who, what, when*, and *where*, used in *wh*-questions and various types of dependent clause. (2.5.1)

word class: a class of words based on grammatical and semantic properties. Two major families of word classes are lexical word classes (nouns, verbs, adjectives, and adverbs) and function word classes (e.g. determiners, prepositions).

yes/no interrogative clause: another term for *yes/no* question.

yes/no question: a type of interrogative clause marked only by subject-operator inversion: ***Is** that right?* (8.11.2)

zero article: the term used where there is no article or other determiner before a noun: *serve **dinner**, drink **wine***. (4.6.2)

zero plural: a plural form which is identical to the singular form: *sheep, deer*. (4.8.4)

zero relativizer: the term used where the relativizer of a relative clause is omitted: *a school ^ I know*. (9.8)

A–Z list of irregular verbs

KEY
The most common verbs are written in **bold**.
Less common verbs are printed in ordinary letters (not bold).
•• Verbs marked like this are **very common** (31 verbs).
• Verbs marked like this are **common** (59 verbs).
Verbs not marked with a bullet point (•) are **less common**.
NOTES: 1 2 3 etc. are explained at the end of the list.

Basic form	Past tense	Past participle
• arise	arose	arisen [see rise]
awake	awoke[1]	awoke[1] [see wake]
•• be	was, were	been
• bear	bore	borne[4]
• beat	beat	beaten
• become	became	become
• begin	began	begun
bend	bent	bent
bet	bet[1]	bet
bid	bade, bid	bid(den)
• bind	bound	bound
bite	bit	bitten
bleed	bled	bled
• blow	blew	blown
• break	broke	broken
breed	bred	bred
•• bring	brought	brought
broadcast	broadcast	broadcast [see cast]
• build	built	built
• burn	burnt[2]	burnt[2]
burst	burst	burst
• buy	bought	bought
cast	cast	cast
• catch	caught	caught
• choose	chose	chosen
cling	clung	clung
•• come	came	come
• cost	cost	cost
creep	crept	crept
• cut	cut	cut
• deal	dealt	dealt
dig	dug	dug
•• do	did	done
• draw	drew	drawn
dream	dreamed, dreamt[2]	dreamed, dreamt[2]
• drink	drank	drunk
• drive	drove	driven
dwell	dwelt[2]	dwelt[2]
• eat	ate	eaten
• fall	fell	fallen
• feed	fed	fed
•• feel	felt	felt
• fight	fought	fought
• find	found	found
flee	fled	fled
fling	flung	flung
fly	flew	flown
forbid	forbad(e)	forbidden [see bid]
forecast	forecast	forecast [see cast]

Basic form	Past tense	Past participle
foresee	foresaw	foreseen [see see]
foretell	foretold	foretold [see tell]
• forget	forgot	forgotten
forgive	forgave	forgiven [see give]
freeze	froze	frozen
•• get	got	got (BrE), gotten (AmE)
•• give	gave	given
•• go	went	gone, been
grind	ground	ground
• grow	grew	grown
• hang	hung[1]	hung[1]
•• have	had	had
•• hear	heard	heard
• hide	hid	hidden
• hit	hit	hit
•• hold	held	held
hurt	hurt	hurt
•• keep	kept	kept
kneel	knelt[2]	knelt[2]
knit	knit[1]	knit[1]
•• know	knew	known
• lay	laid[3]	laid[3]
• lead	led	led
• lean	leant[2]	leant[2]
leap	leapt[2]	leapt[2]
• learn	learnt[2]	learnt[2]
•• leave	left	left
lend	lent	lent
• let	let	let
• lie	lay	lain*
light	lit[1]	lit[1]
• lose	lost	lost
•• make	made	made
•• mean	meant	meant
• meet	met	met
mislead	misled	misled [see lead]
mistake	mistook	mistaken [see take]
misunderstand	misunderstood	misunderstood [see understand, stand]
mow	mowed	mown[1]
overcome	overcame	overcome [see come]
overdo	overdid	overdone [see do]
override	overrode	overridden [see ride]
overrun	overran	overrun [see run]
oversee	oversaw	overseen [see see]
overtake	overtook	overtaken [see take]
overthrow	overthrew	overthrown [see throw]
partake	partook	partaken [see take]
•• pay	paid[3]	paid[3]

*lie meaning 'not telling the truth' is regular: *lie ~ lied ~ lied*

Basic form	Past tense	Past participle
• prove	proved	proven[1]
•• **put**	**put**	**put**
quit	quit[1]	quit[1]
• read	read	read
rid	rid[1]	rid[1]
• ride	rode	ridden
• ring	rang	rung
• rise	rose	risen
•• **run**	**ran**	**run**
saw	sawed	sawn[1]
•• **say**	**said**	**said**
•• **see**	**saw**	**seen**
• seek	sought	sought
• sell	sold	sold
• send	sent	sent
•• **set**	**set**	**set**
sew	sewed	sewn[1]
• shake	shook	shaken
shed	shed	shed
shine	shone[1]	shone[1]
shoe	shod[1]	shod[1]
• shoot	shot	shot
•• **show**	**showed**	**shown**[1]
shrink	shrank	shrunk
• shut	shut	shut
• sing	sang	sung
sink	sank	sunk
• sit	sat	sat
• sleep	slept	slept
slide	slid	slid
sling	slung	slung
slink	slunk	slunk
slit	slit	slit
• smell	smelt[2]	smelt[2]
sow	sowed	sown[1]
• speak	spoke	spoken
speed	sped[1]	sped[1]
spell	spelt[2]	spelt[2]
• spend	spent	spent
spill	spilt[2]	spilt[2]
spin	span, spun	spun
spit	spat, spit	spat, spit
split	split	split
spoil	spoilt[2]	spoilt[2]
• spread	spread	spread
spring	sprang	sprung
•• **stand**	**stood**	**stood**
steal	stole	stolen
• stick	stuck	stuck
sting	stung	stung
stink	stank	stunk
stride	strode	stridden, strode
• strike	struck	struck
string	strung	strung
strive	strove[1]	striven[1]
swear	swore	sworn
sweep	swept	swept
swell	swelled	swollen[1]
swim	swam	swum
swing	swung	swung
•• **take**	**took**	**taken**
• teach	taught	taught
tear	tore	torn
•• **tell**	**told**	**told**
•• **think**	**thought**	**thought**
• throw	threw	thrown
thrust	thrust	thrust
tread	trod	trod
undergo	underwent	undergone [see go]

Basic form	Past tense	Past participle
• understand	understood	understood [see stand]
• undertake	undertook	undertaken [see take]
undo	undid	undone [see do]
• uphold	upheld	upheld [see hold]
upset	upset	upset [see set]
wake	woke[1]	woken[1]
• wear	wore	worn
weave	wove	woven
wed	wed[1]	wed[1]
weep	wept	wept
• win	won	won
wind	wound	wound
withdraw	withdrew	withdrawn [see draw]
withhold	withheld	withheld [see hold]
withstand	withstood	withstood [see stand]
wring	wrung	wrung
•• **write**	**wrote**	**written**

NOTES
[1] means that regular forms are also used.
[2] means that both regular forms and irregular forms exist. The regular spellings are generally more common in AmE, e.g. *leaped*.
[3] *Lay* and *pay* are regular verbs in pronunciation, but the spellings *laid* and *paid* are irregular. (Compare the regular *stayed*, *prayed*.)
[4] **Be born** occurs only as a passive form. It is related to *bear ~ bore ~ borne*.

Index

Note: Page references in *italics* indicate tables; those in **bold type** indicate major references to topics; those in ***bold italic*** indicate terms in the Glossary. Headwords in bold type indicate major topics.

A

a/an 41, 56, 58, 67–8, 72, ***457***
about 29, 126
academic prose
  formality in 287
  information density of 5, 23, 187, 189–90, 268, 269, 297
  lexical density in 19, 105–6
  as register category 3, 5, *9*
  see also discussions of corpus findings in all chapters
activity verb 106–7, 128, 137, 270, ***455***
  and aspect 161, 163, 165
  with *ing*-complement clause 344, 346–7
  multi-word 128, 131–2, 133
  single-word 106–7, 110, 112
  and tense 155–6
'add-on' strategy 228, 436, **438–9**, ***455***
  see also preface; tag
adjectival clause *see* relative clause
adjective 22, **187–93**, **197–204**, ***455***
  absolute meanings 217–18
  v. adverb 195–6
  attributive *see* attributive adjective
  be + adjective 191
  in binomial expression 198–9, 449
  central 188–90, ***455***
  characteristics **188–90**
  as classifier 197–8, 199–200, 201, 278, ***455***
  as clause link 203
  color 188, 197, 277–8
  combinations 198–9, 204–5, 209, 279
  comparative *see* comparative adjective
  compound 22, 192, 209, 278
  degree complement 219
  as descriptor 188, 197–8, 199, 201, 217, 278, ***456***
  as exclamation 203
  with extraposed clauses 318–19
  formation 22, **190–3**, 215–18
  gradable 22, 167, 188, 189, 198, 215, ***457***
    and degree adverbs 209, 210
  modification 23, 196, 202, 204–5, 276, 277, 402
  as modifier *see* modifier; postmodifier; premodifier
  nominalized 89

adjective—*cont.*
  as noun phrase head 22, 42, 188, 202–3
  participial 24, 167, 190–1, 277, ***459***
  peripheral 188, 189, ***459***
  with post-predicate clause 318, **335–6**
  as postmodifier 202
  predicative *see* predicative adjective
  register distribution 23, 187, 191–3, *191*, 198, 217
  syntactic roles 22, 187, 188, 198, 202–4
  with *that*-clause 202, 219, 308, 312, 317–19
  of time 188, 197, 199
  with *to*-clause 219, 335–6, 337–8, 339, 342–3, 351
  see also adjective: semantic domains; binomial expression; comparative clause and phrase; morphology; stance adjective; superlative adjective
adjective complement clause 200–1, 202, 257, 308, 310–11, ***459***
adjective phrase 43–4, ***455***
  with complements 43
  with infinitive clause 259
  with *ing*-clause 260
  as modifier *see* modifier; postmodifier
  as predicative 22, 50, 141, 142
  as stance adverbial 203
  as subject predicative 43–4, 45, 141, 142
  syntactic roles 22, 43–4
adjective: semantic domains 22, 188, **197–9**
  ability/willingness 335, 351
  affect 201, 317, 319, 335
  certainty 202, 318, 319, 335, 338, 341
  ease/difficulty 336, 338, 339, 342
  evaluative 144, *144–5*, 198, 199–200, 201, 217, 434
    in complement clauses 317, 319, 336, 339, 347–8
  habitual behaviour 183
  necessity/importance 202, 319, 339, 351
adverb 22–3, 187, **193–6**, **204–15**, ***455***
  v. adjective 195–6
  as clause element *see* adverbial
  combinations 204–6, 209
  comparative 22, **218**, 258
  as complement of preposition 206, 260
  compound 194
  with degree complement 23, 24, 219–20
  fixed phrase as 194
  formation 22, **193–6**
  interrogative 33
  modification of 205–6, 385

adverb —*cont.*
  as modifier *see* modifier; postmodifier;
    premodifier
  postposed 204
  prepositional 30
  register distribution 23, 187, 194–5, *194*, 204–5,
    211, 214–15, *214*, 431
  relative adverb 33, 282, **460**
  simple 193
  stance 208, **212–13**, 214
  standing alone 207–8
  superlative 22, **218**
  syntactic roles 23, 187, 193, **204–8**
  and word order 277
  see also adverb: semantic domains; adverbial;
    amplifier; binomial expression;
    circumstance adverbial; degree adverb;
    deictic; downtoner; intensifier; morphology
adverb phrase 44, *455*
  as adverbial 44, 51, 207, 219, 358
  head 23, 44
  as modifier 44, 205
  syntactic roles 44
adverb: semantic domains 23, 208–15
  additive/restrictive 211, 415
  courtesy 213
  linking 213, 214–15
  manner 209, 210, 289
  means 213
  place 34, 206, 208, 413
  purpose 213
  time 152, 206, 208, 214
adverbial 23, 50–1, 187, 207, 353–96, 455
  addition/restriction adverbial 366, 371–2
  adverb as 193, 195, 209, 355, 358–9
  adverb phrase as 44, 207, 209, 219, 358
  circumstance *see* circumstance adverbial
  classes 354, **355–7**
    see also circumstance adverbial; linking
      adverbial; stance adverbial
  comparative 364
  ed-clause as 227, 260, 358
  with existential *there* 415
  finite clause as 227, 358
  infinitive clause as 227, 259
  ing-clause as 227, 260, 358
  with inversion **460**
  linking *see* linking adverbial
  multiple 18, 355
  and negation 245
  non-finite clause as 260, 358, 364–5, 376–7,
    380
  noun phrase as 42, 51, 355, 358
  obligatory 50–1, 355, 369
    and copular verb 51, 120, 135, 140
  one-word 372

adverbial —*cont.*
  optional 51, 119, 121, 122–3, 355–6, 357, 370
  peripheral 51, 53
  place *see* circumstance adverbial
  positions 51, 355, **359–60**, 361, 406–7, 415
  prepositional phrase as 45, 51, 130, 269, 290,
    355, 358–9, 416
  register distribution 214, 357, 359, *359*, 360
  scope 361
  semantic roles 354–5, 406
  stance *see* stance adverbial
  syntactic forms 355, **358–9**
  temporal *see* circumstance adverbial
  to-clause as 358, 376, 377, 379
  see also adverbial clause
adverbial clause 257, 455
  as circumstance adverbial *see* adverbial clause as
    circumstance adverbial
  as comment clause 257
  register distribution 375, 439
  as stance adverbial 385
  and subjunctive 261
  and subordinator 31, 257, 374, 376, 380–2
  and *wh*-words 257
**adverbial clause as circumstance adverbial 257,
  373–82**
  as discourse frame 379
  ed-clause 374–5, 377–8
  finite clause 376–7, 380–1
  ing-clause 374–5, 377–8
  non-finite clause 358, 374–5, 376–7, 380
  positions **378–9**
  register distribution 375–6, *375*
  semantic categories 152, 257, 294, **373–6**
  see also contingency adverbial; place adverbial;
    process/manner adverbial; proportion
    clause; time adverbial
  syntactic forms *376*, **376–8**
  to-clause 376, 377, 379
  see also conditional clause; preference clause;
    proportion clause; subordinator;
    supplement clause; *though*
adverbial particle *see* particle, adverbial
affective verb 344
affix 17, **88–90**, 91, 118–19, 191–2, *455*, *456*
  see also prefix; suffix
affixation *455*
after 31, 381
agent *455*
  subject as 48, 106–7, 164–5, 168
  see also passive, long
agreement, subject-verb *see* subject-verb concord
almost 210
American English
  and adverbials 386–7
  and adverbs 196, 205

American English —*cont.*
  and aspect 158–9, 160
  and complement clause 315, 348–9
  and conversational grammar 442–3
  as dialect 5, 6–7
  and inserts 449–53, *449*, *453*
  and modals and semi-modals 174, 253
  and negation 243
  and noun compounds 60
  and premodification 275–6
  and pronoun use 95, 100
  and regular/irregular verbs 117–18
  and subject-verb concord 235
amplifier 209–10, 211, 366, **455**
anaphora *see* reference, anaphoric
and 30–1, 198, 227–8, 229, 233–4, 278, 448
antecedent 95, 97, 257, **455**
anyway 394, 395
apologies 433
apposition *see* linking adverbial, semantic
  categories; noun phrase
approximator 212, **455**
  see also hedge
aren't I 242–3
article 67–72, 455
  definite 56, 70–1, 72, 203, **456**
    and anaphoric reference 70, 72
    as determiner 26, 67, 76
    with genitive 82
    and proper nouns 60
  and generic reference 72
  indefinite 26, 56, 67–8, 71, **457**
  register distribution 67, 71
  zero 67, 68–70, 72, **461**
as
  as adverb complement 219–20, 258, *410*
  in comparative 96
  as preposition *36*
  as subordinator 31, *36*, 381, 404
aspect 21, 156–66, 455
  and passive 173–4
  past perfect 136, 157, 159, 161, 162
  past progressive 163, 165
  perfect 112, 118, **156–62**, 173, 241, *459*
    with modal verbs 28, 115, 183
  perfect progressive 157, 158, *459*
  present perfect 136–7, 157, 159–62
  present progressive 162
  progressive **156–9**, **162–5**, 173–4, *459*
    and *ing*-words 135, 183, 293, 347
    with modal verbs 183–4
    with primary auxiliaries 28, 135
  register distribution 158–9, *158*, 163, 164–5,
    173–4
  simple 158, 161–2, **460**
  stative 112

aspect —*cont.*
  and tense 136, 156–62
  see also direct speech reporting
aspect verb **109**, *461*
  with *ing*-complement clause 109, 344, 346–7
  single-word 109
  with *to*-complement clause 109, *333*, 334
assertion
  in elliptic reply
  in interrogative clause 246, **455**
  in negation 244, 246–7, **455**
attention signal 432, *451*, 453, *453*
attitude verb 155, 163
attributive adjective 44, 188, 189, 191, **199–200**,
  455
  common 199–200, *200*
  and intensifier 199
  as modifier 199, 264, 268, 272
  and peripheral adjective 189
  register distribution 189–90, *190*, 192, 199–200,
    200, 431
  see also adjective; adjective: semantic domains
auxiliary verb 16, **27–8**, 115, **455**
  and aspect 28
  in interrogative clauses 42, 138, 252, 253–4
  v. lexical verb 21
  v. main verb 42, 103–4
  modal 28, 42, 104, 174, 175, 242, 243–4, **458**
  in negative clauses 28, 242
  and operators 238, 239
  and passive 28
  primary 27
  and subject-verb concord 237
  in verb phrase 42, 149
  see also be; do; have

B

backchannel 251, 432, **455**
bare infinitive *see* infinitive clause, bare
base 17, 115, 118, 261, **455**
be 44, 50, **135–7**, 139, 140–1, 232, 323, 360, **456**
  as auxiliary verb 21, 27–8, 135, 166
  with complement clause 141, 317, 334, 338–9
  contraction 237, 240–1, 242–3, 435
  existential 141–2
  with existential *there* 412, 414
  with *it*-cleft 420, 421
  as lexical verb 21, 103–4, 105–6
  as main verb 28, 105–6, 135
  and negation 238, 240
  as operator 238
  with passive 28, 115, 135, 166, 171–2, 331
  and personal pronoun 96
  with progressive aspect 28, 135
  register distribution 105, 141–2

be—*cont.*
  in relative clause 295
  and subject-verb concord 237
  and verb contraction 237, 240–1, 242–3, 435
be going to 28, 175, 182, 184–5
become 50, 109, 145
before 36, 257, 381
binomial expression **448–9**, **455**
  adjective + adjective 198–9, 449
  adverb + adverb 448
  noun + noun 448
  verb + verb 448
blend, syntactic 437–8, **460**
block language 69, 255–6, 262, **455**
body *see* conversation

C

can 21, 28, 104, 174, 177–8, *177*, 179, *179*, 184
  register distribution 435
capitals, initial 59–60
case 79–84, **455**
  accusative 48, 79, 93, 96, **455**
  nominative 48, 79, 93, 96, **458**
  and personal pronouns 93, 96
  see also genitive; inflection
cataphora *see* reference, cataphoric
causative verb **108**, **455**
  and aspect 163
  multi-word 132
  single-word 108, 111
  with *to*-complement clause 108, *333*, 334
choice, and grammar 1, 3–4
circumstance adverbial 194, 207, 354, 355, **362–82**, **455**
  clause as *see* adverbial clause as circumstance adverbial
  common adverbials 368–9
  and dangling participle 377–8
  position 360, *369*, **369–72**
  prepositional phrase as 126, 142, 354, 359
  register distribution 357, 367–9, 375–6, *375*
  scope 355, 361, 366, 370–2
  semantic categories **362–8**, *367*
    additional categories 373–6
    recipient 367
    see also addition/restriction adverbial; contingency adverbial; degree adverbial; place adverbial; process/manner adverbial; time adverbial
  v. stance adverbial 385
  see also finite clause; non-finite clause; noun phrase; prepositional phrase
classes
  open v. closed 15, **16–17**, 104, **455**, **458**
  see also lexical word, class

classifier *see* adjective, as classifier; genitive, classifying
clausal unit in conversation, ellipsis in 441–3
clause 13, **221–62**, **455**
  adjectival *see* relative clause
  coordinated 222, 223, *224*, 227–9, 248
  distribution 222–3
  elements **46–54**, 323
    see also adverbial; direct object; indirect object; object predicative; operator; prepositional object; subject; verb phrase
  embedded 31, 38, 222, 223, 224–7, *224*, *225*, 228
  existential *see there*, existential
  extraposed *see* extraposition
  links 33, 227–9
  main 31, 401, 439, **458**
  negative *see* negation
  v. non-clausal material **222–3**
  peripheral elements 53–4, **459**
  as postmodifier 266
  subordination 31, 222, 223, 224–7, 256
  temporal 246
  types 46–7
    see also adverbial clause; comment clause; comparative clause; complement clause; conditional clause; declarative clause; degree clause; dependent clause; exclamative clause; finite clause; imperative clause; independent clause; infinitive clause; interrogative clause; non–finite clause; relative clause; reporting clause; supplement clause
  verbless 259, **261**, 358, 360, **461**
  see also discourse marker; ellipsis; insert; parentheticals; preface; tag; vocative
clause patterns 46–7, 226–7
  infinitive clauses 329–32
  subject + verb + optional adverbial 121, 122–3
  see also end weight principle; fronting; inversion; postponement; valency patterns; word order
clefting 398, **419–23**, **455**
  demonstrative *wh*-cleft 421, 422–3, 425, *425*
  it-cleft 420, 422
  register distribution 422–3, *422*, *425*
  reversed *wh*-cleft 421
  wh-cleft 420, 421
cognition verb *see* mental verb
cohesion **455**
  and adverbials 366, 379, 388, 407, 415
  and fronting 402, 403, 405
  and information principle 340, 370, 399
  and inversion 406, 407, 408
collective noun 60, **455**
  as countable 61

collective noun —*cont.*
  with genitives 82
  of-collective 61
  and subject-verb concord 235
collocation 18, **455**
  with copular verbs 145–6
  fixed 83
  v. lexical bundle 444
  and negation 245
  with package nouns 61–2, 63–4
combination, word 18
  complex prepositions 29
  v. lexical bundle 444
  verb + noun phrase 134, 329
  verb + particle 128–9
  verb + prepositional phrase 126, 134
  verb + verb 134, 448
  see also free combination; lexical bundle; lexical
    verb, multi-word
come 112, 128, 133, 140, *147*, 152, 346
commands 251, 394, 440–1
  and emphatic *do* 139
  and imperative clauses 255
comment clause 257
  as stance adverbial 439
common noun 20–1, 56, **456**
  and modification 21, 294
  package noun 60–4
  v. proper noun 56, **59–60**
  see also countable noun; uncountable noun
communication verb 107, **316–17**, 363, **456**
  and aspect 160, 163
  with *ing*-complement clause 347
  multi-word 131
  single-word 107, 111
  and tense 156
  with *that*-complement clause *315*, 316–17
  with *to*-complement clause *332*
  with *wh*-complement clause *324*, *325*, 326
  see also speech-act verb
comparative adjective 215–18, *216*, 258, 402
  doubly marked 217
  inflectional 22, 188, 215–16, 217, 219
  phrasal 215–16, 217
  register distribution 217
  repeated 198
  see also comparative clause and phrase;
    superlative adjective
comparative clause and phrase 96, **218–20**, 258,
  456
  assertive v. non-assertive forms 246
  and ellipsis 220, 231
  with inversion *410*
complement **456**
  of adjective 43, 200–1, 219, 307–8, 323–4
  of adverb 219–20

complement —*cont.*
  of copular verbs *143–5*, 146, *147*
  noun phrase as 42, 259
  see also complement clause; prepositional
    complement
complement clause 256–7, **300–6**, **307–52**, *456*
  with adjective phrase 43
  choice of **349–51**
  and clefting 421
  controlled by adjective *see* adjective complement
    clause
  controlled by noun 257, **300–6**, 308
    see also noun complement clause
  controlled by predicate 202, 257, 308, 310
  controlled by verb **307–52**
    see also verb complement clause
  and copular verb 141–6
  as dependent clause 256–8, 308
  and ellipsis 220, **348–9**
  finite *see that*-complement clause; *wh*-
    complement clause
  fronted 401–2
  grammatical positions 172, **310–12**
  infinitival *see to*-complement clause
  with lexical bundle 445–6
  and lexical verbs 108, 109, 121
  as nominal clause 236, 308, 421
  non-finite *see ing*-complement clause; *to*-
    complement clause
  and prepositions 45
  register distribution 350, 431
  structural types 308–9, 349–51
  subordinator *see* if; *that*-complement clause;
    whether
  syntactic role 256
  with verbs 304, 307–8
  see also adjective complement clause; *ed*-
    participle clause; extraposition; *ing*-
    complement clause; noun complement
    clause; *that*-complement clause; *to*-
    complement clause; verb complement
    clause; *wh*-complement clause
complement phrase, and predicative adjective 142
complementation *see* clause patterns; valency
    patterns
complementizer 308, **456**
  infinitive marker *to* 34, 348
  wh-words 31, 33, 326, 348
  see also if; *that*-complement clause
complex transitive *see* valency patterns, complex
    transitive
compounding 17, 18, **91–2**, 209, 277, **456**
  see also adjective, compound; adverb,
    compound; noun, compound; pronoun,
    compound
concord *see* subject-verb concord

condensation 223, **230–2**, 440–1, *456*
  see also directive; ellipsis
conditional clause 257, 373–4, 379
  assertive/non-assertive 246, 374
  hypothetical (unreal) 151, 374, 375, 377, 380, *457*
  with inversion 380, *410*
  open (real) 373, 375
  rhetorical 374
conjunction 30, 53, 258, 408, *456*
  see also coordinator; subordinator
connective 138–9
contingency adverbial 365–6, 373
contraction
  of auxiliary verb 27, 28, 140, 240
  negative 28, 239, 240, 242–3, 244, *458*
  register distribution 241, 242, 243, 434
  of verb 237, 240–1, *240*, 242–3, 435, *461*
  see also be
contrast 138–9, 199, 398, **399**
  by clefting 420, 422
conversation 427–54
  and adjectives 187
  complexity v. simplicity in 436
  dysfluencies 11, 434, **436–8**, *456*
    see also 'add-on' strategy; blend, syntactic;
      hesitator; pause; repair; repeat; utterance,
      incomplete
  ellipsis in 231, 348, 430, 436, 441–3
  functional characteristics 428, **429–35**
  information density in 190
  and inserts 19, 430, **449–53**
  as interactive 5, 252, 388, 430, 431–3, 449
  lexical bundle in 19, 428, 434, 443–9, *444*
  lexical density in 23, 105–6, 430
  negation in 247, 431
  non-clausal units 255–6, 430, 432, 436, **440–1**
  non-elaboration/specification of meaning 430–1
  real-time contruction 428, 434–5, **436–43**
  as register category 3, 4
  restricted repertoire 434–5
  shared context 267, 429, 430
  standard English in 6
  and subject-verb concord 237
  and vernacular grammar 6, 237, 437
  see also direct speech reporting; discourse;
    imperative clause; insert; interrogative
    clause, *yes-no*; politeness; preface; tag;
    vocative
conversion *91*, **91**, *456*
coordination 4, 222, **227–9**, 255, *456*
  with clausal/non-clausal units 30, *224*, 227–8, 248
  and ellipsis 230
  and personal pronouns 94
  phrasal 227–8

coordination—*cont.*
  of premodifiers 278–9
  register distribution 228
  and subject-verb concord 233–4
  see also binomial expression; tag
coordinator 16, **30**, 224, 227, *456*
  v. adverbial 227
  correlative 30, 229, *456*
  sentence-initial v. turn-initial 227, 229
  v. subordinator 225
  see also and; or
copula 47, 120, *456*
copular verb 140–7
  with complement clause *143–5*, 146, *147*, 317, 334, 338–9
  current 140–1, 142–4, *144–5*, *456*
  as existence verb 109, 141–4
  functions 141–6
  with participial adjective 190
  phrasal verb as 128, 129, 141
  as primary auxiliary
  register distribution 144, 145–6
  result 140–1, 145–6, *147*, 198, *460*
  sensory 142–4
  with subject predicative 50, 120, 135, 140–7, 188, 200, 310–11, 313
  with *to*-infinitive 334
  valency patterns 47, 120, *456*
  see also be; subject predicative
corpus-based approach 2, 3–4
countable noun 57–8, 60–4, *456*
  and article 56, 58, 68–9, 70, 72
  and determiner 65, 74, 75–6
  plural 56
  and quantifier 74–5

D

declarative clause 139, **249**, 255, *456*
  as directive 249
  with ellipsis 442
  and existential *there* 413
  and fronting 401
  and intransitive phrasal verb 128
  lexical bundle in 446
  negative 240
  preface with 418
  and tag 53, 258, 419, *456*
definite article *see* article, definite
degree *see* amplifier; comparative clause;
    intensifier
degree adjective *see* comparative adjective;
    superlative adjective
degree adverb 188, 209–11, 214, 216
  see also adverb, comparative; *so*; *that*
degree adverbial 366, 367, 371–2

degree clause 31, 246, 402–3, *456*
deictic 214, 369, 430, *456*
demonstrative *see* determiner, demonstrative
demonstrative pronoun 98–9, *456*
 and anaphoric reference 74
 with demonstrative *wh*-cleft 421
 as determiner 26–7
 with existential *there* 417
 and modification 271
 register distribution 98–9
 as tag 419
 those with postmodifier 271
 see also that; this
dependent clause 256–62, *456*
 with clefting 420, 421
 and ellipsis 231, 262
 embedded 31, 224, 248, 419
 finite 225, 226–7, **256–8**, 308–9, 350, 380–1
 fronting in 404
 interrogative 301–2, 326–8, 409–10
 inversion in 409–11, *410*
 and negation 246
 non-finite 225–6, **259–61**
 and past perfect aspect 162
 register distribution 439
 and simple past tense 151
 and subjunctive verbs 261
 and subordinator 31, **224–7**, 404
 unembedded 262
 see also adverbial clause; complement clause;
  noun complement clause; relative clause;
  that-complement clause; *to*-complement
  clause; *wh*-complement clause
derivation 17, *456*
 adjective 22, **191–2**
 and gender
 noun 20, 85, **88–92**, 108
 verbs 21, **118–19**
 zero 91
 see also adverb, formation; affix; conversion;
  prefix; suffix
descriptive grammar 7
determiner 26, 65–77, *456*
 central 65, 66
 comparative 258
 definite/indefinite *see* article
 demonstrative 26, 65, **73–4**, 98, *456*
 interrogative 33
 v. noun 66
 with noun-head phrase 41, 65, 66, 72, 264
 v. pronoun 66, *67*
 and referential specification 70–2, 80, 272
 register distribution 32, *32*
 relative 33
 semi-determiner 66, **77**, 101, 231, 233, *460*
 wh-determiner 26, 65, **77**, *461*

determiner —*cont.*
 see also article; genitive; numeral; possessive
  determiner; postdeterminer; predeterminer;
  quantifier; reference, generic
dialect
 American v. British English 3, 5, 6–7, 158–9
 and contraction 243
 in LSWE Corpus 3, 5–6, 7–8
 and modals 174
 and negation 247
 regional/social 435
 and register 5, 435
diminisher 210, 366, *456*
direct object 49, *456*
 and adverbial particle 425
 complement clause as 308, 310
 ed-particle as 260
 finite clause as 226–7
 infinitive clause as 226–7, 259
 ing-clause as 226–7, 260
 noun phrase as 125, 126, 130, 172, 330, 424
 with object predicative 50, 201, 424
 of phrasal verb 127–8, 424–5
 postponed 424
 and predicative 50
 and prepositional phrase 423
 of prepositional verb 129–30, 131, 367
 pronoun as 125, 127–8, 423, 424
 pronoun sequence as 423
 semantic roles 49
 and valency patterns 49, 120
 word-order options 423
 see also clause patterns; complement clause; gap
direct speech reporting 192, 328
 and communication verbs 316
 past tense with reporting verb 111, 152–3
 and *that*-complement clause 316
 and zero relativizer 288–9
 see also reporting clause
directive 128, 248–9, *249*, 251, 255, 433, *456*
 condensed 440–1
discourse marker 391, 419, 433, 440, *450–1*, *453*,
 456
 in imperative clause 255
 v. stance adverbial 386
 see also insert; linking adverbial
dislocation **418–19**, *456*
 see also preface; tag, noun phrase
ditransitive *see* valency patterns, ditransitive
do 137–9
 as auxiliary verb 21, 27–8, 42, 104, 138, 240
 do-support 138, 139, *456*
 as dummy operator 138, 238, 239–40, 243–4,
  252, 253–4, 406, 408, *456*
 v. ellipsis 138, 231
 emphatic 138–9, 403

do—*cont.*
  in idiomatic expressions 134
  and imperative clauses 139
  in interrogative clauses 28, 42, 138
  as lexical verb 21
  as main verb 27, 104, 137–8
  in negative clauses 28, 138, 239–40
  as pro-verb 137–8, 139
  as stranded operator 139
  with subject-operator inversion 408
  and subject-verb concord 237
downtoner 210, *456*
dummy operator *see* do
dummy pronoun *see* it
dysfluencies *see* conversation, dysfluencies

E

early 36
echoing 250, 403
ed-participle 116–18, 260, 377, *457*, *459*
  and participial adjectives 190–1
  and passive voice 135, 166, 183, 292–3
  and perfect aspect 11, 118, 160, 183
ed-participle clause 260, *456*
  as adverbial 227, 260, 358, 374–5
  common controlling verbs 309
  as complement clause 309
  as object predicative 227
  as postmodifier 260, 266, 270, 272, 291, 292–3
  register distribution 292
  restrictive and non-restrictive 281
ed-predicate, fronted 404
effort verb
  with *ing*-clause 347
  with *to*-clause 333, *333*
elision 434
ellipsis 230–2, 436, *457*
  in clausal units 222, 223, 441–3
  in comparative clause 220, 231
  in complement clause 220, **348–9**
  in coordinate clause 230
  v. *do* 137–8, 231
  elliptic genitives 81, 97, 231
  final (post-operator) 230, 239, **442**
  initial (situational) 230, **441–2**
  in interrogative clause 231, 251
  medial (operator) 230, **442–3**
  in non-clausal units 440
  in noun phrases 81, 231
  situational *see* ellipsis, initial
  textual v. situational 230
embedding 298–9, *457*
  and complement clause 350
  and coordination 228
  and dependent clause 31, 224, 248, 298–9, 419

embedding—*cont.*
  multiple *298*, 299, 439
  phrases 38, 40, *41*, 45, 265, 299
  and subordination 222, 223, 224–7, *224*, *225*
  that-clause 313, 320
  see also dependent clause; parentheticals
emphasis 98, 138–9, 387, 388, **399**, 403–4, 421
  see also focus; word order
enclitics
end weight principle 398, **400**, 419, *457*
  and adverbials 360, 370
  and clause-end patterns 131, 320, 342, 423
  and fronting 404
  and genitive v. *of*-phrase 84, *84*
  and long passive 169–70
  and subject-verb inversion 406, 407, 411
endearments 433
evaluation *see* adjective: semantic domains,
    evaluative; stance; stance adverbial
exclamation 203, *457*
exclamative clause 248, *249*, 251, **254**, *457*
  and adjectives 203
  and degree adverbs 210
  with fronting 404–5
  indirect 323
  register distribution 253, 433
  and *wh*-words 322–3, 404
  see also expletive; interjection
existence verb **109**, *461*
  and aspect 160
  and copular verbs 109, 141–4, 414
  multi-word 132
  single-word 109
  with *to*-complement clause *333*, 334, 337, 341
expletive 7, 250, 433, *452–3*, *457*
extraposition 259, *457*
  in *that*-complement clause 311, 313, 317, **318–
    21**, 337, 350
  in *to*-infinitive clause 259, 311, 328, **338–42**, 350
  in *wh*-complement clause 311

F

false starts 434
farewells 432, *450*, *453*
feminine *see* gender
fiction
  and dialect 6
  as register category 3, 5, *8*
  *see also discussions of corpus findings in all
    chapters*
finite clause *457*
  as postmodifier 266
  and style adverbial 386
  subject of 376–7
  and subject-verb concord 232, 236

finite clause —*cont.*
  and subordinator 380
  see also dependent clause, finite
focus 399, 400, 416–17, 421, 422
  double 398, 399, 403
  end-**focus** 84, 398, 399, 404, 408, 417, 419, *457*
  and fronting 402, 403, 404, 405
  and inversion 406, 409
  see also emphasis; word order
formality 287
free combination *457*
  v. multi-word lexical verb 124–5, 126, 127, 128–9, 134, 329, 448
fronting 400–5, *457*
  with bare infinitive 403–4
  with clefting 420
  in dependent clauses 404
  in exclamations 404–5
  with inversion 402–3, 404
  in non-finite constructions 403–4
  of objects and other nominals 401–2, 405
  of predicative 402–3, 405
  of prepositional phrase 288
  register distribution 405
  types 401–5, *401*
function, and structure 248–9
function word 16, 19, **26–35**, 273, 447, *457*
  borderline cases 29
  classes 16, 26–32
  register distribution 32, *32*, 430
  special classes 32–5
  see also auxiliary verb; coordinator; determiner;
    not; numeral; particle, adverbial;
    preposition; pronoun; subordinator; *there*;
    to; *wh*-word
future tense *see* aspect; modal verb; tense, and
  time; volition/prediction

G

gap 281–2, 284, *457*
  adverbial 282–3, **289–91**, 293–4
  direct object 282, 283, 293–4
  prepositional object 293
  subject v. non-subject 283, 286–8, 291–2, 293, 301
  see also relative clause
gender 85–8, 93, *457*
  classes 85–6
  personal v. non-personal reference 85, 87–8
genitive 20, **79–84**, *457*
  attributive 83
  classifying 80–1, *455*
  as determiner 65, 80, 93
  double 82, *456*
  elliptic 81, 97, 231

genitive —*cont.*
  form 79–80
  independent 81, *457*
  and modification 80–1, 272
  and *of*-phrases 80, 82–4, *84*
  possessive 83
  register distribution 84, *84*
  specifying 80–1, *460*
  subjective 83
  of time and measure 81
genitive phrase 81
get 7, 111–12, 117–18, 133, 146, 159–60, 309, 346
  get-passive 112, 166, 171–2, 331, *457*
go 103, 112, 117, 128, 140, 146, 152, 346
going to 153, **182**, 184–5
good
  as adjective 142, 198–9, 339
  as adverb 195–6
  as intensifier 198–9, 211
grammatical units
  discourse function 14
  internal structure 13–14
  meaning 14
  syntactic role 14
  types 13
  see also clausal unit; non-clausal unit; phrase;
    preface; tag; word
graphemes 13
Greek words, plurals 79
greetings 432, 433, 443, *450*, 453, *453*
guess 314–15, 348, 349

H

have 104, 309
  and aspect 28, 115, 136–7, 159–60
  as auxiliary verb 21, 27–8, 104, 136–7, 241
  and contraction 240–1, 242, 243
  v. existential *there* 136
  in idiomatic phrases 134
  and interrogative clause 253
  as lexical verb 21, 243, 253
  as main verb 27, 136
  as operator 239, 243, 253, 406
  as possessive 136, 160
  and prepositional phrase 294–5
  register distribution 136
have to 136, 175, 180, *180*, 184–5, 243, 253
head *see* noun phrase head
hedge 210, 212, 229, 384, 431, *457*
  coordination tag as 229
  as stance adverbs 212
here 193, 407
hesitator 434, 449, *452*
honorifics 433

hyphenation
    and compounding 18, 192, 209
    and multiple modification 276, 278

I

idioms 112–13, 123–5, 136, **457**
    with *do* 134
    and free combination 18, 126–7, 130, 134,
        137
    v. lexical bundle 447–8
    register distribution 448
if 31, 152, 257, **326–8**, 368, 375, 381, 385
imperative clause 139, **254–5**, *457*
    discourse function 254–5, 368
    with intransitive phrasal verb 128
    with *let's* 250, 254, 433
    long verb phrase as 52
    negative 240
    and question tags 255
    register distribution 255, 432
    second-person 433
    subject of 254
    and subject-verb concord 232
    and vocative 254
impersonal pronoun *it see* clefting; extraposition;
    it
indefinite pronoun 99–101, *457*
    direct object as 424
    with modifier 202, 271
    and quantifying determiner 27
    and subject-verb concord 234
    see also one; pronoun, compound; quantifier
independent clause **248–56**, *457*
    complex 248
    coordinated 224, 248
    and ellipsis 231
    inversion in 400
    structure and speech-act functions 248–9
    see also clausal unit; declarative clause; directive;
        exclamative clause; interrogative clause;
        question
indirect object 49, 367, *457*
    clause patterns 121
    noun phrase as 330
    pronoun sequence as 423
    semantic roles 49
        recipient 367
    word-order options 423
indirect speech *see* reporting clause
infinitive clause **259**, 328, *457*
    bare 174, 309, 329, 403–4, 421, **455**
    as direct object 227, 259
    post-predicate **328–36**
    as postmodifier 291
    register distribution 328, 329

infinitive clause —*cont.*
    wh-clause 324
    see also raising; *to*-clause; *to*-complement clause
inflection *457*
    of adjectives 22, 188–9, 215, 217, 219
    of adverbs 218
    and lexical words 17
    of nouns 20
    of verbs 115–18
    see also case; gender; genitive
informality 196, 287, 328, 423, 435, 543
information, structuring 379
information-flow principle 84, *457*
    and circumstance adverbial 370, 379
    and clefting 422
    and fronting 402–3, 404
    and inversion 406, 411
    and passive 169–70
    and *that*-clause 320
    and *to*-clause 340, 341–2
    and word order 169, **398–9**, 400, 415, 417
informational density 273
    of academic prose 5, 23, 187, 189–90, 268, 269,
        297
    of conversation 190
    of news 5, 19, 23, 189–90, 274–5, 297
ing-complement clause 45, **259–60**, **344–8**
    controlled by adjective 344, 347–8, 350
    controlled by verb 344–7, 350
    as non-finite clause 350
    as non-finite dependent clause 308–9
    as noun complement clause 301, 305
    as object of preposition 227, 260
    post-predicate **344–8**
    register distribution 292, 344, 346–7, 350
ing-participle 377, *457*
    noun v. adjective 24, 25, 191
    noun v. verb 24–5
    and participial adjectives 190–1
    v. preposition 135
    and progressive aspect 135, 183, 292, 347
        see also aspect, progressive
    verb v. adjective 25
ing-participle clause 151, *457*, *459*
    as adverbial 227, 260, 358, 374–5
    as postmodifier 260, 266, 291, 292–3
    and progressive aspect 293
    restrictive and non-restrictive 281
    with subordinators 226–7
    syntactic role 259–60, 344
    see also ing-complement clause
ing-predicate, fronted 404
insert 428, **449–53**, *450–3*, *457*
    and multi-word lexical units 54
    v. non-clausal unit 440
    polite speech-act formulae 452

insert —*cont.*
  register distribution 16, 19, 430, 433, 449, *449,*
    450–3
  see also attention signal; discourse marker;
    expletive; farewells; greetings; hesitator;
    interjection; response
intensifier *457*
  adjective as 198–9, 211
  degree adverb as 209–10, 399, 403
  degree adverbial as 366
  and inversion 406
  see also emphasis; fronting; *so; very*
interjection 433, 440, *450, 453,* *457*
  see also insert
interrogative clause **249–54,** *457*
  assertive/non-assertive 246, *455*
  with auxiliary *do* 42, 138, 252, 253–4
  condensed question 440
  declarative 249, 252
  dependent 301–2, 326–8, 409–10
  and dummy *do* 253–4
  echo questions 250
  and ellipsis 231, 251, 441–2
  fragments 447
  with inversion 238, 250, 251, 400, 410–11, *410*
  lexical bundle in 446
  and negative 240
  and noun phrase tag 419
  preface with 419
  register distribution 252
  rhetorical questions 250, 252
  and stranded prepositions 45
  who v. *whom* 7, 253
  yes-no 138, 174, 241, 249, 251, 252, 326–7, *461*
  see also question; tag, interrogative; *wh-*
    interrogative
interruption, in conversation 437
intonation, in conversation 16, 249, 251, 280
intransitive *see* valency patterns, intransitive
inversion **405–12,** *457*
  in dependent clauses 409–11, *410*
  discourse functions 406
  fronting with 402–3, 404
  register distribution 411–12, *411*
  in reporting clauses 411, 412
  special cases 409, *410*
  subject-operator 48, 380, 405–6, *406,* **407–9,** *460*
    with degree expressions 408–9
    with interrogative clause 238, 250, 251–2, 400,
      409–10
    with negation 407–9
    and negative scope 408
  subject-verb 48, 236–7, 405, *406,* **406–7,** *460*
    fronting with 402–3, 404
    with initial adverbial 406–7
    with interrogative clause 240, 250

inversion —*cont.*
  subject-verb —*cont.*
    with locative *there* 407
    in short verb-phrases 407
  and verb contraction 242
  see also word order
irony 210, 213, 405
irregular verb **115--18** *and inside front cover*
it 14, 87–8, 98, 378
  as dummy pronoun 48, 49, 95, 311, *456,* *457*
  it-cleft **420,** 422
  see also clefting; extraposition

J

jargon, discourse function 248–9, 250
just 255, **368–9**

K

know 4, 113, 164, 314, 315–16, 324–5, 327–8,
    348

L

Latin words, plurals 79
let 108
let's 250, 254, 433
lexemes 15, 21, *458*
lexical bundle **443–9,** *458*
  v. collocation 444
  common 19, 446–7
  definition 444–5
  grammatical types 445–6
  v. idiom 447–8
  register distribution 19, 296, 428, 431, 434, 443–
    9, *444*
  see also binomial expression; combination,
    word; free combination
lexical density 19, 23, 105–6, 430
lexical expression *see* binomial expression;
    collocation; combination, word; idiom; lexical
    bundle
lexical phrase *see* lexical bundle
lexical verb 21–2, 42, **103–35,** *458*
  formation **118–19**
  irregular *see* irregular verb
  multi-word 21, 104, 112, **123–35**
    fixed v. free combinations 124–5, 126–7
    register distribution 127, *127*
    semantic role 123–4
    v. single-word 124
    types 126–7, 133–4
    see also phrasal verb; phrasal-prepositional
      verb; prepositional verb
  and multiple meanings 110

lexical verb—*cont.*
  v. primary v. modal verb 104
  register distribution 105–6, 357
  semantic role 22
  single-word **106–14**, 130
    common 107, 110–14, *110*, *114*
    inflections 104
    irregular 104, 116–18
    register distribution 113–14
    regular 104, 115–16
    semantic categories 106–10
  syntactic role 21
  see also activity verb; aspect verb; causative verb;
    communication verb; existence verb; mental
    verb; morphology; occurrence verb
lexical word 15–16, 19, 59
  classes 15, **20–6**, *23*, 24–5, 187, *458*
  and lexical density 19, 23
  and morphology 17–18, 20
  see also adjective; adverb; lexical verb; noun
like 4, 164, 348, 386–7
likely/unlikely 216, 337
linking adverbial 207, 354, 356–7, 366, **389–96**,
  415, *458*
  of apposition 390, 393
  common adverbials 393–4, 395
  of contrast/concession 357, 391, 393, 394,
    404
  v. coordinator 227
  v. discourse marker 391, 394
  of enumeration/addition 357, 366, 389
  positions 360, **394–5**, *395*
  as preface 439
  prepositional phrase as 354, 359
  register distribution 357, *392*, **392–4**, 395
  of result/inference 390–1, 393
  scope 361
  semantic categories **389–93**
  v. stance adverbial 386
  v. subordinator 225
  of summation 389–90
  syntactic realizations, *see also* adverb phrase;
    anyway; finite clause; non-finite clause; *so*;
    then; *though*
  of transition 391–2
look 131, 132–3, 142, *144*, 164
LSWE Corpus
  dialect distinctions 3, 5–6, 7–8
  quantitative findings *110*, *177*, 443
  and register 3, 5, 7–8, 180
  size 3, 7–8, *8*

M

main verb 21, 27–8, 103, 105, 136, *458*
  v. auxiliary verb 42, 103–4

make 50, 112–13, 121–2, 134
  make out 424
manner *see* adverb, semantic categories; process/
  manner adverbial
marginal modal *see* semi-modal verb
masculine *see* gender
may 28, 104, 174, *177*, 178–80, *179*, 183, 409
meaning
  and grammatical units 14
  and structure 2, 149–50
measure 206, 362
  and genitive 81
  and quantifying nouns 62–3
  and subject-verb concord 236
mental verb **107–8**, **315–16**, *458*
  and aspect 155, 161, 163–5
  copular verbs 141
  with *ing*-complement clause 344, 346–7
  multi-word 131–2
  register distribution *315*, 316
  single-word 107–8, 110–13
  and tense 155
  with *that*-complement clause 315, 316
  with *to*-complement clause 330, *332*, 341
  with *wh*-complement clause 324–6, *325*
modal verb **174–85**, *458*
  with aspect/voice 183–4
  central 174, 175, 177–8
  v. lexical v. primary verb 104
  marking time 153–4, 175–6, 177, 181–2
  obligation/necessity 153, 175, 176–7, 180–1,
    183–5
  and past time 153–4
  permission/possibility/ability 153, 175, 176–7,
    178–80, 316
  personal v. logical meanings 176–7, 178–82,
    458, *459*
  register distribution 105, 177–83, *177*, *178*, 184–
    5, 431, 435
  sequences 184–5
  and stance 153–4, 174, 175, 176, 178
  and subject-verb concord 232
  and tense 150, 183
  volition/prediction 176–7, 181–2, 185, *461*
  see also auxiliary verb; modality; semi-modal
    verb
modality 28, *458*
  with circumstance adverbials 377
  in complement clause 309, 341
  intrinsic/extrinsic 176
  see also modal verb
modification
  of adjective 23, 43, 193, 196, 202, 204–5, 276,
    277, 402
  of adverb 23, 205–6, 385
  complex 264–5

modification —*cont.*
  and gender 86
  and genitive 80–1, 272
  and head noun types 270–1
  of noun 21, 23, 57, 187, 199, **264–300**, 431
  of noun phrase 41, 206
  of prepositional phrase 45, 206
  of pronoun 199, 206, 270–1
  restrictive/non-restrictive *458*
  see also hedge; postmodification;
     premodification
modifier *458*
  adjective as 22, 23, 57, 187, 195–6, 199, 202–3
  adjective phrase as 22, 43–4, 202
  adverb as 23, 193, 195, 196, 202, 204–6
     degree adverb 188, 205, 210–11
  adverb phrase as 44, 205
  free 203
  hedge as 212
  postposed 202, *459*
  see also modification
morphemes 13, 17, 20, 21, *458*
morphology 13, **17–18**, 20, *458*
  adjectives 22, 188
  adverbs 22
  lexical verbs 21, 104, 115
  of vernacular grammar 434, 435
  see also adjective, compound; adverb,
     compound; derivation; inflection; noun,
     compound
multi-word unit 18, 29, 54, 59, 75, 104, 130, 174
  see also idioms; lexical bundle; lexical verb,
     multi-word
must 28, 105, 174, 176, 180–1, *180*, 183, 184

N

names
  and modification 199
  personal 59
  and subject-verb concord 236
  see also proper noun
negation **239–48**, *458*
  assertive/non-assertive 244, 246–7, *455*
  and auxiliary *do* 28, 138, 239–40
  clausal 238, 239, 240, 245–6
  and contraction 28, 239, 240, 242–3, 244, *458*
  and coordinators 30
  and dummy *do* 243–4
  implicit negative 247
  with inversion 407–8, 409
  in lexical bundle 447
  multiple 6, 246, 247–8, 435, *458*
  and quantifiers 75–6, 244
  register distribution 245, 431
  scope 245–6, 247, 408, *460*

negation —*cont.*
  see also no; not
newspaper writing
  and informational density 5, 19, 23, 189–90,
     274–5, 297
  as register category 3, 5, *9*
  see also discussion of corpus findings in all
     chapters
nice 142, 198–9, 200, 211
no 239, *239*, 244, *458*
  v. *neither* 76
  v. *not* 245, *245*
nominal clause *see* complement clause
nominal element *458*
  fronted 402
  noun phrase as 421
  see also noun; noun phrase; pronoun; reference
nominalization 89–90, 303, 304, *458*
nominative *see* case, nominative
non-assertion *see* assertion
non-clausal unit in conversation 46, 255–6, 432,
     436, **440–1**, *458*
  ellipsis in 440
  syntactic 440–1
  see also insert
non-finite clause 226, **259–61**, *458*
  as adverbial 260, 358, 364–5, 376–7, 380
  and condensation 232
  as postmodifier 266, **291–4**
  and subject-verb concord 232, 236
  and subordination 226, 380
  as supplement clause 374–5, 376
  see also clause, verbless; *ed*-participle clause;
     infinitive clause; *ing*-complement clause;
     ing-participle clause; supplement clause; *to*-
     clause; *to*-complement clause
not 34, 174, 238, 239–40, *239*, 242–3, 244, 247–8,
     349, *458*
  v. *no* 245, *245*
noun 20–1, **56–64**, **77–92**, *458*
  abstract v. concrete 21, 57–8, 89–90
  in binomial expression 448
  collective *see* collective noun
  common *see* common noun
  compound 20, **91–2**
  countable *see* countable noun
  derived 20, 85, **88–92**, 108
  v. determiner 66
  formation *see* conversion; nominalization;
     noun, compound
  and gender bias 86
  head *see* noun phrase head
  modification 23, 44, 187, 199, **265–72**, 431
     see also postmodification; premodification
  package nouns 60–4
  of place 82

noun—*cont.*
plural 20, 63, **78–9**, 80, 275–6
as premodifier 266, 268, 272, 275–6, 277
productivity 275
proper *see* proper noun
quantifying *see* quantifying noun
and referential specification 65
register distribution 5, 23, 430
semantic characteristics 21
species **64**, 460
and stance 302
syntactic characteristics 21
types 56–64
uncountable *see* uncountable noun
unit *see* unit noun
noun + noun sequence 92, 256, 268, **272–6**, 295–6
logical relations 273–4, 278
plural nouns as premodifiers 275–6
see also premodification
noun complement clause 257, **300–6**, 308, *458*
head nouns 41, 302–6
ing-clause 301, 305
v. postmodifier 266–7
register distribution 304
v. relative clause 300–1
restrictive/non-restrictive functions 301–2
and stance 302, 303–4
structural types 301–2
that-clause 301, 303–4
to-clause 301, 303–5
wh-interrogative clause 259, 301–2, 306
noun phrase 41–2, *458*
as adverbial 42, 51, 355, 358
appositive 266, 270, 281, **297–8**, *455*
complex 72, 241, **263–306**
premodification v. postmodification 270–1
with contraction 241
coordinated 233–4, 435
definite 73, 418
as direct object 125, 126, 130, 172, 330, 424
and ellipsis 231
embedded 265
fronted 401, 404
as fronted object 401
head *see* noun phrase head
in idiomatic expressions 124, 125
indefinite 404, 412, 414
as indirect object 330
in lexical bundle 446
modification *see* postmodification; premodification
and multi-word verbs 124–5
as nominal element 421

noun phrase—*cont.*
and notional subject 412–13, 415
as object predicative 42, 48
predicative 42, 50, 69
as prepositional object 129–30
pronoun as 33, 92, 264, 430–1
register distribution *93*
simple 56, 430–1
stand-alone 96
structure 40
see also determiner; noun complement clause; postmodification; premodification
as subject 42, 48, 98, 135, 166, 233–4, 254, 319–20, 330, 345, 412, 414
as subject predicative 50, 141–2, *143*, 338–9
syntactic roles 42
verb + noun phrase combinations 134, 329
and vocative 54, 254
and *wh*-cleft 421
see also case; clause patterns; gender; nominal element; noun, plural; noun + noun sequence; noun complement clause; postmodification; preface; premodification; prepositional complement; reference; tag, noun phrase
noun phrase head 16, 21, *457*
abstract 42
adjective as 22, 42, 188, 202–3
and determiner 41, 65, 66, 76, 80, 264
and end-weight principle 400
and genitives 80
with noun complement clause 41, 302–6
numeral as 34, 35, 76
plural 279
and possessive pronouns 27, 97
with postmodifier 257, 297
pronoun as 42, 264
with relative clause, *see* relative clause
types 270–1
uncountable 279
see also noun complement clause; postmodification; premodification
now 74, 392
number 48, **78–80**, 93, *458*
see also noun, plural
numeral **34–5**, *458*
cardinal 34, 76, *455*
complex 34
as determiner 26, 34, 35, **76–7**
as linking adverbial 389
modification 206
ordinal 35, 76, *458*
plural 20, 34, 35, 63
as premodifier 272
register distribution

O

object 39, 48–9, *458*
  double 132, 133, 167, 172
  fronting 400, 401–2, 405
  see also direct object; indirect object; object
    predicative; prepositional object
object complement *see* object predicative
object predicative **50, 120**, 403, *458*
  adjective as 120, 188, 200, 201
  adjective phrase as 50
  and clause patterns 227
  and direct object 50, 201, 424
  ed-clause as 227
  infinitive clause as 227, 259, 330
  ing-clause as 227
  noun phrase as 120
  to-clause as 330
occurrence verb **109**, *461*
  and copular verbs 414
  multi-word 132
  single-word 109, 112
of-phrase
  with genitive 80, **82–4**, *84*
  with package noun 60, 61, 62, 64, 295
  as postmodifier 71, 271, **295–6**
  with quantifier 100, 234, 295
one **100–1**
  generic 95, 96, 101
  substitute 100, 270–1
only 211, 420
operator **238–48**, *458*
  and auxiliary verbs 138, 238, 239
  and ellipsis 239, 441–2
  and interrogative clause 238, 251
  and negation 238, 240, 242, 243–4
  stranded 139, 239, 442
  see also do, as dummy operator; inversion,
    subject-operator
or 30, 227, 229, 233–4, 278, 327, 448
orthography *see* spelling
outside 36

P

package noun **60–4**
parallelism, structural 69, 409
parentheticals 53, *459*
participle *459*
  dangling (unattached) 377–8, *456*
  past 7
  as premodifier 265–6
  see also adjective, participial; *ed*-participle; *ing*-
    participle
participle clause *459*
  see also ed-participle clause; *ing*-complement
    clause; *ing*-participle clause

particle, adverbial **29–30**, *455*
  in free combinations 128–9
  movement 125, *459*
  with phrasal verb 29, 124, 125, 187, 206, 424–5
  with phrasal-prepositional verb 124, 132–3
  v. preposition 124
  with prepositional phrase 30, 45
  register distribution 32, *32*
  with subject-verb inversion 407
particle, negative *see* not
passive 166–74, 398, *459*
  and aspect 135, 173–4
  and auxiliary verb 28, 135, 166, 171–2
  common verbs 170–2
  and direct object 168, 173
  discourse functions 166, 167–70
  finite constructions 292
  get-passive 112, 166, 171–2, *457*
  and indirect object 49
  long 166–7, 169–70, *458*
  modal verb in 183, 184
  and postmodification 292–3
  and prepositional verb 130, 132, 167, 172–3
  progressive 135, 173
  register distribution 3, 167–70, 171, 173–4, 425,
    425
  and relative clause 292–3
  short (agentless) 166–8, *455*, *460*
  and stranded prepositions 173
  subject of 48, 167, 173
  in *that*-clauses 315, 321–2
  in *to*-clauses 329, 331, 341
  uncommon verbs in 172–3
  and word order *425*
  see also ed-participle; voice
past tense *see* tense, past; tense, present
pause 280, 434
  see also hesitator
perception verb *see* mental verb
perfect aspect *see* aspect, perfect
peripheral clause 258
peripheral elements *see* discourse marker; insert;
    parentheticals; preface; tag; vocative
personal pronoun 53, **93–7**, *459*
  and anaphoric reference 95
  with attributive adjective 199
  and case 93, 96
  coordinated 94
  and copular verb 96
  as direct or indirect object 423
  first person 5, 94–5, 181, 182, 242, 340, 435
  and gender 85, 87–8, 93
  general reference 95–6
  in lexical bundle 446
  with modification 199, 270–1
  nominative v. accusative forms 96

personal pronoun —*cont.*
  non-personal reference 94
  plural 94
  and possessive determiner 72, *93*, 94
  and possessive pronoun 93
  and reflexive pronoun *93*, 97
  register distribution 94–5, 98, 430
  second person 5, 95, 242, 430, 435
  as subject 94, 321, 445
  and subject-verb concord 237
  third person 95, 237
  and zero relativizer 289
  see also it; one
phonemes 13
phrasal verb 123–9, *459*
  and adverbial particles 29, 124, 125, 187, 206,
      424–5
  common 128–9
  as copular verb 128, 129, 141
  direct object of 127, 424–5
  in idiomatic expressions 124–5, 126–7
  intransitive 124–5, 126, 127, 128
  and particle movement 125, 127
  register distribution 127, *127*, 128–9
  semantic domains 124–6
  transitive 124, 125, 127, 129
phrasal-prepositional verb 124, **132–3**, *459*
  register distribution 127, *127*, 133
  semantic role 133
phrase 13, **38–54**, *459*
  embedded 38, 40, *41*
  lexical *see* lexical bundle
  structures 38–9, *39*, 40–1, 400
  syntactic roles 39
  types 41–5
  see also adjective phrase; adverb phrase; binomial
      expression; coordination, phrasal; embedding,
      phrase; noun phrase; prepositional phrase;
      verb phrase
place *see* adverb, semantic categories, place; place
      adverbial
place adverbial 51, 194–5, 207, 289, 294, 354, 367,
      370–1, 373
  adverbial clause as 294, 373, 415
  categories 362–3
  with subject-verb inversion 406, 407
plurals
  irregular 78–9, 233, **457**
  Latin and Greek 79
  regular 78, **460**
  and subject-verb concord 79, 232–4, 235,
      236–7
  and uncountable nouns 20, 58–9, 279
  zero 79, 233, **461**
  see also noun, plural; number; subject-verb
      concord

politeness 7, 151, 176, 251
  markers 213, 255, 433, 441, *452*, *453*
  see also insert, polite speech-act formulae; stance
possessive determiner 26, **72–3**, 93, *93*, 345, 447–
      8, *459*
  with definite noun phrases 73
  v. genitive 80
  v. possessive pronouns 27, 97
  and proper nouns 57
possessive pronoun 27, 82, 93, 97, *459*
  and genitive 81, 93
  v. possessive determiner 27, 97
postdeterminer 65, *66*
postmodification 80, 259, **264–71**, **279–300**, *459*
  with demonstrative pronouns 271
  and genitives 80
  multiple *298*, **298–9**
  of notional subject 415
  v. noun complement clause 266–7, 300–6
  and noun head 257, 270–1, 284
  with proper noun 270
  register distribution 267–8, *268*, 269–70, *269*,
      270, 294, 297, 298
  restrictive/non-restrictive **279–81**, *460*
  types 265–6, 269–70
  see also of-phrase; postmodifier; relative clause;
      relative pronoun
postmodifier 267–72, *459*
  adjective as 202
  adjective phrase as 202, 266
  adverb as 204, 206, 220, 266
  appositive noun phrase as 266–7, 270, **297–8**
  non-finite clause as 266, **291–4**
  participial
      ed-clause 260, 266, 270, 291, 292–3
      ing-clause 260, 266, 291, 292–3
  prepositional phrase as 266, 269–70, *269*, 271,
      288, **294–6**, 299
  pronoun as 270–1
  relative clause as 71, 74, 257, 264, 266, 269–70,
      270, 272, **279–91**, 299, 300, 416
  to-clauses as 220, 266, 291–2, 293–4
  see also noun complement clause
postmodifier complex 264–5, 298–9, *298*, *459*
postponement, of direct object 424
predeterminer 65, *66*, 206, 323
predicate *459*
  adjectival 317–19, 323–4
      see also predicative adjective
  see also verb phrase
predicative 50, *459*
  and adjective phrases 50, 142
  and complement clause 308
  fronted 402–3, 405
  and noun phrase 50, 69
  semantic role 50

predicative—*cont.*
  see also object predicative; subject predicative
predicative adjective 22, 188, 189, **200–2**, *459*
  common 201–2
  and complement clause 200–2, 257, 308, 310
  and copular verb 144, 200
  v. *ing*-participle 191
  and intensifier 198–9
  and passive 167, 171
  and peripheral adjectives 189
  register distribution 189–90, *190*, 201–2, 434
  as stance device 142, 202
  as subject predicative 200–1
  see also object predicative; subject predicative
prefabrication *see* lexical bundle
preface 53, **418–19**, *459*
  register distribution 419, 425, *425*, 439
preference clause 374
prefix 17, *459*
  adjectival 13, 190
  negative 190
  noun 88–9
  verb 118–19
  see also affix; derivation; suffix
premodification 264, **265–79**, *459*
  of adjective 202–3, 276, 402–3
  v. adverb phrase 44
  multiple **276–9**
  and noun head types 270–1
  register distribution 267–8, *267*
  and specific reference 272
  types 265–6, 272–3
  see also attributive adjective; noun + noun
    sequence; premodifier
premodifier 265–72, *459*
  adjective as 264, 265, 268, 272, 277–8
  adverb as 204, 206, 209, 266, 276, 277
  coordinated 278–9
  noun as 266, 268, 272, 275–6, 277
  noun phrase as **267–8**
  participle as 265–6
  plural noun as 275–6
preposition 16, **28–9**, *459*
  and adverb complement 206, 260
  v. adverbial particle 124
  as closed system 17
  complement *see* prepositional complement
  complex 29, *456*
  and free combination 29
  omission 290
  stranded 45, 173, 253, 284, 290, 294, *460*
  v. *which* 290
prepositional complement 44–5, 206, 260, 294,
  323, *459*
  and gap 283
  noun phrase as 28–9

prepositional complement—*cont.*
  wh-clause as 45, 324
prepositional object
  and clause patterns 227
  finite clause as 227
  ing-clause as 227, 260
  noun phrase as 130
  and phrasal-prepositional verb 133
  and prepositional verb 129–30, 131, 167, 173
  and stranded prepositions 294
prepositional phrase 44–5, *459*
  with adjectives 200–1, 219
  with adverbs 30
  and complement clause 42, 45, 142, *143*, 218,
    219, 338–9, 341
  with copular verb 142, *143*
  embedded 40, 45, 299
  extended 30
  fronting 288
  in idiomatic expressions 130
  with *in* 296
  with *of* 295–6
  as predicative 50, 142
  register distribution 294, 359
  v. relative clause 269, 282–3, 284, 294–5
  restrictive and non-restrictive 281
  structure 40
  and word order 423
  see also adverbial; circumstance adverbial;
    modification; postmodifier
prepositional verb 29, 45, **129–32**, *459*
  common verbs 130–2
  v. free combination 125–6
  in idiomatic expressions 124–5, 130
  with *ing*-complement clause 346
  object of 125, 126, 129–30, 324
  and passive 129–30, 132, 167, 172–3
  and prepositional object 129–30, 131, 167, 173
  register distribution 127, *127*, 131–2
  semantic domains 124–6
  structural types 129–30
  with *to*-infinitive clause 331–2
  transitive 126
  with *wh*-complement clause 126, 130, 324
  see also activity verb; communication verb;
    mental verb
prescriptive grammar 7, 218, 284, 345, 371, 435
primary verb 21, 27–8, 42, **135–40**, *459*
  v. lexical v. modal verb 104
  main v. auxiliary functions 104
  register distribution 105, 431
  see also aspect; auxiliary verb; be; copular verb;
    do; have
pro-form 231–2, 233, *459*
  adverbial
  in complement clause 231

pro-form —*cont.*
  in conversation 430
  with inversion 408
  pro-verb 137–8, 139, **459**
  see also pronoun
probability verb *333*, 334, 341
process/manner adverbial 51, 257, 367, 370–1,
    373, 379
  and adverbial gap 290–1, 294
  categories 364–5
progressive aspect *see* aspect, progressive
pronoun 16, 26–7, **92–101**, **459**
  compound **99–100**, 202, **456**
  and condensation 231
  with contraction 241, 242
  v. determiner 66, *67*
  as direct object 125, *127–8*, 423, 424
  discourse role 14
  dummy *see* it
  and gender 87–8
  generic 95–6, 100
  and indirect object word order 423
  interrogative 27, 33, **457**
  in lexical bundle 445, 446
  nominative and accusative case 48, 79
  as noun phrase head 42, 264
  v. noun phrases 92
  with prefaces 418–19
  reciprocal 27, 98, **460**
  register distribution 5, 32, *32*, 67, *93*, 232,
    430
  relative *see* relative pronoun
  sequence as direct/indirect object 423
  substitute *see* one
  types **92–101**
  wh-pronoun 101, **461**
  see also demonstrative pronoun; indefinite
    pronoun; modification; nominal
    element; personal pronoun;
    possessive pronoun; reflexive
    pronoun
proper names 59, 199
  see also proper noun
proper noun 5, 20, 42, 56–7, 83, **459**
  v. common noun 56, **59–60**
  and definite article 56, 57, 60
  and genitive 82
  and initial capitals 59–60
  modification 21, 57, 199, 270
  notional subject as 415
  as noun phrase head 42
  with possessive determiner 57
  with *the* 60
  see also proper names
proportion clause 374, 402
prose, academic *see* academic prose

proximity, and subject-verb concord 236
punctuation, and postmodification 280

Q

quantifier 26, 27, 35, 66, **74–6**, 231, **459**
  of arbitary amount 75–6
  inclusive 74–5
  of large quantity 75
  and negation 75–6, 244
  pronoun as 35, **100**, 234, **459**
  of small quantity 75
  and subject-verb concord 234–5
  types 74–6
quantifying noun 60, **62–4**, 79, **459**
  and *of*-phrase 62
question 248, *249*, **459**
  adverb as 207–8
  alternative 249, 251, **455**
  condensed 440
  indirect 323, 326–8
  rhetorical 250, 252
  see also interrogative clause
question tag *see* tag, interrogative
quotation, and subject-verb concord 236
quoted speech *see* direct speech reporting;
    reporting clause

R

raising **337–8**
  object-to-subject 338, *339*, 342
  subject-to-subject 334, 337–8, 341
real 196, 211
really 196, 211, 385, 387
reason adverbial 257, 289, 354, 376, 420
reduction 175, 434, 454
  see also contraction; ellipsis; pro-form; pronoun;
    relativizer, zero; *that*-complement clause,
    that retention v. omission
reference
  anaphoric 70, 72, 73, 74, 95, 271, **455**
  cataphoric 71, 73, 74, **455**
  co-reference 97, 234, 321, 418–19, **456**
  and gender 85
  generic 68, 71, 72, 95–6, **457**
  personal v. impersonal 94
  situational 73–4
  specific 65, 68, 73, 80, 272, 431
  time 74
  see also gender
referent 26, 73, 267, **460**
reflexive pronoun 97–8, **460**
  as determiner 27
  emphatic 98
  and personal pronoun *93*, 97

register 23, 40
  categories 4–5
  and lexical word classes 23
  in LSWE Corpus 3, 4–5, *4*, 7–8
  and phrase structure 40
  and sub-registers 5, 8
  see also academic prose; conversation; fiction;
    newspaper writing
relationship verb 324, *325*
relative adverb 33, 282–3, 289, *460*
relative clause 192, 257–8, **279–91**, *460*
  v. adjectival compounds 192
  as finite clause 279–91, 292
  head noun 281–2, 284, 286–8, 290, 293–4
  nominal 236, 257–8, 322–3, 326
  v. noun complement clause 300–1
  participle clause as, *see also ed*-participle clause;
    ing-participle clause
  v. prepositional phrase 269, 282, 284, 294–5
  register distribution 269–70, *270*, 280, 284, 290,
    431
  restrictive v. non-restrictive **279–81**, 283, 284,
    287–8, 295, 297
  and stranded prepositions 45, 284, 290
  and subject-verb concord 236
  to-infinitive *see to*-clause
  and *wh*-words 32, 33, 77
  see also gap; postmodifier
relative pronoun 33, **282–9**, *460*
  as determiner 27
  omission *see* relativizer, zero
  register distribution 284–9
  see also relativizer; *that*; *what*; *which*; *who*
relativizer 33, 257, 281, 299, *460*
  discourse function 282–4
  register distribution *285–6*, 287–9
  zero 282–4, 286–7, 288–9, 290, *461*
  see also relative adverb; relative pronoun
repair, conversational 434, *460*
repeats 434
repetition
  and comparative adjectives 198
  in conversation 434, 444, 445
  in fronting 405
  local v. lexical bundle 445
  see also repeats
reporting clause 152–3, 258, 327, 347, 349,
  460
  with inversion *410*, 411
  with subject-verb order 258
  see also communication verb; direct speech
    reporting; speech-act verb; *that*-
    complement clause, as reporting clause
response
  elicitor 249, 432, *451*, 453, *453*
  form *451–2*, 453, *453*, *460*

S

sarcasm 405
say 4, 110, *110*, 111, 131, 152, 165, 237, 313, 316,
  321, 329–30, 350
  + *so* 349
scope
  of adverbial 356, 361, *460*
  negative 245–6, 247, 408, *460*
see 113, 164, 309, 314, 315–16, 325–6, 327–8, 346–
  7
seem 4, 50, 109, 142, *143*, 337, 341
semantic roles 20
  see also circumstance adverbial; direct object;
    indirect object; subject
semi-determiner *see* determiner, semi-determiner
semi-modal verb 28, 112, 136, **174–83**, *460*
  with ellipsis 442–3
  register distribution 177–8, *178*, 182–3, 185
  stance 178
  and time 153, 175, 181, 182, 185
sentence 13, *460*
  see also independent clause
since 31, 381–2
so 209, 211, 219–20, 349, 390–1, **393**, 395, 402–3,
  408
speech
  direct *see* direct speech reporting
  see also conversation
speech act *460*
speech-act functions 248–9, 250, 433
speech-act verb **107**, **316–17**
  and aspect 161
  with *ing*-complement clause 344, 347
  with inversion 411
  with *that*-complement clause *315*, 316–17
  with *to*-complement clause *332*
  with *wh*-complement clause 324, *325*, 326
  see also communication verb
spelling
  and standard English 6
  see also capitals, initial
stance *460*
  attitudinal 146, 155, 212, 317–19, 384
  and complement clause 304, 313, 316, 317–19,
    335–6, 342–3
  epistemic
    of actuality 212, 383, 387
    of certainty 153, 202, 212, 302, 303, 316–17,
      382–3, 387
    of imprecision 384, 387
    of limitation 383–4
    of perspective 384
    of source of knowledge 212, 303, 383
  grammatical devices 142, 151, 153–4, 316
    see also adverb, stance; stance adjective; stance
      adverbial

stance —*cont.*
  and noun complement cause 302–4
  register distribution 433–4
  style of speaking 213, 356
  and substitution 349
  see also modal verb; politeness; stance adverbial
stance adjective 146, 317–19, 335–6, 339
stance adverbial 154, 207, 354–5, **382–8**, *460*
  attitudinal 195, 356, 384, 386, *455*
  v. circumstance adverbial or degree modifier
      385
  common adverbials 386–7
  discourse functions **388**
  v. discourse marker 386
  epistemic 356, 378, 382–4, 386, 387, 388, *457*
  v. linking adverbial 386
  multiple meanings 385–6
  positions 360, 385, **387**
  as preface 439
  prepositional phrase as 354, 359
  as question 207
  register distribution 357, *386*, **386–7**, 434
  scope 356, 361, 387
  semantic categories 382–6
  style 356, 378, 385–6, *460*
  see also adverb, stance
stance verb 347, 414
stand 122, 165
standard/non-standard English 6–7, 160, 195, 217,
      247, 288, 435
  see also grammar, conversational
statement 248, 249, *249*, *460*
  condensed 441
stative verb 108, 112, 163–5, 171, 363, *460*
stem 13, 17, 18, *460*
stress, and fronting 403
subject 39, 48, *460*
  agentive 48, 106–7, 164–5
  anticipatory 33
  clausal 226, 236
  complement clause as 310, 311
  ellipsis 441–2
  as experiencer 164, *457*
  in imperative clause 254
  infinitive clause as 259, 323, 328
  of *ing*-clause 345
  ing-clause as 226, 259, 344
  notional 236–7, 412, **414–15**, 416, 417, *458*
  noun phrase as 42, 48, 98, 135, 166, 233–4, 254,
      319–20, 345, 414
  overt 294, 376
  with passive 48, 167, 173
  semantic roles 48
  that-clause as 312, 319–21
  to-clause as 226, 259, 334–5, 337–8, 340–1
  wh-clause as 323

subject —*cont.*
  see also inversion, subject-operator; inversion,
      subject-verb
subject complement *see* subject predicative
subject predicative 50, *460*
  adjective as 145, 167, 188, 200–1
  adjective phrase as 43–4, 45, 141, 142
  complement clause as 142, 310, 323
  copular verbs with 44, 50, 120, 135, 140, **141–7**,
      188, 200, 313
  finite clause as 226
  fronted 402
  infinitive clause as 226, 259, 323, 328
  ing-clause as 260, 344
  noun phrase as 50, 141–2, *143*, 338–9
  participial adjective as 167
  prepositional phrase as 142, 200–1, 338–9
  that-clause as 201, 312, 313, 334, 350
  to-clause as 200–1, **334–5**, 338–9, 350
  wh-clause as 323
subject-operator inversion *see* inversion
subject-verb concord **232–7**, *456*
  with clausal subject 236
  with collective noun 235
  with coordinated subject 233–4
  and inversion 236–7
  non-standard 233, 237, 435
  notional 235–6, *458*
  and pronoun reference 87, 234–5, 237
  and proximity 236
  with quantifier 234–5
  singular v. plural 79, 232, 233–4, 235, 236–7
  and subjunctive verbs 232, 261
  and tense 232
subject-verb inversion *see* inversion
subjunctive verb 151, 232, **261**, 319, 409, *460*
subordinator 30, **31**, 222, 223, **224–7**, 439, *460*
  with adverbial clause 31, 257, 374, 376,
      380–2
  as clause link 224–5, 394
  common 380–1
  and complement clause 31, 256
  complex 31, 34
  v. coordinator 225
  with degree clause 31
  and dependent clause 31, 224–7, 404
  with fronting 404
  if v. subject-operator inversion 380
  with multiple meanings 381–2
  register distribution 381–2, 422
  subordination signals 225–6
  see also adverbial clause; adverbial clause as
      circumstance adverbial; *as*; embedding; *that*;
      though; *wh*-word
substitution
  in complement clause 348–9

substitution —*cont.*
  pro-form 231, 430
suffix 17, 86, *460*
  adjectival 22, 191–2, 215
  adverb 13, 193, 209
  of gender 85–6
  genitive 20
  noun 20, 63, 88, **89–90**
  verb 115–17, 118–19
  see also affix; derivation; prefix
superlative adjective 22, 188, **215**, *216*, 217, 402
  doubly marked 217
  inflectional 215–16, 217
  phrasal 215–16, 217
  register distribution 217
  see also comparative adjective
supplement clause 260, 374–6, 379, *460*
  register distribution 260, 375–6
sure 142, 318, 338
swearword *see* taboo word
synonym 70, 346
syntactic blend 437–8, *460*
syntactic role *460*
syntax 13, 20, 431, *460*

T

taboo word 7, 54, 203, 211, 347, 368, 429, 433, 452–3
tag 53, *460*
  coordination 94, 229
  declarative 53, 258, 419, *456*
  demonstrative pronoun as 419
  interrogative 53, 251–2, 258, 439, *459–60*
    and auxiliary verbs 139
    and existential *there* 413
    and imperative clauses 255
    as response elicitor 432, *451*
  noun phrase 53, 418, **419**, 425, *425*, *458*
  register distribution 439
tag clause 258
take 49, 112–13, 134
  take up 424
tense 42, **150–6**, *460*
  and aspect 136, 156–62
  with circumstance adverbials 377
  historic present 150, 152, *457*
  and lexical verbs 21, 104, 155–6
  and modal verbs 150, 183
  past 104, 116–17, 151, 155–6, 165, 239, 295
    and present perfect aspect 159, 161–2, 173
    in reported speech 152–3
  present 104, 136–7, 151, 159, 232, 239
    and *say* 111, 152
  register distribution 111, 113, 152, 153–5, *154*
  and time 149–56, 175, 293–4

tense —*cont.*
  see also direct speech reporting
thanks 433
that
  as complementizer *see that*-complement clause
  as degree adverb 402–3
  as demonstrative determiner 73, 74, 98
  as demonstrative pronoun 98–9, 271, 323, 421
  omission *see* relativizer, zero; *that*-complement clause, *that* retention v. omission
  as relativizer 31, 33, 281, 282–3, 284, 286, 290, 300–1
  as subordinator 31, 256
  see also which; whom
***that*-complement clause** 4, 42, 202, 220, **312–22**, *460*
  controlled by adjective 202, 308, 312, **317–19**
  controlled by verbs 308, 314–17, *315*, 350–1
  coordinated 313, 321–2
  as direct object 308
  discourse functions **312–13**, 320–1
  with ellipsis 348
  embedded 313, 320
  extraposed 311, 313, 317, **318–21**, 337, 341, 350
  as finite dependent clause 308–9, 350
  as noun complement clause 301, 303–4
  post-predicate 310–11, 312, 313, **314–18**, 349, 350–1
  register distribution 312, *312*, 313, 320, 321, 328, 350–1, 431, 439
  and relative clause 6, 300–1, 312
  as reporting clause 312, 313, 316
  as stance device 313, 384
  as subject 312, 319–21
  as subject predicative 201, 312, 313, 334, 350
  and subjunctive 232, 261, 319
  and subordinator 31, 256
  substitution with 349
  that retention v. omission 7, 301, **321–2**
the 41, 67, 69, 70–1, 72, 203, 374, 402
  anaphoric use 70, 72
  cataphoric use 71
  with proper nouns 59, 60
  situational use 72
  see also article, definite
then 74, 162, **369**, 391, **393–4**, 395
***there*, existential** 33–4, **412–18**, *457*
  with adverbial 415
  as anticipatory subject 33
  as deictic adverb 369, 430
  discourse functions **416–17**
  grammatical status 413
  v. *have* 136
  and inversion 236–7, 407, 413
  v. locative *there* 407, 413, *413*
  and negation 416

there, **existential** —*cont.*
   in non-finite clause 413
   with notional subject 236–7, 412–13, **414–15**,
      416, 417, *458*
   register distribution 413, *413*, 416, 425, *425*
   simple v. complex clauses **415–16**, *416*
   and subject-verb concord 236–7
   and verb 412, **414**, 416
there, locative 34, **369**, 407, 413–14, *413*
think 4, 113, 151, 164–5, 314–15, 321, 346, 348,
   350–1
this 73, 74, 98–9, 271, 402
though 139, 394, 404
time *see* adjective, time; adverb, semantic
   categories, time; adverbial clause as
   circumstance adverbial; circumstance
   adverbial, semantic categories; modal verb;
   tense
time adverbial 194–5, 207, 252, 257, 289, 294, 354,
   370–2, 373, 379, 415
   and aspect and tense 162
   categories 363–4
   with inversion 406, 408
   marking future time 152
   obligatory adverbial 51
titles, and subject-verb concord 236
to
   infinitive marker 34, 200–1, 324
   see also to-clause; *to*-complement clause
to-clause 34, 42, 151
   as adverbial 358, 376, 377, 379
   as complement clause *see to*-complement
      clause
   as postmodifier 220, 266, 291–2, 293–4
to-**complement clause** 4, 259, 308, **328–43**,
   460–1
   bare infinitive 329
   controlled by adjectives 219, **335–6**, 337–8, 339,
      342–3, 350–1
   controlled by nouns 301, 304–5
   controlled by verbs 329–34, 338–9, 342, 350
   discourse functions 342–3
   with ellipsis 348
   extraposed 259, 311, 328, **338–42**, 350
   meaning variations 329–31
   as non-finite clause 308–9, 350
   as object predicative 330
   and passive 329, 331, 341
   post-predicate **328–33**, *332–3*, **335–6**, 339, 342–
      3, 348
   register distribution 328, 329, 331–4, 340, 341–
      3, *343*, 350–1
   subject predicative 200–1, **334–5**, 350
   with *wh*-cleft 421
   see also raising
   token 15, *461*

topic 48, 419
topicalization *see* fronting
transitive *see* valency patterns, transitive
type 15, *461*

U

uncountable noun 20, 56–8, 62, *461*
   and article 56, 67–8, 70, 72
   and determiner 59, *65*, 74, 75–6
   plural 20, 58–9, 64
unit, clausal *see* clausal unit; non-clausal unit
unit noun **61–2**, *461*
used to 176, **182–3**, 244, 253–4
utterance
   incomplete 437
   launcher 422, 439
      see also discourse marker; fronting; preface

V

vagueness 98, 214, 229, 431, 439
   markers *see* approximator; hedge
valency patterns 110, **119–23**, *461*
   complex transitive 47, 49, 50, 51, 120, 121–2,
      201, 330–1, *456*
   copular verbs 47, 120, *456*
   and direct object 49
   ditransitive 47, 49, 120, 121, 167, 330, 423, *456*
   intransitive 47, 107, 119, 121, 122–3, 124–5, 126,
      140–1, *457*
   main v. auxiliary verb 103–4
   monotransitive 47, 49, 120–1, *458*
   multiple 121–2
   with optional adverbial 119, 121, 123
   transitive 10–57, 107, 124, 140–1, 166, *461*
   see also clause patterns
varieties, English *see* dialect; register; standard/
   non-standard English
verb 102–47, *461*
   auxiliary *see* auxiliary verb
   in binomial expression 448
   concord *see* subject-verb concord
   continuation 129, 141, 142, *143–4*
   derived 21, 118–19
   dynamic 108, 163–5, 177, 270, *456*
   formation **118–19**
   full *see* lexical verb
   irregular 104, 116–18, 260, *458*, *462–3*
   lexical *see* lexical verb
   modal *see* modal verb
   multi-word *see* lexical verb; phrasal verb;
      phrasal-prepositional verb
   nominalized 89
   as operator *see* operator
   phrasal *see* phrasal verb

verb —*cont.*
phrasal-prepositional *see* phrasal-prepositional verb
prepositional *see* prepositional verb
primary *see* primary verb
register distribution 4, 23, 431
regular 104, **115–16**, *460*
semantic domains **106–10**
see also activity verb; affective verb; aspect verb; attitude verb; causative verb; communication verb; existence verb; lexical verb; main verb; mental verb; occurrence verb; perception verb; prepositional verb; probability verb; relationship verb; speech-act verb; stative verb
see also aspect; tense; valency patterns; verb classes
verb classes 103–6
see also clause patterns; copular verb; lexical verb; modal verb; primary verb; valency patterns
verb complement clause 304, 307–8, 310, 349–50
post-predicate position 310
and stance 304
subject (pre-predicate) position 310
verb phrase 42–3, *43*, **148–85**, 232, *461*
and clause grammar 46–7, 48
complex 185, 411
discontinuous 42
finite/non-finite 42, 151, 153, 225, *457*, *458*
in lexical bundle 445, 446–7
long 51–2, *52*, 407, *458*
syntactic roles 21
see also aspect; clause patterns; inversion; modal verb; negation; tense; valency patterns; verb classes; voice
vernacular 6, *461*
very 167, 188, 209, 211, 399
vocative 54, *461*
in imperative clauses 254
noun phrase 54
register distribution 432, 433
and zero article 69–70
voice 166–74, *461*
active 166, 172, 331
and aspect 173–4
lexical verbs 21
and modal verbs 183, 184
passive *see* passive

W

want 4, 113, 151, 164, 309, 331, 348
weight
balance 398

weight —*cont.*
see also end weight principle
well 193, 195, 206
wh-complement clause 45, **322–8**, *461*
and adjectival predicate 323–4
controlled by verbs 323, 324–6, *325*, 349
with ellipsis 348
exclamative 322–3
extraposed 259, 311, 324
as finite dependent clause 308–9, 350
as infinitive 324
as nominal relative clause 257
as object 323, 324
post-predicate **324–6**, 348, 350
as prepositional complement 45, 324
register distribution 325–6, 327–8, 350, 431
structural types 322–4
as subject 323
as subject predicative 323
with *whether* and *if* 326–8
wh-interrogative 1, 32–3, 77, 130, 138, 249, 250, 252, 322–3, *461*
and alternative question 249
formation 126
as noun complement clause 301–2, 306
register distribution 252
and yes-no questions 249, 326
wh-question *see wh*-interrogative
wh-word 32–3, 250, *461*
as adverbial subordinator 31, 225
as clause link 32, 33
in cleft 420, **421**, *425*
as determiner 26, 27, 65, **77**, *461*
as exclamative 254, 404
and fronting 323, 400, 404
as pronoun 101, *461*
as relativizer 32, 33, 77
as subordinator 31, 225, 256–7
see also relative pronoun; *wh*-complement clause; *wh*-interrogative
what 33, 65, 101, 126, 130, 250, 254, 323, 421
as relative pronoun 6
when 33, 126, 130, 250, 257, 282–3, 289–90, 381
whether 31, 33, 302, 323, **325–8**
which 33, 65, 101, 250, 282–3, 284, 293
of which v. *whose* 288
v. preposition 290
v. *that* 6, 287
v. *who* 284–6
who 7, 33, 101, 126, 130, 250, 253, 281, 282–3, 284
v. *that* 7, 286–7
v. *which* 284–6
v. *whom* 7, 253, 286–7
whom 33, 101, 282–3
v. *that* 7, 286–7
v. *who* 7, 253, 286–7

will 21, 104, 150, 152, 153, 174, 175, 177–8, *177*, 181, 184
   register distribution 435
   and verb contraction 28, 240–1, 242
word 13, **14–20**
   grammatical 15
   orthographic 15, 17, 18, 444, *459*
   'stand-alone', *see also* insert
   structure *see* morphology
   types v. tokens 15, *461*
   see also function word; insert; lexeme; lexical density; lexical word; morphology; multi-word unit
word classes 15, **20–6**, *461*
   ambiguities 35–6, *36*
   borderline cases 24–5, 29
   open 15, 16, 104
   single-word 33–4
   special 32–5
   see also function word; insert; lexical word

word order 397–426
   discourse functions 398–400
   and information flow 169, **398–9**, 400, 415
   marked 425, *425*
   register distribution 425
   subject-verb 249, 250, 254, 398
   unmarked 400, 411
   variations 277–8, 423, 424–5
   see also clause patterns; clefting; condensation; dislocation; emphasis; end weight principle; extraposition; focus; fronting; inversion; passive; postponement; reporting clause; *there*, existential

Z

zero article 67, 68–70, 72, *461*

Index compiled by Meg Davies (Registered Indexer, Society of Indexers)